Music Theory
in Concept and Practice

Eastman Studies in Music

The Poetic Debussy: A Collection of His Song Texts and Selected Letters
(Revised Second Edition)
Edited by Margaret G. Cobb

Concert Music, Rock, and Jazz since 1945: Essays and Analytical Studies
Edited by Elizabeth West Marvin and Richard Hermann

Music and the Occult: French Musical Philosophies, 1750–1950
Joscelyn Godwin

"Wanderjahre of a Revolutionist" and Other Essays on American Music
Arthur Farwell, edited by Thomas Stoner

French Organ Music from the Revolution to Franck and Widor
Edited by Lawrence Archbold and William J. Peterson

Musical Creativity in Twentieth-Century China:
Abing, His Music and its Changing Meanings
(includes CD)
Jonathan P. J. Stock

Elliott Carter: Collected Essays and Lectures, 1937–1995
Edited by Jonathan W. Bernard

Music Theory in Concept and Practice
Edited by James M. Baker, David W. Beach, and Jonathan W. Bernard

Forthcoming

Music and Musicians in the Escorial Liturgy under the Habsburgs, 1563–1700
Michael Noone

MUSIC THEORY
IN CONCEPT AND PRACTICE

edited by

JAMES M. BAKER
DAVID W. BEACH
JONATHAN W. BERNARD

UNIVERSITY OF ROCHESTER PRESS

First published 1997

University of Rochester Press
668 Mt. Hope Avenue
Rochester, NY 14620   USA

and at P.O. Box 9
Woodbridge, Suffolk IP12 3DF
United Kingdom

ISBN 1–878822–79–9
ISSN 1071–9989

Library of Congress Cataloging-in-Publication Data

Music theory in concept and practice / edited by James M. Baker, David W.
Beach, Jonathan W. Bernard.
      p.   cm. — (Eastman studies in music; 8)
Includes bibliographical references and index.
ISBN 1–878822–79–9 (alk. paper)
1. Music—Theory.   I. Baker, James M., 1948–   .   II. Beach,
David, 1938–   .   III. Bernard, Jonathan W., 1951–   .   IV. Series.
MT6.M962078   1997
781—dc21   96–53956
                                                                                         CIP

British Library Cataloguing-in-Publication Data
A catalogue record for this book is
available from the British Library

Designed and typeset by Cornerstone Composition Services
Printed in the United States of America
This publication is printed on acid-free paper

for

ALLEN FORTE

on his seventieth birthday
(23 December 1996)

Contents

Part One: Historical and Theoretical Essays

INTRODUCTION   1

HISTORICAL PERSPECTIVES

Jonathan W. Bernard   11   Chord, Collection, and Set in Twentieth-Century Theory

James M. Baker   53   Scriabin's Music: Structure as Prism for Mystical Philosophy

Patricia Carpenter   97   Tonality: A Conflict of Forces

Pieter C. van den Toorn   131   Neoclassicism and Its Definitions

Arnold Whittall   157   Modernist Aesthetics, Modernist Music: Some Analytical Perspectives

THEORETICAL PERSPECTIVES

John Rothgeb   181   Salient Features

David Neumeyer   197   Synthesis and Association, Structure and Design in Multi-Movement Compositions

Elizabeth West Marvin   217   Tonal/Atonal: Cognitive Strategies for Recognizing Transposed Melodies

Joseph N. Straus   237   Voice Leading in Atonal Music

Robert D. Morris   275   K, Kh, and Beyond

Part Two: Analytical Studies

THE TONAL REPERTOIRE

David W. Beach 309 The Submediant as Third Divider: Its Representation at Different Structural Levels

William Rothstein 337 The Form of Chopin's *Polonaise-Fantasy*

Robert P. Morgan 361 Chasing the Scent: Tonality in Liszt's *Blume und Duft*

Steven E. Gilbert 377 Reflections on a Few Good Tunes: Linear Progressions and Intervallic Patterns in Popular Song and Jazz

TWENTIETH-CENTURY MUSIC

Daniel Harrison 393 Bitonality, Pentatonicism, and Diatonicism in a Work by Milhaud

Robert W. Wason 409 Signposts on Webern's Path to Atonality: The *Dehmel Lieder* (1906-08)

David Lewin 433 Some Notes on *Pierrot Lunaire*

Christopher Hasty 459 Form and Idea in Schoenberg's *Phantasy*

Ann K. McNamee 481 Elision and Structural Levels in Peter Maxwell Davies's *Dark Angels*

INDEX 521

CONTRIBUTORS

JAMES M. BAKER is Professor of Music at Brown University.

DAVID W. BEACH is Dean and Professor, Faculty of Music, University of Toronto.

JONATHAN W. BERNARD is Professor of Music Theory in the School of Music, University of Washington.

PATRICIA CARPENTER is Professor Emerita at Barnard College, Columbia University.

STEVEN E. GILBERT is Professor of Music at California State University, Fresno.

DANIEL HARRISON is Associate Professor in the College Music Program at the University of Rochester, and Associate Professor of Music Theory at the University's Eastman School of Music.

CHRISTOPHER HASTY is Associate Professor of Music at the University of Pennsylvania.

DAVID LEWIN is Walter W. Naumburg Professor of Music at Harvard University.

ELIZABETH WEST MARVIN is Associate Professor and Chair of Music Theory at the Eastman School of Music, University of Rochester.

ANN K. McNAMEE is Associate Professor of Music at Swarthmore College.

ROBERT P. MORGAN is Professor of Music at Yale University.

ROBERT D. MORRIS is Professor of Composition and Music Theory at the Eastman School of Music, University of Rochester.

DAVID NEUMEYER is Professor of Music and Director of Graduate Studies in the School of Music, Indiana University.

JOHN ROTHGEB is recently retired from the Department of Music, State University of New York at Binghamton.

WILLIAM ROTHSTEIN is Associate Professor of Music Theory at the Oberlin College Conservatory of Music.

JOSEPH N. STRAUS is Professor of Music at Queens College and the Graduate School of the City University of New York.

PIETER C. VAN DEN TOORN is Associate Professor of Music at the University of California, Santa Barbara.

ROBERT W. WASON is Associate Professor of Music Theory at the Eastman School of Music, University of Rochester.

ARNOLD WHITTALL is Professor (Emeritus) of Music Theory and Analysis at King's College, London.

INTRODUCTION

Music theory as a research discipline—separate and distinct from historical musicology—has gone through a period of notable expansion during the past four decades. This expansion began with the appearance of several new journals and a number of books devoted to issues of a specifically music-theoretical nature. Next came the founding, almost twenty years ago, of an independent professional organization, the Society for Music Theory, which continues to thrive today. And in recent years this burgeoning interest in music theory in all its aspects has spread from its point of origin, in North America, to England and subsequently to the European continent, where the process of disciplinary specialization on our side of the Atlantic, as reflected in histories of publication and in the establishment of professional societies, has been to a considerable extent replicated.

Surely prominent among the reasons for this rapid growth of music theory in the modern (post-WWII) era is a resurgence of attention to areas traditionally associated with the discipline, among them pedagogy, analysis, and the history of theory. As has often been pointed out, music theory is actually a much older discipline than historical musicology: the former extends back to classical antiquity, the latter could not even be said to exist before its first faint stirrings in the mid-eighteenth century. Ironically, the preeminence of historical musicology in the academy during the first half of the twentieth century left music theory the role of upstart, of newcomer, as it began its renascence from the marginalized position it had come to occupy to the status of intellectually respectable activity.

Today, in fact, if music theory seems to be expanding in every conceivable direction, this is probably the inevitable result of its emergence from a narrow and somewhat ignominious niche in the conservatory, where it functioned primarily as a training ground in general musicianship. Having come into its own in the modern university, music theory has been influenced by disciplines such as computer science, linguistics, mathematics, literary theory, gender studies, philosophy, aesthetics, and psychology. Throughout this process, however, three principal areas of study have remained at the heart of the enterprise. One is historical research, which includes efforts to trace the development of theoretical ideas and their philosophical bases. Another is the theory and analysis of common-practice tonality and its associated repertoire (including chromatic and "transitional" music), much though by no means all of it growing out of the work of Heinrich Schenker. The third area comprises the large body of work associated with the theory and analysis of post-tonal music, especially music identified with the "advanced" idioms of atonality and dodecaphony.

With the idea of reflecting these central preoccupations of music theory's recent past—extending, of course, to the present—we have organized the nineteen essays from the nineteen contributors to this volume into two broad categories: historical and theoretical perspectives on important issues in current research; and analytical studies of both tonal and post-tonal music. The following paragraphs provide a summary of what we have assembled, a collection that well represents the considerable diversity of philosophies and methodologies that now operates within the three areas of inquiry identified above.

It is altogether appropriate that several of the contributions dealing with the tonal repertoire engage in some fashion the theories of Schenker, whose work has had a major impact upon our understanding of tonal structure. John Rothgeb's essay, "Salient Features," discusses a basic tenet of Schenkerian theory: that prominent musical features —for instance, those brought to our attention by their rhythmic/metric articulations—are often not the primary carriers of musical content. In fact, quite often the opposite is the case: other features less apparent on first hearing, such as underlying pitch connections or voice leading, are often more important to structure and hence to musical meaning. The message is clear: we must not be led astray by what first catches our ears, but must look beyond the obvious to discover underlying connections. After providing several examples to illustrate this point, Rothgeb concludes with a detailed examination of Beethoven's Bagatelle, op. 126 no. 6.

More explicitly in an analytical vein are three further essays influenced by Schenker's ideas. David Beach studies the progression I-vi-IV(ii6)-V-I at different structural levels from the foreground to the deep middleground. He also considers difficulties that arise in interpreting the function of the submediant harmony in this progression when it is preceded by the dominant. Under what circumstances does the submediant function as a third divider between the tonic and subdominant, as opposed to prolonging the preceding dominant? After considering this question, Beach discusses several examples of this progression at increasingly expanded levels, ending with an analysis of Bach's Prelude in B Major from Book I of *The Well-Tempered Clavier*. The second essay in this group is Steven Gilbert's "Reflections on a Few Good Tunes." In answer to the question of what makes a good tune for improvisation, Gilbert points to the fact that the good ones exhibit two basic structural characteristics—clearly defined linear progressions (*Züge*) and supporting intervallic patterns. He examines excerpts from songs by such composers as Hoagy Carmichael, Duke Ellington, George Gershwin, Dizzy Gillespie, Jerome Kern, Morgan Lewis, Ray Noble, Charlie Parker, and Cole Porter.[1] Third is William Rothstein, whose study of Chopin's *Polonaise-Fantasy,* op. 61, focuses on its formal

---

1. Among its other homages, this essay nods meaningfully in the direction of Allen Forte's recent involvement in the analysis of popular song. See Allen Forte, "Secrets of Melody: Line and Design in the Songs of Cole Porter," *Musical Quarterly* 77 (1993): 607–47; idem., *The American Popular Ballad of the Golden Era, 1924–1950* (Princeton: Princeton Univesity Press, 1995).

organization but also presents a durational reduction of the entire piece (excepting the introduction), with accompanying discussion of phrase rhythm and expansion and graphs of its underlying voice leading. Formally, this work is related to the Polonaise in A♭ Major, op. 53, and to the Fantasy, op. 49; by combining the formal and motivic features of these two works, Chopin created a hybrid form that is "far more complex, ambiguous, and troubling than either of its models." At the largest level the form is based on a simple song form, the quatrain, which is expanded through extensive interpolations.

Two further contributions also reveal the influence of Schenkerian thinking, although in neither case is the connection as explicit as in the four essays enumerated above. David Neumeyer develops a model for describing structural connections in multi-movement works for concert and stage, in functional dance music, and in music for film. After a brief survey of the pertinent literature, Neumeyer considers the mechanisms available in Schenkerian theory for treating the connection of independent units, taking as a point of departure connections between pairs in which the structure of the first unit is either closed or open; from there he progresses to a consideration of relationships within entire collections or sets. Central to his investigation is an examination of several binary oppositions (autonomous piece versus cycle, tonal versus associative connections, issues of structure versus design, and so forth), their logical negations, and their combination into a new synthesis, an approach borrowed in this instance from the field of semiotics. Robert Morgan's contribution is an analytical study of a single piece, Liszt's *Blume und Duft*, a song that has received considerable attention in the literature. Allen Forte's analysis of this work is limited to the consideration of octatonicism in two passages;[2] Morgan, by contrast, is concerned with its overall organization, which as he points out is resistant to either an octatonic or a tonal interpretation. His initial reading shows the prolongation of an A♭ triad throughout (without the aid of its dominant), an interpretation whose problems he then discusses. Features that contradict this initial reading lead to an alternate interpretation and sketch hinging upon the prolongation of A major! Neither is judged by the author to be a satisfactory explanation of the song's crucial features. Morgan concludes that the song's tonal ambiguity is inseparable from its expressive character and, of course, from the text. The two Lisztian features described in Forte's analysis—the one traditional, the other experimental—work hand in hand here: the song is "still (somehow) tonal yet significantly independent of the norms of traditional tonal syntax."

Markedly different from, in some ways even opposed to the Schenkerian view of tonal structure are the theories of Arnold Schoenberg, which have undergone something of a revival within the theoretical community in recent years. Patricia Carpenter explores Schoenberg's concept of tonality as a conflict of forces, of attraction and repulsion. She traces his ideas on this subject throughout his writings and

---

2. Allen Forte, "Liszt's Experimental Idiom and Music of the Early Twentieth Century," *Nineteenth-Century Music* 10 (1987): 209–28.

discusses in some detail his analysis of the first movement of Brahms's Sextet, op. 36, as set forth in *Der musikalische Gedanke und die Logik, Technik, und Kunst seiner Darstellung* (1934).[3]

Of course, it is also highly appropriate that Schoenberg the composer be represented in the present volume. Two of the analytical studies deal with individual compositions by Schoenberg. Like Carpenter, Christopher Hasty takes Schoenberg's own writings—in his case those on form and idea, together with the notion of "comprehensibility"—as a point of departure. More specifically, he takes comments from Schoenberg's late essay, "Brahms the Progressive," as inspiration for his own very detailed examination of the opening measures of Schoenberg's late composition, *Phantasy for Violin with Piano Accompaniment,* op. 47 (1949). Hasty terms his approach "temporal-processive," a type of analysis that attempts to include aesthetic categories (categories of feeling) along with close study of formal and motivic processes. David Lewin's contribution is a detailed analysis of the opening eleven measures of "Mondestrunken," the first song of *Pierrot Lunaire,* op. 21. Like Morgan, Lewin takes comments by Forte as a point of departure for his own analysis, an endeavor which draws on Lewin's own recently published work on musical transformation. Thus his essay, in addition to shedding some new light on the Schoenberg piece, also illustrates the analytical application of Lewin's theories.

Two of the essays in the section on "Theoretical Perspectives" deal with theoretical issues arising from atonal music. Robert Morris presents an extension of Forte's theory of the set complex (as expounded in *The Structure of Atonal Music* [1973]), coupled with a reformulation of his theory of pitch-class-set genera.[4] Morris finds the notion of the set complex, despite the scant attention it has received in the theoretical literature, a useful tool. He proposes a refinement of it, the KI relation, which limits the inclusion relations to the two sets under consideration (thus excluding the complements which Forte's K and Kh relations engage). From this he develops a "KI complex" and applies it to the analysis of "From the Island of Bali," no. 109 in Bartók's *Mikrokosmos,* and of the first movement of Varèse's *Octandre.* The second essay in this category is Joseph Straus's "Voice Leading in Atonal Music," based on a transformational approach in which emphasis "is shifted from the objects to the transformations that connect them." Initially, Straus confines his investigation to mappings (voice connections) between pairs of elements in equivalent sets as "classically" defined—that is, sets of identical cardinality related by T and/or I. The limitations imposed by this condition are then taken to suggest the usefulness of relations termed "near-transposition" and "near-inversion," which obtain between two sets of identical

---

3. This work of Schoenberg's remained unpublished until the recent issuance of the bilingual edition, *The Musical Idea and the Logic, Technique, and Art of Its Presentation,* ed., trans., and with commentary by Patricia Carpenter and Severine Neff (New York: Columbia University Press, 1995).

4. Allen Forte, "Pitch-Class Set Genera and the Origin of Modern Harmonic Species," *Journal of Music Theory* 32 (1988): 187–270.

cardinality when all but one element in each can be mapped into the other by T and/or I. Straus concludes that we should not be seeking in atonal music the type of unified hierarchy set forth by Schenker for tonal music; rather, we should embrace its multiplicity and diversity—speaking not of *the* voice leading, but of voice leading*s*, in atonal music.

Elizabeth West Marvin's study, "Tonal/Atonal: Cognitive Strategies for Recognizing Transposed Melodies," adopts a theoretical perspective not otherwise represented in this book. Reviewing previous studies in the literature of music cognition/perception that have dealt with recognition of both transposed and untransposed melodies of tonal and atonal types, Marvin shows that while valuable information has been amassed about the ways in which musicians and nonmusicians perform such tasks under experimental conditions, certain flaws in the design of these experiments have left questions unanswered about the differences in strategies employed by different segments of the experimental population, especially with regard to atonal melodies. Marvin then offers an experiment of improved design and reports results from its administration which suggest reasons for differences in ability to recognize sameness and difference in tonal as opposed to atonal melodies, as well as reasons for differences in performance between musicians and nonmusicians, between musicians with perfect pitch and those without, and between male and female subjects.

Three essays, though in many respects very different from one another, have in common a concern with the integration of conflicting or, at least, potentially conflicting forces in twentieth-century music. This concern, as the various placements of these essays in this book show, is as much a historical as an analytical matter. In his study of the interaction of pentatonic and diatonic sets within a bitonal context (the first movement of Milhaud's Second Chamber Symphony), Daniel Harrison argues that the family of bitonal set classes and those of 5-cycle (pentatonic and diatonic) set classes do not necessarily operate independently but may work toward reinforcing the same pitch-class structure. That is, they are not to be viewed as competing or unrelated structural parameters but, at least as they occur in the work under analysis here, as mutually supportive elements. Pieter van den Toorn comes to a very different conclusion in his examination of conflicting forces (the old versus the new) in Stravinsky's neoclassic works. We must understand this music, says van den Toorn, not as organic in the sense of tonal or (Schoenbergian) twelve-tone music, but rather in terms of opposition, of superimposition not only of segments, sets, and chords, but of referential collections as well. His development of this argument proceeds by way of consideration of various approaches—both motivic and tonal, informed by the interaction of the octatonic Collection I with the diatonic C-scale—to analysis of the first movement of Stravinsky's *Symphony in Three Movements*. Arnold Whittall grapples with the complex issue of balance between diversity/fragmentation and unity/continuity in modernist music. To demonstrate the wide range of styles that crowds under the umbrella of "modernism," he engages in a comparison of the musical and aesthetic qualities of works by two very different composers, Elliott Carter and Harrison Birtwistle.

One additional contribution to the category of post-tonal analysis is Ann

McNamee's study of Peter Maxwell Davies's *Dark Angels,* a cycle of three pieces for voice and guitar. McNamee discusses the balance between musical and poetic form in each piece; she discusses the use of "structural intervals" and their combination into central motives with multiple forms, as well as the hierarchical structures that result from the interaction of several levels of melodic motives; and she presents evidence of two types of elision operating in this work.

Finally, the three remaining essays are, to varying degrees, historical in nature (though one has enough of an analytical slant to warrant placing it in the second half of the book). James Baker's essay explores the roots of Scriabin's adherence to the Theosophical movement and the influence of this mystical religion on his music. The first part traces the forces that shaped his convictions about the state of the universe; the second part reveals how some of these ideas—for instance, a cosmology based on the number seven—are reflected in the structure of his music. Without an awareness of these beliefs, we cannot have a full understanding of the *meaning* of Scriabin's music—though of course this knowledge should complement, not replace analysis based on purely "musical" criteria. Jonathan Bernard's essay fills a major lacuna in twentieth-century history by recounting the development of ideas, beginning with Schoenberg's *Harmonielehre* (1911) and other treatises published around the same time, that led eventually to Allen Forte's writings on pitch-class set theory. Bernard identifies four principal themes that organize the history of harmonic theory during this period (c. 1900–60): first, a progressive enlargement of the harmonic sphere; second, a growing fascination with exhaustive classification of the structures arising from this enlargement; third, a new kind of organizing principle based on the ordered disposition of the twelve tones of the chromatic scale; and fourth, an increasing tendency to consider melody and harmony as functionally equivalent. And Robert Wason's contribution, an analytic study of Webern's *Dehmel Lieder,* examines an early stage on the composer's path to atonality. In these works, never published during Webern's lifetime, we see the beginning of a process whereby conventional harmonies are replaced by motivically connected "referential sonorities." Though the methodologies differ, the present study is quite clearly patterned on Allen Forte's earlier article treating the transition from tonality to atonality in Schoenberg's music.[5]

*   *   *

The list of individuals who have played important roles in the modern rise of music theory would no doubt fill several pages. It would include both musicologists and composers, as well as others who could not readily be classified as either. But it would be safe to say that no single individual has been more central to these developments than Allen Forte. His early books *Contemporary Tone-Structures* (1955) and

---

5. Allen Forte, "Schoenberg's Creative Evolution: The Path to Atonality," *Musical Quarterly* 64 (1978): 133–76.

The Compositional Matrix (1961) were noteworthy titles on the very short list of theoretically-oriented monographs published during those years. His textbook *Tonal Harmony in Concept and Practice* (1962) was a milestone in contemporary theory pedagogy, the first such book to combine traditional instruction in harmony with insights gained from Schenkerian theory and analysis. Shortly after joining the faculty of the Yale School of Music in 1959, he assumed the editorship of the fledgling *Journal of Music Theory* and, over a period of seven years, brought this journal from the somewhat quirky and tenuous quality of its early issues to professional standards of content and production, and to international visibility. He was among the small group that spearheaded the initiative to found the Society for Music Theory in 1977, and was the natural choice for its first President. And upon moving from the School to the Department of Music at Yale in 1965, he gave crucial impetus to the establishment of a doctoral degree program in music theory—the first of its kind at a major research university—and has since served as advisor to more than sixty successful Ph.D. candidates, many of whom have gone on to notable scholarly careers of their own and have helped establish and sustain graduate programs in theory at universities throughout the United States and Canada.

Last but certainly not least, it is Allen Forte's scholarship, especially the articles and books he has published since the early 1960s, that has largely defined the scope and direction of the field of music theory over the past decades. In the course of the foregoing overview, we had occasion several times to refer to his work. This should hardly be surprising, for its impact, over a wide range of topics, will be clearly evident to all who read the present book. Several of the essays included here are based directly on his work or take his observations as a point of departure, as has been noted. But even where the influence is not obvious, it is most certainly there. On behalf of all his former students and his past and present professional colleagues who are represented in this book, we honor Allen Forte and acknowledge what he has given us.

James M. Baker
David W. Beach
Jonathan W. Bernard
March, 1997

PART ONE:
HISTORICAL AND THEORETICAL ESSAYS

Chord, Collection, and Set in Twentieth-Century Theory

Jonathan W. Bernard

> On a related topic, I also want to say that I did not invent the
> unordered pitch-class set. That was the creation of a far higher
> power—and I don't mean Milton Babbitt.
> —Allen Forte[1]

O ver approximately the past three decades, during a period that can be
said to commence with the appearance in 1964 of Allen Forte's article
"A Theory of Set-Complexes for Music" and to continue with the publication nine years later of *The Structure of Atonal Music*, the discipline
of music theory, developing into its modern (and present-day) form, has come to
accept Forte's formulation of the pitch-class set, together with his enumeration of set
classes and the bases he laid down for relating sets of like and unlike cardinalities
and for applying them to analysis, as a kind of fundamental standard for the study of
the pitch dimension of twentieth-century music: a standard to which various modifications and additions have been proposed, and some even widely adopted, without
altering its essence.[2] The great relevance and multifarious applicability of the pitch-
class set, already amply demonstrated in our professional literature, has understandably left many theorists less curious than they might otherwise be about its prehistory;
having now almost the status of a "paradigm"—to use that term that music theorists

This essay was written during a period of sabbatical leave (1994–95) from the University of
Washington, whose support is hereby gratefully acknowledged. I would also like to express
my thanks to Robert Wason, Daniel Harrison, Elizabeth West Marvin, Catherine Nolan,
and John Covach for their bibliographic assistance and other advice rendered at various stages
of my work on this essay; and to the students of my graduate seminar in the history of theory
at the University of Washington in Spring 1992, in which many of the writings treated in this
essay were read and fruitfully discussed.

1. Allen Forte, "Banquet Address: SMT, Rochester 1987," *Music Theory Spectrum* 11 (1989):
95–99.

2. Allen Forte, "A Theory of Set-Complexes for Music," *Journal of Music Theory* 8 (1964):
136–83; Forte, *The Structure of Atonal Music* (New Haven and London: Yale University Press, 1973).

most love to borrow, not entirely justifiably, from science—its existence is all too easily taken for granted. Especially for those of us who were not "present at the creation," a group that by now includes all but the most senior practitioners of the discipline, what came before the pitch-class set has remained largely obscure. Even now—to say nothing of a generation ago—history-of-theory curricula in graduate theory programs have a way of stopping with Schoenberg's *Harmonielehre* (1911), perhaps in part because it was right around this same time that Heinrich Schenker began to produce his major works, the books that in the modern theoretical world have come to define the end of the history of tonal music theory.[3] This, however, leaves a gap of a good fifty years in the history of theory as it engages music of the post- common-practice period. And it leaves unanswered the question: How did we get from the nineteenth-century theory of harmony (however supplemented with novelties in the first decades of the twentieth) to the theory of the set complex?

It is with the idea that the *Entwicklungsgeschichte* of the intervening years might be worth knowing more about that the present essay came to be written.[4] It is a peculiar history in many ways, hardly a straightforward linear progression: full of duplicated effort, reinventings of the wheel, and seemingly inexplicable conceptual leaps. Perhaps most unexpected is the definite impression that begins to form as to the lack of *inevitability* about the emergence of the pc set, that as late as midcentury the tendency toward comprehensive accounting for pitch combinations in the twelve-note universe might have led to a very different result by the 1960s than the one that actually came about. By tracing this history in the pages that follow, I hope to show: first, that important conceptual groundwork for pc-set theory was being laid even before Schoenberg's *Harmonielehre*, that this process continued throughout the first half of the twentieth century, and that the last pieces of the puzzle, as it were, did not fall into place until relatively soon before pc-set theory emerged full-blown; and second, that this process, and this emergence, may well have been repertoire-driven to a greater extent than previously supposed.

Four principal themes organize the history of harmonic theory during this period. The first is a progressive enlargement of the harmonic sphere, as more and more structures are accepted as fundamental beyond the "stacks of thirds" whose origins can be traced back to the work of Rameau. The second, related to the first, is a growing interest in classifying these new structures, leading eventually to compre-

---

3. This statement, by the way, is by no means meant to denigrate any of the important work done in tonal theory over the past few decades. It is simply an acknowledgment of the present state of graduate theory curricula, and the general tendency within the discipline of theory to regard such books as Fred Lerdahl and Ray Jackendoff's *A Generative Theory of Tonal Music* (Cambridge, Mass.: MIT Press, 1983) as "current events" rather than "history."

4. For two much shorter studies treating some of the same material, see: *Dictionary of Contemporary Music,* ed. John Vinton, s.v. "Theory" (Allen Forte), 753–61; Janet Schmalfeldt, *Berg's "Wozzeck": Harmonic Language and Dramatic Design* (New Haven and London: Yale University Press, 1983), Introduction ("Pitch-Class Set Theory: Historical Perspective"), 1–13.

hensive systems that aimed to organize all possible combinations of pitches and/or intervals into a readily accessible and usable framework. A third theme enters with a new kind of organizing principle, based upon the ordered disposition of the twelve notes of the chromatic scale, which in conjunction with the second theme assured the absolute reign of enharmonic equivalence and the establishment of what Paul Lansky has called "pitch- class consciousness."[5] The fourth theme, finally, is an increasing tendency to regard "harmony" and "melody," rather than as entirely separate musical functions (even if operating in the same musical space), instead as integral and therefore functionally equivalent. In this last development may be witnessed the decided reversal of a trend already well established by the middle of the eighteenth century (and, some might say, even a good deal earlier than that): as the definition of *harmony* coalesced ever more firmly into the concept of *chord* as self-sufficient vertical entity, to be explained in terms of that dimension alone, theories of tonal harmony and counterpoint became ever more rigidly separated. Radical revisions in compositional practice beginning around 1900 served as an impetus to theorists' efforts to reintegrate the vertical and the horizontal.

I

The treatises of the early decades of the twentieth century certainly show that the expanding harmonic vocabularies of the post-Wagnerian period had begun to make it imperative for theorists to find ways of expanding their own vocabularies as well. For the most part, the attempts made in this direction were conceived as supplements to the older harmonic theory that had served for tonal music up to about 1850, and as such did not provide any fundamentally new ideas about pitch combination; however, in important ways they set the stage for developments that were to follow. The works of four authors in the 1900s and 1910s—one French, one English, one

---

5. Paul Lansky, "Pitch-Class Consciousness," *Perspectives of New Music* 13, no. 2 (Spring-Summer 1975): 30–56. Even before the turn of the century, certain theorists in German-speaking countries were providing foreglimpses of such consciousness. In his *Harmoniesystem* (1859), Carl Friedrich Weitzmann renounced the mathematical purity of just intonation in favor of enharmonic equivalence and presented arguments in favor of recognizing previously unfamiliar sonorities as legitimate components of harmonic language once they had become self-sufficient through repeated use—arguments that would be taken up again by Schoenberg half a century later. And H. J. Vincent, in *Ist unsere Harmonielehre wirklich eine Theorie?* (1894), went so far as to recommend a twelve-pc notation and symbology, including numerical designations for intervals that accurately reflected their semitonal size, and cast aspersions on the figured bass for representing only the intervals of a chord in relation to the bass, not all the others contained in the chord as well. See Robert Wason, "Progressive Harmonic Theory in the Mid-Nineteenth Century," *Journal of Musicological Research* 8 (1988): 55–90.

German, and one German-American—will serve us here as examples of this state of affairs.

René Lenormand's *Etude sur l'harmonie moderne* (1912) is the most conservative of the four; even so, it contains some interesting material, especially in Chapter 11 ("Other Harmonies").[6] Lenormand's initial concern in this, the longest chapter in his book is to interpret chromaticism in terms of altered notes within the context of ninth, eleventh, and thirteenth chords. It soon becomes evident that any member of his stacked-third structures may be altered; some examples from actual musical works are also explored in terms of substitution (such as the sixth substituting for the fifth in his Ex. 7).[7] Eventually, even the fifth of a seventh chord becomes eligible for alteration (Exx. 32, 34).[8] Meanwhile, other forces are adduced that suggest contrapuntal rather than strictly harmonic explanations: appoggiatura, retardation (suspension), pedal point, and the generically "linear." None of these is particularly innovative, compared to previous harmonic theory, although the examples of application are somewhat novel— even that of the added sixth, which as a concept is no different from Rameau's identification of it nearly 200 years earlier. More adventurous are the applications of whole-tone harmony, "succession by conjunct degrees" (parallel harmony), and bitonality. A fairly large miscellaneous category, including a series of examples from Satie's works, reveals the author attempting to cover every empirically encountered possibility of vertical formation without, however, showing explicitly how such formations and their temporal succession can be brought under the explanatory umbrella of the old laws of harmonic progression.

More comprehensive, farther-ranging, but equally empirical in approach is Arthur Eaglefield Hull's *Modern Harmony* (1914), a work which evidently aims to be a compendium of modern techniques for the student (since it takes the nominal shape of a textbook, complete with suggested exercises at the end) but which, in part owing to its sheer scope, ends up being a somewhat unwieldy hodge-podge.[9] It is clear that Hull has learned a certain amount from his study of Schoenberg's work, both theoretical and compositional: he has lifted, without attribution, several examples from the *Harmonielehre* into his own book, either exactly as Schoenberg had them or slightly altered, among them the eleven-note chord from *Erwartung*; but Hull on his own initiative has also quoted several passages from the *Kammersymphonie*, the *Drei Klavierstücke*, and the *Fünf Orchesterstücke*, extremely new pieces then and scarcely known—or even known of, one would imagine—in England. His brief analysis of the *Kammersymphonie*, though woefully inadequate and with some examples not

---

6. René Lenormand, *Etude sur l'harmonie moderne* (1912), trans. Herbert Antcliffe as *A Study of Twentieth-Century Harmony* (London: Joseph Williams, 1915).

7. Lenormand, 109.

8. Lenormand, 122–23.

9. Arthur Eaglefield Hull, *Modern Harmony: Its Explanation and Application* (London: Augener Ltd., [1914]).

even accurately transcribed from the score, does have the surprising distinction of predating Berg's famous analysis of this work by several years.[10] Although Hull's choices of illustration tend to favor then-recent French and English repertoire, the Germans and Russians are also well represented; there are even occasional forays into American music.

Apart from a cursory and rather half-hearted attempt, by way of introduction, to explain contemporary practice in terms of loosening of old strictures, Hull's book divides into three main sections, devoted respectively to scales, chords, and modern trends in melody, rhythm, and form. Perhaps predictably, the chapters on scales are devoted to modal, whole-tone, chromatic, and "other," miscellaneous or unclassifiable varieties. In these chapters chord structure is not addressed directly, but only (if at all) as a general function of the global possibilities of the particular scale under consideration. However, at the beginning of Chapter 5 (on the whole-tone scale), Hull remarks that "many of the newer chords, and also the new methods of chord-structure, were first predicted melodically,"[11] in which one detects the germ of the idea that, with the hegemony of the twelve-tone equally tempered scale established beyond question, the horizontal and vertical dimensions of pitch structure might approach some kind of equivalence. At any rate, in this chapter one finds more systematic enumeration of verticalized extractions from the scale (that is, chords) than in any of the other scalar chapters—perhaps only because the number of possibilities within the whole-tone scale is severely limited. Later, in Chapter 6 ("Other Scales"), Scriabin's "favourite chord" (the mystic chord) is explicitly discussed as scalar and chordal phenomenon.[12] Hull further explores this chord's potential as a kind of source set for triads, sevenths, and thirteenth chords (Ex. 1)—structures, that is, with tonal associations, echoing his sentiments, expressed elsewhere in the book, that all the resources of modern harmony ought best be regarded as supplementing, not supplanting, the traditional tonal ones.

The chapters on chords (7–12) proceed from altered triads, sevenths, ninths, and so forth, to chords produced by various additive processes, to alternatives to the traditional standards of third-stacking using intervals both like and unlike in size and quality, to the catch-all categories of "Impressionistic Methods" and "Horizontal Methods," the latter including polytonality. Hull places a high value on empiricism in the discovery of new possibilities; his expository method often seems context-sensitive to a fault, for since practically every example illustrates something different, general principles of structure and application remain elusive. But the sheer

---

10. Hull, *Modern Harmony*, 186-87; Alban Berg, *Arnold Schönberg. Kammersymphonie Op. 9: Thematische Analyse* (Vienna: Universal, [n.d.]). Estimates of the actual date of publication of Berg's analysis range from 1918 to 1921. See Walter Frisch, *The Early Works of Arnold Schoenberg, 1893-1908* (Berkeley and Los Angeles: University of California Press, 1993), 221n.

11. Hull, 53.

12. Hull, 72.

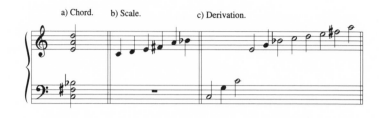

Example 1. Hull, *Modern Harmony*, 72–73.

breadth of repertoire covered is impressive, and one comes away impressed too with the author's courage in grappling with scalar and harmonic vocabulary that had hardly yet even been heard, much less absorbed.

Far more extensive and venturesome than either of these two works is Schoenberg's treatise.[13] Indeed, the difference is almost one of kind rather than of degree: unlike Hull or Lenormand, Schoenberg buttresses his verbal presentation (which is also much more extensive and philosophically discursive than that supplied by either of his contemporaries) with invented, mostly strictly chordal (therefore "artificial") musical examples, with only a few excerpts from actual pieces. This approach lends itself well to a more comprehensive or "encyclopedic" accounting of the possibilities of altered sevenths and ninths, for instance, even if Schoenberg is at pains to point out that his concocted examples illustrate only musical situations that he knows exist or of which he is certain that an example could be found. Such abundance is certainly very far from comprehensive accounting for its own sake, but it is easy to see how Schoenberg's eagerness to uncover myriad new possibilities of harmonic construction and succession (not to mention the remarkable powers of invention he demonstrated in doing so) might have inspired others to take up the second

---

13. Arnold Schoenberg, *Harmonielehre* (1911; 3d ed. 1922), trans. Roy E. Carter from 3d ed. as *Theory of Harmony* (Berkeley and Los Angeles: University of California Press, 1978).

of the four principal themes enumerated above. For his part, Schoenberg is content to proceed empirically, as he makes especially clear in his final chapter, on "chords of six or more tones": to do otherwise could imply a claim to have discovered laws, which he is willing to forego in favor of doing nothing more than "describe."[14]

Schoenberg also goes much further than Hull or Lenormand in supplementing the stacked-third system. His well-known work with the whole-tone vocabulary and chords in fourths remains, in a nominal yet important sense, within the orbit of "tonality," for all of these new chords appear with resolutions to third-based chords, and (usually) eventually to concluding triads. Yet while Lenormand, for example, is content merely to point out that the six-tone whole-tone sonority can be derived from the regular dominant ninth chord by simultaneously flatting and raising its fifth, Schoenberg puts the same whole- tone chord through many permutations and alternatives of preparation and resolution. And in his prose treatment of these supplementing sonorities he reveals a far more capacious vision than either of the other men, explaining the six-member whole-tone chord as the union of augmented triads a step apart and seeing in the chord in fourths a solution to the problem of eventual replication of tones in stacked-third constructions, allowing (of course) as many as all twelve tones in a single chord, if desired. This is no more evidence of a nascent "twelve-tone method" than his many examples are evidence of a yearning for comprehensive accounting, yet surely Hauer, for one, must have been struck by the implications of such "universal" structures as the extendible chord in fourths.[15]

Schoenberg also takes a palpable step towards *collectional* thinking at such junctures; bearing in mind that Rameau's idea of equivalence of function under inversion is already remotely collectional in its implications (compared to figured-bass theory for instance), and that Schoenberg had also freed the ninth chord from the old prohibition against involving the ninth itself in inversion, we must recognize in the new attention to whole-tone chords and chords in fourths the emergence of a collectional sensibility. The very symmetrical nature of these structures must have had something to do with this development: with their limited number of distinctly different configurations, it is easier to think of them as functioning much the same way in *any* orientation, allowing of course for the exigencies of conjunct voice leading and other contextual factors. Finally, the *Harmonielehre* points the way as well toward development of the fourth theme, horizontal-vertical equivalence, without explicitly engaging it. It is apparently enough for Schoenberg to hint that such equivalence is *possible* under the conditions produced by the newly extended vocabulary— without, however, showing in more than a rudimentary way (such as arpeggiation) how such a possibility might actually be realized.

---

14. Schoenberg, *Theory of Harmony*, 421.

15. That Hauer did read the *Harmonielehre* and derive some rather important lessons from it seems clear from the evidence presented in Bryan Simms, "Who First Composed Twelve-Tone Music, Schoenberg or Hauer?," *Journal of the Arnold Schoenberg Institute* 10 (1987): 109–33.

"Advanced" harmonies are also of special interest to Bernhard Ziehn, as is evident in his *Manual of Harmony* (1907) and *Five- and Six-Part Harmonies* (1911).[16] More explicit in Ziehn's work than in Schoenberg's is an encyclopedic bent, a pronounced tendency to work out systematically all the possible ways of resolving a given chord or altering a diatonic harmony.[17] For example, in the *Manual of Harmony*, Ziehn presents a résumé of altered seventh chords in which all the chromatic alternatives for filling the interval of a minor or diminished seventh with stacked thirds (aside from those that would produce the "standard" varieties of sevenths such as major-minor, diminished, and so forth) are laid out (Ex. 2). These formations could be said to anticipate Schoenberg, but in a sense they also outdo him, for they verge on the speculative (not surprising, perhaps, in someone who had more formal training in mathematics than in music), an area into which Schoenberg himself felt little inclination to venture.

In the briefer *Five- and Six-Part Harmonies*, the limited space is taken up mainly by strictly chordal examples, almost entirely of the author's own invention, with even less prose commentary than in the already rather terse *Manual*. In both works, the reader is effectively invited to learn by example rather than precept. Ziehn devotes more attention here than he did in the *Manual* to ninth chords and their alterations. Unlike Schoenberg, he does not treat whole-tone chords as a separate category, contenting himself with pointing out (as did Lenormand) that the dominant ninth chord with augmented and diminished fifth presents "the whole-tone in concert [*im Zusammenklang*],"[18] and he does not treat fourth chords at all. But Ziehn does treat a topic not addressed by Schoenberg: symmetrical (mirror) inversion. Several braces' worth of examples are inverted in this fashion, with dotted barlines connecting the inversion with the original, "upright" forms. Example 3 is a typical illustration of this technique: the axis of inversion is always D4, as it is also in Ziehn's contrapuntal writings, such as the *Canonic Studies* (1912). Ziehn shared with several of his contemporaries, particularly Georg Capellen, a fascination with the new harmonic resources and progressions opened up by symmetric inversion, though he claimed to have hit upon the technique on his own through the study of Renaissance theory and practice. One of the many interesting ironies of theory's historical development is that the idea of symmetrical inversion, which evidently originated in harmonic dualism—specifically in the work of Hugo Riemann—was perpetuated (even popularized, if such a term can be used to characterize music theory) by theorists who were either

---

16. Bernhard Ziehn, *Manual of Harmony* (Milwaukee: Wm. A. Kaun Music Co., 1907), trans. from *Harmonie- und Modulationslehre* (Berlin, 1887/88); *Five-and Six-Part Harmonies and How to Use Them* (Milwaukee: Wm. A. Kaun, 1911).

17. Severine Neff discusses this aspect of Ziehn's work and its later influence on Ernst Bacon in her article, "An American Precursor of Non-Tonal Theory: Ernst Bacon (1898–1990)," *Current Musicology* 48 (1991): 5–26.

18. Like most of Ziehn's books published in the United States, this one was produced as a bilingual edition, with parallel German and English text.

The chromatic Seventh-chords with the diminished Thirds b d♭ and d♯ f.

An inversion of these chords showing the augmented Sixth instead of the diminished Third.

Example 2. Ziehn, *Manual of Harmony*, 22.

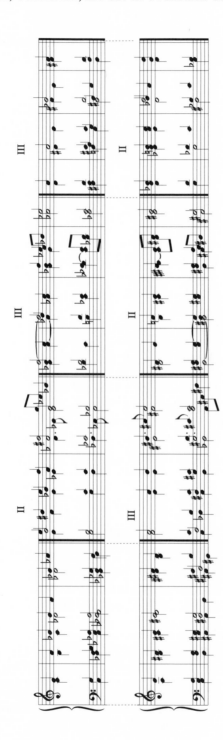

Example 3. Ziehn, *Five- and Six-Part Harmonies*, 11.

skeptical of or openly hostile to Riemann's work.[19] But it would be well not to over-look the fact that something crucial was lost in the translation of symmetrical inver-sion out of the "language" of dualism: namely, that the idea of one "generating" the other in any real, acoustical sense no longer obtained, and consequently there could no longer be any question of *equivalence* between the upright and inverted material. This circumstance may well explain why, as we will see, it apparently never occurred to Ernst Bacon, whose primary musical training was accomplished through study of Ziehn's works, to consider chords related by mirror inversion as equivalent, in the same way as were forms in open and close spacing or in different vertical orderings.

II

After perusing the foregoing attempts to come to grips with the multitudinous pos-sibilities of modern harmony—all, no matter how far afield they range, ultimately informed by nineteenth-century ideas of tonal harmony as augmented by chromati-cism—it comes as something of a shock to encounter the work of Ernst Bacon, who only a few years after the theorists discussed above, in 1917, determined to map out exhaustively the melodic and harmonic possibilities of the twelve-note universe, not only independently of tonal context, but independently of any context at all. That he did this at the age of nineteen, and that his findings withstand the scrutiny of a disci-pline now, eighty years later, far more exacting about such matters, can only be cause for further astonishment. Some of the mystery is dispelled when one learns that Ba-con studied with one of Ziehn's former pupils and apparently was drawn, through this exposure, to the challenge implicit in carrying Ziehn's ideas further, enumerat-ing all conceivable manipulations of pitch materials. Nevertheless, Bacon's decision to attack the problem with algebraic tools, thereby surmounting the hazards of trial-and-error empiricism and the biases endemic to the ingrained habits of tonality, was truly a bold and innovative step.

In his article-treatise, "Our Musical Idiom," Bacon takes an essentially two-pronged approach, investigating first the horizontal dimension (scales), then the ver-tical (harmonies).[20] Imposing what amounts to a criterion of well-formedness, Ba-con excludes all intervals larger than a major third from eligibility as adjacencies in his scales; he does not consider any additional species that might result from exceed-

---

19. For a penetrating treatment of the relationship between Capellen's, Ziehn's, and oth-ers' ideas on the subject, see David W. Bernstein, "Symmetry and Symmetrical Inversion in Turn-of-the-Century Theory and Practice," in *Music Theory and the Exploration of the Past,* ed. Christopher Hatch and David W. Bernstein (Chicago: University of Chicago Press, 1993), 377–407. For an interesting history of dualism in music theory, see Daniel Harrison, *Har-monic Function in Chromatic Music: A Renewed Dualist Theory and an Account of Its Precedents* (Chicago: University of Chicago Press, 1994).

20. Ernst Bacon, "Our Musical Idiom," with an introduction by G. D. Gunn, *The Monist* 27 (1917): 560–607.

ing the bounds of an octave, but within this octave limit counts all permutations of constituent intervals separately. Having determined that there are thirty-four possible *unordered* combinations of eligible adjacent intervals summing to twelve semitones, he arrives at a grand total of 1490 possible orderings, or actual scales. Within this rather large array, Bacon shows special interest in the much smaller class of *equipartite* scales, his term for those exhibiting various degrees of transpositional symmetry, comprising the two basic types, *bipartite* and *tripartite*.[21]

As for harmonies (a term which Bacon prefers to "chords," evidently because, like Ziehn, he associates the latter exclusively with third-stacking), Bacon takes as his purview all cardinalities from two through twelve inclusive. As with the scales, adjacent intervallic content is crucial to identifying and distinguishing entities; unlike the scalar procedure, however, differences in order (in this case vertical, produced by simple rotation of the contents) are of no consequence, since these for Bacon are akin to the equivalences of function produced under (tonal) inversion. Bacon's 350 harmonies correspond one for one to the present-day "T_n types" for these cardinalities—since he does not recognize equivalence under the other ("mirror") type of inversion—and thus, indirectly, to the 222 *set classes*.[22]

Contemplating Bacon's résumé of scalar and harmonic resources, one is struck by a number of things. First, it is clear from his demonstration that *total* interval-class content is not a criterion necessary to the generation of an accurate list (even by modern lights) of set classes—although of course its absence from Bacon's methodology means that such features as inversional equivalence and the Z-relation are also absent. (For example, the two all-interval tetrachords are produced by Bacon from *different* interval combinations; in his accounting, what we now call [0146] and [0137] each have more in common with several other harmonies than they do with each other; see Ex. 4.)[23] Second, it is also clear that the idea of any equivalence between horizontal and vertical dimensions, whether from the point of view of composition or from that of analysis, is completely foreign to Bacon's sensibilities; there are of

---

21. This class obviously includes, among others, the octatonic scale and all of Olivier Messiaen's modes of limited transposition, the second of which is identical to the octatonic. For a more detailed summary of Bacon's article and an interesting discussion of its compositional implications, see Neff, "An American Precursor." I must point out, however, that Neff's characterization of equipartite scales as "inversionally symmetrical" (p. 14) is incorrect. This property is found only in some of the scales, as a by-product of the transpositional symmetry which for Bacon's purposes is the property crucially operative.

22. The terms "T_n-type" and "T_n/T_nI-type"—the latter the same as "set class"—were introduced by John Rahn in *Basic Atonal Theory* (New York: Schirmer Books, 1980). In this essay I follow his notational conventions for these types, using regular parentheses () for the former and square brackets [] for the latter.

23. "Our Musical Idiom," Table III (594–95). In Example 4, the headings "C.7" and "C.8" are Bacon's abbreviations for his serially numbered interval combinations. Bacon labels his interval stacks from bottom to top, with dashes separating the numbers; the T_n-types indicating the all-interval tetrachords and their inversions are my addition.

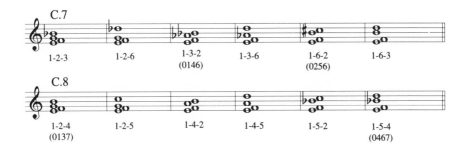

Example 4. Bacon, "Our Musical Idiom," 594–95.

course numerous overlaps between his scales, considered as unordered collections, and his harmonies, but since scales are ordered by definition, such correspondences, if Bacon even noticed them, would be of only trivial interest. Third, the idea of closest available spacing, with the smaller adjacent intervals as near to the bottom of the stack as possible, corresponds quite closely to the later formulation of normal order as a "canonic form" in which to represent set classes.[24]

In summary, Bacon's work is historical evidence that a comprehensive enumeration of harmonies in the twelve-note universe independent of any (later) developments in twelve-tone theory was certainly not impossible. That Bacon's work remained for all practical purposes unknown to anyone outside the "Chicago circle" anchored by Ziehn's former pupils and was eventually forgotten completely, only to be "rediscovered" in recent years, could plausibly be attributed to its publication in an obscure journal rarely if ever consulted by musicians. However, there may be another reason as well: that the significance of what Bacon had done could hardly have been appreciated, since it would not have seemed susceptible of much application to any music being written at that time, at least in the United States. Lacking such potential "usefulness," Bacon's feat perhaps seemed more like a freak, a stunt, than anything else. It would require the advent of the twelve-tone method to make such compilations of possible harmonies, most of them totally unsuited to a tonal context, of real interest to composers and theorists.[25]

---

24. Neff points out this correspondence (p. 18); of course, it is easy to see how such an idea might have occurred independently to different theorists, since it bears such a close resemblance to the representation of tonal harmonies in generic close position for the purposes of enumeration and study. In this connection, Neff's claim that Bacon "does not acknowledge pitch class" (p. 18) is puzzling. Certainly he did not use the term; nor did he convert his pitch notation to numbers (although he did use numbers as an intervallic shorthand). But substantively speaking, the notion of pitch class is integral to Bacon's theory; he could hardly have arrived at his list of harmonies otherwise.

25. Another, related sort of stunt was to be witnessed eight years later in an article by Fritz Heinrich Klein, "Die Grenze der Halbtonwelt" (*Die Musik* 17, no. 4 [January 1925]:

III

Such an advent was not in fact long off, though it occurred half a world away from Chicago. In an article entitled "Sphärenmusik," published in 1922, the Viennese Josef Matthias Hauer proposed a system of *tropes*, intended to regulate musical composition in conformance to the *Nomos*, or twelve-tone law, that he had announced two years previously in his book *Vom Wesen des Musikalischen*.[26] As is well known, Hauer had become convinced through his own researches and activity as a composer that music needed to free itself from the strictures of tonality and strive for an ideal, *atonal* state. To that end, the *Nomos* stipulated that the twelve notes of the chromatic scale be employed in as even distribution as possible to avoid the undue emphasis on any one of them that might create the impression, however fleeting, of a "fundamental" note.[27] Initially, because of its "intuitive" origins, the *Nomos* applied to groups of nine, ten, or eleven notes as well as to twelve, but one of Hauer's principal reasons for

---

281–86). Here the author makes the claim, quite accurate as it turns out, that there are 4095 possible chords (counting all transpositions separately) of cardinalities one through twelve inclusive. In Klein's article these were not actually enumerated beyond cardinality four (although readers were assured that the author had presented complete tables of his chords to the editors of the journal for verification), suggesting even more strongly than in Bacon's case that these constructs had no direct or immediate use. Klein's article is translated in full with extensive commentary by Dave Headlam in "Fritz Heinrich Klein's 'Die Grenze der Halbtonwelt' and *Die Maschine*," *Theoria* 6 (1992): 54–96. This enumeration, rediscovered yet again with a calculation certified by algebraic means, appears almost thirty years later in George Perle's article, "The Possible Chords in Twelve-Tone Music" (*The Score and I.M.A. Magazine* 9 [1954]: 54–58), issued as a corrective to Roberto Gerhard's erroneous reckoning in a previous article but done with no apparent awareness of Bacon's or Klein's work. (Perle's tallies for the separate cardinalities on p. 55 of his article actually total 4094, since he excludes cardinality twelve from consideration.)

26. Josef Matthias Hauer, "Sphärenmusik," *Melos* 3 (1922): 132–33; Hauer, *Vom Wesen des Musikalischen: Grundlagen der Zwölftonmusik* (1920), ed. Victor Sokolowski (Berlin: Robert Lienau, 1966).

27. Schoenberg, of course, was moving in a similar direction at the same time. In his *Harmonielehre* he had already written: "I have noticed that tone doublings, octaves, seldom appear [in new music]. The explanation for that is, perhaps, that the tone doubled would acquire a predominance over the others and would thereby turn into a kind of root, which it should scarcely be." (Schoenberg, *Theory of Harmony*, 420.) Later, he would accuse Hauer of paraphrasing this passage in *Vom Wesen* without attribution (see Simms, "Who First Composed Twelve-Tone Music?," 121–22). Schoenberg's own compositions of the decade 1913–23, both finished and unfinished, reveal a steadily increasing tendency towards the systematic use of the twelve-note aggregate. Finally, Webern in his lectures of the 1930s, collected in *The Path to the New Music*, trans. Leo Black (Bryn Mawr: Theodore Presser, 1963), recounted "the path to twelve-tone composition" as an intuitive process springing in part from the feeling that "when all twelve notes have gone by, the piece is over" (81).

introducing the tropes was to fix the size and configuration of these groups in the form of pairs of hexachords.

For the purposes of the present essay, it will not be necessary to provide a detailed account of the workings of these tropes, only to point out a few of their salient features and implications.[28] In "Sphärenmusik," Hauer referred to the eighty hexachords that he then called tropes. As Bryan Simms has summarized Hauer's approach at that time: "These were usable by the composer in different orderings, different transpositions, and different metric-rhythmic contexts, provided only that each melodic statement of a trope was juxtaposed with another hexachord with which it had no pitches in common. A pair of complementary tropes would thus create a twelve-tone block and satisfy the twelve-tone law."[29] These eighty hexachords, considered as intervallic structures, are congruent to Bacon's eighty six-note chords—and therefore, of course, are congruent to the modern list of hexachordal set classes augmented by the inverted forms of those set classes that are not inversionally symmetrical.

It is undeniably interesting that Bacon and Hauer, working independently, should have come up with results that are, certainly in one very important sense, "the same." (For one thing, the coincidence may show that, once Western musical practice had evolved to the point where the solution to the problem "What are all the possible chords in the twelve-note universe?" had become at least potentially useful to know, this solution was not all that difficult to find.) But that this happened should not distract us from the fact that Bacon's and Hauer's results, are *not*, in other senses, the same. Bacon did not regard his 350 harmonies as the gateway to a new, radical kind of music; he remained a conservative, tonally oriented composer, mostly of songs, throughout his life. For Hauer, the very opposite was true. Furthermore, it is clear from the way he devised his tropes that the point of the whole exercise was to enable him to compose coherently, by his lights, in a twelve-tone context—not simply to give him a whole range of potentially interesting chords to choose from. In fact, his tropes could be presented entirely in linear fashion or, more often, as two-dimensional structures of two or more voices unfolding simultaneously. Hauer's redefinition of the tropes as forty-four pairs of hexachords by the mid-1920s only served to confirm the dodecaphonic basis on which he had been working all along. Example 5 displays two tropes in specific transpositions and their working out in a kind of canonic texture.[30]

---

28. Three important documents pertaining to the tropes, beyond those already cited, are Hauer's further writings on the subject: "Die Tropen," *Musikblätter des Anbruch* 6, no. 1 (1924): 18–21; *Vom Melos zur Pauke: Eine Einführung in die Zwölftonmusik* (Vienna: Universal Edition, 1925); *Zwölftontechnik: Die Lehre von den Tropen* (Vienna: Universal, 1926). For an indepth study of Hauer's work, see John R. Covach, "The Music and Theories of Josef Matthias Hauer" (Ph.D. diss., University of Michigan, 1990).

29. Simms, "Who First Composed Twelve-Tone Music?," 117.

30. In Example 5, the tropes are transcribed into standard notation from Hauer's own invented notation, which employs an eight-line staff that emulates the physical spacing of a

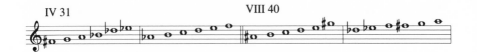

Example 5. Hauer, *Zwölftontechnik*, 10–11.

This two-dimensional character implies already that the horizontal and vertical musical dimensions were beginning to be thought of as a single entity, as in fact the same aspect presented in different ways. This, combined with the fact that the pitches constituting the separate hexachords of Hauer's tropes could be presented in any order, in any combination of simultaneous and successive configuration without affecting their identity as tropes, certainly suggests a species of "setlike" thinking, in the modern sense. On this front, too, Schoenberg's trajectory had begun to converge

---

piano keyboard. (Hauer did not use this notation for his canonic "resolutions.") The arabic numeral refers to the position of the trope in a chart of the forty-four pairs at the back of the *Zwölftontechnik*; the roman numeral refers to the transpositional level (at level I the initial pitch is always E♭; thus IV 31, for instance, means the thirty-first trope beginning on F♯). In the resolutions, each articulation of a trope occupies two successive beats of the complete texture, corresponding to the two hexachords that constitute that trope. Measures 1–2 are devoted to trope 31, mm. 3–4 to trope 40. Accidentals affect only the notes they immediately precede.

with Hauer's, though they would never follow exactly the same path. But some years would lapse before Schoenberg's own writings on the subject reached print: his major statement on "Composition with Twelve Tones," originating in lectures given during the 1930s and put in more formal prose in 1941, was not published until the first edition of *Style and Idea* in 1950.[31] Here one finds the famous declaration in capital letters, "THE TWO-OR-MORE-DIMENSIONAL SPACE IN WHICH MUSICAL IDEAS ARE PRESENTED IS A UNIT," and all that it entails, including: "The elements of a musical idea are partly incorporated in the horizontal plane as successive sounds, and partly in the vertical plane as simultaneous sounds. The mutual relation of tones regulates the succession of intervals as well as their association into harmonies."[32] Even as early as 1923, Schoenberg committed to paper a few paragraphs on twelve-tone composition (unpublished until 1975), in which he noted that "the weightiest assumption behind twelve-tone composition is this thesis: Whatever sounds together (harmonies, chords, the result of part writing) plays its part in expression and in presentation of the musical idea in just the same way as does all that sounds successively (motive, shape, phrase, sentence, melody, etc.), and it is equally subject to the law of comprehensibility."[33] Naturally, it was the Basic Set, or "twelve-tone row," with its canonical transformations, that received the greatest share of attention when Schoenberg introduced it as a means of organizing what went on in this "unitary" space—and that also seemed most clearly to distinguish Schoenberg's approach, with its completely ordered set and the integration of inversion into the compositional method, from Hauer's. Yet among Schoenberg's earliest twelve- tone compositions one might mention the *Suite*, op. 25, with its tetrachordally subdivided row in which the order of the tetrachords, and even the order within the tetrachords, exhibit a certain freedom from what one would expect to be the strict dictates of the row. Such "collectional" treatment of row segments was a part of the twelve-tone method from the start.

IV

Hauer's devising of the tropes was one response to the challenge of organizing compositional exploitation of the vast (479,001,600) permutational potential of the chro-

31. Arnold Schoenberg, *Style and Idea* (New York: Philosophical Library, 1950).

32. Schoenberg, "Composition with Twelve Tones (I)" (1941), in *Style and Idea*, ed. Leonard Stein (London: Faber & Faber, 1975), 220.

33. Schoenberg, "Twelve-Tone Composition" (1923), in *Style and Idea* (1975 edition), 207. Another early book on twelve-tone resources and methods of composition, Herbert Eimert's *Atonale Musiklehre* (Leipzig: Breitkopf & Härtel, 1924), takes this two-dimensionality for granted, though the idea is represented in rather more prosaic terms ("Die Resultierende der zwölftönigen horizontalen und der zwölftönigen vertikalen Komponente ist eine Linie, die Melodie und Harmonie zugleich ist," 11).

matic scale; during the 1920s there were other responses too, however, that had nothing much to do with twelve-tone music as Hauer, Schoenberg, and their respective associates were coming to think of it. One notable example came in the form of a treatise translated into German from Czech and published in 1927: Alois Hába's *Neue Harmonielehre*.[34] Hába, in fact, was not content to stop with the resources of the semitonal scale, devoting large sections of his book to the harmonies possible in third-, quarter-, sixth-, and twelfth-tones. The sprawling scale of the *Neue Harmonielehre*—so titled, one must guess, to position it as the natural successor to all the works of the past several decades known as *Harmonielehren*, and perhaps especially to Schoenberg's by then quite well-known work—seems at first perusal a bit excessive, its contents vitiated by frequent redundancy. To appreciate fully what Hába has done, it helps to realize that he has contracted the urge to comprehensiveness in a particularly virulent form. He is determined to explain, not only how the new, wholly chromatic practice had evolved out of the diatonic system, but also how in the new chromatic system *everything is related to everything*: not only can any chord follow or be followed by any other chord (as Reger attested was already true by the end of the previous century), but any chord succession can be interpreted as a melodic/polyphonic combination and any polyphony as organized by the harmonic principle—that is, the horizontal and vertical principles are really one and the same.[35] Further, just as chord construction through interval stacking tends toward the total chromatic, the total chromatic can be broken into components to produce all possible harmonies—or at least any that one would care to think of. At the same time, Hába takes it upon himself to enumerate as many as possible of the scales and harmonies available in the chromatic system, an ambition which leads him to produce fantastic lists and tables of inverted scales and chords derived and then respaced by various different procedures. What appears to us now, and perhaps appeared even to some readers of the time, to be overkill is for Hába simply the route to a convincing demonstration.

For the purposes of the present essay, the portion of Hába's treatise that is of greatest interest begins about two-thirds of the way through Part I, where the author declares that "every chord is susceptible of interpretation as a unity or as the combination of smaller groups of sounds."[36] There is no reason, Hába continues, to take construction in thirds or fourths as the *a priori* basis for all harmonic thought; rather, all intervals, in all possible combinations, should be admitted. Over the next fifteen pages, with some discursive breaks, are presented lists of chords from cardinalities two through eleven inclusive: eleven dyads, fifty-five trichords, 195 tetrachords, 176 pentachords, 119 hexachords, thirty-one heptachords, twenty-one octachords, thirteen nonachords, seven decachords, and three undecachords. Example 6 displays the derivation of dyads and part of the derivation of trichords.

---

34. Alois Hába, *Neue Harmonielehre des diatonischen, chromatischen, Viertel-, Drittel-, Sechstel-, und Zwölftel-Tonsystems* (Leipzig: Kistner & Siegel, 1927).

35. See, for example, p. 53.

36. Hába, *Neue Harmonielehre*, 94.

There is nothing about this account to remind us of the cool elegance of Bacon's reckoning. By comparison, Hába's is messy, and also incomplete. It does not start out that way: the list for cardinality two is certainly complete, that for cardinality three as complete as could be imagined (every one of the nineteen transpositionally equivalent ("T_n") trichords appears thrice, except for the augmented triad, which comes up only once); but the tetrachords are more puzzling. Perhaps the total of 195 really would cover every one of his possibilities of combination, but it is difficult to be certain from Hába's presentation, for he lists only 165 on pp. 98–99, mentioning then in passing that the others have already been given in the section on construction in thirds. Just which thirty chords he might mean, though, is left unexplained.[37] As the cardinalities increase, the method that at first served Hába so well, systematically adding a pitch to an interval in all the different possible ways by placing it by turns in the different available semitonal positions (see trichordal derivations in Ex. 6), becomes less and less satisfactory. Seemingly in recognition of this, and perhaps also because he has begun to suspect that his procedure is yielding a high degree of redundancy, his enthusiasm for the project he has undertaken begins to flag, as fewer and fewer possibilities are shown.

From this somewhat peculiar exercise, we come to understand that Hába, even if he is striving for comprehensiveness, never expects actually to achieve it. Quite evidently, he considers the "new harmony" an effectively inexhaustible sea, and means only to set his readers to voyaging upon it, not to supply them with maps guaranteed to get them to some particular destination. After all, even if every possible chord could be listed, there would still be all the different inversions and spacings to consider, not to mention the infinitude of compositional applications that any chord would have in relation to any other.

Treatises published in the United States over the next two decades (by native-born citizens and immigrants both) reveal several very different approaches to the problem of comprehensiveness. Henry Cowell's *New Musical Resources* (1930) is the earliest of those we will consider here; it was apparently written even earlier (1917–19), when the author was barely into his twenties, than its date of publication would suggest. By the time the book was being prepared for the printers, Cowell had at least heard of Hába as the promulgator of a quarter-tone system;[38] whether he ever

---

37. In fact, among these 165 harmonies each of Bacon's forty-three tetrachords appears at least once and as many as five times. It is possible that Hába's figure of 195 is a corruption of 165 that somehow became embedded in his text as he was writing it. Eimert (*Atonale Musiklehre*, 12–13) arrives at a total of 165 four-note chords using a procedure similar to Hába's, although he does not provide an exhaustive enumeration.

38. See author's introduction, evidently written soon before publication, in Henry Cowell, *New Musical Resources* (1930), repr. ed. with a preface and notes by Joscelyn Godwin (New York: Something Else Press, 1969), xx. Hába was in fact among those to whom Cowell wrote asking for a pledge of support in the form of a purchase order for his book (see Godwin's preface, xi).

Example 6. Hába, *Neue Harmonielehre,* 95.

actually consulted the *Neue Harmonielehre* is unknown, but in any case such exposure would have come too late to have had any effect on his own book, and Cowell's work certainly bears no discernible sign of any such influence. It is more likely that he knew of contemporary theoretical work in Central Europe mainly by rumor, and that for all intents and purposes he was proceeding quite independently in his efforts to codify modern practice.

Not that Cowell was unschooled in music theory: he cites the harmony books of Hull and Schoenberg as works that are to varying degrees unsatisfactory as explanations of *why* modern practice permits so many new combinations of tones and proposes to remedy that deficiency in his own book. In fact, Cowell goes Schoenberg's "emancipation of the dissonance" one better, not only by detaching dissonant chords of all sorts from the seemingly mandatory resolutions they receive in the *Harmonielehre*, but also by suggesting that modern practice might fruitfully be explained, at least in part, by a *reversal* of the old consonance-dissonance hierarchy, with what were formerly stable sonorities becoming unstable, dependent upon "dissonant" sonorities for their coherence.[39] Cowell's justification for this exaltation of dissonance is essentially the same as Schoenberg's—that the dissonant intervals, deriving from the more remote overtones of the harmonic series, are different only in degree from the consonances and therefore do not deserve to be rigidly segregated from them—but Cowell diverges from Schoenberg at that point in seizing upon the overtone (and, eventually, the "undertone") series as the main structural principle controlling his new harmonic resources. Of course, the naive, "gee-whiz" style of presentation, including the unqualified acceptance of the validity of undertones, is rather a departure from Schoenberg as well.[40]

The two chapters of Cowell's book devoted to "Tone Combinations" and "Chord Formation" reveal the author to be much more interested in treating the means of combination and formation than in enumerating all the imaginable results of such processes. Like Hába, he regards modern harmony as effectively limitless in its possibilities; unlike Hába, he fills very few pages giving examples of them. There are really just two categories of harmony: *polychords*, dissonant harmonies assembled from triads built on roots a fifth, third, or second apart (and usually spaced so that these components remain clearly distinguishable aurally); and harmonies whose constitution is explained more directly in terms of adjacent intervals: (1) fifths, fourths, and tritones; (2) thirds and sixths; and (3) seconds, also called *tone clusters*. This satisfies, if only rather loosely, the requirement imposed by the author on himself at the outset that the various intervals determined by the overtone series play an integral

---

39. Cowell, 38–39; see Schoenberg, *Theory of Harmony*, 20–21. Here the *idea* of "emancipation of the dissonance" appears in clear form, though the term itself is not used; it occurs, apparently for the first time in Schoenberg's writings, in the essay "Opinion or Insight?" (1926; see *Style and Idea,* 1975 ed., 258–64).

40. The experimental results of Nicolas A. Garbusov reported by Cowell (21–23) would presumably be explained today by difference tones or sympathetic resonance. Like Ziehn's symmetrical inversion, Cowell's appropriation of undertones can be interpreted as another echo (though in this case fainter) of harmonic dualism, again in the service of a basically empirical investigation.

role in the theory of harmony.[41] Only very general advice about the application of these harmonies is supplied for the reader's benefit; whatever is to be made of them, however simple or complex, is up to the prospective user.

The 1940s saw further notable efforts in the direction of comprehensive accounting, at the hands of two Russian émigrés to the United States. Joseph Schillinger, who arrived in 1928 and subsequently gained a certain measure of fame as the teacher of George Gershwin, reveals in his *Kaleidophone* (1940) and in *The Schillinger System of Musical Composition* (1946) an enormous energy for describing and classifying a huge range of musical phenomena.[42] Always a somewhat controversial figure, his reputation today is marred by the mechanical nature of his ideas about musical structure and their pseudomathematical presentation, in the context of a far- fetched theory of "the mathematical basis of the arts."[43] Still, numerous composers of his time, especially of popular music, swore by the efficacy of Schillinger's teachings; and it is possible to trace their influences in some music of that era.[44]

The *Kaleidophone*, much the briefer of the two treatises, claims on its title page to be about "Pitch Scales in Relation to Chord Structures." Schillinger's approach to this topic, though not at all anomalous in terms of concurrent twentieth-century music- theoretical developments, does turn out to be highly idiosyncratic. There does not seem to be much of a distinction made between scale and chord, since a scale can consist of any collection of pitches—as few as three—distributed within an octave in a constantly ascending direction. One might guess that this blurring of identity is in

---

41. It is interesting that for Cowell the coordination and unification of horizontal and vertical dimensions is a question, not of the relations between scales and chords, but of physical ratios that can be expressed either harmonically (as intervals) or temporally (as rhythmic/metric relationships). Cowell's ideas about relating pitch and rhythm, as their recurrence in Karlheinz Stockhausen's writings of the 1950s demonstrates, were destined to become another of music theory's reinvented wheels, the manufacturing history of which will not detain us here.

42. Joseph Schillinger, *Kaleidophone: New Resources of Melody and Harmony* (New York: M. Witmark & Sons, 1940); *The Schillinger System of Musical Composition* (New York: Carl Fischer, 1946).

43. Schillinger actually wrote a treatise called *The Mathematical Basis of the Arts* in the late 1930s; it was not published until 1948, some years after his death. See Elliott Carter's review of *The Schillinger System* for an early, unsympathetic response to Schillinger's work ("Fallacy of the Mechanical Approach," *Modern Music* 23, no. 3 [Summer 1946]: 228–30; repr. in *Elliott Carter: Collected Essays and Lectures, 1937-1995*, ed. Jonathan W. Bernard [Rochester, N.Y.: University of Rochester Press, 1997], 15–16).

44. See Paul Nauert, "Theory and Practice in *Porgy and Bess*: The Gershwin-Schillinger Connection," *Musical Quarterly* 78 (1994): 9–33. In his article, "Gershwin's Art of Counterpoint" (*Musical Quarterly* 70 [1984]: 423–56), Steven Gilbert briefly discusses some recognizably Schillingeresque techniques in Gershwin's *"I Got Rhythm" Variations*; Schillinger's influence on the composition of this work and *Porgy and Bess* is addressed as well in Gilbert, *The Music of Gershwin* (New Haven and London: Yale University Press, 1995).

a way deliberate, part of the coordination (though hardly equivalence) of horizontal and vertical. However, because in Schillinger's schemata scales are "developed" out of chords by inserting new notes between the chords' vertically adjacent members, not *every* scale, verticalized, would make a usable chord: the adjacent notes must be at least a whole step apart to allow an insertion. Further, apparently only scales of odd cardinalities (three, five, seven, up to a maximum of nine members) may be produced this way, from dyads, triads, tetrads, and pentads respectively. Chords of higher cardinalities may well be subsumed under scalar identities, but this is not made clear, any more than it is made clear whether scales of four, six, or eight notes are entirely inadmissible or simply missing from this account.

Other gaps in the supposedly comprehensive coverage become visible upon scrutiny of Schillinger's tables. Table I is designed to allow "instantaneous locating of scales which correspond to any given chord" (p. 12); as an example, Schillinger presents the tetrad consisting of adjacent intervals 2, 3, and 5 (intervals given throughout in numbers of semitones) and shows that these intervals may be permuted six ways to produce six different chords. (These form a *family* and are listed together in Table II, about which more in a moment.) Each of the six may be looked up separately in Table I, some fifty-seven pages in extent; at these different sites each of the six chords receives three new notes (according to the process of insertion described above). For each chord, this can be done eight different ways, for a total of forty-eight seven-note scales in all. Example 7 shows this process for the first of the six chords. These forty-eight scales are, indeed, all different, in the same sense that Bacon's are. Some are circular permutations of one another, a fact which is not immediately apparent because Schillinger, unlike Bacon, does not include the "round-the-corner" interval in his scale forms. Thus, considered as horizontalized chords, these forty-eight scales can be subsumed under just twenty-eight of the sixty-six T_n classes of heptachords.

It is easy to imagine, of course, that among all the numerous such families of scales, most or all of the sixty-six heptachords would eventually be found. It is also easy to predict a high incidence of redundancy, but what we might now call duplication of effort could not have concerned Schillinger very much: for one thing, scales would have a compositional application different from that of chords; for another, in a tonal context there would be some value in considering them as all distinct; and third, the method which Schillinger taught and encouraged his students to use consisted largely in trying out many, many permutations of pitch and rhythmic elements until one hit upon something that seemed to "work." It was *systematic* in that one learned a mechanism by which to invent various possibilities to consider, and a means by which to exhaust them— but beyond that it was merely trial-and-error.

In all, despite the presentation of the *Kaleidophone* as a neutral source of information, susceptible of application to any compositional task, the book reflects a compositional stance not very compatible with most of the other works treated so far in this essay. The omissions from Table II, from a more chromatic or twelve-note point of view, are telling. Here, in the final three pages of the *Kaleidophone*, are Schillinger's

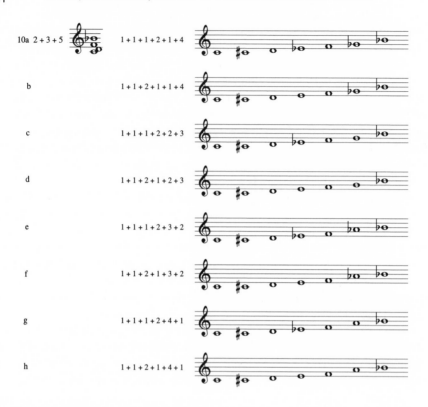

Example 7. Schillinger, *Kaleidophone,* 38.

families of triads, tetrads, and pentads; one notices among the triads that several of the nineteen T_n-types are given thrice over, while two, (012) and (048), are not found at all. Among the tetrads, thirteen of the forty-three are absent. By Schillinger's criteria, these are not omissions or oversights: chords of all equal intervals are excluded unless they can be arranged differently within an octave, otherwise their potential for scale generation is too limited for his purposes; the same goes for any chord with only a semitone between adjacent members, since no note can be inserted at such points. Type (0158), for example, can be respaced 4 + 3 + 4, but nothing can be done with (0124).

As for the massive, two-volume *Schillinger System,* comprising some 1640 pages, it probably deserves an article in itself. Here I will confine myself to remarking that in this work, specifically in Book II ("Theory of Pitch Scales") and Book IX ("General Theory of Harmony"), Schillinger takes a rather different approach to the subjects covered in the *Kaleidophone,* an approach which could be regarded at times as a supplement to the earlier book, at other times as a replacement. Scales are divided into four groups, two of which classify those exceeding an octave (hence not accounted for at all in the *Kaleidophone*); the third of these groups comprises symmetrical scales springing from the five equal divisions of the octave. Among the "Diatonic and Related Scales," seven-member scales receive special attention; here too they are built from tetrachords, but the method of construction is completely different from that of the *Kaleidophone*, based as it is on "conjunct tetrachords"— that is, as actual scale segments, remotely resembling the Greek practices of antiquity. In an interesting chapter near the end of Book II, "Melody-Harmony Relationships in Symmetric Systems," Schillinger verticalizes scales, then extracts chords of various cardinalities. This technique seems to foreshadow modern subset relations, but the resemblance is rather faint: the tonic is repeated at the double octave in each example, yet is treated as a separate member of the chord; and all extracted chords are segmental adjacencies in the scales. As for the harmonies of Book IX, Schillinger takes a greater interest in listing absolutely every possibility arising from interval combinations, including those left out of the *Kaleidophone*.[45]

The other Russian émigré contributor to the literature of what might be called "encyclopedic music theory" is Nicolas Slonimsky, who arrived in the United States a few years before Schillinger and outlived him by over half a century. His *Thesaurus of Scales and Melodic Patterns* (1947) reveals certain preoccupations that are markedly similar to those of Schillinger, though the form he put them in has proved more durable: while the *Kaleidophone* and *The Schillinger System* have long since fallen into disuse, the *Thesaurus* is still in print and continues to find new readers with each successive generation of jazz musicians.[46] This popularity owes something to the fact that the *Thesaurus*, besides its value to composers and theorists, serves instrumentalists and improvisers equally well as an exercise book.

When the *Thesaurus* was first published, Slonimsky sought and received comments about it from various eminent musical personages—including Schoenberg, who wrote that he "was very interested to find that you have in all probability organized every possible succession of tones"—calling this however a mere "feat of mental gymnastics" and adding that "as a composer, I must believe in inspiration rather than mechanics."[47] The very title *Thesaurus* does suggest that it was conceived essentially as a compendium in which the user may cast about until coming upon "just the right collection" of notes. In this it resembles the permutational style of Schillinger's work. Surely, however, if Schoenberg had reflected a moment longer on the contents of Slonimsky's book he would have realized that it hardly includes "every possible succession of tones," even if one were to discount a listing of the 479,001,600 twelve-tone rows as a realistic goal. Slonimsky himself points out in his introduction that what he terms "melodic patterns"—sequences of notes that, rather than ascending or descending uniformly, develop little bumps or excrescences, effectively ornament-

---

45. See, for example, the tetrad list, 1124–26.

46. Nicolas Slonimsky, *Thesaurus of Scales and Melodic Patterns* (New York: Charles Scribner's Sons, 1947).

47. Nicolas Slonimsky, *Perfect Pitch: A Life Story* (Oxford and New York: Oxford University Press, 1988), 178–79.

ing an underlying scale or other framework, such as a symmetrical partitioning of the octave—are for all practical purposes limitless in number. As for the scales themselves, an examination of the pentatonic and heptatonic listings quickly dispels any illusion that the chromatic resources have been exhausted: only twenty-four of the sixty-six T_n classes of pentachords and twenty-one of the corresponding sixty-six heptachords are employed (many in multiple forms, thus in circular permutation of their adjacent interval content).[48] To a certain extent this limitation appears to spring from practical considerations, since most of the excluded collections would distribute the pitches less evenly throughout the octave, owing to the presence of wholly chromatic groupings within the collection, and therefore might lie less gracefully under an instrumentalist's fingers. But it may also signify a lingering tonal bias, despite Slonimsky's stated aim of doing away as much as possible with fixed key associations by adopting a newly invented terminology for intervals as well as somewhat fanciful names for the embellishment of the symmetrical divisions to form scales (interpolation) and melodic patterns (infrapolation and ultrapolation).

The bulk of the *Thesaurus* is a highly eclectic mix of materials. Roughly the first half is devoted to development of scales and patterns from the symmetrical partitioning of one or more octaves—very much reminiscent of the third and fourth categories of scales in Schillinger's *System*. Then, after the heptatonic and pentatonic scales, comes a veritable olio, evidently the miscellaneous accumulation of several years' reflection and invention: quadritonal arpeggios, division of twelve tones into four mutually exclusive triads, mirror interval progressions, complementary scales, and so on. As the title of the book implies, harmony per se is really a side issue here, very much in the service of the scales and patterns, not at all an equal partner in the enterprise. Triad and seventh- chord progressions (the latter called "master chords") are provided to harmonize nearly everything. The final pages present, as if only curiosities, several examples of post-tonal chordal vocabulary, for two of which in particular Slonimsky has recounted his process of discovery: the "Chord of the Minor Twenty-Third" and the "Grandmother Chord."[49] The former arose from an effort to build a chord of stacked thirds that would include all twelve pitch classes without (octave) duplication. Hába had in fact already done this more than a decade before Slonimsky got around to it; Slonimsky's version (Ex. 8a) is the same as the second of four different such chords listed by Hába (Ex. 8b).[50] The "Grandmother Chord" arose from further speculation on the "Mother Chord" (*Mutterakkord*), as Berg had jokingly called the twelve-note chord, invented by his pupil Fritz Heinrich Klein and employed in Klein's composition *Die Maschine* (1921), which encompassed

---

48. *Thesaurus*, 160–68 and 137–54 respectively.

49. Slonimsky, *Perfect Pitch*, 176–77.

50. See *Neue Harmonielehre*, 90. Schoenberg, by contrast, claimed that third-stacking would yield a maximum of nine different tones before an octave duplication was produced (*Theory of Harmony*, 407); however, Schoenberg set more stringent limits on his stacks, allowing only contiguous major and minor triads.

**Chord
of the Minor 23rd**
Containing All Twelve
Chromatic Tones and
Four Mutually Exclusive
Triads

Example 8a. Slonimsky, *Thesaurus,* 242.

Example 8b. Hába, *Neue Harmonielehre,* 90.

all eleven intervals between the adjacent pairs of pitches (Ex. 9a).[51] Slonimsky's version put these intervals in a particular symmetrical arrangement, such that from the
bottom to the top of the chord even intervals (counted in numbers of semitones)
alternated with odd, and the odd intervals decreased (11,9,7,5,3,1) while the even
intervals increased (2,4,6,8,10) (Ex. 9b). It is indeed unlikely that anyone had yet made
use of this as a literal chord by 1947, let alone by the date on which Slonimsky "invented" it.[52]

The prose works of Cowell, Schillinger, and Slonimsky, though all "comprehensive" in their own terms, by more general standards fall short of being exhaustive
accounts of the pitch resources of the chromatic universe. Other composers' books of

51. See Headlam, "Fritz Heinrich Klein's 'Die Grenze der Halbtonwelt,'" 68, and note
25 above. Berg borrowed this idea for several compositions, including the *Lyric Suite* (1926),
where at the opening of the first movement such a chord appears in mm. 2–4 in the first
violin, "horizontalized," which of course turns it into an all-interval series.

52. This was 13 February 1938, according to the *Thesaurus,* vii.

Example 9a. Klein's *Mutterakkord* (from Headlam, 68).

Grandmother Chord
Containing All Twelve
Chromatic Tones and
Eleven Symmetrically
Invertible Intervals

Example 9b. Slonimsky, *Thesaurus*, 243.

the same era with some aspirations to comprehensiveness reveal an even more blinkered approach; brief mention will be made here of two prominent examples. Paul Hindemith's *Unterweisung im Tonsatz*, vol. 1 (1937) offers a sexpartite table of classification which sorts chords according to two principal criteria: presence or absence of tritone and presence or absence of seconds and/or sevenths. Superficially considered, this table provides an objective assessment of intervallic makeup; in reality, it provides Hindemith with an avenue of attack on those composers who failed to heed his dictum that music "will always take its departure from the tonic triad and return to it."[53] For one thing, all of these classifications are colored by the fact that every chord has a *root* in Hindemith's estimation; thus the whole system has a

---

53. Paul Hindemith, *Unterweisung im Tonsatz* (1937), trans. Arthur Mendel as *The Craft of Musical Composition* (Mainz, New York, and London: Schott, 1942), 22.

built-in tonal bias, however differently it may operate from the system of common-practice harmony. For another, according to Hindemith's theory, chords are characterized by varying degrees of tension, depending on their positions in his table, and a control of the flow from lesser to greater tension and back again is essential to coherent shaping on all levels, from phrase to overall form. In light of such criteria, the intent behind Hindemith's harmonic analysis of an excerpt from Schoenberg's *Klavierstück*, op. 33a—undertaken in deliberate disregard of the twelve-tone technique in which it was written—is all too clear: the progression consists of almost nothing but chords from categories III and IV, the tensest of all, and is thus, by implication, quite incoherent.[54]

It is worth noting that Hindemith carries out his analysis of melody in nearly complete independence from that of harmony; the two meet only in his analytical graphs and even there are confined to separate braces. In fact, throughout his book melody and harmony are treated essentially as opposites, although of course such positioning also implies a certain complementarity. In Olivier Messiaen's *Technique de mon langage musical* (1944), more modest in its goals than the Hindemith treatise, a similar separation obtains: melody and counterpoint, often in conjunction with rhythm, are dealt with almost entirely apart from harmony.[55] But that Messiaen's thinking, at least in some areas, was more explicitly *collectional* than Hindemith's is evident from the one common ground in Messiaen's treatise for the vertical and horizontal: the seven modes of limited transposition, so called by the composer because of their symmetrical properties, which limit to two, three, four, or six the number of distinct transpositional levels. Messiaen describes these modes as an aspect of the mysterious "charm of impossibilities" that informs his work. But Messiaen is less than informative about how these seven collections, ranging in size from six to ten members, were chosen out of all the other, similarly symmetrical possibilities, or why mode 1 (the whole-tone scale) is included in his numbering if, as he asserts, he does not even use it. At any rate, where these modes hold sway, the way in which chords go together to constitute the complete contents of particular modal transpositions is always quite clear, even if the choices made in forming the individual chords are not. For Messiaen, harmony is otherwise a plethora of forms, only very loosely defined (though not, compositionally speaking, loosely used), except for certain specific sonorities such as the chord on the dominant. Some are only qualitatively defined (such as the chords of inferior and superior resonance); others are named after an element coupled with an already familiar sonority (added sixth or augmented fourth), or after a process of embellishment (appoggiatura, suspension, pedal point).

In their mature phases, both Hindemith and Messiaen, though in vastly different ways, could be considered tonal composers, the last major figures of this persuasion in the twentieth century until much more recently. Their separation from the

---

54. This analysis appears in Hindemith, *Craft*, 217–19.

55. Olivier Messiaen, *Technique de mon langage musical* (1944), trans. John Satterfield as *The Technique of My Musical Language* (Paris: Alphonse Leduc, [1956]).

mainstream, as defined by twelve-tone and other advanced styles that dominated new music during the years following the Second World War,[56] is a measure of the lack of relevance that their theoretical work came to have during this period. Composers—and theorists too, to the extent that they can be separately identified—were beginning to look for *general* answers to questions of structure in post-tonal music, answers susceptible of widespread, "objective" application, and clearly these were not to be found in writings conceived as personal credos, coming from composers whose music, in the view prevalent at that time, looked so unrepentantly backward.

V

Meanwhile, however, to return for a moment to the 1930s and '40s, even during the heyday of neoclassicism news of Schoenberg's twelve-tone method had begun to get around. Schoenberg himself, as mentioned, had as yet published no writings on the subject, but he had given a few lectures since emigrating to the United States in 1933, and some of his associates and former students had been helping to increase musicians' awareness and understanding of the details involved. An article by Richard Hill published in 1936, "Schoenberg's Tone-Rows and the Tonal System of the Future," was apparently widely read.[57] Two composers—one, a native-born American, the student of the other, an Austrian émigré—would eventually cite the article in their own important efforts at further developing the twelve-tone method.

From his lessons with Ernst Krenek—as he was to recall fifty years later— George Perle learned that his youthful grasp of the twelve-tone method, arrived at independently through study of the few scores of Berg that he was able to find, was actually faulty in Schoenbergian terms. Lacking any guidance, and not yet having come across Hill's article (one of the very few sources of information about Schoenberg available in English at the time), Perle was under the impression that any element in a twelve-tone series had available to it, as its next "move," the element that came next in *any* of the four canonic forms (prime, retrograde, inversion, retrograde inversion). Krenek, of course, set him straight but, as Perle has recounted the story, "was generous enough to call what I had come up with a 'discovery'"—as indeed it was, or at least the germ of one—especially since the Schoenbergian method, even if not perfectly understood at the time, was understood well enough to make it obvious that what Berg had done in his *Lyric Suite* (among other works) was impossible to parse out according to the standard set of transformations of a single row.[58] Subsequently,

---

56. Messiaen's brief involvement in such matters, evinced by his *Etudes de rythme*, excepted.

57. Richard S. Hill, "Schoenberg's Tone-Rows and the Tonal System of the Future," *Musical Quarterly* 22 (1936): 14–37.

58. George Perle, *The Listening Composer* (Berkeley and Los Angeles: University of California Press, 1990), 126–33.

in an article published a few years later, Perle set forth the basis of what he had come to regard as the next logical step in the evolution of the twelve-tone method: interpreting the all-interval series of the *Lyric Suite* as a circle of fifths delineated in both directions at once—which he called "*the* twelve-tone scale"—he constructed a matrix of progressions using each of the tones of the row in succession as an axis.[59] Thus, as Krenek explained in an article of his own published two years after Perle's, "Perle arrives at a complex set of regularly shaped tone clusters which he soon goes on to treat as chords."[60] Under this revision of technique, "Perle has the series as good as completely absorbed by the texture and minimizes its influence on the melodic outline," thus freeing the row from the necessity of supplying motivic relationships, to which in Perle's view it was ill suited in any case.

Krenek saw that Perle, in turning the "classical" twelve-tone technique, fundamentally *polyphonic* in its original conception, to the task of systematizing chords, had accomplished something significant. Indeed, in retrospect it can be regarded as a further and highly original step in the direction of setlike thinking about dodecaphonic materials, in the way that the neighboring tones cluster about their respective axes in Perle's matrices. This discovery has served as the impetus for a long and fruitful compositional career, sparked periodically by further additions to and expansions of the technique, in particular those undertaken in collaboration with Paul Lansky in the late 1960s that led to the codification detailed in *Twelve-Tone Tonality* (1977). That hardly any other composers have followed Perle's lead, and that no one else of any appreciable stature now employs this approach to twelve-tone composition, must be regarded as one of the more baffling outcomes of recent musical history.

Krenek himself, meanwhile, stimulated by Perle's work, by Hill's speculations as to the suitability of the twelve-tone method for development in a modal or "extra-motivic" direction, and by his own analyses of Schoenberg's music, undertook not so much a fundamental revision of the very basis of the Schoenbergian method as a radical loosening of the strictures binding musical progression to the order of presentation in the row and its transformations, while still—paradoxically—continuing to respect the canonical function of that row. Krenek's exposition of his method in his *Symphonic Piece for String Orchestra* (1939) and the *Lamentatio Jeremiae Prophetae* (1942) shows, in the former, a row not explicitly stated until late in the work yet, in the process of being formed, generating all sorts of motivic relationships through such techniques as the extractions of series of tones from the contoural extremities of other series, the coalescing of a series of tones into chords, the resultant voice leading of which spins off other series, and so forth. In the latter work, the two hexachords of the row are induced to behave somewhat like the modes of antiquity and the Medi-

59. George Perle, "Evolution of the Tone Row: The Twelve-Tone Modal System," *Music Review* 2 (1941): 273–87.

60. Ernst Krenek, "New Developments of the Twelve-Tone Technique," *Music Review* 4 (1943): 81–97.

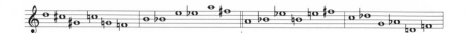

Example 10. Excerpt from Schoenberg Violin Concerto cited by Krenek ("New Developments of the Twelve-Tone Technique," 86).

eval era, being subjected to circular permutation ("diatonic" species) and to retransposition from these permutations to the original starting tone ("chromatic" species). The resultant six-note groups are then treated as unordered collections in various combinations and juxtapositions even as their order of succession continues to reflect their twelve-tone derivation.

It should be stressed that in adopting such techniques, which in contemporary critical accounts were often designated "free" applications of the twelve-tone method, Krenek saw himself simply as following Schoenberg's lead. After all, the very concept of hexachordal combinatoriality (as it was later called) emphasized *content* as much as *order* in the relationships between row forms and their constituent hexachords; and Krenek had been able to find passages in works such as Schoenberg's Violin Concerto in which row forms seemed to have been separated, not only into independently operating hexachords, but even into trichords (Ex. 10). In going "still further in breaking down the integrity of the series," as he put it, in his own compositions, Krenek was really only responding to the potential for collectional application that had been embedded in the twelve-tone method from its inception.[61]

---

61. Krenek, "New Developments of the Twelve-Tone Technique," 86–7. Krenek mistook the inverted form of the row for its prime, and vice versa (in a footnote he acknowledged that his choice of prime was largely arbitrary). To Krenek's excerpt from the Violin Concerto, I have added brackets indicating trichords from the row and its inversion, given as deduced by Krenek at the head of the present example.

Some years later, Krenek would formalize the technique of circular permutation employed in the *Lamentatio* into the principle of *rotation* of hexachords.[62] This
way of delineating segments of the row as independently functioning entities attracted the attention of Stravinsky (among others), who subsequently adapted it for
his own use beginning with *Movements for Piano and Orchestra* (1959). This and the
other ways devised by Krenek of getting beyond the purely linear and ordered aspect of the row can be grouped with all the other myriad techniques, invented by
other Americans and by the members of the so-called Darmstadt School of the 1950s,
through which the row's compositional control was at once extended and diffused—
to such extremes, eventually, that some composers came to feel that, once the row
was everywhere, it might as well be nowhere at all. This part of the history of twentieth-century music is beyond the scope of this essay, but it is worth noting in passing
that the pitch-manipulative techniques alone that arose from such preoccupations—
including Boulez's troping and pitch multiplication, Stockhausen's pitch bands, and
Babbitt's arrays—had the very definite effect of emphasizing the collectional properties of row segments and other derivatives far more than any order that could be
traced back to a row source.[63]

VI

It was, in fact, twelve-tone-oriented composers and theorists of a strongly mathematical bent who provided the final impetus for the development of an explicit
theory of pitch-class sets. At this juncture, the work of two individuals was particularly important.

First, in three articles that are still required reading for doctoral students in
theory everywhere, Milton Babbitt promulgated and rigorously worked out what
Janet Schmalfeldt has termed his "outstanding contribution": namely, that "the well-

---

62. Krenek, "Extents and Limits of Serial Techniques," *Musical Quarterly* 46 (1960); repr.
in *Problems of Modern Music*, ed. Paul Henry Lang (New York: Norton, 1962), 72–94.

63. A considerable literature has accumulated on these developments of serialism. For
more on Boulez's work, see: Pierre Boulez, *Boulez on Music Today*, trans. S. Bradshaw and R.
R. Bennett (London: Faber & Faber, 1971); Boulez, *Stocktakings from an Apprenticeship*, trans.
S. Walsh (Oxford: Clarendon Press, 1991); Lev Koblyakov, *Pierre Boulez: A World of Har-
mony* (London and New York: Harwood Academic Publishers, 1990); Stephen Heinemann,
"Pitch-Class Set Multiplication in Boulez's *Le Marteau sans maître*" (D.M.A. diss., University
of Washington, 1993). Jonathan Harvey's book, *The Music of Stockhausen* (Berkeley and Los
Angeles: University of California Press, 1975), provides a helpful introduction to the adapta-
tions of serialism at the hands of that composer. For Babbitt, see: Joseph Dubiel, "Three
Essays on Milton Babbitt," Parts One, Two, and Three, respectively in *Perspectives of New
Music* 28, no. 2 (Summer, 1990): 216–61; 29, no. 1 (Winter, 1991): 90–122; 30, no. 1 (Winter,
1992): 82–131; Andrew Mead, *An Introduction to the Music of Milton Babbitt* (Princeton:
Princeton University Press, 1994).

known concept of *group* in mathematics may be effectively used as a model for the twelve-tone system, since the rules of formation and transformation within the latter are sufficiently analogous to those of the former."[64] For the subsequent literature of twelve-tone theory these articles serve collectively as a kind of *locus classicus*; already in an article by Donald Martino published just one issue later in the *Journal of Music Theory* than the third of Babbitt's articles, the three were explicitly recognized as a body of knowledge, an understanding of which on the part of anyone who wished to pursue twelve-tone theory further (or, at least, follow it at a safe distance) simply *had* to be assumed.[65] The focus in these articles on the varieties of combinatoriality meant, of course, that hexachords which could be transposed, inverted, or both to yield their twelve-note complements, irrespective of order, received a good deal of attention.

Second, in two articles of remarkable concision, David Lewin—not yet out of his twenties, identified on the contributors' pages as composer and Junior Fellow at Harvard, also the possessor of an undergraduate degree in mathematics—presented generalized ways of describing (1) "the intervallic relations between two collections of notes" (thus using the term *collection*, in its modern music-theoretical sense, for the first time) and (2) "the intervallic content of a collection of notes" and "intervallic relations between a collection of notes and its complement."[66] The form of the "interval function" in the first of these played no role in pitch-class set theory as eventually laid out by Forte, since in Forte's work all relations between collections were handled in terms of their set types (or "set classes")—though of course it has played a mighty role in Lewin's own subsequent work. In the second article, Lewin's interval function applied to the content *of* a single collection (or, as he puts it, "the interval function between [a collection of notes] P and itself") is the conceptual predecessor of the interval-class vector (called "interval vector" for short) in Forte's work. Lewin's interval function between a collection of notes and itself is in turn a special case of the interval function as set forth in the first article.[67] Using this "reflexive" form of the

---

64. Janet Schmalfeldt, *Berg's "Wozzeck"*, 3. The three articles by Babbitt are, of course: "Some Aspects of Twelve-Tone Composition," *The Score and I.M.A. Magazine* 12 (June 1955): 53–61; "Twelve-Tone Invariants as Compositional Determinants," *Musical Quarterly* 46 (1960), repr. in *Problems of Modern Music*, ed. Paul Henry Lang (New York: Norton, 1962), 108–21; and "Set Structure as a Compositional Determinant," *Journal of Music Theory* 5 (1961): 72–94.

65. Donald Martino, "The Source Set and Its Aggregate Formations," *Journal of Music Theory* 5 (1961): 224–73. The term "source set" was taken from the first of Babbitt's three articles—where, significantly, it refers to "a [twelve-tone] set considered only in terms of the content of its hexachords, and whose combinatorial characteristics are independent of the ordering imposed on this content" ("Some Aspects of Twelve-Tone Composition," 57n).

66. David Lewin, "Intervallic Relations between Two Collections of Notes," *Journal of Music Theory* 3 (1959): 298–301; "The Intervallic Content of a Collection of Notes, Intervallic Relations between a Collection of Notes and Its Complement: An Application to Schoenberg's Hexachordal Pieces," *Journal of Music Theory* 4 (1960): 98–101.

67. The interval vector differs from Lewin's interval function in that it collapses intervals

interval function, Lewin is able not only to find a general relation between complementary collections but also to establish the general conditions under which two collections may have identical interval content, and that these conditions do not always entail that one collection can be inverted and/or transposed to obtain the other. This was the first discussion in print of the property eventually to be named the "Z-relation" by Forte.[68]

The study of the multitudinous ways in which the combinatorial operations of twelve-tone theory could be carried out, and the kinds of relationships they established between different collections, along with the investigation of interval content within and between collections not necessarily operating within a twelve-tone context—all dependent principally upon the *total* (not simply the adjacent) interval content of the collections, and all described in formal (that is, mathematically emulative) terms—soon drew the attention of theorists who lacked any pronounced interest in twelve-tone music but wondered whether such formalization might not be extended to collections of any number of notes (as Lewin's work had already begun to accomplish) and whether additional relationships between them could be described with a rigor equaling that of twelve-tone theory, yet not reliant on twelve-tone rows or the aggregates formed between them as frames of reference. While it was goals of this sort that led directly to the initial formulations of Forte's "Theory of Set-Complexes" article, not until the revision and considerable refinement in his *The Structure of Atonal Music* did it become clear that pc-set theory as Forte envisioned it was designed principally to address questions of structure in the music of Schoenberg, Berg, and Webern from the years ca. 1908–23, with a few side-excursions to Scriabin, Stravinsky, and Bartók to indicate a potentially greater scope of application.[69]

In light of this history, it is intriguing to find certain properties of pitch-class collections, and some of the relations between them, described and explored in

---

into interval classes, which means necessarily that it counts tritones at exactly half the frequency that the interval function does; it also ignores unisons, since the number of these is the same as the cardinality of the collection and is already evident as the prefix in Forte's set name. See Lewin, "Forte's Interval Vector, My Interval Function, and Regener's Common-Note Function," *Journal of Music Theory* 21 (1977): 194–237.

68. Lewin, in his 1960 article, specifically identifies the one tetrachordal pair and two pentachordal pairs (overlooking one) that share this relation; he does not enumerate the hexachordal pairs.

69. A distinctly different message is sent in Perle's book, *Serial Composition and Atonality* (Berkeley and Los Angeles: University of California Press, 1962), where the music of what is termed "'free' atonality" remains essentially a marginal phenomenon. Perle's approach to this repertoire is definitely collectional, but it quickly becomes obvious that he sees little point in attempting, beyond a certain rudimentary extent, to formalize pitch(-class) relationships in music whose principal function, historically speaking in his view, was transitional, paving the way for the twelve-tone method but not a route much worth traveling for the sake of its own scenic beauties.

Howard Hanson's *Harmonic Materials of Modern Music: Resources of the Tempered Scale* (1960), in a form that might almost be dubbed "proto-set theory." Evidently the product of long gestation, like Babbitt's work, stretching back to the 1940s, the ideas in Hanson's treatise seem to have been developed in complete independence from those of the twelve-tone-oriented composers and theorists.[70] Hanson himself was not a twelve-tone composer and apparently bore a certain animosity towards practitioners of that method; yet his working assumptions, outlined at the outset of his book, are remarkably similar to those which operated in the work of his more "advanced" brethren: the twelve-note scale in equal temperament as the "logical basis" for study of modern practice; equivalence of the vertical and horizontal dimensions (Hanson calls his groups of notes "sonorities" to avoid the vertical bias of words like "chord" and "harmony"); total interval content of collections; pitch class as a primary defining factor. The concept of *interval class* is effectively established by the observation that "an interval and its inversion . . . perform the same function in a sonority."[71] Shortly thereafter, a résumé of interval-class content is proposed, in which the order of interval classes differs from that of Forte's later formulation in the interval vector (the implications of this will be discussed shortly). Consistent with the adoption of inversional equivalence for intervals is its extension to sonorities of three or more notes, where it is called *involution* and comes in three varieties: *simple* (for asymmetrical sonorities, producing a "different sound" when involuted); *isometric* (for symmetrical sonorities); and *enharmonic*, a special variety of the isometric that yields the same pitch classes as the original form. Hanson then proceeds to define a further phenomenon, not classifiable as involution but (one gathers) somehow related in his mind: the *isomeric* relation, which denotes the relationship between sonorities identical as to total interval content but not derivable from one another by inversion and/or transposition. This is of course the Z-relation again, arrived at, one must infer, by a very different route from that taken by Lewin.

The greater part by far of Hanson's book is devoted to derivation of all the possible sonorities in the twelve-note universe, one by one, largely by means of *interval projection*. First the "six basic tonal series" are enumerated, each based on one of the interval types. These series involve both simple concatenation of the interval in question and an expansion of the procedure in those cases where simple concatenation begins to yield octave duplicates before the twelve tones are exhausted—a tone foreign to the accumulated sonority is then introduced and built upon again by concatenation. Example 11 reproduces Hanson's summary of this process for the major second.[72] Further possibilities are derived by means of triadic projection, by simulta-

---

70. Howard Hanson, *Harmonic Materials of Modern Music: Resources of the Tempered Scale* (New York: Appleton-Century-Crofts, 1960). According to Robert Sutton, Hanson's book was essentially complete by 1955. See Sutton, "Howard Hanson, Set Theory Pioneer," *Sonus* 8, no. 1 (Fall, 1987): 17–39. The claim made in this title will be examined later in the present essay.

71. Hanson, *Harmonic Materials*, 9.

72. The right-hand column of Example 11 provides Hanson's summary of interval classes for

C D	s
C D E	ms^2
C D E F♯	m^2s^3t
C D E F♯G♯	$m^4s^4t^2$
C D E F♯G♯A♯	$m^6s^6t^3$
C D E F♯G G♯A♯	$p^2m^6n^2s^6d^2t^3$
C D E F♯G G♯A A♯	$p^4m^6ns^7d^4t^3$
C D E F♯G G♯A A♯B	$p^6m^7n^6s^8d^6t^3$
C C♯D E F♯G G♯A A♯B	$p^8m^8n^8sd^8t^4$
C C♯D D♯E F♯G G♯A A♯B	$p^{10}m^{10}n^{10}s^{10}d^{10}t^5$
C C♯D D♯E E♯F♯G G♯A A♯B	$p^{12}m^{12}n^{12}s^{12}d^{12}t^6$

Example 11. Hanson, *Harmonic Materials*, 93.

neous projection of two intervals, and by "projection by involution and at foreign intervals." A presentation of complementary sonorities and scales rounds out the book. As one would anticipate, Hanson's methods produce a certain amount of re-dundancy; but unlike Hába, for instance, Hanson always makes accurate note of such redundancy—accurate, that is, with respect to the criteria for identity of sonor-ity established by total interval content and inversional equivalence—acknowledg-ing that it is possible to construct quite a number of his sonorities in more than one way. In modern terms, then, Hanson's list of possible sonorities, as finally shown by the summary chart at the back of his book, is complete without duplication; its con-tents match, one for one, the now standard 220 pitch-class sets of cardinalities two through ten inclusive.

Hanson's book, the first full-length account of the "resources of the tempered scale," was indeed "an important breakthrough," as it has been described.[73] Why, then, was it not immediately accepted as the basis for a new theory of twentieth-century musical structure? Why does it languish in such obscurity today? The an-swer is partly a matter of substance, partly one of historical circumstances. As to the latter, Hanson's book had the misfortune to appear at a time when, in academic circles at any rate, neoclassical composers were falling out of fashion and quickly being supplanted by their twelve-tone-oriented counterparts. One suspects, even without access to sales figures or printing histories, that whatever market there may have been for *Harmonic Materials* was soon commandeered by Perle's *Serial Compo-sition and Atonality*, published just two years later, which must have seemed much more up-to-date in its outlook. Even those who managed to get past the very fact of the author's name, indelibly associated with compositional conservatism, and actu-

---

each sonority. The letters p, m, n, s, d, t stand for the interval classes now numbered 5, 4, 3, 2, 1, 6 respectively; the numeric superscript indicates the frequency of occurrence of each in that sonority.

73. Schmalfeldt, *Berg's "Wozzeck,"* 9.

ally examine Hanson's book would have been put off almost immediately by his dismissal of "the atonal theory in which all twelve tones of the chromatic scale are used in a single melodic or harmonic pattern" on the grounds that "such patterns tend to lose their identity, producing a monochromatic effect with its accompanying lack of the essential element of contrast."[74] They would also have looked askance at the musical illustrations, which by the tenor of the times must have seemed old-fashioned, even reactionary: true, Schoenberg and Berg are (just barely) represented, but so are Britten, Shostakovich, Holst, and Roy Harris. In these aspects, *Harmonic Materials* comes across as a work hoping vaguely to be useful to composers of the future yet clinging desperately to the past.

Much more serious obstacles to the success of Hanson's book, however, were posed by its substance. Inextricably bound up with the author's musical preferences was a distaste for the systematic and the abstract, in his view qualities associated with the twelve-tone method. According to Robert Sutton, Hanson never called himself a theorist, in fact regarded theorists as "'they'—somebody else."[75] And Hanson was at pains in the preface to his book to deflect the words "method" and "system," in case any reader might feel inclined to attach them to his work, calling it instead simply "a compendium of harmonic-melodic material" for the use of the composer.[76] It is precisely this attempt to maintain a neutral stance towards what he has discovered that dooms his work *as theory*, for there is no larger *raison d'être* to organize an exploration of its implications.[77] Hanson's demurrals notwithstanding, his book *is* organized, after a fashion, systematically—but ultimately it is a system that no one else could use. As an example of this inadequacy, consider inclusion relations, to which a good deal of attention is drawn in the chapters on projection of intervals, and in the summary chart. Many inclusion relations are shown in these projections, but the derivational chains alone cannot tell us what *other* sonorities are embedded in these progressively larger sonorities; in fact, the chains lend the impression that, because the sonorities are derived one from the other in such fashion, *this is their primary meaning*, an impression that persists even when alternative derivations turn up. Among these progressively larger sonorities, only hexachords are extensively analyzed for their inclusion of other sonorities. As for the summary chart, it does take account, it is true, of the universal field of inclusion relations: one can start anywhere

---

74. Hanson, *Harmonic Materials*, 33.

75. Sutton, "Howard Hanson, Set Theory Pioneer," 17.

76. Hanson, *Harmonic Materials*, xi.

77. For this reason, I cannot agree that Hanson was a "set theory pioneer," as he is identified by Robert Sutton in the article previously cited. His book is not about "unordered pitch-class sets of all sizes"; it is about *sonorities*, as Hanson himself calls them, from two to ten notes in extent. Sutton claims that the two are "the same thing," but a sonority cannot be a *set* until it is defined unambiguously as one and the implications of that definition explored in appropriately rigorous terms. And since no thesis is presented in Hanson's book concerning the function of these sonorities in music that might be written or that already has been written, his work cannot properly be called a *theory*, either.

and, given sufficient patience, amass a list of all sonorities smaller by one member, smaller by two members, and so forth, and, by the same token, all sonorities larger by one, larger by two, and so forth in which the initial sonority is itself included. But the data remain inchoate: no indication is given of possible compositional applications (quite deliberately, of course) any more than possible analytical ones (which, to be fair, there was evidently never any desire on the author's part to address).

Finally, it has to be said that any modern reader with even a modicum of scholarly expectations for a book titled as Hanson has titled his would be made uneasy by the complete absence of reference to the work of any other musical thinker. One ends up impressed that the author did all this himself, but distressed that it apparently isn't connected to anyone else's efforts. The few detectable influences on Hanson seem, not surprisingly, to reach back to well before the 1950s: the separation of consonance and dissonance, and the way in which this distinction is embedded in the order of his interval tabulations (using modern ic numbers: 5,4,3,2,1,6), evoke Hindemith, and are of course part of the old-fashioned aura given off by this book.

But for all the shortcomings of *Harmonic Materials*, and for all its isolation from the mainstream of theoretical formalization adequate and appropriate to the study of the progressive music of our century, it is clear that Hanson's work belongs squarely in the line of development according to the themes outlined at the beginning of the present essay, specifically those of comprehensiveness, inversional equivalence, and vertical-horizontal unity, all of which are fully integrated into his presentation of the material. Furthermore, certain features of the book—ranging from larger issues, such as the close attention given to complementation (especially as manifested by nonhexachordal sonorities) and the idea of weighting of intervals within a sonority as a means both of associating and differentiating sonorities, to such odd details as the "maverick" sonority, known to us today as 5–Z12 [01356], the only set class with fewer than six members not included in its own complement—are quite clearly reflected in Forte's subsequent work, especially in *The Structure of Atonal Music*, where, somewhat ironically in light of Hanson's antipathy towards atonality, a theory incorporating many of his insights was put in the service of explaining structure in the early music of the Second Viennese School.

VII

Forte's contribution, finally, to the development of twentieth-century theory was really twofold: first, a consistent *terminology* for pitch-class collections based on the mathematical properties of the set, together with consistent definitions of inclusion and similarity relations (between sets of unlike and like cardinalities respectively) and segmentation procedures for analytical application; second, the *set complex,* knit together by the network of K and Kh relations, which serves as a kind of capstone to these definitions and manipulations. At least as important to observe, however, is that the motivation for these inventions is firmly *analytical*, springing from a truly

fervent desire to uncover the secrets of an at times laconic, always enigmatic repertoire. Without this desire, *The Structure of Atonal Music* probably could never have
been written. This realization, in turn, focuses one's attention on the great extent to
which repertorial considerations have affected and directed the evolution of harmonic thinking throughout the twentieth century. In the earliest decades, the approach was basically analytical, proceeding with reference to the tonal music of the
recent past as supplemented by work closer to the present and not so readily expli-
cable in terms of tonal models. Further into the century, work was carried on mostly
at the hands of those whose agenda was essentially compositional—whether explicitly engaging their own music (Hauer, Messiaen, Schoenberg, as well as Krenek and
Perle) or implicitly doing so (Hába, Hindemith, Cowell), or tending to emphasize a
certain kind of approach (neotonal or "pantonal" in the case of Schillinger and
Slonimsky). In the years since 1945 the emphasis has been more on the analytical
once again, even if with some underlying, personal compositional implications.
Babbitt's passionate interest in the dodecaphonic Schoenberg has been amply demonstrated, Lewin's scarcely less so; Perle's corresponding advocacy of Berg is certainly well known. (Likewise, the "integral serialism" of the Darmstadt School and
associated publications in *Die Reihe* grew in great part out of a deep absorption with
the music of Webern.) With Forte's work, the compositional "angle," already having
reached a considerable degree of obtuseness (I mean this strictly in the geometrical
sense), flattens out completely. The very fact that Forte is not himself a composer has
changed the field of theory considerably. Not that there has been a sudden influx of
"perfect objectivity": indeed, Forte's great love for the atonal repertoire, to which
others had given short shrift in their preoccupation with the twelve-tone repertoire,
comes across vividly in *The Structure of Atonal Music*. But it has been his example,
and his tutelage, that have given rise to a whole generation of theorists many of
whom are not composers or, at least, do not regard any composing they may do as
competing significantly with their theoretical activity.[78]

Who did invent the pitch-class set? The question has no single answer. Forte's
comment quoted as the epigraph to this essay, though of course delivered in a certain
jocular spirit, nevertheless makes a serious point. Whoever it was who first used the
term in its modern sense (and it may well have been Forte[79]), it could hardly have

---

78. This observation, of course, is not meant to slight those contemporary theorists who
do happen to be composers and are happy about it, some of whom are among the contributors of the finest work being done in theory today.

79. In a footnote early on in *The Structure of Atonal Music*, Forte gives credit to Babbitt
for introducing the term and the concept. Yet one scans Babbitt's articles of the 1950s and
early '60s in vain for any use of the word *set* apart from its *original* meaning, denoting an
ordered twelve-note set. (Babbitt does use the term *subset* at one point in his article "Set
Structure as a Compositional Determinant.") Forte himself, by contrast, begins his article on
set complexes with the statement, "For the moment let us regard a 'set' as any collection of
notes" ("A Theory of Set-Complexes for Music," 136).

assumed the meaning it now has without the development, at the hands of many others, of its contributory concepts over time: that any collection of notes, not just those called chords in the venerable (pre-1900) literature of the theoretical discipline, had the potential to function independently and meaningfully; that criteria might be identified that would enable one to find all possible combinations of notes and also, at the same time, classify them into a manageable number of distinct types; that the concept of tonal inversion could be extended, once tonality itself had been superseded, to complete inversion of the intervallic content of a combination of notes, with the resultant regarded as equivalent in function to the original; and that the essential opposition of melody and harmony, so much insisted upon in nineteenth-century theory, could be broken down in favor of functional entities that would be comparable to one another whether presented horizontally, vertically, or as some hybrid of the two. Without all this as preparation, the notion of the pitch-class set would have made no sense at all. Further, it is doubtful that the pc set could have been invented, let alone come into the prominence it now enjoys, without first the advent and then (especially) the post-War resurgence of twelve-tone music, with its vital contributions of horizontal-vertical and inversional equivalence. Had the twelve-tone method met the early demise that its detractors were already predicting for it by the 1930s, perhaps we would still be sorting chords à la Hindemith, or using the cumbersome, ad hoc approach of Vincent Persichetti's *Twentieth-Century Harmony*.

Without question, pc-set theory will continue to develop, and change as it does so; indeed, this has already been happening, thanks to important work by Lewin, John Rahn, Robert Morris, and Forte himself, among many others. Even the set complex may one day be "replaced" by general consensus. But whatever shape the music theory of the twenty-first century may assume, it will owe a considerable debt to the emergence of the pc set in the twentieth. And it is safe to guess that the pc set and its accumulated theoretical superstructure (which for many theorists represent a kind of crux of the modern discipline of theory unmatched in importance even by that other significant contender, the work of Heinrich Schenker) will always seem to "belong"—as, when all is said and done, they should—to Allen Forte.

SCRIABIN'S MUSIC:
STRUCTURE AS PRISM FOR
MYSTICAL PHILOSOPHY

JAMES M. BAKER

Alexander Scriabin's place in music history has never been fully understood or appreciated. Stravinsky's famous rhetorical questions—". . . Scriabin . . . Where does he come from? And who are his forebears?"[1]— whether posed out of naiveté or a more complex motivation, reflect the general perception of Scriabin as a figure set off from the mainstream of musical developments. Scriabin scholars themselves have frequently contributed to the notion that the composer was simply a megalomaniac who had no interest in furthering a musical tradition.[2] The reasons for these misapprehensions are understandable, for Scriabin was perhaps the only major composer whose creative work seems to have been totally motivated by deeply held philosophical and mystical convictions about the state of the universe and his particular purpose within it. It is precisely his mystic beliefs, however, that most clearly define Scriabin's place in the history of culture, both Russian and Western European. For he partook of a mystical outlook which was in fact shared by a broad range of artists and poets working in Russia at the turn of the century. This essay begins with a description of the development of Scriabin's mystical beliefs in relation to those of his Russian contemporaries in art and literature. It concludes with a consideration of the impact of Scriabin's mysticism on the structure of his music.

An abbreviated version of the latter part of this article was presented at the Scriabin Museum in Moscow on the occasion of a festival celebrating the composer's 120th birthday, 7 January 1992. Examples 1 through 8 and Table 1 are reprinted, with permission, from: James M. Baker, *The Music of Alexander Scriabin* (New Haven and London: Yale University Press, 1986).

1. Igor Stravinsky, *Poetics of Music,* trans. Arthur Knodel and Ingolf Dahl (New York: Vintage Books, 1947), 100–01.

2. Hugh Macdonald, for instance, begins his concise study of Scriabin's works with the following comment: "Skryabin is one of those few composers who made no attempt to be versatile, let alone universal. His first music was for the piano; later he moved into orchestral music, and he was content with these, the piano and the orchestra, for the rest of his life. The horizons of his art never widened. Instead they grew gradually and inexorably narrower, his gaze focused more and more closely on himself, and a clearer example of artistic monomania—in his case egomania—is not easy to find in the chronicles of music." See his *Skryabin,* Oxford Studies of Composers, 15 (London: Oxford University Press, 1978), 7.

In a real sense, Scriabin was a product of his times, a period of frenzied creative activity known to historians of art and literature as the Silver Age. In the 1890s, after a period of relative stagnation, Russia was experiencing social, political, economic, and technological changes at a drastically accelerated pace. After the death of Alexander III in 1894, contacts with the West were greatly increased.[3] The advances in science and philosophy which had taken place in the latter part of the nineteenth century had completely altered the common understanding of humanity's place in the universe. The human species appeared to be on the threshhold of unprecedented technological, material, and even psychological and biological advances. The spirit of Prometheanism—confidence in human capability to conquer and transform the world—pervaded all fields of endeavor, including the arts.[4]

Yet progress came at a price. While most educated Russians felt relieved of the burdens of traditional religion, they were anxious about what the future held in store politically and socially. Many feared that Russia was destined to become merely another bourgeois industrialized state annexed to Western Europe. Many artists and intellectuals were alarmed at what progress meant with regard to the status of the individual in society. In his essay "The Crisis of Consciousness and Henrik Ibsen" (July 1910), Andrei Bely categorized five essential contradictions in contemporary society, the first being a description of the problem in general: consciousness vs. feeling, contemplation vs. will, individual vs. society, science vs. religion, and morality vs. beauty.[5]

During this highly materialistic and positivistic age, there appeared Russia's first great philosopher, Vladimir Solovyov, who, although not opposed to the scientific outlook, insisted that the rational intellect was inadequate to the task of comprehending human experience. His aim was to reconcile science and Christian revelation in a sort of "transcendental logic."[6] Many Russian artists, in particular the poets who grouped together under the banner of Symbolism, were more overtly distrustful of positivism, in that it denied the ideal and metaphysical aspect of existence. The poet Dmitri Merezhkovsky complained that

> although experience has led in its ultimate synthetic conclusion to the idea of world evolution, the metaphysical significance of this idea for the future has been blocked out by its empirical content gleaned from investigations of natural laws. . . . Suddenly

---

3. William Richardson, *"Zolotoe runo" and Russian Modernism: 1905–1910* (Ann Arbor: Ardis, 1986), 13–14.

4. For a thorough discussion of Prometheanism in turn-of-the-century Russia, see James H. Billington, *The Icon and the Axe: An Interpretive History of Russian Culture* (New York: Vintage Books, 1970), 478–92. Billington considers Prometheanism one of three trends characteristic of the age—the other two being sensualism and apocalypticism (see 492–518)—and he uses Scriabin's *Prometheus,* op. 60 as his chief example of the phenomenon.

5. J. D. Elsworth, *Andrey Bely: A Critical Study of the Novels* (Cambridge: Cambridge University Press, 1983), 10.

6. James West, *Russian Symbolism: A Study of Vyacheslav Ivanov and the Russian Symbolist Aesthetic* (London: Methuen, 1970), 36.

overwhelmed by the mass of inductive knowledge about what was and is, the horizons of deductive knowledge about what might and ought to be have been blocked out. The great realities of external, perceptual experience have muted the creative possibilities of inner, mystical experience. We know and understand more and more, and we want and create less and less.[7]

Another symbolist, Alexander Blok, taking the eruption of Mt. Etna in 1908 as an omen of terrible things to come, was skeptical of the ability of science to grasp the forces of nature:

Every promoter of culture is a demon, cursing the earth and devising wings in order to fly away from it. The heart of the advocate of progress breathes vengeance on the earth, on the elements; on the earth's crust not yet sufficiently hardened; vengeance for all its difficult times and endless spaces, for the rusty onerous chain of cause and effect, for the injustice of life and the injustice of death. Persons of culture, advocates of progress, choice intellectuals, foaming at the mouth, construct machines, move science forward in secret spite, trying to forget and not to hear the rumbling of the elements, subterranean and terrestrial, which are stirring, now here now there. . . .[8]

For many artists in those days, external appearances seemed barely to contain a much more vibrant deeper reality. The painter Vasily Kandinsky described the epoch as "a time of tragic collision between matter and spirit . . . for a few people . . . a time of presentiment or of precognition of the path to Truth."[9] And Valery Bryusov declared in 1903 that in these exceptional days "fundamental matter is beginning to tremble with life in the depths of our souls."[10] In particular, these artists felt that the spirit of positivism thwarted the development of humankind to its fullest potential. Blok, in his essay "The Decline of Humanism," declared that

man's entire being is in revolt; he has risen from a century-long stupor of civilisation. Spirit, soul and body have been caught up by the storm and, in the turmoil of the spiritual, political and social revolutions which have their causes in the cosmos, there takes place a transformation—the birth of the new man. [11]

---

7. Dmitri S. Merezhkovsky, "Sword," in *A Revolution of the Spirit: Crisis of Value in Russia, 1890–1918*, ed. Martha Bohachevsky-Chomiak and Bernice Glatzer Rosenthal (Newtonville, Mass.: Oriental Research Partners, 1982), 209.

8. Alexander Blok, "Nature and Culture," in Blok, *The Spirit of Music,* trans. I. Freiman (Westport, Conn.: Hyperion Press, 1973), 51.

9. Rose-Carol Washton Long, "Kandinsky's Vision," in *The Life of Vasilii Kandinsky in Russian Art: A Study of "On the Spiritual in Art,"* ed. John E. Bowlt and Rose-Carol Washton Long (Newtonville, Mass.: Oriental Research Partners, 1980), 44.

10. Valery Bryusov, "A Review of K. D. Balmont's 'Let's Be Like the Sun'," in *The Russian Symbolists: An Anthology of Critical and Theoretical Writings,* ed. and trans. Ronald E. Peterson (Ann Arbor: Ardis, 1986), 43.

11. Alexander Blok, "The Decline of Humanism," in Blok, *The Spirit of Music,* 69–70 (italics his).

Kandinsky believed that the world was entering an "epoch of great spirituality" in which art would "serve the development and refinement of the human soul."[12]

The Russian symbolists demanded more of poetry than their French predecessors, although as a rather loosely formed group they were themselves not entirely in agreement on the aims of the movement. While the French symbolists concentrated on evocation of mood and refinement of poetic technique, the Russians had the more grandiose goal, in the words of Vyacheslav Ivanov, of "liberation of the soul *(katharsis)* as a development of inner experience."[13] Bryusov declared the highest purpose of symbolism to be "the world's cognition beyond rational forms, beyond thinking about causality."[14] Ivanov stressed the synthetic effect of symbolism:

> ... One could say of Symbolist art that the principle of its activity is, above all, union. ... Not only does it unite, it also combines. Two are combined by a third, the highest. The symbol, this third, resembles a rainbow that has burst into flames between the ray of the word and the moisture of the soul which reflected the ray ... [15]

The symbolists believed that their art was hastening the evolution of humankind to a transcendental state of aesthetic and spiritual awareness.

For most symbolists, striving toward the ideal culminated in true religious mysticism. In this regard, their direct predecessor was Solovyov, who envisioned government by theocracy and aspired toward a knowledge of the ultimate reality which would embrace nature, divine principle, and human individuality. Solovyov believed in the prophetic role of art.[16] The poet Georgy Chulkov, who originated the symbolist schism known as "mystical anarchism," declared that the goal of art is "to find that common soil on which it is possible to break the circle of solitary experience and together with this to find the path that leads to a religious society."[17] For Ivanov, another mystical anarchist, "Symbolism ... seems like the first, vague reminiscence about the sacred language of the priests and magi, who at one time gave the words of national language a special, secret significance. ... "[18] In penetrating the mysteries underlying the fragmentation of contemporary life, the symbolists hoped to restore the human race to a primordial state of oneness with the universe. From this point of view, the role of the poet is crucial. According to Alexander Blok, "a Symbolist from the very beginning is a *theurgist,* that is, a possessor of secret knowledge, behind which secret action stands. But he looks upon this secret, which only later turns out to be universal, as his own. ... "[19] And Bryusov states:

---

12. Long, "Kandinsky's Vision," 45.
13. Vyacheslav Ivanov, "Thoughts About Symbolism," in Peterson, 188.
14. Bryusov, "Keys to the Mysteries," in Peterson, 63.
15. Ivanov, "Thoughts," 182.
16. James West, 39–41.
17. Georgy Chulkov, "The Veil of Isis," in Peterson, 92.
18. Ivanov, "The Precepts of Symbolism," in Peterson, 147.
19. Blok, "On the Present Status of Russian Symbolism," in Peterson, 158.

We demand from a poet that he tirelessly bring his "holy sacrifices," not only with his verses, but with every hour of his life, with every feeling—his love, his hate, accomplishments and failures. Let the poet create, not his books, but his own life. Let him keep the altar fire burning, like Vesta's fire, let him kindle a great bonfire, unafraid of burning himself and his life in it. We throw ourselves on the altar of our divinity. Only a priest's knife, cutting our breasts, gives us the right to be called a poet.[20]

Later Blok was to pronounce his involvement with mysticism "childish," placing his faith instead in the Russian people,[21] and some of his fellow symbolists never subscribed to a specifically religious view of poetry. Regardless of their individual beliefs, however, the symbolists generally recognized the element of mystery as essential to their art.

Before proceeding to a discussion of Scriabin's mystical beliefs, it will be useful to summarize his connections with the aforementioned poets and artists and others as well. According to his biographer, Boris de Schloezer, Scriabin was not an avid reader, except when it came to the poetry of the Russian symbolists, for which he had an ardent interest.[22] Schloezer cites in particular the poets Konstantin Balmont and Ivanov as having a special attraction for Scriabin. Of Ivanov, Scriabin said, "I am close to him . . . we are alike."[23] After Scriabin's death, Balmont wrote an essay entitled "Light and Sound in Nature and the Color Symphony of Scriabin," which was published by Serge Koussevitzky in 1917. Scriabin was introduced to Dmitri Merezhkovsky in June 1907,[24] and after Scriabin returned to Moscow in November 1912, Merezhkovsky was one of a number of artists who attended evenings at the Scriabin apartment. Scriabin wrote a sonnet to Bryusov on the occasion of his safe return from the front in January 1915.[25] Evidently Scriabin knew Andrei Bely as early as the period 1900–04. After an enthusiastic review of Bely's Second Symphony (a literary work) by the critic Emil Medtner, brother of the composer, Bely became friends with the Medtner brothers, and it was at the Medtners' studio that Bely met Scriabin, Koussevitzky, and other luminaries. Bely mentions Scriabin several times in his memoirs.[26]

---

20. Bryusov, "A Holy Sacrifice," in Peterson, 69.

21. Blok quoted in Bohachevsky-Chomiak and Rosenthal, introduction, 32.

22. Boris de Schloezer, *Scriabin: Artist and Mystic,* trans. Nicolas Slonimsky (Berkeley and Los Angeles: University of California Press, 1987), 94–95.

23. Faubion Bowers, *Scriabin: A Biography of the Russian Composer, 1871–1915,* 2 vols. (Tokyo and Palo Alto: Kodansha, 1969), 2:239.

24. Bowers, *Scriabin, Russian Composer,* 2:170.

25. *Muzika,* no. 229 (1915); reprint, *Russian Musical Gazette,* no. 17/18 (1915).

26. Ada Steinberg, *Word and Music in the Novels of Andrey Bely* (Cambridge: Cambridge University Press, 1982), 38–39. Scriabin was invited by Emil Medtner, music editor for the Moscow-based symbolist journal *Zolotoe runo (The Golden Fleece),* to be a regular commentator, to which Scriabin replied (15 February 1906) that he would have to postpone offering any commentaries until sometime in the future, because "the realms where I now study have no

Prince Sergei Trubetskoi, professor of philosophy and first elected president of Moscow University, was a friend and admirer of Scriabin. Trubetskoi, who considered himself a mystical Christian, was President of the Moscow Philosophical Society, and at his behest Scriabin joined the organization and attended a number of sessions. Through Trubetskoi, whose works include *Metaphysics in Ancient Greece,* Scriabin most likely first encountered Classical Greek drama and ritual, which certainly influenced his grandest conception, the *Mysterium.*[27]

Scriabin's patroness, Margarita Morozova, was the widow of a wealthy landowner and member of the large and close-knit Morozov clan, the liberally minded merchant-industrialist family responsible for importing to Moscow the finest impressionist and post-impressionist paintings from France. Scriabin, however, seems to have had little interest in the visual arts. He admired the work of Lithuanian artist M. K. Ciurlionis, whose efforts to paint according to principles of musical structure may have been inspired in part by Scriabin's synaesthetic aims, and he was an enthusiastic supporter of the French sculptor Rodo (pseudonym of August Niederhäusern), with whom he reputedly had lengthy conversations on theosophy. While in Brussels around 1908, he was associated with the artist Jean Delville, who created the famous frontispiece for the score of *Prometheus,* replete with theosophical iconography. He might have had the opportunity to become acquainted with the paintings of Kandinsky, since his friend and biographer Leonid Sabaneev published an article on *Prometheus* in Kandinsky's famous *Blauer Reiter* almanac (Munich, 1912), but there seems to be no documentary evidence that Scriabin knew Kandinsky's work.

From his youth onward, Scriabin had a religious bent. His diaries concentrate heavily on religious and philosophical aspects of his development. At age sixteen, he wrote of humanity's aspiration toward God, of human resemblance to God.[28] In 1906, looking back at his religious attitudes in early childhood, Scriabin recorded: "Naive belief in the Old Testament. Prayers ... A very serious participation in the mystery of the Eucharist ..." And at age twenty: "The first earnest attempt at philosophy; the beginning of self-analysis. . . . First reflections on the value of life, religion, God. Continued strong faith—in God the Father rather than Christ. Ardent, long prayers, constant church attendance ... Reproaches addressed to fate and to God."[29] At age

---

direct connection with music" (Bowers, *Scriabin, Russian Composer,* 2:128–29). Although a staunch advocate of the German tradition (as personified by Wagner), Medtner seems to have had a genuine respect for Scriabin's music. He was involved in a fascinating debate which raged in the pages of the *Golden Fleece* concerning the music of Max Reger, whose music Medtner deplored. Oddly enough, Reger's defender in this battle was Karatygin, a loyal Scriabinist who, as organizer of the famous Petersburg Evenings of Contemporary Music, had seen to it that Scriabin was virtually the only Russian represented on their programs; see Richardson, 79–80.

27. V. V. Rubtsova, *Aleksandr Nikolaevich Skryabin* (Moscow: Muzika, 1989), 335–37.

28. Manfred Kelkel, *Alexandre Scriabine: Sa vie, l'ésotérisme et le langage musical dans son oeuvre,* 2 vols. (Paris: Editions Honoré Champion, 1978), 2:4.

29. Schloezer, 115.

twenty-one the young composer evidently experienced a religious crisis, from which he emerged with new-found confidence and a sense of mission:

> I thank you for all the trials and tribulations to which you subjected me, for you gave me the knowledge of my endless power, my unbounded strength, my invincibility. You endowed me with creative power. I will go forth to carry to all humanity the message of strength and power, tell them they should not despair, that nothing is lost.[30]

The theme of overcoming a spiritual crisis is important in several of Scriabin's earlier projects. In the poetic text of the final movement of his First Symphony (1900), the speaker does not address God directly but rather the "sublime laws of harmony," which he calls "pure symbols of the living God": "In the dark, hopeless hour/ When the soul falls into vain torments,/ Torch of the arts, you bring to light/ The new day which consoles us./ Our strength failing in combat/ You rekindle with your flame." Scriabin's outline for a projected opera dating from this time contains a similar theme, but with the significant difference that he finds freedom not in God but in himself:

I.   Beatitude. Ideal, Truth. The goal outside me. Faith in God, which fills me with longing for high ideals and a hope of their attainment through divine power.
II. Disillusion in the possibility of this attainment; reproaches to God.
III. Search for the ideal in my own self. Protest. Freedom.
IV. Scientific justification of freedom.
V.   Religion[31]

Attempting a quasi-scientific approach to self-examination, Scriabin, like most symbolists, was led to religion. Indeed, this outline could be a summary of the composer's quest over his entire lifetime.

At about age twenty-one Scriabin read Renan and Schopenhauer, and later he became familiar with the writings of Johann Gottlieb Fichte (1762–1814), Kant, and Hegel. Never a systematic reader, Scriabin seems to have picked up a good deal of his knowledge from secondary sources, such as Windelband's *Geschichte der Neuen Philosophie*. His readings of the German idealist philosophers played a crucial role in the formation of his artistic persona. From Schopenhauer he gleaned the notion of music as the art through which the absolute truth can be revealed, and the themes of individual will and the play of creative activity so prevalent in Scriabin's "Poem of Ecstasy" owe something to Schopenhauer as well. In his diaries, Scriabin shows an awareness of the Hegelian dialectic in speaking of a synthesis of his states of consciousness. Manfred Kelkel believes that the strongest influence on Scriabin was the philosophy of Fichte, from which Scriabin gleaned two ideas basic to his creative role: the principle of the "I" which is both that which acts and at the same time the

---

30. Schloezer, 118.
31. Schloezer, 117.

product of the action; and the concept of the "not-I" determined in the process of the assertion of the "I."[32] Fichte's idea that "art introduces an actually transcendental view into life itself" was an important precedent for the Russian symbolist aesthetic.[33]

The works of Friedrich Nietzsche exerted a very powerful influence on Scriabin's writings and music, as on the poetry of the Russian symbolists. James P. Scanlan describes Nietzsche's impact on the artists of the Russian renaissance as follows:

> Friedrich Nietzsche . . . showed them the sanctity of paganism and classical antiquity. . . . The earthly and the heavenly, long divorced in Russian cultural life, began to come together for these thinkers in a strange blend of paganism and Christianity. They read of the twice-born Dionysus, and were reminded of the resurrected Christ; they studied the Christian scriptures, and found a Dionysian, fleshly spectacle, the Apocalypse. The result was an intoxicating new vision of the world and its future—a "new religious consciousness" which not only made the body the equal of the soul, but prophesied an imminent golden age, in which that equality would transfigure the earth.[34]

Scriabin freely acknowledged his debt to *The Birth of Tragedy* for its Dionysian concept of ecstasy,[35] and the persona of the artist-superman which Scriabin so carefully cultivated was obviously based on *Also Sprach Zarathustra*. The opera on which Scriabin worked from 1900 to 1903—a project which he ultimately abandoned—was based on Nietzschean themes. His hero, the philosopher-warrior-musician-poet, calls himself the "goal of goals" and teaches the princess ecstasy through dance.[36] His aim is to free the masses of humanity, to illumine their lives and bring hope for the future.[37] Scriabin's text for the *Poem of Ecstasy* is replete with Nietzschean subjects: the sun, the heights, beauty, acceptance of both suffering and joy, desire to be God.[38]

---

32. Kelkel, 2:4, 22, 29–33.

33. Chulkov, in Peterson, 88.

34. Quoted in Mihajlo Mihajlov, "The Great Catalyzer: Nietzsche and Russian Neo-Idealism," in *Nietzsche in Russia,* ed. Bernice Glatzer Rosenthal (Princeton: Princeton University Press, 1986), 130.

35. Bowers, *Scriabin, Russian Composer,* 2:214.

36. Ann M. Lane, "Bal'mont and Skriabin: The Artist as Superman," in Rosenthal, *Nietzsche,* 212–13.

37. Schloezer, 165.

38. Lane, 215. Konstantin Balmont, a member of the so-called first generation of Russian symbolists, was particularly affected by Nietzsche's ultra-individualistic poetic stance: "If there were gods, how could I endure not to be a god!" Like Zarathustra, Balmont composed odes to his own soul. For Balmont, the artist is free, lord of the world. In his poem "The Scorpion," Balmont expressed the Nietzschean theme of *amor fati* (love of fate), an important theme in Scriabin's writings as well, as reflected in the above-cited diary entry: "[T]hank you for all the trials and tribulations. . . ." The sun imagery which pervades much symbolist poetry, including that of Scriabin, is taken directly from *Zarathustra*. For Balmont, whose best-known collection *Let's Be Like the Sun* was published in 1903, Nietzsche was the very

An aspect of Scriabin's artistic persona which connects him with Nietzsche and the Russian symbolists is his solipsism, particularly evident in his diaries, as witnessed by this excerpt from 1905:

> . . . I am God!
> I am nothing, I am play, I am freedom, I am life.
> I am the boundary, I am the peak.
>
> . . . I am God!
> I am the blossoming, I am the bliss,
> I am all-consuming passion, all engulfing,
> I am fire enveloping the universe,
> Reducing it to chaos. . . . [39]

This language, so foreign to modern notions of identity, is no doubt the source of the commonly held impression that Scriabin was psychopathically egocentric. He may well have been, but many other artists of the time shared the same sorts of delusions. For example, in 1900 Balmont wrote, observing passers-by: "They will all finally merge into one common stream, directed by your thoughts, and having perceived the beauty and complexity of your soul, they will form with you one unbroken unity, like radii from a center. The world will become a phantasmagoria. . . ."[40] And in much more apocalyptic tones, Fyodor Sologub wrote in 1908: "There are no different people, there is only one person, only one *I* in the whole universe, willing, acting, suffering, burning in an unquenchable fire, and from the fury of a horrible and ugly life saved in the good and joyful embrace of the universal comforter—Death."[41]

The obsessive use of the poetic "I" by the Russian symbolists certainly reflects the crisis of identity which afflicted many younger artists during the Silver Age. Although the Nietzschean influence is clear, the solipsistic focus of Scriabin's language may have derived from a more traditional source, the development of the theory of knowledge in German idealistic philosophy. Scriabin's diaries were, in fact, the means he used to work out the complex theories of cognition explored in his readings and discussions. The "I" that he employs in the diary notes is not equivalent to the individual ego, but is rather the result of synthesis in a dialectical process:

---

model of the refined artist, who must perish because of his refinement. In speaking of Nietzsche, Balmont evokes the myth of Icarus, "who was able to make himself wings but not able to give his wings the strength to endure the heat of the scorching sun" (Lane, 195–201). Even those symbolists, such as Blok, who were not especially attracted to the notion of the superman were nevertheless drawn to the Dionysian concept of orgiastic, communal celebration; see Evelyn Bristol, "Blok between Nietzsche and Soloviev," in Rosenthal, *Nietzsche,* 150.

39. Bowers, *Scriabin, Russian Composer,* 2:61.

40. Konstantin Balmont, "An Elementary Statement About Symbolist Poetry," in Peterson, 38.

41. Fyodor Sologub, "The Theater of One Will," in Peterson, 111.

By identifying "I" with "non-I," I annex "non-I." From this point on, the consciousnesses of all men are dissolved in my individual consciousness. I become for them the fulfillment of all their yearnings; the world becomes a unified action, an ecstasy.... Everything in the world is the result of mankind's creative activity, because everything is my creation. Mankind, that is, I, is the Deity. Strife and death will be vanquished, and universal joy without measure will spring forth in a triumphant torrent of life.[42]

In 1908 Merezhkovsky employed precisely the same philosophical model, based on Hegel and Fichte, to describe the evolution of mystical cognition.[43] All of the symbolists were quite sensitive to the use of the poetic "I," and their writings are often concerned with critiques or explanations of its use in particular works. Innokenty Annensky, writing of Zinaida Gippius's poetic voice, states: " . . . there is only an immeasurable *I* in her lyrics, not her *I* of course, not Ego at all. It is the world and it is God. . . . "[44] In differentiating his poetical/philosophical persona from himself as individual, Scriabin used the terms "greater I" and "little I."[45] At roughly the same time that he was recording his philosophical musings in the diaries, Scriabin was defending his concepts in conversations with his close friend Georgi Plekhanov, the father of Russian Marxism.[46] It is safe to conclude that he was aware of a general skepticism toward his artistic stance. In fact, his sensitivity may be reflected in the fact that his statement "I am God" from the private diaries becomes in the concluding lines of the published "Poem of Ecstasy" the much more generally acceptable "And the universe resounds/ With joyful cry/ I am!"

Scriabin's concept of ecstasy is bound together with the Fichtean notion of the play of the creative activity, important for all of the Russian symbolists. Play is the means for liberating the creative forces within us, as indicated by Vladimir Markov's statement that "in playing, we express our "I" more vividly and unconstrainedly and emerge no longer as the masters of forces hidden within us, but as their slaves."[47] Thus the individual "I" is released, becoming one with the universe. For Scriabin, ecstasy is the product of this synthesis: "Ecstasy is the highest exaltation of action; ecstasy is a summit. . . . Intellectually, ecstasy is the highest synthesis; emotionally, it is the greatest happiness."[48] In Scriabin's view, ecstasy is essentially erotic, as is evident in his declaration, "I want to take the world as [a man] takes a woman."[49] In this regard, Scriabin was clearly heir to the philosophy of Solovyov, who extolled sexual

42. Schloezer, 197.
43. Merezhkovsky, in Bohachevsky-Chomiak and Rosenthal, 212–13.
44. Innokenty Annensky, "On Contemporary Lyrism," in Peterson, 142.
45. Schloezer, 125.
46. Bowers, *Scriabin, Russian Composer,* 2:95–96.
47. Vladimir Markov, "The Principles of the New Art," in *Russian Art of the Avant-Garde: Theory and Criticism, 1902–1934,* ed. and trans. John E. Bowlt (New York: Viking, 1976), 31.
48. Schloezer, 149.
49. Schloezer, 131.

pleasure as intimating mystical union with Sophia, the eternal feminine principle. For Solovyov, art afforded a means to achieving an ecstatic state of "total-oneness." The symbolists were among the many young artists who seized upon Solovyov's ideas, exploring sensuality in their poetry and plunging into sexual experimentation in their personal lives. Scriabin may have been acquainted with Solovyov's notions through Trubetskoi, who was the author of a major study of his philosophy.[50]

The historical context of Scriabin's *Poem of Ecstasy* sheds light on the meaning of this grandiose work. This symphony is the only one of Scriabin's completed compositions which originated as a literary project. As early as 1904, Scriabin was making notes for a literary work entitled "Poème orgiaque," which was published privately in Russian in May 1906. He began composing music on the same subject in early 1905, completing the sketch of the work in draft by December 1906. The *Poem of Ecstasy* had its world premiere in New York in December 1908, and was first played in Russia one month later, in St. Petersburg. The creation of this work coincided with years of social and political turmoil in Russia. When war broke out with Japan in February 1904, there was initially little concern among the intelligentsia, since a Russian victory was assumed. The subsequent revolution of 1905 generated great excitement among the intellectuals. Blok led a demonstration brandishing a red banner, and Chulkov was imprisoned for his activities.[51] Many others, however—including Diaghilev, Benois, and Balmont—departed for Western Europe. Since he was already out of the country when the war began and did not return until 1909, Scriabin was minimally affected by these events, although he followed them as closely as possible. The symbolists initially hailed the revolution as bringing on the next phase of human evolution. By the end of 1906, however, with the reestablishment of government control, they had become pessimistic about the extent to which things had really changed. In the next several years they would become increasingly factionalized over matters of aesthetic and philosophical doctrine. The poet Ellis blamed the crisis within the symbolist movement on the ill-defined literary and ideological groupings in "our culturally too young society," and on the "excessive chaos and individuality of the main leaders, generally characteristic of undisciplined Russian life."[52] In 1910, looking back on the revolution, Blok wrote: "We have lived through the madness of other worlds, demanding a miracle too soon . . . the violet worlds of revolution burned [the miracle] to ashes."[53]

Ironically, at the very time the symbolists were finding themselves divided against one another, the public discovered and took a fancy to their poetry. This was due in large part to the fact that the government was slow to reimpose censorship. Having been disappointed in their political aspirations, after the revolution the pub-

---

50. W. Bruce Lincoln, *In War's Dark Shadow: The Russians before the Great War* (New York: Simon and Schuster, 1983), 351–52.

51. Richardson, 181.

52. Ellis, "Symbolism and the Future," in Peterson, 178.

53. Alexander Blok, "Present Status," in Peterson, 164.

lic sought to escape in a wave of pornography, eroticism, and debauchery, and it happened that the so-called decadent poetry suited popular taste perfectly.[54] While Scriabin's attempts at sensualism in the poetic text to the *Poem of Ecstasy* come across as naive in comparison to much of the literature of the time, and while he surely never intended to cater to public demand, his orchestral work reflects the erotic fascination then welling up in contemporary Russian society.

Scriabin's biographer Boris de Schloezer records that in 1902 Scriabin regarded mysticism as superstition, rejecting the mystical philosophies of Solovyov and Trubetskoi (even though he was a friend and admirer of the latter).[55] If this is true, it is unclear at what point he altered his opinion and turned toward mystic philosophy. In any event, it is apparent from the philosophical speculations in his diaries that his beliefs pointed in the direction of mysticism from the beginning. The central concept of mysticism is union, always Scriabin's abiding concern, even if earlier on he was likely to describe this union, in the language of German idealism, as the synthesis of the "I" and "not-I". Scriabin's "I am God" declarations are strikingly close to certain sayings from Eastern religions, for instance "Thou art that" and "I am Brahman" from the *Upanishads,* although it is impossible to trace the origin of his usage to Eastern sources.[56] With his confidence in his own special creative powers, Scriabin could well have found it appealing to assume the role of the Adept, a highly evolved human being who has been initiated into the secrets of the universe.

We do know that in May 1905 Scriabin was reading and was impressed by Madame Blavatsky's *Key to Theosophy.*[57] The theosophical movement had arisen in the peculiar cultural context of nineteenth-century America, characterized by its eclectic traditions of anti-institutionalism, social liberalism, transcendentalism, and belief in the efficacy of individual effort, as well as a very lively interest in occultism. Founded in New York City in 1875 by Blavatsky, Col. Henry Olcott, and others, the

---

54. Richardson, 183.

55. Schloezer, 65.

56. Geoffrey Parrinder, *Mysticism in the World's Religions* (New York: Oxford University Press, 1976), 13–15.

57. See his letters of 5 and 8 May 1905 (new style), written from Paris to Tatyana Schloezer, in A. Scriabin, *Pis'ma,* ed. A. V. Kashperov (Moscow: Muzika, 1965), 367–69. In the latter he writes, "*La Clef de la Théosophie* is a remarkable book. You will be surprised how close it is to my thinking" ("Ti budesh' udivlena, do kakoi stepeni blizko ko mne"). This statement would appear to indicate that Scriabin was just becoming acquainted with Blavatsky's writings at this time.

The circle of seemingly disparate influences on Scriabin becomes nearly closed when one learns that Helena Blavatsky was indirectly connected with the philosopher Vladimir Solovyov through his elder brother, Vsevolod, the novelist. Initially an ardent Theosophist, Vsevelod subsequently disingratiated himself by writing *A Modern Priestess of Isis* (1895), intended to expose Blavatsky as a charlatan. See Sylvia Cranston, *HPB: The Extraordinary Life and Influence of Helena Blavatsky, Founder of the Modern Theosophical Movement* (New York: G. P. Putnam's Sons, 1993), 298–309.

Theosophical Society had the avowed purpose of reconciling science—in particular, the theory of evolution—with religion. Claiming to tap ancient sources of wisdom, theosophists aimed at synthesizing all religions, including Eastern religions, in the belief that all faiths have a single primitive source. Theosophists assert a primal unity and the physical devolution of man from higher spirits.[58]

In a highly complex and elaborate cosmogony based largely on the number seven,[59] Theosophy describes a universe in which the Absolute is differentiated on seven planes. Man is said to have a sevenfold constitution: body, vitality, astral body, animal soul, human soul, spiritual soul, and spirit, the first four of which make up the physical body, the last three the immortal spirit. The universe will evolve through seven cycles, the first three effecting materialization culminating in a state of crystallization in the fourth. The last three cycles will involve the reverse process of dema-

---

58. Bruce F. Campbell, *Ancient Wisdom Revived: A History of the Theosophical Movement* (Berkeley and Los Angeles, and London: University of California Press, 1980), 9, 20, 36–37.

59. Helena Blavatsky, co-founder of the Theosophical Society, explained the significance of numbers, and the special significance of the number seven as follows:

All systems of religious mysticism are based on numerals. . . . The sacredness of numbers begins with the great First—the ONE—and ends only with the nought or zero—symbol of the infinite and boundless circle which represents the universe. All the intervening figures, in whatever combination, or however multiplied, represent philosophical ideas . . . relating either to a moral or a physical fact in nature. They are a key to the ancient views on cosmogony, in its broad sense, including man and beings, and the evolution of the human race, spiritually as well as physically.

The number *seven* is the most sacred of all, and, as such, is undoubtedly of Hindû origin. . . . This number reappears likewise on almost every page of *Genesis* and throughout the Mosaic books, and we find it conspicuous . . . in the *Book of Job* and the Oriental Kabala. . . . It . . . again reappeared in Christianity with its *seven* sacraments, *seven* churches in Asia Minor, *seven* capital sins, *seven* virtues . . ., etc.

Have the *seven* prismatic colors of the rainbow seen by Noah no other meaning than that of a covenant between God and man to refresh the memory of the former? To the Kabalist, at least, they have a significance inseparable from the seven labors of magic, the seven upper spheres, the seven notes of the musical scale, the seven numerals of Pythagoras, the seven wonders of the world, the seven ages, and even the seven steps of the Masons. . . . (H.P. Blavatsky, *Isis Unveiled: A Master-Key to the Mysteries of Ancient and Modern Science and Theology*, 2 vols. [1877; 3d ed. rev., Point Loma, Cal.: The Aryan Theosophical Press, 1919], 2: 407–8)

The Russian symbolists held numbers sacred as well. Valery Bryusov wrote:

I kneel down before you, I eagerly seek you, numbers!

Free and fleshless, incorporeal shadows,

You hang, reaching across like an arching rainbow,

Down to one's thoughts from the peak of inspiration!

Quoted in F. D. Reeve, "On Some Scientific Concepts in Russian Poetry at the Turn of the Century," Monday Evening Papers No. 6 (Middletown, Conn.: Wesleyan University Center for Advanced Studies, 1966), 15.

terialization. We are said to be at present just past the midpoint of the fourth cycle. Human beings will evolve through seven root races. Most Europeans living at the turn of the century were thought to be members of the fifth, Aryan race, although the beginnings of the sixth race were said to have been observed in America. The theosophical doctrine of evolution includes the concept of recapitulation—that is, at each stage of evolution, each organism must first repeat the course of its previous evolution before advancing. The concept of karma, "reaping the effects of past actions," is basic to theosophical teachings on evolution, as is, of course, the concomitant notion of reincarnation.[60]

Scholarly opinion has been split on the question of whether Scriabin was significantly influenced by Theosophy. As evidence that he never seriously subscribed to theosophical doctrine, Manfred Kelkel cites the fact that Scriabin's voluminous correspondence contains only four mentions of Theosophy and introduces only one word—*Manvantara*—from the specialized theosophical vocabulary.[61] Kelkel is satisfied that Scriabin's background in German philosophy, particularly the works of Fichte, is a logical and sufficient basis for his personal system of beliefs.

Scriabin's use of the word "Manvantara" warrants close inspection. This term denotes the cycle of cosmic evolution from the Unifying Principle to the material world, followed by involution to the Absolute, a process taking place over many millions of years. The passage in question comes from Scriabin's second notebook, dating from 1904–05, roughly the time he was reading Blavatsky:

> An impulse disturbs divine harmony and thereby creates the substance upon which divine thought is imprinted. Equilibrium is then reestablished *for an instant a degree lower* and then is broken by a new impulse, and so on, until all the accumulated force is spent in the activity of the *entire manvantara*. But with respect to what follows, this manvantara can itself be considered an impulse which disturbs divine equilibrium; and so on.[62]

Scriabin's reference here is no mere allusion to an esoteric concept. Rather, his thought here is complex and bears striking similarities to certain of Madame Blavatsky's pronouncements on cosmogony, as, for example, these excerpts from the *Secret Doctrine*:

---

60. Campbell, 43–44, 46, 63, 66; Elsworth, 43.

61. Kelkel, 2:2–3, 35.

62. His italics; English translation by the author from the French translation by Marina Scriabine: "L'élan trouble l'harmonie divine et par cela crée le matériau, sur lequel sera empreinte la pensée divine. L'équilibre sera rétabli *pour un instant un degré plus bas* et ensuite, par un nouvel élan, il sera rompu à nouveau, et ainsi de suite, jusqu'à ce que toute la force accumulée ne trouve une issue dans l'activité de *tout le manvantara*. Mais par rapport à celui qui le suit, ce manvantara peut être considéré aussi comme un élan qui trouble l'équilibre divin et ainsi de suite" (Alexandre Scriabine, *Notes et réflexions: Carnets inédits,* trans. and ed. Marina Scriabine [Paris: Editions Klincksieck, 1979], 22).

The Primordial Substance had not yet passed out of its precosmic latency into differentiated objectivity, or even become the . . . invisible Protyle of Science. But, as the hour strikes and it becomes receptive of the Fohatic impress of the Divine thought . . . its heart opens. . . .

Manvantaric impulse commences with the reawakening of Cosmic Ideation (the "Universal Mind"), concurrently with, and parallel to, the primary emergence of Cosmic Substance—the latter being the manvantaric vehicle of the former—from its undifferentiated *pralayic* state. Then, absolute wisdom mirrors itself in its Ideation; which, by a transcendental process, superior to and incomprehensible by human Consciousness, results in Cosmic Energy (*Fohat*). Thrilling through the bosom of inert Substance, *Fohat* impels it to activity, and guides its primary differentiations on all the Seven planes of Cosmic Consciousness.[63]

Two aspects of Scriabin's statement resonate particularly strongly with theosophical teachings. First, the process he describes entails levels, or planes of existence. Second, and even more striking, Scriabin asserts that, at another level, an entire manvantara can become an initiating impulse for a much greater manvantara. This accords with Blavatsky's teaching: "The full period of one *Manvantara* is 303,448,000 [mortal] years. . . . 14 "Manvantaras" *plus* the period of one *Sâtya Yuga* make ONE DAY OF BRAHMA, or a complete Manvantara and make 4,320,000,000 years."[64]

Given the correspondence of Scriabin's musings with these special theosophical teachings, one is inclined to accept Schloezer's testimony that Scriabin read broadly in Theosophy and enjoyed engaging in conversation on the subject.[65] Scriabin would have been most closely involved with Theosophists while he was in Brussels in 1908. Bowers speculates that Scriabin was enrolled in the Theosophical Society at that time through Emile Sigogne, a professor of elocution who was planning to collaborate with the composer on a new language for the *Mysterium* to be rooted in San-

---

63. H. P. Blavatsky, *Collected Writings 1888: The Secret Doctrine*, 3 vols., 7th ed. (Wheaton, Ill.: Theosophical Publishing House, 1979), 1: 58 and 328.

64. Blavatsky, *Secret Doctrine*, 2:69.

65. Schloezer writes: "Scriabin first became acquainted with theosophy in Paris in 1906 [but note, Scriabin's correspondence indicates 1905; see n. 57], when a friend told him that his vision of *Mysterium*, of the union of humanity with divinity and the return of the world to oneness, had much in common with theosophy. Here we can definitely speak of an influence, for when I saw Scriabin a few months later in Switzerland he was deeply engaged in reading works by Mme. Blavatsky, Annie Besant, C. W. Leadbeater, and other theosophists. His conversation was full of theosophical allusions to Manvantara, Pralaya, Seven Planes, Seven Races, and the like; he used these terms volubly as if they were familiar to all and as if they reflected incontrovertible truths. With the intransigence of a neophyte, he dismissed my doubts about theosophical postulates. 'Read it,' he would say, 'I refuse to discuss the subject until you have read, even if superficially, the first volume of *The Secret Doctrine* of Mme. Blavatsky'" (Schloezer, 66–67). See also: Bowers, *Scriabin, Russian Composer,* 2:117.

skrit.[66] Perhaps because the Belgian headquarters of the Society was destroyed in 1914, no documentation of Scriabin's membership has yet been located.[67] Bowers states that Jean Delville, designer of the highly symbolic cover of the score of *Prometheus,* was a member of a Theosophical cult, the Sons of the Flames of Wisdom, and he speculates that Scriabin might have joined this group as well, in view of the fact that they worshipped Prometheus.[68]

Scriabin's last and largest work for orchestra, *Prometheus: The Poem of Fire,* has been called "the most densely Theosophical piece of music ever written."[69] The figure of Prometheus, to whom Scriabin alternately referred as Lucifer (the light bringer), was especially important to Theosophists, symbolizing the illumination and elevation of human consciousness. (*Lucifer,* in fact, was the title of a Theosophical magazine published by Madame Blavatsky.[70]) The orchestral forces—huge orchestra, solo piano, and wordless chorus—evidently represent in turn the cosmos, the individual soul, and unified humanity, in a musical drama depicting the evolution of the soul toward union with the Absolute. The spirit of this work is entirely different from that of the *Poem of Ecstasy,* perhaps reflecting a more mystical outlook resulting from Scriabin's discovery of Theosophy. In particular, the more thoroughly complex and dissonant harmonic language which Scriabin created specifically for this work is relatively abstract, less sensual, less of this world. (In this regard, it is helpful to recall that Kandinsky aimed for abstraction in order to liberate art from the material.[71]) Finally, Scriabin's revolutionary coordination of lights and music is a move in the direction of a totally synaesthetic experience mirroring the ultimate unification of the universe.[72]

---

66. Bowers, *Scriabin, Russian Composer,* 2:187.

67. I am greatly indebted to the following officials of various branches of the Theosophical Society for their recent attempts to locate documentary proof of Scriabin's membership in the Society: Mrs. Radha Burnier, President, and Mr. Conrad Jamieson, Head of the Archives, International Headquarters of the Theosophical Society, Madras, India; Mr. John Algeo, National President, the Theosophical Society in America, Wheaton, Illinois; and Mr. Kirby Van Mater, International Headquarters, the Theosophical Society, Pasadena, California. Mrs. Burnier reports that "records of the French Section of our Society were taken away by the Nazis, 'and were recently found to be in Russia.' But we have not recovered them. There is therefore no saying where the records of the Belgian TS may be!" (letter to the author, 1 November 1995).

68. Bowers, *Scriabin, Russian Composer,* 2:206.

69. Faubion Bowers, *The New Scriabin: Enigma and Answers* (New York: St. Martin's Press, 1973), 192.

70. Campbell, 48.

71. John E. Bowlt, "Vasilii Kandinsky: The Russian Connection," in Bowlt and Long, 7–8.

72. For a discussion of the first performance of *Prometheus* with color organ, as well as Scriabin's ties with other artists striving for "color-music," see James M. Baker, "*Prometheus* in America: The Significance of the World Premiere of Scriabin's *Poem of Fire* as Color-Music, New York, 20 March 1915," in *Over Here: Modernism, The First Exile, 1914–19,* ed. Kermit Champa et al. (Providence: David Winton Bell Gallery, Brown University, 1989), 90–111.

A number of Russian artists and intellectuals were attracted to Theosophy during the first decade of the twentieth century, including the critic Emil Medtner, the painter Kandinsky, and the poets Ellis and Bely. In his essay "On the Spiritual in Art," Kandinsky mentions Blavatsky but places even more emphasis on Rudolf Steiner, who developed Theosophy into his own brand of Christian mysticism in Anthroposophy. For Kandinsky, Steiner's appeal was based primarily in his emphasis on artistic experience as one of the most effective means of grasping the spiritual.[73] Steiner's focus was on the Book of Revelations, and he believed a *parousia,* an "appearance of Christ in the etheric sphere," would take place in the twentieth century, resulting in a series of calamitous events which would lead to a new phase of human evolution.[74] Steiner predicted that Russia would play a crucial role in bringing together East and West. For this reason, and because they viewed his philosophy as continuing the teachings of Solovyov, the Russian symbolists came very much under Steiner's sway. Andrei Bely, who throughout the teens was a devoted disciple of Steiner, stated that "from 1910, Steiner entered into a special and rare contact with all of us."[75] Steiner's continual evocation of sun imagery in conjunction with Christ (he called him the "Great Sun Spirit") may well have been borrowed from the Russian symbolists.[76]

The first decade of the twentieth century was permeated with apocalyptic premonitions, nowhere more desperately felt than in Russia. In 1900 Solovyov had warned of the threat of Mongol hordes and the impending end of civilization.[77] Hopes for a new society had been dashed with the failure of the 1905 revolution, but everyone seemed to know that a more violent upheaval would follow. In 1908, Chulkov, writing about the French Revolution as "the bearer of a myth about the incarnation of freedom on earth," stated that "in our time people live by faith in the approaching social revolution."[78] As a symbolist, Chulkov believed that this revolution would have theurgic, spiritual significance. Indeed, symbolists were likely to believe that a revolution was in process on all planes of existence throughout the universe. Thus Blok, also writing in 1908, was able to see the most portentous significance in the eruption of Mt. Etna:

> [W]e are living through a terrible crisis. We still do not know exactly what events await us, but, in our hearts, the needle of the seismograph is already deflected. Already we see ourselves, as if against the background of a glow, flying in a light, rickety

---

73. Long, in Bowlt and Long, 45.

74. Alfred Heidenreich, "The Rediscovery of the Cosmic Christ," in *The Faithful Thinker: Centenary Essays on the Work and Thought of Rudolf Steiner, 1861–1925,* ed. A. C. Harwood (London: Hodder and Stoughton, 1961), 63–64.

75. Long, in Bowlt and Long, 46–47.

76. Heidenreich, 64.

77. Lincoln, 385.

78. Chulkov, in Peterson, 92–93.

aeroplane, high above the earth; but beneath us is a rumbling and fire-spitting mountain, and down its sides, behind clouds of ashes, roll streams of red-hot lava.[79]

In his novel *Petersburg* (completed in 1912), Bely took up Solovyov's warning:

> Once it has soared up on its hind legs, measuring the air with its eyes, the bronze steed will not set down its hooves. There will be a leap across history.... Great will be the strife, strife the like of which has never been seen in this world. The yellow hordes of Asians will set forth from their age-old abodes and will encrimson the fields of Europe in oceans of blood.... Earthborn creatures once more will sink to the depths of the oceans, into chaos, primordial and long-forgotten.[80]

Scriabin never succumbed to this brand of doomsday pessimism, although he explored the darker regions in the Ninth Sonata and certain of the shorter pieces; rather, he took the outbreak of the World War as evidence of developments on the spiritual plane that would bring about an era of spiritual renewal.[81]

The expectation of apocalypse looms large over Scriabin's last, most grandiose, and unfinished project—the *Mysterium*. According to Schloezer, Scriabin began talking about this project as early as 1902.[82] There is no doubt, however, that his plans for the work changed over the years in conjunction with the evolution of his philosophical and mystical beliefs. For example, Scriabin fully believed that he was commencing work on the *Mysterium* immediately following the completion of the *Poem of Ecstasy* and the Fifth Piano Sonata, although the product of that work proved to be *Prometheus*—but *Prometheus* anticipates the apocalyptic aims of the *Mysterium* only very weakly. Understandably, Scriabin had in fact pushed the *Mysterium* indefinitely into the future, deciding to concentrate first on a project more immediately within grasp, a *Prefatory Action* to the *Mysterium*. And at the time of his death in April 1915, Scriabin had completed only the text to the *Prefatory Action* and sketches of a very limited amount of musical material.

Convinced that the culmination of cosmic evolution was at hand, and equally certain of the spiritual power of his art, Scriabin aimed in the *Mysterium* not only to trace the history of the individual soul, the human race, and the cosmos but also to push the evolutionary process to its completion.[83] He envisioned his work culminating in a burst of ecstasy in which all disparate matter would return to its spiritual source, the Unifying Principle. The *Mysterium* was to be a production of unprecedented dimensions (as it certainly would have had to be!), combining all arts and appealing to all senses. Scriabin fully intended to specify and control dance, lights,

---

79. Blok, "Nature and Culture," 55.

80. Andrei Bely, *Petersburg,* trans. Robert A. Maguire and John E. Malmstad (Bloomington: Indiana University Press, 1978), 65.

81. Lane, 217.

82. Schloezer, 177.

83. Schloezer, 263–66.

perfumes—in fact all aspects of the environment, including the architectural design of the theatre. He conceived of this work not so much as a performance, but rather as a mystical rite in which he, as artist-creator, would officiate.

Even in light of the evolution of Scriabin's creative philosophy and the general grandiosity of many composers' aspirations in the post-Wagner era, Scriabin's concept of the *Mysterium* and of his own artistic powers seems absurdly deluded. In earlier discussions of Scriabin's poetic voice, the term "persona" was introduced to differentiate between an artistic fabrication—a posture assumed by the artist—and the artist as human being. It is possible that Scriabin, in setting forth his concept of the *Mysterium,* was speaking as a poetic persona. Perhaps by this time his identity had actually fused with a prophetic persona. As with many artists beginning about this time, Scriabin had become more interested in living the life of an artistic visionary than in creating specific works of art. In 1913, in a document entitled "Why We Paint Ourselves: A Futurist Manifesto," Ilya Zdanevich and Mikhail Larionov proclaim: "We have joined art to life."[84] Scriabin could surely have made the same claim.

Scriabin's concept of the *Mysterium* may well have been influenced by theories of the theatre being developed at that time by the Russian symbolists. As early as 1902, Bely was asserting the need to reinfuse drama with the religious spirit of the medieval mystery play.[85] Ivanov proposed in 1904 a new type of theatre based on Greek tragedy which would reunite "the crowd" and "the poet."[86] In effect, the symbolists sought in the theatre a substitute for the church, an institution which would embody the beliefs and values of the Russian nation. Sologub anticipated the concept of the *Mysterium* when he wrote in 1908: "[W]e come to look at the spectacles [of the theater] and the hour is approaching when, in the transformation of mind and body, we will come to true unity in liturgical action, in a rite of mystery."[87]

Although certainly one of the pioneers of synaesthetic art in the twentieth century, Scriabin was not alone in calling for a union of the arts, an idea which goes back of course to Wagner. In an article entitled "Free Art as the Basis of Life: Harmony and Dissonance (On Life, Death, etc.)," written in 1908, Nikolai Kulbin jotted the following, coming quite close to the spirit and content of Scriabin's then unwritten *Prometheus:*

> *Ideology.* Symbol of the universe. Delight. Beauty and good. Love is gravity.... Art is the quest for gods. Creation is the myth and the symbol. Freedom. The struggle of Titans and Olympus. Prometheus and Hercules. Painting and servitude.
> A single art—of the word, music, and the plastic arts.[88]

---

84. Ilya Zdanevich and Mikhail Larionov, "Why We Paint Ourselves: A Futurist Manifesto," in Bowlt, *Avant-Garde,* 81.

85. George Kalbouss, "Echoes of Nietzsche in Sologub's Writings," in Rosenthal, *Nietzsche,* 183.

86. James West, 141.

87. Sologub, in Peterson, 107.

88. Nikolai Kulbin, "Free Art as the Basis of Life: Harmony and Dissonance (On Life, Death, etc.)," extracts translated in Bowlt, *Avant-Garde,* 16.

Kulbin was a close associate of Kandinsky and presented the latter's famous "On the Spiritual in Art" in St. Petersburg in 1911. In an essay, "Form and Content," written in 1910, Kandinsky set forth the idea that each art possesses its own peculiar form. He therefore concludes that there is "the possibility of, and the need for, the appearance of a *monumental art* . . . [which] represents the unification of all the arts in a single work."[89] The cubofuturist painter David Burliuk, describing the new painting in 1912, evoked virtually every sense: "Previously painting only Saw, now it Feels. . . . [It has] a Sense of *Visual ponderability*—A Sense of color Smell. A sense of *duration of the colored* moment."[90] Kandinsky wrote a play, "The Yellow Sound," in which "music is as expressive as the action on the stage."[91] The symbolist poets, decrying the fragmentation of modern perception, likewise favored a synaesthetic approach to art in the belief that "poetry, knowledge, music and speech were at first a unity."[92]

For most of the artists striving for a fusion of the arts in the first decade of the twentieth century, music was of special significance. In his quest for an abstract art, Kandinsky valued music because it is the most nonmaterial of the arts and as such has greater potential for immediate communication with the spiritual aspect of humanity: "The musical tone has direct access to the soul."[93] He admired the holistically unified, self-consistent structure of music: "[M]usic is an art which never uses its media to make a deceptive reproduction of natural phenomena. On the contrary, music always uses its own media to express the artist's emotional life, and, out of these media, creates an original life of musical tones."[94] The symbolist poets believed that the laws of music underlie all of the arts. Chulkov wrote in 1908: "Music . . . as the objectification of what is innermost—this is the central theme of Symbolism, if we broaden the principle of music to include all the other arts and most of all poetry."[95] Music signified breadth and continuity, and its laws seemed to correspond to laws of nature. For Blok, music has the power to restore the communion of man and nature:

> There exist, as it were, two kinds of time and two kinds of space; one is the historical, the calendar time; the other the incalculable, the musical time. To the civilised consciousness only the first kind of time and space is immanent; in the other we can only dwell when we feel ourselves as part of nature, when we immolate ourselves in the waves of music which rise from the world's orchestra.[96]

---

89. Vasily Kandinsky, "Form and Content," in Bowlt, *Avant-Garde*, 21.

90. David Burliuk, "Cubism (Surface-Plane)," in Bowlt, *Avant-Garde*, 73.

91. Bowlt, "Kandinsky," in Bowlt and Long, 10.

92. Andrei Bely, "The Magic of Words," in *Symbolism: An Anthology,* ed. and trans. T.G. West (London and New York: Methuen, 1980), 124.

93. Vasily Kandinsky, "On the Spiritual in Art," in Bowlt and Long, 73–74.

94. Kandinsky, "On the Spiritual in Art," 71.

95. Chulkov, in Peterson, 87.

96. Blok, "The Decline of Humanism," 60.

Bely believed that "music is an attempt to express through form the quintessence of the processes of creation."[97]

In effect, for artists striving for a spiritual, mystical, or theurgical effect, music must be of paramount interest because, even as Plato said, its laws correspond to those governing the cosmos. Art created in accordance with those principles makes it possible for humankind to transcend material existence and to enter spiritual realms. Thus the Silver Age witnessed a number of attempts to regulate and control artistic creation according to musical rules of structure, or to develop theoretical systems for other arts analogous to theories of music. The most fascinating case of this phenomenon—and one closely connected to Scriabin—is that of Andrei Bely. Bely's father was the famous mathematician Nikolai Bugayev, and his mother was a talented pianist. Himself a graduate in mathematics from Moscow University, Bely was concerned all his life with reconciling the scientific and artistic aspects of his personality—and he succeeded in finding a certain synthesis in the study of music theory and acoustics. He studied counterpoint with Sergei Taneyev, the author of a very systematic algebraic theory of counterpoint, who earlier had taught Scriabin at the Moscow Conservatory. Bely's first literary works, entitled *Symphonies,* are attempts to apply the sonata form to prose fiction. As a result of his sophisticated knowledge of musical structure, Bely was able to devise a theory of orchestration for poetry, whereby vowels, consonants, references to colors, and other poetic elements are employed systematically as leitmotives in counterpoint to the external meaning of the text.[98] Bely valued music because of the precision of relations among its parts:

[T]he sounds of music are simple, like a melody, determined, always the same; they are virtually numbers. Music is the mathematics of the soul, so to speak. With respect to the diversity of thoughts and images it arouses, it is somehow the law they evoke. With respect to that which it evokes in the soul, music is the unity of a solution, but the thoughts and images of music in us are crystals. Music is the source of the birth of certain very complicated formations of the soul in us . . . Music is deeper than everything it engenders in us; it awakens in us the not simple but the more complex and precise.[99]

In developing a quasi-musical theory for poetry, Bely believed that he was enlarging its capacity for profundity and revelation.

Many of the artists associated with mysticism around the turn of the century embraced the advances of science and attempted to relate them to their art. Valery Bryusov was an avid reader of science publications, including the writings of Einstein, and used science and technology as subjects for his poetry. After 1909 he argued for a scientific poetry for which the poet "will no longer run confusedly all over the

97. Andrei Bely, "Revolution and Culture," in Bohachevsky-Chomiak and Rosenthal, 295.

98. See Part II of Steinberg.

99. Bely, "Revolution and Culture," in Bohachevsky-Chomiak and Rosenthal, 294–95.

world after impressions but, like the scientist, will produce carefully prepared works, make observations and experiments, study and think."[100]

The scientific outlook extended to the visual arts as well. In his essay "On the Spiritual in Art" of 1911, Kandinsky posited the bases for a theory of counterpoint for painting. By means of this systematic theory, "painting, too, will become composition and, as an authentic, pure art will be able to serve the divine. And the same steadfast guide will lead art to supreme heights: to the *principle of inner necessity*."[101] Like Bely, Kandinsky believed that a system of structural relations would heighten the mystical effect of the artwork. Kandinsky also advanced a theory of color, examining the psychic and mystical associations of certain colors, as well as their musical qualities.[102] In this regard, he more or less duplicated Scriabin's efforts to associate particular colors with notes of the diatonic scale. In 1908 Kulbin, a close associate of Kandinsky who was similarly interested in Theosophy, reported on his research concerning the relation of musical scales to the spectrum and how the relations between adjacent elements in either scale or spectrum affect subjective experience.[103] In his 1913 manifesto on "Rayonist Painting," Mikhail Larionov noted a movement known as Orphism, which "is inclined toward a literal correspondence of musical to light waves, which stimulate color sensation—and . . . constructs painting literally according to musical laws."[104] The Lithuanian painter Ciurlionis, who was close to the Russian symbolists, particularly Ivanov, is notable for his attempts to "fuse time and space" and to "paint music."[105]

For the artists of the Silver Age, music was valued for its powerful precision, for its capacity for complexity within a well-proportioned framework. Thus music appeared to vibrate in tune with the harmonies of the cosmos, to offer a means for tapping into other, more spiritual planes of being. It would be difficult to imagine that this belief, to which Scriabin certainly subscribed, did not have an impact on the content and structure of his music. The remainder of this essay is devoted to the question of the relation between Scriabin's mysticism and his music. The aim here is not simply to trace through his music programmatic depictions of particular concepts, although this might be possible—for instance, his use of melodic leitmotives

100. Reeve, 16–17.

101. Kandinsky, "On the Spiritual in Art," 80–81.

102. Ibid., 85. After the Revolution of 1917, Kandinsky was appointed to head the Moscow Institute of Artistic Culture (INKHUK), a laboratory for the investigation of artistic properties and media, but because his colleagues were not in agreement with his intuitive approach, he left soon after the project began. In 1924, Kandinsky's old friend Leonid Sabaneev set up a physico-psychological lab as part of the Russian Academy of Artistic Sciences, implementing in part a plan which had been drawn up by Kandinsky in 1921 before his departure for Berlin. Sabaneev was a close friend and an important biographer of Scriabin. See Bowlt, "Kandinsky," in Bowlt and Long, 31–32.

103. Kulbin, in Bowlt, *Avant-Garde,* 13–14.

104. Mikhail Larionov, "Rayonist Painting," in Bowlt, *Avant-Garde*, 96.

105. Bowlt, "Kandinsky," in Bowlt and Long, 6.

Example 1a. "Poem," op. 32, no. 2.

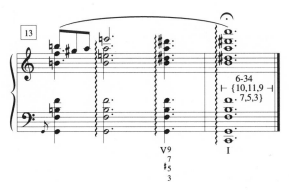

Example 1b. "Désir," op. 57, no. 1.

in the manner of Wagner. Rather, the discussion that follows is based on the premise advanced by Boris de Schloezer in his biography of Scriabin, that the work of art and the artist's ideology are independent reflections of the artist's intuition.[106]

In turning to the question of mysticism in Scriabin's music, what better place to begin than the famous mystic chord? Example 1 shows two instances of the chord, the first from the "Poem," op. 32, no. 2, a fairly early work dating from 1903, and the second a very significant appearance at the end of "Désir," op. 57, no. 1 (1907). In the examples, both are labeled 6–34, the name of the chord in Allen Forte's set nomenclature.[107] It is often reported that this chord was used as an independent harmony for the first time in *Prometheus,* and it has often been explained as derived

---

106. Schloezer, 76–77.

107. In addition to Forte's set names, in the discussion that follows, pitch classes will be indicated (usually in curly brackets) in standard integer notation, with pc 0 signifying B♯, C♮, or D♭♭, 1 equal to C♯ or D♭, and so on.

WT I (C#, D#, F, G, A, B)   mm. 0–2 5–7   10–14
WT II (C, D, E, F#, G#, A#)   2–5 8–9   14–(15)

Example 2. "Poème fantasque," op. 45, no. 2.

from the upper partials of the overtone series or as the product of superposed fourths. In fact, the harmony was widely used throughout Scriabin's earlier tonal works. The most typical occurrence is as a whole-tone dominant chord suspended over the tonic root, as is the case in both excerpts in Example 1. In Example 1a the suspension chord resolves by the end of the measure to a consonant D-major tonic harmony. In Example 1b, the mystic chord is the concluding harmony of the piece, thus lingering and fading away unresolved. Because this is the closing gesture of the piece, and especially because of the highly evocative registral disposition of the chord, the harmony in "Désir" has a completely different effect from its appearance in the earlier piece. It could be said that the composition ends not by establishing closure in the material world, as would be entailed in the progression demanded by the bass, but rather by opening into a spiritual realm.

The whole-tone scale is an important nontraditional component in Scriabin's tonal music. The two forms of this scale, in their symmetrical partitioning of the twelve-tone chromatic into two complementary groups of six, often suggest opposing planes of existence. A shift of whole-tone planes typically occurs at important

Example 3. "Ironies," op. 56, no. 2.

cadence points. Example 2, the "Poème fantasque," op. 45, no. 2 (1905), illustrates this phenomenon. The opening measures contain a whole-tone dominant chord progressing to the tonic. In m. 3, the initial gesture is transposed up seven half steps (or down five), so that a modulation to the dominant is accomplished. In conjunction with the transposition, maximum contrast is obtained by shifting to the plane of the complementary whole-tone scale. The shift actually occurs gradually and before the transposition, for in m. 2, when the tonic enters in the bass, notes from the preceding dominant are suspended over it, effectively mingling elements of both whole-tone harmonies. A "resolution" of the suspension occurs at the beginning of m. 3, however—not to a consonant harmony but to a full-fledged whole-tone chord, a subset of the complement of the original whole-tone scale. The middle section of this little piece (mm. 7–12) involves several shifts between the two whole-tone planes at a more rapid pace, before the first material returns to conclude the composition.

Example 2 illustrates in a relatively simple way a remarkable innovation in musical structure which constitutes Scriabin's most significant contribution to the creation of new musical forms and procedures. For here two very different types of procedures, which might ostensibly be considered mutually exclusive—one the traditional tonal language as conveyed especially by the bass progression, the other the exploitation of a symmetrical non-tonal pitch collection, the whole-tone scale—actually operate in an integrated manner to create a unified composition. This type of structure corresponds strikingly to the Theosophical teaching concerning interpenetrating planes of existence.

Scriabin was able to work out extra-tonal relations of the most abstruse sort in his tonal music. Example 3 shows a phrase from "Ironies," op. 56, no. 2 (1907) which in tonal terms basically effects a cadence in C♯ major. The first measure of the phrase contains an eight-note superset of the whole-tone scale, identified as Forte's 8–24. (The numbers in parentheses indicate the pitches *not* present here.) The phrase concludes with a verticality comprised of precisely these pitches, {5,7,9,1}, a form of set class 4–24. (The numbers in curly brackets represent the pitches present here.) Thus the nontonal relation of complementation governs the beginning and ending of the

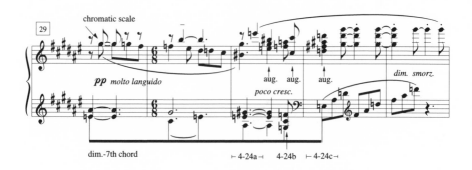

Example 4. Fifth Sonata, op. 53.

phrase, lending a special kind of unity to the gesture. According to Theosophy, the Unifying Principle is understood to have been differentiated into various planes of matter and spirit. One can well imagine that to a mystical composer, the complementation relation would signify this differentiation, embodying within the microcosm of the universe of twelve pitch classes the aspiration toward unification.

Example 4 contains examples of abstract, symmetrical apportionments of the twelve-tone universe. It features a passage from the Fifth Sonata, a phrase labeled *molto languido* which one would hardly expect to evince precise mathematical relations. Nonetheless, the highly chromatic passage entails the interpenetration of various types of symmetrical pitch-class collections—the augmented, whole-tone, and diminished-seventh chords, the latter structurally unrelated to the others. Of special interest are the whole-tone tetrachords (forms of 4–24) labeled a, b, and c. Together a and c form the full whole-tone aggregate, while b (the harmonization of a passing tone in the melody, from the point of view of whole-tone structure) shares no pitches with a or c.

Example 5 shows the overall formal scheme of the Prelude, op. 59, no. 2 (1910), which may be regarded as Scriabin's first nontonal composition. An annotated score of the opening measures of the piece is offered as Example 5d. Example 5a traces the progression of set 6–27, the first hexachord of the piece, throughout the composition. (This progression is governed by successive transpositions up three half-steps.) In Example 5b the elements are organized to demonstrate pitch retention among forms of 6–27. Over the course of this progression, an aggregate is produced which is identified as 8–28, the complement of the diminished-seventh chord, otherwise known as the octatonic scale. Example 5c shows the complement of this 8–28, {2,5,8,11}, delineated in a conspicuous way as the sum of the high, accented melodic notes which occur immediately after the statements of 6–27. The transposition scheme which governs the structure of this Prelude thus exhausts and symmetrically partitions the universe of twelve tones. At this point, Scriabin has abandoned overall tonal structure in favor of a structure which has the geometrical proportions of a crystal. Such a structure might well have mystical ramifications.

For Theosophists the crystal is the perfect reflection of cosmic principles. One Theosophist author writes that crystals remind us

> that the highest geometrical form, and perfect symmetry, are one and the same thing; that "Nature geometrizes universally in all her manifestations" (*The Secret Doctrine,* Vol. I, p. 124), the basis of Cosmic Architecture being geometrical; and that each human soul which evolves at all, is evolving, even if indirectly, toward a more perfect symmetry, a more evenly sustained consciousness which, symbolically at least, one may think of as represented by a more perfect geometrical form.[108]

The author goes on to say that crystals give us the sense that "we have in some mysterious way penetrated to a plane higher than the purely physical."[109] In the text to the *Prefatory Action,* a work designed as a kind of purification rite to prepare the audience for the *Mysterium,* Scriabin's metaphor conveys precisely this Theosophical outlook:

> Be bold, drink from these cups, O Mortals!
> And enter your Father's portals!
> Then let the rainbow crystals of your souls
> Reflect the secrets of the distant goals![110]

---

108. D.[author anonymous], "The Dawn of Individuality in the Mineral Kingdom," *Theosophical Quarterly* 24 (1926–27): 207.

109. D., "Dawn of Individuality," 210.

110. Translated in Schloezer, 306. Scriabin's fascination with crystals is still more evident in the following lines from the text to the *Prefatory Action:*
> Each stone falls like a magic and singing star,
> Flaming, from strings of the solar lyre
>> Each stone has fallen
>> Like a sounding crystal,
>> Like a gleaming sound,
>> Full of sweet tortures.
>> They gleam like topaz,
>> Hyacinth, chrysoprase,
>> Carbuncle, opal, sardonyx,
>> Like emerald, malachite,
>> Chalcedony, chrysolite,
>> Like the heavenly sapphire,
>> Like the world's caress.
> It burns like a unique diamond glittering with a thousand fires,
> This temple—our life, our blossoming, our ecstasy.

These lines are translated by the author into English from Marina Scriabine's. French translation:
> Chaque pierre comme une étoile magique et chantante
> Tombe, enflammée, des cordes de la lyre solaire

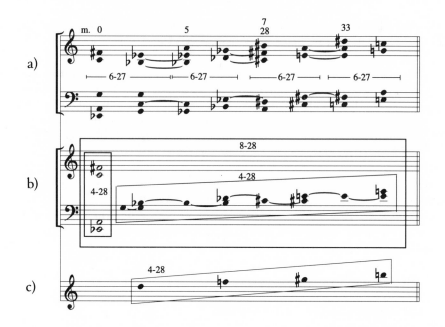

Example 5. Prelude, op. 59, no. 2.

Schloezer remarked very aptly that "all Scriabin's works, beginning with the Third Piano Sonata and ending with the Tenth Piano Sonata, are built according to a uniform succession of states—languor, longing, impetuous striving, dance, ecstasy, and transfiguration."[111] This formal process corresponds to the spiritual progress of the soul toward ecstatic union with the Divine Principle. Very often, one may trace

---

Chaque pierre est tombée
Comme un cristal qui sonne,
Comme un son qui brille,
Plein de douces tortures.
Elles brillent comme la topaze,
L'hyacinthe, la chrysoprase
L'escarboucle, l'opale
Le cristal de la sardoine
Comme l'émeraude, la malachite
La calcédoine, la chrysolithe
Comme le céleste saphir
Comme la caresse du monde.
Il brûle comme un diamant unique étincelant de mille feux
Ce temple—notre vie, notre épanouissement, notre extase.
See Scriabine, *Notes,* 117–18.
111. Schloezer, 97.

Example 5 cont'd. Prelude, op. 59, no. 2, Sauvage, belliqueux

Example 6. Fifth Sonata, op. 53.

this progress with regard to the transformation of distinctive pitch-class collections. Example 6 shows three occurrences of the same five-note set class, identified as 5–27, at the beginning, middle, and conclusion of the Fifth Sonata. In m. 7, this sonority arises out of the mire of chaos, and by m. 59 it has been activated as part of the main subject of the piece. At the ecstatic conclusion, in m. 441, this harmony reappears in an explosion which results in a return to chaos, as at the beginning. An instance of a transposed form of 5–27 is shown at m. 114, in conjunction with the victorious *quasi trombe* motive. This form of the chord is rooted on E♭, a tritone away from the three forms discussed earlier, which are based on A. Actually, the form on E♭ was heard in immediate juxtaposition to the 5–27 in m. 59 (see m. 6l), a very dramatic contrast since the two forms have no pitches in common. In fact , the A/E♭ juxtaposition was itself evident in the chaotic bass rumblings of the introduction (spelled D♯/A). What is significant here is that the spiritual process is not mirrored merely in the external drama of the music. On the contrary, Scriabin the creator takes formless matter, molds it, breathes life into it, and sends it on its flight to the sublime.

Although the *Poem of Ecstasy* conforms to the tripartite division of sonata form, its procedures and form are dramatically different from those associated with the earlier piano sonatas (the First through the Fourth), depending as it does to a much greater extent on thematic transformation. This is true especially with regard to the most important theme, identified in the following analysis as Theme D.[112] The transformation of this theme throughout the piece is at least as strong a factor in the determination of the form as the development and recapitulation of other themes. By way of providing an overview of the process of transformation of Theme D, a chart containing brief descriptions of its occurrences is provided as Table 1.

The sole presentation of this material in the exposition is in section D1, a very tentative statement where little of the potential of the material for expansion is indicated. Consisting of two transpositionally equivalent phrases in succession, this statement quickly loses momentum, fading to a quieter section. It is based on V/V. When Theme D returns in D2 at the beginning of the development, it is presented more energetically. Here the second phrase does not parallel the first, but rather is an opening gesture directed to new material. The harmonic support for this statement is E♭, a rather distant area from the C major tonic. The expansiveness of Theme D is fully realized in D3 at the height of the development. Its phrases are freely derived and are spun forth in sequence and in imitation. In this section harmony changes continually, progressing at a fairly rapid pace. This section is not harmonically closed, but rather ultimately progresses to V/V, leading to V in the remaining section of the development.

The first statement of Theme D in the recapitulation—D4—thwarts our expectations since it is not a genuine restatement but is instead part of a freely composed developmental episode recalling section D2. Like D4, D5 is based on V, but this section contains a literal, though somewhat transformed, repetition of D1 (transposed up a fourth). Like D1, however, D5 is inconclusive. Section D6 entails the first statement of Theme D in the tonic, yet this presentation proves to be only a slight expansion of D5 with precisely the same weaknesses in dramatic impact. Only at the very end of the *Poem of Ecstasy* does Scriabin provide a completely satisfying recapitulation of Theme D. A unique feature of the final section, D7, is the aspect of closure, both harmonic and melodic. Based on a tonic pedal, it is the only statement which provides consequent melodic material to resolve the tensions inherent in the theme itself. At the moment of apotheosis, concentration is on the theme itself, with-

---

112. This analysis accords with the more complete discussion of musical structure in the *Poem of Ecstasy,* in James M. Baker, *The Music of Alexander Scriabin* (New Haven and London: Yale University Press, 1986), 216–35.

Table 1. *Poem of Ecstasy:* Transformation of Main Theme (Theme D).

Section	Measures	Harmony	Comments
D1	102–10	D(V/V)	two transpositionally equivalent phrases; fades away
D2	181–92	E♭	opening, slightly expansive, no conclusion
D3	260–96	E♭–V–1 (thwarted)– V/V	Sequential progression from E♭ to V (m. 277); deceptive cadence (m. 285); further sequence leads to V/V (m. 295); expansive climax of development; imitative writing; not conlcusive
D4	415–22	V	developmental episode (compare D2), not the expected recapitulation
D5	468–76	V	literal recapitulation of D1 at T_5
D6	490–506	I	like D1, though constructed to be twice as long; fades away
D7	553–605	I	apotheosis; true recapitulation; theme in augmentation; first two phrases are the same as corresponding phrases of D2 (at T_4); closure

out the agitated syncopations or imitative counterpoint of other sections. The rich orchestration, complete with bells and organ added only at this point, and especially the grandiose statement of the theme in augmentation give this finale great weight.

The peculiar progress of this theme through the piece, which creates a kind of ebb and flow of tension, actually corresponds closely to the shape of Scriabin's verse "Poem of Ecstasy," in which several times the spirit "is ready to sink into oblivion." Each time weariness threatens, however, something unexpectedly happens, signaled by such interjections as "but then . . ." or "but suddenly . . ." The result in the music is a sensuously undulating form which projects the erotic aspect of the soul's striving for union with the Divine Principle.

Scriabin's large-scale forms, particularly those of his later works, appear to reflect a mystical conception of the universe. A particularly remarkable instance of such a correspondence is the form of the Fifth Sonata, graphed in a Schenkerian scheme in Example 7. The Sonata is definitely a tonal work in the key of F♯ major. Yet, as we observed in Example 6, it begins chaotically with E♮ in the bass, a note outside the key. Governing the structure overall is a stepwise bass ascent shown in Example 7 beginning with the tonic root . The bass ascent carries the harmony up a fourth to the key of B major by the time of the recapitulation, and the initial material is in fact restated in this key. Since the remainder of the piece amounts to a sequential repetition of what has already taken place, the bass ascends another fourth to E♮. At this point the music has come full cycle through ecstasy back to chaos. The most problematic aspect of this form is the tension between the key areas of F♯ major

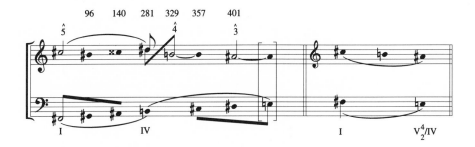

Example 7. Fifth Sonata, op. 53.

and B major. On the one hand, B major can be understood as the subdominant of F♯; but in light of the ascent from F♯ to E♮, it seems as if F♯ could well be the dominant of B. The form is obviously a perpetual cyclical form—one which might be seen to project the evolution from the F♯ tonic, the area of pure spirit, to the material plane of B major.[113] The subsequent involution back to F♯ completes a motion which in Theosophical terms corresponds to the cosmic cycle of the manvantara, or Day and Night of Brahmâ.[114]

Example 8a contains sketches of the bass progression of *Prometheus*. (The upper staff is a more detailed graph, while the lower staff demonstrates the most essential bass progressions.) With respect to the bass progression, *Prometheus* has a tonal structure with F♯ major as tonic, as shown in the reduction in Example 8b.[115] (This explanation provides the only sensible accounting for the concluding F♯-major triad, the only consonant harmony in the piece!) However, the harmony which is supported by this bass progression is consistently rich and dissonant, with a focus on the mystic chord, set 6–34. Beneath the staff systems are traced levels of transposition of occurrences of the mystic chord, with the chord associated with the F♯ tonic root labeled as transposition level T_0. By this method, one discovers that the bass progression and the sequence of transpositional forms of the mystic chord are coordinated (although in a complex way), so that the atonal surface harmonies progress in accordance with tonal laws. It is clear that in the harmonic context it is virtually impos-

113. The interpretation of F♯ major as representing the absolute spiritual realm accords with the symbolic use of this harmonic region in *Prometheus;* see discussion of Example 8.

114. Mme. Blavatsky explained the Day and Night of Brahmâ as follows: "The former represents a certain period of cosmical activity, the latter an equal one of cosmical repose. In the one, worlds are being evolved, and passing through their allotted four ages of existence; in the latter, the 'inbreathing' of Brahmâ reverses the tendency of the natural forces; everything visible becomes gradually dispersed; chaos comes, and a long night of repose reinvigorates the cosmos for its next term of evolution" (Blavatsky, *Isis Unveiled*, 2:421–22).

115. For a complete discussion of musical structure in *Prometheus*, see Baker, *The Music of Scriabin*, 235–67.

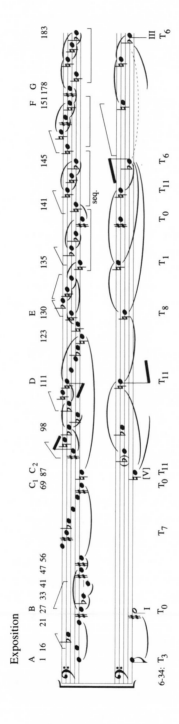

Example 8a. *Prometheus*, op. 60: Underlying Bass and Harmonic Progressions.

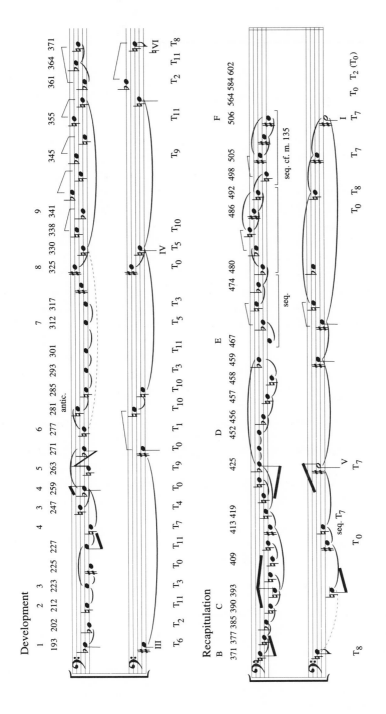

Example 8a cont'd.

Example 8b. *Prometheus*, op. 60: Underlying Tonal Design.

sible to hear the piece as conventionally tonal. The bass progression may be simply a vestige of traditional form, a means of organizing this grandiose post-tonal conception in the absence of other means at a composer's disposal in 1909. On the other hand, Scriabin's mystical beliefs provide another perspective within which the unique structure of this work might be grasped. For one might understand the bass progression as corresponding to the material plane of existence and the atonal surface to reflect the spiritual plane. The form could then be understood to employ on a very grand scale—yet in a quite obvious manner—the same sort of differentiation of planes we observed in Example 2.

Schloezer reports that Scriabin told him: "You may not accept the doctrine of Seven Planes as the ultimate truth, but to me it serves as a convenient framework for classifying natural phenomena and for creating order out of the chaos of factual data."[116] If the composer was in fact involved to any extent with Theosophy, one would expect to find the number seven projected in various ways in the structure of his music. Schloezer maintains that Scriabin's formal plan for the *Mysterium* was based on seven:

> The *Mysterium* unfolds before us the evolution of the cosmos, mankind, and the individual; all three traverse the trajectory from incoherent homogeneity to specific multiplicity, returning to pristine unity. This history was to be enacted in the *Mysterium*. In accordance with the number of human races in Mme. Blavatsky's doctrine, the *Mysterium* was divided into seven parts. The performance of each part was to occupy a whole day, and the entire *Mysterium* was to last a period of seven days or multiples thereof.[117]

The text of the *Prefatory Action* would appear to bear out the importance of this number in Scriabin's final project:

> Strong, you must vanquish seven temptations,
> Accomplish seven glorious exploits.
> You will achieve seven victories,
> Sacrifice seven victims, large and precious sacrifices.

---

116. Schloezer, 67.
117. Schloezer, 263.

. . . .
Seven angels in ethereal robes
Seven heralds of your imperishable glories,
Seven burning pillars, seven white faces,
Heads of powerful lights
Will aid you in your labors.[118]

The *Poem of Ecstasy* offers powerful evidence of the number seven as the basis for overall formal design, for the progress of its main theme through seven stages (already observed in conjunction with Tab.1) may be easily understood as depicting the human evolution through seven races, culminating in ecstatic union with the Divine Principle. Although the extreme motivic complexity of *Prometheus* makes analysis more difficult, a similar sevenfold evolution of the main theme may be discerned, as demonstrated in Table 2.

In Scriabin's later works, the number seven is evident as a defining principle at more local levels of structure as well. Example 9a shows a passage from the Seventh Piano Sonata (the composer's favorite, to which he attributed sacerdotal properties, naming it the "White Mass"). This passage is especially rich in septenary features. The most significant "contrasting" idea in the sonata is the seven-measure theme introduced in mm. 29–35 with special performance instructions: "avec une céleste volupté; très pur, avec une profonde douceur." The main melodic phrase of this material (mm. 29–32) is a sequence of seven tones (attacks). In mm. 39–41 this phrase is repeated, set against a seven-note countersubject in faster values (stated twice). The number seven is important in vertical components as well. The passage begins with a sonority comprised of intervals of sevenths in both hands (G♯-F♯ and B♯-A[♯]). The clangorous chords entering in m. 36 ("mystérieusement sonore") owe their effect largely to the major seventh formed between outer elements. They make up a bell motive, a basic succession of seven chords (attacks) in mm. 36–37, extended by varied repetition in m. 38.

The Ninth and Tenth Piano Sonatas have strikingly similar conclusions, each closing with a seven-measure phrase harking back to the opening (see Exx. 9b and 9c

---

118. Translated by the author from the French translation by Marina Scriabine:
   Fort, tu dois vaincre sept tentations,
   Accomplir sept glorieux exploits.
   Sept victoires sur toi remporter,
   Sacrifier sept victimes, grands et précieux sacrifices.
   . . . .
   Sept anges aux robes éthérées
   Sept hérauts de tes gloires impérissables
   Sept piliers embrasés, sept faces blanches,
   Chefs des puissances de lumière
   T'assisteront dans les périls.
(Scriabine, *Notes,* 88–89)

Table 2. *Prometheus,* op. 60: Transformation of Main Theme (Theme A)

Section	Measures	Performance Directions
A1	1–12	lento; foggy [*brumeux*] (low brass)
A2	130–38	grand majestic theme [*thème large majestueux*] (solo piano)
A3	236–41	defiant; bellicose; stormy; with a splendid flash [*avec défi; belliqueux; orageux; avec un splendide éclat*] (low brass)
A4	325–28	suave, enchanted [*suave, charmé*] (solo violin)
A5	341–63 passim	sparkling; increasingly animated; victorious [*étincellant; de plus en plus animé; victorieux*] (violins)
A6	467–503	apotheosis; with a dazzling flash [*avec un éclat éblouissant*] (theme sung by wordless chorus)
A7	522–90	dematerialization; prestissimo; winged dancing; waves of light, vertiginous [*ailé, dansant; flot lumineux; dans un vertige*] (condensed version of A2; theme in horn, then oboe and piano)

respectively). The final phrase of the Tenth, a condensation of the opening eight-measure gesture, contains seven pitch classes (forming Forte's 7–28). On a slightly larger level, the final sections of the Ninth and Tenth Sonatas, spanning twelve and nineteen measures respectively, are each comprised of seven hypermeasures defined primarily on the basis of direct or sequential repetition (also shown in Exx. 9b and 9c).

The opening of the Ninth Sonata (dubbed the "Black Mass" sonata by a friend of the composer—a title to which Scriabin did not object), is based on seven at two metrical levels.[119] The main theme ("légendaire") spans seven full measures, overlapping in m. 7 with the beginning of a contrasting, somewhat ominous idea ("mystérieusement murmuré"), spanning seven half-measures (see Ex. 9d). On the broadest level, the ten-measure phrase, embracing both main ideas, breaks down into four phrases balanced in accordance with the proportion 4 + 3 + 2 + 1. For Theosophists these numbers held special significance, for they are the numbers associated with the Pythagorean Triangle. This figure, as described by Mme. Blavatsky,

---

119. The juxtaposition of "White" and "Black Mass" Sonatas in Scriabin's oeuvre very much reflects the thinking of the time. Artists felt an urgent need to explore both beatific and satanic realms. Merezhkovsky wrote, for example: "If 'divine ecstasy' (sex) is not satisfied, the soul seeks the 'satanic ecstasy' of war" (quoted in Lincoln, 351).

Example 9a. Seventh Sonata, op. 64, mm. 29–43.

Example 9b. Ninth Sonata, op. 68, closing measures.

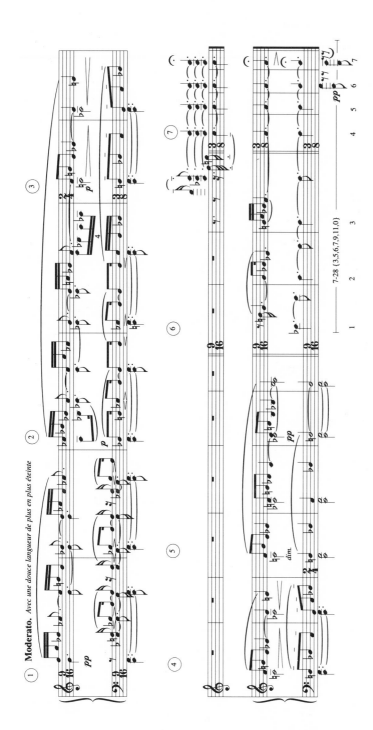

Example 9c. Tenth Sonata, op. 70, closing measures.

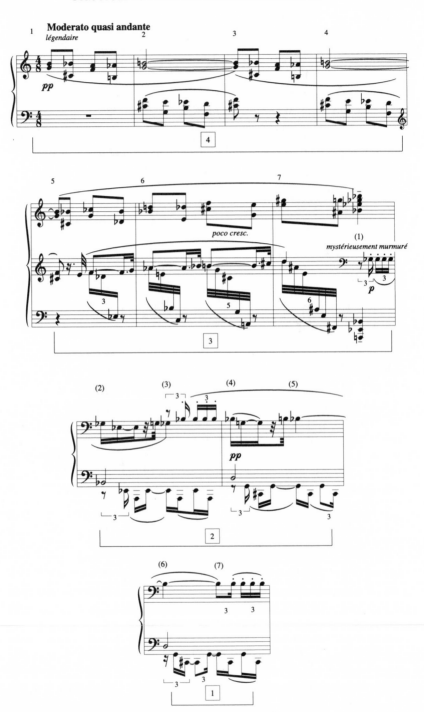

Example 9d. Ninth Sonata, op. 68, opening measures.

consists of *ten points* inscribed pyramid-like (from one to the last four) within its three lines, and it symbolizes the Universe in the famous Pythagorean Decad. The upper single dot is a Monad, and represents a Unit-Point, which is *the* Unity from whence all proceeds, and all is of the same essence with it. While the ten dots within the triangle represent the phenomenal world, the three sides of the equilateral triangle which enclose the pyramid of dots are the barriers of *noumenal* Matter, or Substance, that separate it from the world of Thought.[120]

In the *Secret Doctrine,* Mme. Blavatsky had declared that the numbers contained in this Triangle, "along with the plane cube and circle, are more eloquent and scientific descriptions of the order of the evolution of the Universe, spiritual and psychic, as well as physical, than volumes of descriptive Cosmogonies and revealed *"Geneses."*[121] It seems probable that a composer with Scriabin's theurgical aims would want to avail himself of the powers of this proportion. After all, in the Fifth Sonata he had placed as an epigraph the following excerpt from his "Poem of Ecstasy": "I call you to life, oh mysterious forces!" It is easy to imagine that he might have consciously built the opening of the Ninth Sonata on the Pythagorean proportion to accomplish this same purpose. In point of fact, the mysterious passage from the Seventh Sonata previously analyzed offers powerful corroboration of the presence of the Pythagorean Triangle in Scriabin's music, for the ten-measure phrase in mm. 29–38 in the Seventh (see Ex. 9a) likewise breaks down into phrases based on the sacred proportion: 4 (mm. 29–32, "avec une céleste volupté") + 3 (mm. 33–35, "très pur, avec une profonde douceur") + 2 (mm. 36–37, "mystérieusement sonore") + 1 (repetition/extension).

Schloezer relates that Scriabin, in his grapplings with mysticism, was greatly troubled by one problem in particular.[122] Theosophy teaches that we are presently in the fifth of seven races which must evolve before we return to union with the Absolute. Since each stage of this process takes place over millions of years, it was evident to Scriabin that, at least according to these teachings, in his present life he would not have a role in the ultimate unification of the universe. Yet so convinced was Scriabin of his own destiny to bring on the apocalypse through his art, that he developed a theory that the pace of involution back to unity from the material would be tremendously accelerated in its final stages, so that what formerly took place over millenia would be compacted into seconds of time.[123] *Prometheus* gives us musical evidence of Scriabin's theory of accelerated involution (as indeed do all of Scriabin's extended works completed after 1910—the Sixth through the Tenth Piano Sonatas). After the apotheosis of the main theme of the work (mm. 467–503)—the culminating event which concludes all of Scriabin's previous large-scale forms from the Third Sonata on—Scriabin appends a codetta which in effect recapitulates the substantial

120. Blavatsky, *Secret Doctrine,* 1:616.
121. Blavatsky, *Secret Doctrine,* 1:612.
122. Schloezer, 215.
123. Schloezer, 216.

closing material from the exposition, but condensed and accelerated in a delirious dance of dematerialization (see Tab. 2). Ultimately, the material simply evaporates into the Unifying Principle, in this case the triumphant F♯-major chord which concludes the piece.

The music itself provides strong evidence that Scriabin held certain mystical beliefs which he most likely came to know through his readings in Theosophy and his close contacts with Theosophists. This evidence amounts to a convincing preponderance of structural features which seem to reflect or correspond to mystical conceptions of the universe. Taken individually, these correspondences may seem purely coincidental, but considered together they would seem to corroborate a view of the music as having a mystical significance. It is crucial to recognize that the mystical aspects we have observed do not negate or even alter analyses based on purely musical criteria. On the contrary, the mystical content of the music seems to bear out and to depend upon musical structure. What a knowledge of mysticism brings to the study of this music, then, is a notion of the ultimate *meaning* of the music, at least as far as the composer might have been concerned. Especially for the bigger, more overtly mystical works, in particular *Prometheus*, a true mystical belief on the part of the listener may be required in order to receive the music as Scriabin intended. For those of us today who find ourselves unable to meet this expectation, the music still stands as a marvel of musical construction and sonorous beauty, fully capable of appreciation in purely musical terms.

Tonality: A Conflict of Forces

Patricia Carpenter

As a rule, the articulation of a perceptual image comes about
rapidly and below the level of consiousness. We open our
eyes and find the world already given. Only special circumstances make us realize that it takes an intricate process to
form an image. When the stimulus situation is complex,
unclear, or ambiguous, we consciously struggle for a stable
organization, one that defines each part and each relation
and so establishes a state of finality.

—Rudolf Arnheim, *New Essays in the Psychology of Art*

Consider tonality. To define it, as Tovey observed, is as difficult as to describe the taste of a peach.[1] These two—concept and phenomenon—are
the two sides of all experience, constituted, as it is, by a dialectic between
subject and object. We may consider a tonal theory in regard to practice
or composition, or to a single piece of music or the history of musical works.[2] Concerned with the adequacy of concept to phenomenon, we might investigate the phenomena, tonal musical works; for example:

> To extract historically relevant criteria from theories that present themselves simply as
> universal musical systems, it is necessary first to narrow the range of their validity.[3]

---

1. James C. Kidd begins an essay on different "senses" of tonality with Tovey's "wonderful
choice of simile, involving the sense of taste . . . a mode of direct, bodily and vivid knowing."
To describe and explain tonality fully may lie beyond the reach of words, Kidd says, but the
mode by which one preceives tonality may not. "Tonality in a New Key," in *Explorations in
Music, the Arts, and Ideas: Essays in Honor of Leonard B. Meyer*, ed. Eugene Narmour and Ruth
A. Solie (Stuyvesant, N.Y.: Pendragon Press, 1988), 375.

2. Currently, "music theory" as a field of study distinguishes in itself these various kinds of
experience to which it can apply, for example: "In recent years the discipline of music theory
has developed into a diverse field of inquiry encompassing a variety of subdisciplines. What
is particularly striking about the present state of the discipline is its independence from the
other principal branch of musical scholarship—historical musicology. . . . Now, however, the
time may have come to encourage the dialectical process and to test the value of merging the
two disciplines." (*Music Theory and the Exploration of the Past*, ed. Christopher Hatch and
David W. Bernstein [Chicago and London: University of Chicago Press, 1993], 1).

3. Carl Dahlhaus, *Studies on the Origin of Harmonic Tonality*, trans. Robert O. Gjerdingen

Or we might trace the term, "tonality," and the varied concepts it has signified, thereby unfolding the life of an idea; for example:

> The history of harmonic theory in the eighteenth century can be viewed as a struggle between figured bass theory and the revolutionary ideas of Rameau. Apparently, Rameau was the victor. . . .The history of harmonic theory in the nineteenth century seems at first to be a complex matter. Apparently, we cannot speak of a single theory— or even of two competing theories of harmony. Rather, there appear to be almost as many methodological approaches as there are theorists. . . .Yet the student of eighteenth-century theory easily detects the ghosts of Rameau and the figured bass theorists lurking behind our nineteenth-century authors.[4]

In this paper I shall explore one concept of tonality—that of Arnold Schoenberg. In confronting such a concept, I shall not assume some "real" tonality, but rather, suspending the question of whether his concept of tonality is "correct," adequate to what tonality "really" is, I shall emphasize its character as an individual thought. Tonality, he says, is conflict. The lines through a tonal work are lines of attraction and repulsion. A tonal work is a battlefield of forces.

Schoenberg sometimes differentiates old from new tonality, but always emphasizes their continuity:

> I . . . have the hope that in a few decades audiences will recognize the *tonality* of this music today called *atonal*, [and] would not then be compelled to attempt to point out any other difference than a gradual one between the tonality of yesterday and the tonality of today. Indeed, tonal is perhaps nothing else than what is understood *today* and atonal what will be understood in the *future*.[5]

In a recent article, Allen Forte lays out his assumptions underlying the analytic work in his study: a primary assumption, he says, is that the delay in a long overdue study of linear features in Schoenberg's music may be attributed to, among other factors, "the persistence of the atonal-tonal dichotomy as a presumably viable area of discourse."[6] Although I approach Schoenberg's music and musical thought from a different perspective than Forte, I too am concerned to overcome that dichotomy.

(Princeton: Princeton University Press, 1990), 3. The issues regarding tonal theory that I only sketch here have been presented with great clarity by Thomas Christensen in his review of Dahlhaus's study in *Music Theory Spectrum* 15 (1993): 94–111.

    4. Robert W. Wason, *Viennese Harmonic Theory from Albrechtsberger to Schenker and Schoenberg* (Ann Arbor: UMI Research Press, 1985, 1982), xi.

    5. Arnold Schoenberg, *Style and Idea. Selected Writings of Arnold Schoenberg,* ed. Leonard Stein, trans. Leo Black (New York: St Martin's Press, 1975), 283.

    6. "Concepts of Linearity in Schoenberg's Atonal Music: A Study of the Opus 15 Song Cycle," *Journal of Music Theory* 36 (1992): 285–382.

1. Schoenberg and Traditional Theory

It has never been the purpose and effect of new art to suppress the old, its predecessor, certainly not to destroy it. Quite the contrary: no one loves his predecessors more deeply, more fervently, more respectfully, than the artist who gives us something truly new; for respect is awareness of one's station and love is a sense of community.

—Schoenberg, *Harmonielehre*

Schoenberg's theoretical concepts, like his compositions, are rooted in tradition. He uses "tonality" in its earliest sense, to mean modern tonality, "from Bach to Wagner," the sense by which Fétis distinguished major-minor tonality—*tonalité moderne*, from *tonalité ancienne*, the modality of the old modes.[7] Since its introduction, the term "tonality" has provoked an unending debate, acquiring meanings that seemed to change with each of its advocates. That debate, often represented by the opposing views of Fétis and Riemann, centers on two main issues: the origin of tonality and its basis. Does tonality originate in the mind of man, or in natural laws?[8] Is its basis the scale or the chord?[9]

Schoenberg participates in this ongoing argument in interesting ways. His concept of tonality gathers up, expands, and synthesizes many notions prevailing at the beginning of this century.

Tonality, he maintains, orginates in both the musical material and the listening mind. He considered it to be a possibility of the fundamental tone, but only one such possibility. It is not a natural law existing without the effort of the composer, and therefore cannot claim to be the automatic result of the nature of sound. Nevertheless, it is one of the most apparent possibilities arising from the tone, a simple exploitation of the most evident natural characteristics of the tone. (*Style and Idea*, 270)

---

7. F.-J. Fétis, *Traité complet de la théorie et de la pratique de l'harmonie contenant la doctrine de la science et de l'art* (Paris: Braudus et Cie, 1844).

8. According to Fétis, "For the elements of music, nature provides nothing but a multitude of tones differing in pitch, duration, and intensity by the greatest or least degree. . . . The conception of relations that exist among them is awakened in the intellect" (*Traité complet*, 11f.). Riemann maintains that tonality originates by natural law, in an acoustic fact, the overtone series. Dahlhaus summarizes these issues in *Studies*, 7–18.

9. Fétis maintained that the basis of tonality is the diatonic scale. "Tonality is formed from the set of requisite relationships, simultaneous or successive, among the tones of the scale" (*Traité complet,* 22). Riemann declared this to be the cardinal error of our generally accepted theory of harmony, that it takes as its point of departure the scale and not the chord. He defined tonality as the special meaning [or "functions"] that chords receive through their relation to a fundamental sonority, the tonic triad. See Hugo Riemann, *Musik–Lexicon*, 7th ed. (Leipzig, 1909), s.v. "Tonalität."

Tonality's origin is found—and rightly so—in the laws of sound. But there are other laws that music obeys, apart from these and the laws that result from the combination of time and sound: namely, those governing the working of our minds.[10]

Schoenberg also mediates the nineteenth-century argument concerning a scale-based or chord-based theory:

> Now if we are short-sighted enough—and we are—always to regard only the momentary result as the goal, to consider now the chord, now the melody as the *Motor* that produces musical movement, then the possibility of perceiving and comprehending the whole vanishes. (*Harmonielehre*, 315)

He bases his concept of tonality on an acoustical fact: the musical sound. This is the source of both scale and chord.

> Whenever all chords of a complete piece of music appear in progressions that can be related to a common fundamental tone, one can then say that the idea of the musical sound (which is conceived as vertical) is extended to the horizontal plane. Everything following it springs from this fundamental postulate, refers back to it, even when antithetical to it, elaborates and complements it, and finally leads back to it, so that this fundamental is treated in every respect as central, as embryonic. (Ibid., 28)

The diatonic scale, he claims, was discovered; it can be explained as having been "found" by imitating nature.

> Intuition and inference assisted in translating the most important characterstic of the tone, the overtone series, from the vertical . . . into the horizontal, into separate, successive tones. (Ibid., 23)

Chords are also an imitation of nature.

> If the scale is imitation of the tone on the horizontal plane, that is, note after note, then chords are imitation on the vertical, notes sounded together. . . . The triad is without doubt similar to the tone, but it is no more similar to its model than, say, Assyrian reliefs are to their human models. (Ibid., 26)

Schoenberg denies priority to either vertical or horizontal dimension. It is hardly appropriate, he maintains, to present chords as if they had germinated and devel-

---

10. Schoenberg, *Style and Idea*, 259. Cf. "The material of music is the tone; what it affects first, the ear. The sensory perception releases associations and connects tone, ear, and the world of feeling. On the cooperation of these three factors depends everything in music that is felt to be art" (Schoenberg, *Harmonielehre,* rev. ed. [Vienna: Universal, 1922]; translated as *Theory of Harmony*, trans. Roy E. Carter [Berkeley and Los Angeles: University of California Press, 1978], 19). References to Carter's translation shall henceforth be given in the text.

oped spontaneously, or to explain polyphony as nothing else but voice leading that merely follows certain conventional rules without considering the chords resulting from their coincidence. Each is determined by the other.

> Whether the chords were created through voice leading, or voice leading became possible only through our recognition of chords, is of no consequence here; for—whichever was first—they both spring from *one* impulse: to bring the natural material, the tone, into proper relation with the organ of perception, and with all secondary and tertiary functions contributing to perception, both associative and physical. Both procedures are consistent with this impulse; they both fulfil the purpose, even if by different routes, of creating the truest possible imitations of the material. (Ibid., 313)

Schoenberg agrees with most theorists that the essential property of tonality is centricity.

> Though the development of tonality was by leaps and bounds, though it has not signified the same thing at all times, its function has, nevertheless, been one and the same. It has alway been the referring of all results to a centre, to a fundamental tone, to an emanation point of tonality. (*Style and Idea*, 270)

The concept of tonality, he says,

> coincides to a certain extent with that of the key, in so far as it refers not merely to the relation of the tones with one another, but much more to the particular way in which all tones relate to a fundamental tone, especially the fundamental tone of the scale, whereby tonality is always comprehended in the sense of a particular scale. (Ibid.)

The pitch content of the scale may be vastly extended, but one thing is certain.

> All chords that in any way turn to a key, no matter how dissonant they may be, fall within the domain of the old harmony and do not disturb tonality. (Ibid., 282)

2. TONALITY AND HARMONY

> The paths of harmony are tortuous; leading in all directions, approaching a starting point and leaving it again and again, leading astray, as they lend to a different point a momentary meaning that they soon take back again, producing climaxes that they know how to exceed, calling forth gigantic waves that ebb without coming to a standstill. Nevertheless, this seemingly random progress is based on a profound meaning that can be easily verified in music governed by tonality and assumed in music free of tonality.
> —Schoenberg, *Der musikalische Gedanke*

Unlike most of his nineteenth-century predecessors, Schoenberg does not equate tonality and harmony: both are essential properties, if different aspects, of the whole musical work. Ordinarily, however, Schoenberg means by harmony one of the pedagogical divisions in the teaching of composition, along with counterpoint and form.

> The subject matter of the doctrine of musical composition is usually divided into three areas: harmony, counterpoint, and the theory of form. Harmony is the doctrine of chords and their possible connections with regard to their tectonic, melodic, and rhythmic values and relative weight. Counterpoint is the doctrine of the movement of voices with regard to motivic combination. . . . The theory of form deals with the disposition for the construction and development of musical thoughts.[11]

To consolidate these into a unified theory of musical composition was his persistent goal, formulated as early as 1911 in a letter to his editor, Emil Herzka, and pursued throughout his life.[12]

Over the years, Schoenberg developed a striking image to represent the musical whole: the unity of the musical space. In a lecture written in 1934 he described this concept, beginning with the traditional view of the two dimensions of music, the vertical and horizontal, which he had taken such great pains to unify.

> In formulating the notion concerning the *unity of the musical space* I relied on an assertion that had already been made by previous theoreticians, namely: chords are the vertical product of the overtones, but the scale is the horizontal product. I carried this thought to its conclusion and consequently arrived at the concept whereby the vertical and the horizontal, harmonic and melodic, the simultaneous and the successive were all in reality comprised within one unified space.[13]

---

11. *Harmonielehre*, 13. Translated in Rudolf Arnheim, *Art and Visual Perception: The New Version* (Berkeley and Los Angeles: University of California Press, 1974), 349.

12. "I would perhaps be ready to draw up a contract for my entire activities as a writer on music." He projects books on counterpoint, instrumentation, a preliminary study of form, form analysis, and finally a theory of form. "All of these books are textbooks or teaching aids. They form in their entirety an 'Aesthetic of Music', under which title, I wish to write a comprehensive work." Text and translation in Bryan R. Simms's review of Schoenberg, *Theory of Harmony*, trans. Roy E. Carter, in *Music Theory Spectrum* (1982): 156–57.

Schoenberg dealt with this issue especially in his series of manuscripts written between 1923 and 1936, the so-called *Gedanke* manuscripts (housed in the Archives of the Arnold Schoenberg Institute at the University of Southern California). For example: "At present, the theory of harmony, counterpoint, and theory of form mainly serve pedagogical purposes. With the possible exception of the theory of harmony, the individual disciplines completely lack even a truly theoretical basis emanating from other external criteria. On the whole, the consequence is that three different disciplines, which together should constitute the theory of composition, in reality fall apart because they lack a common point of view" ("Der musikalische Gedanke; seine Darstellung und Durchfuehrung" [undated], trans. Charlotte Cross, 3).

13. "Vortrag/ 12 T K/ Princeton," ed. Claudio Spies, *Perspectives of New Music* 13 (1974): 83–87.

He was concerned with this idea as early as *Harmonielehre*, maintaining that the essence of music is not the chord, nor counterpoint, nor chords in conjunction with counterpoint, but something different:

> Instead of seeing that both [chord and melody] serve only one purpose . . . we take now the one, now the other to be the essence of music; whereas, in reality, this essence is not even the third, but rather some fourth that cannot be more closely examined here. . . . Art is in reality a fourth [dimension] which these great ones have always given.[14]

Schoenberg's notion of a unified musical space was crucial to his development of his new method. In a manuscript written in 1925, contrasting tonal and twelve-tone composition, he observes that the use of the musical space aims at accelerating the presentation of the idea. Roughly stated, the following happened in tonal composition: the relationship of each occurring tone to the fundamental tone was expressed in both the vertical and the horizontal; the idea was presented in such a way that certain problems were worked out not only in one dimension but in others as well.

> In the new music, the relationship of the twelve tones to each other is expressed in such a way that in both dimensions of the musical space that we are aware of up till now, the same thing is said. Simultaneity is merely an extremely rapid succession.[15]

Is it possible, he asks, to invent a technique that makes the comprehension of the vertical succession of tones as easy as that of the horizontal, for which we have more time?

Ultimately Schoenberg describes the two-or-more dimensional musical space in which ideas are presented as a unit; the unity of musical space demands an absolute and unitary perception.[16] The musical space is a metaphor for the work as both gestalt and discourse.

---

14. *Harmonielehre*, 315–16. Schoenberg observed that he achieved such a unified musical space in 1906, in his *Kammersymphonie*, op. 9, where a very intimate reciprocation between melody and harmony is established; see *Style and Idea*, 84.

15. "On the Presentation of the Idea," written November 6, 1925. Unpublished, Arnold Schoenberg Archives [104a].

Felix Greissle comments on the dimensions of musical space in an unpublished biography of Schoenberg: "Twelve tone composition; tonality is not abandoned; Schoenberg in his later compositions of traditional harmony never *returned* to tonality, because in his twelve tone composition he *never left* it. In the latter he has proceeded into a new form of tonality which represents a new concept of time and space in music, as Einstein's Theory of Relativity in science. . . . Considering the *diatonic tonality* as being *two-dimensional*, that is, polyphonic (horizontal) and proceeding in harmony (vertical), we are now, with Schoenberg's hexachordal twelve tone tonality entering a *third dimension*, the simultaneousness of two interacting, yet in itself consistent with two-dimensional elements." R. Wayne Shoaf, "From the Archives; The Felix Greissle Collection," *Journal of the Arnold Schoenberg Institute* 10 (1987): 80–81.

16. "Vortrage." These notes for a lecture at Princeton University (March 6, 1934), were

One of Schoenberg's definitions of music reflects his concern for the whole:

Music is a simultaneous and successiveness of tones and tonal-combinations, which are so organized that its impression on the ear is agreeable, and its impression on the intelligence is comprehensible, and that these impressions have the power to influence occult parts of our soul and of our sentimental spheres and that this influence makes us live in a dreamland of fulfilled desires, or in a dreamed hell.[17]

3. THE TONAL FIELD

Done, finished, over. *Consummatum est. La commedia e finita.*
...We tend to speak of conclusions when a sequence of events
has a relatively high degree of structure, when, in other
words, we can perceive these events as related to one another
by some principle of organization or design that implies the
existence of a definite termination point. . . . The sense of
closure is a function of the perception of structure.
—Barbara Herrnstein Smith, *Poetic Closure*

The unit of musical space that Schoenberg describes is a framed field, with characteristics of its own. It is not unstructured; a frame creates a specific field of

---

expanded and published as "Composition with Twelve Tones (I), 1941," in which his well-known description of musical space appears:

> Music is not merely another kind of amusement, but a musical poet's, a musical thinker's representation of musical ideas; these musical ideas must correspond to the laws of human logic; they are a part of what man can apperceive, reason and express. Proceeding from these assumptions, I arrived at the following conclusions:
> THE TWO-OR-MORE DIMENSIONAL SPACE IN WHICH MUSICAL IDEAS ARE PRESENTED IS A UNIT. Though the elements of these ideas appear separate and independent to the eye and the ear, they reveal their true meaning only through their co-operation, even as no single word alone can express a thought without relation to other words. All that happens at any point of this musical space has more than a local effect. It functions not only in its own plane, but also in all other directions and planes, and is not without influence even at remote points. (*Style and Idea*, 220)

I have explored aspects of musical space in "Temporal Form Regained," *Journal of Philosophy* 62 (1967): 56–87, "The Musical Object," *Current Musicology* 5 (1967): 116–125, and "Aspects of Musical Space," in *Explorations in Music*, 341–374.

17. A definition of music requested by Dr. Walter E. Koons, cited in H. H. Stuckenschmidt, *Schoenberg. His Life, World and Work*, trans. Humphrey Searle (New York: Macmillan Publishing Company, 1977), 383.

forces. Barbara Smith, discussing closure in poetry, suggests that in the common land of ordinary events, we create or seek out "enclosures," that is, structures that are highly organized and separated as if by an implicit frame from a background of relative disorder. Closure need not be temporal, she observes; it is not always a matter of endings.

> Indeed, the term has been used most frequently by psychologists to refer to a quality of visually perceived forms, spatial structures which exhibit relatively clear, coherent, and continuous shape. In such forms no particular point is experienced as the *last* one.[18]

The importance of a frame has been observed by the art historian, Meyer Shapiro. A monkey's scribble on a sheet of paper, he has remarked, is closer to a modern painting than the cave paintings, because the sheet becomes in effect a framed field.[19] Such a visual field is described by Rudolf Arnheim:

> A visual figure such as the square is empty and not empty at the same time. The center is part of a complex hidden structure, which can be explored by means of a disk, somewhat as iron filings will reveal the lines of force in a magnetic field. If the disk is put in various places within the square, it may be found that at some points it looks solidly at rest; at others it exhibits a pull in some definite direction, or its situation may be unclear and wavering. Investigation reveals that the disk is influenced also by the diagonals of the square as well as by the cross formed by the central vertical and horizontal axes. The center is established by the crossing of these four main structural lines.[20]

Gestalt structure extends in the time dimension as readily as in the space dimensions, and the principles governing time and space are similar. In temporal constructs the phenomenon analogous to the visual centricity described by Arnheim would seem to be a heightened sense of beginning, middle, and end. In modern Western music this has been achieved to a remarkable degree by triadic tonality.

Schoenberg considers tonality to be one of the easiest and most effective means of achieving musical form; a formal possibility of attaining a certain completeness or closure [*Geschlossenheit*] by means of a certain uniformity emerges from the tonal material (*Harmonielehre*, 125–29).

---

18. Barbara Herrnstein Smith, *Poetic Closure: A Study of How Poems End* (Chicago: University of Chicago Press, 1968), 2.

19. Class lecture, Columbia University, 1962. And see his discussion of the function of the frame in the development of western art, in *Theory and Philosophy of Art: Style, Artist, and Society. Selected Papers* (New York: George Braziller, 1994), 1ff.

20. *Art and Visual Perception*, 2f. The consequences of this field of forces in painting is further explored in his *The Power of the Center: A Study of Composition in the Visual Arts* (Berkeley and Los Angeles: University of California Press, 1982).

By form, in an aesthetic sense, Schoenberg means the organization of a whole in which the parts function like those of an organism.

> The form of a composition is achieved because (1) a body exists, and because (2) the members exercise different functions and are created for these functions. He who from the outside forces through some function on them all reminds one of the bad craftsmen who, to hide faults of construction, over-upholster, over-daub, over-lacquer, cover with nickel and so on. (*Style and Idea*, 257)

Tonality's formal function begins to exist, he says, if the phenomena that appear can, without exception, be related immediately to a tonic and if they are arranged so that their accessibility is a matter of sensory perception, or if one uses methods that allow those phenomena farther away to become accessible.

> In a piece so constructed the internal relationships acquire such cohesion that it is guaranteed in advance a certain formal effectiveness. The listener of a certain degree of comprehension, through the unity of relationships, must inevitably perceive a work so composed to be a unity. (Ibid., 261)

Tonality serves musical form in a dual way. Unifying is one, articulating is another of its formal functions.

> I perceive in both these functions, the conjoining and the unifying on the one hand, and on the other the articulating, separating, and characterizing, the main accomplishments of tonality. (Ibid., 282)

Tonality assists in determining not only the position of parts, but also their function.

> Who can say today how a principal subject must be built up? What must one do that it may hold together, so that one does not find oneself suddenly on the wrong track? Who can say how a fluid form is solidified, how an introduction or a development must be evolved? . . . Whether something be principal or subordinate idea, introduction or transition, episode, bridge, connecting link, embellishment, extension or reduction, whether independent or dependent, and, further, at which moment it begins or ceases to express one of these formal characteristics—all this is possible for masters of form to make manifest through harmony. Characteristic kinds of beginnings and endings, basic and concentrated or resolving and liquidating dispositions of the harmony and many other means of art have accomplished that great clarity necessary to formal ends. (Ibid., 257, 278)

Tonality has given the real composer a subconsciously functioning sense of form, an almost somnambulistic sense of security in creating, with utmost precision, the most delicate distinctions of formal elements. (Ibid., 218)

The unity of the whole that tonality effects pervades the concrete work, from smallest element to tonal plan.[21] Pursuing that unity, Schoenberg expanded his concept of tonality to conform to the unified musical space, ultimately formulating his concept of a "monotonality," in which all pitches, chords, and key areas are related to each other and to the centric key area.

> Every digression from the tonic is considered to be still within the tonality, whether directly or indirectly, closely or remotely related. . . . There is only one tonality in a piece.[22]

Schoenberg realized his concept of monotonality by extending the same principle he had originally used to generate the musical material from the tone: imitation.

> Most essential is the following psychological assumption: The development of the harmonic resources is explained primarily through the conscious or unconscious imitation of a prototype; every imitation so produced can then itself become a prototype that can in turn be imitated. (*Harmonielehre*, 385)

By these means, every tone can be related to every other tone—so long as its relation to the fundamental is clear.

> In one way or another all chords are naturally related to one another, as are all men. Whether they make up a family, a nation, or a race is certainly not without interest; but it is not an essential question if we place it beside the idea of species, which gives perspectives other than those admitted by the special relationships. (Ibid., 228)

The concept of an expanded and unified tonality can be traced back through Schoenberg's theoretical writings. It is foreshadowed in an early manuscript, where he stresses both stabilizing and digressive possibilities of key.

> The key is indicated by means of an appropriate succession of its scale tones, as well those not belonging to its scale in such an order that any digressions arising can promptly be brought under control by countermeasures.[23]

---

21. I have illustrated this tonal unity in a sonata of Beethoven in "Grundgestalt as Tonal Function," *Music Theory Spectrum* 5 (1983): 15-38, and in "A Problem in Organic Form: Schoenberg's Tonal Body," *Theory and Practice* 13 (1988): 1-19.

22. Arnold Schoenberg, *Structural Functions of Harmony*, rev. ed., ed. Leonard Stein (New York: W. W. Norton, 1969), 19. Future references to this work appear in the text.

23. Arnold Schoenberg, *Zusammenhang, Kontrapunkt, Instrumentation, Formenlehre* (1917); ed. Severine Neff, trans. Charlotte Cross and Severine Neff as *Coherence, Counterpoint, Instrumentation, Instruction in Form* (Lincoln: University of Nebraska Press, 1994), 46. Reference is to the English edition.

In *Harmonielehre* this idea is apparent in his treatment of modulation, where he works through the possible relations of keys to a fundamental. Here he uses the traditional circle of fifths, on which distances among keys are indicated by the number of sharps or flats in the key signatures. The circle, he maintains, expresses relationship of two keys only to a certain extent, not completely. (*Harmonielehre*, 154)

He refines this idea in *Der musikalische Gedanke*.

> From now on I shall employ a new terminology for harmonic progressions.
>
> According to my well-known presupposition that there is only one key in a movement, all so-called modulations are to be comprehended only as expansions of a key, and every establishment in a so-called "foreign" tonality should be regarded only as the *xth degree that is carried out as if it were a key*.
>
> But since the relationships *of the "more remote parts"* should be compared with those in other parts . . . for the purpose of recognizing what is the same, similar, and different, I have decided on this manner of terminology. My method of terminology has the purpose of attributing all phenomena to the fundamental scale and the tendencies of an harmonic nature governing it.[24]

The full concept of monotonality is presented in *Structural Functions of Harmony*. Here Schoenberg explains his concept of region, which he defines as a "segment of the tonality carried out as if it were a key," that is, what had formerly been considered a contrasting key area. The "chart of regions" as presented here comprises relative and parallel minor relations, as well as the fifth relations of the circle. Schoenberg's terminology for regions is contrived to clarify that network, indicating relation of the regions to the tonic and classifying them accordingly.[25] Far regions are reached by analogy to close ones: for example, T:t (tonic minor to tonic major) affords access to mediant major and submediant major (M:m, SM:sm), or sm:T (submediant minor to tonic major) accesses flat mediant and flat submediant (t:♭M, sd:♭SM). Thus "registration" of regions in a piece traces the tonal path through it.

Consider, as an example, the tonality of the first movement of Brahms's String Sextet, op. 36.[26] I have roughly sketched the tonal plan of this movement in Figure 1, and traced its path on both the circle of fifths (Fig. 2) and the chart of regions (Fig. 3).

---

24. Schoenberg, "Der musikalische Gedanke und die Logik, Technik, und Kunst seiner Darstellung" (unpub. ms., Archives of the Arnold Schoenberg Institute), ed. and trans. Patricia Carpenter and Severine Neff as *The Musical Idea, and the Logic, Technique, and Art of Its Presentation* (New York: Columbia University Press, 1995), 330–31. Henceforth, references to this work (as *Gedanke*) will appear in the text.

25. His classifications are: direct and close, indirect but close, indirect, indirect and remote, distant (*Structural Functions*, 20). Figure 3 reproduces Schoenberg's chart in major, with his explanation of his terminology for the regions.

26. Schoenberg discusses this movement in "The Constructive Function of Harmony," an essay in *Gedanke*. I shall return to this discussion below.

Figure 1. Brahms: Sextet, op. 36, mvt. 1: Tonal Plan

Introduction		mm. 1-2	tonally ambigous
Exposition			
Main theme	Tonic	a 3-32	borrows from ♭SM
		b 33-52	" " SM
		a' 53-95	" " ♭SM
Bridge	to Dominant	95-135	
Subsidiary theme	Dominant	135-213	borrows from v:M
Closing theme		213-230	
Development			
Link	v-minor	229-239	
I	v-minor	239-249	to v:V
II	SMsm (C♯-)	249-285	to SMsm/♭mM
III	roving	285-315	
Retransition	t to V	315-343	
Recapitulation	tonic	343-547	
Coda		547-605	

How can one describe the "monotonality" of this movement? The tonality is G major, with its dominant as the customary main contrast. What marks the individuality of this tonality, its particular characteristics? Two further main contrasts: the flat submediant major (E♭+) and the tritone area (C♯+/D♭+). In the figures, I have noted five large-scale tonal movements. (1) Both main contrasts are set up in the initial theme (a b a'): flat submediant (E♭+) in the first segment, submediant major (E+) in the middle segment (preparing for the contrast, C♯-/+). (2) The subsidiary theme moves to the dominant, and to mediant major of its relative minor (F+). (3) The first development section moves from v minor through its flat submediant, to a deceptive cadence on its V (A+). (4) Development II turns abruptly to and elaborates the submediant major's submediant minor (C♯-), the tritone area and farthest distance. (5) Development III instigates an enharmonic change (C♯/D♭), which reinterprets the tritone area as the flat-mediant minor's mediant major (D♭+). From here, through a series of roving sequences, the tonal movement returns, at the retransition, to the tonic minor. The exposition recapitulates the tonic major.[27]

How will this somewhat fragmented tonality be unified?

---

27. In each of the large Brahms movements I know, there is only one actual enharmonic equivalence on which the structure turns. In this work, for example, B major is enharmonically equivalent to C♭, the flat submediant of the flat submediant (E♭), but C♭ is not approached as such. (Schoenberg, however, in his version of the Coda, does exploit this relationship.) In the Sextet, C♯ is reached clockwise, as the mediant minor/major of the dominant of the dominant (A+); D♭+ is left counterclockwise though its mediant (F-).

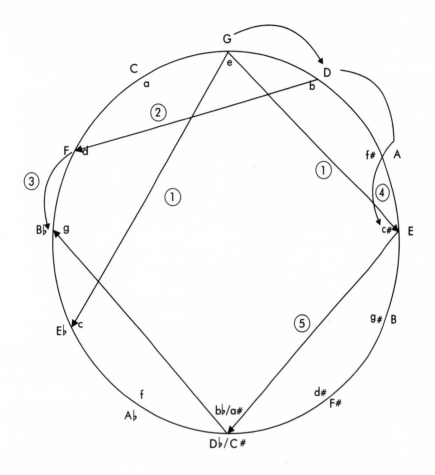

1 Main theme, a, b
2 Subsidiary theme
3 Development I
4 Development II
5 Development III, retransition

Figure 2. Tonal Plan of Brahms's op. 36, mvt. 1, traced on the circle of fifths

Chart of the Regions

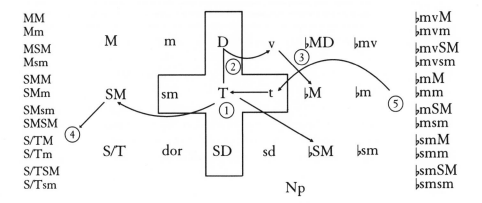

Abbreviations

T means tonic   **Np** means Neapolitan
D dominant   **dor** Dorian
SD subdominant   **S/T** supertonic
t tonic minor   **♭M** flat mediant major
sd subdominant minor   **♭SM** flat submediant major
v five-minor   **♭MD** flat mediant major's dominant
sm submediant minor   **♭m** flat mediant minor
m mediant minor   **♭sm** flat submediant minor
SM submediant major   **♭mv** flat mediant minor's five
M mediant major

[N.B. All symbols in capitals refer to major keys; those in small letters to minor keys.]

The first symbol always indicates the relation to the tonic. The second symbol shows the relation to the region indicated by the first symbol. Thus: **Mm** reads "mediant major's mediant minor" (in **C**, a minor region on **g♯**); SMsm reads "submediant major's submediant minor" (in **C**, a minor region on **f♯**); **♭smSM** reads "flat submediant minor's submediant major" (in **C** a major region on **F♭**), etc.

1 Main theme, a, b
2 Subsidiary theme
3 Development I
4 Development II
5 Development III, retransition

Figure 3. Tonal Plan of Brahms's op. 36, mvt. 1, traced on Schoenberg's chart of the regions (From *Structural Functions of Harmony*, 20)

4. CONFLICTING FORCES IN A FRAMED FIELD

> Every chord that is set beside the principal tone has at least
> as much tendency to lead away from it as to return to it. And
> if life, if a work of art is to emerge, then we must engage in
> this movement-generating conflict. The tonality must be
> placed in danger of losing its sovereignty; the appetites for
> independence and the tendencies toward mutiny must be
> given opportunity to activate themselves; one must grant
> them their victories, not begrudging them an occasional ex-
> pansion of territory. For a ruler can only take pleasure in
> ruling live subjects; and live subjects will attack and plunder.
> —Schoenberg, *Harmonielehre*

Unrest, maintains Schoenberg, is inherent in the very material of music; his
development of the tonal material is based on that assumption.

> The primitive ear hears the tone as irreducible, but physics recognizes it to be com-
> plex. In the meantime, however, musicians discovered that it is *capable of continuation*,
> i.e., that *movement is latent in it*. That problems are concealed in it, problems that clash
> with one another, that the tone lives and seeks to propagate itself. They had heard in it,
> and extracted from it, the octave, the fifth, and the third. (*Harmonielehre*, 313)

In *Harmonielehre* Schoenberg begins his elaboration of tonal material with a
striking image of opposing forces—attraction to or repulsion from the fundamental.

> If C is taken as the midpoint, then its situation can be described by reference to two
> forces, one which pulls downward, toward F, the other upward, toward G. (Ibid., 24)

He likens this situation to that of a man hanging by his hands from a beam and
exerting his own force against the force of gravity. The man pulls on the beam just as
gravity pulls him, and in the same direction. But the effect is that his force *works
against* the force of gravity, and so in this way one is justified in speaking of two
opposing forces.

This somewhat desperate image, embodying the dynamic play of forces in the
tonal field, represents Schoenberg's notion of centricity. Although the model he uses
here, for deriving the just diatonic scale from its three consonant triads, goes back at
least to Zarlino, Schoenberg's image personifies the forces at work. One feels the
tension in muscles and joints. The tone lives.

A force is an action. Here the energy inherent in the tone is directed toward, or
away from, a goal: the fundamental. Schoenberg terms the opposing forces "centripetal," those close to or having the potential to move towards the tonic, and "centrifu-

gal," those far from or moving away from it. The fundamental tone would be relatively lifeless if it did not itself contain in its overtones those centrifugal and centripetal forces. It is inherent in its nature to allow those forces that are unified and contained within it to develop and strive away from each other, as is their nature. (*Gedanke*, 120–21)

Centrifugal, key-dissolving elements may be nondiatonic pitches, modulations, even ambiguities. Centripetal tendencies are exerted by stopping centrifugal tendencies, that is, by establishing a tonality through the conquest of its contradictory elements. For example, he explains the basic I – IV – V – I cadence (and he considers a piece to be an extended cadence) in terms of conflicting forces: a statement, challenge, contradiction and confirmation. (Schoenberg 1934, 310–11) The statement of IV after I not only functions in the tonic but also has the potential to act as a challenger, to become a tonic on its own. The introduction of V, with its natural leading tone, however, contradicts any power of IV and instead confirms the tonic.

Musical forces have been seen as generated by a few basic means: motion and rest—Fétis's *tendence* and *repose*, dissonance and consonance (dissonance, notes Rameau, motivates the motion toward the goal); leading tones, Kurth's "original tonal energy"; or the tensions holding among roots. The network of tonal forces is a kinship, a companionship (*Verwandschaft*) of pitches and their functions. The function of a root, interval, or single pitch is its specific relation to the fundamental, defined by its scale degree. Function gives meaning to force.

Schoenberg's theory, continuing the Viennese tradition based on the diatonic scale degrees, is also fundamentally diatonic. Tonal motion is governed by root progression.

> The structural meaning of a harmony depends exclusively upon the degree of the scale.... Structural functions are exerted by *root progressions*. (*Structural Functions*, 6)

He emphatically objects, for example, to speaking of a "C-major triad," because this tells nothing about its function, its meaning. A C-major triad is I in C major, IV in G major, V in F major—and Neapolitan II in B major/minor, III in A minor, or III with raised third in A♭ major, and so forth. Thinking about musical elements in this way focuses attention on their multiple meaning.[28]

The concept of monotonality is rooted in multiple meaning and tonal ambiguity. Although based on diatonic root progressions, the collection is extended to include all pitches. Any pitch in an infinite spiral of fifths can be "borrowed" from a region and "substituted" for its diatonic equivalent—again, so long as its diatonic

---

28. As beginners in Schoenberg's classes, we were encouraged to practice such exercises with single tones, intervals, and chords in all keys. This practice apparently went back through Viennese theory at least to Vogler. For a study of multiple meaning see Janna Saslaw, "Gottfried Weber and the Concept of Mehrdeutigkeit," Ph.D. diss., Columbia University, 1992.

degree is made clear.[29] Altered chords, or "transformations," can be built on all degrees of all regions.[30] "Some may be impossibly harsh, others dangerous but possible" (*Structural Functions*, 35). Most are "vagrants" because of their multiple meaning, for example, diminished-seventh and augmented-sixth chords. Any major triad can function as a Neapolitan chord, any dominant-seventh as an augmented-sixth. Thus the entire pitch collection becomes accessible to a single fundamental. Schoenberg's vivid image for such a tonality introduces the study of modulation in *Harmonielehre*.

> We can assume that tonality is a function of the fundamental tone, that is, everything that makes up tonality emanates from that tone and refers back to it. But, even though it does refer back, that which emanates from the tone has a life of its own—within certain limits; it is dependent, but to a certain degree also independent. What is closest to the fundamental has the most affinity with it, what is more remote, less affinity. If, roaming over the domain of the fundamental, we follow the traces of its influence, we soon reach those boundaries where the attraction of the tonal center is weaker, where the power of the ruler gives way and the right of self-determination of the half-free can under certain circumstances provoke upheavals and changes in the constitution of the entire structure. (*Harmonielehre*, 150–51)

How is such a tonality made manifest in a musical work? In his essay, "The Constructive Function of Harmony," Schoenberg, using examples from Brahms, demonstrates how tonal forces work in structuring a piece. (*Gedanke,* 308ff.) The first movement of Brahms's Sextet, op. 36, for example, unfolds from a wonderfully ambiguous changing-note figure (Ex. 1). Schoenberg observes that

> the viola figure, resembling a pedal point, has a dual meaning: in one case it is the G, in the other it is the F♯ that is "changing-note" for three different chords. (Ibid., 322–23; see Ex. 2a)

This ambiguous figure motivates the expansion of the movement (Ex. 2b): (1) In the main theme, projected to $\hat{5}$ and inverted, it links the two fifths of the

---

29. In general, two procedures yield this expansion: any tone can be raised or lowered to create an "artificial" leading tone, thereby forming an "artificial" dominant; any dominant allows the interchange of its major and minor, thereby giving immediate access to the subdominant minor, from which other elements are borrowed.

30. The second degree (progressing to V) is Schoenberg's model for transformations. Most appear as seventh or ninth chords, with or without the root (as the diatonic diminished triad on VII usually functions as V). All members of a chord can be altered: the third can be raised to create a leading tone to V; the fifth lowered for the same reason; the ninth lowered, forming (without its root) the diminished-seventh chord; or almost any combination of these substitutions can be made.

Schoenberg indicates a transformation by a slash through the degree number: for example, II̸.

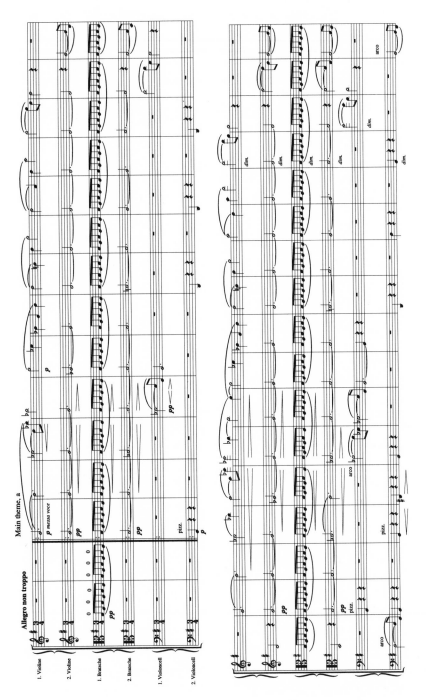

Example 1. Brahms: Sextet, op. 36, mvt. 1, opening measures.

a)

b)

Example 2. a) Schoenberg's analysis of changing-note figure in Brahms's op. 36, mvt. 1; b) The figure motivates the tonal expansion of the movement.

Example 3. Brahms: Sextet, op. 36, mvt. 1: Schoenberg's illustrations of the link to Development.

Grundgestalt, thereby acquiring elements from flat submediant major (E♭+). (2) In the turn to the contrast section, the tonic becomes ♭6̂, thereby accessing submediant major (E+), by transformations on III and VI. (3) Transposed to v minor (D-), it is the source of the development section. (4) And it effects the movement to the tritone area, the farthest distance in this movement.

Schoenberg illustrates how the development of this movement is based on ♭V̶I̶-V.

> Op. 36 . . . shows the characteristic modulation to a VI of the minor subdominant region (E♭-major triad). . . . The entire elaboration section is constructed on this. (Ibid.)

Example 4a. Brahms: op. 36, mvt. 1: Development I.

In the link to the development section, Schoenberg points out a small change Brahms made to the initial theme, producing a major second (Ex. 3). He sketches the first theme (mm. 7–13, his Ex. 211a) and its transposition to the dominant (Ex. 211c), then indicates the change Brahms has made mm. 226–29, Ex. 211b).

> In measure 12 after the repeat sign [m. 228], a change arises in the layout of the theme. According to this [layout], bars 11–15 would sound as in 211c, returning to D major; here (211b) bar 12 immediately brings the dominant, followed by D minor. In so doing, the principal voice (Vl. 1) takes the ascending step of a second, D – E (bars 11–12) which will later be developed further. (Ibid.)

He then indicates how the development unfolds from this change.

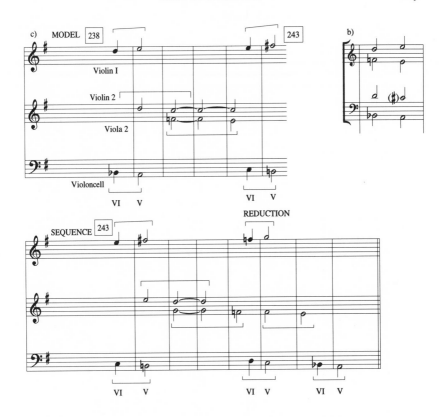

Example 4b and c. Brahms: op. 36, mvt. 1: Development I.

The course of the modulation in the following measures of the elaboration is then (211d) based on the fundamental step VI V and returns to a V on A (m. 33) [m. 249]. (Ibid., 324–25)

This passage (Development I) is shown in Example 4a. In Example 4b and 4c I have sketched this section of the development. Brahms constructs a model, sequence and reduction, using the voice leadings of the ♭VI–V progression, shaping the outer voices as upbeat figures, the inner voices as suspensions, and projecting the tonal motion from the VI–V in v minor, by means of the ascending major second, to a deceptive cadence on V on A.

Playing again with the ambiguity of the changing-note figure (A–G♯) and an ambiguous third (C♯/E), Brahms interprets A as ♭6, turning abruptly to the tritone area (C♯) (Ex. 5a), repeating the fundamental progression (VI–(I)–V) in this distant region (Ex. 5b). This is the farthest point reached in this movement, the point of greatest imbalance (Development II).

Let me continue Schoenberg's political metaphor.

Example 5a. Brahms: op. 36, mvt. 1: Development II.

Example 5b. Brahms: op. 36, mvt. 1: Development II.

To establish boundaries in a district where there are so many interchanges may be a futile undertaking. . . . It is important for us to recognize that in tonality there are regions that will remain neutral, so long as they are forced to do so, but that, as soon as the rule of the fundamental is even momentarily relaxed, are ready to submit to the inticements of a neighboring tonality. . . . From this situation, and from the tendency of every degree either to become a fundamental or at least to gain a more significant position in another district, a competition emerges, which constitutes the excitement of the harmonic events within tonality. (*Harmonielehre*, 151)

In Brahms's Sextet, I should think, we are now in this situation.

The climax of the tonal motion is reached in Development III, which effects the enharmonic change, C♯/D♭ (Ex. 6a). Schoenberg, in his Example 211e, illustrates that this section shows "the same thing"—that is, like the first two sections, it is based on the fundamental VI–V progression. Again Brahms constructs a model and sequence, moving by descending semitones from the tritone (D♭) to a deceptive cadence on V of the dominant. (I have sketched this in Ex. 6b, indicating the roving VI–V progressions.) This passage has turned back from D♭, along the counterclockwise half of the circle, as abruptly as it turned clockwise away, toward C♯.

The appetite for independence shown by the two strongest subordinates in the district, the mutiny of the more loosely connected elements, the occasional small victories and gains of the competing parties, their final subjection to the sovereign will and their meeting together for a common function—this activity, a reflection of our own human enterprise, is what causes us to perceive as life what we create as art. (Ibid.)

How, in the Sextet, will these competing forces come together for a common function?

5. STRIVING TOWARD BALANCE

Music, like drugs, is intuition, a path to knowledge. A path?
No—a battlefield.
The game of music . . . resembles the game of power: monopolize the right to violence; provoke anxiety and then

Example 6. Brahms: op. 36, mvt. 1: Development III.

provide a feeling of security; provoke disorder and then propose order; create a problem in order to solve it.

—Jacques Attali, *Noise*

Schoenberg believed that the musical work, like the material itself, originates
in unrest. In his *Gedanke* manuscript he describes the musical idea in these terms.

> Through the connection of tones of different pitch, duration and emphasis (intensity??),
> unrest comes into being: a state of rest is placed in question through a contrast.
>   From this unrest a motion goes out, which after attainment of a *climax* will
> again lead to a state of rest or to a . . . new kind of consolidation that is equivalent to a
> state of rest. (*Gedanke*, 15)

Those elements of "unrest" or "imbalance" which, to use his political metaphor, challenge the sovereignty of the tonic he considered to be the problem.

> Every succession of tones produces unrest, conflict, problems. . . . Every musical form
> can be considered as an attempt to treat this unrest either by halting or limiting it, or
> by solving the problem.[31]

Contrasting tonal and twelve-tone composition, Schoenberg defines tonality itself
with respect to the musical idea and tonal problem.

> The question of tonality can only be judged according to the laws of presentation of
> the musical idea. Compositions executed tonally proceed in every sense so as to bring
> every occurring tone into a direct or indirect relationship to the fundamental tone,
> [so] that doubt about how a tone is related can never last for a long time. . . . Twelve-
> tone composition does not involve the tonal problem. Composition with twelve
> tones related only to one another . . . *presupposes the knowledge of these relationships*,
> and does not see in them a problem still to be solved and worked out. ("On the Presen-
> tation of the Idea," 1)

Schoenberg's several representations of musical dynamics—centrifugal and
centripetal forces, inherent unrest, imbalance and balance—converge in his concept
of the musical idea. In his well-known description of the musical idea, he describes
the production of imbalance in terms of the multiple meaning of tones.

> Every tone which is added to a beginning tone makes the meaning of that tone doubt-
> ful. If, for instance, G follows after C, the ear may not be sure whether this expresses C
> major or G major, or even F major or E minor; and the addition of other tones may or
> may not clarify this problem. In this manner there is produced a state of unrest or

---

31. *Fundamentals of Musical Composition*, ed. Gerald Strang and Leonard Stein (London:
Faber and Faber, 1967), 102.

imbalance which grows throughout most of the piece and is enforced further by similar functions of the rhythm. (*Style and Idea*, 122–23)

The method by which balance is restored, he says, is the idea of the composition. More broadly, he defines the idea as the totality of a piece: the idea which its creator wanted to present. By this he would seem to mean the manner in which the challenge to the fundamental is concretely manifested and sustained across the work, and how its conflicting elements are ultimately assimilated into the tonic.

> Each composition raises a question, puts up a problem which in the course of the piece has to be answered, resolved, carried through. It has to be carried through many contradictory situations; it has to be developed by drawing conclusions from what it postulates . . . and all this might lead to a conclusion, a pronunciamento.[32]

In Brahms's Sextet, Schoenberg shows us the problem: the same flat submediant that brought about imbalance in the movement is the means by which balance is restored.

> Op. 36 . . . shows the characteristic modulation to a VI of the minor subdominant region (the major triad on E♭). The entire elaboration section is constructed on this and, in the recapitulation the turn to the tonic of the subsidiary theme comes about by means of a small variation (the seventh, D♭) of this triad on E♭. (*Gedanke*, 322–23)

The tonality of this movement is unified, and balance restored, by an old device—the ambiguous augmented six-five chord—manipulated in an elegant way. In the recapitulation (Ex. 7), D♭ added to ♭VI moves as dominant to ♭II (A♭+), while C♯, reinstated in the initial changing-note figure, now on the dominant, effects another transformation on II, the augmented six-five.

> In the recapitulation . . . the E♭ chord is expanded to the Neapolitan sixth-chord (on II) leading to the seventh chord (2 on E♭): D♭ E♭ G B♭ (which is identical with the augmented 6/5 chord on the second degree: D♭ + C♯ E♭ G B♭). The Neapolitan sixth-chord is again followed by I 4/6, so here the chord progression (directly) II (I) V is a lovely variant, (indirectly, though, it remains VI (II – II) – (I) – V) and one only regrets that it remains a *variant* instead of serving as the basis for consequences. (Ibid.)

In his last example (211f), Schoenberg indicates what he means by drawing consequences from the tonal material (Ex. 8a):

---

32. Jean and Jens Christensen, *From Arnold Schoenberg's Literary Legacy: A Catalogue of Neglected Items* (Warren, Mich.: Harmonie Park Press, 1988), 99.

Example 7. Brahms: op. 36, mvt. 1: (a) recapitulation; (b) return to Main Theme.

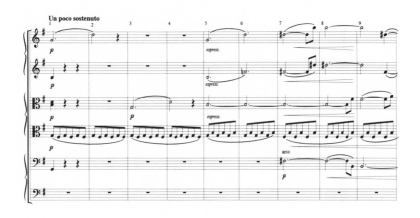

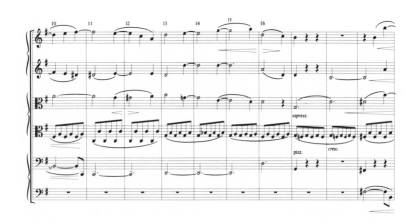

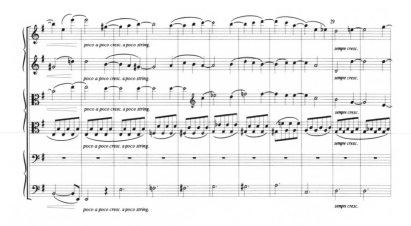

Example 8a. Brahms: op. 36, mvt. 1: Coda.

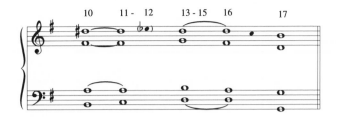

Example 8b. Brahms: op 36, mvt. 1: Coda.

Still another beautiful variant appears in the Coda (page 27, Un poco sostenuto), where (in place of VI) III is used, though also without having any consequences at all. For example, *211f*, which Brahms, had he done it at all, would naturally have executed much more beautifully, which is shown here only to illustrate what it means to draw consequences. (Ibid.)[33]

In the Coda, Brahms repeats the move to the mediant major that was so striking in the main theme (m. 33). Here (m. 552, m. 6 of the *Un poco sostenuto*) Brahms enhances that progression with an augmented six-five (I in the tonic; II in mediant major), rather than simply relying on the reinterpretation of G as $\flat\hat{6}$. In mm. 10–12 he creates a dominant-seventh, then a diminished-seventh on III, reinterpreting it as V in the tonic, leading directly to the cadence (m.17; Ex. 8b). The move is repeated, extended to VI (as in the main theme), leading to II and again to the cadence.

Schoenberg, in his version, avoids any dominant function on III, moving on to VI of the mediant major (G#-), which, with a raised third, becomes ♭HH in the tonic (m. 13, Ex. 8c). This effectively ties in any loose ends. The ♭HH is shown to be the enharmonic pivot point, approached not only from the one contrast, the flat submediant (and the counterclockwise side of the circle), but also from the other, the mediant major and its submediant (and the clockwise side of the circle). The transformed HH (B+) is shown to be the ♭VI (C♭) of the ♭VI (E♭). All the phenomena are indeed clearly related to the fundamental.

Schoenberg spent many years in an attempt to formulate his concept of the musical idea. Following his work, I have come to see him as "a human being painfully stirred by the search for inward harmony."[34] As he himself struggled to form-

33. Severine Neff discusses Schoenberg's reworking of the Coda in "Schoenberg and Analysis: Reworking a Coda of Brahms," *International Journal of Musicology* 3 (1995):187–201.

34. In the phrase of Karl Kraus. See my "Musical Form and Musical Idea: Reflections on a Theme of Schoenberg, Hanslick, and Kant," in *Music and Civilization: Essays in Honor of Paul Henry Lang*, ed. Edmond Strainchamps and Maria Rika Maniates, with Christopher Hatch (New York: W. W. Norton, 1984), 427.

Example 8c. Brahms: op. 36, mvt. 1: Coda.

ulate his thoughts about music, some of his most important ideas were synthesized: concrete musical form, the musical idea, the tonal problem, and what he took
to be the very essence of tonality. None of these, I think, can be adequately grasped
singly; all must be ultimately understood within the context of the totality of his
thought.

NEOCLASSICISM AND ITS DEFINITIONS

PIETER C. VAN DEN TOORN

How does neoclassicism manifest itself? Do parts or features readily identified as Baroque or Classical, tonal or adhering to tonally conceived forms and shapes, draw attention to themselves as such? And if they do, do they then defy integration? Are they then incapable of being assimilated by the individual context, incapable of acquiring a sense of motivation by way of that assimilation, a sense of integrity? (Are neoclassical wholes never wholes, in other words, never "organic"?) Or are questions of this kind questions of degree after all? Can neoclassical works have it both ways (which would seem to be the established view)?

Some of these questions do not lend themselves all that well to analysis. They touch to too great an extent on the immediacy of the experiencing subject. The organic character of, say, Stravinsky's neoclassical works cannot be proved one way or the other. Only as impressions do musical works manifest themselves in this way, do they become organically whole or "total" (as Schoenberg might have expressed it);[1] only on the basis of what is sensed and felt, given directly in experience, can a musical train of thought appear as a whole rather than in parts, can parts assume a transparency in the service of that whole; only on such a basis is there a reciprocity with parts both defining and being defined by the whole. And even then, the manner in which such impressions are tied to aesthetic responses of one kind or another, favorable or not, adds yet another dimension to the puzzle. All of which is not to question the metaphor itself or its usefulness in practical analysis, the metaphor of organic unity or wholeness. Elusive and at times overly deterministic in its effect,[2] it can

---

1. Arnold Schoenberg, "Gustav Mahler" (1912, 1948), in *Style and Idea,* ed. Leonard Stein, trans. Leo Black (Berkeley and Los Angeles: University of California Press, 1984), 449. According to Schoenberg, a sense of the context as a whole, an "impression" of its "totality," emerged gradually in the listening experience, even if it could be anticipated and later invoked in a moment's time. For a survey of the origins of the metaphor of organic life, see Ruth A. Solie, "The Living Work: Organicism and Musical Analysis," *Nineteenth-Century Music* 4 (1980): 147–56. Its application to Schoenberg's writings is discussed in Severine Neff, "Schoenberg and Goethe: Organicism and Analysis," in *Music Theory and the Exploration of the Past,* ed. Christopher Hatch and David W. Bernstein (Chicago: University of Chicago Press, 1993), 409–33; it is discussed with reference to Schenker's writings in William Pastille, "Music and Morphology: Goethe's Influence on Schenker's Thought," in *Schenker Studies,* ed. Hedi Siegel (Cambridge: Cambridge University Press, 1990), 29–44.

2. See, for example, Joseph Kerman, "How We Got into Analysis, and How to Get Out," *Critical Inquiry* 7 (1980): 311–331. Kerman's critique of organicist thought in music analysis

nonetheless underscore the lifelike rather than mechanical quality of musical wholes, the natural and effortless rather than arbitrary or forced manner in which parts can be felt to cohere.[3] It can help sustain a sense of the experience of music.

But if analysis can offer little proof in these matters, it can offer evidence. And of immediate concern is the established view of neoclassicism, the contradiction embedded in that view, the idea, on the one hand, of an unbridgeable gap between the old and the new and that, on the other, of an assimilation or transcending contextuality.[4] The assumption would seem to be that traditions both remote and long since spent, no longer capable of functioning authentically, only anachronistically, are put to use on behalf of the new; neoclassical works can make a point by way of that use and we as listeners can respond accordingly.[5] But that point is made, bits and pieces of the nonimmediate past are revived even as the individual neoclassical context makes a point of its own, emits a sense of integrity that overrides the very traditions upon which rests the initial point of departure.

This may oversimplify the established view, of course, by treating each side of the contradiction independently of the other. Applying the idea of a transformation of the old by the new, both sides could presumably be taken into account,

---

has been reprinted in Joseph Kerman, *Write All These Down* (Berkeley and Los Angeles: University of California Press, 1994), 12–32.

3. These particular implications of the organic model were always an important part of its message: see Kevin Korsyn, "Schenker's Organicism Reexamined," *Intégral* 7 (1993): 91. Korsyn remarks that "organicism must also be seen in relation to mechanistic and materialistic trends, as a response to everything that threatened to reduce human beings to mere mechanisms."

4. For a recent manifestation of this traditional view of neoclassical music, see Joseph N. Straus, *Remaking the Past: Musical Modernism and the Influence of the Tonal Tradition* (Cambridge: Harvard University Press, 1990), 44–73. Straus underscores the "non-organic" character of Stravinsky's neoclassical "recompositions," their "dual structures" of old and new, "continuous conflict," and absence of "larger resolution or synthesis." At the same time, however, he insists that a transcending "new meaning" is realized, one in which "traditional formations [are] heard in a novel way." Moreover, according to Straus, the new or post-tonal in Stravinsky's "recompositions" is distinguished by motivic processes involving abstract pitch-class sets and their relations. Here, however, such processes and relations are heard and understood to straddle the tonal and post-tonal worlds. See note 20.

5. The extent to which aspects of the nonimmediate past manifest themselves anachronistically (and in this way neoclassically) in several contexts from the music of Stravinsky, Bartók, and Schoenberg is discussed in illuminating detail in Martha Hyde, "Neoclassic and Anachronistic Impulses in Twentieth-Century Music," *Music Theory Spectrum* 18 (1996: 200–35). The influence of jazz may also be felt in the harmonic and rhythmic configurations in the first movement of Stravinsky's *Symphony in Three Movements,* undoubtedly a product of the composer's arrival in the United States in 1939 and of his reacquaintance at that time with varieties of American popular music. See, in this connection, the triplets and offbeat patterns of punctuation at Rehearsal 7–13, as condensed in Example 2.

nonimmediate tradition as well as newly constructed context. Viewing the latter as a transformation of the former, old and new could figure as part of the same overriding process.

Observe, however, that such a perspective does not eliminate the contradiction. On the contrary, a before-and-after scenario remains in place, one in which the new is defined to some extent by the old, by an awareness of what it is that is being transformed. And the approach would therefore continue to segment and isolate what for the critic stands isolated by its own accord, namely, the past which resists integration. So, too, application in analysis is likely to be partial and incomplete; not all of the data covered by, say, a tonal reading of a neoclassical context is likely to overlap or intersect with the data of the new, an interpretation of the new. (Here, the "data" might include the manner in which pitches, intervals, and rhythms are grouped as well as the pitches and intervals themselves. In passages to be examined here from Stravinsky's *Symphony in Three Movements*, classes of pitches and intervals which figure as part of a diatonic and even tonal segmentation are not included in an octatonic arrangement—one, however, which is no less specific and cohesive in its articulation.)

And this is where the difficulty lies, of course, in the apparent absence of a unifying design or synthesis, one specific enough to be of use in embracing conflicting components of this kind. Instead, such parts and the traditions they embody attract too much attention; they are felt as insufficiently transparent in a reading of the whole, insufficiently motivated from the standpoint of the whole. All of which has tended to manifest itself in the following practical terms: Analysis can either accept the high degree of non-integration or conflict as a defining attribute of this music, devoting its energies accordingly, or it can pursue a transcending ideal by retreating to relations of greater abstraction and, for the specifics of the conflict, less definition. It can either attend to the conflict or, pursuing the whole, adopt relations of an increasingly abstract nature precisely in order to override conflict. In the latter case, however, it will override that which defines the underlying rationale of its subject matter. And it is in the irreconcilable duplicity of these options that analysis reflects the contradiction that lies at the heart of the traditional approach to the study and understanding of neoclassical music.

Indeed, many familiar forms of analysis have proceeded along just such lines. What may work with a convincing degree of specificity for the part is imposed on the whole; alternatively, a highly abstract reading of various parts, one involving, say, pitch-class sets and their relations, is imposed on the whole in like fashion, and with results too watered down to be of consequence. In each case, the issue of the whole is forced; parts which conflict at relatively low levels of abstraction (parts representing the old and the new, for example) are made to relate and intersect at higher levels (with the old either cancelling out the new or vice versa). And the larger issue thus becomes not relatedness as such but, rather, its kind and degree, not intersection but the manner of its articulation. (Given a sufficient degree of abstraction, in other words, all parts can be made to relate.) And what may therefore be sensed and felt of the past and present, what, indeed, may seem to define the character of Stravinsky's neoclassical works, is lost. This is not to suggest that such a predicament is peculiar to the analysis of this particular music, only that its effects can seem unusually severe and problematic.

Thus, theories of tonality as sophisticated as Schenker's are apt to make for an uneasy fit. Many of Schenker's terms work best as an outside foil, in fact, a way of setting neoclassical processes in relief; stretched beyond that point, they lose much of the explanatory power they wield for the repertory for which they were intended. Indeed, by way of a Schenkerian analysis, very little of Stravinsky's neoclassical idiom is likely to come to the fore; by such means, a piece such as the *Symphony in Three Movements* can relate only rather poorly (or irrelevantly) to such exemplars of the tonal past as the symphonies of Haydn, Beethoven, and Brahms.

But here again, to dismiss the tonal tradition altogether is to dismiss a point no less crucial to neoclassicism; the tonal tradition requires acknowledgment, even if the evidence in support of the Schenkerian model is too incomplete to allow for a convincing application. What tends to emerge from such application, in fact, is a residue, one manifesting itself discontinuously in bits and pieces, here and there, without much in the way of a connective tissue. (For Schenker himself, of course, fragmentary evidence of this kind would have ruled out the possibility of tonality or of an organic structure altogether.) And it is in just this fragmentary respect that Stravinsky's (neoclassical) uses of the past can indeed seem far from disciplined, even within single, individual pieces; varied in their individual effects, they are scattered and too contextualized from one piece to the next to be judged the product of a methodically applied technique or system abstracted from the classics. The composer himself might have argued differently, to be sure, and by insisting repeatedly on the craftlike nature of his art, the need for received rules, discipline, and so forth.[6] And there is little question but that, between the two world wars, Stravinsky's aesthetic as well as political views grew increasingly conservative and even reactionary, driven apparently by images of a chaotic present and the need for the restoration of an idealized order. Richard Taruskin has documented a number of aesthetic and institutional implications that would seem to bear this out.[7] Yet the music speaks very differently, it seems to me, not of method or system but of far-reaching freedom in both the borrowing and the uses to which that borrowing is put; it speaks of a

6. See, for example, Igor Stravinsky, *Poetics of Music,* trans. Arthur Knodel and Ingolf Dahl (Cambridge: Harvard University Press, 1947), 65. "My freedom will be so much the greater and more meaningful the more narrowly I limit my field of action and the more I surround myself with obstacles . . . The more constraints one imposes, the more one frees one's self of the chains that shackle the spirit."

7. See Richard Taruskin, "Back to Whom? Neoclassicism as Ideology," *Nineteenth-Century Music* 16 (1993): 287–93. Taruskin documents some of the conservative aesthetic and sociopolitical currents with which Stravinsky seems to have identified himself during the early years of his neoclassicism in France.

great variety of references whose sources are numerous, varied and conflicting even within individual pieces and movements.

On the other hand, analytical methods having to do with motives and pitch-class sets are capable of more extended treatment. In the case of motives and their development, this has to do with the highly contextualized nature of the motivic process. Defined by its rhythms and successions, the melodic life of a particular work can still be very much its own. And this is because, although relatively nondescript in and of themselves, motives can reflect all the various aspects of a context, including its melody, harmony, rhythm, and instrumentation. Motives can result from an interaction of those aspects, and can reflect not only the sum but the transcending context itself. And it is their initial nondescriptness that allows for such a reflection, allows motives both to mold and to be molded in such a comprehensive fashion, and to become so entirely both instruments and reflections of the individual context.

It was Schoenberg who sought to define a repertory along such lines (his own repertory, of course, twelve-tone as well as tonally "extended"), identifying his music with the Classical and Romantic traditions of the eighteenth and nineteenth centuries—"homophonic" music, as he described it at one point, music which adhered to "the style of 'developing variation.'"[8] And he identified his music accordingly, connecting it with various tonal traditions by way of the motive and its development, at the expense of other repertories, including Stravinsky's neoclassical. In its relations with the past, neoclassicism was deemed a fraud, indeed, "fashionable foolishness."[9] In contrast, Schoenberg's twelve-tone works escaped the neoclassical label for much of the century, notwithstanding the obvious and elaborate transfer they often entailed not only of Baroque and Classical forms but of various types of phrases, themes, and accompanimental figuration which were no less tonal in origin. Even today, with much of the earlier polemic subsided, efforts persist in the demonstration of the organic character of that transfer, the extent to which the inherited forms in Schoenberg's music can be heard and understood as forming an integral part of the twelve-tone structures, indeed, as having been motivated by those structures.[10]

But other critics have continued to insist on the significance of that restoration, and on the extent to which Schoenberg's twelve-tone idiom was made intelligible by

---

8. Arnold Schoenberg, *Fundamentals of Musical Composition*, ed. Gerald Strang and Leonard Stein (London: Faber and Faber, 1970), 8. "Homophonic music can be called the style of developing variation. This means that in the succession of motive-forms produced through variation of the basic motive, there is something which can be compared to development, to growth."

9. Schoenberg, "Igor Stravinsky: *Der Restaurateur*" (1926), in *Style and Idea,* 482. In another article, Schoenberg referred specifically to *Oedipus Rex:* "I still believe this work is nothing," he averred. ("Stravinsky's *Oedipus*" [1928], in *Style and Idea,* 483.)

10. See, for example, Andrew Mead, "'Tonal' Forms in Arnold Schoenberg's Twelve-Tone Music," *Music Theory Spectrum* 9 (1987): 67–92; and Martha Hyde, "Dodecaphony: Schoenberg," in *Models of Musical Analysis: Early Twentieth-Century Music,* ed. Jonathan Dunsby (Oxford: Oxford University Press, 1993), 56–80.

it.[11] The presumption motivating this view has been that, once made aware of the given forms and types, listeners can apply some of the logic that accompanied their tonal unfolding; in however incidental or qualified a fashion, listeners can impose a borrowed sense of location and direction. At the same time, the need for constraints on the part of both composer and listener can also be said to have been satisfied, so that, from any number of perspectives, the old forms and their employment become linked inextricably to their tonal origins. And it has been in opposition to this rationale that other enthusiasts, including Milton Babbitt, have chosen to sidestep the idea of a transformation altogether.[12] If Schoenberg's twelve-tone music was to prevail, then it would have to do so on its own—not, as was imagined in neoclassical music, through a logic that lay outside of itself, one which could not be made organically a part of itself.

And so the familiar complaint about the non-organic character of Stravinsky's neoclassical works, about the inability of such works to blend old and new in the interests of a whole, was also Schoenberg's complaint. Parts or features were perceived as resisting assimilation, refusing an intrinsic role. Either the new was judged incapable of absorbing the old or, in reverse, the old was judged incapable of absorbing the "impurities" or "wrong notes" of the new. Either way, neoclassical works were little more than hybrids, neither tonal or atonal but "half-measures," compromises destined to fall short; they followed a meek and nostalgic path, a "middle road," to follow Schoenberg's account, one which could never be expected to reach a suitable destination.[13] (Here as elsewhere in his criticism, Schoenberg ignored the restored forms in his own twelve-tone music, the extent to which those forms were susceptible to the same kinds of arguments about assimilation and the demands of the individual context.) And analysis was made to fall short as well. Relying on tonal or atonal models, it could proceed only with a good deal of qualification; either analysis was judged incapable of doing justice to neoclassical works, or its inadequacy was judged the reflection of an inadequate music.

---

11. See Leonard Meyer, "A Pride of Prejudices; or, Delight in Diversity," *Music Theory Spectrum* 13 (1991): 247. "Contemporary composers have employed 'borrowed' forms and procedures not solely (or even primarily) because they considered themselves to be heirs to the great tradition of European art music, but because they had virtually no alternative. They could not do without some way of deciding how the motivic variants they invented should be combined with or succeed one another."

12. See Milton Babbitt, "Some Aspects of Twelve-Tone Composition," *The Score* 12 (1955): 55. Babbitt insists on "a completely autonomous conception of the twelve-tone system . . . in which all components, in all dimensions, would be determined by the relations and operations of the system." He ignores, therefore, the "transference to twelve-tone composition" of the forms (rondo, gigue, sonata, and the like) belonging to "triadic music."

13. Arnold Schoenberg, Foreword to *Drei Satiren*, op. 28. The Foreword is reproduced and translated in full in Scott Messing, *Neoclassicism in Music from the Genesis of the Concept through the Schoenberg/Stravinsky Polemic* (Ann Arbor, Mich.: UMI Research Press, 1988), 144.

In this way, too, the underlying issues of neoclassicism can be seen to lead back to immediate experience. For they involve our experience of the nonimmediate past as well as of the new and the individual context; even more crucially, they involve the extent to which we are obliged to recognize that nonimmediate past for what it might authentically have been. (Even with the evidence discontinuous and in bits and pieces, whole images of the past may be invoked in the mind of the listener.) How substantially are we compelled to look back in this music, to recall the old for the sake of the new? How extensive is this dependence on a familiarity with styles, idioms, and repertories long since past? And if indeed extensive (as has been implied), does it inhibit the individual context (as has also been implied)? Is this what neoclassicism is, in fact, inhibition with a distancing and alienating effect of this kind? Does the idea of a split between the tonal and atonal worlds, the pillarlike existence which those worlds have assumed in much critical discourse, encourage such an interpretation of neoclassicism? Has the suggestion been too pronounced, above all in the critical reception surrounding Schoenberg's music and that of Schoenberg's immediate and nonimmediate schools, that it is only the fully committed sides of that split that are capable of genuine musical expression, not the half-hearted spaces in between?

Such questions can bring society and politics into play. What is more concretely apparent, however, is that, typically, the borrowing of tonal or stylistic features involves the nonimmediate past, traditions presumed dead rather than living; that the degree of relatedness and intersection, of unity sensed or demonstrated superficially, is far less than in the music of the various nonimmediate pasts; and that the resultant heightened sense of conflict is in no way eased by the idea of a transformation or that of the individual context, by the contradictory claim of an overriding sense of purpose. A more tangible consideration of these issues will be pursued in the analysis which follows.

MOTIVES

The opening section of the *Symphony in Three Movements*, Rehearsal Nos.0–34, is without question a "developing variation," consistent with the many attempts to pin down this elusive if suggestive concept of Schoenberg's. Illustrated in Example 1, the principal theme appears in two parts, the second as a "continuation" of the first. The first part, labeled Motive A, consists of a lower pitch G standing in opposition to its tritone-related triad (D♭–F–A♭); crucial is the upper-lower disposition of the two components, a fixed registral spacing that is transposed and repeated variously throughout the first movement and from which a quality of superimposition and ultimately of opposition emerges. Additional segments include the separate grouping of G with A♭, arising from the G–A♭ "minor ninth" span that opens the movement. G is grouped with F as well, forming the "minor seventh" G–F. And if we assume "octave displacement," the latter three pitches may be joined as a descending "minor-third" motion A♭–G–F, a part not only of Motive A but of its "continuation" in the form of Motive B as well.

Example 1. Stravinsky: *Symphony in Three Movements,* I.

The preceding segments are motivic, of course, and as such hinge on repetition, on what follows in the way of a continuing development. In the case of Motive A, subsequent transpositions and transformations project the idea of a *Grundgestalt,* or "basic shape," along the lines indicated by Patricia Carpenter and Severine Neff in their recent studies of this elusive yet suggestive Schoenbergian concept.[14] Reduced to the common thread of a pitch-interval succession, Motive A as "basic shape" may be defined by a lower pitch standing in tritone-related opposition to an upper triad, most often major, sometimes minor. Traced in Example 2, the transition at Nos. 5–7 leads to a further transposition at Nos. 7–13: the A of an A–C–A basso ostinato stands in opposition to an upper (E♭–G–B♭) triad. The configuration at No. 13 is less clear-cut in this regard, although it too involves a whole-step transposition, this time to B and (F–A–A♭–(C)); lacking its fifth, the triad has become incomplete. The conclusion of this section at No. 34 is marked by a similar configuration, only transposed to C♯ and (G–B–B♭–(D)). Tritone-related to the initial thematic statement, this final transposition allows for a reversal of the initial opposition; C♯ (D♭) now stands

---

14. Patricia Carpenter, *"Grundgestalt* as Tonal Function," *Music Theory Spectrum* 5 (1983): 15–38; Neff, "Schoenberg and Goethe."

Example 2a and 2b.

Collection II

Example 2c.

Collection I

Example 2d.

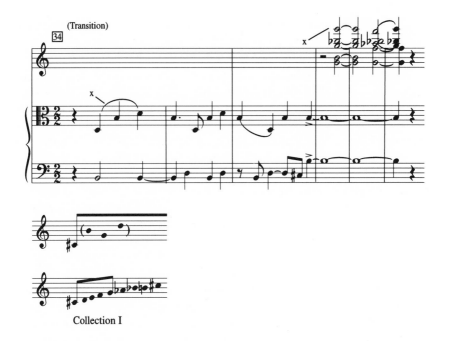

Example 2e.

Example 2f.

opposed to its incomplete tritone-related triad (G–B–B♭–(D)). So, too, the successive transpositions of Motive A yield a larger pattern of ascending whole steps; as shown in Example 3, only the transposition back to G (D♭–F–A♭) at No. 22 upsets this pattern.

Observe, too, that the sense of an opposition between tritone-related components is far less evident at No. 34 than in earlier passages; the lower of the two components, C♯(D♭) in the bass, is scarcely more than an inflection at this point, a V-of-V chromatic tendency tone (or chromatic neighbor) to the D; it asserts itself with far less independence. And while the C♯–B "minor seventh" at No. 34 + 3 is unmistakably motivic, referring back to the G–F "minor seventh" of Motive A in the opening measures, the opposition itself is defined not so much by the tritone relationship as by that most pervasive of all neoclassical "clashes," the major-minor third, conceived here in terms of the two incomplete major and minor triads rooted on G. Incomplete with roots doubled and fifths missing, the two triads magnify the effect of a clash, reflecting at the same time an even more pervasive motivic function than that defined by Motive A and its segments.

Motive B follows as a "continuation" of Motive A: shown in Example 1, it includes the entire thematic stretch beginning with the upbeat to m. 4 and ending with the upbeat to m. 9. Ultimately more significant, however, are the octaves contained within this scale-like stretch of material, octaves which are split on either side by a third, most often minor but occasionally major. Labeled motive x in Examples 1 and 2, octaves split in this way (forms of the incomplete triad, as suggested already) permeate this music as "building blocks" or "basic motives," to use Schoenberg's terms, elementary units of vocabulary or "smallest common multiples."[15] In the transition at Nos. 5–7, motive x appears linearly in the horns and trumpets in terms of G–B♭–G and B♭–G–B♭; it identifies harmonically with the diminished-seventh chord, (C♯–E–G–B♭). Subsequently, at Nos. 7–13, it is transposed to A–C–A, appearing as a basso ostinato; the configurations at Nos. 7, 13, and 34 all make reference to the incomplete triad. In its final appearance at No. 38 it is transformed as the principal theme of a new section.

In schematic form, then, such are the motivic paths of this music, to the extent that such paths lend themselves to systematic analysis. Briefly read, they can be shown to differ little from the more familiar paths traced by Schoenberg and others in the music of Beethoven, Brahms, and Schoenberg himself. And the manner of their developing variation can likewise be shown to differ little. Indeed, only very weakly can a distinction be drawn along these lines, can the concept of developing variation be used to distinguish the music of the earlier and more familiar sources from this present Symphony and other excluded repertories such as the neoclassical; only very weakly can the claim of a distinct critical tradition be made, in other words, confined as this has been to the "homophonic" music of Schoenberg's particular choice.[16]

---

15. Schoenberg, *Fundamentals*, 8. "Since [the basic motive] includes elements, at least, of every subsequent musical figure, one could consider it the smallest common multiple."

16. I refer specifically to Walter Frisch, *Brahms and the Principle of Developing Variation*

Example 3.

This would not be to dismiss the many other distinctions which have been brought to the fore in this connection. Schoenberg set the "style of developing variation" against that of the model and its sequence, against the unvaried repetition that was attributed to the music of Liszt, Wagner, and the New German School, or to composers such as Tchaikovsky and Rimsky-Korsakov. He judged the exact or merely embellished repetition in these latter repertories shallow and too easy for composers and listeners alike: "It was the Brahmsian School which fought violently against the sequences of the New German School. Their attitude was based on the opposite viewpoint that unvaried repetition is cheap."[17] And he set the same "style" against that of various "folkloristic symphonies" as well: he judged borrowed folk material unable to imply continuation, unable to remain incomplete so as to suggest eventual completion; he thought folk material unable to pose questions that required answers, answers that could lead to further elaborations.[18] (The folksong was judged too complete in and of itself.) Yet, the motivic processes he examined are far more pervasive

(Berkeley and Los Angeles: University of California Press, 1984). But see also the discussion of motives and motivic development in Straus, *Remaking the Past*, 21–73.

17. Schoenberg, "Criteria for the Evaluation of Music" (1946), in *Style and Idea*, 129.

18. Schoenberg, "Folkloristic Symphonies" (1947), in *Style and Idea*, 164.

than he allowed, more integrally a part of a great many styles, idioms, and repertories. In the case of Stravinsky's music, for example, the ostinato-like repetition characteristic of the melodic invention is unvarying only from the standpoint of pitch-interval succession. From that of accent and metrical placement, it is neither unvarying nor devoid of a sense of development.[19]

By way of illustration: as a basic motive, the idea of motive x, of an octave split on one side or the other by a minor or major third (the idea of an incomplete triad, more traditionally), is no less active in the first movement of Stravinsky's Symphony than, say, in the first movement of Brahms's Third Symphony (see Ex. 4). It is no less the subject of a developing variation in the former than in the latter. What separates the two sides is not motivic process but tonal organization, the absence (or near absence) of tonal constraints in the post-tonal Stravinsky, their presence in the tonal Brahms. Indeed, constraints in Stravinsky's music are more readily octatonic or octatonic-diatonic; in the principal theme of the opening measures (Ex. 1), both Motive A as the *Grundgestalt* G (D♭–F–A♭) and the "continuation" of Motive B are confined to a single transposition of the octatonic set; the successions of motive x in this stretch, octaves enclosing major or minor thirds, are constrained accordingly. Alternatively, in the Brahms symphony the motive's minor third is chromatic in relation to the F-major tonality, a circumstance whose consequences are immediately at hand in the flat-side modal mixture of the opening measures, the common-tone diminished-seventh chord of m. 2, and the chord of the lowered submediant in m. 8.

But neither, on an even broader scale, can motivic processes, Schoenbergian or other, be used to distinguish the post-tonal from the tonal. Defined by means of pitch, shape, interval, or rhythm, motives and their variants are no more pervasive in, say, Schoenberg's atonal or twelve-tone music (indeed, in the first movement of Stravinsky's Symphony) than in Bach's chorale preludes, Beethoven's symphonies, or Brahms's chamber music. And when reduced to unordered pitch-class sets (sets of interval classes, for the most part), they do not figure as part of a post-tonal "common practice" which could distinguish the post-tonal from the tonal.[20] Rather, sets tend to

---

19. See the discussion of accentual displacement as it effects two types of rhythmic-metric construction in Pieter C. van den Toorn, *The Music of Igor Stravinsky* (New Haven and London: Yale University Press, 1983), 214–51; and van den Toorn, *Stravinsky and "The Rite of Spring"* (Berkeley and Los Angeles: University of California Press, 1987), 97–114. More specifically, the subject concerns reiterated motives or fragments in Stravinsky's music and their patterns of accentual displacement in relation to a steady meter, notated or concealed.

20. Such a case is made in Straus, *Remaking the Past,* 22–27, 57–64. Straus argues that the manipulation of motives, reduced in turn to abstract pitch-class sets, became a "common practice" in post-tonal music, one that can distinguish the post-tonal period generally from the tonal. In my estimation, however, motives based on the recurrence of unordered sets of varying degrees of determinacy are no less prevalent in tonal music than they are in post-tonal music (which includes the music of Bartók and Stravinsky as well as that of the Second Viennese School); the distinction rests with a negative, in other words, with the absence, in varying degrees, of tonally functional relations, not with any increased motivic "saturation,"

Example 4. Brahms: Symphony No. 3.

change while the motivic processes themselves remain intact; the latter processes overlap the post-tonal and tonal worlds, uniting rather than separating those worlds. This is the whole point of the ties Schoenberg sought to project in his own music, of course, the point of a tradition of motives and of motivic development preserved.

In Stravinsky's Symphony, the octaves of Motives A, B, and x do not allow for

"density," "richness," or the like. The issue is discussed at greater length in Pieter C. van den Toorn, *Music, Politics, and the Academy* (Berkeley and Los Angeles: University of California Press, 1996), 157–68. See also Richard Taruskin, review of Straus, *Remaking the Past, Journal of the American Musicological Society* 46 (1993), 129–34.

extensive reduction. Consisting of an upper-lower tritone opposition, Motive A is a registral idea. And the specifics of its articulation, of two components standing in a tritone-defined opposition or polarity, are deeply reflective not only of this present Symphony but of Stravinsky's music as a whole. Relations of significance can thus be defined fairly determinately. For our purposes, that more determinate definition has seemed preferable to the further abstraction of the unordered pitch-class set—which in the case of Motive A would have involved reducing G (Db–F–Ab) or A (Eb–G–Bb) to [0137], set class 4–Z29, to follow Forte's nomenclature.

POLYCHORDS; C-MAJOR TONALITIES; OCTATONIC SETS

The above analysis can point not only to a good deal of consistency in Stravinsky's use of motives, but also, from the same standpoint, to a good deal of motivation on the part of the individual context. For if, as has been indicated, motives can be non-descript and a part of processes which are hugely general, they can also, in their ultimate realizations, reflect considerable detail and hence individuality; as part of a continuing development, they can reflect all aspects of a specific context. This is the nature of the process, of developing variation, properly speaking, not static or iso-lated identification but a process of dynamic framing, one of motives being joined to form larger configurations from which new motives are made to evolve. There is an element of growth, as Schoenberg insisted.

Alternatively, however, motives carry no inherent sense of succession, no gov-erning rationale as to why one variant would necessarily precede or follow another. Beyond general processes of liquidation, there is no syntax of motivic succession, however much Schoenberg might often have imagined that there was, treating mo-tives as if they were units of vocabulary within larger phrases, sentences, and para-graphs. Tonal functions provide for such a sense, of course, one of "directed mo-tion," as has often been indicated. And this may be possible even when such func-tions are severely qualified.

Tonality, then, stands somewhat apart from strictly "motivic" considerations, as becomes clear from an examination of Felix Salzer's Schenkerian interpretation of Stravinsky's first movement.[21] Two of Salzer's graphs are reproduced in Examples 5 and 6: Example 5 refers to the theme itself and its accompaniment in the bass; a dissonant "polychord" (Salzer's term) is prolonged, consisting in the main of the tritone-related major triads rooted on G and Db.[22] Of these triads, G is judged primary, Db secondary. Yet Salzer treats the polychord as a stable sonority; Ab and F in the theme are "chord tones" while G and E are subsidiary. In the second graph of Ex. 6, a "gigantic prolongation of G" is inferred at Nos.1–27.[23] Enclosed are

---

21. Felix Salzer, *Structural Hearing* (New York: Dover, 1982), 248, 296 (Exx. 417, 472).
22. Salzer, *Structural Hearing,* 218.
23. Ibid.

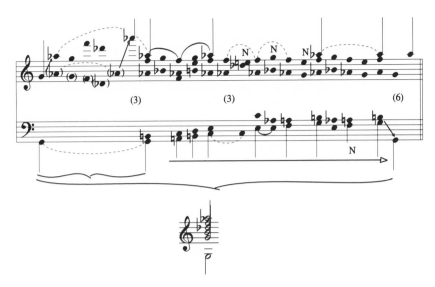

Example 5.

smaller prolongations, including a neighbor motion involving A (in the bass) at Nos. 7–13.

To some extent, of course, the idea of a polychord prolonged corresponds to that of a basic shape transformed. Motive A in terms of G and its tritone-related triad (Db–F–Ab) may be compared to Salzer's polychord, successive transpositions of Motive A to various stages of Salzer's prolongation. At Nos. 7–13, for example, Motive A is transposed up a whole step to A(Eb–G–Bb); A in the bass (see Ex. 2) stands in opposition to a reiteration of (Eb–G–Bb) in the strings. In Salzer's account, this transposition is interpreted as a large-scale motion surrounding G and involving A as a neighbor note; a return to G and the (G–B–D) (Db–F–Ab) polychord is noted at No. 22.

In the large, then, motives and basic shapes are transformed into polychords, transpositions into prolongations. In turn, the latter prolongations may be reinterpreted as well. For the areas marked off for interpretation by Motive A coincide with transpositions of the octatonic set.

Indeed, as mentioned already, the principal theme is octatonic, accountable to a single transposition of that set. Plotted in Example 1, Motive A followed by Motive B and its subsequent successions of motive x in the treble part are all confined to Collection I, one of three content-distinguishable transpositions of the octatonic set.[24]

---

24. See the discussion of the octatonic set in van den Toorn, *The Music of Igor Stravinsky*, 31–98; and in van den Toorn, *Stravinsky and "The Rite of Spring,"* 119–31, 143–48. As a reflection of its symmetry, the set is limited to three transpositions, beginning at C♯ with the semitone-tone ordering of the scale. I have labeled these Collection I (at C♯), Collection II (at D), and Collection III (at E♭).

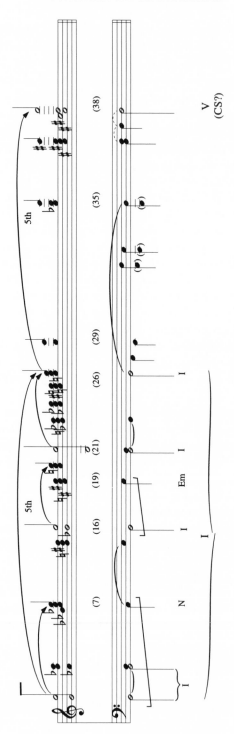

Example 6.

So, too, the transposition up a step from G(D♭–F–A♭) to A(E♭–G–B♭) at Nos. 7–13 (see Exx. 2 and 3) involves not only Motive A or a neighbor motion but the octatonic set as well: Collection I is succeeded by Collection III. And the diminished-seventh chord (C♯, E, G, B♭) shared by those two collections is isolated in a passage of transition at Nos. 5–7. A smoother octatonic maneuver would be hard to imagine. Indeed, the octatonic relations which follow are extraordinarily evident.

But such an octatonic reading brings us no closer to the nonimmediate traditions underlying this music than the motivic paths traced in Examples 1–3 or, in Examples 5 and 6, Salzer's idea of a prolongation of a dissonant polychord. The octatonic interpretation refers only to the new, in other words, not to the old or, indeed, to the idea of a transformation of the old by the new; it ignores the context as a whole as, at the very least, an interaction of conflicting components. Prolongation is a Schenkerian term, to be sure, but Salzer's polychord fuses and to some extent negates tonal function. Indeed, tonality can best be acknowledged by changing Salzer's quasi-tonic from G to a C, interpreting G as the dominant in C major. In this way, and as illustrated in Example 7, an octatonic theme with G at its center is placed in interaction with the diatonic white-note collection centered on C, the latter represented most conspicuously in the opening measures by the G–A–B–C ascending motion in the bass. The tonal implications of this interaction are shown in Example 8: superimposed over G, a Neapolitan chord is succeeded by a dominant minor ninth with A♭ as the degree of the lowered submediant. And this interpretation would seem to be confirmed by the return of the opening theme at the end of the movement, a return which does in fact resolve to a type of C-ending. (See Ex. 9, where the continuation of the theme as Motive B is in augmentation.) There, the presence of tonal degrees is unmistakable.

But how convincingly does this C-ending work as a confirmation of the earlier suggestion of C major? To what extent do the later degrees confirm the earlier ones? By virtue of the C-ending, in other words, is the sustained G of the opening section that much more a dominant, (D♭–F–A♭) that much more a Neapolitan, and A♭ a lowered submediant? Is the C-major tonality that much more authentic, the movement as a whole that much more integrated from a tonal standpoint? Or does the C-ending fail as a resolution of conflict? Is it a convenience at this point?[25] In a way typical of Stravinsky's music, of the statically sustained blocks of material and of the abrupt shifts which can often replace a more traditional sense of progression, do the reiterations of Motives A and B followed by the C-ending merely rehearse what has been rehearsed all along, indeed, from the beginning of the Symphony?

In concrete form, of course, problems of this kind are typical of those arising from Stravinsky's neoclassicism. Specifically of concern here is the C-major tonality, the point at which tonal expectations conflict not only with the symphony's octatonicism but also with the motivic paths traced in Examples 1–3.

---

25. See the discussion of this in my earlier treatment of Stravinsky's Symphony (van den Toorn, *The Music of Igor Stravinsky*, 362–64).

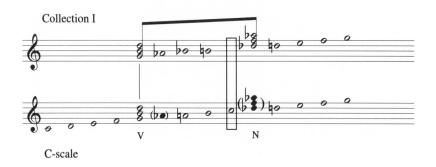

Example 7.

Example 8.

The C-ending is anticipated to some extent by the principal theme of the opening measures, by the G–A–B–C motion in the bass at mm. 3–5 and by the repeated Cs at m. 5. It is not without impurity: Bs are positioned in such a way as to give vent to earlier assertions of priority on the part of both E and G (E and E/G/E at No. 29). (The large-scale relationship of G to E, the octatonic as well as diatonic C-scale implications of that relationship, can also bring to mind the first movements of the *Symphony of Psalms* (1930) and the Symphony in C (1940)). And this positioning can readily reflect the individual context, a form of assimilation. By such means, the transformation of the old by the new makes itself felt in the final measures of the movement. Not to acknowledge such assimilation and transformation, to interpret

Example 9.

B as a true impurity, is to interpret solely in terms of the C-major tonality, an option which seems to have been followed not only by Schoenberg but also by early critics of similar passages in Stravinsky's neoclassical works. That option rules out the possibility of a segmentation: as an integral component, B may be grouped with (E–G–B) and (G–B–D) within the final simultaneity, reflecting earlier assertions of priority and acquiring in this way a sense of motivation. As an impurity or "wrong note," however, it is detached from the C-major triad, isolated and without the reflection of a context.

CONTINUING CONFLICTS

There are obvious hazards in dredging up the Stravinsky-Schoenberg wars of the 1920s and '30s. Schoenberg viewed neoclassicism as merely facile and clever, an idiom lacking in substance or "idea," wholly superficial in its relations with the past; Stravinsky complained of "modernists" who worked with "formulas instead of ideas."[26] Yet, with the exception of *Pierrot Lunaire* for Stravinsky and *Oedipus Rex* for Schoenberg, the two composers knew little of the music about which they expressed such contempt.[27] Moreover, while we can point to the compelling nature of the motive and its developing variation in Stravinsky's Symphony, we need not question

26. Quoted in Messing, *Neoclassicism in Music,* 141.

27. See Messing, *Neoclassicism in Music,* 145. "Like that of Stravinsky, Schoenberg's assess-

the nature of the process itself or, indeed, the legitimacy of the ties Schoenberg sought to invoke. Indeed, were we to ignore motivic processes altogether, the first movement of Stravinsky's Symphony would group only very awkwardly with Schoenberg's "extended," atonal, and twelve-tone repertories, or with the rhythmic and melodic aspects of those repertories; in their progressive and forward-moving impulses, the latter aspects can seem antithetical to the statically maintained blocks and sections characteristic of the Symphony. On a more comprehensive basis, the two sides are better distinguished than likened; the contrast they afford is more compelling than the similarity.

Moreover, the persuasiveness of the individual context is hard to miss in the present case. Parts or features identified as Baroque, Classical, or tonal do not draw a great deal of attention to themselves as such, the sort of attention likely to impede integration and prevent, on the part of the individual context, the emergence of an overriding sense of integrity. Rather, a sense of purpose is everywhere immediately felt; embedded in the context, bits and pieces of the past do not create the sorts of separations likely to force the listener into a distanced form of dependence. Consistent with the idea of a removed sense of the nonimmediate past, neoclassical issues of this kind can seem skirted for the most part.

On the other hand, each of the four interpretations in the above analysis was given its due. As Motive A, for example, G was grouped with (D♭–F–A♭), a compound sonority which was first interpreted as a *Grundgestalt*, second as a polychord prolonged, and third, in C major, as the superimposition of a Neapolitan triad over a sustained dominant. Subsequently, the same sonority was located within an octatonic framework, a single transposition of that set, an interpretation which introduced yet another set of circumstances.

The trick of such an analysis would be to avoid the piecemeal, presumably by pointing once again, however provisionally, to the idea of a transformation. Thus, as illustrated in Example 7, the boundaries of the two interacting octatonic and diatonic sets overlap: with G and its major triad as the principal points of intersection, the two sets intersect more readily than they conflict. Indeed, the only nonoctatonic pitch classes in the opening thematic section are A and C in the accompaniment in the bass; illustrated in Example 1, A–C–A is a form of motive x at m. 4 while C is reiterated at m. 5. And while A and C are involved in a variety of clashes—A against the A♭ at m. 4, C harshly against the D♭ at m. 5—there are mitigating circumstances. Apropos of the C-major interpretation of this passage, A♭ and D♭, however octatonic in relation to the principal theme, are not without tonal implications.

But the intersection and transformation of these varying interpretations, of the segmentations implied in each case, cannot, it seems to me, erase the sense of conflict that is at the heart of this music, the sense of a superimposition of segmenta-

---

ment of his contemporary was gleaned from what he read, not from what he heard: contemporary reviews and essays of their music made up the evidence upon which the composers made their aesthetic conclusions."

tions never entirely reconciled, of a clashing of forces locked in confrontation. And that conflict may be traced to the very first measure, indeed, to the opposition defined by Motive A, the lower G which stands in opposition to its upper tritone-related triad. For although Motive A's two opposing components intersect with both the octatonic Collection I and the diatonic C-scale (the latter by virtue of the Neapolitan interpretation of (D♭–F–A♭)), they are kept apart registrally; in the bass, G groups with the diatonic motion G–A–B–C while, in the treble, (D♭–F–A♭) groups with the octatonic set (see Ex.10). Hence the ensuing conflict between registers as well as sets, between lower diatonic components which move contrary to upper octatonic ones, reflects, at the outset, the compound nature of Motive A; although motivically whole (indeed, a *Grundgestalt*), Motive A is split into opposing components.

And the ensuing separation of those components as referential sets is remarkably cohesive. In the opening thematic stretch shown in Example 10, the nonoctatonic pitches A and C are not isolated as such. In the bass at mm. 4 and 5, they are grouped first with G and then with the ascending motion G–A–B–C, above all with the successions of motive x that articulate that motion; they form relations with the pitch classes of that motion, with G and B, for example, relations which, although partially intersecting with the octatonic set of the theme above, are effected accordingly. Those nonoctatonic relations, including the reiteration of C at m. 5, are diatonic, even tonal apropos of C major, however extensive the intersection with the octatonic theme and the deployment of motive x on both sides of this referential fence.

In other words, A and C group with other pitch classes in the accompaniment which, even if intersecting with the octatonic set, are affected by their nonoctatonicism; larger diatonic C-scale components are formed. Indeed, the static and to some extent irreconcilable superimposition of an octatonic theme over a diatonic accompaniment is unmistakable at the outset of the Symphony, as it is in later sections: C and (C–E–G) are not accounted for—and are hence made to clash and conflict with—the octatonic Collection I at the outset (see Ex. 10), while, later at Nos. 4 and 22 (see Ex. 11), Collection I triads and motive x successions are superimposed over white-note, diatonic scale passages. These relations are typical of Stravinsky's neoclassical contexts, from the variation movement of the *Octet* (1923), where an octatonic Collection III theme with A at its center is placed in opposition to a tonic D, to the third movement of this present symphony: while tonics and tonic triads tend to conflict with interacting octatonic sets, dominants and dominant triads intersect.[28]

Inevitably, then, we are led back again to the contradiction of the conventional view of Stravinsky's neoclassicism, even if the terms of that contradiction may be addressed more tangibly in terms of specific motives, sets, segments, and their interactions; an impression of conflict, of a high degree of nonintegration coexists with one of transcendence. The opposing forces in the Symphony, right and left hands of

---

28. See the further discussion of this in van den Toorn, *The Music of Igor Stravinsky*, 330–71.

Example 10.

the principal theme at mm. 1–9, the octatonic Collection I theme and its diatonic, C-scale accompaniment, are kept apart registrally. At the outset, they assume the character of a superimposition which, as has been noted, is a matter of conflicting sets and of the cohesiveness exhibited by those sets. And although not examined here, there are rhythmic metric definitions as well: fixed in register and instrumentation, motives of the kind traced in Examples 1–3 may repeat according to cycles which vary independently of each other; they can stand opposed in this respect, with a sense of movement coming only by way of the resultant shifts in their coincidence.

On the other hand, it has also been noted that conflicts of this kind are not absolute. In addition to the intersections plotted in Example 7, the two forces sound together; the meaning of one derives in part from the relationship it forms with the other. The point of the octatonic top at mm. 1–9 is defined to some extent by its superimposition over a diatonic bottom.

It is here, in matters having to do with opposition and superimposition, matters effecting all aspects of context, that Stravinsky's music is most appropriately

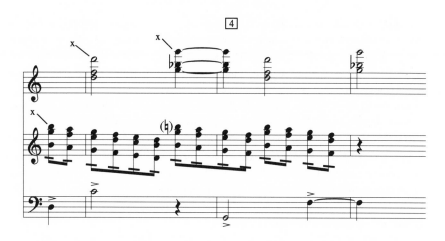

Example 11.

addressed, that it can be distinguished convincingly from, say, much of Schoenberg's, a repertory which, in its vertical or harmonic grouping, tends to invite integration to a far greater extent. (By reason of that integration, the issue of segmentation, of determining the legitimate parts of Schoenberg's music, is far more problematic). For the referential interaction detailed here can easily be related to other octatonic-diatonic interactions in Stravinsky's music, indeed, to forms of conflict that operate at all levels of structure and as an integral part of each of the three celebrated stylistic periods: Russian, neoclassical, and serial.

So, too, it may be best to confront the contradiction of Stravinsky's neoclassical works, features of a familiar yet nonimmediate past and the problem of their assimilation, on the elementary basis of segments, sets, and their union or separation. Neoclassicism can thus be related to manifestations of conflict more generally. For the interaction between the octatonic Collection I and the diatonic C-scale in the Symphony figures as one of many interactions involving the octatonic and diatonic sets, while Motive A together with its subsequent transformations is but one of many tritone polarities that emerge from such interactions. To begin with segments and sets in this fashion, with what may be characteristic of their use in Stravinsky's music as a whole, allows the analyst to move with greater certainty to the issue of tonality and its residue, inevitably, to the problem of assimilation. Thus, the tritone polarity between G and (Db–F–Ab) need not be confined to the idea of a dominant and a Neapolitan chord. Its behavior can also be dealt with in terms of basic shapes (motivically, that is), prolongations, and transpositions of the octatonic set. While the impression gained of such an analysis is likely to be one of nonorganicism, there are, as has been suggested, few alternatives.

In acknowledging neoclassicism, analysis must deal with ideas which are often partial in themselves or which can only be applied partially. But to deal differently is to ignore the issue itself, that of neoclassicism, its character and rationale. Hence the next step is likely to consist of another confrontation with the familiar contradiction, another attempt to reconcile partiality with the demands of the individual context. The solution may remain beyond the analyst's grasp, yet one hopes that the process can serve as a continuing source of illumination.

Modernist Aesthetics, Modernist Music: Some Analytical Perspectives

Arnold Whittall

I

One of Adorno's many memorable sayings is that "the true language of art is speechless."[1] The point could only have been made in words, and Adorno struggled for a lifetime to find the appropriate verbal form for his musical insights. As far as I am aware, he never attempted to argue that a single, model structure for technical commentary on music might be possible, and since such writing could hardly hope to emulate the speechlessness of art, it could scarcely expect to mirror its artistic qualities either. Even so, a model of a kind emerges from Adorno's consideration of a "particular problem for the musical work in the modernist period": how "to construct a unity which does not conceal the fragmentary and chaotic state of the handed-down musical material, and yet which does not simply mirror fragmentation through identification with it, but which is able to embody, negate and transcend it."[2] How better, then, to write about modernist music than in a way which aspires to reflect, however awkwardly and partially, its particular structures and aesthetic perspectives?

The most obvious way in which this essay embodies fragmentation, or at any rate diversity, is in dealing with two composers of different generations and nationalities: Harrison Birtwistle (born Accrington, England, 1934) and Elliott Carter (born New York, 1908). Yet that separateness is immediately countered by my assumption that something is shared by Carter and Birtwistle, and that "something" is modernism. At the outset, therefore, it is necessary to consider two general questions: what is modernism, and why does music analysis need it?

---

1. Quoted in Max Paddison, *Adorno's Aesthetics of Music* (Cambridge: Cambridge University Press, 1993), 114.

2. See Paddison, *Adorno's Aesthetics,* 158.

Like most exponents of word-based interpretation, music theorists tend to prefer certain terms because of the resonances they set up, the associations with particular authorities which they create. It is not possible here to present a comprehensive history of modernism as a concept, or of its musicological interface with other concepts—atonal, post-tonal, contemporary, avant-garde. For better or for worse, modernism has acquired the implication of something cultural rather than merely technical: the assumption has grown up that we use the word when we want to talk about a nineteenth- or twentieth-century composition in its historical context, as well as about its more specifically musical identity. There is a particularly valuable discussion of modernism in this sense in Paddison's study of Adorno. Paddison argues that Adorno's aesthetic is an "aesthetic of modernism," because it "seeks to understand the fragmentation and alienation which characterizes Western art in the twentieth century."[3] Yet just as Adorno's own work has a consistency in its use of concepts which, as Paddison puts it, is "the necessary counterpole to the fragmentation which characterizes its mode of expression,"[4] so, in my view, modernist art at its most interesting and successful is not simply a reflection of what is often apocalyptically described as the chaos of modern society, but an expression of the special and unprecedented tension between the attempt to embody fragmentation and the impulse to transcend it. Modernist art in these terms is a response to modern life and modern civilization, rather than just a reflection of them, although I am well aware that social theorists and even ordinary citizens might claim that what is special about many twentieth-century societies is the nature and strength of the tension between those very same opposing tendencies. As I have written elsewhere:

> Social theorists argue that "the very dissonances and fragmentations of society *do* compose a larger coordinating structure, and that historical change, in its very rapidity, is strengthening this structure," and cultural historians may also conclude that it is the degree and nature of dissonance and fragmentation in art that makes it modern, or modernist, and not the total absence or suppression of any coordinating or integrating formal processes.[5]

---

3. *Adorno's Aesthetics,* 3.

4. *Adorno's Aesthetics,* 14.

5. See "British Music in the Modern World," in Stephen Banfield, ed., *The Blackwell History of Music in Britain, 6: The Twentieth Century* (Oxford: Blackwell, 1995), 10. My quotation is from a book review by Richard Sennett in the *Times Literary Supplement,* 8 February 1991, 6.

II

Given that the concept of modernism has wide currency, in a musicological context that seems increasingly concerned to interpret musical compositions as phenomena infiltrated by culture, history and ideology, how does music analysis respond? Since modernism as a term has been used more explicitly in connection with Carter than with Birtwistle, I will begin with Carter.

The topic of Carter's modernism has been aired with particular pertinence by David Schiff in an article which is, so far, the most ideologically charged of his various supplements to his invaluable book on the composer.[6] Schiff's own position is determined by the perception that while "Carter's recent works sound as resolutely modernist as ever" (115) he finds evidence in those works—from the Triple Duo (1983) onwards—of a "classicism which has absorbed modernism."[7] (119) Clearly Schiff is seeking to qualify, even adulterate, what he regards as modernism in order to do justice to what he hears as a change of character in Carter's later music. So it is important to establish what Schiff understands by modernism itself.

Schiff's theory of modernism evidently derives not from Adorno but from the French post-structuralist Roland Barthes. Barthes's notion of the "plural text" is Schiff's starting point,[8] but this, as Schiff describes it, seems to lack the play with concepts of coherence and integration that Adorno provides. In Schiff's words, what is "missing from Barthes's account are the ideas of order which actual modernist texts—literary or musical—create out of their very plurality." Schiff asserts that Joyce's *Ulysses* and Berg's *Lulu* "epitomize the modernist enterprise because they counterbalance a pervasive fragmentation with an obsessive demand for organization. Carter's [later] music . . . demonstrates the interconnection of plurality and order . . . every difference is also a connection; every disjunction creates a new continuity," and this is the outcome of a concern on Carter's part to "correct" the essential formal archetype employed in most of the works spanning the seventeen-year period between the Second String Quartet (1959) and *A Symphony of Three Orchestras* (1976).[9] In many of these works "stratified texture was used to heighten the alien-

6. David Schiff, "Carter's New Classicism," *College Music Symposium* 29 (1989): 115–22; Schiff, *The Music of Elliott Carter* (London: Eulenberg and New York: Da Capo, 1983). The two most recent publications on Carter that are relevant to the present essay are Jonathan W. Bernard, "Problems of Pitch Structure in Elliott Carter's First and Second String Quartets," *Journal of Music Theory* 37 (1993): 231–66, and the "Carter 85th" issue of *Sonus* 14, no. 2 (Spring 1994).

7. Schiff, "Carter's New Classicism," 115, 119.

8. Schiff refers primarily to Barthes's *S/Z,* trans. Richard Miller (New York: Farrar, Straus, and Giroux, 1974).

9. Schiff, "Carter's New Classicism," 119-20.

ation of the protagonists, the sense that they were playing different pieces at the same time without mediation." And while Schiff does not deny that there are moments of convergence, even of fusion, in these works, he regards such moments as embodying all that is most negative, like the "vision of mechanized brutality" in the *Symphony*'s conclusion. Here, "disjunction was not only presented, it was privileged; the diversity of elements became an emblem of freedom while their convergence appeared as a form of tyranny." The more recent compositions, by contrast, "reverse this relationship of disjunction and order by making the possibility of connection both explicit and desirable–if never entirely attainable." So, in the Oboe Concerto, "the freedom the soloist represents is the imaginative freedom of modernism; its power to transform reality derives from the form-creating impulse which I would term 'classic.'" [10]

Schiff offers an eloquent and persuasive interpretation which, as usual in his writing, makes much use of the clues Carter himself has provided about the meaning of his music in terms of the psychological and social attributes of twentieth-century civilization. There is less sustenance for the analyst in Schiff's narrative, however, primarily because his favored technique is to summarize what usually amounts to the nature of certain precompositional materials (intervals, rhythms), and to identify a formal or generic model, but then to stand back from much in the way of detailed explication. While I can sympathize with anyone for whom Schiff provides sufficient detail, I believe that analysis has to dig deeper, not least to test the validity of Schiff's interpretations.

One can of course simply disagree with Schiff in his own terms, through a critically informed reaction to the work in question. In an earlier discussion of one of the most substantial of Carter's works of the 1980s, *Penthode*, Schiff interprets this "vision of a musical utopia" in terms of a process whereby the modern becomes classic.[11] As he argues, "The modern side of the piece appears as an entropy-haunted collage, fragmented, unpredictable, and at times chaotic." Yet,

> out of all the apparent fragmentation ... the music evokes that most classic of classical forms, the *aria da capo*, a form which explains the consistent melodic nature of the piece and which supports its extraordinary cadential gesture, an operatic cadenza soaring to an impossible high note. The music journeys from the private musing of the opening viola to the piccolo's extravagant public display, as the modern becomes classic.[12]

My own response to *Penthode*, especially as the "sequel" to *Triple Duo*, which also explores the possibility of resolution winning out over dissolution, is to hear a strong degree of resistance to "classicism."[13] In particular, I find less a sense of the

10. Ibid., 120, 122.

11. Schiff, "Elliott Carter's Harvest Home," *Tempo* 167 (December 1988): 5.

12. "Carter's Harvest Home," 6.

13. See my review of the score in *Music and Letters* 72 (1991): 344–5.

modern becoming classic than of the two remaining powerfully and productively at odds. Carter's own note, published in the score, describes *Penthode* as concerned with "the experiences of connectedness and isolation ... while the five groups oppose or combine with each other, one long continuous line passed from one instrument to another binds the first and third sections of the score together." Even so, what I hear as a sustained dialogue between similarity and difference, rather than any decisive shift from difference to similarity, suggests that the composition's "vision of a musical utopia" (surely in utopia connectedness is all?) has most to do with the practical skills of the Ensemble InterContemporain and its director Pierre Boulez, who commissioned the work and gave its première. In advancing from a Triple Duo to a quintuple quartet, Carter elaborated the dialogue between individual and collective in ways which make Schiff's metaphor of "private" yielding to "public" seem far too simple. In *Penthode* a formalist "background"–a typical Carter grid of salient intervals and a polyrhythm, shared between the groups—becomes inexhaustibly flexible in the "foreground," and this flexibility intensifies as the work proceeds. Whether "isolated" or "connected," the five groups sustain a modernist equilibrium between fragment and continuum without, to my ears, suggesting some kind of classical synthesis, which would be incongruous, and even banal, in such a context. If the *aria da capo* is evoked, therefore, it is only to provoke resistance, and while melody is certainly consistent enough to prevent the music from collapsing into an arbitrary jumble of disparate fragments, I cannot feel that the increasing exuberance of mood in the final section is achieved at the cost of allowing the collective decisively to override the essential independence of the five contributing ensembles. Carter may have become classical enough to compose finales which embody a strong sense of intensification and cumulation: but his actual endings are still matters of release rather than of resolution.

A fully detailed analytical demonstration of how that "modernist equilibrium between fragment and continuum" actually functions in *Penthode* is far beyond the scope of the present essay, but an analytical discussion of a shorter but not unrepresentative Carter work, *Enchanted Preludes* for flute and cello (1988), may serve to indicate what issues are at stake.

In his brief note on *Enchanted Preludes*, Schiff draws attention to the way in which, despite the fact that the sounds of flute and cello "do not blend when superimposed," the two instruments "find a common ground" towards the end of the piece.[14] This is undoubtedly true: as Example 1 shows, flute and cello converge on G in m. 120, while the cello adds the A which preceded (a higher) G in the flute in the piece's first two notes (also shown in Ex.1). At first glance, this ending may appear to be as close to a "resolution" as Carter has come, but it will be no less clear that this final convergence is effected by way of a final assertion of intervallic individuality, the result of Carter's familiar technique of parceling out intervals between the instruments on the basis of inversional complementation: the flute tends to focus on 1,

---

Example 1. Elliott Carter: *Enchanted Preludes*, mm. 1–4, 119–21. © Copyright 1988 by Hendon Music, Inc. Reprinted by permission.

3, 5, 8, and 10 semitones, the cello on 2, 4, 7, 9, and 11 semitones. In mm. 119-20, therefore, the predominance of 1 (and 13), 5, 8, and 10 reinforces what is personal to the flute, while emphasis on 2, 4, 7, 9, and 11 does the same for the cello. No less familiar, here, is the distinction of rhythmic profiles within the common quarter-note meter—the flute making use of triplet subdivision while the cello sticks to multiples of two.

Given the use of what I once termed "interval-class thematicism"[15] in Carter—as distinct from the more traditional kind of motivic process—the type of motivic interaction detected in patterns where the flute focuses on permutations of the [015] collection and the cello on [026] might be expected to be, at best, fleeting (see m. 4). It is there, nonetheless, and the hint of it in m.119 suggests that this final convergence is also closural in a recapitulatory sense. To be specific, m.119 alludes to mm. 3 and 4, where the cello's Ab, Bb, D♮ echo of the flute's D♯, E♮, G♮ is rather more strongly asserted.

The balance of similarity (contour, interval "type"—that is, second plus third) and difference (rhythmic profile, modes of articulation and, above all, actual pitch interval) deserves its status as a modernist technique by virtue of being so fundamental to Carter's way of writing. There could scarcely be a more striking instance of this quality in his entire output than the way in which the two "sets" (cello mm. 43-45, flute mm. 45-47), both using "white-note" cells, present complementary retrograde inversions of their constituent intervals (see Ex.2). In context, as Carter once commented in notes on the Double Concerto and the Duo for violin and piano, there is "a stratification of sound, so that much of the time the listener can hear two different kinds of music, not always of equal prominence, occurring simultaneously."[16] Yet these "two different kinds of music" are the source of a dialogue within which "style exchanges," like those between cello and flute in mm. 43-47, are crucial.

Such a dialogue of opposition and complementation can be explored a little more thoroughly in a characteristic context like that of mm. 5–7 (see Ex.3). Here the initial major seventh in the cello and minor second in the flute combine to form an inversionally symmetrical pitch collection (Bb, Eb, E, A) which can be represented as two intersecting trichords, the second an inversion of the first. This brief moment of stability is then exploded, if only as far as register is concerned. The collection in the second half of m. 5—G♯, B, C, D♯—is still symmetrical in pitch-class terms, and the flute dyad which ends the phrase in m. 7 (F/F♯) symmetrically divides the cello's C/B, and also the C♯/A♯. Divergence of contour or register from a literally symmetrical base, like that in m. 5, need not represent the total abandonment of interactive sym-

---

15. "The Theorist's Sense of History: Concepts of Contemporaneity in Composition and Analysis," *Journal of the Royal Musical Association* 112 (1987): 18.

16. Carter, "Double Concerto for Harpsichord and Piano with Two Chamber Orchestras (1961); Duo for Violin and Piano (1974)," in *The Writings of Elliott Carter,* ed. Else and Kurt Stone (Bloomington: Indiana University Press, 1977), 330.

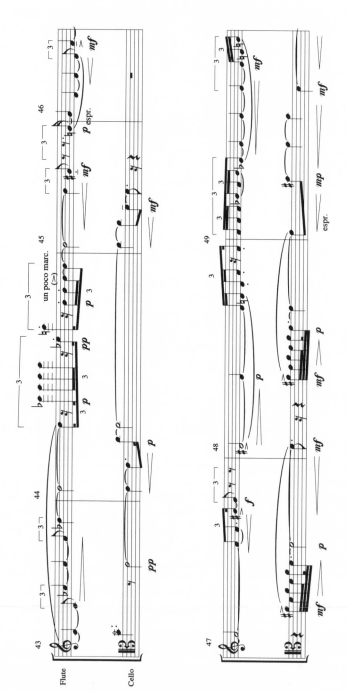

Example 2. Carter: *Enchanted Preludes*, mm. 43–49. © Copyright 1988 by Hendon Music, Inc. Reprinted by permission.

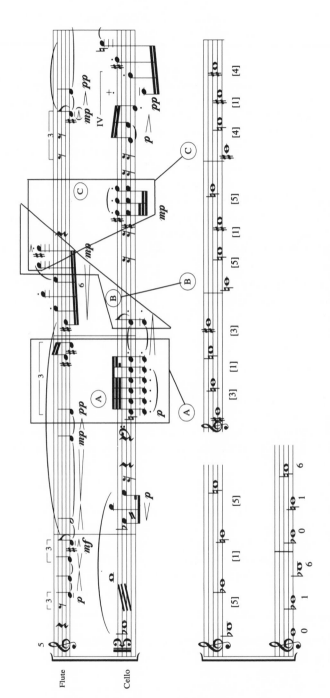

Example 3. Carter: *Enchanted Preludes*, mm. 5–7. © Copyright 1988 by Hendon Music, Inc. Reprinted by permission.

metry as a post-tonal compositional principle. What it does is increase the distance, and enhance the dialogue, between literal and dispersed instances of the same structural principle.

One further instance of the particularly striking interaction of similarity and difference may be found in mm. 111-13 (see Ex.4). The texture here evidently anticipates the ultimate convergence, yet subtle but crucial differences in interval and rhythm are enhanced by the sharing of actual pitches, notably the Gb/F#–C, and F/ Db, which provide the boundary pitches of the melodic segments.

These comments on *Enchanted Preludes* are offered in support of the argument that Carter's modernism takes the form of a consistent commitment to resisting the siren call of decisively resolving convergence: as in *Penthode*, so in *Enchanted Preludes* we observe what I have described as "a sustained dialogue between similarity and difference, rather than any decisive shift from difference to similarity." What Carter himself termed in the score of *Penthode* "the experiences of connectedness and isolation" continue to interact, and it is this interaction that Schiff tends to discount.

Schiff's search for a new classicism in the later Carter seems to be motivated by what he perceives as a change of musical tone—a shift from epic, tragic concerns to a contentment with the utopian vision of ideal equality. Yet the absence from Schiff's discourse of any theoretically grounded concept of tonal classicism creates difficulties. After all, the "enchantered space / within which the enchanted preludes have their place"—the lines of Wallace Stevens which preface the score of *Enchanted Preludes*—is not a hierarchically layered and synthesized classical space. Jonathan Bernard may be stating the obvious when he observes that

> the mosaic-like qualities of both pitch and rhythmic organization suggest also that "structural levels" in Carter's music are quite a different matter from both those of tonal music as construed by Schenkerian theory and those of theories of "transitional" or post-tonal music based, however generally or partially, on Schenkerian models.

Yet it still needs to be said, as Bernard continues, that "one cannot assume Carter's conception of a work as 'one large motion including many inner ones' to imply a highest level of motion that is simply a greatly magnified version of events on the local level".[17] It is not that a tonal composition exploiting the dialogue of relatively stable and relatively volatile ideas is inconceivable: rather that the hierarchically differentiated levels within which that dialogue would play itself out are not employed by Carter. Even in *Enchanted Preludes* where, as shown above, the flute's initial focus on D#, E, G is recalled at the end, at the same time as the cello's relatively stable D/A fifth from m. 3 is also picked up again (mm. 119–20), this creates a form-spanning association: there is no consistently demonstrable span from one to

---

17. See Bernard's review of David Harvey, *The Later Music of Elliott Carter,* in *Music Analysis* 9 (1990): 354.

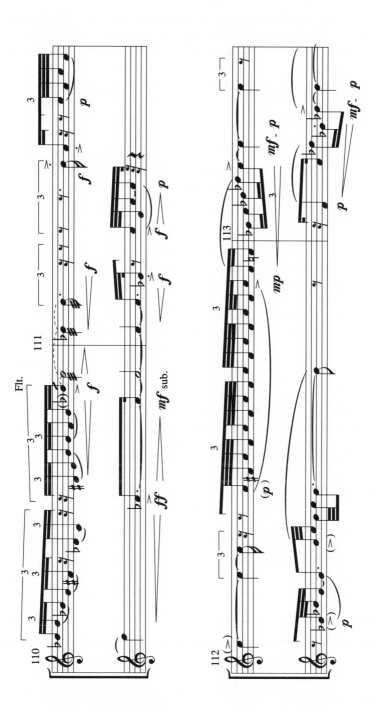

Example 4. Carter: *Enchanted Preludes*, mm. 110–13. © Copyright 1988 by Hendon Music, Inc. Reprinted by permission.

the other, creating what Bernard terms "a highest level of motion." Moreover, this remains the case even when one observes that the flute creates a further association by returning to its D♯/E/G material during the central stages of the piece (mm. 48ff.: see Ex. 2).

It is precisely because genuinely classic music's most powerful structural quality is missing that any discussion of Carter's later music in terms of a dialogue between modernism and classicism, rather than as a modernist dialogue between tendencies to continuity and discontinuity, is both technically and aesthetically problematic. The "journey" embodied in *Enchanted Preludes* is not a progression from separation to synthesis, but a sequence of events which presents the similarity/difference dialogue from ever-changing angles, and with different emphases.

III

In this context, the following description of a composition might well seem familiar. The composer

> divides the texture into six layers or "strata," each occupying a specific register and having a specific interval or set of intervals to define it. Not all the layers are in play at the same time: each fades in and out of the proceedings so that the whole affair seems to be slowly pulsating. Inevitably there is a dramatic climax when the various layers are equalized and a "non-symmetrical balance" is achieved.

Given a further comment about the music going to extremes, and having an "elemental, almost barbaric quality," we might almost be dealing with Carter's *A Symphony of Three Orchestras*. But this narration comes from Michael Hall's discussion of Harrison Birtwistle's large-scale orchestral work *Earth Dances* (1986).[18]

Elsewhere, Hall has provided an excellent general account of Birtwistle's modernism, without actually using the term. Hall's central concept is embodied in a paradox: the "perpetual recurrence" of a process like isorhythm, which need have neither beginning nor end, is combined with the principle of organic growth—a "goal-orientated process" which is "circumscribed and unique."[19] For "combined with" in this phrase we should perhaps substitute "superimposed on," given the associated paradox we can deduce from Hall's discussion. Birtwistle is described as a composer who "takes monism to extreme lengths" and whose thought is essentially "centripetal." Yet he nevertheless works by superimposing on an "absolutely regular and uniform pattern . . . a pattern which is its extreme opposite" on the grounds that "protagonist and chorus, the capricious and the staid, chance and necessity are sym-

---

18. Michael Hall, "The Sanctity of Context: Birtwistle's Recent Music," *Musical Times* 129 (January 1988): 15.

19. Michael Hall, *Harrison Birtwistle* (London: Robson Books, 1984), 11.

biotic. They need each other."[20] In comments like this, Hall reveals Adorno-like perceptions, even though Adorno is not specifically invoked.

Birtwistle himself is, on the face of it, disarmingly consistent in the way he describes his form-building concerns: for example, in a discussion of the opera *The Mask of Orpheus*, he claims that "throughout the piece I've made a distinction between a series of closed forms which define the stage action, and a much more organic, through-composed substructure belonging exclusively to the orchestra."[21] This model was similarly described in comments about his later opera *Yan Tan Tethera*: "I have a strophic substructure as foregound and an organic substructure as background which are independent, or largely independent, of each other."[22] For one critic, at least, this superstructure/substructure model is something of a problem, since it embodies the "paradox" of "a scarcely graspable macrostructure and an intricately detailed microstructure";[23] and it could be added that for the adequate analytical explication of this model in Birtwistle we have all too little of the kind of information—primarily about precompositional dispositions—that is available in Carter's case.

There is nevertheless plenty to be said about appropriate analytical strategies in the light of a musical modernism as powerful and individual as any on the current compositional scene. In his comments on *The Mask of Orpheus* Birtwistle claimed that in order to find a narrative to match his approach to composition, he had to turn to myth, "for only in myth do you find narratives which are not linear. Myths are multi-dimensional narratives containing contradictions and ambiguities,"[24] and this appeals to him because as a composer he is essentially concerned with "repetition, with going over and over the same event from different angles so that a multi-dimensional object is created, an object which contains a number of contradictions as well as a number of perspectives. I don't create linear music, I move in circles; more precisely, I move in concentric circles."[25]

In remarks such as these can be seen the source of the paradox identified by Clements, and that source is an analytical language—Birtwistle interpreting his own musical methods—which certainly contains ambiguities, if not outright contradictions. One might, as it were, square the circle by noting that even movement round the circumference of a circle is in a sense, linear: the process obviously occupies more

20. Hall, *Harrison Birtwistle*, 12, 13, 16.

21. Harrison Birtwistle and David Freeman, "Composer and Producer Speak," in the English National Opera program book for *The Mask of Orpheus* (London, 1986, n.p.).

22. Hall, *Harrison Birtwistle*, 145.

23. Andrew Clements, in notes with the recording of *Earth Dances* issued in 1991 (Collins Classics 20012).

24. Birtwistle and Freeman, "Composer and Producer Speak."

25. Birtwistle and Freeman, "Composer and Producer Speak." See also Jonathan Cross, "Lines and Circles: on Harrison Birtwistle's *Punch and Judy* and *Secret Theatre*," *Music Analysis* 13 (1994): 203–25.

than an instant of time. But what Birtwistle means is that, like Carter, he does not create the kind of linear music that requires globally functioning goal-directedness, and in which those "contradictions and ambiguities" are subsumed into a higher unity, dissolved by the integrating force of that most constraining of musical languages, tonality. Even so, "circling through time" may indeed involve a powerful resistance to a strong sense of musical progress, and the effect—perhaps most palpable in the original version of the "Turning of the Seasons" episode which ends Act I of the opera *Gawain*–is to create a tension between the music's temporality and its resistance to a linearity which, if not "goal-directed" in a tonal sense, still needs to embody change, and to do so whether or not change is of the evolutionary variety, or more a matter of suddenly juxtaposed contrasts.

We can find a simple example of a structure embodying evolutionary change, and therefore raising the possibility that the ending is a "goal," in "Urlar," the first of Birtwistle's *Duets for Storab*, written early in 1983 when work on *The Mask of Orpheus* was entering its final stages.[26] In a dialogue which I would describe as a counterpoint of reaction and interaction, "Urlar" moves from the shared D to the single C♯ which also happens to be the twelfth different pitch class in Flute 1's line (see Ex.5). That word "line" has not crept in by accident, for it is difficult to avoid the conclusion that the music is as it is on account of an interaction between the spatially connected, or adjacent, and the spatially dispersed; and that is as it should be if we apply the Birtwistle form-plan of disjunct substructure and "organic" superstructure to "Urlar." The four stages of the superstructure can be regarded as determined by the four pause marks indicating the points of maximum change (mm. 5, 14, 17 and 26). But elements of an organic substructure can be discerned in each voice separately, as well as in the two voices together. For Flute 1 the process involves the unfolding of all twelve pitch classes, five in two octave positions and two (D and E♭) in three. The resulting continuum (see Ex.6) is exploited by Birtwistle to underline the contrasts between lower, middle, and higher registers, in the sense that, while Segments 1 and 2 gradually widen the distance between the low, centripetal D and the other pitches, and Segment 3 confines itself to the pitch space immediately above that D, Segment 4 exploits a dialogue between middle and higher registers which is then radically reinterpreted in Segment 5 to focus on high and middle Ds and their immediate neighbors, ending on the "non-D," C♯.

The music for Flute 2 offers a more selective approach to the same registrally stratified continuum, the main difference being that in Segments 3 and 4 it confines itself to the pitch space immediately around the middle D, and in Segment 5 its dialogue is between middle and high Ds and their neighbors. At the end, therefore, the two instruments settle in different registral strata, and the whole work offers a

---

26. Storab was a Viking prince who, according to legend, was shipwrecked on the Hebridean island of Raasay, Birtwistle's home when these pieces were composed (January 1983). An "urlar" is the theme of a pibroch; pibroch is the "classical" category of Scottish highland bagpipe music, of which the best-known class is the lament.

Example 5. Harrison Birtwistle: *Urlar*. © Copyright 1983 by Universal Edition (London) Ltd. Reprinted by permission.

Example 6. Birtwistle: *Urlar*: pitch materials.

dialogue of registral interaction (Segments 1 and 2) and registral separation (Segment 3), which is reshaped in Segments 4 and 5 as part of an ascending dynamic curve which provokes the textural fragmentation evident in the final measures.

In its modest way this is a subtle and characteristic piece, whose "dialogic" emphasis is perhaps most evident in Segment 4, as Flute 1 gives particular attention to the pitch classes which Flute 2 never uses. "Urlar" also offers particularly explicit evidence of Birtwistle's propensity for a post-Stravinskian notion of gravitational attraction, which here, admittedly, comes close to a kind of extended tonality. More usually, Birtwistle's points of focus make their impact, and exercise their influence, without creating the incongruous prospect of Schenkerian hierarchies which, even in the orchestral work *Nomos* (1968), are countered rather than confirmed.[27] It is one thing to have, as is the case with *Nomos*, a "through-composed" cantus firmus, moving overall from G down to C. It is something else again to control that motion by means of prolongational procedures which Schenker would have recognized and approved. Birtwistle's apparent allusion to a Schenkerian concept in *Nomos* is, therefore, further evidence of a modernist perspective, promoting disparity and tension rather than unity and integration. Even so, when Birtwistle's major works are surveyed in general, there is a clear contrast between an emphasis on mechanisms, with consequent suppression of the organic, and what I would regard aesthetically as a richer model in which mechanisms and organisms either confront one another, in music of supreme tension and black moods, or else achieve a more genial equilibrium—not exactly stable, but not anxiously disturbed either.

When I reviewed the newly published score of *Carmen arcadiae mechanicae perpetuum* (1978), I suggested that the relative absence of melody was a limitation.[28]

27. In the 1960s Birtwistle "studied the analytical methods of Heinrich Schenker" at the University of Colorado at Boulder. *Nomos* was composed at that time (see Hall, *Harrison Birtwistle*, 49, 60).

28. This paragraph derives from my review in *Music and Letters* 63 (1982): 376–77.

Birtwistle calls the piece "a homage to Paul Klee, and the title is a fantasy contrivance of a title he could have invented." Birtwistle also describes the piece as consisting of "six musical mechanisms which are juxtaposed many times without any form of transition." No organic substructure, then, but not narrowly circular music of a perpetual present, either. This work is an energetic, exuberant fantasia on ostinatos in which the superimposed blocks, each line often very restricted in range, some blocks more homogeneous in rhythm than others, "mark time" with a repetitive irregularity which could scarcely be more different from normal time succession, as marked by the ticking of clocks. It is this rhythmic diversity and pitch density, as well as the large-scale use of variational development, which makes it inappropriate to call such music "minimalist." Even if it is more essentially mechanistic than organic, the process of change and interrelation (coherently contrived) is vital and explicit.

If *Carmen arcadiae mechanicae perpetuum* is the jocular, unbuttoned Birtwistle, *Melencolia I*–to quote Michael Tippett's text for *A Child of Our Time*—turns the world "on its dark side." I referred earlier to David Schiff's description of Carter's *Penthode* as the "vision of a musical utopia," and while I am skeptical about Schiff's argument, I would not wish to deny that Carter's music—despite occasional glimpses into the abyss (the Piano Concerto)—has often been extraordinarily positive and outgoing in effect, ever since he decided in the 1950s to turn his back on neoclassicism and confront the world and its problems "in a less oblique and resigned way."[29] *Melencolia I*, for clarinet, harp and two string orchestras, is tribute to a friend which turned into a response to the image of the "dark side of utopia" as defined by Günter Grass in his book *From the Diary of a Snail*. This concludes with a section headed "On Stasis in Progress. Variations on Albrecht Dürer's engraving *Melencolia I*."[30]

Grass's book has its own genre-challenging identity: part fiction, part autobiographical report on the 1969 Federal German election campaign, fought in the year of the first moon landing and an atmosphere unusual even for the 1960s in the intensity of its alternations between hope and fear. Dürer's melancholic is "a thinking being in perplexity" confronting "a problem which cannot be solved."[31] The melancholic's inertia is that of a being renouncing what it could reach because it can't reach what it longs for, and these associations are significant for Grass as he

---

29. See Allen Edwards, *Flawed Words and Stubborn Sounds: A Conversation with Elliott Carter* (New York: Norton, 1971), 61.

30. Günter Grass, *From the Diary of a Snail*, trans. Ralph Manheim (London: Secker & Warburg, 1974), 286–310.

31. Erwin Panofsky, *The Life and Art of Albrecht Dürer* (Princeton: Princeton University Press, 1971), 163; cited in Hall, *Harrison Birtwistle*, 92–93. For a wide-ranging discussion referring (in very different terms from those used here) to music's ability to provide "a narrative of melancholy" as well as to respond to "the utopian impulse," see Lawrence Kramer, *Music as Cultural Practice, 1800–1900* (Berkeley and Los Angeles: University of California Press, 1990).

moves through a society "whose fringe groups were beginning to take desperately extreme attitudes of resignation or euphoria."[32] In these terms the euphoria of uto- pian visions and the lapses into melancholic withdrawal are two sides of the same coin, and while Grass's humanistic engagement may still have its attractions, it does not in itself seem particularly stimulating to musical thought, nor does it create the kind of associations likely to have struck Birtwistle when he read the book with his composition well under way. Those associations seem to have come from other pas- sages in *From the Diary of a Snail*: for a melancholic "only order, a universally re- peated system, offers security" and "only those who know and respect stasis in progress, who have once and more than once given up, who have sat on an empty snail shell and experienced the dark side of utopia, can evaluate progress."[33] The first can be related to compositional procedure—structure; the second to compositorial attitude—psychology. Both appear to support that celebrated propensity of Birtwistle's to reject intuition, and in a powerful passage Michael Hall declares that "absolutely fundamental to Birtwistle . . . is the conviction that he is an inventor, someone who constructs . . . What survives is not man but the systems man invents. The tighter, the more rigorous the system, the more likely it is to endure."[34] But that sounds more like the formalist gospel according to Milton Babbitt than anything relevant to the British love of paradox and compromise. It could even be said in response that the ability to think and feel beyond system is the decisive step out of melancholy and the best way to celebrate a properly modernist plurality. That is not to dismiss system, but to locate it in either superstructure or substructure: not— classically—in both.

As for *Melencolia I*, we can easily forget 1969, or even 1976, when it was com- pleted, and respond to the work as the journeyings of a Don Quixote (the clarinet cantus) with his Sancho Panza (harp), in a world without a Dulcinea, an unremit- tingly dark world in which there are only degrees of divergence, while hints of convergence prove illusory and provoke more extreme conflict. This state is memo- rably established at the outset of the work, where the disparities between the clarinet's sustained cantus, the tugging motions of the strings and the flowing continuities of the harp are all instantly detectable (see Ex.7). Birtwistle's reliance on very slowly expanding explorations of narrow areas of pitch space in this cantus carry all the risks, in a modernist context, of an idea which might be perceived as too obvious, too primitive, and lacking adequate potential to sustain a large-scale structure. Yet the expressive intensity of a line which seems to embody with remarkable direct- ness a character's search for security (or stasis) makes the risks worth taking. As with Carter, we can hear "different kinds of music . . . occurring simultaneously."[35] But Birtwistle's method of generating an extended line in slow motion as we listen

---

32. *From the Diary of a Snail*, 287.
33. *From the Diary of a Snail*, 294, 310.
34. Hall, *Harrison Birtwistle*, 97.
35. See note 16, above.

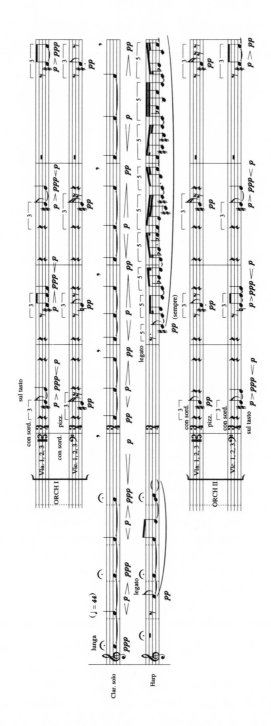

Example 7. Birtwistle: *Melencolia I*, beginning. © Copyright 1977 by Universal edition (London) Ltd. Reprinted by permission.

Example 8. Birtwistle: *Melencolia I*, mm. 4–2 before rehearsal N. (score, p. 18). © Copyright 1977 by Universal edition (London) Ltd. Reprinted by permission.

is worlds away from Carter's volatile euphoria. (That Birtwistle, in lighter mood, can come closer to Carter's spirit is evident, for example, at the beginning of *Secret Theatre*.) The opening of *Melencolia I* remains the archetypal instance in Birtwistle of what I described earlier as the "model in which mechanisms and organisms . . . confront one another." Yet even here there is the inevitable prospect (since this is a work of art) of equilibrium, or resistance to instability, consequent on the fact that the concise rhythmic mechanisms (those features of Birtwistle's music which suggests links with Stockhausen's concept of *Momentform*) also evolve, their clear-cut cadences intersecting with particular points of repose in the cantus line. Indeed, in order to sustain the substantial twenty-five-minute structure of the work, Birtwistle from time to time raises the possibility that the orchestra might be "won over" to the clarinet's slowly unfolding style of lyric melancholy (see the music between Letters E and G). There is even a sense of relative convergence—of positive musical sharing (see Ex.8)—which makes the eventual, ultimate breakdown of communication the more powerful and poignant.

Melencolia I reaches its climax (Letters S–T) with the clarinet shrieking despair and defiance into a dense curtain of quiet string sound which settles on to a thirty-one-note chord after a passage in which the two orchestras are in rhythmic canon (Ex.9). The clarinet's lack of complexity here is, one supposes, a kind of metaphor for the catatonic silence of clinical melancholia, but in any case this is a musical expression of conflicting impulses—to preserve stasis, to provoke progress—which goes to the heart of Grass's discourse as it transcends it. The music then shatters the chordal unanimity of the strings, dissolving into a welter of soft ostinatos—society's

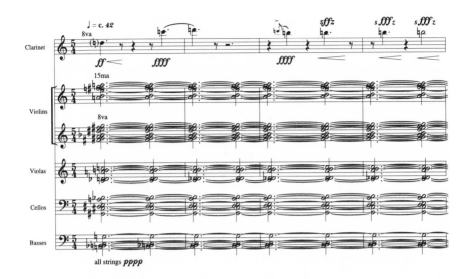

Example 9. Birtwistle: *Melencolia I,* mm. 5–2 before rehearsal T. (score, p. 29). © Copyright 1977 by Universal edition (London) Ltd. Reprinted by permission.

last, melancholy words. Then a long crescendo from the clarinet grows out of the silence. Is this a circle or a line? Its growth in time appears positive, affirmative, but all it leads to is the clarinet's own mechanical ostinato, which is cut off by the harp as if the faithful servant has put his mad master out of his misery and has become the last living thing on earth (Ex.10).

My language here is a long way from the kind of discourse that would point out that the [0167] pc set of the harp's last chord is a subset of the clarinet's [01367] collection (though no actual pitches are shared)—a discourse which would therefore set up a characteristically modernist dialogue of similarities and differences which achieve equilibrium rather than synthesis. Such talk would move us away from hermeneutic interpretation back into an analytical domain where we could debate, in appropriate depth, the question of just how rigorous or non-rigorous the various systems are which we can deduce from, or impose on, Birtwistle's musical materials in *Melencolia I.* On the more general level of argument preferred here, it is necessary rather to reinforce the point that it is in the rich variety of dialogues informing his music that Birtwistle's modernism achieves its fullest realization.

IV

It is inevitable that the act of bringing Carter and Birtwistle together within one piece of interpretive prose promotes observations about similarities and differences.

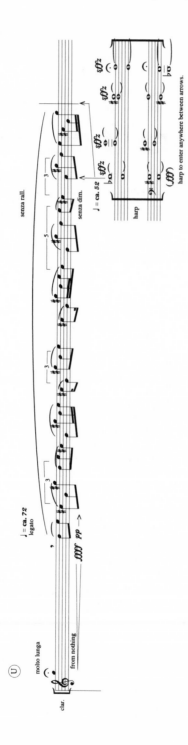

Example 10. Birtwistle: *Melencolia I*, ending. © Copyright 1977 by Universal edition (London) Ltd. Reprinted by permission.

If we take the two "duet" pieces, one basic difference is that Carter proceeds to convergence, Birtwistle to divergence. Another is that Birtwistle's "post-tonal" language is distinctly more centripetal than Carter's—Birtwistle gives more explicit emphasis to D than Carter does to G or any other pitch class. A basic similarity is that the duet genre does not promote the preservation of exclusive registral strata—even in Carter's case, where the two instruments have so many obvious differences. Carter's concept of complementation (of interval type, of rhythmic pattern) may represent the kind of schematic framework which Birtwistle avoids on principle, yet in Birtwistle, too, there is the kind of dialogue that involves reaction and interaction, not merely the superimposition of strong contrasts. After all, the "Urlar" principle, of two different approaches to the same continuum of pitches, is not entirely different from the *Enchanted Preludes* principle of two approaches to the continuum of intervals which are, as interval classes, the same. And simply because a strong initial pitch focus (as on A in *Melencolia I*) tends to be displaced rather than reinforced at the structure's end a fundamental divergence can be discerned in this piece too.[36]

Writing of Carter's *Syringa* in 1983, I declared that:

> The primitive and sophisticated clash constantly, and the flow of time is itself split so that the urgings of unbridled instinct persistently challenge and provoke the smooth rationality of the conscious mind. The work is disturbing not just because of its feverish intricacy but because it holds integration at bay and obliges the listener to confront unresolved oppositions which are not simply two distinct halves of the same whole.[37]

If, for Carter, *Syringa* is a "pre-classical" work in Schiff's terms, it follows that, in the later music which forms the primary focus for my present discussion, Carter does not simply "hold integration at bay" but brings converging and diverging tendencies into an ever more subtly interactive relation. His persistent yet increasingly refined modernism is fueled by the kind of paradox to which he alludes (in the score) with reference to Petrarch's poem "Scrivo in vento," whose title he eventually attached to his solo flute piece of 1991. The playfulness of the poet's confession—"I plow the waves and found my house on sand and write on the wind"—is not without its melancholy tinge: the euphoria of creativity is offset by the perceived ephemerality of what is created. Yet Petrarch's poem is not ephemeral at all, and the poet himself lives on: as Carter mentions in the score, *Scrivo in vento* was first performed on Petrarch's 687th birthday.

If one possible cause of intense melancholy is the conviction that any action—even writing music—is futile, Birtwistle's *Melencolia I* embodies as profoundly as any twentieth-century work the paradox of using creative activity (building artistic

---

36. See my discussion of a comparable rejection of an earlier focused pitch in Birtwistle's *Earth Dances,* "Comparatively Complex: Birtwistle, Maxwell Davies, and Modernist Analysis," *Music Analysis* 13 (1994): 139–59.

37. See my review of the score, *Music and Letters* 64 (1983): 317–18.

ideas into structures) to paint a portrait of utter inertia. Perhaps only a composer who is not by nature "oblique and resigned" could successfully undertake such a task. Musicological attempts to place Birtwistle exclusively on the "dark side of utopia" and Carter on the bright side are therefore futile, and just as the two composers can be said to "share" an association with modernism (as defined in this essay) so this might seem to reinforce the ultimate unity of the intellectual enquiry surrounding them. What must not be forgotten, therefore, is the complementary fragmentation. "Unity," for Carter and Birtwistle alike, is more a matter of balance than of synthesis. Among many other things, we owe to Allen Forte the perception that post-tonal compositions may exemplify "connected" structures which are not inconsistent with "pronounced changes in the underlying structure."[38] This is the creative tension between connections and changes which remains at the heart of modernist music, and analysis of that music, however hard it tries, cannot wholly escape the consequences.

---

38. Allen Forte, *The Structure of Atonal Music* (New Haven and London: Yale University Press, 1973), 128.

SALIENT FEATURES

JOHN ROTHGEB

Recent assessments of musical analytic practice and its criteria often invoke the notion of *salience*. It is alleged, for example, that one or another analytical approach overlooks or disregards features that manifest this quality.[1] Certainly, any analytic approach that disregarded truly salient features should be considered deficient. The criteria for musical salience, however, are far from obvious and are scarcely susceptible of generalization. In particular, they have far less to do with immediate noticeability than is commonly supposed. This article will examine several musical contexts in which the most readily apparent characteristics are not the primary conveyors of musical content but must instead recede in importance in comparison to others less apparent at first glance. Since rhythm is justly considered one of the primary vehicles of salience, it is appropriate to begin by observing a few of its modes of interaction with other dimensions.

The distinction has been made in rhythmic analysis between "rhythm-to-pitch" and "pitch-to-rhythm" strategies.[2] The former assume that rhythmic factors (chiefly the patterning of durations) influence pitch significance, the latter that pitch configurations are capable of creating rhythmic entities. Both directions of influence are exhibited in the chorale melody "Ach Gott, wie manches Herzeleid" as it is set by Bach in Example 1. Measures 6–8 of this version of the melody strongly suggest a fifth-progression within the triadic fifth of a tonicized G-major chord, and they are set as such by Bach. From the perspective of pitch alone, d^2, b^1, and g^1, measured against the prevailing G sonority, would count as stable and therefore primary elements, with c^2 and a^1 serving as subordinate passing notes. But the mere distribution of durations (agogic "accent") enhances the significance of both c^1 and a^1 relative to b^1. Thus the "rhythm-to-pitch" direction of influence would, even in defiance of the meter, tend to project b^1 as a passing tone between c^1 and a^1 as the boundaries of a third-progression. In Bach's setting, the pitch dimension elegantly collaborates in realizing this tendency: Bach's bass, with its upward leap of a fifth from the root of IV, unequivocally demotes the b^1 to the status of a passing note (albeit with consonant support).[3]

This article is an expanded version of a paper delivered March 27, 1992, under the title "Misleading Associations," at the Second International Schenker Symposium at the Mannes College of Music in New York.

1. For example, "Schenkerian analysis repeatedly slights salient features in the music" (Joseph Kerman, Contemplating Music [Cambridge, Mass.: Harvard University Press, 1985], 82).

2. This useful terminology was introduced and defined by Maury Yeston in *The Stratification of Musical Rhythm* (New Haven and London: Yale University Press, 1976), 4ff.

3. The rhythm of this version of the melody itself, of course, is also by Bach. In the absence

Example 1. Bach: Chorale No. 217, "Ach Gott, wie manches Herzeleid."

If rhythmic factors can influence pitch significance (whether or not they are supported, as in Example 1, by other contextual features), it is equally certain that pitches can be shaped into entities that resist, indeed override, any parsing of musical continuity suggested by rhythm alone. A very simple instance is provided by the next example, mm. 13–16 of Schubert's Impromptu op. 142, no.2 (see Example 2). Of the five bass notes in this phrase, the shortest and metrically weakest one (E♭ in m. 15) serves as the boundary of the definitive pitch space, the descending fourth from I to V. For an impressive verification, one might experiment by imagining the passage first with the bass notes G and F suppressed, and then with those notes restored but with the E♭ omitted. The priority of E♭ here is partly—but only partly—due to its decisive position as dominant of the key; that advantage alone could be overridden by a different continuation. It is in addition the overall pitch formation—the contour and the arrangement of the stepwise motion and the leap—that defines the E♭ as a boundary element.

A considerably more intricate case in which pitch factors supersede rhythm is found in the opening bars of the Rondo movement from Beethoven's Piano Sonata op. 90. An interpretation by Hugo Riemann appears as at *a* in Example 3.[4] Beethoven's own notation of the music is given at *b* in the example.[5] (Riemann's designation of it as "überlieferte Bezeichnung"—"traditional marking"—is surely an understatement.) Central to Beethoven's conception of the passage is the association among tonal shapes—in particular, the parallelism of the rising thirds e–f♯–g♯ (leading into m. 1) and f♯–g♯–a (leading into m. 3). His portato marking in m. 2 makes it clear that a

---

of Bach's bass, mm. 6–8 might well be considered ambiguous: the established meter would support the "pitch-to-rhythm" interpretation, while the durational pattern would favor "rhythm-to-pitch." In any case, the viability of the rhythm-to-pitch direction of influence is established.

4. This example, from Riemann's *Präludien und Studien*, 3 vols. (Frankfurt am Main: Bechhold, 1895), 1:94, is quoted and discussed briefly in Oswald Jonas, *Introduction to the Theory of Heinrich Schenker*, trans. and ed. John Rothgeb (New York: Longman, 1981), 10–11.

5. See Ludwig van Beethoven, *Klaviersonate E-moll op. 90. Faksimile-Ausgabe mit Einführung von Michael Ladenburger* (Bonn: Verein Beethoven-Haus, 1993).

Example 2. Schubert, Impromptu, op. 142, no. 2, mm. 13–16.

a) mit Phrasierungsbögen.

b) überlieferte Bezeichnung.

Example 3. Riemann on Beethoven, Piano Sonata, op. 90, mvt. 2, mm. 1–4.

musical entity (that is, a unit of diminution) begins with the third eighth-note of that bar rather than with the fourth (as would be required by a strict metric repetition of the opening half-phrase), so that corresponding elements of the parallelism are not assigned to corresponding metric positions. (The parallelism of the two half-phrases is confirmed by the preservation, up to the fifth note of the second half-phrase, of the pitch contour of the first.)

Riemann's reading of the music was different: what was salient for Beethoven was not so for Riemann. For him the metric correspondence (which, for the purpose of this discussion, falls into the general category of rhythm) outweighed—indeed, evidently obliterated—the musical content defined by tonal shape. In choosing between the readings at *a* and *b* in Example 3, it is surely appropriate to be guided by the opinion of Beethoven, which fortunately is not in doubt, rather than by that of Riemann. In several examples of competing and even conflicting associations to be discussed below, it may be in order to hear both associations but to assign priority to one of them. Here, however, it seems that Beethoven's parallelism wipes out the entities implied by Riemann's parsing of the music: if we hear Riemann's metric (rhythmic) parallel, we will not hear Beethoven's composition. It is not so much that a pitch association here overrides a rhythmic one, but rather that pitch *defines* a rhythmic relationship far richer than any that could be produced by purely durational and metric factors: as the pitch shape undergoes enlargement, the rhythmic feature—the upbeat—is necessarily expanded, and this is part of the artistic yield. Beethoven's marking supports this enrichment of the rhythmic content; Riemann's vitiates it.

Of the two associations implicit in Example 3, then, we must hear the one at *b* to the exclusion of the one at *a*. The norm in art music, however, is saturation of the musical surface with associations that are "genuine" (rather than "spurious" as in Example 3*a*) and that compete, each of them with some degree of legitimacy, for the ear's attention. Consider the first two bars of the first of Bach's Six Small Preludes, of which the treble voice is given in Example 4. The association of the two anacrusis-formations shown by square brackets at *a* is more than merely salient: it literally cannot be missed. But a different association—the one marked by the square brackets at *b*—will elude the ear that is too easily seduced by the first one.[6] This second association is forged by the pitch dimension, with little if any assistance from rhythm. Of the two associations, the one at *b* must be considered artistically primary. The association at *a* operates in a somewhat paradoxical way: it is certainly "there" as an inseparable component of the musical object, but to the extent that it suggests a parsing of the continuity in which the last note of m. 1 is detached from what precedes and grouped instead with what follows, it distracts the ear from a relationship that enriches the content vastly more than it alone could possibly do.

When a "misleading" rhythmic association of this kind is allied with specific motivic shape, the potential for deception is greater still. In Schumann's third "* * *" piece (no. 30) from the *Album for the Young* (see Example 5), the association of the dotted rhythm in the fourth quarter of m. 2 with that in the upbeat to m. 1 cannot fail to attract the ear's attention, especially as it is coordinated with the third-leaps f^2 -d^2 and c^2-a^1. Pitch and rhythm combine here to create motifs of the lowest order— the ones that usually make the strongest case for interpretation as salient features. These motifs, however palpable, once again have the effect of obscuring a still more important feature of content. The a^1 of the opening motif, after being suspended as a seventh, moves down a step to g^1 as part of a third-progression aiming for f^1; this is at first thwarted, and a second attempt is made (thus, twice a^1–g^1). The third melodic entrance begins with f^2 at the end of m. 2, as though to fall from a greater height and thus avoid a third failure. It finally achieves f^1 (albeit only as a passing note prolonging g^1), which, like its linear antecedent g^1, is approached by the descending third-leap c^2–a^1 (Example 6). Although these latter notes as they appear in m. 3 do not preserve the original dotted rhythm, and although they are further disguised as a seemingly insignificant component of a complete triad-arpeggiation, they should in

---

6. The association of the two broken sixths—above and beyond intervening rests in the first of them—needs to be brought out in performance; one way to do this is by applying (at least conceptually if one is playing the harpsichord) the dynamic shadings shown at *b*.

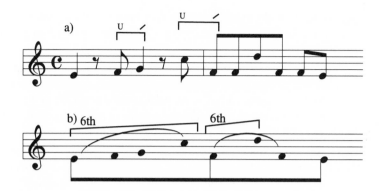

Example 4. Bach: Prelude, *BWV* 933, mm. 1–2.

Example 5. Schumann: *Album for the Young,* op. 68, no. 30, mm. 1–4.

Example 6. Interpretation of Example 5.

fact be heard as an exact quote—in augmentation—of the opening third. As such, they represent a feature of the composition that must be described as more expressive or meaningful than the relatively "incidental" allusion provided by the rhythm-preserving third f^2–d^2 that serves them as upbeat. In this example it is not just tonal shape but exact pitch content that is important, and once again the deeper association is *not* supported by or correlated with the most salient metric and durational features of the surface.

Against active opposition from the most obviously salient features of the surface, a particular deployment of tonal shapes in the variation-theme of Schubert's Impromptu op. 142, no. 3 breaks the back of the rigidity that would have attended a merely schematic repetition. Example 7 quotes the first thirteen bars. Apart from a brief coda, the Theme comprises sixteen bars in the form a_1–b–a_2 (where a_1 is subdivided as antecedent-consequent); it is articulated almost consistently into two-bar segments with the rhythm ♩♫♩♩. The beginning of the b section is melodically identical to that of both antecedent and consequent phrases within the a_1: thus it represents a *third* two-bar segment beginning with the same notes, and the fifth segment with the same rhythm. The potential for monotony is clear. Schubert avoids this pitfall not only through reharmonization but also, more subtly, by drawing parallel tonal shapes that cut across the two two-bar groups of the b section as shown in Example 8, and he applies an accent to demarcate the beginning of the parallelism. The first descending fifth, d^2–g^1, is compressed so that the second one, c^2–f^1, can begin "prematurely."[7] A literal parallelism might have appeared as in Example 9, where tonal shape is exactly coordinated with rhythmic association. Once again a feature salient by conventional standards is found to be actually subordinate to a more subtle association defined by pitch—one that should be heard in spite of its apparently inferior degree of salience.

If it is now established that salient features can mislead the ear, the next example, longer and far more complex, shows deceptions of still greater consequence. The music of Beethoven's Bagatelle, op. 126, no. 6 is given in Example 10.[8] Although the framing Presto sections relate in interesting ways to the main body of the bagatelle,[9] we shall concentrate here on the latter, the Andante amabile e con moto beginning in m. 7. Measures 7-21 are organized in five three-bar segments,[10] of which the first four are grouped into two pairs. From the perspective of design, mm. 7-12 seem to present a self-contained whole whose first segment is answered by a second one that preserves not only the very individual rhythm of the first but also an important

7. These two composed-out descending fifths were undoubtedly motivated by the descending fifth-leaps in mm. 3–4, which become inverted to ascending fourths in the consequent, mm. 7–8.

8. Janet Schmalfeldt treats this bagatelle in "Towards a Reconciliation of Schenkerian Concepts with Traditional and Recent Theories of Form," *Music Analysis* 10 (1991), 233–87. Although Schmalfeldt and I are in agreement on several points, our divergences are fundamental, and germane to my present topic.

9. These relationships eluded Sieghard Brandenburg, who writes in Sieghard Brandenburg, ed., *Ludwig van Beethoven, Sechs Bagatellen für Klavier, Op. 126. Facsimile der Handschriften und der Originalausgabe mit einem Kommentar herausgegeben von Sieghard Brandenburg* (Bonn: Verein Beethoven-Haus, 1984), *Teil 2: Originalausgabe, Übertragung, Kommentar*, 62, that "the six bars [of the Presto] prepare the slow section neither in mood nor in themes and motifs. . . ."

10. More exactly, three-bar hypermeasures; the fourth of these, mm. 16-18, constitutes an entity only by the criterion of hypermeter, not by that of content. This will be amplified in the following discussion.

Example 7. Schubert: Impromptu, op. 142, no. 3, mm. 1–13.

Example 8. Interpretation of Example 7, mm. 9–12.

textural feature, the pattern of alternating thirds and sixths in the right-hand part. These two segments, mm. 7–12, constitute what will be called the first phrase. The patterning of the two segments causes their respective third bars to associate in such a way as to suggest that g^2, the obvious apex-note of the first arpeggiation, returns as g^1 at the end of the second segment—as though the end-result of the six bars were an octave coupling or register-transfer with $\hat{3}$ prolonged by two applications of reaching-over. These two apparent reaching-over figures are designated x^1 and x^2 in Ex-

Example 9. Interpretation of Example 7, mm. 9–12, with hypothetical literal parallelism.

ample 11. Indeed, if only the first phrase of the Andante were taken into consideration, this reading would be inescapable. But we do not hear this phrase in isolation: the meaning of its elements is determined by the overall environment. The music continues; m. 13 repeats the motif of the first segment (mm. 7–9) in a new rhythm and beginning a third lower, on the g^1 that ended the first phrase.

Because this repetition preserves the exact contour of the head of the motif (rising fourth plus rising third), it now outlines a C-minor triad. The sixth g^1–$e\flat^2$ that it unfolds associates not only with the initial rising sixth $b\flat^1$–g^2 but also with the descending sixth between the f^2 that concludes x^1 and the $a\flat^1$ that initiates x^2. (The integrity of this latter sixth as an entity, and not just as an incidental byproduct of other processes, is of course underscored already in the second segment by the appearance of the two pitches f^2 and $a\flat^1$ in direct succession across the barline of mm. 11/12.) The tonal parallelism between mm. 13–14 and mm. 7–9 supersedes the rhythmic and contour parallelism between figures x^1 and x^2, which is now subsumed within a pair of coordinated linear progressions moving in sixths unfolded by arpeggiations in alternating directions (see Example 12).[11]

These associated tonal shapes and the linear progressions they define cut across such salient features as rests, rhythmic entities, design groups, and formal boundaries. They illustrate Oswald Jonas's dictum that "the masters want to make us forget the barline [read also: hypermeasure, formal division] for the sake of higher-order connections."[12]

If the figures marked x^1 and x^2 in Example 11 act in a certain sense as red herrings that mask more fundamental continuities, the group beginning in m. 13 sends a signal that is potentially even more misleading. Its second segment, beginning in m. 16, repeats the motivic contour of mm. 7–9 *at the original pitch level*. In so

---

11. Had the initial vertical third of the second segment, $a\flat^2$ above f^2, been stated an octave lower, the association of the sixths and the continuity of the two linear progressions would have been more obvious. Such a "clarification" would have been pedantic, however, and would have excessively underscored the already palpable segmentation. Beethoven's use of the higher octave provides a simple linkage (see the curly-bracketed figures in Example 12) between the two segments. It should be added that the second segment thereby *begins* with downward motion, which immediately gives the general impression that it is a free inversion of the first. Only later does it become clear that it is specifically the descending *sixth* f^2–$a\flat^1$ that relates by inversion to the rising sixth of the first segment.

12. Jonas, *Introduction*, 14.

Example 10. Beethoven: Bagatelle, op. 126, no. 6.

Example 10 cont'd.

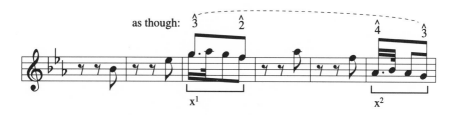

Example 11. Interpretation of Example 10, mm. 7–12.

Example 12. Interpretation of Example 10, mm. 7–14.

doing, it delineates an E♭ harmony, apparently as a direct successor, by virtue of parallelism, to the C-minor harmony of m. 13. The origin of this latter sonority is now clear as a consequence of the voice-leading and motivic design of mm. 7-14; but at least two perplexing questions arise from the restatement of the motif apparently in the tonic E♭ in mm. 16–18: (1) Does the parallelism of m. 16 to m. 13 define an upward progression by the interval of a third? and (2) Is the E♭ of m. 16ff. to be understood as a *return* of the original tonic? If not, what is its meaning? Two decisive clues point to the answers.

The first, and more superficial, clue is that the appearance of the motivic statement "in" E♭ of m. 16ff. is but the second of three occurrences within mm. 13–21 of the same general shape of an ascending arpeggiation followed by a stepwise descent (see Ex. 13).

This by itself gives the impression that the E♭ of m. 16ff. is not to be understood as a reappearance of the opening tonic: if it were so understood, mm. 7-16 would have to be heard as circumscribing motivic entrances in E♭, C minor, and E♭ respectively—that is, as defining a progression I–VI–I. Such a progression, or more accurately succession of sonorities, is sometimes encountered, but it always supports an explicit neighbor-note formation $\hat{5}$–$\hat{6}$–$\hat{5}$, usually in the treble; here it would have to be understood simply as defining motion down a third and then back up a third, which would be musical doggerel. Successions of this kind might be found in very simple sectionalized forms in which consecutive self-contained segments present completely parallel statements in major, "relative minor," and major. The point of such a procedure is merely to contrast major and minor colorings without actually employing modal mixture. This emphatically is not Beethoven's purpose in the

Example 13. Beethoven: Bagatelle, op. 126, no. 6: motivic recurrences.

passage under discussion. The function of the E♭ area of m. 16ff. is not one of inclusion or circumscription: it is itself included within and circumscribed by a larger formation.

The second clue, which alone can completely clarify matters, lies in the radical difference of effect between the apparently analogous measures 15 and 18. The most immediately obvious difference is perhaps that between the effects of the respective downbeats of those bars: the former presents a local change of harmony, while the latter merely prolongs the harmony of m. 17. But the contrast goes far deeper. The initial statement of the motivic contour, in m. 7ff., at first appeared to include an ascending arpeggiation followed by a single descending step; the stepwise continuation of f^2 to $e\flat^2$, yielding as a totality a descending third-progression, emerged only in mm. 13-14. (The resulting total contour—up one step and then down three—is one feature explicitly prepared by the framing Presto; Beethoven improvises on this contour in an elaborate way in mm. 54–62.) As the motif is transposed to C minor in mm. 13–16, the descending-third component is completed immediately: d^2, the analog of f^2 in m. 9, moves directly to c^2 in bar 13. Despite its metrically weak position, this c^2 above IV represents the end of a voice-leading entity, a third-progression ($e\flat^2$– d^2–c^2). That is by no means true of the analogous $e\flat^2$ in m. 18. A decisive change of harmony at the second chord of m. 18 rules out any possibility of reading f^2 of that bar as a passing note in a linear progression ending with the $e\flat^2$ at the last beat of the bar. Far from being the goal of a linear progression, $e\flat^2$ of m. 18 is itself a passing note *within* a third-progression: f^2–$e\flat^2$–d^2.[13] It is ironic but true that the parallelism of the two genuine third-progressions—the first one ending and the second one beginning above one and the same a♭ bass—is more powerful than the apparently far more prominent parallelism between the motivic statements of mm. 13–15 and mm. 16–18 respectively. It is as though the two third-progressions belonged together in direct succession, with the sixth-chord in m. 18 arising from a 5–6 replacement above the bass a♭.

13. The weight of the change of harmony on the second beat of m. 18, and the attendant effect of f^2 as the primary note of a third-progression, is greatly enhanced by the aforementioned continuation of the harmony of m. 17 into the first beat of m. 18. Beethoven's articulation-slur, of course, ends with the passing note $e\flat^2$. To have drawn a slur encompassing the third-progression would have been unthinkable. The downbeat of m. 19 is an elision: it is defined as an ending by a voice-leading entity (the linear progression) and as a beginning by the change of design. It is probably a rule without exception that in such cases articulation-slurs and dynamics will give priority to the latter function, since the former is ensured by stronger forces.

Example 14. Beethoven: Bagatelle, op. 126, no. 6, mm. 7–21.

The answer to each of the two perplexing questions raised earlier, therefore, is no: the parallelism of m. 16 to m. 13 does not define an upward progression through a third, and the E♭ triad composed out in m. 16ff. is not an incarnation of the original tonic. The apparent ascent of a third from m. 13 to m. 16 suggested by motivic parallelism is overridden by the more fundamental ascent of a step (5–6 above a♭) defined by the third-progressions; and the relationship of the E♭ harmony of mm. 16-18 to that of mm. 7-12 is one of (almost ironical) allusion or recollection rather than structural connection. In its transposition to E♭, the motif—especially the third bar of its three-bar segment—has undergone a dramatic reinterpretation very much in keeping with its significance as a *parenthetical interpolation* between the third beat of m. 15 and the second beat of m. 18.

The content of mm. 7–21 is displayed in the direction from background to foreground in Example 14. At level *a*, the most fundamental voice-leading stratum presents a motion from $\hat{3}$ to $\hat{2}$ above I moving to V. Level *b* shows a prolongation in which the treble moves through a linear progression ending with e♭² in m. 12 (14). From the perspective of the background, this necessitated the use of one or another device of prolongation to attain f², the $\hat{2}$; level *b* shows this accomplished with the

Example 14 cont'd.

aid of a 5-6 motion above IV. At level *c*, the 5–6 replacement is enhanced by means of two reaching-over progressions departing from e♭² and f² respectively. The approach to IV is moreover intensified by a chromatic passing b♮, set as the upper third of a major III. (In the foreground, this III♮ pretends to be V of C minor.)

Level *d* shows two new features. Two octave couplings appear in the bass, the first within the opening I and the second (very much compressed) with the passing III♮.[14] Above the first of these, a 5–6 replacement gives rise to what will emerge as the C-minor harmony of mm. 13–14. (From the middleground perspective, it also avoids a direct chromatic succession by intervening between b♭ and b♮.) And finally, the more fundamental 5–6 replacement above IV is negotiated with the aid of an 8–7–6 progression; the dissonant passing note is transferred up an octave and is supported (made consonant) by a bass E♭. This passing note with its bass support provides the

---

14. This latter coupling did not appear in an earlier draft, in which Beethoven wrote the bass of m. 15 as F♯–G–A♭ (with an explicit "7" above the F♯), thus altogether in the lower (great) octave. See Brandenburg, *Beethoven, Sechs Bagatellen für Klavier, Teil 1*, 60, and *Teil 2*, 38. A sketch associated with the same draft shows a bass a♭–a♭–a♮ in eighth-notes for bar 18. These earlier attempts seem to me to support, in a way, the reading presented here of the final version; they would have established the continuity described above, but in a manner all too obvious and to the detriment of the great subtlety of the finished product.

Example 15. Beethoven: Bagatelle, op. 126, no. 6, mm. 7–51.

framework for the parenthetical motivic statement of mm. 16–18. That statement, accordingly, is parenthetical by two different standards that operate simultaneously: it is the middle member of a three-stage patterning process (see Ex. 13), and it is set within the span of a transient voice-leading event.

This same interpolation (with its ending modified, but recognizably the same entity by virtue of its inclusion of the appoggiatura—now $b\flat^3$—in its second bar) returns beginning in m. 48. It is again an interpolation (supporting a passing note, g^3), but now in a *comparatively* conventional way: it does appear a step below (seventh above) the immediately preceding motivic statement to which it forms a paral-

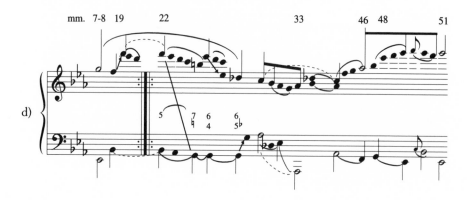

Example 15 cont'd.

lel and from which it defines a progression downward by step. Example 15 summarizes the content of the whole of mm. 7–51, again in the direction from background to foreground; the appearance of our interpolation in m. 48 is marked with an asterisk at level *d*, which explains its voice-leading significance.

All of the examples discussed share the characteristic that features salient according to conventional standards are *not* the ones that are decisive in projecting the musical message. In each case these "salient" features recede in significance by comparison to tonal shapes that are less obvious but, once perceived, more powerful. These less obvious shapes, indeed, *are* the salient features of high musical art.

SYNTHESIS AND ASSOCIATION, STRUCTURE AND DESIGN IN MULTI-MOVEMENT COMPOSITIONS

DAVID NEUMEYER

This article addresses the question of tonal design (specifically, synthesis on a harmonic/voice-leading model) in multi-movement compositions. A brief survey of pertinent literature is followed by discussion of the mechanisms in Schenkerian theory for joining together independent pieces or movements of a cycle. A theoretical model then arises gradually from the examination of several binary oppositions (autonomous piece versus cycle, tonal versus associative, ordered key relations versus design in extra-musical components of a texted work), along with their logical negations and the combinations of the resulting sets of terms. The model is consistent with Schenkerian theory and offers a framework for resolution of cyclic design issues in music for concert and stage, and also in some unexpected repertoire, including functional dance music and music cues for cinema.

Some years ago I wrote an article which took a skeptical view of those interpretive projects which find in multi-movement compositions a coherent, overarching "organic" design based on harmonic/voice-leading structures.[1] It is generally acknowledged that compositions with more than one movement, such as the sonata, dance series, song cycle, or character-piece set of the eighteenth and nineteenth centuries, pose special problems for musical analysis precisely because methodologies have been designed to work on individual, closed pieces, not on groups of such pieces. The analyst-interpreter is thus left to mark, with some wistfulness, certain obvious features like main-key relations, thematic recurrence, or other motivic-cyclic connections, without being able to refer these intriguing items in anything other than ad hoc fashion to an overarching (and preferably stereotypical) logic of design. The lack of a theory of multiple structures is all the more galling in that a large portion of the traditional musical repertoire consists of such works.

The obstacles that confront anyone proposing such a theory are daunting. It is, for example, by no means obvious that instrumental and vocal cycles can be subsumed under a single theory, their histories being essentially separate and their inter-

---

1. David Neumeyer, "Organic Structure and the Song Cycle: Another Look at Schumann's *Dichterliebe*," *Music Theory Spectrum* 4 (1982): 92–105.

nal characteristics different. Nor is it clear that models of artistic synthesis (such as Schenker's) can be expanded beyond the bounds of the individual movement, as I observed in connection with the music of Schumann:

> Neither key unity (i.e., beginning and ending in the same key) nor intra-cycle key succession patterns support the idea that an expanded harmonic-contrapuntal structure in itself represents or generates organic structure in the keyboard or song cycles of Schumann. This is plain from the fact that those sets which most people would be willing to agree are merely collections . . . or that have the barest sort of narrative integration . . . do not differ in any significant way with respect to key unity or succession from those works which most people would probably agree are in fact integrated cycles. . . . The constant, shifting tension between "collection" and integrated "cycle" one feels not only in Schumann's work but also in that of his contemporaries cannot be resolved on the tonal-harmonic plane alone.[2]

Nevertheless, I proposed a way to read *Dichterliebe* in terms of an "expanded but closed" methodology in which "organic structure [is regarded] as a balanced interaction of narrative and tonal progression."[3] This methodology, however, was merely adumbrated, certainly neither sketched nor demonstrated.

A few years later, Joseph Straus wrote in a similarly skeptical vein about the question of prolongation in atonal music. In a statement closely parallel to my claim that "Analytic methods based on procedures (or presumed ideals) of harmonic design and phrase structure in eighteenth-century instrumental music will not bear extension to multipart, cyclic vocal forms," Straus asserts that "Analytical observations based on incorrect assumptions about prolongation can lead to distorted and— in a strict sense—meaningless assertions about music."[4] His definition of tonal music is closely constrained to match Schenker's, and therefore he argues that the post-tonal middleground, under most circumstances, involves at best a "mimicry of the prolongational types of tonal music without their original significance," even as he grants the possibility that post-tonal music may "contain carefully organized large spans."[5] Precisely what "span" means in this context is left to conjecture. Thus, Straus's argument with respect to the middleground is similar to my argument with respect to the background, differences in the pertinent repertoire notwithstanding.

Straus's method of escape from this dilemma is to construct a binary opposition between the "prolongational" and the "associative." He establishes four conditions which must be satisfied in order for a pattern to be a true prolongation. These are: "A consistent, pitch-defined basis for determining relative structural weight, . . . a consistent hierarchy of consonant harmonies, . . . a consistent set of relationships

---

2. Ibid., 95–96.

3. Ibid., 97.

4. Ibid.," 104; Joseph N. Straus, "The Problem of Prolongation in Post-Tonal Music," *Journal of Music Theory* 31 (1987): 7–8.

5. Straus, "The Problem of Prolongation," 19, 17.

between tones of lesser and greater structural weight, . . . and a clear distinction between the vertical and horizontal dimensions."[6] Association, on the other hand, need not conform to such strict requirements (according to which "dissonant prolongation" is impossible). Analogously to my narrative controls, association is a loose, mostly undefined device of grouping which relies on "similarities in register, metrical placement, duration, dynamics, instrumentation, and so forth. These groupings may contain notes widely separated in time."[7]

Although the state of research at the time justified the pessimistic assessments made by Straus and myself, subsequent work has shown that the situation in our respective topic areas did not thereby reach a dead end. In 1988, Allen Forte demonstrated that, having begun with Straus's careful distinctions, one may nevertheless develop effective methods for analyzing post-tonal music in terms of a (non-Schenkerian) theory of structural levels (or "strata") which emphasizes the relations between "the large-scale horizontal dimension [and] the motivic structure of the music."[8] This notion of "linear analysis" was later reinterpreted and integrated with Forte's construct of pc-set genera and, more recently, with the transformational technology of David Lewin.[9]

Similarly, Patrick McCreless has accepted my limitation of the Schenkerian voice-leading model to individual, closed movements, as well as the equating of textual/narrative patterning with tonal design as a structural determinant, but he is nevertheless able to draw on autograph sources and other information to arrive at a convincing reading of Schumann's *Liederkreis*, op. 39, as a (tonally) unified song cycle. (In fact, the discussion covers both versions of the work, each of which has interesting cyclic features.) Although he is careful not to overstate his case, McCreless uses a familiar historical process as his main justification for arguing the possibility of a significant key plan (but not a harmonic/voice-leading structure) in a mid-nineteenth-century song cycle: European instrumental music gradually evolves from the Baroque suite and concerto, with their tableaux of affects, to "works such as those by Wagner, Bruckner [et al.], where complex tonal plans unfold over the course of a number of movements to create a single, coherent structure."[10] It is therefore reason-

6. Ibid., 2, 4–5.

7. Ibid., 21n.

8. Allen Forte, "New Approaches to Linear Analysis," *Journal of the American Musicological Society* 41 (1988): 315–48. The quotation is from p. 346.

9. Allen Forte, "Pitch-Class Set Genera and the Origin of Modern Harmonic Species," *Journal of Music Theory* 32 (1988): 187–270; "Concepts of Linearity in Schoenberg's Atonal Music: A Study of the Opus 15 Song Cycle," *Journal of Music Theory* 36 (1992): 285–382. For work which allies pc-set theory more closely with traditional Schenkerian analysis, see James Baker, "Schenkerian Analysis and Post-Tonal Music," in *Aspects of Schenkerian Theory*, ed. David Beach (New Haven and London: Yale University Press, 1983), 153–86; and "Voice Leading in Post-Tonal Music: Suggestions for Extending Schenker's Theory," *Music Analysis* 9 (1990): 177–200.

10. Patrick McCreless, "Song Order in the Song Cycle: Schumann's *Liederkreis*, Op. 39," *Music Analysis* 5 (1986): 10.

able to find the creation of the song cycle (Beethoven, Schubert) at the same historical moment as the birth of "organic relations" in multi-movement instrumental music.

Pertinent to my discussion below is McCreless's distinction between "ordered" and "unordered" processes, or more narrowly, the "processive" and the "cross-referential," which are essentially the same as Straus's "prolongational" and "associative." Of particular interest is the mechanism by which motivic cross-references can become processive: McCreless's example is the "familiar technique of nineteenth-century music, in which a chromatic note or chord occurs on the surface at the beginning of the piece, and then is later expanded into a fully-fledged tonicization."[11] Clearly, such points of contact between the individual movement and the cyclic design, between the motive and the harmonic/voice-leading structure, between a word and a note, must necessarily be the focus of attention in any tonally based theory of multi-movement structures.

Christopher Lewis argues much as McCreless does, but he assigns more importance to patterns of relations between text and key, and therefore to potential functional relationships between keys and large-scale tonal designs.[12] With respect to *Dichterliebe*, he is willing to go so far as to claim that "the textual structure . . . , articulated by events of the plot, by symbol, and by the sense of narrative time, is exactly matched by a tripartite tonal scheme, the idea behind each section of which is an actual progression in the usual harmonic sense of the term."[13] Lewis illustrates this scheme with a figure showing whole notes for the main keys of each song, functional labels, and a beam which connects the C♯ seventh chord in song 1 with the C♯/ D♭ tonality of the final song. The latter is in fact an instance of McCreless's mechanism of functional change: C♯ is motivic in song 1 but processive in song 16. The awkward element is the open beam, which forwards suspicion that even a tentative conflation of harmonic plan and motivic cross-reference will bring us well down the path toward rehabilitating the Schenkerian apparatus for use with multi-movement works.

Peter Kaminsky goes farther than Lewis, arguing that the early piano cycles may have established models which influenced Schumann's views on "principles of cyclic structure [achieved through] essentially musical means." Using McCreless's device of cross-reference, specifically "the repetition of motives, themes, and/or har-

---

11. Ibid., 9. McCreless uses the notion of harmonic-motivic cross-reference with especially fruitful results in reading works by Beethoven, Schubert, and Brahms in "Schenker and Chromatic Tonicization: A Reappraisal," in *Schenker Studies*, ed. Hedi Siegel (Cambridge: Cambridge University Press, 1990), 125–145. For his extensions of the idea to opera, see "Schenker and the Norns," in *Analyzing Opera*, ed. Carolyn Abbate and Roger Parker (Berkeley and Los Angeles: University of California Press, 1989), 276–97; and "Motive and Magic: A Referential Dyad in *Parsifal*," *Music Analysis* 9 (1990): 227–65.

12. Christopher Lewis, "Text, Time, and Tonic: Aspects of Patterning in the Romantic Cycle," *Intégral* 2 (1988): 37–73.

13. Ibid., 51.

monic progressions across movements," Kaminsky examines features of *Papillons*, *Carnaval*, and *Davidsbündlertänze*. Particularly for the latter, Kaminsky's analyses reveal a number of striking cross-references of harmonic/voice-leading patterns, but for *Carnaval* the simplicity and narrowly diatonic range of the key successions lead him to interpret them with a Schenkerian bass-line sketch, complete with a tonic prolongation consisting of a nested full functional cycle (I–ii–V–I).[14]

Despite the interpretive virtuosity shown by McCreless, Lewis, and Kaminsky, and despite the insights their demonstrations give us into questions of text/music relationships in song cycles and the patterns of Schumann's compositional development, the cause of a theory of tonal synthesis for multi-movement works has not been significantly advanced. All these authors beg the question whether it is indeed desirable that multi-movement patterns of key relation (and prolongation?) conform to the familiar rules for chord progressions. Kaminsky is on slightly more solid ground in that he is dealing with the keyboard cycles, which are grounded in historical instrumental cycles or sets, but he does not explain specifically how the structures found there are supposed to have influenced the song cycles.[15] Neither Lewis nor McCreless succeeds in defining the specific conditions which would allow inter-movement cross references to be interpreted in processive (that is, tonal-functional) terms. And none of the authors defines the level at which one may abandon the two-voice counterpoint of the *Ursatz* for more abstract bass-only backgrounds. The goal of this essay is to address at least some of these open questions.

We will begin with the mechanisms available in Schenkerian theory for the connection of independent musical units. Arthur Komar takes Schenker to task for failing to clarify this point in *Free Composition*, since the extension from single movement to cycle should presumably be both direct and obvious in a theory whose central tenet is organic synthesis.[16] Apparently this is another of those issues left unresolved because Schenker died before he could fully work out his theory of form. In the chapter as it stands, he briefly discusses two instances of inter-movement connection, but these are slow-fast pairs in a keyboard suite by Handel, and both slow movements are tonally incomplete (the suite follows the four-movement *sonata da chiesa* plan). Schenker is given pause by the mismatch between structural significance and length in the first pair ("the short Allegro would seem almost too brief to constitute a main

---

14. Peter Kaminsky, "Principles of Formal Structure in Schumann's Early Piano Cycles," *Music Theory Spectrum* 11 (1989): 207–25. The quotations are from pages 207 and 208 respectively. The graph referred to is Example 3 (212).

15. Lewis ("Text, Time, and Tonic," 40, 42) argues that key plans are essential to cycles because critics of the time routinely mention key relations in reviews, but that argument is hardly convincing in itself.

16. Arthur Komar, "The Music of Dichterliebe: The Whole and its Parts," in *Schumann: Dichterliebe*, ed. Arthur Komar (New York: W. W. Norton, 1971), 65.

movement"), but he decides that "the density of its voice-leading gives musical ears so much to hear that much time seems to elapse in the listening."[17]

As Schenker's example suggests, two movements or pieces may easily be linked to one another if the tonal structure of the first is open; that is, if it does not end in the primary key.[18] The fundamental structure of the second piece takes precedence because the closure of the fundamental structure is the primary indicator of artistic synthesis. Thus, a sequence of events occurs as a result of which the relative structural significance of the first piece is reinterpreted. During the course of the first piece, we assume from experience that its tonal structure will be closed (since this is true of most pieces in the traditional tonal repertoire), and we treat the deepest level of its tonal structure as a background (for sake of example, imagine $\hat{5}$ in E minor). When the piece ends without the correct tonal closure, its deepest level is tentatively reinterpreted as middleground, an impression confirmed when the second piece ends (thus, continuing the hypothetical example, if the second piece expresses an *Urlinie* from $\hat{3}$ in A minor, the $\hat{5}$ of E minor becomes a middleground incomplete neighbor to the $\hat{3}$ of A minor—and presumably somewhere mixture would have changed E minor to E major in order to smooth the harmonic transition). It is such processes of change in interpretation which I will call "background-middleground transfer": what is originally perceived to be a tonal background becomes the middleground, or, to put it another way, the material of the (initial and apparent) background is transferred to the middleground.

Perhaps the most familar instance of this phenomenon cited in the Schenker literature is the "Introduzione" which replaced the original second movement of Beethoven's "Waldstein" Sonata. David Beach has shown the mechanism by which this is to be interpreted (see Ex. 1).[19] An apparent *Urlinie* from $\hat{3}$ in F major moves toward an interruption on its dominant (with $\hat{2}$) with an intermediate applied dominant—as in Example 1a. But the dominant and its $\hat{2}$ are reached only at the beginning of the Rondo, where they are revealed as the tonic of C major and $\hat{5}$, the first tone of the Rondo's *Urlinie* (Ex. 1b). As a result, the truncated *Urlinie* of this second movement becomes a middleground element in the larger structure controlled by the *Ursatz* of the finale.

A similiar, also well-known instance occurs in Schumann's *Dichterliebe*, songs 1 and 2. The ambivalent first song, "Im wunderschönen Monat Mai," emphasizes the upper-voice tone C♯, but whether that C♯ is really $\hat{3}$ of A major or $\hat{5}$ of F♯ minor is

---

17. Heinrich Schenker, *Free Composition*, ed. and trans. Ernst Oster, 2 vols. (New York: Longman, 1979), 1:130.

18. The importance of closing key is addressed in connection with independent compositions by Harald Krebs, "Tonal and Formal Dualism in Chopin's Scherzo, Op. 31," *Music Theory Spectrum* 13 (1991): 48–60.

19. David Beach, "Beethoven, Piano Sonata Op. 53, Introduzione: A Schenkerian Analysis," in *Readings in Schenker Analysis and Other Approaches*, ed. Maury Yeston (New Haven and London: Yale University Press, 1977), 213–15 and Ex. 13.7.

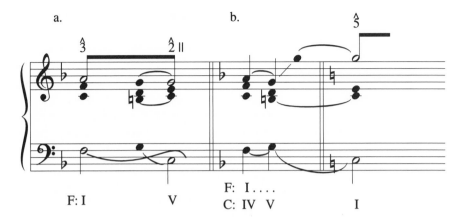

Example 1. Ludwig van Beethoven: "Waldstein" Sonata, II, III (after David Beach); a: expected fundamental structure for II (in F major); b: actual tonal structure for II, linked to III.

cause for debate.[20] In any case, the song ends on the dominant of F♯ minor, and the whole of the piece is readily heard as a middleground to the complete fundamental structure of song 2, "Aus meinen Thränen spriessen," despite the fact that no explicit connection between the songs is demanded by the composer (unlike Beethoven's *attacca subito*).

When both pieces or movements have closed fundamental structures, yet we wish to understand them as connected, the procedure involved is no more difficult. We may take as a model the Baroque dance pair or Classical minuet and trio. In these closely related schemata, each dance is closed, but the da capo subordinates the second to the first in performance. Therefore the fundamental structure of the trio belongs to the middleground. Examples of such readings in *Free Composition* include the minuet and trio which constitute the second movement of Mozart's Sonata in A Major, K. 331.[21] Properly, the first note of the minuet's fundamental line (C♯— that is, A: $\hat{3}$) and the second and third of the reprise ($\hat{2}$, $\hat{1}$) make up the *Urlinie*: the other notes which Schenker shows as "open" notes are first middleground elements, that is, the $\hat{4}$–$\hat{3}$ in the neighbor-note figure $\hat{3}$–$\hat{4}$–$\hat{3}$ (the $\hat{4}$ is the controlling structural tone in the trio, from which tone runs a middleground "fundamental line" of the octave spanning the entire trio). Even if the trio's own "*Urlinie*" had run from, say, F♯ (D: $\hat{3}$), the fundamental structure of the minuet would take precedence, and the

20. See my "Organic Structure and The Song Cycle," 103–04.

21. Schenker, *Free Composition*, 2:Fig. 35,1; see also Fig. 20,4. Similar examples (pieces with trios, as indicated by Schenker) are: Fig. 30, a (Chopin, Mazurka in A♭ Major, op. 17, no. 3); Fig. 40,1 (Chopin, Polonaise in A Major, op. 40, no. 1); Fig. 40,6 (Beethoven, Piano Sonata in A♭ Major, op. 26, III); Fig. 76,5 (Chopin, Mazurka in B♭ Major, op. 17, no. 1).

deepest-lying structural tone of the trio would still be D (in that case, the final tone of its fundamental line).

In those situations where the hierarchy of the musical components is not obvious (or if we choose to withhold judgment about such potential hierarchies), the background-middleground transfer can still be used as a way to connect song pairs or to "chain" groups of songs in a series. For example, in *Dichterliebe*, since songs 1 and 2 insist on the listener's construction of a single tonal structure, the immediate impression at the beginning of the third song might very well be that it, too, belongs to the middleground. See the box graphic in Example 2, which depicts this situation with closed notes and the query "$\hat{4}$?" The mistaken impression is eventually corrected: by the end of the song we know it is a closed tonal structure with an *Urlinie* from $\hat{8}$. Thus, in the box graphic an arrow points from the closed notes to the open notes d^1 and d^2, or D: $\hat{8}$ over I, the beginning of the *Ursatz* for song 3.[22] Note, incidentally, that the "direction" of the background-middleground transfer is reversed when it is used for such "chaining" strategies. The background of song 1 becomes middleground once we recognize the stable tonal structure of song 2, but the potential middleground of song 3 becomes background once we accept that song as a closed structure of equal stature with song 2.

The upper-voice connections between songs 2 and 3 were easily made, but between songs 3 and 4 the task is slightly more difficult, since the latter moves from b^1 (G: $\hat{3}$). The best linkage is to a^1 (D: $\hat{5}$), the division of song 3's octave line; see Example 3, which shows the middleground-to-background exchange in another box graphic.[23] The voice part holds a motive which anticipates this relationship: its final three notes are $b^1-a^1-d^1$, which gesture combines the closure of the octave line ($d^1 = \hat{1}$) with boundary play expressing the melodic link between songs 3 and 4 (b^1-a^1). The fourth song, as it happens, repeats this gesture in the form of a later middleground interruption in its opening phrase (or b^1-a^1 as G: $\hat{3}-\hat{2}$ over I–V).

Given such a "chaining" capability, the background-middleground transfer may be applied to entire collections or sets, where it models an aural process of grouping (under a Schenkerian mode of hearing) rather than a true fundamental structure as envisioned by the composer. For example, the *Valses sentimentales*, op. 50 (D. 779), obviously cannot constitute a cycle in the sense of the standard five- or six-waltz cycle established near the end of Schubert's lifetime by Josef Lanner. Indeed, the thirty-four waltzes of D. 779 can be understood to form at least two sets following the conventions of functional dance music in early nineteenth-century Vienna.[24] The

---

22. This analysis of song 3 is based on an analysis by Schenker as given by Komar in "The Music of Dichterliebe," 107–08.

23. The background of song 4 is based on Schenker's analysis in *Free Composition*, 2:Fig. 152,1.

24. Tilden A. Russell discusses the performance practices in Viennese *Redouten* (balls) in his "Minuet, Scherzando, and Scherzo: The Dance Movement in Transition, 1781–1825" (Ph.D. diss., University of North Carolina, 1983), 59–60. On the question of authenticity of

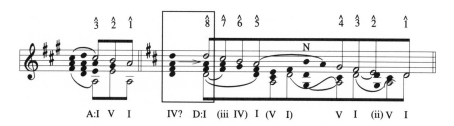

Example 2. Robert Schumann: *Dichterliebe,* songs II, III, fundamental structures and background-middleground transfer.

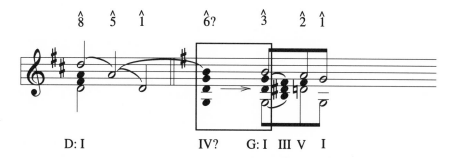

Example 3. Schumann: *Dichterliebe,* songs III, IV, background-middleground transfer.

first forty waltz sets of Lanner—any or all of which Schubert might well have heard[25] —average five to six waltzes per set; a very few have introductions, and most but not all have codas of varying length (codas in Lanner's earlier waltz sets tend to be shorter). The key schemes of most sets are closed; in most instances, the final waltz and the coda are in the main key. Key relations are close—the majority of waltzes are in the home key, with diversions normally restricted to dominant or subdominant. A typical example is Lanner's opus 34 (*Ankunfts-Walzer*), whose six waltzes are laid out in the key scheme E, E, A, E, B, E (all major keys). When performed in concert, the cycles were usually played straight through, but when used for dancing, the individual waltzes were grouped and repeated in a dance/trio or even rondeau fashion:[26] the dance sets of Hummel, for instance—many of which were intended for use in the Apollo-Saal, one of the great Viennese dance halls—always include trios, often several. Hummel's sets, all of which were published before 1820, also employ more

the groupings in Schubert's dance sets, see David Brodbeck, "Dance Music as High Art: Schubert's Twelve Ländler," in *Schubert: Critical and Analytical Studies,* ed. Walter Frisch (Lincoln: University of Nebraska Press, 1986), 32, 37, 45n.

25. Paul Nettl, *The Story of Dance Music* (New York: Philosophical Library, 1947), 265.

26. These practices are echoed in the recurrent strains characteristic of the waltzes of Chopin—who heard the orchestra of Johann Strauss Sr. in Vienna.

adventurous key relations and often do not end in the key in which they began. For example, the Six German Dances, op. 29 (1809), all with trios in the same key, use the major-key scheme C, F, D, B♭, E♭, G.[27]

On these terms, the *Valses sentimentales* might be speculatively partitioned as follows: Collection 1: a sequence of dances with trios mostly in the same key: nos. 1–2 (C), 3–4 (G), 5–7 (B♭), 8–9 (D), 10–11 (G), 12–14 (D-A-D), 15 (isolated) (F), 16–17 (C); Collection 2: a sequence of dances mostly with two trios: 18–20 (A♭), 21–23 (E♭), 24–26 (doubtful if these are to be grouped: B♭, G, C), 27–29 (E♭), 30–32 (C); and a final dance with trio (A♭). Note that both of these hypothetical plans more nearly resemble Hummel's collections than they do Lanner's published waltz sets, which fact tends to support the generally accepted view that Schubert's dance sets are not concert pieces but functional music intended for dancing.

If we allow the grouping of numbers 12–14 as a dance (12) with two trios (13, 14), the design works as outlined in Example 4. In this context, the familiar Waltz in A Major (no. 13) expresses a prolongation of an interruption on e^2, or $\hat{2}$ of D major, a reading which resonates with—though it flips the structural priorities of—a statement by Carl Schachter as he seeks to explain the prominence of $\hat{5}$ in the A-major waltz:

> A curious feature of the upper line is its beginning on [f♯²] . . . A glance at the Waltz that precedes this one helps to explain: . . . Op. 50, no. 12 is in D major with [f♯²] as its most prominent melodic tone. The [f♯²] forms a link between the two Waltzes; such links occur fairly often in a chain of short pieces.[28]

The background-middleground transfers that would occur between nos. 10 and 12 (recall that no. 11 would act as a trio to no. 10) and between nos. 12 and 15 follow different models altogether. In the first instance, a fundamental line from $\hat{5}$ in G major closes on g^2; the subsequent $f♯^2$ (beginning no. 12) would first be taken as a middleground leading tone (G: $\hat{7}$) before being reinterpreted as D: $\hat{3}$. The move from D major to F major between nos. 12 and 15 is a bit more complicated: Initially, F (as D: $\hat{3}$) would undergo mixture (the tone F♮² is heard in the first measure of no. 15), but subsequently this would have to be understood as an inner voice as it becomes clear that the fundamental line moves from a^2 (= F: $\hat{3}$).

As the preceding discussion of dance collections should have made clear, the background-middleground transfer is no more than a mechanism which reflects in terms of linear-harmonic structure the perceptual process of linking that a person would employ in a Schenkerian mode of hearing. Thus, the background-middleground transfer cannot help us in deciding whether a work is an integrated

---

27. The piano arrangements of these dances have been reprinted in Johann Nepomuk Hummel, *Dances for Piano Solo; Music for Piano Four-Hands and Two Pianos*, ed. Joel Sachs (New York: Garland, 1989).

28. Carl Schachter, "Rhythm and Linear Analysis," *Music Forum* 5 (1980): 223.

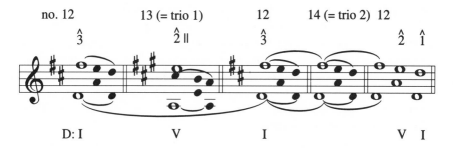

Example 4. Franz Schubert: *Valses sentimentales,* nos. 12–14 (read as a waltz with two trios), fundamental structure.

cycle, and, if so, what kinds of hierarchies may be involved. No claims are made about the stylistic and other musico-aesthetic judgments that would influence one's decision to regard movements or pieces as connected (no claims, that is, other than the obvious ones of sensitivity to historical context and of adherence to what might be called musical common sense).

In particular, the background-middleground transfer does not address the question of whether "connection" or "contrast" is the real aesthetic goal in joining movements. It is entirely possible that some of the inter-movement links which occur in works throughout the period of traditional tonality are designed not to merge, but to contrast. By "artificially" drawing together essentially separate, equal movements of differing character, tempo, and material, by forcing the performer to connect where he or she might otherwise take a considerable pause, the composer insures maximum dramatic impact. Beethoven's "Emperor" Concerto, to cite one famous example, has a mysterious "tag" which connects the slow second movement to the rapid finale. By demanding this connection, Beethoven prevents the performers from stopping, perhaps tuning again, wiping their brows, adjusting their seats, and so on—in other words, from constructing a thick "frame," to use Edward T. Cone's term, about the second movement, thus disarming any aural connections between it and the finale.[29] But the effect in this case is not to create a single enormous structure; it is to generate the greatest possible contrast between two essentially separate structures through contrast of tempo (*adagio un poco mosso* versus *allegro ma non troppo*), key (B major versus E♭ major), and material (long spun-out melodic lines, richly harmonized, versus a sharply accentuated, short-breathed rondo theme emphasizing arpeggiations).

As the background/middleground transfer by itself will not resolve questions of tonal design in cyclic and other multi-movement works, we must consider other possible tools, in particular any which would allow us to incorporate McCreless's

---

29. Edward T. Cone, *Musical Form and Musical Performance* (New York: W. W. Norton, 1968), 16.

"cross-reference" and Straus's "association." To begin this task, let us further constrain the notions connected to "cycle" and "set" by mapping them out as terms in a semiotic square or "square of logical oppositions" as the semiotician A. J. Greimas has revived and exploited that ancient device.[30] The initial term in Figure 1 is the traditionally autonomous, tonally closed musical composition, such as Chopin's E-Major Scherzo, op. 54. To the right we set an opposing term, the cycle, or a multi-movement composition whose parts are connected by conventional schemata (as in the symphony), by narrative (as in the song cycle), or by some other device. Examples from Beethoven symphonies to Lanner's *Steyrische Tänze* and Schumann's *Dichterliebe* would be placed here. For my purpose, it is irrelevant if the cycle is tonally closed—it is the transcendence of the bounds of the individual work which sets the cycle in opposition with the initial term, which emphasizes the necessity of closure in all its important structural aspects. "Cycle" is not the logical contrary of "autonomous individual composition": that category is represented at the lower right of the figure as "not-autonomous" and "not-[tonally]-closed." Here we would refer the several forms of recitative, the "Introduzione" of the "Waldstein" Sonata, the German melodrama, and melodramatic passages and cues for stage and cinema.[31] Finally, the lower left corner contains the logical negation of "cycle," or "not-cycle," that is, a set or collection, which lacks a significant (non-arbitrary) thread connecting the parts. Most, perhaps all, of the Hummel and Schubert dance sets belong here, as do song collections that are not cyclic.

Following Fredric Jameson, we may use the semiotic square not only to define terms, but also to explore the dialectical process that is set into play by the resulting oppositions. In other words, the ability of the semiotic square "to articulate the workings of binary oppositions" also permits it "to model ideological closure"; "a dialectical reevaluation . . . intervenes, however, at the moment this entire system of ideological closure is taken as the symptomatic projection of something quite different, namely of social contradiction."[32] This "reevaluation" is accomplished by examining

---

30. A. J. Greimas and F. Rastier, "The Interaction of Semiotic Constraints," *Yale French Studies* 41 (1968): 86–105. My specific use of it here, with the combined terms, is indebted to Fredric Jameson; see his *The Political Unconscious: Narrative as a Socially Symbolic Act* (Ithaca: Cornell University Press, 1981), 46–49, 82–83, 253–57, 275–77. See also the comparison between the agendas of Greimas and Schenker in Richard Littlefield and David Neumeyer, "Rewriting Schenker: Narrative—History—Ideology," *Music Theory Spectrum* 14 (1992): 49.

31. By "German melodrama," I mean the stage genre which was in fact initiated by Jean-Jacques Rousseau in *Pygmalion* but which was especially associated with German composers, such as Georg Benda (*Ariadne auf Naxos, Medea, Pygmalion*), and to which Mozart, Beethoven, and Schubert also contributed. By "melodramatic passages and cues," I mean the conventional music written for entrances and exits, pantomimes, action scenes, and so forth in the nineteenth-century stage melodrama and later transferred to music for cinema. See my "Melodrama as a Compositional Resource in Early Hollywood Sound Cinema," *Current Musicology* 57 (1995): 66–79.

32. Jameson, *The Political Unconscious*, 83.

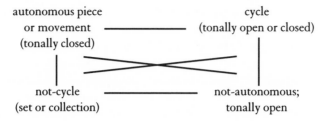

Figure 1. Diagram of a binary opposition (autonomous work versus cycle) with logical contraries.

the syntheses of adjacent terms in the square. The conflict between the Romantics' urge toward "organic" unity, represented here by the autonomous work, and the inherited model of the eighteenth-century sonata cycle, with its series of affect "tableaux," finds a resolution—a synthesis of the terms—already in works such as Beethoven's *An die ferne Geliebte*, Schubert's "Wanderer" Fantasy (whose cyclic theme takes on the qualities of a lonely Romantic poet wandering through a series of emotional or affective situations), and Berlioz' *Symphonie fantastique* (with its narrative program and an *idée fixe* which certainly represents a specific individual). Jonathan Dunsby's notion of the "multi-piece" in Brahms may be subsumed under this synthesis as well, as could Charles Rosen's notion of a universalized sonata principle, and therefore compositions such as Mozart's later operas, in which the composer attempts an integration at the level of compositional materials that is uncharacteristic of the eighteenth-century number opera, whether *seria* or *buffa*.[33]

The combinations of terms in the square can show more, however. Just as the act of defining a concept like that of the autonomous work necessarily generates its logical negation, the conflict between the aesthetic ideal of organic unity and the inherited cyclic schemata provoked other oppositions whose syntheses found expression in nineteenth-century music. Moving clockwise about Figure 1, we can see in the synthesis of the cycle and the "not-autonomous" work the impulse toward "endless melody"—that is, the blurring of distinctions between components of the number opera for the sake of better dramatic integration. Another quite different genre to be included here are the published (or improvised) capriccios and fantasias produced by the piano virtuosi in Paris and Vienna during the earlier part of the century. Liszt's Sonata in B Minor, which might at first seem to be the "ideal" synthesis of the cycle and the autonomous movement, in fact should be placed here as well, because the conventional designs of the individual movements have been so compromised that they have lost any serious claim to autonomy. Among later reper-

---

33. Jonathan Dunsby, "The Multi-Piece in Brahms: *Fantasien*, Op. 116," in Robert Pascall, ed., *Brahms: Biographical, Documentary, and Analytical Studies* (Cambridge: Cambridge University Press, 1983), 167–89; Charles Rosen, *The Classical Style: Haydn, Mozart, Beethoven* (New York: W.W. Norton, 1972), 302.

toires, the longer symphonic poems of Richard Strauss may be referred here, too, as can those among Max Steiner's film scores which consist primarily or entirely of melodramatic cues tied together by a leitmotivic network (his music for Bette Davis films such as *Dark Victory* [1939] or *Now, Voyager* [1942] fits this description well).

The synthesis of the two negations, not-cycle (collection) and not-autonomous, represents not only minor repertoires in the nineteenth century, such as the potpourri (a genre of which Johann Strauss Sr. was quite fond), but also the pastiche scores compiled for stage melodramas and later for silent-film performances—as well as some sound films (particularly serials). Finally, the combination of the autonomous work and the (arbitrary) collection plainly reflects the practices of nineteenth-century concert programs and recitals, with their free mingling of arias, rondos, sonatas, improvised variations, and even choruses.

Thus we must recognize that the aesthetic and compositional issues Schumann faced in writing the piano and song cycles which are most often discussed in the literature were only a subset of the potential issues before him, resolutions for which may be represented in his oeuvre. If, for example, the sonata-like construction of *Faschingsschwank aus Wien* (1839) barely moves beyond the sonata-cycle schema by virtue of its title and sub-title (the latter is *Phantasiebilder*), *Kreisleriana* (1838) barely attempts, by the same means, a synthesis of collection and (organically unified) autonomous work. But the *Davidsbündlertänze* (also 1838), mainly through ingenious recurrences of harmonic/voice-leading progressions, as Peter Kaminsky has shown, succeed in the same synthesis at which *Kreisleriana* fails.[34] *Carnaval* (1835), in this sense, is the logical negation of the *Davidsbündlertänze* in that it combines aspects of cyclic and not-autonomous components. Cyclic in the same sense as the previously mentioned works, by virtue of its title (but also because of the referential set A.S.C.H.), *Carnaval* contains several movements which are tonally open ("Eusebius," "Florestan," "Lettres dansantes," "Pause") or which are musically incomplete, either because they are too short ("Chopin," "Aveu"), because they have unusual and inconclusive ending gestures ("Arlequin," "Reconnaissance"), or because they are linked to an adjacent movement ("Replique," "Paganini," "Pause"). *Papillons* (1831) attempts the same synthesis in a different way, by taking the familiar schema of the waltz cycle as the frame (introduction and no. 1; extended coda in which no. 1 is quoted) and reinforcing it in a minimal fashion (no. 8 is a German dance; all numbers except the second are in triple meter), Schumann inserts into that frame an apparently miscellaneous collection of short character pieces. The result is an oddly schizophrenic work—a set prevented from being a wholly arbitrary collection by the waltz-cycle frame.[35]

Thus, the character of nineteenth-century composers' solutions to the problem of the individual movement and multi-movement cycle varies widely, and, just as the aesthetic agendas differ, it is reasonable to suppose that the significance of

---

34. Kaminsky, "Principles," 216–24.

35. The remaining combination—set and not-autonomous—is not represented in Schumann's piano or solo vocal works.

factors such as tonal design may differ. In other words, to repeat my earlier skeptical arguments, the mere fact that a multi-movement composition begins and ends in the same key signifies nothing in itself about the structural weight of key plans and certainly implies nothing about overarching harmonic/voice-leading structures. One must be able to position the composition at hand in relation to the single-tonality autonomous work.

In order to consider more closely how such positioning might affect Schenkerian theory, we may separate the harmonic and generic aspects of the binary opposition that we have been considering and construct a new semiotic square (see Fig. 2). Here the initial term is "tonal," by which I mean the tonal design of traditional European music, a teleological model with a fixed hierarchical system of harmonic relationships here construed as consistent with Schenker's theory (or controlled by a harmonic/voice-leading structure—an *Ursatz*—in a system of structural levels). The theory's treatment of other aspects—form, register, motive, and so forth—is also assumed. The opposing term is Straus's "associative": that is, relationships established outside of—and functioning independently of—the harmonic/voice-leading structure of the traditional tonal system, including motivic references, poem or libretto design, private symbols, and so on. "Associative" in this sense is synonymous with McCreless's "cross-references" and consequently is implicated in his binary pair "systemic/extra-systemic," into the latter term of which he folds "cross-references" as part of a defense of Schenker against Leo Treitler's criticisms.[36] Additionally, the binary pair "tonal/associative" is close to Leonard B. Meyer's "primary and secondary parameters," the former being syntactic, the latter statistical (that is, organized by patterns of increase/decrease).[37]

The logical negations needed to complete the semiotic square in Figure 2 are "not-tonal," or atonal in the common sense of the term, and "not-associative," which might be taken to mean music whose design elements are unusually open and direct (as in minimalist compositions) or music whose relationships are established in a strict teleology, without consistent or meaningful hierarchic patterning (as might happen in the key successions of eighteenth-century number operas or collections of dances, for example).

Since "associative" includes "motivic," the ideal goal of a pragmatic Schenkerian analysis—to integrate a reading of the tonal structure with hidden repetition, or motivic design at different structural levels—is itself the ideal combination of the initial binary terms, "tonal" and "associative." The commonly held view about compositional evolution from tonality to atonality could also be understood as charting a path from the first term to the second. Leonard Meyer shares this view, as he assumes that a gradual process of "'foregrounding' of syntactical relationships" resulted in harmony ceding its form-creating powers to motivic unity and to the sec-

---

36. McCreless, "Chromatic Tonicization," 126–27.

37. Leonard B. Meyer, *Style and Music: Theory, History, and Ideology* (Philadelphia: University of Pennsylvania Press, 1989), 14–16, 209.

ondary parameters, including tempo, dynamics, and timbre. However, he claims that this process began earlier than is generally believed and was more drastic in its suppression of the significance of harmonic hierarchy.[38] In that sense, then, his views are not compatible with Figure 2.

The term "not-tonal," or "atonal," assumes a system of organization comparable and parallel to traditional tonality, a level of design which to date has been best explicated through the help of pitch-class set theory and the transformational technology of David Lewin. Thus, the combination of the terms "not-tonal" and "associative" charts Allen Forte's cultural positioning of "atonal" as a force equal to and opposing tonality and as ideally merging motivic and systemic, or cross-referential and pitch aspects. The remaining combinations (tonal/not-associative and not-associative/not-tonal) simply model the (arbitrary) aspects of tonal design in potpourris, pastiche scores, or concert programs—and possible listener responses to such designs.

Narrowing the range of discussion again to tonal music, we can rewrite the square once more, allowing the less specific "ordered key relations" to stand in for "tonality" (Fig. 3). The reason for this change is to permit bass-line sketches or other ways of representing patterns of harmonic design without invoking questions of upper-voice prolongations or counterpoint. The distinction I am making between "ordered key relations" and "tonality" is essentially the same as the one made by David Beach between "tonal design" ("the layout of keys in the course of a composition") and "tonal structure," or harmonic/voice-leading structure.[39] For multi-movement compositions, this distinction is necessary because no one has demonstrated convincingly that motivic cross-references occurring beyond the range of the tonally autonomous individual movement do in fact have the same status as motives embedded in the harmonic/voice-leading structure within such movements. The term "ordered key relations" applies to Kaminsky's bass-line sketch for *Carnaval*, Arthur Komar's key scheme for *Dichterliebe*, and other ways of representing key relations without making any claims about a relationship to tonal structure (in Beach's sense). In the rewritten square of Figure 3, then, the opposing term (which was "associative" in the earlier diagram) becomes the logic of all "non-tonal" elements, whether that logic be a network of motivic cross-references independent of tonal structure or the design constraints imposed by conventional form schemata, poem, libretto, or film scene.[40] To the extent that tonal plans are invoked, this juxtaposition is also

38. Meyer, *Style and Music*, 208–11, 300–03, 330. As radical proponents of motivic unity, the Schoenberg-Réti school of analysts also hold views which are not compatible with Figure 2—unless of course one reinterpreted "tonal" to mean "developing variation in a major/minor-key context." A representative analysis of a cyclic work (Schumann's Third Symphony) from a Schoenberg-Réti stance may be found in David Epstein, *Beyond Orpheus: Studies in Musical Structure* (Cambridge: MIT Press, 1979), 148–57.

39. David Beach, "Schubert's Experiments with Sonata Form: Formal-Tonal Design versus Underlying Structure," *Music Theory Spectrum* 15 (1993): 3.

40. For the present purpose, this is enough, and I leave it to the reader to explore the logical negations and the possibilities that arise from the combination of terms.

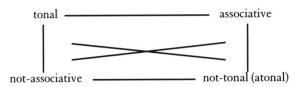

Figure 2. Diagram of a binary opposition (tonal versus associative) with logical contraries.

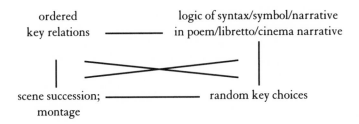

Figure 3. Diagram of a binary opposition (ordered key relations versus logic of "non-musical" components) with logical contraries.

consistent with Beach's proposal, in which a "traditional hierarchical notion of form" is opposed to the harmonic/voice-leading structure.

However, the extension of the design/structure opposition to multi-movement compositions introduces another level (literally) to the problem. Ordered key relations (which are an aspect of tonal design in the autonomous work) cannot have the same status for the multi-movement composition as did the harmonic/voice-leading structure for the individual movement. Therefore, the separation of the motivic from the structural (or cross-references from harmonic/voice-leading structure) and, subsequently, of ordered key relations from harmonic/voice-leading structure (or harmonic design from the *Ursatz*) has implications for the Schenkerian theory of structural levels. Specifically, it suggests that the domain of the *Ursatz* is limited, and that in multi-movement works large-scale aspects of design must necessarily take precedence in a structure/design hierarchy. Taking the optimistic position that organic synthesis may be found at these higher levels, too, I propose in Figure 4 a revised scheme of structural levels. Here, "background" (at the upper left) is represented by the broadest design elements of a multi-movement composition, whether that be a conventional form schema, opera libretto, or the loose narrative of a song cycle. "Middleground" is then a hierarchical series of design levels interacting with a variety of associational types. At some (for now undefined, but probably varying) point in this series of levels, the *Ursatz* and first middleground level of tonal structure for individual movements would form a connection to the design hierarchy and the Schenkerian mode of hearing would take over (the latter is represented by the bracketed series of levels at the lower right of Fig. 4).

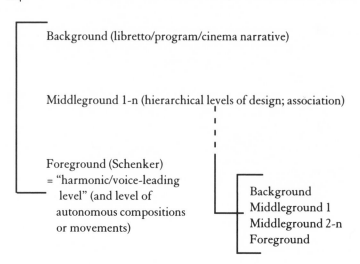

Figure 4. Diagram of a hierarchical model of design/structure in a "texted" work.

Given this design hierarchy, inter-movement cross references would never be interpreted in "processive" (that is, tonal) terms. In general, I believe that result to be entirely appropriate—the notion of a vast *Ursatz* reaching across the entirety of the "Waldstein" Sonata, for example, really is too grotesque to contemplate. Nevertheless, there can be exceptions. The first several songs of *Dichterliebe*, for example, are quite short, and we know, furthermore, that Schumann wrote them all on the same day, so that it might not be unreasonable to consider them as a closed group with a single controlling fundamental structure, if only the problem of the main key could be resolved.[41] (It is symptomatic of the difficulties involved that the tonal design schemes devised by Komar and Lewis for this cycle are based on completely different premises and parse the cycle in different ways.)

Except for the much more cautious position taken with regard to tonal design and structure, nothing in Figure 4 contradicts McCreless's or Lewis's claims about the song cycle.[42] Lewis's own Figure 1, for example, distinguishes between poetry and music, which would be situated as background and middle/foreground in my Figure 4. He divides his "poetry" heading into two subheadings, the poem's meaning and the composer's reading of it, which pairing constitutes a background/middleground 1 succession in my Figure 4. And so on. Only in the unusual significance he grants to coherent key-relation schemes as evidence that a set of songs is a cycle, and in his willingness to blur the edges of the distinction between tonal design

---

41. David Loeb explores a potentially parallel situation in four adjacent movements of Bach's St. John Passion in "Dual-Key Movements," in *Schenker Studies*, 76–78.

42. McCreless makes statements that appear directly to contradict mine here, but the contradiction disappears when one realizes that he is talking about tonal design, not tonal structure ("Song Order," 7–8).

(as represented in key relations) and harmonic/voice-leading structure, does Lewis's view differ significantly from my own.[43]

The conspicuous absence of mention, to this point in the present essay, of the literature on tonal relations in opera may now be remedied. The tension between interpretive priorities—tonal design versus a vaguely defined contextuality or intertextuality—is at the forefront in Carolyn Abbate's and Roger Parker's introduction to *Analyzing Opera*, though it is somewhat less apparent in the actual essays themselves.[44] The authors resolve this tension to their satisfaction by denigrating tonal readings and praising an "inevitable eclecticism in analyzing opera." In an anti-positivist move that now, only ten years later, seems rather dated, they demonize tonal analysis for its alleged anti-contextuality and false scientism and then valorize its opposites: "If [analyzing opera] shows us how to recognize [the imperfect, the ambiguous, the illogical], perhaps it can also teach us to face them without uneasiness or fear."[45]

It would seem more productive—and would represent recent literature more accurately—to think in terms of a model in which a historically (that is, contextually) contingent awareness influences the interaction of the two foreground/middleground/background structures in Figure 4. The two binaries, tonal/associative and "full narrative"/"tableau-montage" (the latter being analogous to structure/design in representing degrees of integration) may be understood as continua, or combinations of terms emphasizing the path or motion between a term and its opposite, as was discussed above in connection with Figure 2. As these continua interact, like freely moving axes within a field, the character of the analytic enterprise changes. The extreme cases—where the endpoints of the continua meet—are, on the one hand, a pastiche of scenes with arbitrary key successions (perhaps a vaudeville or a potpourri involving programmatic elements such as battle codas), and, on the other, a libretto written by the composer, who also created a fully integrated tonal structure. (Whether the later operas of Wagner fit the second instance is still a matter for debate.) As the continua change positions, the nature of the relations between tonal and narrative design changes with them. For example, Mozart's allusions to instrumental music in the tonal plans of finales or his habit of beginning and ending an opera in the same key are mostly associative; thus tonal structure is situated at a relatively low level of the overall design, exactly as Figure 4 has it. Much the same could be said of Beethoven's *Fidelio* or the operas of Weber. Richard Strauss, to cite a quite different case in a different era, seems to have linked his readings of libretti

---

43. Lewis, "Text, Time, and Tonic," 40–42 and *passim*.

44. Carolyn Abbate and Roger Parker, "Introduction: On Analyzing Opera," in *Analyzing Opera*, 1–24.

45. Abbate and Parker, "Introduction," 23, 24. A critic who actually does work out the "anti-unity" argument is Alan Street in "Superior Myths, Dogmatic Allegories: The Resistance to Musical Unity," *Music Analysis* 8 (1989): 77–123.

with the formation of networks of tonal associations, which in turn had the capacity to dictate tonal design.[46]

Thus, for Strauss, tonal design—and, potentially, tonal structure—moves up the hierarchical levels of design (Fig. 4, at the left) perhaps as far as its first middleground, which implicates tonality very deeply in all aspects of the opera. Rather than vilifying tonal analysis of opera, then, it would seem a more useful strategy to encourage interpretation that is sensitive to the changing relationships of tonality, counterpoint, and libretto—keeping in mind, of course, that it is usually easier to locate patterns of tonal relations than it is to prove that they are significant.[47]

Finally, the theoretical constructs offered here have been intended to continue the conversation begun several years ago by Allen Forte, a conversation centered on what he called "the advantages as well as the shortcomings of linear approaches to the study of music."[48] Where Forte was concerned with the interplay between prolongational structures, motivic design, and tonal or non-tonal referential collections, and David Beach has more recently been occupied with righting the balance between formal/tonal design and tonal structure, I have here proposed ways to clarify the conceptual framework that can guide interpretative projects involving close musical-technical criticism of multi-movement compositions. In general, my object has been the same as it was nearly fifteen years ago—to sound a note of caution while at the same time suggesting ways in which the work can proceed.

---

46. See Bryan Gilliam, "Strauss's Preliminary Opera Sketches: Thematic Fragments and Symphonic Continuity," *Nineteenth-Century Music* 9 (1986): 176–88; Gilliam, *Richard Strauss's Elektra* (New York: Oxford University Press, 1991), 68–69. Strauss was Max Steiner's godfather and a close friend of the Steiner family; he may very possibly have influenced Steiner sometimes to create key schemes of the sort I explore tentatively in "Film Music Analysis and Pedagogy," *Indiana Theory Review* 11 (1990): 20–23.

47. Among essays which exemplify or approach this attitude, I would cite McCreless, "Schenker and the Norns"; Warren Darcy, "The Metaphysics of Annihilation: Wagner, Schopenhauer, and the Ending of the *Ring*," *Music Theory Spectrum* 16 (1994): 1–40; and Rudy T. Marcozzi, "The Interaction of Large-Scale Harmonic and Dramatic Structure in the Verdi Operas Adapted from Shakespeare" (Ph.D. diss., Indiana University, 1992). Clearly, this notion of a contextual analysis is also my point of contact with the work of Kevin Korsyn—see, for example, his "Towards a New Poetics of Musical Influence," *Music Analysis* 10 (1991): 3–72.

48. Forte, "New Approaches to Linear Analysis," 315.

Tonal/Atonal: Cognitive Strategies for Recognizing Transposed Melodies

Elizabeth West Marvin

Introduction

One of the beauties inherent in musical structure is the potential for recasting segments of pitches (realized musically as melodies or successions of chords) in new harmonic, formal, or tonal contexts. Recognition of melodic transposition—a transformation that generally preserves rhythm, contour, and interval size—is a crucial element in perceiving formal structure in musical compositions. Perception of the sonata form's structural design, for example, hinges upon the listener's recognition that material in the recapitulation is a transposed replication of music introduced previously in the exposition. Transformations that preserve a melody's contour and rhythmic profile, but alter interval size are also common to tonal forms. The sonata's development section, for instance, may feature sequential treatment of melodic fragments from the exposition without maintaining interval-for-interval transpositional equivalence.

Perception of structural coherence in music written in what is commonly called the "atonal" idiom (without a hierarchical relationship of pitches and harmonies to a stable tonal center) also relies upon the listener's recognition of transposed melodies, motives, or chords. In fact, many analysts of this repertoire, following principles set forth in Allen Forte's *The Structure of Atonal Music*,[1] would argue that other opera-

The author wishes to acknowledge the University of Rochester for its support in the form of a Bridging Fellowship for cross-disciplinary research in the psychology department during the spring semester of 1993. In particular, I wish to thank Thomas G. Bever, who was instrumental in guiding this project through the analysis of data and the interpretation of results; his work on sex differences in spatial navigation inspired several follow-up experiments of my own. In addition, I want to acknowledge the input of John Trueswell, who co-taught the psychology course at the University of Rochester for which this experiment was originally designed.

1. Allen Forte, *The Structure of Atonal Music* (New Haven and London: Yale University Press, 1973).

tions upon melodic segments and unordered pitch-class sets provide structure in this music as well, though the extent to which these transformations may be perceived by listeners remains a topic for empirical investigation.[2]

Melodic transformations that do not maintain interval-for-interval transpositional equivalence, yet preserve contour, occur in atonal music just as they do in tonal compositions. Recent theories developed for the analysis of contour, particularly in their formulation by Robert Morris,[3] demonstrate that contour equivalence also plays a structural role in atonal composition. Analyses of Arnold Schoenberg's and Anton Webern's music by Michael Friedmann, Elizabeth West Marvin, and Paul Laprade likewise illustrate the function of contour in structuring atonal works.[4] The implicit assumption in both tonal and atonal analyses is that melodies that have invariant contours, but differ with respect to their scale-degree or set-class identity, will be recognized by listeners not as replications, but as variants of the original. Yet empirical support for this statement has until now been far from clear, since early research in this area suggested that listeners were unable to discriminate between exact transpositions and same-contour variants.

In a series of music-cognitive experiments dating from the 1970s to the present, several investigators—notably W. Jay Dowling, Lola Cuddy, and their collaborators—tested listeners' abilities to distinguish between an exact repetition and a transformation of a melody in tonal and atonal contexts. At the root of these experiments

---

2. At least one textbook, Michael Friedmann's *Ear Training for Twentieth-Century Music* (New Haven and London: Yale University Press, 1990), is devoted to teaching musicians to hear transformations upon pitch-class sets or ordered segments. Music-cognitive experiments that systematically explore the perceptual issues involved in atonal music listening are relatively few in number. Among those published in recent years, but not discussed or cited elsewhere in this essay, are Nicola Dibben, "The Cognitive Reality of Hierarchic Structure in Tonal and Atonal Music," *Music Perception* 12 (1994): 1–25; Michel Imberty, "How Do We Perceive Atonal Music? Suggestions for a Theoretical Approach," *Contemporary Music Review* 9 (1993): 325–37; Mariko Mikumo, "Encoding Strategies for Tonal and Atonal Melodies," *Music Perception* 10 (1992): 73–82; and Cheryl Bruner, "The Perception of Contemporary Pitch Structures," *Music Perception* 2 (1984): 25–39.

3. Robert Morris, *Composition with Pitch Classes: A Theory of Compositional Design* (New Haven and London: Yale University Press, 1987), and "New Directions in the Theory and Analysis of Musical Contour," *Music Theory Spectrum* 15 (1993): 205–28. For an overview of various approaches to contour analysis, see Elizabeth West Marvin, "A Generalization of Contour Theory to Diverse Musical Spaces: Analytical Applications to the Music of Dallapiccola and Stockhausen," in Elizabeth West Marvin and Richard Hermann, eds., *Concert Music, Rock, and Jazz Since 1945: Essays and Analytical Studies* (Rochester: University of Rochester Press, 1995), 135–71.

4. Michael Friedmann, "A Methodology for the Discussion of Contour: Its Application to Schoenberg's Music," *Journal of Music Theory* 29 (1985): 223–48; Elizabeth West Marvin and Paul A. Laprade, "Relating Musical Contours: Extensions of a Theory for Contour," *Journal of Music Theory* 31 (1987): 225–67.

Strategy	"Are You Sleeping?"
1. Contour plus pitch class sequence	< + + -> plus C, D, E, C
2. Contour plus scale degrees in a key	< + + -> plus do, re, mi, do
3. Contour plus interval sequence	< + + -> plus M2, M2, M3
4 Contour plus scale type	< + + -> plus major scale
5. Contour alone	< + + ->

Figure 1. Possible Strategies for Melodic Encoding Based on Dowling (1986). [See note 15.]

is the very basic question of how listeners represent melodies in memory. Several possible strategies are summarized in Figure 1, though this is clearly an oversimplification of a complex perceptual issue. Indeed, listeners may frequently switch from one strategy to another while listening, based upon musical characteristics of the stimulus and upon their own musical experience and predispositions. One perceptual hypothesis is that listeners remember melodies as collections of pitch classes; this strategy would explain the ease with which listeners recognize a melody's untransposed repetition or its replication in a higher or lower octave. It would not account, however, for the ease with which listeners can recognize and produce exact transpositions of tonal melodies to distant keys sharing few common pitch classes, nor for their relative difficulty in performing the same tasks with atonal melodies. This hypothesis also fails to explain the difficulty listeners experience when asked to recognize familiar melodies in which random pitches have been octave displaced.[5] Researchers have shown that melody recognition is markedly improved if the contour of the original is preserved in conjunction with the octave displacement of pitches; thus pitch class information alone is usually not sufficient for melody recognition.[6]

A second hypothesis is that listeners retain melodic structure in terms of contour plus scale degrees. This strategy is available to listeners only if the melody conforms to the principles of tonal composition familiar to them from the music they hear habitually in their culture; these principles in Western tonal music favor certain

---

5. Diana Deutsch has undertaken a series of experiments in which she examines listeners' abilities to recognize melodies with octave displacement; among the first was "Octave Generalization and Melody Identification," *Perception and Psychophysics* 23 (1972): 91–92. For an overview of her work, see her "The Processing of Pitch Combinations," in Diana Deutsch, ed., *The Psychology of Music* (New York: Academic Press, 1982), 271–316. See also W. Jay Dowling, "Musical Experience and Tonal Scales in the Recognition of Octave-Scrambled Melodies," *Psychomusicology* 4 (1984): 13–32.

6. W. L. Idson and D. W. Massaro, "A Bidimensional Model of Pitch in the Recognition of Melodies," *Perception and Psychophysics* 24 (1978): 551–65.

scale degrees and tonal patterns over others, thus facilitating recognition and retention of familiar patterns. A third possibility is that listeners remember melodies as
contours plus pitch-interval sequences. This method has a presumed cognitive advantage over the scale-degree strategy in that it should work equally well for tonal
and atonal melodies. Finally, Dowling's early experimentation led him to propose a
two-component model, whereby melodic contour is retained independently of pitches
or intervals, and melodies are reconstructed in memory retrieval by "hanging" the
remembered contour upon a scale type.[7] The two-component theory explains
Dowling's finding that listeners have difficulty distinguishing in short-term memory
between a tonal melody and a same-contour imitation that begins on a different
scale degree, since the two melodies represent an identical contour hung upon an
identical scale (but in a different position on that scale). It also explains the difficulty
some listeners experience in remembering atonal melodies, since they cannot infer a
tonal scale upon which the remembered contour may be hung.

What experimental evidence exists to support or refute these hypotheses?
Among the first experiments on recognition strategies for atonal melodies was
Dowling's 1971 investigation with Diane Fujitani, in which the experimenters asked
subjects to make same-different judgments between an atonal standard melody (different for each trial) and a comparison melody that might be an exact untransposed
repetition, an exact transposition, a same-contour imitation, or a randomly generated melody.[8] In the nontransposed condition, the experimenters concluded that subjects used pitch recognition in making judgments, whereas in the transposed condition subjects seemed to rely upon contour information alone. Dowling subsequently
repeated this design using tonal melodies and eliminating the untransposed condition.[9] In both studies, same-contour comparison melodies that contained intervallic
alterations were frequently confused with exact transpositions of the standard melodies.

These studies raise important (even disturbing) questions for the music theorist. Can it be that structural features of music that have long held interest for music
analysts—such as thematic transformations—are generally not perceived by listeners because melodic encoding in memory does not preserve intervallic information,
but only contour and scale, as Dowling's early study would suggest? Or could it be
that skilled listeners remember melodies using entirely different strategies from other
listeners?

Let us address each of these questions in turn. First, more recent experimentation has shown that perception of intervallic changes in transposed comparison melodies depends upon the length of delay time between hearing the stimulus and the
comparison, as well as the strength of tonal implication inherent in the melody.

---

7. W. Jay Dowling, "Scale and Contour: Two Components for a Theory of Memory for
Melodies," *Psychological Review* 85 (1978): 341–54.

8. W. Jay Dowling and Diane S. Fujitani, "Contour, Interval, and Pitch Recognition in
Memory for Melodies," *Journal of the Acoustical Society of America* 49 (1971): 524–31.

9. Dowling, "Scale and Contour," *passim*.

W. L. M. Croonen and P. F. M. Kop found, in contrast to Dowling's early studies, that moderately experienced listeners were able to distinguish between exact transpositions and tonal imitations at very short retention intervals, but that this was due in part to the "tonal clarity" of their melodic stimuli.[10] Likewise, Lola Cuddy reported in a series of articles that subjects were more accurate in identifying comparison melodies that contained a single altered or mistuned pitch in melodic stimuli that ranged from highly tonal to atonal, if the standard melody was constructed according to strongly tonal principles (an implied I–V–I chord progression and a final cadence of scale-degrees 7 to 1, for example).[11] She found this ability to infer strongly tonal harmonic progressions from melodic stimuli—and to make use of this information to identify the altered melodies—even among subjects who were nonmusicians. Finally, in Dowling's more recent work, he has rejected his earlier hypothesis that contour is an entirely separable feature of melody because of subsequent studies in which tonal context affected subjects' memory for contour.[12] For example, in an experiment designed to test listeners' ability to discriminate exact transpositions from same-contour imitations and different-contour test melodies, James Bartlett and Dowling found that the "tendency to falsely recognize different contour lures was markedly affected by tonality, being lowest for strong tonal melodies" and highest for atonal melodies; thus "listeners' ability to reject a different-contour test item depended on tonal tontext, and not just on its difference of contour."[13] They also found that after short delays (between the standard melody and its comparison), listeners distinguished between exact transpositions and different-contour lures better than they did between exact transpositions and same-contour lures in both the tonal and atonal conditions. With increased delay time, however, listeners' discrimination between exact transpositions and same-contour lures improved significantly in the tonal condition only, and not in the atonal.[14] This suggests that cognitive processing occurred for the tonal melodies during the delay time, processing that was ineffective for encoding the atonal melodies in memory.

---

10. W. L. M. Croonen and P. F. M. Kop, "Tonality, Tonal Scheme, and Contour in Delayed Recognition of Tone Sequences," *Music Perception* 7 (1989): 49–68.

11. See, for example, Lola L. Cuddy, Annabel J. Cohen, and D. J. K. Mewhort, "Perception of Structure in Short Melodic Sequences," *Journal of Experimental Psychology: Human Perception and Performance* 7 (1981): 869–83; Lola Cuddy and H. I. Lyons, "Musical Pattern Recognition: A Comparison of Listening to and Studying Tonal Structures and Tonal Ambiguities," *Psychomusicology* 1 (1981): 15–33; and Lola L. Cuddy, "On Hearing Pattern in Melody," *Psychology of Music* 10 (1982): 3–10.

12. James C. Bartlett and W. Jay Dowling, "Scale Structure and Similarity of Melodies," *Music Perception* 5 (1988): 285–314.

13. W. Jay Dowling, "Melodic Contour in Hearing and Remembering Melodies," in Rita Aiello with John A. Sloboda, eds., *Musical Perceptions* (New York and Oxford: Oxford University Press, 1994), 186.

14. Ibid., 186–87. See also W. Jay Dowling and James C. Bartlett, "The Importance of Interval Information in Long-Term Memory for Melodies," *Psychomusicology* 1 (1981): 30–49.

What of the second question: to what extent do cognitive strategies differ between musicians and nonmusicians? Dowling has also addressed this question in a 1986 study that showed clear effects of musical experience; in fact, he demonstrated that different subject groups used different cognitive strategies for representing melodies in memory.[15] His results suggest that inexperienced listeners represent melodies as a series of (directed) pitch intervals, moderately experienced listeners represent melodies as scale-degree patterns, and professional musicians use a flexible system that takes advantage of both interval and scale-step information. To this, we might caution that strategies may vary even among professional musicians, depending in particular upon the type of melodies heard and the musicians' experience with tonal and atonal musical idioms.

EXPERIMENTAL DESIGN

What the experiments summarized here fail to do adequately is to explore how musically experienced listeners recognize transformations upon idiomatic atonal melodies if contour is completely removed as a cue. In recent years, experimenters have begun to refine their methods for generating tonal melodies so that they conform to the idiomatic principles of harmonic progression found in music literature—in contrast to stimuli in earlier studies, which might begin and end on the tonic but draw intervening pitches quasi-randomly from the diatonic collection.[16] The experiment reported here attempts to construct idiomatic atonal melodies as well, in order to approximate the style of composition found in some atonal music literature—unlike previously cited studies, which created atonal stimuli by adding "foreign" accidentals to diatonic melodies or by generating random pitch collections within limited intervallic constraints.[17] In addition, this experiment controls for the powerful effect of contour perception by holding contour invariant between the standard and comparison melodies in all conditions, thus forcing subjects to rely upon other perceived structural features for discrimination.

---

15. W. Jay Dowling, "Context Effects on Melody Recognition: Scale-Step versus Interval Representations," *Music Perception* 3 (1986): 281–96.

16. Cuddy's research on the perception of tonal melodies (note 11) stands out positively in this regard, as sensitive to the logic and cognitive power of implied harmonic progression.

17. This discussion excludes experimental work in which melodies (or entire textures) are drawn from actual atonal compositions, such as Carol L. Krumhansl, Gregory J. Sandell, and Desmond C. Sergeant, "The Perception of Tone Hierarchies and Mirror Forms in Twelve-Tone Serial Music, *Music Perception* 5 (1988): 31–78; Carol Krumhansl and Mark Schmuckler, "The *Petroushka* Chord: A Perceptual Investigation," *Music Perception* 4 (1986): 153–84; and Irene Deliège and Abdessadek El Ahmadi, "Mechanisms of Cue Extraction in Musical Groupings: A Study of Perception on *Sequenza IV* for Viola Solo by Luciano Berio," *Psychology of Music* 18 (1990): 18–44.

The experiment reported here draws features of its design from Dowling's 1971 and 1978 studies. It uses both tonal and atonal melodies, but differs from the earlier studies in its treatment of contour, in the compositional constraints placed upon its stimuli, and in the nature of its subject pools. In the tonal condition, this experiment reexamines perception of what Dowling calls the "tonal answer"—that is, a same-contour imitation that is "slid" along the diatonic scale to begin on another scale degree. While Croonen and Kop demonstrated listeners' abilities to distinguish between exact transpositions and "tonal answers," they did not do so for atonal stimuli. The hypothesis here, then, is that listeners can indeed distinguish between the transposed repetition of a melody and its same-contour imitation—in both tonal and atonal contexts—but that accuracy will be greater in tonal contexts and will vary depending upon the musical experience of subjects.

Ninety-three University of Rochester undergraduates participated as subjects; fifty-nine were drawn from the University's Eastman School of Music and thirty-four were liberal arts students (all non-music majors). Figure 2 summarizes information about the subjects, whose data were divided into three distinct subject groups: nonmusicians, musicians, and absolute-pitch (AP) musicians.[18] Musicians were members of randomly chosen freshman aural-skills courses, which means that they were engaging in the initial stages of explicit training in aural perception of tonal music but had received no training in atonal music perception. AP subjects (all Eastman School of Music students) were identified by self-disclosure on an information sheet.[19] Nonmusicians were volunteers from an introductory psychology course.

Subjects were tested in groups using a prerecorded tape played over high-quality loudspeakers in a classroom, with their responses circled ("same" or "different") on an answer sheet. On each trial, subjects heard a sample melody followed by a comparison melody: either a "target" or a "lure." Target melodies (to be correctly identified as "same") were exact transpositions of the given sample melody, while lures

---

18. Of those surveyed here, only Cuddy's work has previously explored perceptual strategies employed by AP musicians in a similar task.

19. Absolute pitch will be understood here as a listener's ability to identify the pitch class of a tone by ear without reference to any standard pitch that has been sounded and identified by name. Anecdotal evidence shows that absolute pitch facility may vary among those who claim to have this ability; it may be restricted to particular timbres or registers in some individuals, for example. In this experiment, no AP pretest was given; subjects were grouped entirely by self-disclosure. Interestingly, those claiming AP had a higher mean number of years studying an instrument, and thus began this study at a younger age. Some theories of absolute pitch acquisition posit a "critical period" during early childhood, similar to that for language, during which AP may be acquired if children are studying an instrument and associating pitch names with sounds. See, for example, Ken'ichi Miyazaki, "Absolute Pitch as an Inability: Identification of Musical Intervals in a Tonal Context," *Music Perception* 11 (1993): 55–72; and Annie Takeushi and Stewart Hulse, "Absolute-Pitch Judgments of Black-and White-Key Pitches," *Music Perception* 9 (1991): 27–46.

Subject Group	N	Mean Age	Gender M/F	Mean Years Instrumental Study
Musicians	49	18.4	23/26	8.34
AP Musicians	10	18.3	4/6	11.35
Nonmusicians	34	18.8	22/12	3.28
Totals/Means:	93	18.5	49/44	7.66

Figure 2. Subject Information.

("different") were modified from the target as described below. A total of forty-eight trials were recorded using twelve melodies in each of four conditions: tonal-target, tonal-lure, atonal-target, atonal-lure. Tonal and atonal stimulus pairs were both heard in this randomly ordered sequence of forty-eight trials, rather than being segregated into blocks by type. Each melody was recorded at a tempo of quarter-note equals M.M. 46, with two beats between the standard melody and comparison melody, and three beats between trials. Comparison melodies were always in a different key from the standard, sharing few common tones. The experimental trials were preceded by instructions with examples played at the piano, then three practice trials with feedback; no feedback was given during the experimental trials.

Twenty-four six-note melodies were composed (twelve tonal and twelve atonal) according to the specifications given in Figure 3, with twenty-four corresponding lures for each. The six-note length was chosen to conform to the stimulus length in the Dowling work which inspired it, and to Miller's oft-cited limit on the capacity of short-term memory to seven elements plus or minus two.[20] Twelve distinct contours were used for the tonal melodies; the same contours, with one exception, were retained for the atonal.[21] Tonal melodies conformed to rules of common-practice harmonic progression; this assures that scale-degree $\hat{7}$, for example, leads functionally up to scale-degree $\hat{1}$, and so on. Unlike previous experiments, half of the tonal stimuli were in major keys, and half in minor. Lures were composed to begin on a different scale degree in the new key, but otherwise conformed to all the same compositional constraints as the standards. Atonal melodies specifically avoided triadic leaps, and featured patterns that do not commonly occur in tonal melodies, such as consecutive leaps by dissonant intervals. Lures followed the same compositional guidelines, maintaining the targets' contour without altering any interval by more than a third.

Example 1 presents two tonal and two atonal melodies and their transformations. The contour label above each pair of melodies follows Morris's contour desig-

---

20. Dowling, "Context Effects on Melody Recognition," and G. A. Miller, "The Magic Number Seven, Plus or Minus Two," *Psychological Review* 63 (1956): 81–97.

21. The exception was simply due to the experimenter's error and not to any conscious manipulation of the experimental design.

Tonal Standard Melodies:

- identical rhythm for all melodies
- 6 major, 6 minor keys
- all constructed of leaps in I, IV, V^7 chords plus stepwise embellishment
- ended on a member of the tonic triad, but not always scale-degree $\hat{1}$
- conformed to principles of common-practice progression and voice leading

Tonal Lures:

- each lure had identical contours to its tonal standard melody
- began (and continued) on different scale degrees from the standard
- followed same harmonic and voice-leading constraints as the standard
- transpositions chosen to minimize common tones with the standard

* * * * * * * * * * * *

Nontonal Standard Melodies:

- identical rhythms to tonal stimuli
- 11 of 12 had identical contours to corresponding tonal stimuli
- featured nondiatonic patterns that generally do not occur in tonal music
- featured rare intervals of the diatonic collection: m2, tritone, M7

Nontonal Lures:

- same contours as the corresponding standard nontonal melodies
- generally 4 to 5 intervals altered (each by no more than minor 3rd)
- same compositional guidelines as the atonal standards
- transpositions chosen to minimize common tones with standard

Figure 3. Characteristics of Experimental Stimuli

nations in assigning 0 to the lowest pitch and $(n - 1)$ to the highest, where n represents the number of distinct pitches in the contour; this representation conveys more information about relative height within the contour than the commonly used sequence of "+'s" and "-'s", which is also given.[22]

Example 2 shows stimuli from the two earlier studies for comparison. One crucial difference between the results of these earlier studies and the one reported

---

22. One of the tonal lures in this example contains only two changes of interval in comparison to its standard melody. This is atypical; all but two of the tonal lures contained 4 to 5 changes. There was not a strong correlation, however, between number of intervals changed and listeners' abilities to discriminate.

Example 1. Melodic Contour Realizations: < 0 1 2 3 4 1 > and < 4 3 1 0 2 1 >.

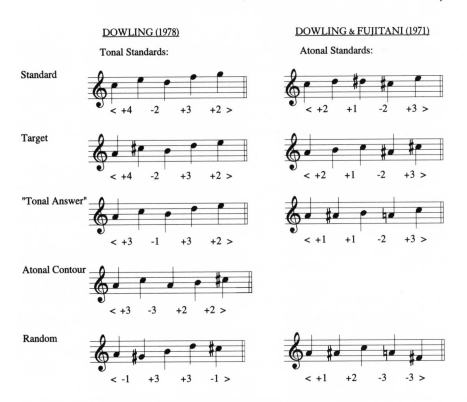

Example 2. Stimuli from Previous Experimental Research.

here lies in how "tonality" and "atonality" are defined, and how these tonal contexts are reflected in the musical stimuli. In Dowling's 1978 study, all standard stimuli were generated by a random walk on the C-major scale, using randomly selected contours, and probabilities of .67 for a diatonic step (up or down) and .33 for two steps, giving a mean interval size for the melodies overall of 2.3 semitones. The problem here is that a random walk on the diatonic collection may produce a diatonic melody, but it may not produce a strongly tonal melody, particularly when intervals are so highly constrained.

Diatonicism is not equivalent to common-practice tonality; the latter implies a hierarchical relationship of each scale degree to the tonic. For this reason, the "tonal answer" in the left-hand column of Example 2 presents a problem. It is intended as a same-contour lure that is "hung" upon the C-major scale beginning on a different note from the standard. By choosing A as the beginning note (as roughly half of his lures did) and using the diatonic C-major pitch class collection, musically experienced listeners will hear the lure not in C-major but rather in A minor. (Dowling acknowledges this as one possible listening strategy.) If listeners use a scale-degree strategy, then this standard melody and its tonal answer lure are functionally identical; the standard represents scales degrees $< \hat{1}\ \hat{3}\ \hat{2}\ \hat{4}\ \hat{5} >$ in C major while the lure presents $< \hat{1}\ \hat{3}\ \hat{2}\ \hat{4}\ \hat{5} >$ in A minor, thus explaining in part listeners' difficulty in distinguishing between them.[23] Finally, the "same-contour" atonal melody of this example actually differs in its contour from the standard if Morris's definition of contour is used. Even though the tonal standard and atonal lure share the same pattern of "ups" and "downs," the atonal contour contains a repeated note while the standard does not. To control for these possibly confounding factors, care was taken in the current experiment to use Morris's more sensitive measure of contour equivalence, and to create unambiguously tonal melodies with strong harmonic focus.

The compositional constraints upon atonal melodies also differed between this study and the 1971 Dowling and Fujitani experiment, in order to minimize the possibility of tonal interpretation. The stimuli for the earlier study were generated by computer, with up and down intervals equally probable between successive notes. Each five-note standard melody began on C; succeeding notes were selected according to a second-order Markov chain with the probability of a half step .50 and of a whole step or minor third, .25. Careful examination of the sample stimuli for that experiment (right-hand column of Ex. 2), reveals that the atonal standard melody actually may be interpreted tonally. As Helen Brown has pointed out, nondiatonic tones in tonal melodies usually result from mixture between parallel keys and tonicization of various scale degrees, as is the case here.[24] With enharmonic respell-

---

23. If listeners quickly infer a tonic as they listen to the comparison melody, even the "atonal contour" of the example drawn from Dowling's 1978 study may be heard functionally in a minor, since the C♯ with which the melody ends may be interpreted as a "Picardy third," $< \hat{1}\ \hat{3}\ \hat{1}\ \hat{2}\ ♯\hat{3} >$.

24. Helen Brown, "Cognitive Interpretations of Functional Chromaticism in Tonal Mu-

ing, this standard becomes C–D–E♭–C♯–E, which could be heard in C minor (beginning unambiguously with scale degrees $\hat{1}$–$\hat{2}$–$\hat{3}$) with the C♯ and E♮ representing a secondary dominant of D. In the experiment reported here, no constraints were placed upon interval size within the octave, but successions that implied a tonality were avoided; special attention was given to the rare intervals of the diatonic collection (the minor second, tritone, and major seventh) whose resolutions might otherwise strongly imply a key.

Results

Figure 4 summarizes this experiment's mean percentage correct for the tonal and atonal contexts in each subject group. The bold numbers show the percent of "hits": correct identification of targets. The other mean given is the percent of "false alarms": false positive identifications of lures as targets. The percent of false alarms reflects subjects' uncertainty or possible guessing; not surprisingly, the false alarm rate is highest for nonmusicians in both conditions. One statistical method to correct for possible bias in the data due to subjects' guessing strategies is to plot hits against false alarms, then to convert to d′ values using conversion tables.[25] D-prime values extend from -4.64 to +4.64, where 0 represents no discrimination.

Figure 5 presents d′ means for each condition and subject group. For all three subject groups—even for the nonmusicians—in both the tonal and atonal conditions, d′ means differed significantly from 0, confirming subjects' discrimination at above chance levels (using a one-tailed sign test, $p < .01$).[26] In addition, one-tailed t-tests on d′ differences showed a significant difference in subjects' discrimination between tonal and atonal stimuli (all p values $< .01$); listeners in all subject groups were better able to distinguish targets from lures in the tonal condition. There were also significant differences between paired subject groups—both in their ability to distinguish tonal targets from lures (all p values $< .05$) and in the extent to which their performance in the tonal condition exceeded the atonal (all p values $< .01$).

Of interest are the results obtained for the absolute-pitch subjects. The most

---

sic," in Mari Reiss Jones and Susan Holleran, eds., *Cognitive Bases of Musical Communication* (Washington, DC: American Psychological Association, 1992), 139–60. While this is familiar territory for music theorists, others might appreciate examples: the common usage in a major key of chromatic tones "borrowed" from its parallel minor (for example, C major/C minor) is known as "mixture"; chromatic tones that mimic the half-step ascent of scale degree $\hat{7}$ to $\hat{1}$ on other degrees of the scale help to define "tonicization."

25. P.B. Elliott, "Tables of d′," in J. A. Swets, ed., *Signal Detection and Recognition by Human Observers: Contemporary Readings* (New York: John Wiley & Sons, Inc., 1964), 651–84.

26. P values denote the degree of probability that the experimental results are due to chance factors; that is, if $p < .01$, we are 99% sure that our results are due to the effect of our dependent variable, and not due to chance factors.

Tonal Context

Subjects:	Average Hit Rate		False Alarm Rate	
	Mean	SE	Mean	SE
Musicians	**.80**	.02	.39	.03
AP Musicians	**.88**	.05	.32	.08
Nonmusicians	**.67**	.03	.52	.03

Atonal Context

Subjects:	Average Hit Rate		False Alarm Rate	
	Mean	SE	Mean	SE
Musicians	**.56**	.02	.39	.02
AP Musicians	**.58**	.05	.38	.04
Nonmusicians	**.53**	.02	.48	.02

Figure 4. Mean Percentage Correct by Subject Group.

surprising result is that any cognitive "advantage" that AP subjects had over non-AP musicians in the tonal condition virtually disappeared in the atonal condition. There was no significant statistical difference between the AP musicians' performance compared with non-AP musicians, nor even between AP musicians compared with nonmusicians. The only significant difference in the atonal condition (p < .01) occurred between regular musicans and nonmusicians.

DISCUSSION

Dowling's 1978 study found that subjects performed at chance levels in a task that required them to distinguish between exact transpositions of comparison melodies and melodies that shifted their contours along the same diatonic scale as the standard. In the tonal condition of the present experiment, however, all three subject groups performed above chance in a similar task. There are at least two possible explanations for this discrepancy in results. The first is the difference in the principles by which the musical stimuli were constructed, as discussed previously. The second is the dual factor of age and musical experience among subjects. Dowling's experienced group had a mean of five years musical training, but a mean age of 30.4 years; it is possible that this training may have occurred as many as fifteen years previously. In contrast, the subjects in the present experiment were generally twelve years younger and had at least three years more of musical experience—even in the nonmusician group. I define subjects as "musicians" if they are currently active in

Subjects:	Tonal		Atonal		Difference (Tonal–Atonal)	
	d' Mean	SE	d' Mean	SE	d' Mean	SE
Musicians	1.28	.11	.48	.09	.79	.13
AP Musicians	1.98	.37	.54	.15	1.44	.32
Nonmusicians	.36	.10	.15	.08	.22	.11

Figure 5. D-Prime Analysis by Subject Group.

professional music-making, as Dowling did in his 1986 study (his experienced group in this later experiment was made up of professionals). The differences in subjects' ages and musical experience may also account for the fact that subjects in this experiment performed slightly better than those in Dowling and Fujitani's experiment using atonal melodies.

To summarize, the combination of stimuli that are unambiguously tonal or atonal, together with the differences in subject groups, seems to account for the differences in results between this study and its predecessors. These results support Dowling's 1986 conclusion that subjects with extensive experience listening to and performing music may use cognitive strategies different from those of inexperienced listeners to remember unfamiliar melodies in short-term memory. In particular, he concludes that experienced musicians employ a flexible system that uses information from both scale degrees and interval successions.[27] The results also suggest that the nature of the stimulus itself contributes to the choice of mental representation, since scale-degree information cannot be encoded for atonal stimuli.

That discrimination of targets from lures was so much more accurate in the tonal than the atonal context, across all subject groups, suggests: (1) that listeners are better at the tonal task simply because they have more experience listening to tonal music, or (2) that listeners are better at this task because they use a different and more effective method of encoding melodic information in memory. Both alternatives may contribute to this finding. Testing of the first premise is reported below, using subjects drawn from a pool of graduate music students and professional musicians skilled in atonal music listening, performance, composition, or analysis, compared with a control group of comparably experienced musicians without specialized expertise in atonal music. It may be that the "experienced" musicians in the present experiment were in fact inexperienced listeners in the atonal idiom, who were unable to form an effective strategy "on the fly."

Let us consider the other premise: that scale-degree representation has a cognitive advantage because it requires less memory due to the chunking of familiar tonal patterns. Listeners experienced with tonal music can chunk leaps within the

27. Dowling, "Context Effects on Melody Recognition," 293–94.

tonic triad ($\hat{1}$–$\hat{3}$–$\hat{5}$, $\hat{3}$–$\hat{5}$–$\hat{1}$, $\hat{5}$–$\hat{3}$–$\hat{1}$, etc.), for example, by remembering the scale degree of first note, the implied harmony, and contour. Thus listeners need not remember a string of five unrelated intervals to complete this task; rather, they may remember the leaps as patterns within the underlying context of a familiar harmonic progression of just two or three chords. But is it not possible that to musicans skilled in atonal music listening, these are not "five unrelated intervals"? Instead, these musicians may perceive the atonal melodies by their succession of two familiar trichord types, or by identifying other familiar set-class types within the tunes. Indeed, it may be that subjects' ability to perform better in the tonal condition may be due in part to the effect of training, which favors skill development in Western tonal music in the early years of the musician's education over training in atonal, modal, or non-Western musics.

To test the hypothesis that musicians trained in atonal music listening might develop equally effective cognitive strategies for atonal melodic discrimination, this experiment was subsequently run on sixteen graduate music students (thirteen male, three female) who were considered expert in atonal composition, analysis, or performance. The atonal experts' performance was significantly higher than the earlier subject group in the atonal condition, though there was no difference between the two subject groups in the tonal condition. Experts' mean percentage correct in the tonal condition was .84 (SE .03) and in the atonal was .72 (SE .04); see Figure 4 for comparison data. As in the previous subject pool, the expert subjects were significantly better at discrimination in the tonal condition than in the atonal ($p < .0005$). Of interest, however, is a subgroup of seven highly skilled expert listeners (six male, one female), who showed no significant difference in discrimination between the two conditions ($p < .119$). Their mean percentage correct for tonal stimuli was .86 (SE .04) and for atonal was .87 (SE .05). Although two of the expert subgroup were AP musicians, their results did not differ significantly. These data suggest that some musicians (with and without AP) are able to develop cognitive strategies for aural discrimination of atonal melodies that are as effective as those for tonal melodies. The identification of these strategies and their implication for musical training remain topics for further study.

Musicians are trained to chunk tonal melodies by harmonic function—both explicitly in music-theory classrooms and implicitly when they practice arpeggios on their instruments. Continued involvement with the harmonic language of tonal music in performance, sight reading, and memorization enables experienced musicians to infer not only a tonal center but also an implied harmonic progression from a melody as it is heard, without necessarily being aware of this strategy. The fact that nonmusicians were able to perform significantly better in the tonal than the atonal condition suggests that they, too, are able to infer some principles of harmonic structure to assist them in remembering the tonal patterns. Lola Cuddy has come to similar conclusions in her research, stating that the "ability to detect and implement harmonic structure exists in the average non-musician and this is a finding...that deserves further exploitation in adult music education."[28]

---

28. Cuddy, "On Hearing Pattern in Melody," 3.

The cognitive strategy of chunking by harmonic function probably holds true even for AP musicians on some level. The common perception that AP listeners hold an advantage in musical memory—that they can simply recall strings of pitch classes as absolutes without interpreting them tonally—is probably an overstatement. These data suggest that AP musicians also rely upon a flexible system, one that uses pitch-class and scale-degree information primarily, with less reliance upon memory for strings of interval relationships than regular musicians and nonmusicians. Thus, in the transposed recognition task in the tonal condition, memory for a string of pitch classes may have been reinforced by its tonal interpretation within a key. Upon hearing a transposed lure, AP subjects might transpose the target's pitch classes in real time to a new key or—more likely—shift to a scale-degree recognition strategy that would remain invariant across the key change. This strategy will not work in the atonal condition, however.

Recall that in Figure 5, the d′ means' difference (tonal minus atonal) for AP musicians was nearly double that of regular musicians, showing a marked decrease in AP subjects' abilities to discriminate when the context shifted from tonal to atonal. It may be that AP subjects retained the atonal stimuli in short-term memory as pitch-class collections. They were unable because of the atonal context to use scale-degree information, and less able than those in the other subject groups to use interval information. If this were the case, discrimination would require either real-time transposition of the collection to the new key so that pitch-by-pitch comparisons could be made as the comparison melody was heard, or memorization of both the standard and the target—twelve notes total—so that transposition and comparison between melodies could be made in memory. Miller's research suggests that the latter strategy would be unlikely due to the sheer number of elements to be remembered.[29] AP subjects in this experiment may simply have had difficulty transposing quickly enough and may not have had confidence in their transposition. Subjects who noticed just one wrong note in the lure, for example, might attribute this to a transposition error rather than to the comparison melody's identity as a lure. In any event, it is fairly clear that at least some of the AP subjects were unable to use a flexible retrieval system that incorporated interval information, since their ability to discriminate declined so markedly in the absence of a tonal context.[30]

Finally, statistics were compiled for each of the target-plus-lure stimulus pairs. For each pair, the percentage of subjects scoring hits and the percent scoring false alarms were converted to d′s. In this analysis, subjects were sorted not only by musical experience but also by gender to determine whether certain stimuli or classes of stimuli were better discriminated by one gender. Research has shown that ability to complete certain cognitive tasks is correlated to subjects' gender; Doreen Kimura's

---

29. Miller, "The Magic Number Seven," see note 20.

30. It should be noted that the AP subject pool (n = 10) was smaller than the other two pools and possible variation in the results might occur with a larger pool.

1992 article in *Scientific American* provides a concise summary of these experimental results.[31] In related research, Thomas G. Bever has shown that the strategies by which subjects complete a spatial navigation task differ by gender.[32] In his study, no significant differences were found in subjects' ability to navigate from one end of a maze to another; however, the strategies by which they completed this task did differ. Males were significantly better at drawing from memory a map of the route just traversed, while women were better at remembering the landmarks that had been seen along the maze's route. Thus males seemed to create a global spatial representation of the maze using directional vectors, while women used local landmarks as navigational aids. This gender difference for spatial representation may have a direct analogy in memory for melodies, if memory for contour is considered a spatial strategy of directional vectors and recognition of distinctive local melodic features is considered a landmark strategy.

In order to generalize to a population of melodies whose distribution is unknown, nonparametric one-tailed sign tests were used in the analysis of this data. Some significant gender differences were found, but only in the atonal condition. Nonmusician females' discrimination exceeded males' ($p < .02$), but more striking is the fact that when the data for musicians and nonmusicians were combined (omitting only the data for AP musicians), there was still a significant gender difference in the atonal condition, with women's discrimination exceeding men's ($p < :003$). One possible explanation is that in the absence of the more efficient tonal encoding discussed above, subjects relied on "spatial" strategies such as contours (vectors) or aural landmarks (perhaps distinctive interval patterns). In this case, the (male) vector strategy was less effective than the (female) landmark strategy, because contour was held invariant between the standard melody and comparison.

No significant differences by subjects' sex were found for discrimination in the tonal condition. However, an informal examination of the tonal stimulus pairs showing the greatest difference between females' and males' performance reveals that melodies with distinct characteristics stand out. Example 3 shows the two tonal melodies discriminated best by females and the two discriminated best by males, with their associated lures beneath. Note that in the tonal condition of the melodies discriminated best by females both melodies consist entirely of leaps within I and V chords, and that the lure may imply more than one possible harmonic background. Further, both lures contain a leap to a dissonance—that is, a leap to a pitch outside the implied harmony. It may be that a leap away from the anticipated harmonic background may have stood out to female listeners as a distinctive landmark, thus enabling them to identify correctly the melody as a lure. The tonal stimulus pairs

31. Doreen Kimura, "Sex Differences in the Brain," *Scientific American* 267 (1992): 119–25.

32. Thomas G. Bever, "The Logical and Extrinsic Sources of Modularity," in M. Gunnar and M. Maratsos, eds., *Modularity and Constraints in Language and Cognition* (Hillsdale, NJ: Lawrence Erlbaum and Associates, 1992), 179–211.

Melodies favoring discrimination by females:

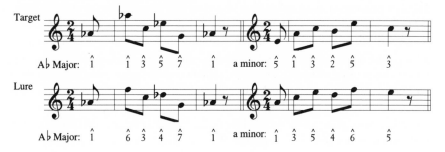

Melodies favoring discrimination by males:

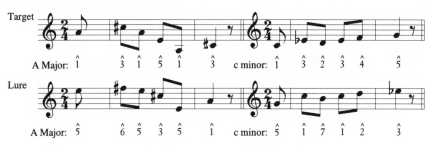

Example 3. Tonal Stimuli Suggesting Differences by Subjects' Sex.

better discriminated by males appear at the bottom of Example 3. The harmony implied by these melodies could be interpreted as just a single tonic triad (with stepwise embellishments in the case of the C-minor example), or alternatively as a tonic plus dominant. In contrast to the melodies just discussed, comparison of these lures with their targets shows no leaps to dissonances but rather only stepwise embellishment, which may not stand out so markedly as the leaps to dissonances seen above.

What conclusions may we draw about how listeners perceive and process tonal and atonal melodies? First, these data suggest that different classes of listeners may use entirely different strategies in completing a task such as that described here. Second, although the results do not tell us precisely which strategies listeners employed, the striking difference in subjects' performance between the tonal and atonal conditions suggests that subjects did not use an intervallic strategy in both contexts, since that strategy should be equally effective across stimulus types. Because scale-degree patterns—chunked by triadic function and following accepted patterns of harmonic expectation—are a more efficient means of encoding melodies in tonal contexts, and because performance in all three subject groups was significantly better in the tonal condition, we conclude that scale-degree representations were used for the tonal melodies with a switch to another type of representation for the atonal melodies. Further experimentation remains to be run to determine what strategies musicians with extensive experience in atonal music use to remember atonal melodies. If evidence were found of effective strategies among these listeners, then more effective pedagogical reinforcement of these strategies might be devised for music instruction (in much the same way as moveable-do solfège reinforces scale-degree relationships and harmonic function in tonal music). Finally, the experiment demonstrates that while the nature of the melody—tonal or atonal—has profound implications for cognitive strategy, listeners can and do make fine discriminations between similar melodies in either context, even in the absence of rhythmic or contour cues.

Voice Leading in Atonal Music

Joseph N. Straus

I t is possible at present to distinguish three models for atonal voice leading. The first, which I will call *prolongational*, has its roots in the theories of Heinrich Schenker.[1] The second, which I will call *associational*, has its roots in

---

Earlier versions of this paper were presented at Florida State University (February 1993), Columbia University (September 1993), and the Eastman School of Music (February 1995). It has benefited greatly from questions raised by audience members on those occasions, and from the incisive comments of Charles Burkhart, Henry Klumpenhouwer, Robert Morris, and the students in two recent seminars at the Graduate Center of the City University of New York.

1. Schenkerian discussions of atonal voice leading begin with Schenker himself, in particular with his well-known analysis of a passage from Stravinsky's Concerto for Piano and Wind Instruments. See Heinrich Schenker, "Resumption of Urlinie Considerations," from *Das Meisterwerk in der Musik*, vol. 2 (Munich: Drei Masken Verlag, 1926), trans. Sylvan Kalib in "Thirteen Essays from the *Three Yearbooks 'Das Meisterwerk in der Music'* by Heinrich Schenker: An Annotated Translation" (Ph.D. diss., Northwestern University, 1973), 196–216. Schenker's students, and their students, have created a distinctive tradition of Schenkerian studies of atonal voice leading, some maintaining Schenker's disapproving tone, others celebrating new musical developments. See Allen Forte, *Contemporary Tone Structures* (New York: Bureau of Publications, Teacher's College, Columbia University, 1955); Adele Katz, *Challenge to Musical Tradition: A New Concept of Tonality* (1945; reprint, New York: Da Capo, 1972); Edward Laufer, "Review of Schenker's Free Composition," *Music Theory Spectrum* 3 (1981): 158–184, and extensive unpublished graphic analyses of music by Schoenberg, Sibelius, and others; Felix Salzer, *Structural Hearing: Tonal Coherence in Music* (New York: Dover Publications, 1962); and numerous publications by Roy Travis, including "Directed Motion in Schoenberg and Webern," *Perspectives of New Music* 4 (1966): 84–89; "Toward a New Concept of Tonality?" *Journal of Music Theory* 3 (1959): 257–84; and "Tonal Coherence in the First Movement of Bartók's Fourth String Quartet," *Music Forum* 2 (1970): 298–371. Important recent work in the Schenkerian tradition, often incorporating extensive revisions and modifications, includes James Baker, "Voice-Leading in Post-Tonal Music: Suggestions for Extending Schenker's Theory," *Music Analysis* 9 (1990): 177–200, and "Post-Tonal Voice-Leading," in *Models of Musical Analysis: Early Twentieth Century Music*, ed. Jonathan Dunsby (Oxford: Basil Blackwell, 1993), 20–41; Steve Larson, "A Tonal Model of an 'Atonal' Piece: Schoenberg's Opus 15, Number 2," *Perspectives of New Music* 25 (1987): 418–33; Fred Lerdahl, "Atonal Prolongational Structure," *Contemporary Music Review* 4 (1989): 65–87; Joel Lester, "A Theory of Atonal Prolongations as Used in an Analysis of the Serenade, Op. 24, by Arnold Schoenberg" (Ph.D. diss., Princeton University, 1971); Robert P. Morgan, "Dissonant Prolongations: Theoretical and Compositional Precedents," *Journal of Music Theory* 20 (1976): 46–91; Charles Morrison, "Prolongation in the Final Movement of Bartók's String Quartet No. 4,"

the pitch-class set theory of Allen Forte and others.[2] The third, which I will call *transformational,* has its roots in recent theoretical work by David Lewin.[3] Example 1 applies each model to a simple chord progression.

Music Theory Spectrum 13 (1991): 179–96; David Neumeyer and Susan Tepping, *A Guide to Schenkerian Analysis* (Englewood Cliffs, N.J.: Prentice-Hall, 1992), 117–24; Edward Pearsall, "Harmonic Progressions and Prolongation in Post-Tonal Music," *Music Analysis* 10 (1991): 345–56; Paul Wilson, "Concepts of Prolongation and Bartók's Opus 20," *Music Theory Spectrum* 6 (1984): 79–89, and *The Music of Bela Bartók* (New Haven: Yale University Press, 1992). It should be acknowledged that Schenker's theory is not exclusively prolongational; it has a strong motivic or associational component as well. See Heinrich Schenker, *Free Composition,* trans. Ernst Oster (New York: Longman, 1979), Figs. 118 and 119; Charles Burkhart, "Schenker's Motivic Parallelisms," *Journal of Music Theory* 22 (1978): 145–76; and John Rothgeb, "Thematic Content: A Schenkerian View," in *Aspects of Schenkerian Theory,* ed. David Beach (New Haven: Yale University Press, 1983), 39–60. For an evaluation of the sometimes uneasy relationship in Schenkerian theory and practice between prolongational and motivic structures, see three articles by Richard Cohn: "Hierarchical Unity, Plural Unities: Toward a Reconciliation," co-authored with Douglas Dempster, in *Disciplining Music: Musicology and its Canons,* ed. K. Bergeron and P. Bohlman (Chicago: University of Chicago Press, 1992), 156–81; "The Autonomy of Motives in Schenkerian Accounts of Tonal Music," *Music Theory Spectrum* 14 (1992): 150–70; and "Schenker's Theory, Schenkerian Theory: Pure Unity or Constructive Conflict?" *Indiana Theory Review* 13 (1992): 1–20.

2. The basic texts of pitch-class set theory include Allen Forte, *The Structure of Atonal Music* (New Haven: Yale University Press, 1973); Robert Morris, *Composition with Pitch Classes: A Theory of Compositional Design* (New Haven: Yale University Press, 1987); and John Rahn, *Basic Atonal Theory* (New York: Longman, 1980). Applications of that theory to the linear organization of atonal music include Alan Chapman, "Some Intervallic Aspects of Pitch-Class Set Relations," *Journal of Music Theory* 25 (1981): 275–90; Allen Forte, "New Approaches to the Linear Analysis of Music," *Journal of the American Musicological Society* 41 (1988): 315–48, and "Concepts of Linearity in Schoenberg's Atonal Music: A Study of the Opus 15 Song Cycle," *Journal of Music Theory* 36 (1992): 285–382; Christopher Hasty, "On the Problem of Succession and Continuity in Twentieth-Century Music," *Music Theory Spectrum* 8 (1986): 58–74; and Joseph N. Straus, "A Principle of Voice Leading in the Music of Stravinsky," *Music Theory Spectrum* 4 (1982): 106–24.

3. David Lewin, "Transformational Techniques in Atonal and Other Music Theories," *Perspectives of New Music* 21 (1982–83): 312–71; *Generalized Musical Intervals and Transformations* (New Haven: Yale University Press, 1987); *Musical Form and Transformation: 4 Analytic Essays* (New Haven: Yale University Press, 1993). See also John Roeder, "A Theory of Voice Leading for Atonal Music" (Ph.D. diss., Yale University, 1984); "Harmonic Implications of Schoenberg's Observations of Atonal Voice Leading," *Journal of Music Theory* 33 (1989): 27–62; "Voice Leading as Transformation," *Essays in Honor of David Lewin* (Boston: Ovenbird Press, 1995, 41–58); and Henry Klumpenhouwer, "A Generalized Model of Voice-Leading for Atonal Music," (Ph.D. diss., Harvard University, 1991). Lewin has elaborated aspects of Klumpenhouwer's work in "Klumpenhouwer Networks and Some Isographies that Involve Them," *Music Theory Spectrum* 12 (1990): 83–120; and "A Tutorial on Klumpenhouwer Networks, Using the Chorale in Schoenberg's Opus 11, No. 2," *Journal of Music Theory* 38 (1994): 79–102. My own approach has been heavily influenced by that of Klumpenhouwer. I have also

The prolongational analysis (Ex. 1a) identifies some tones as structural and others as embellishing. It uses stems and slurs to assert that a structurally superior D in the bass is embellished by a structurally inferior lower-neighbor C♯, and that a structurally superior C♯ in the soprano is embellished by a structurally inferior upper-neighbor D. The three-chord progression as a whole projects in time a single harmony with D in the bass and C♯ in the upper voice, a harmony that is embellished and elaborated, that exerts structural control even when not literally present, in other words, that is prolonged.

The analysis looks attractive, but is fraught with problems, of which it is appropriate briefly to mention two.[4] First there is the problem of harmonic support: unless we know which harmonies are consonant and which are dissonant, we will not be able to determine reliably which notes are structural and which are embellishing. Atonal music, including the chord progression in Example 1, does not systematically distinguish between consonance and dissonance. As a result, deciding which notes are structural and which embellishing becomes arbitrary. In the soprano line, for example, Example 1 gives greater weight to the C♯, due to its position at the end of the progression, but the D might equally well have been privileged, due to its registral prominence. In the absence of a distinction between the level of harmonic support of the two tones, it becomes impossible to resolve analytical disputes of this kind in a principled way.

The second problem is that of embellishment: there are three traditional embellishment types—passing notes, neighboring notes, and arpeggiations—but atonal music, including the chord progression in Example 1, makes it impossible to identify these embellishments with any assurance. In traditional tonal music, with its diatonic underpinning, a neighbor note is an adjacent scale degree. When the underlying reference changes from the diatonic scale to the twelve-note chromatic scale, the concept of adjacency may come to seem overly restrictive or arbitrary. In the bass line, for example, if the C♯ were a C♮, could it still be a neighbor note, despite its nonadjacency within the referential twelve-note collection? If the C♮ would seem to be a kind of common-sense neighbor if not a strict neighbor, then how about a B♮? Is that close enough to be considered a neighbor? And there is a related problem in this example: D and C♯ are both members of the hypothetically prolonged chord. Perhaps, then,

been influenced by an important but, unfortunately, unpublished article by Allen Forte, "New Modes of Linear Analysis," paper presented at the Oxford University Conference on Music Analysis (1988), particularly its concept of "unary transformation," which I will discuss in more detail below. It is appropriate in the context of the current volume to note that Forte has made significant contributions to the development of all three models for atonal voice leading.

4. For a more extended critique of the prolongational approach to atonal voice leading, see Joseph N. Straus, "The Problem of Prolongation in Post-Tonal Music," *Journal of Music Theory* 31 (1987): 1–22. See also James Baker, "Schenkerian Analysis and Post-Tonal Music," in *Aspects of Schenkerian Theory*, ed. David Beach (New Haven and London: Yale University Press, 1983), 153–88. An interesting recent study has offered some empirical support for the critique offered in these articles and in the following discussion; see Nicola Dibben, "The Cognitive Reality of Hierarchic Structure in Tonal and Atonal Music," *Music Perception* 12 (1994): 1–25.

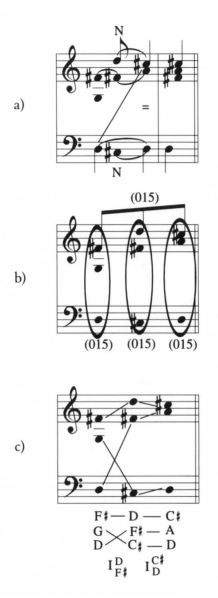

Example 1. Three models for atonal voice leading: a) prolongational; b) associational; c) transformational.

the bass motion from C♯ to D should be considered an arpeggiation, and not a neighboring motion at all. In this musical context, and in atonal music generally, it is often impossible to give precise, reliable, systematic descriptions of embellishing functions.

If one cannot distinguish the structural tones from the nonstructural tones or determine the means by which the nonstructural tones embellish the structural tones, then one cannot produce convincing prolongational analyses. In offering this critique, I do not wish to enact an absolute ban on prolongational language—surely it can be useful in discussions of atonal music to refer casually to apparent passing notes and neighboring notes. I do wish to suggest, however, that prolongation may not be a reliable basis for sustained analytical inquiry, or for structural levels beyond the immediate musical surface.[5]

If the prolongational analysis fails in many ways, however, it is notably successful in capturing the unmistakable tonal echo in the progression, its D majorish feel. In the atonal repertoire, permeated as it is with tonal echoes, that may be a useful function. For dealing with the more idiomatically atonal musical features, however, the prolongational model is unsatisfactory.

In the associational analysis in Example 1b, the three chords are shown to represent the same trichord-type: [D,F♯,G], [C♯,D,F♯], and [A,C♯,D] are all members of set-class 3–4 (015). Furthermore, the highest notes of each chord, F♯–D–C♯, taken together, form the same type of harmony and, indeed, linearize the notes of the middle chord. The highest registral line thus presents, in a linear fashion, the intervallic content of all three chords and the actual pitch-class content of the middle chord.

Associational analyses generally take this form, finding linear projections of harmonies or harmony-types from the musical surface. Musical tones separated in time may be associated by any contextual means, including register, timbre, metrical placement, dynamics, and articulation. Tones associated in this way may form coherent linear structures.

This means of describing the linear organization of atonal music is theoretically straightforward and analytically revealing. It is important to note, however, that the entities under discussion in this model are *lines*, not *voices*. A line is a series of notes, heard one at a time, that share some distinctive musical quality (for example, they are all in the highest register, they are all played by the contrabassoon, they are all played pizzicato, or they are all played pianisissimo). To adapt Christopher Hasty's terminology, notes may cohere into a line if they have an identical value in some musical domain.[6] A voice, in contrast, is a manifestation of an underlying

---

5. For an interesting recent discussion of these issues, see Jack Boss, "Schoenberg on Ornamentation and Structural Levels," *Journal of Music Theory* 38 (1994): 187–216.

6. Christopher Hasty, "Segmentation and Process in Post-Tonal Music," *Music Theory Spectrum* 3 (1981): 54–73. "A change of value in a particular domain creates a discontinuity—a difference which isolates distinct objects for our attention. . . . Such elements thus differentiated may, however, come to be heard as a unity if in some domain they possess identical values. . . . [A structure] must have a unitary value in some domain, that is, there must be no

pitch-class counterpoint.[7] In tonal music, for example, sevenths resolve down by step, and they do so irrespective of the register, instrumentation, articulation, or dynamic of their occurrence. Lines are entirely dependent on the contextual means by which they are established. Voices are generally more robust, better able to maintain their integrity in the face of contextual disruptions, the familiar register transfers of tonal theory being a case in point. In Example 1b, the beamed upper line links F♯ to D to C♯. But that connection is an exclusive function of the registral placement of the notes. If the D were transferred an octave lower, the line would be destroyed, because there is no underlying pitch-class counterpoint that leads from F♯ through D to C♯. F♯–D–C♯ is a registral line, not a voice-leading voice.[8]

In the transformational model, we gain a sense of an underlying pitch-class counterpoint, one relatively immune to the vagaries of the contextual surface (see Ex. 1c). This model shifts our attention from the chords themselves to the operations, the transformations, that connect them. The first chord inverts onto the second, and the second inverts onto the third.[9] When the first chord moves to the sec-

---

change of value in this domain which would cause it to be broken up into subcomponents. It must be distinguished as an object of our attention by possessing a difference of value in the same domain compared with another object" (58).

7. The phrase "pitch-class counterpoint" is taken from William Benjamin, "Pitch-class Counterpoint in Tonal Music," in *Music Theory: Special Topics*, ed. Richmond Browne (New York: Academic Press, 1981), 1–32. "As I understand it, a harmonic progression is not a succession of vertical complexes so much as it is a counterpoint of lines. What separates such a counterpoint from what we ordinarily call counterpoint is that the lines in a harmonic progression are PC lines. Whereas the structures of traditional counterpoint—such as Fuxian species counterpoint—are defined in pitch-specific terms, the structures of harmony are here, by definition, conceived of in PC terms, that is, without reference to the octave placement or irreducible elements—scale degrees—in an individual harmonic progression. Therefore, whereas traditional counterpoint distinguishes between the bass voice and upper voices, or between perfect fourths and perfect fifths, harmony as I conceive it makes no such distinctions and regards even the matter of melodic contour, so basic to counterpoint, as foreign" (4).

8. A similar distinction between voice and line is generally maintained in studies of array-based compositions, like those of Milton Babbitt. There, analysts routinely imagine that the precompositional "lynes" of the array are voices that define the voice leading of a composition. These voices are often reinforced compositionally, that is, are realized as lines (usually in register, dynamics, or articulation), but they need not be. Voices, then, are operational—they result from the workings of the system—while lines are contextual. For a discussion of these matters, and a clear sense of the ways in which a precompositional array may recede from the contextual surface, see Joseph Dubiel, "Three Essays on Milton Babbitt," Part 1: *Perspectives of New Music* 28 (1990): 216–61; Part 2: *Perspectives of New Music* 29 (1991): 90–123; Part 3: *Perspectives of New Music* 30 (1992): 82–131.

9. Inversion is commonly described as a compound operation, T_nI, where I means "invert around C" and T_n means "transpose by some interval n." In this paper, I will use instead Lewin's convention of describing inversion as I_v^u, which means "invert around an axis of symmetry defined by pitch-classes u and v," or "perform the inversion that maps u and v onto each other." Pitch-classes u and v may be any pitch classes and they may be the same

ond, the D and F♯ map onto each other in a voice exchange that frequently, in atonal music, suggests pitch-class inversion. The same inversion maps G onto C♯. When the second chord moves to the third, C♯ and D have a similar kind of voice exchange, and the inversion specified by that exchange sends F♯ onto A.

This analysis identifies three real voice-leading voices, D–F♯–A, G–C♯–D, and F♯–D–C♯, each of which is traced on the example.[10] Within each voice, the underlying transformation can be heard as motivating the movement from note to note. When the first chord moves to the second, for example, $I^D_{F♯}$ sends each note in the first chord onto a corresponding note in the second. The inversion of G onto C♯ and D onto F♯ can be heard to push the F♯ onto D, as each note is urged onward by the behavior of the other two. No chord, by itself, implies any particular continuation (as dominant-seventh chords, for example, do in tonal music) and the voices are thus not lines of realized implications, as they often are in tonal contexts. They nonetheless form a pitch-class counterpoint for the passage, one which may or may not be reflected in the actual registers. The three high notes really do comprise a voice: F♯ goes to D because the chord inversion sends it there; D goes to C♯ because a different inversion sends it there. In the lower parts, the voices cross, but the pitch-class counterpoint asserts their integrity. Of course, it is still easy to hear in the lowest register a registral line that goes D–C♯–D, but, as in tonal music with its transfers of register and its covering voices, although the voice leading may coincide with the actual registers, it need not do so. Tracing the pitch-class counterpoint, and hearing it in relation to variously formed contextual lines, can reveal much about the linear organization of atonal music. I do not suggest that voices are structurally superior to lines. Indeed, a voice, in the sense I am giving the term, is simply a special kind of line, one created by relevant transformations. It is in the interaction of voices and lines, not in the subordination of one to the other, that so much of the interest of the linear organization of atonal music lies.

The kind of pitch-class counterpoint I am describing has always been implicit in atonal set theory. Any time we say that two chords are related by transposition or inversion, we are also saying that each note in the first chord maps onto a corresponding note in the second, thus creating a network of linear connections between the chords. In that sense, we have been doing voice-leading analyses all along, but without explicitly acknowledging it. The transformational model I am describing can thus be

---

pitch class. See Lewin, *Generalized Musical Intervals and Transformations*, 50–59. In Example 1c, I have labelled the operation that leads from the first chord to the second $I^D_{F♯}$, in order to emphasize the movement of the upper voice, F♯ to D, and its exchange with the motion from D to F♯ below it. I could just as well have chosen $I^G_{C♯}$, $I^{C♯}_C$, I^A_B, I^B_B, I^E_F, or I^E_E. All of these labels are equivalent.

10. My sense of atonal voices as the pitch-class counterpoint induced by certain transformations, and my notation for expressing that sense, are both derived from Klumpenhouwer "A Generalized Model of Voice-Leading for Atonal Music." Whereas Klumpenhouwer is primarily concerned with the registral permutations that result from the motion of the voices, I will focus instead on the integrity of the voices themselves, over potentially large musical spans, and their interaction with contextual lines.

thought of as set theory in which the focus has been shifted from the objects to the transformations that connect them, in which a sense of linearity and movement, implicit in the ideas of transposition and inversion, has been brought to the fore. It can be thought of as set theory with an attitude, specifically, with a "transformational attitude."[11]

Example 2 traces the voice leading between pairs of chords related by transposition. In Example 2a, the pitch-class counterpoint is supported by register and instrumentation, as each instrument simply ascends eight semitones. Examples 2b, 2c, and 2d present slightly more complicated situations in which the pitch-class mappings may or may not be coincident with register or instrumentation. In 2b, the highest three lines move down four semitones, strongly confirming the T_8 relationship between the chords as a whole. The lower lines ascend by two semitones, but the pitch-class voices cross, each moving by T_8. In 2c, all but one note in the first chord has a counterpart three semitones higher in the second chord. The E♭ in the first chord, however, finds its partner twenty-one semitones lower. In 2d, the sense of moving down two semitones from the first chord to the second is felt strongly in the highest registral line (violin and cornet), less so in the other instrumental or registral parts.[12]

Example 3 traces the voice leading between chords related by inversion. In Example 3a, the first chord literally inverts onto the second in pitch space, then descends a semitone, again in pitch space. In Examples 3b, 3c, 3d, and 3e, the inversion takes place in pitch-class space—the second chord is not the literal pitch inversion of the first—but the mappings are confirmed by the instrumentation and registration of the chords. In 3f, as in 3c and 3d, a single note is held in common between the two chords, and that note forms the axis around which the first chord inverts onto the second. In 3g, as in 3b and 3e, two notes are held in common between the chords, and they describe a voice exchange. As a general matter, voice exchange in atonal music usually suggests not harmonic prolongation, as it would in a tonal context, but pitch-class inversion: the exchange defines the axis around which the first chord inverts onto the second.

---

11. The phrase is David Lewin's: "To some extent for cultural-historical reasons, it is easier for us to hear 'intervals' between individual objects than to hear transpositional relations between them; we are more used to conceiving transpositions as affecting *Gestalts* built up from individual objects. As this way of talking suggests, we are very much under the influence of Cartesian thinking in such matters. We tend to conceive the primary objects in our musical spaces as atomic individual 'elements' rather than contextually articulated phenomena like sets, melodic series, and the like. And we tend to imagine ourselves in the position of *observers* when we theorize about musical space; the space is 'out there,' away from our dancing bodies or singing voices. . . . In contrast, the transformational attitude is much less Cartesian. Given locations s and t in our space, this attitude does not ask for some observed measure of extension between reified 'points'; rather it asks: 'If I am *at* s and wish to get to t, what characteristic gesture should I perform in order to arrive there?'" (*Generalized Musical Intervals and Transformations*, 158–59).

12. Because the chord-type in Example 2d is inversionally symmetrical, the chords might be understood as related by either T_{10}, as shown, or I_A^A, which would induce a different set of mappings. Voice leading between symmetrical chords will be discussed below.

a)

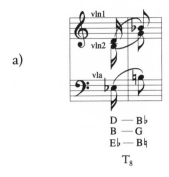

$$D — B\flat$$
$$B — G$$
$$E\flat — B\natural$$
$$T_8$$

b)

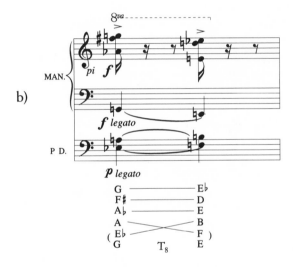

G ——————— E♭
F♯ ——————— D
A♭ ——————— E
A ✕ B
(E♭ ✕ F)
G T_8 E

Example 2. Chords related by transposition: a) Webern: Movements for String Quartet, op. 5, no. 3, mm. 1–2, upper strings; b) Messiaen: "Les Mains de l'abîme" from *Livre d'orgue,* m. 12.

A special kind of voice exchange, one in which the exchanged voices do not literally move, is illustrated in Example 4. In 4a, the second chord is the pitch inversion of the first: within a fixed frame of C4–E4, the second violin moves from C♯4 to its symmetrical partner D♯4. That motion from C♯ to D♯ changes the relationship between C and E. In the first chord, the C has notes one and four semitones away from it while the E has notes three and four semitones away; in the second chord, their roles are reversed—now C is in the invervallic position previously occupied by E and vice versa. The C and E, that is, change places, despite not moving at all. That reversal of intervallic position induced by the single moving voice is what lends the

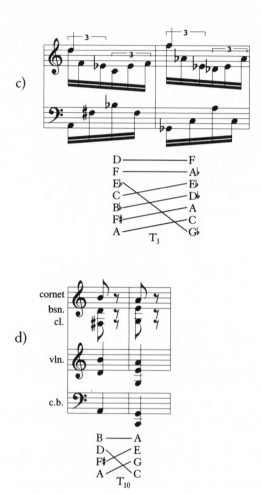

Example 2 cont'd. c) Roslavets: Piano Piece, mm. 1–2; d) Stravinsky: *A Soldier's Tale,* conclusion of "The Soldier's March."

sense of a voice exchange to this progression. In 4b, the motion from C to A in the upper voice can be heard retrospectively to cause the sustained G♯–C♯ in the bass to exchange positions. Conversely, the sustained G♯–C♯ can be heard as causing the first upper-voice note C to move to its symmetrical partner, A. In other words, the imbalance in the first chord pushes the C downward to A, which balances it with respect to the sustained G♯–C♯. All of the progressions in Example 4 involve voice exchanges in which an asymmetry in the first chord is rectified by the second, as each note in the first chord finds its inversional partner. This kind of movement, from an unbalanced state to a balanced one, is common in atonal music and often, as in the progressions of Example 4, signifies the end of a phrase or structural unit.

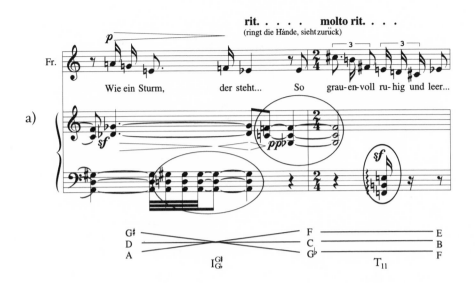

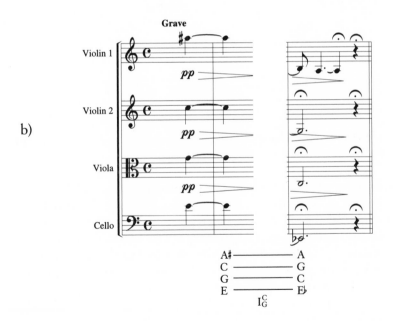

Example 3. a) Schoenberg: *Erwartung*, mm. 13–14; b) Beach: String Quartet, mvt. 1, first and last chords.

Example 3 cont'd. c) Webern: Movements for String Quartet, op. 5, no. 3, m. 3, upper strings; d) Jolivet: "Danse initiatique" from *Cinq danses rituelles*, m. 1.

Inversionally symmetrical harmonies may be understood as related by either transposition or inversion (see Ex. 5). In 5a, imagining the chords as related by T_1 correlates strongly with motion of the highest registral line, but fails to capture the static nature of the progression, with the repeated pizzicato C in the cello. Imagining the chords as related by I_B^G depicts the repeated C as part of a C-E♭ voice exchange, and calls attention to the temporal ordering of the notes: the first note of the first chord maps onto the last note of the second chord; the second note onto the second-to-last, and so on. The inversional symmetry of the voice leading is thus reinforced by the retrograde symmetry of the ordering of the notes. On balance, then, the inversional interpretation offers a richer hearing of the passage, although the transpositional hearing also has its merits. The progression lends itself to either interpretation.

The same is true in Example 5b: the transpositional interpretation captures the descending motion in the first violin and viola, but the inversional interpretation captures the static, balanced quality of the progression, where notes flip around a

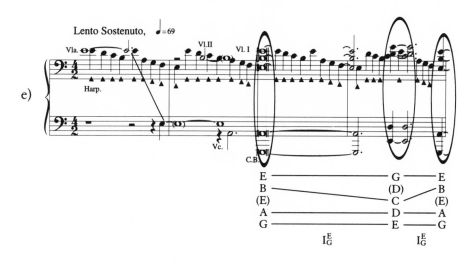

e)

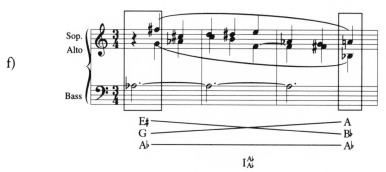

f)

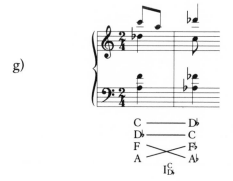

g)

Example 3 cont'd. e) Stravinsky: *Orpheus*, mm. 1–4; f) Crawford: Chant No. 2 ("To an Angel"), mm. 5–7; g) Scriabin: Prelude op. 74, no. 4, mm. 11–12.

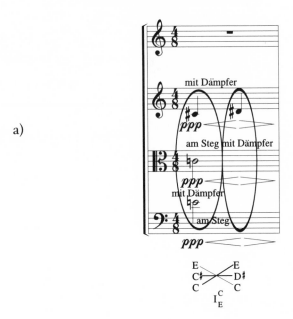

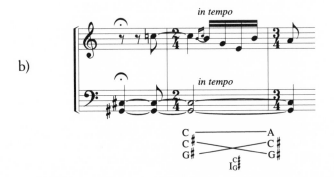

Example 4. Chords related by inversion with static voice exchange: a) Webern: Bagatelles for String Quartet, op. 9, no. 5, m. 1; b) Stravinsky: *Rite of Spring*, Introduction, mm. 6–8.

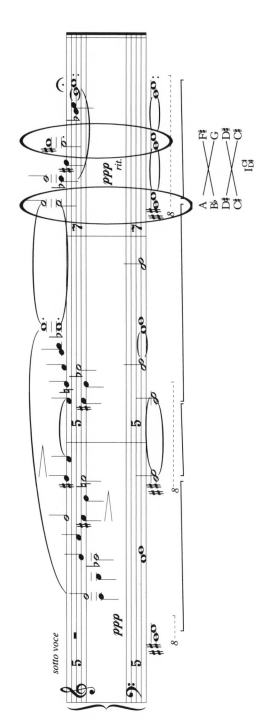

Example 4 cont'd. c) Crawford: Prelude No. 9, mm. 23–24.

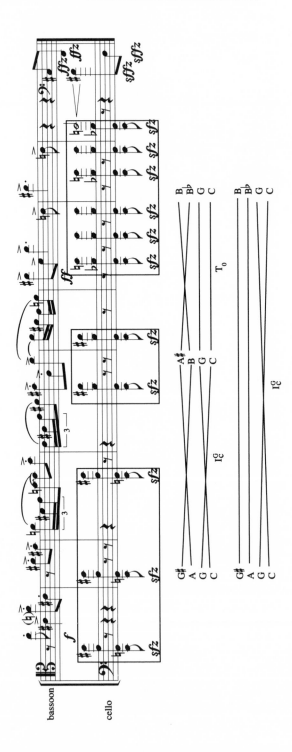

Example 4 cont'd. d) Crawford: Diaphonic Suite No. 2 for Bassoon and Cello, mvt. 3, mm. 36–43.

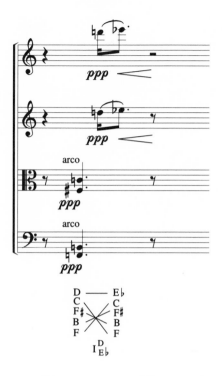

Example 4 cont'd. e) Webern: Movements for String Quartet, op. 5, no. 2, m. 5.

retained A and E.[13] 5c and 5d show similar multiple interpretations.[14] The same symmetrical trichord-type from 5d, 3–9 (027), accounts for virtually every simulaneity in 5e. In the progressions in that passage, the inversional interpretation often seems more compelling, because of the persistence of A–E as a harmonic frame, but the frequent motions up or down by five semitones tends to support the transpositional interpretation.

Over longer passages, it becomes possible not only to trace the voices from harmony to harmony but to discover movements of larger scale, a transformational middleground. In Example 6, the circled chords are all members of set-class 3–5 (016), and the immediate connections among them are shown in Level 1. Level 2 simplifies the progression into two inversional moves, each of which exchanges the voice part

13. Forte discusses this passage in *The Structure of Atonal Music*, 30. He points out that the two notes held invariant between the chords, A and E, are isolated in mm. 4–5.

14. The notes of Example 5c are written in score order rather than registral order and the B in the second chord, doubled between cello and viola, is written only once. Forte discusses another movement of this piece in "An Octatonic Essay by Webern: No. 1 of the *Six Bagatelles for String Quartet*, Op. 9," *Music Theory Spectrum* 16 (1994): 171–95. In Example 5d, the notes in the oboe parts are duplicated by the other instruments, and are omitted from the analysis.

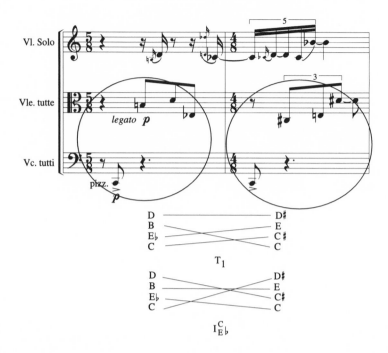

Example 5. Symmetrical chords related by either transposition or inversion: a) Stravinsky: *Agon*, mm. 421–22.

with the lowest sounding part. Finally, Level 3 describes the progression as the transposition at T_8 (actually a pitch transposition at T_{-4}) of the first chord onto the last chord.

In the passage in Example 7a the lower three registral lines form an augmented triad, transposing it up or down by semitone, while the melody moves about somewhat more freely.[15] Every time the four lines attack simultaneously, as they do on virtually every beat, they create a form of set-class 4–19 (0148). An associational description of the passage would point out that, after an initial alternation of two chords, the melody linearizes five forms of the same set class (shown with beams), all of which occur as verticals at least once somewhere in the passage.

A transformational description views the melody somewhat differently (see Ex. 7b). Level 1 shows the transformations connecting adjacent chords, each of which is mirrored in the upper voice. When the upper voice moves at T_7, so does the chord as a whole, and when the upper voice moves by semitone, the chord inverts around the axis defined by that semitone. Throughout the entire passage then, the highest

---

15. George Perle describes this passage in terms of the "simultaneous unfolding of different cyclic progressions," and likens it to the compositional practice of Alban Berg. See "Scriabin's Self-Analyses," *Music Analysis* 3 (1984): 116.

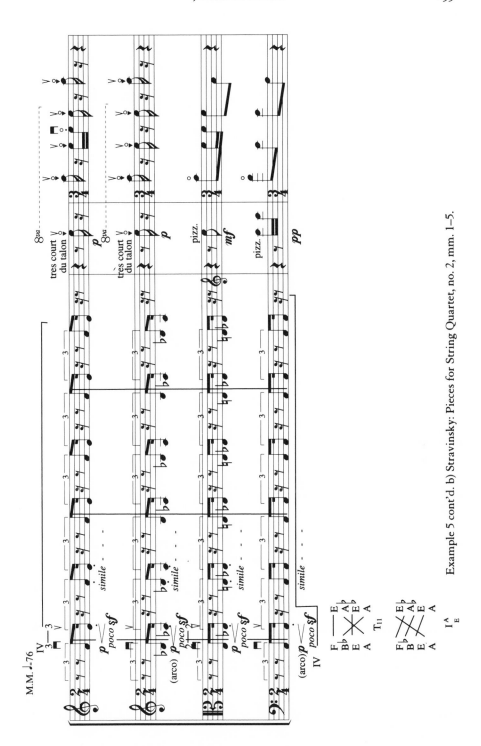

Example 5 cont'd. b) Stravinsky: Pieces for String Quartet, no. 2, mm. 1–5.

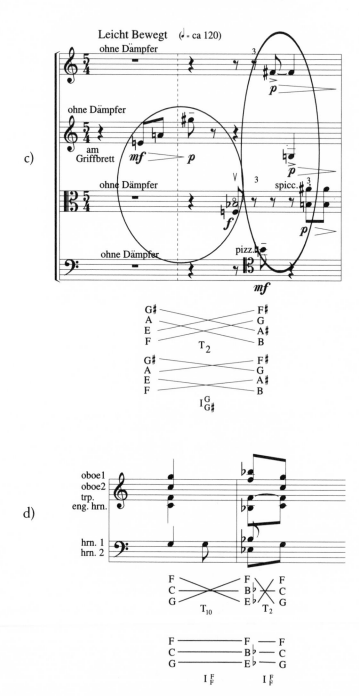

Example 5 cont'd. c) Webern: Bagatelles for String Quartet, op. 9, no. 2, m. 1; d) Stravinsky: *Agon*, mm. 39–40.

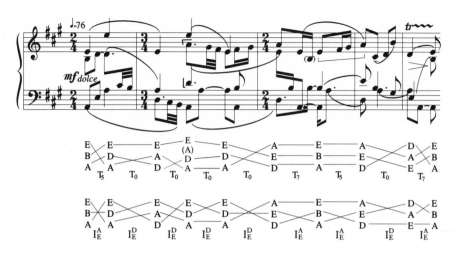

Example 5 cont'd. e) Stravinsky: *The Rake's Progress,* act I, sc. 1, mm. 1–5.

sounding part maintains its integrity not only as a registral line but as a contrapuntal voice. It has the same integrity at the deeper structural levels, including Level 4, which shows the first and last chords in mm. 13–17 connected by T_0.

Despite its appearance, this multilevel analysis is hierarchical only in a casual sense. The chords omitted from the deeper levels cannot be said to prolong the chords that are retained. Conversely, the chords at the deeper levels do not organize the music into prolongational spans. As a result, chords must earn their membership in the deeper levels by virtue of contextual cues: like the chords at the surface level they must be associated in some way. In Example 7b, Level 1 selects chords that occur on each beat. Level 2 retains the chords that are accented both by the duration of the melody note and by their metrical position within the prevailing hemiola. Level 3 retains the first and last chords in each of the two transpositionally related phrases that make up the longer period, and Level 4 retains the first and last chords of the period. There is no sense in this analysis that the passage is "in" [C, D♭, F♭, A♭], merely that the passage moves from one statement of that harmony, along a certain path, to another statement of it.

In Example 7, the motivic/associational reading and the voice-leading/transformational reading are distinct, but the voice leading may itself follow a motivic path. The passage in Example 8 consists of groups of two or three chords, all members of set-class 3–3 (014), interspersed with canonic interjections. The instrumentation of the chords reflects their voice leading to a remarkable degree, exclusively so in the first violin, and with one brief voice crossing in the second violin and viola. In other words, whatever each instrumental line does, moving via transposition or inversion, that is what the chord as a whole does, and vice versa.

Level 2 isolates one chord from each group of chords: the first chord from the first group, and the last chord in each group thereafter. The intervals of transposi-

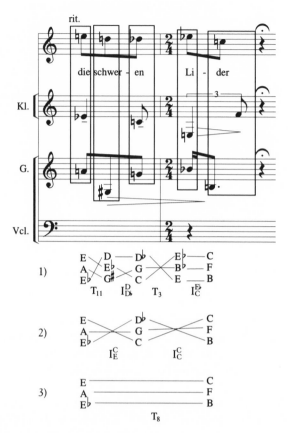

Example 6. Webern: Songs, op. 14, "Die Sonne," mm. 23–24: transformational analysis in three levels.

tion—T_1, T_3, and T_4—are the same as the intervals contained within the chord-type being transposed. The voice leading at this level thus follows a motivic path.[16]

In Example 9a, Level 3 shows a passage spanned by two statements of the same trichord, the second voiced as the registral inversion of the first. Those two trichords are connected, at Level 2, by a transpositional path that reflects the intervallic content of the trichord itself: the trichord contains intervals 6, 8, and 10, and at Level 2 it is transposed by just those intervals. Level 1 accounts in a more detailed way for the path between the second and third chords of Level 2.[17]

It will be apparent that, in Examples 7b, 8, and 9a, many notes are uncircled and thus entirely ignored in the analysis. Indeed, the analyses ignore any notes that

16. For an interesting recent study of this work, one that shares some of the concerns and conclusions of this analysis, see Eric Lai, "Transformational Structures in Webern's Opus 5, No. 3," *Indiana Theory Review* 10 (1989): 21–50.

17. My description of this passage relies heavily on David Lewin's in "Transformational Techniques."

do not form the set-class whose transformations are being traced: 4–19 (0148) in Example 7b, 3–3 (014) in Example 8, and 3–8 (026) in Example 9a. These analyses tease out of the musical fabric a single strand and describe the voice-leading connections that may be heard to bind it. The fabric of the music as a whole, however, is comprised of many interwoven strands of varying content and length, no one of which endures from beginning to end, or reaches from top to bottom. The remaining notes belong to other strands, other transformational networks, each with its own internal voice leading.

In the spirit of that observation, Example 9b offers a different voice leading analysis of the passage from Example 9a, now tracing the occurrences of set-class 3–11 (037), the major or minor triad.[18] Its motions consist of T_3 and $I^D_{F\sharp}$, which combine into I^D_D. In more traditional language, D, which is the root of the initial minor chord, becomes the fifth of the concluding major chord.[19] Neither the (026)-oriented reading of Example 9a nor the (037)-oriented reading of Example 9b is hierarchically superior. Neither subsumes the other or embellishes the other. Rather, they are independent strands that intertwine, with each other and with other strands not mentioned, to create the larger fabric.[20]

It is evident, then, that the voices in these analyses do not have the identity and continuity of voices in tonal compositions. There, one expects to speak particularly of outer voices that are continuous from the beginning to the end of entire works. In contrast, atonal transformational voices come and go, entering and exiting. Transformational analyses, then, do not purport to describe the voice leading of entire passages, much less entire pieces. Indeed, I don't think that the post-tonal repertoire lends itself to single, all-encompassing readings of that kind. I believe we must content ourselves with describing the multiple voice leadings (plural), knowing that for each transformational path we traverse, there will be others that run alongside or intersect it, each with its own points of interest.

The transformations may remain the same even as the objects being transformed change. In Example 10, mm. 4–9 are analyzed with respect to 3–4 (015) while mm. 10–12 are analyzed with respect to 3–9 (027). The trichord stated at the beginning of m. 4, A♭–D♭–C, is transposed twice at T_6, via a series of smaller transpositions and inversions, leading to its return at the end of m. 6. There, over a sustained G♯–C♯, the opening melody returns, and its descending motion from C to A is interpreted in relation to $I^A_{G\sharp}$: the transformation that sends C onto A sends C♯ and G♯ onto each other.[21] In mm.

18. This set class is not particularly prominent in this passage, but becomes so when the same music is varied in its recapitulation at the end of the movement. See Joseph N. Straus, *Remaking the Past: Musical Modernism and the Influence of the Tonal Tradition* (Cambridge: Harvard University Press, 1990), 93–95, for an account of major and minor triads in this work.

19. This view confirms David Lewin's sense of the passage as notably involved with inversion around D (see "Transformational Techniques").

20. John Roeder analyzes this movement in terms of transformations of (026) and (037), as well as several other trichord-types, in "Voice Leading as Transformation," 52–53.

21. This passage was discussed earlier, with respect to Example 4b, as a static voice ex-

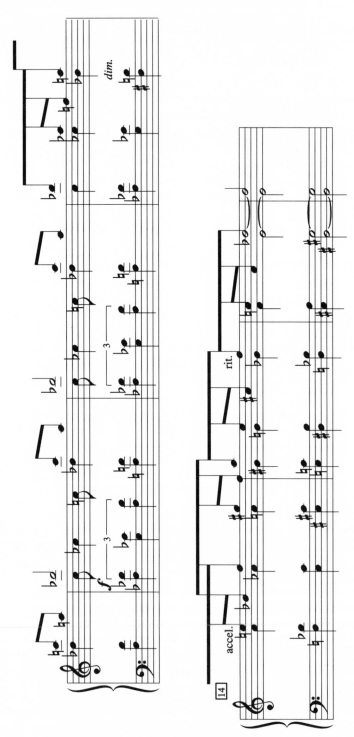

Example 7. Scriabin. Prelude, op. 74, no. 4, mm. 10–17: a) associational analysis with linear forms of set-class 4–19 (0148).

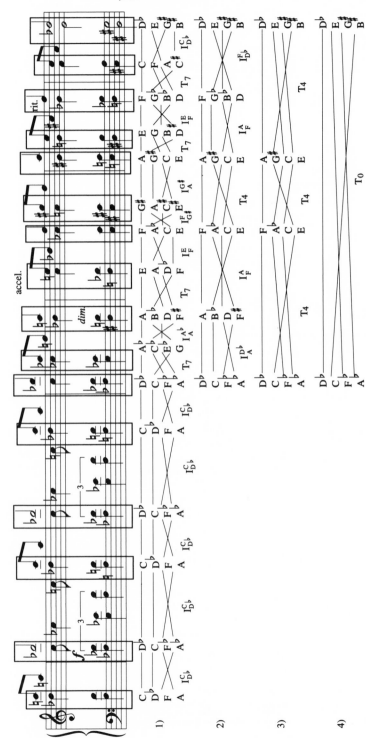

Example 7 cont'd. b) transformational analysis in four levels.

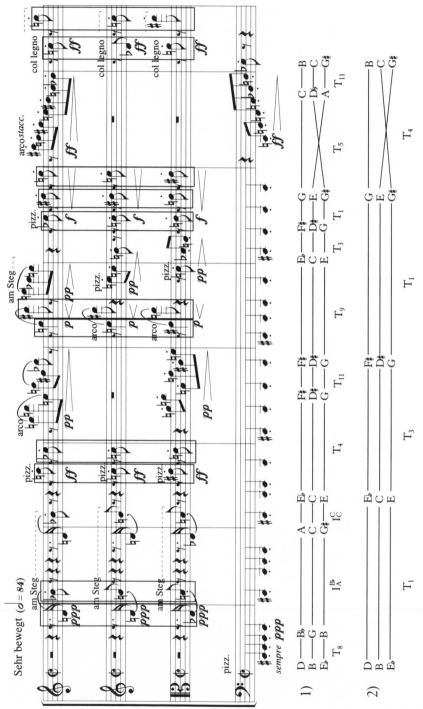

Example 8. Webern: Movements for String Quartet, op. 5, no. 3, mm. 1–8: transformational analysis in two levels.

10–12, the G♯ and C♯ are still sustained in the bass, but the melody changes, and with it the structure of the simultaneities. The transformation I$^9_{G♯}$ remains active, however, now sending F♯ onto D♯ in the melody.[22] The content of the harmonies changes in mm. 10, but the means of moving from harmony to harmony remains the same.

The structure of the passage in Example 11 is remarkably similar to that of mm. 7–9 of Example 10, which was written a few years earlier. Both passages involve a static voice exchange in which a melodic descent causes the notes of a sustained bass interval to invert onto each other. In Example 10, I$^9_{G♯}$ mapped a melodic C onto A, and then F♯ onto D♯, the melody moving down by three semitones each time. In Example 11, I$^9_{F♯}$ motivates a similar melodic motion from F down to D, a motion that occurs both from the first chord to the second (Level 1) and, in transformational enlargement, from the first chord to the fifth (Level 2).

In Examples 10 and 11, tonal references, particularly as embodied in the melodic minor thirds, coexist with the atonal transformations, and this is a persistent feature of twentieth-century music.[23] Prolongational analyses have tended to be best suited for teasing out implicit tonal structures, with Schenker's own analysis of a passage from Stravinsky's Concerto for Piano and Wind Instruments a striking case in point (see Ex. 12a).[24] Schenker analyzes the passage in A minor, and shows that it begins with a third-span in the upper voice, A–G♯–F♯, within a prolonged subdomi-

---

change. It is instructive to compare my transformational analysis with Roy Travis's prolongational analysis ("Toward a New Concept of Tonality?" *Journal of Music Theory* 3 [1959]: 257–63) and Allen Forte's associational analysis ("New Approaches to the Linear Analysis of Music," *Journal of the American Musicological Society* 41 [1988]: 315–22). Travis analyzes the passage with respect to a "tonic sonority," which is the same member of set-class 3–4 (015) that my analysis traces. He considers the melodic descent from C to A a third-span, but is unable to show how it prolongs, or relates in any clear way, to his tonic sonority. Forte shows how the passage linearizes a number of significant sets, and considers the melodic descent from C to A as part of a linear statement of 4–17 (0347), itself part of a larger octatonic collection. Forte's lines are motivic entities, not voices as I am using the term here.

22. Not incidentally, the upper voice as a whole descends C–A–F♯–D♯, tracing a diminished-seventh chord and linking the passage, at this deeper level, to the octatonic concerns of *The Rite of Spring* as a whole. See Pieter van den Toorn, *The Music of Igor Stravinsky* (New Haven: Yale University Press, 1983), 100–37 and *Stravinsky and The Rite of Spring: The Beginnings of a Musical Language* (Berkeley: University of California Press, 1987), 115–214, for an extended discussion of these matters. Christopher Hasty (in "Succession and Continuity") describes a similar large-scale statement of a descending diminished-seventh chord in the opening section of *Symphonies of Wind Instruments*, another of Stravinsky's octatonically inflected works.

23. The relationship between tonal and post-tonal structures in this repertoire is the subject of a number of recent studies, including Straus, *Remaking the Past*; Chandler Carter, "The Progress in The Rake's Return" (Ph.D. diss., City University of New York, 1994); Pieter van den Toorn, "Neoclassicism Revised," *Music, Politics, and the Academy* (Berkeley: University of California Press, 1995), 143–78; and Martha Hyde, "Neoclassic and Anachronistic Impulses in Twentieth-Century Music," *Music Theory Spectrum* 18 (1996), 200–235.

24. Schenker's analysis appears in "Resumption of Urlinie Considerations." This is

Example 9. Webern: Movements for String Quartet, op. 5, no. 2, mm. 1–3: a) transformational analysis with respect to set-class 3–8 (026).

nant harmony and concludes with a long octave-descent in the upper voice. Schenker's principal criticism has to do with Stravinsky's handling of these spans: "Is it not true that Stravinsky contradicts this outline everywhere he possibly can, through the progression especially of the lower voice, which obstructs every formation in spans?... He allows the tones to constantly appear in dissonances against each other.... In bar 3, the first third span, A–G♯–F♯, draws to a close, but this effect is nullified by the B of the middle voice."[25] Schenker claims, quite reasonably in my view, that his analysis

_____

Schenker's only analysis of a post-tonal piece, and is intended as a negative example, an object lesson in how not to compose.

25. Schenker, "Resumption of Urlinie Considerations," 214.

Example 9 cont'd. b) transformational analysis with respect to set-class 3–11 (037).

"could stand for what Stravinsky might have had in mind."[26] There is clearly a sense in the passage that Stravinsky is writing against an implicit tonal model, and Schenker has recovered a likely candidate for that role.[27] Schenker is also right to point out that Stravinsky corrupts the tonal model and violates the integrity of the linear progressions every chance he gets.[28] In fact, as Robert Morgan has observed, Stravinsky thwarts the tonal implications in a very consistent way: at the beginnings and end-

---

26. Ibid., 213.

27. Schenker's sense that Stravinsky's music can be understood in relation to an implicit tonal prototype is confirmed in part by Stravinsky's own frequent compositional practice. In many of Stravinsky's "neoclassical" works, the earliest compositional sketches tend to be relatively square rhythmically and conventional harmonically, thus comprising a traditional tonal model that he transforms as he composes. See Joseph N. Straus, "The Progress of a Motive in Stravinsky's *The Rake's Progress*," *Journal of Musicology* 9 (1991): 165–85.

28. Stravinsky's persistent misalignment of apparent linear spans, in this and other works,

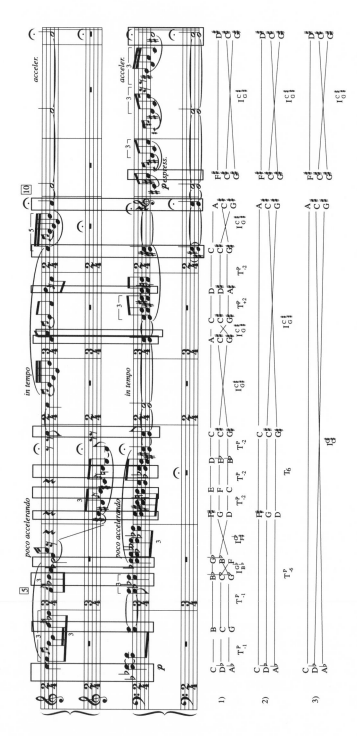

Example 10. Stravinsky: *Rite of Spring*, Introduction, mm. 4–12: transformational analysis in two levels with respect to two set-classes, 3–4 (015) and 3–9 (027).

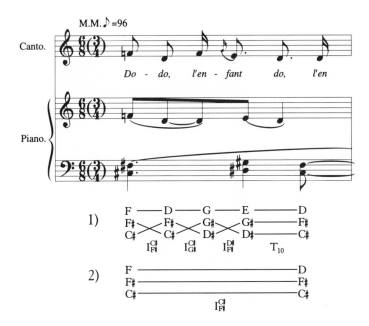

Example 11. Stravinsky: *Berceuses du chat,* no. 3 ("Bay-bay"), m. 1: transformational analysis in two levels with enlargement.

ings of linear spans, Stravinsky generally employs not the triads that occur in Schenker's analysis, but members of set-class 3–4 (015).[29]

The passage can be understood as a perverse kind of A minor, as Schenker has shown, but it can also be understood in relation to that set-class, exclusive of tonal implications. In Example 12b, Level 4 shows the passage spanned by an octave transfer of C♯–D–A. What Schenker described, using the language of tonal prolongation, as an *Octavzug* in A minor, I am describing, using the language of atonal transformation, simply as a transposition at T_{-12}. Level 3 shows T_{-12} as divided up into a T_{-3} and a T_{-9}. Level 2 shows the T_{-9} as divided into a T_0 followed by two inversions, first an inversion around F♯, and then one that exchanges C♯ and D. In Level 1, the second of those inversions is divided into three moves. All the transformations, both the transpositions and the inversions, are reinforced by the actual registers, that is, the registral lines and the voice-leading voices coincide.

In all of the analyses so far, the harmonies have progressed by either transposi-

has been termed "phrase staggering" by Lynne Rogers in "Stravinsky's Alternative Approach to Counterpoint" (Ph.D. diss., Princeton University, 1989).

29. Morgan, "Dissonant Prolongations." This is also the set class traced in Example 10 with regard to the opening of the *Rite of Spring*, and identified by Travis as the "tonic sonority" for that passage.

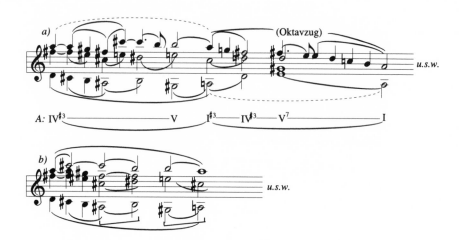

Example 12. Stravinsky: *Concerto for Piano and Wind Instruments,* mvt. 1, 16 mm. at rehearsal no. 34: a) analysis by Heinrich Schenker, divided by him into (a) and (b).

tion or inversion, those familiar interval-preserving operations. But harmonies may be heard to progress in other ways, and any operation that maps notes in one harmony onto notes in another may be understood to create a counterpoint of pitch classes. There are a potentially infinite number of such operations, limited only by our musical imaginations.[30] One such operation that I have found particularly useful I will call *near-transposition* or *near-inversion*. Two harmonies are related by near-transposition or near-inversion if all but one of their notes are related by actual transposition or actual inversion.[31]

In Example 13, the first four chords are repeated throughout the passage. The second and fourth chords are related by transposition, but that is the only actual transposition or inversion in the passage. The first two chords, for example, are not related by transposition as a whole, but three out of the four notes move down by semitone from the first chord to the second. That relationship is identified as $*T_{11}$, with the asterisk denoting that not all of the notes participate.[32] The notes not related by transposition are connected by a dotted line. The second chord moves to the third, and the third to the fourth, by near-inversion. Those two near-inversions combine, as shown in Level

---

30. Lewin's *Generalized Musical Intervals and Transformations* is a fertile source of musical operations suggested by local contexts.

31. My concept of near-transposition and near-inversion is related to considerable earlier and ongoing theoretical work. In discussing the similarity of sets that are not related by transposition or inversion, Forte describes an R_p relation, defined as follows: two sets of cardinality n are in the relation R_p if they share a common subset of cardinality n–1 (*The Structure of Atonal Music,* 47). Any two sets relatable by near-transposition or near-inversion must be in the R_p relation, and vice versa. Forte suggests a disadvantage of his R_p, and my near-transposition and near-inversion, when he observes that "R_p is not especially significant since many sets are so related to a large number of other sets" (48).

Example 12 cont'd. b) transformational analysis in four levels (by the present author).

2, into an actual transposition down two semitones. Finally, Level 3 shows the motion from the first chord to the last chord as a near-transposition down three semitones and, in fact, all of the instruments except the viola actually do descend by three semitones.[33] Indeed, in this passage, the near-transpositions and near-inversions are usually, but not always, confirmed by the actual instrumental and registral lines.

In Example 14, it is easy to sense some kind of connection among the four circled chords, but hard to describe that connection in the usual set-theoretic way, as they represent four distinct chord-types. None of them is related to any of the others by actual transposition, but they are nonetheless connected by a network of near-transpositions. The first chord moves to the second by near-transposition at $^*T_4$.[34] The lower two voices actually move up four semitones, but the highest voice moves up only two semitones. In the motion from the second to the third chord, it is now

---

More recently, Forte has described what he calls a "unary transform": "A unary voice-leading transformation results in the mutation of one pitch-class set into another by a change of a single element" ("New Modes of Linear Analysis"). For Forte, then, two sets may be related by unary voice-leading transformation if all but one of their pitch classes are held in common (that is, are related by T_0 or whatever I_n maps them onto themselves). My near-transposition and near-inversion generalize this idea to include other intervals of transposition and indexes of inversion.

The possibility that one note may be the "odd man out" when two sets are nearly related by transposition or inversion is a central concern of Lewin in "Transformational Techniques." In situations of what I am calling near-transposition and near-inversion, Lewin asks the question, "what if the wrong note were made right?" and offers a series of intriguing answers with respect to the opening chords of Schoenberg's Little Piano Piece, op. 19, no. 6. He speaks of the "urge" and the "lust" that a note in one set might feel to become the transpositional or inversional partner of a corresponding note in another set: "I find it suggestive to think of these generative lusts as musical tensions and/or potentialities which later events of the piece will resolve and/or realize to greater or lesser extents" (341). My near-transposition and near-inversion are Lewin's "what if" operations.

The possibility of relating sets by the simultaneous application of two or more operations (for instance, some notes move by T_n, some by T_{n+x}) is explored in detail by Shaugn O'Donnell in "Transformational Voice Leading in Atonal Music" (Ph.D. diss., City University of New York, forthcoming).

32. In Lewin's terms, the relationship between the chords is "fairly T_{11}-ish" (see "Transformational Techniques," 338–44).

33. Due to limitations of space, I will not be concerned in this brief discussion with the "odd note out," that is, with the note that does not participate in the prevailing transformation. A more thorough account would assess the extent to which the "wrong" note was felt as wrong, and would explore the musical implications of "correcting" it, as Lewin does in "Transformational Techniques." Such an account would also consider closely the extent to which the wrong note is off the mark: Is it off by one semitone? two semitones? more than two semitones? Do these distances affect the perception of the wrong note? Are the distances motivic in some sense (for example, is the wrong note always off by the same interval)?

34. All of the near-transpositions in Example 14 could also be understood as near-inversions, with corresponding changes in the voice leading.

Example 13. Stravinsky: Pieces for String Quartet, no. 3, mm. 3–5: transformational analysis with "near-transposition" and "near-inversion."

the higher two voices that move by the same interval (down five semitones), while the lowest voice moves down only four semitones. When the third chord moves to the fourth, again two voices move by the same interval, in this case, ascending by one semitone, while the third voice does not. Level 2 summarizes the entire progression. It shows that *T_4 followed by *T_7 and *T_1 combine to create the *T_0 that spans the passage. The F and B in the first chord are retained in the last chord.

The registral bass line in Level 1 also rewards an associative analysis. Its notes— G♭, G, and B♭—are related by transposition to the first three notes of the melody, and this same trichord-type, 3–3 (014), occurs many times in the passage. In that sense, the bass line may be thought of as a linearization and a composing-out of a pervasive surface motive. That is certainly true, and interesting. The transformational analysis claims something more, however, namely that the bass line is not only a registral line, but an actual voice-leading voice. G♭ goes to B♭, to G♭, and to G because the transformations impel it to do so.

In Examples 13 and 14, near-transposition and near-inversion mimic the group structure of actual transposition and inversion in their ability to combine in arithmetically predictable ways. In Example 13, $^*T_3$ followed by $^*I_{E♭}^D$ followed by $^*I_C^{B♭}$ was equivalent to $^*T_9$, just as though the operations were actual, not near. Similarly in Example 14, $^*T_4 + {}^*T_7 + {}^*T_1$ was equivalent to $^*T_0$. This need not be the case, however. In Example 15, the near-transpositions combine in an unexpected way: $^*T_0 + {}^*T_2 + {}^*T_2 = {}^*T_3$. Near-transposition and near-inversion thus permit us to trace voice leading, and even to construct transformational middlegrounds, in passages in which the harmonies differ, and which do not necessarily end up where they began.

By defining the concept of transformation broadly, to include any significant means by which one musical object moves to and thus becomes another, we inevitably increase the number of viable voice-leading interpretations. As a general matter, there will be as many different voice-leading interpretations as there are different transformations that could plausibly take us from harmony to harmony. In the case of inversionally symmetrical harmonies, one can imagine them as related by either transposition or inversion (see the discussion of Ex. 5, above). In some cases, actual transposition or inversion at some interval or index might also be modelled as near-transposition or near-inversion at some other interval or index.[35] And, of course, the voice-leading possibilities multiply with the length of the progression.

This is not to suggest that atonal voice leading is a world where absolutely anything goes. Rather, each of the possible voice leadings follows a distinctive, well-marked transformational path, and the transformations "jockey one with another for priority in potential network-formation," in Lewin's phrase.[36] The musical coherence that emerges from transformational analyses, particularly those that invoke ad hoc operations like near-transposition and near-inversion, is thus quite different from the unified hierarchy of traditional tonal music. There, a single fundamental structure may be understood to generate and control all the diversity of the musical surface. In a tonal structure, one can imagine the fundamental structure as God brooding over his creation, the musical foreground (the language is Schenker's).[37] In atonal music as imagined here, God is dead. There is no single privileged position from which to perceive the entire structure. No *Urlinie* spans the musical work from beginning to end; instead, voices come and go. The music can be richly imagined as a network of networks, each rewarding close attention. I think it is futile to seek *the*

---

35. For example, the trichords C–E–G and E–G–B might be understood as related by I_G^E or near-T_0 (with E and G mapping onto themselves and C moving to B). Sets with what Richard Cohn has dubbed the "PP-property"—the ability to move to at least two other sets in the same set-class by retaining all notes except for a single one which moves by the minumum distance—will often be susceptible to modelling by both actual and near transposition or inversion.

36. Lewin, "Transformational Techniques," 341.

37. "Included in the elevation of the spirit to the fundamental structure is an uplifting, of

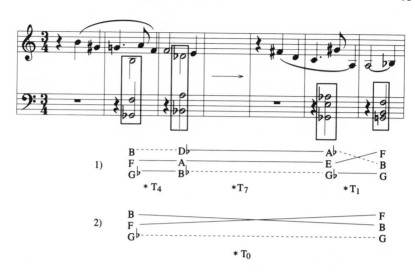

Example 14. Schoenberg: Piano Piece, op. 11, no. 1, mm. 1–3 and 9–11: transformational analysis with "near-transposition."

voice leading of an atonal piece, because atonal works generally resist that kind of unified, hierarchically conceived linear structure. Instead, we should speak of the voice leadings of an atonal piece, of the various strands that intersect, divide, and intertwine to form the fabric of the piece.

Indeed, I think that analysts of twentieth-century music may have spent too much time seeking a single vantage point from which to hear a piece whole, as an integral organism with all its details functioning in the service of a central idea. We have often sought, like Gawain searching for the Grail, a single unifying concept or generating source for each piece we study. But atonal voice leading, and atonal structure more generally, is more diverse, multivalent, and discontinuous than some of us may initially have thought or wished were the case. I think the time has now come to embrace the multiplicity and diversity of atonal music, to accept the tensions and discontinuities that form part of our listening experience, and to reflect them in our theoretical models. The multiple and discontinuous voice leadings I have described here can never be harmonized into unified, piece-spanning *Ursätze*, but instead of bewailing that fact, let us recognize it as a deep and, to my way of thinking, deeply appealing aspect of atonal music.

---

an almost religious character, to God and to the geniuses through whom he works—an uplifting, in the literal sense, to the kind of coherence which is found only in God and the geniuses. Between fundamental structure and foreground there is manifested a rapport much like that ever-present, interactional rapport which connects God to creation and creation to God. Fundamental structure and foreground represent, in terms of this rapport, the celestial and the terrestrial in music" (Schenker, *Free Composition*, 160).

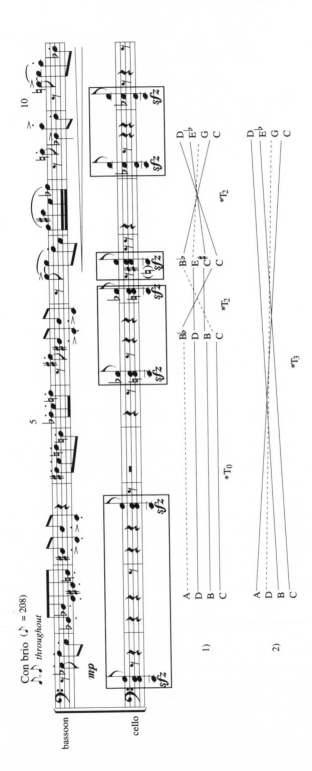

Example 15. Crawford: Diaphonic Suite No. 2 for Bassoon and Cello, mvt. 3, mm. 1–10: transformational analysis with "near-transposition."

K, Kh, and Beyond

Robert D. Morris

Introduction

I n his important and influential book of 1973, *The Structure of Atonal Music*,
Allen Forte offered music theorists a new and useful tool, the K and Kh
relations.[1] These relations and their attendant complexes not only help organize and relate the pitch-class universe of setclasses, but provide a model for
the analysis of "atonal" music.[2] Yet today the K and Kh relations have fallen, if not
by the wayside, at least in frequency of use. To be sure, some scholars have written
accounts of twentieth-century music using K/Kh complex methodology,[3] but Forte
and his students have moved on to consider other approaches to post-tonal music,
especially those involving voice leading and/or transformation. In addition, aside
from reviews of Forte's book, there has been scant theoretic elaboration on the K and
Kh relations in the literature.[4] And the reviews have raised questions about the scope
and character of the relations: Can one methodology address all or most of atonal
music, no matter how wide a net the definition of the word "atonal" casts? What
constitutes a "good" model for post-tonal music and how do we determine its adequacy? What kind of relations are the K and Kh? And even if complexes of set
classes (SCs) do provide important analytic substance, what about the transformations that relate the members of SCs, or possibly relate SCs one to another?

While I cannot answer all of these questions in this paper directly, I hope to
show that Forte's relations and their underlying concepts remain useful to theorists
involved in the study of twentieth-century music. To this end, I will review the K

---

1. Allen Forte, *The Structure of Atonal Music* (New Haven and London: Yale University
Press, 1973).

2. "Atonal music" is Forte's label for nontonal music circa 1910 to 1925, written primarily
by Alban Berg, Arnold Schoenberg, and Anton Webern.

3. For instance, see James M. Baker, *The Music of Alexander Scriabin* (New Haven and
London: Yale University Press, 1986).

4. See Robert Morris, *Composition with Pitch-Classes: A Theory of Compositional Design* (New
Haven and London: Yale University Press, 1987), 98–103, and Richard A. Kaplan, "Transpositionally Invariant Subsets: A New Set Subcomplex Relation," *Intégral* 4 (1990): 37–66.

and Kh relations in theoretic contexts somewhat independent of Forte's. Along the way, I shall analyze two rather different pieces and suggest some theoretic extensions and new analytic applications.

Terms and Concepts

Before I proceed, let me review and introduce a few important terms and concepts. A pc set is an unordered collection of pitch classes (pcs). Set classes (SCs) are collections of pc sets related by transposition and/or inversion. I shall use Forte's labels for SCs.[5] These involve two numerals separated by a hyphen, the first the number of pcs in each pc set in the SC and the second the position of the SC on Forte's list. For instance, SC 6–2 stands for the second SC on Forte's list of SCs containing pc sets of cardinality 6. Two SCs are Z-related if their pc sets have the same interval vector but the pc sets of one SC are not the transpositions and/or inversions of the pc sets in the other.

The sign "#" will the be cardinality operator: for example, #{024} = 3. We shall use "relation notation" of the form "a R b" when we wish to assert that entity a is in the relation R to entity b. For example, for pc sets x and y x ⊂ y says that the pc set x is included in pc set y. We use the following symbols for set-theoretic relations: ∪ for union, ∩ for intersection, ⊂ for (proper) inclusion, ⊆ for inclusion up to identity, and ∈ for membership.[6] The complement of a set S is denoted by S'. The abbreviation iff stands for "if and only if."

It is important to distinguish *literal* from *abstract* relations in atonal theory. Literal relations are among pc sets, abstract relations among SCs. "There are 220 trichordal pc sets" is a literal statement about pc sets; "There are 12 trichordal SCs" is abstract because it is about SCs. Pc set x is *literally included* in y iff x ⊆ y. Let x ∈ SC X and y ∈ SC Y. If x is literally included in y, then SC X is *abstractly included* in SC Y. Now let x and y be pc sets such that y = x'; x and y are literal complements. Abstract complementation obtains between SCs X and Y when x ∈ SC X and y ∈ SC Y and x is the literal complement of y. Two SCs that are abstract complements but not mutually related by abstract inclusion are *ZC-related*. Formally: for SC X and X', X ZC X', iff X ⊄ X', and X' ⊄ X.

A SC list is a list of SCs. The SCs may be randomly collected, found in a piece, or related in some way such as abstract inclusion. The SC list of the Bartók composition we will study is given in Example 5.

---

5. But I drop the "z" designating Z-related SCs in Forte's names.

6. Relational operators <, >, ≤, ≥ (respectively, less than, more than, less than or equal to, more than or equal to) are also used.

The KI relation

Forte's K and Kh relations rest on abstract inclusion. I shall use "KI" for "$\subseteq$".[7] Thus, S KI H iff S $\subseteq$ H for SCs S and H. KI differs from K in that KI relates two SCs whereas K relates two pairs of SCs. For example, 3–5 KI 4–9 means that SC 3–5 is abstractly included in SC 4–9. This in turn means that there is a pc-set member of SC 3–5 that is literally included in a member of SC 4–9; for example, {127} $\in$ 3–5 {1278} $\in$ 4–9.

We can display a group of pc sets related by literal inclusion or SCs related by abstract inclusion by list or lattice. Each item on the list is related via inclusion to at least one other on the list. The lattice is more definitive because it indicates which pc sets or SCs are included in which. Examples 1 and 2 provide lists and lattices for literal and abstract inclusion.[8]

Given a SC list Z containing SC Y, if for all SC X $\in$ Z such that X KI Y, then Y is the KI nexus of the list. The list is called a KI list for Y. If a KI list for Y contains every (abstract) subset of Y, it is called "the KI complex about Y" and denoted by KI(Y). Two KI complexes are given in Example 3. The second contains the abstract subsets of the octatonic scale.

It is instructive to consider a compositional scenario that would generate a piece amenable to analysis with the KI relation. Imagine that a composer has a core idea of only a handful of notes—a tune, motive, chord, or some such—from which she wishes to compose. The notes of the core may be subjected to independent octave transpositions producing various spacings and contours. The core may be cut into smaller parts or elaborated by transformations of itself. The transformations include pitch-class transposition and inversion. The resulting piece will include abstract subsets and supersets of the core's SC. If the transformations are not too complex or bizarre, the analyst will find the SC of the core is related by KI relations to other SCs in the piece. Furthermore, it is likely that KI relations to the core will be more extensive and frequent than KI relations among other SCs. It is important to note that the twelve-tone aggregate need not play a special role in the piece; in fact, the piece may employ fewer than all twelve pcs. The methodology to accomplish KI analysis involves comparing the SC list of the piece with various KI complexes. One could consider the SC list of the piece to be an incomplete KI list; but, since it is likely that the list for the piece will have a few SCs not in the KI relation, it is better to keep the lists for the piece and complex separate.

---

7. The capital I in KI is to distinguish this relation from Kaplan's Ki relation. See Kaplan, "Transpositionally Invariant Subsets."

8. The KI relation is reflexive, antisymmetric, and transitive. It is a "partial ordering" and distinguished from an "equivalence" or "similarity" relation.

Literal inclusion list for pc set {0125}

{0125}
{012} {015} {025} {125}
{01} {02} {05} {12} {15} {25}
{0} {1} {2} {5}
{ }

Abstract inclusion list for SC 4–5[0125] (KI-complex about 4–5)

4–5 [0125]
3–1 [012] 3–3 [014] 3–4 [015] 3–7 [025]
2–1 [01] 2–2 [02] 2–3 [03] 2–4 [04] 2–4 [05]
1–1 [0]
0–0 [ ]

Example 1. Literal inclusion list for pc set {0125}.

A Brief Analysis Using the KI Relation

Béla Bartók's "From the Island of Bali," number 109 from his piano set *Mikrokosmos* provides an analytic vignette.[9] Example 4 provides the pitch and pc relations of the piece. As the double bars show, the piece is in ABA' form. The first section (mm. 1–11) uses two pc sets from the 4–9 SC related by both transposition and inversion. The combination of the 4–9s yields the octatonic scale, SC 8–28. The B part introduces some new pcs into the piece, pc 7 in m. 12 and pc 10 in m. 20. The first addition expands the 4–9 in m. 12 to a 5–7 SC. The second addition results in the pc set {9 10 2 3} of SC 4–8, introducing pc 10 in m. 20; this can be regarded as a transformation of the opening pc set of the piece, substituting 10 for 8. The A' section uses the same material as the A but transposes the right hand in mm. 33–34 down a perfect fourth so that the two SC 4–9s now form 8–9. As a result, a new pc, 1, is introduced. The chords of the coda articulate the ubiquitous 8–28 in a new way, as two 4–26s. In sum, 4–9 is the dominant SC at the beginning, transformed later into 5–7 and 4–8. 8–28 and 8–9 are the large SCs while 4–26 plays a minor role at the end. There is a move toward completing the aggregate that misses its goal by one pc. However, the next piece of *Mikrokosmos* begins with a upbeat gesture that culminates in a clear "cadence" on E♮—the missing pc.

Considering the number of measures in "From the Island of Bali" that employ the octatonic scale (30 out out 43), one might scarcely hesitate to deem it octatonic.

---

9. For a contrasting approach to this piece see Richard Cohn, "Properties and Generability of Transpositionally Invariant Sets," *Journal of Music Theory* 35 (1991): 1–32.

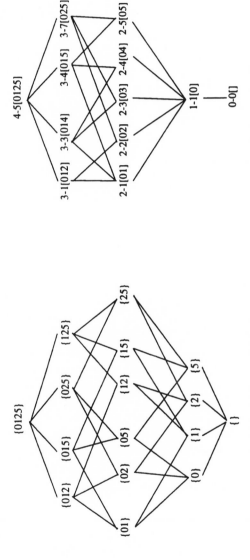

4-5[0125]

3-1[012]   3-3[014]   3-4[015]   3-7[025]

2-1[01]   2-2[02]   2-3[03]   2-4[04]   2-5[05]

1-1[0]

0-0[]

Abstract inclusion lattice for SC 4–5
(KI-complex lattice about SC 4–5)

{0125}

{012}   {015}   {025}   {125}

{01}   {02}   {05}   {12}   {15}   {25}

{0}   {1}   {2}   {5}

{}

Literal inclusion lattice for pc set {0125}

Example 2. Inclusion lattices for pc set {0125} and SC 4–5.

KI complex about 8–9 [0 1 2 3 6 7 8 9]

8–9

7–7   7–19

6–5   6–6   6–7   6–18   6–29   6–30   6–38   6–41   6–42   6–43

5–4   5–5   5–6   5–7   5–14   5–15   5–18   5–19   5–20   5–28   5–29   5–31
5–38

4–1   4–4   4–5   4–6   4–7   4–8   4–9   4–12   4–13   4–14
4–15   4–16   4–18   4–20   4–23   4–25   4–26   4–27   4–28   4–29

3–1   3–2   3–3   3–4   3–5   3–6   3–7   3–8   3–9   3–10   3–11

2–1   2–2   2–3   2–4   2–5   2–6

1–1

0–0

KI–complex about 8–28 [0 1 3 4 6 7 9 10]

8–28

7–31

6–13   6–23   6–27   6–30   6–49   6–50

5–10   5–16   5–19   5–25   5–28   5–31   5–32

4–4   4–9   4–10   4–12   4–13   4–15   4–17   4–18   4–25   4–26   4–27   4–28
4–29

3–2   3–3   3–5   3–7   3–8   3–10   3–11

2–1   2–2   2–3   2–4   2–5   2–6

1–1

0–0

Example 3. KI Complexes about 8–9 [0 1 2 3 6 7 8 9] and 8–28 [0 1 3 4 6 7 9 10].

But how octatonic is it? If we compare its SC list with various KI complexes we can answer that question. See Example 5 for the piece's SC list. While 8–28 is formed by two 4–9s often enough, what about the SCs 4–8, 5–7, or 8–9, none of which has a KI relation with 8–28? In addition, the move toward the aggregate surpasses the octatonic scale {8 9 11 0 2 3 5 6} of the piece. These objections are underscored when we compare the SC list with the KI set complexes about 8–9 and 8–28. Of the seven SCs on

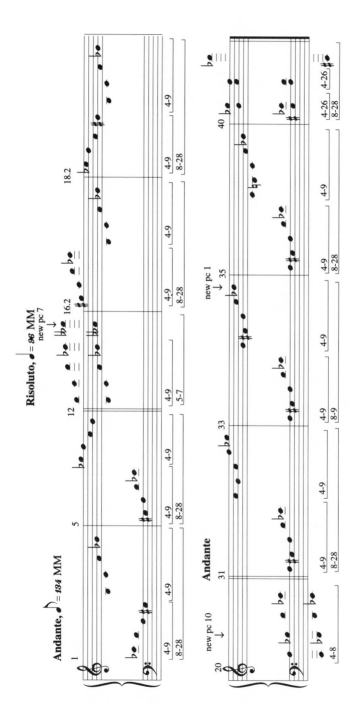

Example 4. Analytic précis of Bartók's "From the Isle of Bali" (*Mikrokosmos*, no. 109).

$$8\text{–}9 \quad 8\text{–}28$$
$$5\text{–}7$$
$$4\text{–}8 \quad 4\text{–}9 \quad 4\text{–}26$$
$$3\text{–}5$$

Example 5. List of SCs in Bartók's "From the Isle of Bali."

the SC list five are found in the 8–9 complex, whereas four are found in the 8–28 complex. So, from a KI point of view the Bartók piece would seem to be slightly more connected to an 8–9 vocabulary than one of 8–28. On the other hand, the pcs outside of the octatonic scale could be seen as embellishing pitches since they can only be one ic 1 away from an octatonic pc. In any case, I shall leave the question of whether a single SC dominates this piece open until later.

The K and Kh Relations

Relations such as partitioning within and among aggregates induce complementation. Pieces that contain (fairly local) aggregates will usually yield complementary SC relations. In addition, it can be shown that the "complement theorem" suggests strong similarity between SC complements.[10] Since only 32 out of the 223 SCs have ZC relations, abstract complement relations form an important resource for the composer; a member of a SC X can be musically articulated as a literal subset of a pc set in the abstract complement of X. Indeed, Forte has shown that "embedded complement" relations often occur in atonal music.

To animate these observations, we revisit our composer who often derives material by appending extra pcs to her compositional core. This may come about in a number of ways: progressing with minimum pitch and pc intersection; combining various versions of the core that have little or no pc intersection; embellishing the core with complementary pcs; or taking the pcs of the core out of the aggregate and working with the complementary pc set.[11] Given these compositional tactics, analysis requires more than the KI relation. KI will have to be supplemented by K and Kh, relations that are sensitive to both literal and abstract complementation.

I define the K and Kh relations as follows:

For SCs S, S′, T, and T′:
K relation: S/S′ K T/T′ iff $S \supset \subset T$ or $S \supset \subset T'$.

---

10. See Robert Morris, "A Similarity Index for Pitch-Class Sets," *Perspectives of New Music*, 18 (1980): 445–60.

11. If the core is a hexachord, the composer may find that two transformations are mutually disjunct and produce an aggregate.

The SC pair S and S' is K-related to the SC pair T and T' if and only if S is included or includes T *or* S is included in or includes T'.

Kh relation: S/S' Kh T/T' iff S $\supset$ $\subset$ T and S $\supset$ $\subset$ T'.

The SC pair S and S' is Kh related to the SC pair T' and T' if and only if S is included or includes T *and* S is included in or includes T'.[12]

Note that these relations are between *pairs* of abstract complementary SCs. Forte stipulates that #S or #S' may not equal #T (or #T'). We call this condition F.1. However, #S may equal #S' or #T may equal #T'. [13]

I shall also use the two following propositions:

P.1: #S $\leq$ #T iff #T' $\leq$ #S'.

P.2: S $\subseteq$ T iff T' $\subseteq$ S'.[14]

The cardinalities of S, S', T, T' are not given in the definitions. We know that #S = 12 − #S' and #T = 12 − #T'. Each of four relations may then obtain or not: #S < T; #S < #T'; #S < #S'; #T < #T'. Only 8 of the total 16 combinations are logically consistent. Four of the consistent combinations order the four SCs according to cardinality: S (S'), followed by T and T' in either order, followed by S' (S). The remaining four combinations are derived by exchanging S and T.[15]

To avoid such complications, given two pairs of complementary SCs in a K or Kh relation, assign the smallest SC to S, the next smallest SC to T, the complement of the smallest to S' and the remaining SC to T'. Thus, #S $\leq$ #T $\leq$ #T' $\leq$ #S'. I reformulate the definitions accordingly.[16]

---

12. Forte's original K and Kh relation definitions were formulated as follows. K relation: S/S' $\in$ K(T,T') iff S $\supset$ $\subset$ T | S $\supset$ $\subset$ T'. (The SC pair S and S' is included in the K complex about SC pair T and T' if and only if S is included in or includes T *or* S is included in or includes T'.) Kh relation: S/S' $\in$ Kh(T,T') iff S $\supset$ $\subset$ T & S $\supset$ $\subset$ T'. (The SC pair S and S' is included in the Kh complex about SC pair T and T' if and only if S is included or includes T *and* S is included in or includes T'.) I have recast Forte's definitions into relation notation and removed the "complex about" notation. See Forte, *The Structure of Atonal Music*, 93–95.

13. Without F.1, the $\subset$ and $\supset$ in the definition would be $\subseteq$ and $\supseteq$.

14. P.2 is found in Forte, *The Structure of Atonal Music*, 94.

15. An example of an inconsistent combination: assert (1) #S < T, (2) #S < #T' and (3) not (#S < #S'). (3) implies (4) #S' < #S. Now, both #S and #S' < both #T and #T', so we have (5) #S' < #T'. But by P.1 (1) implies (6) #T' < #S' and (6) contradicts (5).

16. For theoretical reasons it can be profitable to drop condition F.1. Then $\subset$ becomes $\subseteq$ in the definitions. Without F.1 the K relation is reflexive; S/S' K S/S' for all S since S is trivially included in itself. If S is not ZC-related then S $\subset$ S'. For instance, 3–1/9–1 K 3–2/9–2 since 3–1 $\subset$ 9–2. On the other hand, even without F.1, the Kh relation is not reflexive in a general sense; if S is ZC-related to S', then S/S' Kh S/S' is not true. The omission of F.1 does not affect other aspects of the Kh relation, for if #S = #T and S $\neq$ T, then perhaps S $\subset$ T or perhaps S $\subset$ T' but not both.

K relation:

S/S′ Kh T/T′ iff ((S ⊂ T or S ⊂ T′) and by P.2 (T′ ⊂ S′ or T ⊂ S′))

Kh relation:

S/S′ Kh T/T′ iff ((S ⊂ T and S ⊂ T′) and by P.2 (T′ ⊂ S′ and T ⊂ S′))

Note that if S and/or T are hexachordal (but not ZC-related), S = S′ and/or T = T′.

I now discuss the relations separately, beginning with K. The K relation is *not* the same as the KI relation. First, while two individual SCs are related with KI, *pairs* of complementary SCs are related with K. Second, KI relates SCs by ⊆ not ⊂, as in K.[17] Third, if S/S′ K T/T′ then either S KI T or S KI T′, but not both (unless S/S′ Kh T/T′). To illustrate the implications of the third point, consider the following two K relations: (1) 3–1/9–1 K 5–20/7–20; (2) 3–1/9–1 K 5–12/7–12. In (1), the trichordal SC is abstractly included in the septachordal SC, but not the pentachordal SC. In (2), the trichordal SC is abstractly included in the pentachordal SC, but not the septachordal SC. This difference has implications for analysis. If only two of the four SCs in a K relation are articulated in a piece, the two may not be KI-related and we may be misled by citing a K relation; we cannot tell from the assertion of a K relation alone whether S ⊂ T or S ⊂ T′. In sum, K is only relevant in the context of complementary relations between SCs. KI can work with or without complementation.

In the Kh relation, if (S/S′ Kh T/T′) then (S/S′ K T/T′). Conversely, a K relation can sometimes imply a Kh relation. If T is not ZC-related to T′, S is not ZC-related to S′, and S ⊂ T, then (S/S′ K T/T′) implies (S/S′ Kh T/T′).

Given a Kh relation, S ZC S′ is false. Let (a) S ⊂ T and (b) S ⊂ T′. By P.2 (b) implies (c) T ⊂ S′; (a) and (c) imply S ⊂ S′. Thus, S must not be ZC-related to S′. The converse is also true. An example: SC pair 5–12/7–12 has no Kh relations with hexachords since 5–12 ZC 7–12.

The K and Kh Complexes

I will represent K and Kh complexes as lists of SCs arranged in complement pairs called *SC-comp lists*. These list each SC and its (abstract) complement separated by a slash. When a hexachordal SC is its own complement, it is listed alone, as in the following SC list: 4–2/8–2 6–5 6–8/6–38.

For a SC-comp list Z, if there is a S/S′ ∈ Z such that for all[18] Y/Y′ ∈ Z Y/Y′ K S/S′, then S/S′ is the K nexus of Z. Such a list is called a K list. If this list contains all possible Y/Y′, it is called, using Forte's name, a "K complex about S/S′." K(S/S′)

---

17. Of course, if X KI Y and X ≠ Y, then X ⊂ Y.

18. Note that we assume here that condition F.1 is dropped so that S/S′ can equal Y/Y′.

designates the K complex. The definition applies to the Kh relation mutatis mutandis.[19] See Example 6 for the Kh complexes about 8–9 and 8–28.

Like the KI complex, K and Kh complexes can be displayed in a lattice representation. Example 7 displays the lattice for KI(8–28) while the left side of Example 8 shows the lattice for Kh(4–28/8–28). The difference in the number of SCs between the two lattices illustrates the greater selectivity of the Kh relation. The KI lattice has 8–28 on the top with its included SCs below, while the Kh lattice has the nexus 4–28/8–28 in the middle. This might seem to imply that the KI relation is hierarchic, its lattice having a topmost node, whereas the Kh relation is not since the Kh nexus in is the middle of its lattice. However, the hierarchy implicit in a Kh (or K) complex is easily shown by rewriting its lattice as a tree as on the right of Example 8. As mentioned above, trees and lattices are partially ordered sets many of which can be interpreted as hierarchical structures.[20]

ANALYSIS WITH THE K AND KH RELATIONS

Analysis with K and Kh relations proceeds by comparing a SC list of a piece (or section thereof) with various K and Kh complexes. Forte provides a useful methodology for determining the best fit between the piece list and a K/Kh complex. He constructs a table, often called a "K/Kh chart," to list the K and Kh relations between SCs on the piece list.[21] The chart shows which SC pairs have the most K and Kh relations to the other SCs. Nevertheless, it is not clear when the analyst can assert that a K or Kh relation is functioning in the music from merely comparing the piece's SC list with a complex or consulting a K/Kh chart. For instance, given a particular Kh relation, what if only S (or S′) and T (or T′) occur in the music, is the Kh relation contributing to the piece's structure, or do we have just a KI relation? For instance, just because 3–1 and 8–2 occur in a piece does not imply that 3–1/9–1 Kh 4–2/8–2 also occurs. Worse, given a K relation, what if S and T occur in a piece, S′ and T′ do not, and S ⊄ T? Then no inclusion relation occurs in the music at all! For example, if 3–1 and 4–27 occur in a piece (note that 3–1 ⊄ 4–27), there is no KI relation between these SCs even though 3–1/9–1 K 4–27/8–27 is true.

---

19. A list of all KI (and K) complexes is found in "Appendix 2. Set-Class Inclusion Table" in Robert Morris, *Class Notes for Atonal Music Theory* (Hanover, N.H.: Frog Peak Music, 1991), 112–55. "Appendix 3. The Subcomplexes Kh" lists the Kh complexes in Forte, *The Structure of Atonal Music*, 200–208.

20. It is therefore possible to interpret the KI, K, or Kh nexus as "controlling" the network of SCs and pc sets in analogy to the way the tonic triad or scale degree, or *Ursatz* "controls" harmony and melody in tonal music.

21. A K/Kh chart is found in Example 101 of Forte, *The Structure of Atonal Music*, 98. Forte discusses this table on p. 101.

Kh Complex about 4–9/8–9

3–5/8–9
5–7/7–7   5–19/7–19
6–5   6–6/6–38   6–7   6–18   6–30

Kh Complex about 4–28/8–28

3–10/9–10
5–31/7–31
6–27   6–30

Example 6. Kh complexes about 4–8/8–9 and 4–28/8–28.

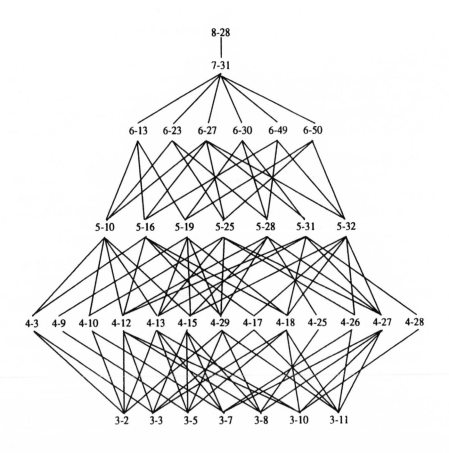

Example 7. Abstract inclusion lattice for SC 8–28 ("Octatonic Scale") (KI-inclusion lattice about SC 8–28).

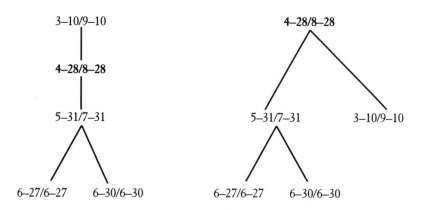

Example 8. Two ways of writing the Kh complex around 4–28/8–28.

To avoid these difficulties in analytic application, I suggest the following distinctions and guidelines.

All four SCs in S/S′ K T/T′ or S/S′ Kh T/T′ must occur in the music to articulate an *explicit* K or Kh relation.

If three of the four SCs are articulated, the Kh relation is *implicit*.[22] In K, the presence of three of the four SCs asserts only the KI relation. We may call this a *partial* K relation, but only the presence of all four SCs portrays an unconditional K-relation.

In the case where only two of the four SCs occur, there is either a KI relation or nothing (no inclusion). Forte uses "K*" in his K/Kh charts to show that two SCs have a KI relation.

So to compare a SC list X of a piece with a Kh (or K) complex about T/T′ (SC-comp list) called Y, for each candidate for S (and S′) a match is determined according to the following rules.

(1) If both Y and X contain S, S′, T, and T′, then there is an explicit match.
(2) If both Y and X contain T and T′ and either S or S′, then there is a implicit match.
(3) If X contains only T or T′ or neither, then there no match.
(4) The higher the number of matches, the better Y models X.

We now return to Bartók's "Isle of Bali" to decide if it is dominated by one SC. The complementary context determined by the 4–9/8–9 SC pair and the move to-

---

22. However, cases involving non ZC-related hexachords need have as few as three SCs for implicit K or two for implicit Kh. For #S < #T or #T′ if T or T′ is non-ZC hex, and S ⊂ T and S ⊂ T′ are the same because T = T′. So S, S′, and T (or T′) asserts a partial K and S and T asserts an implicit Kh relation.

ward aggregate completion justifies the analytic use of K and Kh in addition to KI alone. When we compare the SC list with the Kh complex about 4–9/8–9 we have two (implicit) matches: 3–5 Kh 4–9/8–9 and 5–7 Kh 4–9/8–9. There are no matches of the piece list with the 4–28/8–28 complex since 4–28 does not occur in the music. In addition, the greater KI relations with 8–9 confirm the greater emphasis on a 4–9/8–9 than on 8–28. So I conclude that the piece is dominated by the 4–9/8–9 pair. One could go on to note that the 8–9 SC occurs at a special place in the movement, at the last deviation from the 8–28 SC and the introduction of the last non-octatonic pc, clearly suggesting a possible aggregate completion with pc 4. The position of the 8–9 can also be heard in a tonal manner; it temporally bisects the right hand's 4–9s by inserting a 4–9 a fourth below and fifth above its 4–9 neighbors. The low D♯ pedal (after the 4–8 in mm. 20–30) helps establish this reading.

Indeed, there is a story to be told here—one that involves register, rhythm, tonal reference, and SC relations. To be sure, the KI and Kh relations that define the piece's harmonic character and partitioning cannot serve a narrative purpose alone. Besides, my analysis is provided primarily for illustration. But this does not mean that such relations are irrelevant to musical process either in principle or practice. In fact, I provide the following analysis to makes this very point.

An Analysis of Varèse's *Octandre*, first movement

Despite some claims to the contrary, a good deal of the music of Edgard Varèse can be well served by Forte's methods. Indeed, Forte uses two chords from Varèse's *Intégrales* to illustrate the Z-relation. And since Varèse's music is only weakly connected to the so-called Second Viennese School, the fact that K and Kh relations abound in *Octandre* makes a good case for their general applicability to a wide variety of post-tonal music.[23]

If *Octandre* [24] has any connection to the atonal music of the 1910s, the locus is probably Stravinsky's *Rite of Spring*. Octandrious flowers of eight stamens suggested by Varèse's title have some resonance with the Stravinsky. The instrumentation of the Varèse is also reminiscent of the introductory section of the *Rite*—both are scored for woodwinds and brass accompanied by the low strings. Moreover, both works open with a pensive solo for a double-reed instrument: bassoon in the Stravinsky, oboe in the Varèse. Texture contributes to the comparison as well. The contrasts of aperiodic rhythm with pulsation and parlando-rubato with repetitive folk-like melodies suggests the arabesques of Middle Eastern music, which of course highly influenced the Russian folk music on which Stravinsky drew. These stylistic considerations

---

23. In this connection, I have shown that the I-type combinatoriality of Schoenberg's twelve-tone works is the literal counterpart of Forte's Kh relation. See *Composition with Pitch-Classes*, 102.

24. *Octandre* was composed in New York in 1923.

Introduction (mm. 1–9), oboe solo
A section (mm. 10–15)
transition (mm. 16–18)
Center (mm. 19–21)
B section (mm. 22–24)
Closing section (mm. 25–29) and coda (mm. 30), oboe solo

Example 9. Form of Varèse's *Octandre*, mvt. 1.

are of significance in our analysis since they will help guide our search for a possible Kh nexus for the entire movement.

Overview

Like all of *Octandre*, the first movement is in three parts.[25] As Example 9 indicates, the piece begins with an introduction for oboe solo (mm. 1–9), followed by an "A section" (mm. 10–15). The oboe solo unfolds a single aggregate from its first G♭ (pc 6) to its last extreme high G (pc 7). This aggregate is only one of many to come and suggests that literal and abstract complementation are found at all levels of the piece. The oboe solo also introduces the main melodic cell of the piece—what I call the <310> motive—found in m. 1 as the registrally articulated sequence G♭, E, D♯. The A section is framed by a flute ascent before and bassoon descent after. The section's brash intensity is capped with a climactic pyramid at m. 15.

A transition (mm. 16–18) leads to a short but vivid centerpiece at mm. 19–21. The transition subtly recalls music found in the introduction and A sections while the center section introduces new gestures; the fanfare motive in the horn is accompanied by the first clear pulse of the work.

A "B section" (mm. 22–24) reintroduces the <310> motive and continues the pulse and repetitions introduced in the center section. It culminates in a "closing section" (mm. 25–29) which contains something like a folk melody in the bassoon in m. 27. The piece ends with a return to the opening oboe solo transposed by a tritone.

Introduction (mm. 1–9): oboe solo

As mentioned above, the introduction introduces a complete aggregate from pc 6 to pc 7. Motion toward aggregate completion is apparent from the onset as the opening descending motive of the four pcs <6 5 4 3> (stated three times) is followed by its T_8 transposition producing the pc sequence <6 5 4 3 2 1 0 11> (see Ex. 10). This "de-

---

25. *Octandre* is the only piece of Varèse in three movements.

scending" pc sequence could have been completed by chromatically progressing to pc 7. However it is broken off in m. 4 with a jump to F♯ followed by an embellished F, a return to the opening two notes of the piece. Nonetheless, two new pcs are also introduced, 8 and 9. The delay of the chromatic descent is also marked by the introduction of the clarinet and bass in m. 5 which divides the solo in half. The second part of the oboe solo focuses on the third and fourth notes of the opening tetrachord, pcs 4 and 3. As the clarinet has already introduced the next-to-last pc of the aggregate, pc 10, the oboe has only to add pc 7 strikingly articulated by its last G♮ marked *ffff*.

When we look more closely at the opening measures we see how Varèse projects the <310> motive with the chromatic descent. The motive is isolated by register, therefore playing down the chromatic adjacencies in the pc sequence.[26] The registral partitioning induces the SCs 6–10 and 2–4, SCs of an ic 4 flavor. The imbricated trichords of the upper register are all 3–2s except for the <432> which bridges the move from the first 4–1 to its T_8 image. The first two imbricated tetrachords are of SC 4–2, the last of 4–3. The move from pc 5 to 1 in the lower register highlights the passage's T_8 relation with the last, predicting the clarinet's first note.

In m. 4 the oboe skips over pc 10—the pc that would have been the next pc in the descent—and lands on pc 9. Nevertheless pc 10 is found in m. 5 at the end of the clarinet's <310> motive. This deviation from the chromatic descent is further softened by another 4–3 SC in the oboe's <6859> in mm. 4–5. The last two pcs continue the ic 4 connections from before. The clarinet's <310>, spanning the pcs 1 and 10, is the first adjacent presentation of that motive, with its characteristic rhythmic profile "medium, short, long," the last note rearticulated aperiodically. The basic SCs here are 3–2, 4–1, and 8–1, inducing obvious Kh relations to 4–1/8–1. 8–1 has KI relations with the 4–2, 4–3, and 6–10 SCs.

The clarity of the SC relations is continued and embellished in the second part of the introduction (mm. 6–9). The sustained notes of the oboe, clarinet, and bass {9 10 11} in m. 6 is a 3–1 containing the pcs that continue the oboe's descent. But as soon as the bass enters on its B♮, the oboe continues its soliloquy. These notes together with sustained pcs form a member of SC 7–7. The unaccompanied melody in m. 7, somewhat simplified in the example, introduces a new trichord, 3–5. The C𝄪 grace note enlarges a 3–5 to a 4–6 tetrachord. The 4–6 is answered by its abstract complement, 8–6, which occurs as the last eight notes of the solo. The highest notes of the solo—the G♯ of m. 7 and the closing G in m. 9—complete the aggregate. As the example shows, a number of new SCs are introduced here. The 9–1 embeds its own abstract complement; SC 6–7 articulated by two non-overlapping 3–1s will appear later. The SC-list of this passage includes 3–1, 3–2, 3–5, 4–6, 6–7, 7–7, 8–6,

---

26. The oboe's registral partitioning makes a subtle but telling reference to the *Rite's* beginning. The bassoon's notes C, B, G, E, B, A project the retrograde inversion of the <310> motive (here < C B A >) via registral disjunction. The use of inverted mordants written as double grace notes also makes this connection.

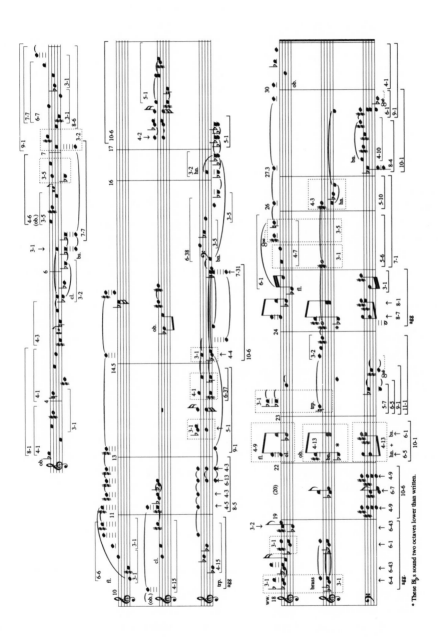

Example 10. Analytic précis of Varèse's *Octandre*, mvt. 1.

* These B♭s sound two octaves lower than written.

and 9–1. Most of these SCs emphasize ic 1; all of cardinality 4 or greater include 3–5. The SC list is totally included in the Kh complex about 4–6/8–6.

Our division of the introduction into two parts is further underlined by the Kh complexes that model each. The opening 4–1/8–1 complex contrasts with 4–8/8–8; the former is chromatic, the latter based equally on two ics, 1 and 6.[27] The two Kh complexes are respective instances of two harmonic strains, one associated with the (abstract) supersets of the 3–1 trichords, the other based on 3–5. The strains will both clash and combine throughout the movement.

A Section (mm. 10–15)

The A section is framed by flute and bassoon gestures. Like the end of the oboe solo, the gestures end on "extreme" notes; the flute ascends to its highest C♯ while the bassoon descends to its lowest note, B♭.[28] The extreme pcs, 1 and 10, are the same pcs that framed the <310> motive in the clarinet entrance in m.5. The flute's 6–6 and bassoon's 6–38 are Z-related. The 6–6 is partitioned both registrally and temporally into two 3–1s. This connects the flute gesture to the 6–7 SC in the oboe solo. (Both SCs emphasize ics 1 and 5, and both can be partitioned into two 3–1s or two 3–5s.) The imbricated pentachords of the flute form two pc sets from SC 5–5, connecting via complementation with the 7–7 of the oboe solo. The bassoon's 6–38 emphasizes 3–5s in contrast to the 3–1s in the flute solo. Aside from the Z-relation connecting 6–6 and 6–38, these SCs have other properties relevant to our analysis. Both participate in the 3–1 and 3–5 strains. Each can be partitioned into two 3–5s. While 6–6 can be trichordally partitioned into 3–1s, 6–38 cannot. On the other hand, 6–38 can be partitioned into an ic1 and a 4–1, thus connecting it to the 4–1s and ic 1s of the oboe solo.[29]

The flute ascent in m. 10 is accompanied by the oboe high G, the clarinet, and the first entrance of the trumpet. The result is an aggregate. The oboe and clarinet form a 4–15 SC answered by the same SC in the trumpet. The choice of 4–15 might reflect on the aggregate, since 4–15 is an all-interval tetrachord.[30]

---

27. That both nexi involve SCs of eight pcs reflects on the title of the work.

28. It is important to remember that at the time of its composition, *Octandre* made severe demands on its instrumentalists. The high oboe G and the flute C♯ were beyond the grasp of most players of the time.

29. Moreover, the two hexachords are related under the M/MI relation, the same relation which exchanges diatonic (ic 5–based) sets with chromatic (ic 1–based) sets. The M relation is useful to connect certain diatonic sets in the work (especially in the third movement) to the chromatic SCs found elsewhere.

30. The instrumental/registral partitioning of the aggregate is interesting. Trumpet {9 10 1 3} ∈ 4–15; clarinet and oboe {2 4 7 8} ∈ 4–15; flute inside/middle pcs {5 6 11 0} ∈ 4–9. The 4–15s are inversionally related and form 8–9 in union. The 4–9 buried in the flute hides its connection to the blatant 4–9s of m. 19 and elsewhere.

Measures 11–12 contain four overlapped and rhythmically active chords. The SCs are 4–5, 4–3, 6–13, and 4–3 in the sequence-pattern ABCB. The chords in union form SC 8–5, the abstract complement of the opening chord, 4–5. The 4–3s are not new, but the 6–13 is anomalous. It appears to be quite unrelated to any harmony that has appeared so far, but the instrumental partitioning helps uncover its role in the piece. The flute, clarinet, and oboe attack the G♯, F, and F♯ at once, while the bassoon and horn (of similar timbre) simultaneously attack the B and C joining the sustained trumpet A♮. The two groups each form a 3–2 sonority. When we look at the prime form of 6–13 we see that it is imbricated by only one trichord, 3–2: {013467}. 6–13 is KI related to 4–9 (containing four 3–5s). We can therefore regard 6–13 as generalizing the combination of 3–2 and 3–5 trichords. This indicates that a third trichordal strain may be at work in the piece, one based on generalizations of SC 3–2.[31]

Measure 13 returns us to the chromatic strain. SC 3–1 is embedded in the 9–1 that comprises the entire measure. The 4–1 and 5–1 point back to the beginning of the piece as does the sustained ic 4 in the flute and horn. The 4–1 at the end of the measure forms the very pc set of the first measure and the low F and F♯ remind us of m. 5. The 6–37 is highly chromatic but has affinity with ic 4, through its abstract complement, 6–4. The climax in the middle of m. 14 starts with 3–1 embedded in 4–4 and quickly expands to a 7–31. SC 7–31 is the unique seven-pc octatonic subset. Since the octatonic scale (8–28) is made out of overlapping 3–2s, we understand the 7–31 as a continuation of the 3–2 strain. The earlier 6–13 can now be interpreted as heralding the climax, for it is an abstract subset of 7–31.

The presence of 6–13 and 7–31 amid the other chromatic SCs prevents closure, even if both are KI-related to 9–1. If we omit them as interruptions in the flow of highly related SCs we still have problems determining an unequivocal Kh complex. Using 3–1/9–1 or 2–6/10–6 as the nexus is a kind of overkill since both of these complexes have too many members that are not articulated in the music. 4–5/8–5 is also a candidate but does not address the presence of 4–1, 4–3, or 4–4. Another possibility is 6–6/6–38, the framing pair. While 4–1 and 4–4 are KI-related to 6–38 and 6–6 respectively, this choice leaves out 5–1. Despite this drawback, 6–6/6–38 is a much smaller Kh complex than 3–1/9–1, so the A section is best modeled by Kh(6–6/6–38).

Transition (mm. 16–18)

The transition is linked to the previous section by the bassoon low B♭. The addition of the horn's C D♭ produces a clear articulation of 3–2. The sustained notes B♭ C♯ are the extreme pcs of section A and occur in association with the <310> motive in the clarinet in mm. 5–6.

---

31. See for instance the bassoon melody at the opening of the third movement for a diatonic chain of 3–2s.

Backward references to the opening and the rest of section A continue in m. 17. The chromatic SCs, the two 5–1s and 4–2, form the same configuration of pitches as in m. 14 which connected back to the opening oboe solo. Yet the reference to the solo is stronger in m. 17, since the last 5–1 is articulated by < {76} 543 >, which resembles m. 1 with the last pc of the solo prepended. But the total SC for m. 17 is 10–6, so there is also a reference to the 3–5 strain.

Measure 18 introduces another aggregate. Four vertical SCs produce the ABCB pattern of SC membership of m. 11. Here too are new SCs, this time within both the 3–1 and 3–5 strains. The first SC 6–4 is composed out of two 3–1s at ic 4. The 3–1s are differentiated by instrumental color, brass versus woodwinds. Once again the pcs 1 and 10 are boundary notes. The 6–4 is the Z correspondent of the 6–37 at the end of m. 13, but, even more remarkably, they are literal complements: the two chords articulating the 6–4/6–37 pair produce an aggregate. The third chord of m. 18 is of SC 6–1 partitioned into two 3–1s. The 6–4 and 6–1 both confirm the 3–1 strain. SC 6–43 occurring twice articulates the 3–5 strain since any member of 6–43 can be constructed by taking two members of 3–5 at ic 4 in union. The ic 4 and 3–5 connect the 6–43 not only to the opening oboe solo but also to the 6–4/6–37 chords nearby. A member of 6–4 can be constructed by taking two 3–1s at T_4. These observations imply that the function of this measure is to connect ic 4 to the 3–1 and 3–5 strains. But 3–2 is also implicated in the last 6–43 chord. The instruments partition the chord into a 3–1 plus 3–2, and this last 3–2 frames the section with the horn/bassoon 3–2 in m. 16.

No single complex models these measures. The absence of SC complements within the large SCs—10–6 and the aggregate—plus the use of T_4 to build larger sets subverts a Kh or K nexus. This, together with the reminiscence of earlier passages, suggests that the section functions as a transition.

Center (mm. 19–21)

The Center stands out from the rest of the composition in a number of ways. Its clear internal ABA structure and rhythmic pulsations contrast with the complex, parlando-rubato rhythms of the previous music. The contrast of brass and woodwinds is now highlighted by temporal alternation. The double-tongued C♯ fanfare in the horn is another instance of pc 1 in a boundary role, connecting back to the first clarinet note in m. 5. The ABA structure can be traced back too. The framing gestures in the A section and the ABCB SC patterning without the first A serve as referents. Of course, the Center itself is the B of a large but rough ABA structure for the whole movement. This larger ABA is formed by the A, Center, and B sections. It is articulated by SCs, for the Center is an undeniable and pure instance of the 3–5 strain. It is surrounded by mixtures of the 3–1 and 3–5 strains, while the chromatic world alone dominates the very edges of the movement. The Center's 6–7 and 4–9 form a 10–6, the abstract complement of a tritone. The 10–6 here has the same content of the previous 10–6 in m. 17, omitting pcs 2 and 8. Kh(6–7) models the section.

B Section (mm. 22–24)

Measure 22 continues the pulse and alternation of the center section. Here the alternated chords are of SCs 6–5 and 6–1 which together produce SC 10–1, a chromatic context. 6–5 represents the 3–5 strain while 6–1 is of 3–1 affiliation. The two chords are articulated by three strata, two of which are inversionally related. This is reminiscent of m. 10. The double reeds play 4–13, as do the horn and bass, while the other woodwinds (of smoother timbre) play 4–9. The pcs 6 and 7 are absent. The boundary pc 10 is articulated in the bassoon low B♭, as in the bassoon descent of m. 15.

Measure 23 builds a climactic pyramid not unlike the one in m. 14. The pulsation and alternation of the surrounding measures is absent as the music builds an 11–1 SC (all the pcs except 5), starting with 3–3 and traversing through 6–5. The trumpet plays the <310> motive ending on pcs 6 and 7.

Measure 24 is a repetition of m. 22 with rhythmic variations. The same 6–1 and 6–5 chords alternate but over the missing pcs of m. 22. The trumpet F♯ and the low bass G complete the aggregate. These pcs connect back to the beginning, since pcs 6 and 7 were the first and last pcs of the oboe solo. The 6–5 and 6–1 of before with the added pcs become 8–7 and 8–1 respectively. The 8–1 is of course the opening SC of the work, while the 8–7 looks forward. It is followed by its abstract complement, 4–7, in the next measure. The ic 1s in the flute and bassoon combine to produce a 3–1 with a common pc 2, which was one of the two pcs absent in the center section. The flute's ic 1 is formed between the first two pcs of the rising gesture that begins the next section.

6–1 and 6–5 of the alternating chords are candidates for a Kh nexus, but 6–1 does not include 4–9 or 4–13. On the other hand, 6–5 serves very well, having Kh relations with all other SCs (except 6–1) in the section. In addition, 6–5 has an affinity with all three strains, 3–1, 3–2, and 3–5. In this regard and others it has a high degree of similarity to the Kh nexus of section A, SC 6–6/6–38.

Closing Section (mm. 25–29)

The flute's ascent (upbeat to m. 25) and bassoon melody (m. 27) remind one of the A section. The flute soars up to touch the same high C♯ as before in m. 10 but settles on the C a ninth below. The gesture articulates a similar SC too, this time 6–1, but the trichordal partitioning is different; the first trichord is 3–1, the last is 3–4. The last four pcs yield SC 4–7, the pcs of which in pairs form SCs 3–1 and 3–5 with the sustained trumpet F♯.

The end of this section (mm. 27–28) is framed by the bassoon but not with a descent. Instead, the bassoon plays something like a folk-tune fragment. The SC is 4–10, a SC with diatonic and octatonic as well as chromatic affiliations. The accompaniment is in two strata; the clarinet, trombone, and bass pulse a 3–5 in quarter notes while the flute and horn sustain D and C. The C is the end of the rise and the D is the end of a statement of the <310> motive. The entire texture up to the end of the bassoon melody is 8–4, followed by a 6–1 chord. These SCs participate in a pc set of SC 10–1 that omits pcs 5 and 6.

The music between the flute and bassoon (m. 26) involves the horn's <310> gesture under the flute's C and trumpet's F♯. The F♯ is sustained from the end of the <310> in m. 23. The entire measure is of SC 5–10, a new harmony, but one that contains a 4–3 in the brass under the flute's C.

The bassoon folk fragment in m. 27 helps provide a consequential SC segmentation. In addition to the bassoon's 4–10, the passage is highlighted by its "primeval" style. Example 11 shows that the bassoon (3–2) and the pulsed accompaniment (3–5) combine to form a 6–38 SC. This combination of trichords relates the 3–2 strain to the 3–5 strain so that all combinations of the three strains (3–1, 3–2, 3–5) have appeared. The 6–38 connects crucially with the bassoon descent using the same SC in section A. This is because the descent in A and the passage in B play the same framing role. Thus 6–38 connects nonadjacent passages of similar function but contrasting style.

As for finding a core for the SCs of the closing section, there is no clear KI or Kh complex. There are far too many SCs without their complements in the passage, such as the 6–38 (without 6–6). However, the section is not out of character except for the 4–10 in the bassoon. The 8–4 refers to the 4–4 at the beginning of the pyramid in the middle of m. 14.

Coda (m.30)

The oboe plays the opening solo tetrachord a tritone higher. The final chord (6–1) of the closing section (m. 29) together with the final measure forms a 9–1. Missing pcs are significant once again. Two of them are used in the piccolo figure that begins the second movement. Since that figure is the retrograde of the first three pitches of the opening oboe solo, the missing pcs of mm. 29–30 suggest yet another backward reference.

Overall Structure

There can be no doubt that this piece is well-structured by pc relations involving complementation. The local omissions of certain pcs result in large sets such as 9–1 and 10–6 that are complements of important small SCs. Moreover, there are at least

Example 11. Measure 27 of *Octandre*, mvt. 1.

	9–1			8–1			8–6		7–1	7–7			6–38	
	3–1	3–2	3–5	4–1	4–2	4–3	4–6	4–9	5–1	5–7	6–1	6–5	6–6	6–7
3–1/9–1				Kh	Kh	K	Kh	K	Kh	Kh	Kh	Kh	Kh	Kh
3–2				Kh	Kh	Kh	K	K	Kh	K	Kh	Kh	K	
3–5				K	K	K	Kh	Kh	K	Kh		Kh	Kh	Kh
4–1/8–1	Kh	Kh	K						Kh	K	Kh	Kh	K	
4–2	Kh	Kh	K						Kh		Kh			
4–3	K	Kh	K						Kh		Kh			
4–6/8–6	Kh	K	Kh						Kh			Kh	Kh	Kh
4–9	K	K	Kh						Kh			Kh	Kh	Kh
5–1/7–1	Kh	Kh	K	Kh	Kh	Kh					Kh			
5–7/7–7	Kh	K	Kh	K			Kh	Kh				Kh	Kh	Kh
6–1	Kh	Kh		Kh	Kh	Kh			Kh					
6–5	Kh	Kh	Kh	Kh			Kh	Kh		Kh				
6–6/6–38	Kh	K	Kh	K			Kh	Kh		Kh				
6–7	Kh		Kh				Kh	Kh		Kh				
	3–1	3–2	3–5	4–1	4–2	4–3	4–6	4–9	5–1	5–7	6–1	6–5	6–6	6–7
	9–1			8–1			8–6		7–1	7–7			6–38	

Example 12. K/Kh Chart for *Octandre*, mvt. 1.

three examples of relatively long-range aggregate completion: the opening oboe solo; the B section, where pcs 6 and 7 (the framing pcs of the oboe solo) are added in repetition; and the last six bars, where the absence of F♯, G, then F and F♯ are balanced by the piccolo figure of the second movement, <456>.

If SCs such as 6–13, 7–31, 6–43—the referential expansions of 3–2 with ic 3 or 4, ics not found in 3–1 or 3–5—and a few other (local) SCs are omitted, the entire piece shows strong Kh closure. A Kh chart for the basic SCs is found in Example 12.

There initially appear to be many candidates for Kh complexes that model the piece, but most of them fail upon closer inspection. The 3–1/9–1 complex would cover most of the SCs, but is very large and contains many SCs that do not occur in

Kh(6–6/6–38)

3–1/9–1   3–4/9–4   3–5/9–5   3–8/9–8   3–9/9–9
4–5/8–5   4–6/8–6   4–8/8–8   4–9/8–9   4–16/8–16
5–7/7–7
6–6/6–38

Example 13. Kh Complex about 6–6/6–38.

the Varèse. The 4–1/8–1 complex leaves out 3–5, 4–9, and 6–7, SCs of the 3–5 strain so clearly articulated in the center section. A better complex is 5–7/7–7, but it omits too many members of the 3–1 strain. In addition Kh(5–7/7–7) does not model any local passage.

The last two complexes suggested by the chart are 6–5 and 6–6/6–38. In addition to their sonic similarity, both have K/Kh relations with same SCs in the piece, form a local nexus, and include SCs of both the 3–1 and 3–5 strains. There are differences too. A 6–5 hexachord cannot be partitioned into two 3–1s or 3–5s; but, as mentioned above, 6–6 partitions into two 3–1s or 3–5s. (6–38 partitions into an ic 1 and 4–1, like 6–5.) 6–5's participation in the piece is limited to the B section, whereas 6–38 connects the A and closing sections. Furthermore, the size of the Kh complexes of each is different; Kh(6–5) has thirty-one members while Kh(6–6/6–38) has twelve.

On the basis of this reasoning, the piece is perhaps best modeled by the 6–6/6–38 complex. Still, this complex omits 5–1, 6–1, and 6–7. Of course similarity relations can help relate these SCs to others in the 6–6/6–38 complex. And while 6–1 and 6–7 are exemplars of 3–1 and 3–5 strains, they alone do not unify the two into a complete whole.

When we compare the SC list of the piece as derived from the column heads of the K/Kh chart with the Kh complex about 6–6/6–38 (in Ex. 13) we confirm our choice. Half the SC pairs in the complex are found on the SC list. Four other SCs on the SC list have a KI relation with 6–6 or 6–38. Thus ten out of the fourteen items on the SC list connect to the Kh nexus. The SCs that remain unconnected have already been noted: 5–1, 6–1, 6–5, and 6–7. Of the items in the Kh complex that are not in the SC list, some of them *do* occur in the Varèse, but in minor roles; these are 3–4, 3–8, 4–5, 4–8/8–8. So only 4–16/8–16 and 3–9/9–9 from the complex do not contribute to the music.

To summarize this analysis, two strains of SCs dominate the music. The 3–1 strain frames the piece. The 3–5 strain is strongly represented by the center section. The moves from the beginning to the center and from the center to the end are marked by different combinations of the two strains. Along the way there are a few digressions from the strains involving ic 4 and members of a third strain based on 3–2. Most of the sections are modeled by clear Kh complexes. The justification for using Kh complexes comes from the presence of adjacent and embedded complementary SCs as well as the frequent use of aggregate completion. I have argued that

6–6/6–38 can be chosen as the Kh complex for the whole piece, but I will modify this assertion slightly below.

I should also point out that the pc sets that represent the SCs of our analysis are not hidden to audition. All can be plainly heard as pcs having some form of musical adjacency, usually in time and/or timbre. Pc sets and pcs that lie on the boundaries of clearly delineated passages (top, bottom, first, last) contribute to the cogency of the analysis and help produce a sense of continuity and form. In addition, even if we take the view that there is no pressing need to identify a Kh nexus for the entire work, there can be no doubt that the KI, K, and Kh relations help identify many of the factors that unify or differentiate local passages as well as forge connections among nonadjacent sections.

Generalizations of the SC-List Concept

The KI, K, and Kh relations generate only one class of SC lists—the class of SC lists derived from SC abstract-inclusion lattices. While such lists are useful in providing a relatively small group of models (the K and Kh complexes) for analytic purposes, we need not think of these lists as being the only ones available—especially when we widen our scope from early twentieth-century analysis to twentieth-century composition, in both its analytic and speculative guises. Nevertheless, the lattice idea is appealing and intuitive, so we will begin by examining extensions of the Kh-complex idea.

The results of the Varèse analysis suggest one obvious direction: what about the set theoretic combinations of SC lists?[32] After all, when we compare a passage's SC list to a complex, we register its "fit" by taking the intersection of the two lists. The higher the cardinality of the intersection, the more completely does the piece fit the complex, or vice versa. We can also determine the size of the symmetric difference of the two lists—the smaller it is, the greater the correspondence.[33] We implicitly utilized the latter comparison when we threw out large complexes (like 3–1/9–1) that contained the piece's SC list but had too many other SCs that did not figure into the piece.

Taking the union of two complexes only increases the number of SCs with which one must contend, so this move is often not useful. The intersection of two lists seems a more fruitful path, especially in the presence of a conflict between two complexes. If one is forced to choose between two complex nexi, one complex will be dropped. Then similarity relations will be the only way to include the losing nexus in the analysis.[34] An intersection complex solves this neatly; it has two or more nexus SCs, each of which abstractly includes all of the other SCs. The problem here is that

---

32. Forte proposed such set-theoretic combinations in his article, "A Theory of Set-Complexes for Music," *Journal of Music Theory* 8 (1964): 136–83.

33. The symmetric difference between two sets is the complement of the intersection with respect to the union of the two.

34. In one sense this is not a problem, since, with the omission of F.1 and F.2 conditions,

Kh(6–7) ∩ Kh(6–5) ∩ Kh(6–6/6–38)

3–1/9–1	3–4/9–4	3–5/9–5	3–8/9–8	3–9/9–9
4–5/8–5	4–6/8–6	4–8/8–8	4–9/8–9	4–16/8–16
5–7/7–7				
6–6/6–38				

Example 14. Intersections of Kh Complexes around 6–7, 6–6/6–38, and 6–5.

the SCs that are not found in all of the combined complexes will not be found in the intersection complex.

Let us apply intersection complexes to the Varèse. Can we model the combination of the 3–1 and 3–5 strains better than with 6–6/6–38? When we take the intersection of the Kh complexes of the hexachordal exemplars of 3–1 and 3–5, 6–1 and 6–7, the resulting complex contains only 3–1, 3–4, 6–1, and 6–7. Clearly this will not do. Better results occur with Kh(6–7) ∩ Kh(6–5) ∩ Kh(6–6/6–38) (see Ex. 14). This combination ends the conflict between 6–5 and 6–6/6–38 as potential nexi. It also allows 6–7 (which does contain 3–1) to contribute as a nexus as well, for 6–7 is clearly presented in the center section. The result is that, aside from the nexus SCs, the intersection complex is the same as for 6–6/6–38. Thus, we have the same SC list as before, but our model now also includes 6–5 and 6–7. Nevertheless, the question of combining the 3–1 and 3–5 strains remains, not to mention the 3–2 strain.[35] The complex defined by Kh(3–1/9–1) ∩ Kh(3–5/9–5) would seem to be a likely candidate for relating SCs from the 3–1 and 3–5 chains, except that it is quite large when compared to the Varèse SC list; the degree of repletion between the intersection complex and the list is too small. This problem and others is addressed by another of Forte's major contributions to atonal pc-set theory, the pitch-class-set genera.

Forte's Genera

On the face of it, the genera seem different in kind from the KI, K, or Kh complexes.[36] First of all, Forte puts them to different ends. Unlike the K and Kh relation used in the analysis of atonal repertory, the genera establish a much more global classification scheme of "harmonic species." In fact, their function is to group rather than to differentiate pieces. This accommodates Forte's goal to describe the historical development of harmonic materials from late-tonal to post-tonal Western art

the KI, K, and, to some extent, the Kh relations are similarity relations—that is, they are reflexive, symmetric, but lack transitivity.

35. For instance, SC 5–1 is not a member of any proposed Kh complex except Kh(6–1).

36. See Allen Forte, "Pitch-Class Set Genera and the Origin of Modern Harmonic Species," *Journal of Music Theory* 32 (1988): 187–270.

music. In addition, the genera seem structurally different from Kh complexes. First, Forte defines only twelve genera (and four supragenera) versus the 102 Kh complexes. Second, a genus is based on one or two trichordal progenitors and not on individual SC-complement pairs with cardinalities greater than 3 as explicitly specified by Forte's F.2 condition. Thus the genera appear to be "bottom-up" as opposed to "top-down" or "middle-out" structures (like the Kh or KI lattices). Third, the genera's inclusion rules are more selective than in KI, K, and Kh complexes. Yet, regardless of these differences, I will show that Forte's genera and others can be generated as set-theoretic operations on KI and Kh complexes.

Once again, it may be helpful to consider a compositional scenario which would result in a piece amenable to analysis with genera. Our composer would use the members of one or two small SCs in any kind of local linkage and combination to make larger (longer) materials. As a result, the surface of the music would be saturated by the sonorities of the generating SCs.

Forte's genera are built from either one or two trichords he calls progenitors.[37] When a genus has a single progenitor, the trichord has an ic vector with a unique combination of ics. For instance, Forte's genus G1 has 3–5 as its progenitor. This trichord's ic vector includes ics 1 and 6; no other trichord has these two ics in its vector. Since trichords 3–8, 3–10, and 3–12 have the same property, there are four genera with a singleton progenitor. With genera based on two trichords, the progenitors must be as similar as possible in both pc and ic. Thus progenitor pairs have two out of three ics in common and enjoy the R_p relation.[38] There are ten cases possible but only eight are used, since two produce genera that are subsets of the others.[39]

Forte's rules for constructing a genus are reformulated below. A SC list is a genus iff the following hold:

GR1. The list contains the progenitor(s).

GR2. Both members of each complementary SC pair on the list include both the progenitors. This means the progenitors have the Kh relation with all other SCs on the list (without condition F.2).

GR3. Excepting the progenitor(s), all SCs of cardinality C on the list contain at least one SC of cardinality C - 1 on the list. For example, as Forte points out, 6–18 is not a member of G5 (based on 3–1 and 3–2), even though 6–18 includes both progenitors (thereby satisfying GR2).[40] 6–18 is omitted because it does not include any of the pentachordal SCs in the genus.

---

37. Forte's genera differ from those of Richard Parks. Parks uses the term "genera" for his lists of SCs arranged according to abstract inclusion. See Richard S. Parks, *The Music of Claude Debussy* (New Haven and London: Yale University Press, 1989).

38. Forte's R_p relation is an abstract relation between two SCs X and Y of cardinality n. Let pc set x ∈ X and pc set y ∈ Y. Iff there is at least one x and one y, such that #(x ∩ y) = n - 1, SCs X and Y are R_p related. See Forte, *The Structure of Atonal Music*, 47–48.

39. Forte's G1 (based on 3–5) subsumes a genus based on (3–3 and 3–4). G2 includes the genus based on 3–6 and 3–8.

40. Forte, "Pitch-Class Set Genera," 194.

Before continuing with more theory, let us attempt to use Forte's genera to model the SC list of the Varèse. Unfortunately, we cannot model the combination of the 3–1 and 3–5 strains with one genus since there is no Forte genus with these progenitors. This is because 3–1 and 3–5 do not have two out of three ics in common. When we compare the piece's SC list with G1, based on 3–5, we find that the hexachords 6–5, 6–6/6–38, and 6–7 intersect with G1, but the genus has sixty-three members, so any kind of repletion is far off. We can also compare G5 (3–1 and 3–2) with the list.[41] Here the genus has only twenty-nine members and the intersection set contains seven SC complementary pairs: {3–1/9–1, 3–2/9–2, 4–1/8–1, 4–2/8–4, 5–1/7–1, 6–1, 6–5}. The presence of 6–5 is a boon, but the lack of other SCs of the 3–5 strain compromises a good fit.[42]

Up to now, I have used Forte's names for his twelve genera, the letter G followed by a numeral from 1 to 12.[43] In the sequel, I will identify Forte's genera and others by the letter G followed by the list of progenitors in parentheses. Thus Forte's G1 is identified as G(3–5).

A General Formalization of Genera

If we drop the unique ic combination requirement, there are twelve genera with a single progenitor. These are the Kh complexes about 3–x/9–x. As we noted above, genera with two progenitors are not simply the intersection of two Kh complexes with trichordal nexi. This is prohibited by rule GR3. But the same rule suggests a way of generating any genus via the intersection and union of Kh and K complexes—that once all the tetrachords in a genus are established, all larger SCs must include them.

More general rules for constructing a genus follow.

H1. A genus may have any number of progenitors of the same cardinality Q.
H2. The progenitor SCs must have mutual R_p relations. (They must form a transitive tuple under R_p.)[44]
H3. The *continuity SCs* of a genus are those of cardinality Q + n (n usually equals 1). They are in the intersection set of all the Kh complexes about the progenitors.
H4. The genus is the intersection of the Kh complexes of each progenitor intersecting with the union of the KI complexes of the continuity SCs.

41. The question of quantitatively comparing Forte's genera is handled by Forte's difference quotient (or DIFQUO) measure. Forte uses a different measure, the Status Quotient or SQUO, when he compares SC lists and genera. See Forte, "Pitch-Class Set Genera."

42. It should be noted that the special (local) SCs (not on the Varèse SC list) such as 6–4/6–37, 7–31, and 6–13 are found in either G1 or G5.

43. Forte also uses nicknames such as such "dia" for G11 (based on 3–7 and 3–9). See Forte, "Pitch-Class Set Genera."

44. We could also demand that the progenitors have mutual maximal similarity under some pc-similarity measure such as Forte's R_1 or R_2.

As an example, let us generate G(3–1,3–2), Forte's G5. The progenitors are 3–1 and 3–2 so Q = 3 (H1). The progenitors are in mutual R_p relation (H2). The continuity SCs are of cardinality 4 (Q + 1 = 4). The Kh complex about 3–1 and the Kh complex about 3–2 both contain 4–1 and 4–2. Thus the continuity SCs are 4–1 and 4–2 (H3). G(3–1,3–2) is Kh(3–1) ∩ Kh(3–2) ∩ (KI(4–1) ∪ KI(4–2)) (H4).

Now we can construct new genera: for instance, G(3–1,3–5) = Kh(3–1) ∩ Kh(3–5) ∩ (KI(4–5) ∪ KI(4–6)). The SC list for this genus is given in Example 15. This genus has twenty-four members whereas the intersection of Kh(3–1) and Kh (3–5) is much larger. As a model for the Varèse, the genus is disappointing, since SCs such as 4–1, 4–9, 5–1, and 6–1 are absent. From another point of view the genus is very useful, for it identifies those SCs that are in both the 3–1 and 3–5 strains. This enables us to return to the music and definitively quantify passages on a continuum from those totally affiliated with 3–1 to those totally affiliated with 3–5, with those affiliated with both in between. This is accomplished by checking the degree of intersection and symmetric difference between the SC list of a passage and G(3–1), G(3–5), and/or G(3–1,3–5).

Genera with progenitors higher than cardinality 3 can be very exclusive. For instance, G(4–1,4–3) contains only four SC pairs: {4–1/8–1, 4–3/8–3, 5–1/7–1, and 6–1}. It is also possible to produce more genera from trichords by dropping the R_p requirement of the H2 rule. Example 16 lists the the SCs in G(3–1, 3–10). 3–1 and 3–10 do not have the R_p relation. There are no tetrachordal SCs in the genus because the continuity SCs are of cardinality 5 (n = 2). So the definition of the genus is Kh(3–1) ∩ Kh(3–10) ∩ (KI(5–4) ∪ KI(5–8)). The omission of a level of cardinality should not alarm us, for many Kh complexes omit a level. For example, the Kh complex about 6–4/6–37 has no SCs of cardinality 5 or 7.

COMPARING SC LISTS IN ANALYSIS

Up to now, analysis with the KI, K, or Kh relations or the genera has involved comparing a piece's SC list with a complex or set-theoretic combination of complexes. Since the complexes list all of the abstract inclusions possible for its nexus and the SC lists are unordered sets of SCs drawn from the piece, there has been an analytic propriety to model a piece with a complex. But, in point of fact, we do reverse the analytic direction from complex-to-piece to piece-to-complex when we are interested in testing the empirical utility of the complexes. If no complex was modeled by a piece, so to speak, then the SC complex concept would not be used in analysis. In addition, we have generalized complexes to SC lists whose content need not be derived from a lattice. Thus there is no necessity always to model pieces with a complex. We could use one piece's SC list to model another's. Or in composition, we might compose a piece by traversing a path through a complex or compositional space.[45] The SC list of

---

45. Compositional spaces are out-of-time networks of pc sets and the like. See Morris,

G(3–1, 3–5)

3–1   3–5
4–5   4–6
5–4   5–5   5–6   5–7   5–13   5–14   5–15   5–36
6–5   6–6/38   6–7   6–9   6–11/40   6–12/41   6–15   6–16   6–17/43   6–18   6–21   6–22

Example 15. Genus generated by 3–1 and 3–5.

G(3–1, 3–10)

3–1   3–10
5–4   5–8
6–2   6–3/36   6–5   6–10/39   6–21

Example 16. Genus generated by 3–1 and 3–10.

the path, not the complex or space, would model the resulting composition. Such analytic actions might produce a better fit between model and piece with respect to completion and repletion.

To illustrate such a notion, let us compare the SC list from the outer sections of the fourth movement of Webern's Five Movements for String Quartet, op. 5, and the Varèse list. The Webern has been analyzed more than once from the SC complex point of view.[46] The SC list for its outer sections is given in Example 17. Its SCs all intersect with Kh(6–5). Except for three SCs, 5–6, 7–5 and 8–9, the Webern list is a subset of the Varèse list. This means there is a considerable resemblance between the two works. Whether Varèse knew the Webern or not is not the issue here, although the question is intriguing. The point is that one work can serve as the model for another—an ordinary state of affairs in all the arts, if especially so in literary fields.

OTHER KINDS OF SC LISTS

SC lists need not follow from abstract inclusion, but proceed by positing special equivalence operators to collect SCs into "set-groups."[47] This is accomplished by inventing pc-set operations that are one-to-one and onto and transforming each member of a

---

"Compositional Spaces and Other Territories," *Perspectives of New Music* 33 (1995), 328–58.

46. See Forte, "A Theory of Set-Complexes"; David Beach, "Pitch Structure and the Analytical Process in Atonal Music: An Interpretation of the Theory of Sets," *Music Theory Spectrum* 1 (1979): 7–22; and Kaplan, "Transpositionally Invariant Subsets."

47. See Morris, "Set Groups, Complementation, and Mappings among Pitch-Class Sets,"

SC list of Webern Op. 5/4.

3–5
4–4   4–8   4–9
5–6   5–7
6–5
7–7   7–5
8–9

Example 17. SC list of Webern, Five Movements for String Quartet, op. 5, mvt. 4.

Equivalence under M (or MI)

9 trichordal set-groups:
3–1/3–9   3–2/3–7   3–3/3–11   3–4   3–5   3–6   3–8   3–10   3–11

Equivalence under M and α_3

6 trichordal set-groups:
3–1/3–2/3–7/3–9   3–3/3–4/3–11   3–5/3–10   3–6   3–8   3–12

$M = (0)$ (3)   (6)   (9)   (1 5)   (2 10)   (4 8)   (7 11)
$\alpha_3 = (0)$ (2)   (4)   (6)   (8)   (10)   (1 3 5 7 9 11)

Example 18. Equivalence under M (or MI) and equivalence under M and α_3.

SC under the operation. This amounts to transforming the prime form (or any other member) of a SC under the operation preceded by T_n or T_nI. SCs may pair up under the operation such that every member of SC X is a member of SC Y under the operation. Or the operation may even map the members of the SC into each other so the SC is invariant under the operation. A familiar example of such pairings and invariance under a nonstandard pc operation involves the multiplicative operation called M or M_5 which groups SCs together in pairs or keeps them invariant.[48] Under M the twelve trichordal SCs are merged into nine set-groups (see Ex. 18). On the other hand, SC members may map to many different SCs forming a network of SC affiliations under the operator. Perhaps the most often cited example of this state of affairs is my α_3 operation (equivalent to Andrew Mead's O_z operation).[49] The operation

Journal of Music Theory 26 (1982): 101–44; and "Pitch-Class Complementation and its Generalizations," *Journal of Music Theory* 34 (1990): 175–246.

48. The M operation multiplies each pc by 5 mod 12. For instance, pc 1 goes to 5 and 5 maps to 1; 0 remains invariant, as do 3, 6, and 9; and so forth.

49. See Andrew W. Mead, "Some Implications of the Pitch/Order Number Isomorphism Inherent in the Twelve-Tone System: Part I," *Perspectives of New Music* 26, no. 2 (1988): 96–163.

involves mapping the pc 0 to 2, 2 to 4, 4 to 6, 6 to 8, 8 to 10, and 10 to 0; all other pcs remain the same. The trichords form six set-groups under α_3 as shown in the example.

Conclusion

The utility or value of the comparison of SC lists to analyze or compare pieces and/ or theoretic structures is determined by one's purposes and underlying philosophy of analysis. Today, many analysts are interested in exploring the implication of transformations between musical entities such as pc sets and SCs as well as identifying their inclusion in a composition. While a transformational approach has many virtues, if one works with the standard transpositional and inversional operations, the identification of SCs helps determine which entities may be so connected or transformed. Thus the SC forms a starting place for transformational analysis. Conversely, identifying families of SCs helps define the canonic context within which nonstandard transformations may act.

From this point of view, the KI, K, and Kh relations are perfectly useful tools. No doubt they are associated with the music theory of the 1960s and 1970s which tended toward more global, totalizing accounts of music. But today in our poststructuralist world, where the discovery or explanation of musical unity is not the only driving force, Forte's tools and their generalizations can be appropriate to determine the degree of fit between pieces, musical structures, and their contexts.

PART TWO:
ANALYTICAL STUDIES

The Submediant as Third Divider: Its Representation at Different Structural Levels

David W. Beach

One of the most common means of expanding the fundamental tonal progression I–IV–V–I is to divide the tonal space between the tonic and subdominant into descending thirds: I–vi–IV (ii⁶)–V–I. Under normal circumstances, this progression—there must be literally thousands of examples of it in the literature, ranging from the Classical period to the present—is perfectly straightforward and thus requires no special comment. However, there are circumstances requiring interpretation—where either the function of the submediant is potentially ambiguous, or the progression itself occurs only at some deeper level of structure and thus may not be easily recognized. The purpose of this study is to examine several such examples. We will begin with two well-known examples at the phrase level that present a particular problem of interpretation and progress from there through several others occurring on increasingly deeper levels of structure. The final section of this study is devoted to the detailed examination of a single work, the Prelude in B Major from Book I of J.S. Bach's *Well-Tempered Clavier*.[1]

A potential ambiguity arises in the progression I–vi–IV/ii⁶–V–I when the submediant is preceded by the dominant: I–V–vi–IV/ii⁶–V–I. Without benefit of additional information, two different interpretations are possible. In the first, the initial dominant elaborates the underlying bass arpeggiation from the tonic to $\hat{4}$, perhaps as harmonization of a passing tone within an embedded linear progression. The other possibility is that this dominant, the second chord, is prolonged by a double neighbor-note configuration in the bass supporting the harmonies vi and IV/ii⁶ before its restatement and resolution to the tonic. Both interpretations are feasible, and we must consider the specific musical context to make an informed choice. As an initial example, let us take a look at the opening phrase from Haydn's *Chorale St. Antoni,* which is reproduced in Example 1. This relatively simple phrase is more complex than it first appears, and before the issue of underlying voice leading can be addressed, we must make some basic decisions about how it might be divided (that

---

1. Several years ago I studied this piece with the late Ernst Oster, and my analysis is strongly influenced by his insights. His sketch of the overall structure of the prelude is reproduced in Figure 13. His notes on the piece, along with his other unpublished sketches, are in the possession of Gail Rehman.

Example 1. Haydn: *Chorale St. Antoni* (piano reduction), mm. 1–5, from Divertimento in B♭ (Hob. II:46).

is, to determine its grouping structure[2]) and whether or not we can consider these five measures as an expansion of four (and if so, how). Let us take up the latter of these questions first, since the answer may shed light on the former. The most obvious reading of the underlying metric structure is to regard the second measure as an expansion of the neighbor-note figure expressed at a lower level within the first measure—in short, to interpret the underlying pattern as 1–2 3 4. The only other possibility with any merit is to regard the third measure as parenthetical (that is, to read the underlying metric group as 1 2 [-] 3 4), a solution that works with respect to the overall voice leading of the phrase but is less logical than the first reading because it entails omission of new material as opposed to interpretation of m. 2 as an expansion of a previously stated relationship. In either case, the last two measures of the phrase remain intact as a unit, supporting the division of five into three plus two. This corresponds to the natural division of the melody into two thirds, the initial descending third d^2–c^2–b♭^{1} in mm. 1–3 and the answering e♭^{2}–d^2–c^2 in mm. 4–5, as shown in Figure 1a.[3] In this interpretation, the underlying progression is I–vi–ii^6–V, and the dominant chord on the downbeat of m. 3 is interpreted as offering local support to the passing tone c within the initial descending third. Despite the logic of this interpretation, one might counter with the following arguments: 1) that it makes no sense to hear these five measures as an expansion of four; 2) that it is just as logical to consider the division of five into two plus three as three plus two; and 3) that the underlying voice leading is something like that shown in Figure 1b. Regarding the first point, it should be noted that the interpretation given in Figure 1a, while incorporating the notion of metric expansion, does not depend on it. And the problem with point two is that it leads to an interpretation (point three) that ignores the natural tendency of the melodic c on the downbeat of measure three to be a passing tone— it is harmonized on the offbeat as the seventh of a secondary dominant—within the descending third d^2–c^2–b♭^{1}. One could arrive at this second interpretation only by considering the harmonic progression in isolation of its context.

2. See Fred Lerdahl and Ray Jackendoff, *A Generative Theory of Tonal Music* (Cambridge: MIT Press, 1983), 13–17 and 36–67.

3. See Heinrich Schenker, *Free Composition*, trans. and ed. Ernst Oster (New York: Longman, 1979), Figures 42.2 and 138.3.

Figure 1.

A far more complex representation of the same progression can be found in the opening phrase of the *Introduzione* from Beethoven's "Waldstein" Sonata.[4] Here again, we are faced with two possible interpretations: 1) that the dominant reached in m. 6 is prolonged by a double neighbor-note figure (supporting the harmonies vi and ii^6) before its resolution in m. 9; and 2) that the dominant in m. 6, though indeed the goal of the preceding chromatic progression, functions on a larger level to introduce vi, which is part of a long-range descending bass arpeggiation connecting the tonic (m. 1) to ii^6 in preparation for the real structural dominant. One can muster arguments in support of either interpretation, and thus the choice is by no means a simple one. Regarding the first, note that much of the phrase is occupied with the chromatic descent from the tonic to the dominant in m. 6, which coincides with the dynamic and registral highpoint of the phrase. Thus it is very easy to hear what follows as an extension of this dominant until its resolution in m. 9. However, a careful look at the progress of the voice leading, particularly the primary melodic line, may force us to reevaluate our initial impression. Note that the goal of the melodic motion generated from the beginning is not in m. 6 (the g^2 over b♭^{1}) but in m. 7 (the f^2 over a^1), after which there is an abrupt shift in register for the closing cadential pattern. Thus we have a basic conflict. Examination of the harmony alone leads to

4. This phrase has been the subject of an extended debate between this author and Charles Smith. See the following sequence of articles: David Beach, "Analysis Symposium," *Journal of Music Theory* 13 (1969): 188–203; Charles Smith, "The Functional Extravagance of Chromatic Chords," *Music Theory Spectrum* 8 (1986): 94–139; Beach, "On Analysis, Beethoven, and Extravagance: A Response to Charles Smith," *Music Theory Spectrum* 9 (1987): 173–85; Smith, "A Rejoinder to David Beach," *Music Theory Spectrum* 9 (1987): 186–94.

our first interpretation, but reexamination of the harmony in relation to melodic goals suggests that the motion pushes through this dominant to the submediant harmony in m. 7. As shown in Figure 2, level a,[5] this dominant offers support for the passing tone g^2 within an initial embedded descent of the fundamental line. That is, despite the emphasis given to it, this dominant chord eventually functions on a much lower level than one might initially suspect. It introduces vi, the second member of the descending bass arpeggiation from F (I) to B♭ (ii⁶).

There are, of course, instances where a structural dominant is prolonged by a double neighbor-note figure supporting the harmonies vi and IV/ii⁶. A particularly clear example occurs in the third movement of Beethoven's Piano Sonata in E♭ Major, op. 7. As shown in Example 3, this progression occurs twice in this passage, extending the cadential $^6_4$ until its resolution to the $^5_3$ in m. 85. Examination of the voice leading, an interpretation of which is provided in Figure 3, reveals that the motion to vi supports an initial descent of the fundamental line, which is repeated an octave lower before the final descent to closure in an inner voice. Considered in its larger context, this passage (mm. 80–86) occurs at the end of a greatly expanded phrase beginning in m. 51.[6] As shown in Figure 3, the opening progression i–V–♭VI harmonizes an initial descent of the fundamental line, but in the parallel minor mode. In the larger context, the function of ♭VI in mm. 54ff. is to form the middle member of a large-scale descending arpeggiation to the subdominant, which is finally reached in m. 80. The two sets of parentheses in Figure 3 represent parenthetical insertions/expansions. Here, within a single expanded phrase, we have multiple functions of the dominant and submediant harmonies. The initial dominant (m. 53) supports a passing tone within the initial descent ♭3̂ 2̂ 1̂, and ♭VI, while locally avoiding closure, becomes part of the large-scale descending third-progression to IV. The $^6_4$ in mm. 70ff., which might initially be heard as cadential,[7] is passing, leading to the subdominant in m. 80, which Beethoven has clearly marked as the climax of the phrase. The structural dominant, which follows, is then prolonged by the above-mentioned double neighbor-note figure supporting the harmonies vi and IV.

Another example of the use of the submediant to prolong the dominant occurs in the closing section of Mozart's Fantasy in D Minor, K. 397, mm. 63–70 of which are provided in Example 4. As shown in Figure 4, the structural dominant is reached in the fourth measure of this eight-measure phrase, which is the second part of a sixteen-measure period, and subsequent events—the passing vii⁶/V as well as the later submediant and immediately following subdominant prolong this dominant

---

5. Figure 2 is a slightly modified version of Example 3 from Beach, "On Analysis, Beethoven, and Extravagance," 177.

6. A discussion of the processes underlying the expansion of this phrase is contained in David Beach, "Phrase Expansion: Three Analytical Studies," *Music Analysis* 14 (1995): 27–47.

7. The function of this $^6_4$ is addressed in David Beach, "More on the Six-Four," *Journal of Music Theory* 34 (1990): 281–90.

Example 2. Beethoven: "Introduzione," Piano Sonata, op. 53, phrase 1.

Figure 2. Beethoven: "Introduzione," mm. 1–9.

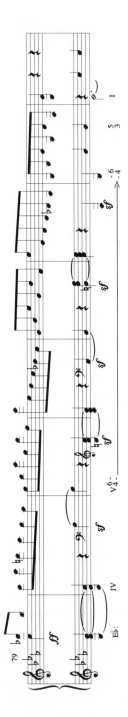

Example 3. Beethoven: Piano Sonata, op. 7 (III), mm. 79–86.

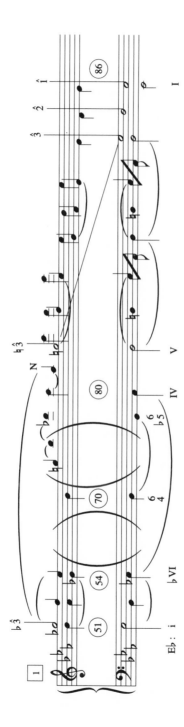

Figure 3.

Example 4. Mozart: Fantasy, K. 397, mm. 63–70.

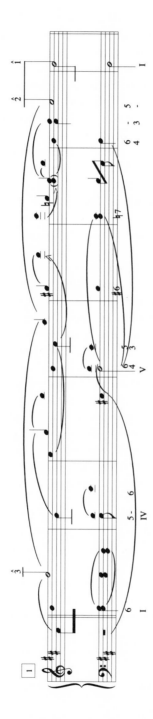

Figure 4.

before its resolution to the tonic and local closure in m. 70. The function of these prolonging chords is to provide support for the chromatic descending line from the high a, a primary motivic idea of the piece.[8]

The function of the submediant is perfectly clear in these last two examples, because there can be no doubt as to the structural importance of the preceding dominant. In the expanded phrase from Beethoven's op. 7, the structural dominant is approached through a large-scale descending arpeggiation, but once the dominant is reached (m. 81), the subsequent statements of the submediant serve to prolong that dominant—in essence to extend the phrase further by avoiding closure. Likewise, the submediant in the excerpt from Mozart's Fantasy prolongs the structural dominant, in this case not to extend the phrase by avoiding closure but to offer support for a motivic idea within the dominant *Stufe*. But the situation is very different when the submediant functions as a third divider between the tonic and the subdominant (or ii[6]). By definition the dominant that introduces this submediant cannot be structural, but rather must function at a more local level, perhaps to offer support for a passing tone. This is the situation in the phrases taken from the *Chorale St. Antoni* and from the "Waldstein" sonata. Though one might argue the contrary from a purely theoretical perspective, most musicians would agree with the interpretation of the first of these provided in Figure 1a, because it follows the natural division of the phrase and the melodic statement of the two thirds d^2–c^2–b♭[1] and e♭[2]–d^2–c^2. However, as noted above, interpretation of the dominant in m. 6 of the Beethoven phrase (and the subsequent submediant as well) is more problematic because that dominant is heard as the goal of the preceding chromatic descent. If considered solely in terms of the harmony, that dominant would seem to qualify as the structural dominant, which is subsequently prolonged. But considered in terms of the melodic line—that is, in terms of the melodic thirds a^2–g^2–f^2 and g^2–e^2 shown in Figure 2, level a—that dominant chord cannot be interpreted as structural, but only as offering support to the passing g^2 within the initial descending third. The difference in interpretation rests on the perceived relationship of the harmony to the melodic gesture.

Like all tonal progressions, the motion by descending third from tonic to subdominant (or supertonic in $^6_3$ or $^6_5$ position) can occur in a wide variety of circumstances and is subject to expansion at various levels. Rather than attempting to provide an exhaustive listing of the possibilities, we will examine two additional examples at the phrase level, both by Schubert, before considering the representation of this progression at the deep middleground. The first example is the opening phrase of the Piano Trio in B♭, D.898 (see Fig. 5). Here the submediant harmony plays a particularly important role: it offers local support for the delayed entrance of the *Kopfton* $\hat{3}$, the goal of the ascending melodic motion, in m. 10.[9] As indicated by the broken beam

---

8. For additional information on this work, see Edward Laufer, "On the Fantasy," *Intégral* 2 (1988): 99–133.

9. This interpretation agrees with the analysis of this passage by Gordon Sly in "An Emerg-

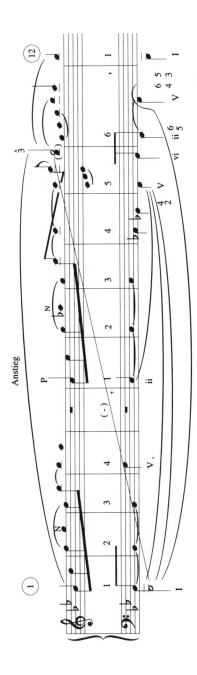

Figure 5. Schubert: Piano Trio in B♭ (I), mm. 1–12.

and lowest slur in the bass, the basic progression is I . . . vi–ii$^6_5$–V–I. The dominant harmony in mm. 4–5 supports the phrase division, and the progression ii . . . V in mm. 5–10 supports the passing tone c^2 and the overlapping to e♭^{3} that lead to the *Kopfton*. A further explanation of the notation of the bass line in these measures is warranted. The upper two slurs and direction of the stems indicate that the bass notes A♭ and G♭ may be understood not only in the local context of connecting ii to V (mm. 6–10) but also as forming a more inclusive stepwise motion from the opening tonic to this dominant. While the A♭ and G♭ are not particularly important in this local context, they assume considerable significance in the development section.[10]

Our second example, taken from the second movement of the "Trout" Quintet (see Fig. 6), illustrates one way in which the progression I–vi–IV can be expanded at the phrase level. We might understand this expansion to occur in two stages. First, the basic harmonies are elaborated by secondary dominants, where initially each chord in the progression occupies a single measure. However, rather than completing this pattern, Schubert further expands the V^7 of IV by extending it an additional measure and then by an eight-measure insertion, clearly divided by compositional articulation into two metric groups of four. The apparent reason for extending the phrase in this way is to stabilize the subdominant, which is subsequently extended for an additional eight measures, in preparation for the sudden shift to A♭ major in conjunction with the return of the opening theme.[11] As indicated by the metric groupings shown in parentheses above the music, one might hear the expansion begin-

---

ing Symbiosis of Structure and Design in the Sonata Practice of Franz Schubert" (Ph.D. diss., Eastman School of Music of the University of Rochester, 1994). A different reading is given by Felix Salzer in *Structural Hearing* (New York: Dover, 1962), Example 389.

10. The development section can be divided into three large sections, the first beginning in the tonic minor and progressing to V of V. The second begins in A♭ major, which, following a sequential chain of descending major thirds, leads to the dominant, which is extended for several measures. The third begins in G♭ (♭VI) with a statement of the opening theme, which might at first be mistaken for the beginning of the recapitulation. From a structural perspective, this G♭ functions as a neighbor note to the dominant, to which it returns just before the true recapitulation. At the same time, it is also possible to hear this G♭ as part of a large-scale descending motion from tonic to dominant following the above-mentioned compositional design of the development section. That is, it is tempting to explain (and to hear) the appearance of G♭ at this point in the composition—following clearly articulated sections in B♭ and A♭—as a parallel to the corresponding motion in the opening phrase of the movement. This explanation, based on the compositional design, is intended to supplement but not replace our structural interpretation of the G♭ as neighbor note to the preceding dominant.

11. At the corresponding place in the recapitulation (mm. 100ff.), each one of these harmonies occupies a single measure, and it is the following dominant that is expanded by an eight-measure insertion. Both of these passages are discussed in Beach, "Phrase Expansion: Three Analytical Studies."

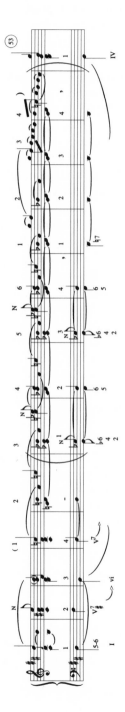

Figure 6. Schubert: "Trout" Quintet (II), mm. 40–53.

ning in the fourth measure, since it is at this point that the imitation between the piano and first violin parts (not represented in Fig. 6) is initiated.[12] Though one can interpret the expansion in slightly different ways, this is a relatively straightforward example of phrase expansion. We have already encountered a far more elaborate expansion of this same progression, though in the minor mode, in the third movement of Beethoven's op. 7 (see Fig. 3).

This brief consideration of phrase expansion leads quite naturally into a consideration of the progression I–vi–IV–V–I as represented at the deep middleground, where the individual steps—particularly I, vi, and IV—are greatly extended and often represented locally as keys. Consider, for example, the second movement of Schubert's Piano Sonata in B♭, D.960, a graph of which appears as Figure 7. A motivic feature of the first part is the prolongation of $\hat{5}$(g♯¹) by its upper neighbor (not shown in Fig. 7), which is subsequently prolonged throughout the B section before its return to g♯, harmonized by the dominant, in preparation for the return to the opening material and the tonic harmony (A′). The upper neighbor is first supported by the local key of A major (VI in the main key), and only at the last minute is the progression directed toward an F♯-minor harmony (at the return to the upper neighbor a¹), completing the large-scale descending arpeggiation from tonic to subdominant. Meanwhile the melodic a¹ is prolonged by its upper third c♯², picking up the persistent covering pedal tone of the opening section, and the return to the prolonged motivic a is elaborated by the neighboring third d♮²–b♮¹.

This same progression can also be found in movements written in sonata form, typically where the submediant is the second key area of the exposition and the subdominant falls somewhere in the development section, prior to the dominant. The return to tonic then coincides with the restatement of the opening material. Oswald Jonas, Ernst Oster, and Heinrich Schenker have mentioned a number of examples of this progression in first movements by Beethoven and Brahms: from Beethoven, String Quintet op. 29, Piano Trio op. 97, Piano Sonata op. 106, Piano Sonata op. 111, and the Ninth Symphony op. 125; from Brahms, Piano Quintet op. 34.[13] Oster also mentions a Sonata in B♭ (Longo 500, Kirkpatrick 545) by Domenico Scarlatti and the first movement of Beethoven's Piano Sonata in G, op. 79. In the latter, the submediant (VI) appears at the beginning of the development section and the preceding dominant (second key area of the exposition) is interpreted as a divider within the larger structural progression.

Sometimes arrival at the subdominant is delayed to coincide with the reintroduction of the opening material (the thematic recapitulation), as one finds in the

---

12. I credit William Rothstein for this observation.

13. Oswald Jonas, *Introduction to the Theory of Heinrich Schenker*, trans. and ed. John Rothgeb (New York: Longman, 1982), 49–50; Ernst Oster, extensive footnote to his translation of Schenker's *Free Composition*, 139–41; Schenker, *Harmony*, trans. Elisabeth Mann Borgese (Chicago: University of Chicago Press, 1954), 248–49. These examples in all cases refer to the first movement only.

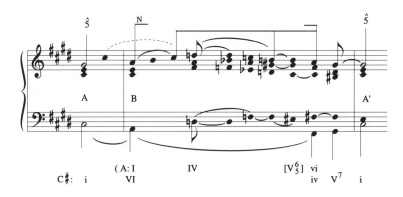

Figure 7. Schubert: Piano Sonata in B♭ (II).

first movement of Schubert's Piano Sonata in A Minor, D. 537. Here the large-scale bass arpeggiation spans from the beginning of the exposition (A minor) through the second key area (F major) to the beginning of the recapitulation (D minor); thus the progression i–VI–iv–V–i encompasses the entire movement.[14] An even clearer example occurs in the second movement of Schubert's Piano Trio in B♭, D.898, a sketch of which is provided in Figure 8. The first section, which is locally closed in the tonic key of E♭, prolongs (g^2), and this pitch continues to receive consonant support in the B section, first by C minor (vi) and then by C major (VI). Arrival at the subdominant, which supports the upper neighbor note a♭^{2}, coincides with the return of the opening material (A'). At this point Schubert embarks on a characteristic sequence by descending major thirds, extending the subdominant; however, the third statement (C Major) is cut short after two measures and the tonic harmony is abruptly reintroduced, from which point the movement progresses to closure.[15] In a certain sense there is a parallel between this structure and the one discussed earlier from the second movement of the B♭ Piano Sonata (see Fig. 7). In the excerpt sketched in Figure 8 the steps in the descending arpeggiation are even more clearly articulated, each being stated at the onset of a major formal division of the movement.

---

14. Oster, in Schenker, *Free Composition*, 140.

15. Another possible way to interpret the closing section is to hear the return to the tonic and $\hat{3}$ as passing between IV and V, thus:

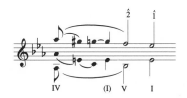

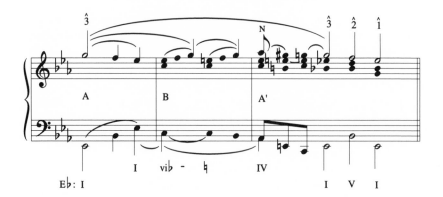

Figure 8. Schubert: Piano Trio in B♭ (II).

Finally, it should be noted that there are instances where the progression I–vi–IV occurs across an apparent return to the tonic—that is, where the tonic that falls at the beginning of the restatement/recapitulation becomes an applied dominant to the subdominant. Such a situation can be found in the second movement of Schubert's "Unfinished" Symphony, which is divided into two parts (exposition and recapitulation) without a development section. The first theme is in the tonic key, E major, and the second in the submediant, C♯ minor. Following a brief connecting passage (no dominant), the initial theme returns in the tonic, which subsequently leads to a statement of the second idea in A major, thus completing the arpeggiation to the subdominant. The overall harmonic structure of the movement can be represented as follows: I–vi–(I)–IV–V–I, where (I) falls at the beginning of the restatement.[16] A similar pattern occurs in the slow movement of Mozart's Piano Concerto in C Minor, K. 491, a five-part Rondo with the following design:

A[1]	B	A[2]	C	A[3]	Coda
I	vi	(I)	IV	I	

The return to the opening idea and the tonic (A[2]) is sufficient to establish the formal design (rondo), but, as noted by Carl Schachter, its brevity (only four measures in length), together with important motivic and orchestrational links between the B and C sections, suggest that the structural connection goes beyond this return, resulting in the descending arpeggiation to the subdominant.[17] One can find several sonata movements by Schubert that follow this same procedure, namely, where the

---

16. A sketch of this movement is provided in David Beach, "Schubert's Experiments with Sonata Form: Formal-Tonal Design Versus Underlying Structure," *Music Theory Spectrum* 15 (1993): 1–18 (Ex. 11).

17. Carl Schachter, "Either/Or," in *Schenker Studies*, ed. Hedi Siegel (Cambridge: Cambridge University Press, 1990), 165–79.

sense of tonal-thematic return is satisfied, yet combined with Schubert's penchant for moving to the subdominant in the recapitulation, from which point the motion to closure parallels the tonal motion of the exposition.[18]

In J.S. Bach's Prelude in B Major—a wonderful example of his free imitative writing in three parts—surface coherence and continuity are achieved by the repetition of a rhythmic-motivic figure, initially stated in the top voice in the first half of m. 1 and re-stated in one form or another and in one part, then another, every half-measure. Most repetitions follow the intervallic pattern of the initial statement, which is an elabora-tion of an ascending step progression in quarter notes. (These statements and vari-ants are indicated by brackets in Ex. 5.) There are notable exceptions: The first type of variant occurs almost immediately, in the first half of m. 2, where the expected descending third is replaced by a fourth, counteracting the ascending tendency of the line and redirecting it to the d♯² (3̂); the same variant, transposed, occurs in the middle part in the first half of m. 12. A second type of variant occurs in the bass in the first half of m. 5 and again in the equivalent place approaching the tonic (the first half of m. 14); these two are indicated by dotted brackets in Example 5. The final type of variant is the inversion of this surface motive, which, with one exception (second half of m. 12, bass voice), is reserved for the final phrase, beginning in m. 15.

The prelude is divided by cadences into four phrases, and the following dis-cussion of voice leading will follow these natural divisions. The first phrase (mm. 1–6) progresses from tonic to dominant, and the second (mm. 6–10) cadences on vi. The third phrase, beginning from vi and progressing to IV (m. 12), is directed through the dominant toward closure, which is avoided at the last minute, as so often hap-pens in Bach's music, on the downbeat of m. 15. The final phrase, extending from this point, achieves closure in m. 19.

A metrical reduction of the initial phrase, resulting from the removal of all submetrical displacements and embellishments, is given at level a of Figure 9. The asterisks point to the repetition of the 7–6 suspension over B (with the upper parts inverted), an association that is made immediately audible by their similar articula-tions. In m. 2 the elaboration of the suspension figure by the surface motive suggests that the 7 progresses to the 8 (which it does in the immediate context), but its contra-puntal meaning as a displacement of 6 is made clear by the continuation and in the repetitions of the figure at the same pitch level in mm. 4 and 8. A simplification and rhythmic normalization of this material, involving adjustments in mm. 3 and 4, is provided at level b. The purpose of these changes and the repetition of the bass de-scent from b to f♯ (in parentheses), which suggests that the sounding bass at this point can be understood as added (as a product of free composition), is to show the origin of this material in strict invertible counterpoint, which is indicated by the exchange

---

18. Two movements that fall under this category are the initial movements from the String Quintet in C, D. 956 and the String Quartet in G, D. 887.

Example 5. J.S. Bach: *Well-Tempered Clavier* (I), Prelude in B Major.

Example 5. J.S. Bach: *Well-Tempered Clavier* (I), Prelude in B Major, cont'd.

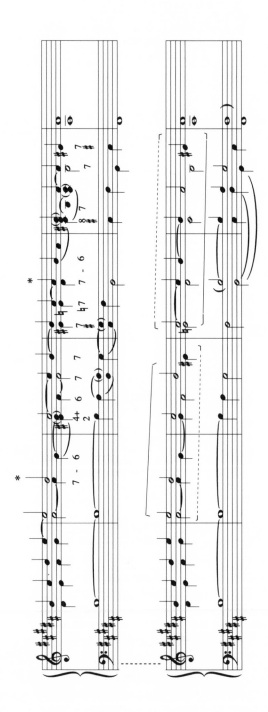

Figure 9.

of solid and dotted brackets.[19] The significance of the motivic descending fourth e–d♯–c♯–b will become apparent as we progress with the analysis.

The voice leading of the second phrase—with its multiple voice exchanges, registral shifts, and transfers of resolution—is more complex than the first. A metric reduction is provided at level a of Figure 10, and, though the reduction itself is self-explanatory, there are certain added features that require clarification. First, references to the preceding phrase—the descending fourth motive (see bracket) and the 7–6 suspension (see asterisk)—are indicated. The first of these is initiated by the registral shift and rearticulation of the bass note e on the second quarter of m. 7. The completion of this idea is somewhat obscured by the voice leading in the second half of m. 8 and the first half of m. 9 (the voice exchange between the B and G♯ and the subsequent transfers of their resolutions shown in the system added above level a), but the clear reference here to the second half of m. 2 (the statement of the half note d♯² in the top voice and the motivically elaborated suspension figure in the middle part) helps us hear the controlling bass note as B. Thus, despite the change of context and the complexity of the voice leading, the reference to earlier events seems quite clear. Second, the numbers 1. and 2. have been added above level a to show that the leap of a sixth above the c♯² in m. 8 is answered by the leap of a sixth from b¹ in m. 10. The repetition of this idea signals their association, suggesting that intervening material (including restatement of the d♯) is embedded within this larger connection.

A simplification of this material is given at level b of Figure 10. One rhythmic adjustment has been made, namely that of shifting the entrance of the D♯⁷ chord (V♯⁷ of vi) to the third quarter of m. 7. Though this change is justified as a rhythmic normalization, it should be noted that it is precisely the interaction of the left- and right-hand parts as written (and as notated at level a) that helps us hear the entrance of the descending fourth motive from the rearticulated e. Finally, note the interpretation of the harmony in m. 9 as V⁹/vi ([d♯]–f×–a♯–c♯–e). Thus the voice exchange shown at level a (m. 9) is not prolonging a subdominant harmony in vi, but its dominant, in which case the g♯¹ in the inner part is heard as a neighbor note to the f× leading tone.

A sketch of the first two phrases (mm. 1–10) is provided in Figure 11. The initial melodic gesture, the ascent to e², is shown as introducing the *Kopfton* d♯² (3̂) in m. 2, from which point the top voice descends a sixth to f♯¹ at the cadence in m. 6. If one conceives of the inner voice tone a♯¹ in m. 2 as coming from the initial b¹ (as well as from below), as shown here, the inner part descends a ninth from b¹ to a♯. (The solid and dotted/broken brackets used in Fig. 9 have been retained here to show the exchange of parts.) In the second phrase, the top voice progresses from the f♯¹ up to the c♯² on the downbeat of m. 8, which is harmonized as the seventh of the dominant of G♯ (vi). As noted above, the melodic leap of a sixth from this c♯² is answered by the

---

19. A similar reduction of this phrase, involving an intermediate stage, is given in David Beach, "Schenker's Theories: A Pedagogical View," in *Aspects of Schenkerian Theory*, ed. David Beach (New Haven and London: Yale University Press, 1983), 1–38.

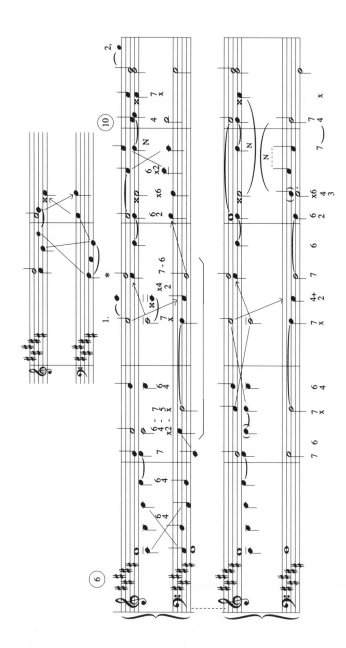

Figure 10.

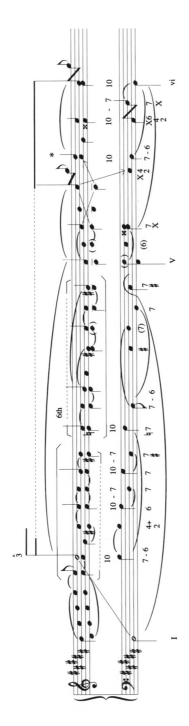

Figure 11.

leap of a sixth from b^1 at the cadence, articulating the larger connection between these two events. This point of arrival completes a preliminary descent of the fundamental third $d\sharp^2$–$c\sharp^2$–b^1, harmonized by the progression I–V^7/vi–vi. However, in the more immediate context, the resolution of the dissonant $c\sharp^2$ in m. 8 is transferred to the bass, allowing the top voice to move momentarily back up to the $d\sharp^2$, the arrival at which is marked by the clear reference to the $d\sharp^2$ ($\hat{3}$) of m. 2. The result is a lower-level copy of the third $d\sharp$–$c\sharp$–b embedded within the $c\sharp$–b of the controlling statement.[20] Stated another way, Bach has summarized the tonal motion of the piece so far as a diminution in the final approach to the cadence on vi.

The third phrase, beginning from the cadence on vi in m. 10 and leading to the downbeat of m. 15, is divided into two parts, a sequence connecting vi and IV (m. 12) and a varied repetition of the material leading to the cadence at the end of the initial phrase, transposed up a fourth. As shown in Figure 12, the outer voices of the sequence move in octaves with intervening tenths. However, in the music it is only the last of these that is stated on the beat, marking it as an important point of articulation of arrival and departure within the phrase. Note, too, that arrival at the subdominant, which is subsequently prolonged, coincides with the only inverted statement of the above-mentioned surface rhythmic-motivic figure prior to the final phrase, and it is from this point that the line descends toward closure, resulting in the clearly articulated statement of the descending fourth motive e^2–$d\sharp^2$–$c\sharp^2$–b^1.[21] It is only by the avoidance of the b that the statement of this motive is left incomplete and closure is averted, making continuation necessary.

Figure 13 is a transcription of Ernst Oster's unpublished sketch of the overall structure of the prelude, which shows the function of the cadence on vi as a third

---

20. From a purely logical point of view, the graph of mm. 8–10 given here conveys conflicting information. Specifically, the lower-level third $d\sharp^2$–$c\sharp^2$–b^1 conflicts with the larger connection shown, which suggests that the $d\sharp^2$ should be read instead as an upper neighbor note to the controlling dissonant $c\sharp^2$. At the same time, the motivic connection between this $d\sharp^2$ and the one in m. 2 is clearly articulated, suggesting a return—though indeed not a structural—return to $\hat{3}$, from which point the line descends through the $c\sharp^2$ to the b^1 at the cadence. The conflict (to the extent that there is one) results from the use of a slur to show a motivic idea within a structural voice-leading graph, where slurs otherwise denote structural connections. Perhaps the use of a bracket type not already employed for some other purpose might be more appropriate and would deflect potential confusion without eliminating what is an important motivic reference.

21. As shown in Figure 12, the subdominant/supertonic harmony is prolonged through the third beat of m. 14. One might describe this process as occurring in two stages. First, the IV is transformed into ii^6 by the melodic motion from e through d$\sharp$ to c$\sharp$ over the bass note e, the return to which is articulated by the 7–6 suspension figure that plays such an important role elsewhere in this composition. Second, the supertonic harmony is prolonged through the progression ii^6–V–vi–ii (as it was in mm. 4–5), which supports the lower-level third c$\sharp$–b–a$\sharp$ prolonging the c$\sharp$.

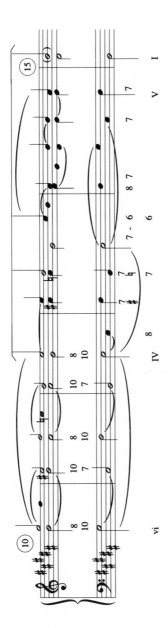

Figure 12.

Figure 13.

divider between the initial tonic and the subdominant of mm. 12–14.[22] Oster's notation of the melodic structure, in particular the various levels of third-progressions, is
interesting. The downward-stemmed and beamed thirds indicate a parallel between
the initial descent, supported by the motion to vi, and the third e^2–$d\sharp^2$–$c\sharp^2$ (8–7–6)
over the subdominant. At the same time, his secondary notation of these thirds (the
upward-stemmed notes and the slurs) show differences in the manner in which
they have been embellished. Finally, one might note how he has been careful to
distinguish between these thirds and the approach to the e^2 from above. It is instructive to note how Oster has used graphic notation in a creative way to convey subtle
differences in his interpretations of musical events.

Oster's sketch of the overall structure implies that closure is to be understood
at m. 15, where it is clearly implied, but at the last minute avoided, thus propelling
the motion forward. At the deepest level, this final phrase, the coda, can be understood as a prolongation of the final tonic. However, at a more immediate level, the
initial tonic is made unstable by the addition of the lowered seventh ($a\natural^1$), which
directs the motion toward the subdominant. As shown in Figure 14, a middleground
sketch of this phrase, the goal of this motion is the dominant (m. 17), which is approached through its diminished seventh chord. The solid and dotted brackets indicate the references in these measures to the invertible lines from the opening phrase
(cf. Fig. 9, level b). To be sure, the context has changed and here we have an $a\natural$ rather
than an $a\sharp$, yet the recall of the opening measures is perfectly clear. At this point the
texture changes from three to four parts. (Note also the momentary switch to four
parts in m. 6.) Beginning with the dominant harmony in m. 17, there are three clearly

---

22. Note that within this overall structure the function of the dominant in m. 6 is assigned a lower-level status, namely that of offering temporary consonant support for the
melodic c$\sharp$ and indirectly introducing vi. (This interpretation in no way diminishes the importance of the cadence on V as articulating a phrase boundary.) There is a parallel between
this reading and the interpretation of the opening phrase of the *Chorale St. Antoni* provided
in Figure 1a.

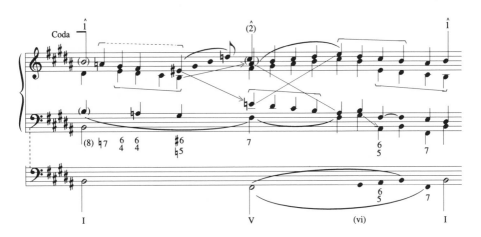

Figure 14.

articulated statements of the descending fourth motive e–d♯–c♯–b. The first occurs in what might be described as the tenor voice, and the other two (in stretto) follow immediately in the upper parts. What has happened here is that an idea that had occurred earlier only in disguised form has emerged in the final phrase as a clearly articulated motive. Only here, in the final phrase, is the importance of this motivic fourth made clear to the listener.

There are various ways one might expand on this study of the submediant as a third divider connecting the tonic and subdominant harmonies in the basic progression I . . . IV(ii⁶)–V–I. For example, one could consider it as a subset of a more inclusive study of the different functions of the submediant, which would include consideration of those circumstances under which the submediant extends the tonic or substitutes for it, prolongs the dominant, and so forth. We have, in fact, touched on these issues in our discussions of the selected phrases from Haydn's *Chorale St. Antoni*, the *Introduzione* from Beethoven's "Waldstein" Sonata, Mozart's Fantasy in D Minor, and from the third movement of Beethoven's Piano Sonata, op. 7. We also see the submediant functioning at two different levels and in two different ways—at a deep level as third divider between tonic and subdominant, and at the surface level as offering consonant support for a passing tone within a dominant prolongation (see Fig. 14)—in Bach's B-Major Prelude. And, as noted above, one could supply additional interesting examples of this basic progression from the tonal repertoire. But that is unnecessary. What we have here is sufficient to demonstrate at least two important points: 1) that this basic idea is represented in the literature at multiple levels of structure, from the surface to the deep middleground; and 2) that our interpretation of the role of the submediant depends on the musical context. This latter point is particularly important as a basic tenet of musical analysis.

The Form of Chopin's
Polonaise-Fantasy

William Rothstein

I

C hopin's *Polonaise-Fantasy*, op. 61, is a work that has challenged commentators from the beginning. Franz Liszt found the piece repellent—
ironically, because nowhere does Chopin's style seem closer to Liszt's.[1]
Hugo Leichtentritt's pioneering analysis (1921) is not very illuminating.[2] The 1960s saw a few studies of op. 61, notably a motivic analysis by Paul Hamburger.[3] Since 1984 there has been a seeming explosion of interest in the work: studies
have appeared by Eero Tarasti, Jeffrey Kallberg, Jim Samson, Nicholas Cook, John
Rink, and Anthony Newcomb.[4] Tarasti's article explores questions of semiosis and
narrativity. Kallberg and Samson focus on the work's tangled compositional history.
Cook examines Chopin's use of motivic transformation, adding important insights
to those of Hamburger; he also offers an idiosyncratic voice-leading analysis. Rink

---

1. Liszt's judgments are expressed in his biography of Chopin (*Frédéric Chopin*; Paris,
1852). Liszt later changed his mind about op. 61 and other of Chopin's late works, as Anthony Newcomb notes in "The Polonaise-Fantasy and Issues of Musical Narrative," in John
Rink and Jim Samson, eds., *Chopin Studies 2* (Cambridge: Cambridge University Press, 1994),
84–101. See p. 86n.

2. Hugo Leichtentritt, *Analyse der Chopin'schen Klavierwerke*, 2 vols. (Berlin, 1921–22),
1:110–21.

3. Paul Hamburger, "Mazurkas, Waltzes, Polonaises," in Alan Walker, ed., *Frédéric Chopin:
Profiles of the Man and the Musician* (London: Barrie & Rockliff, 1966), 105–13. For a list of
other studies (with a brief comment on each), see Jeffrey Kallberg, "Chopin's Last Style,"
Journal of the American Musicological Society 38 (1985): 264–315.

4. Eero Tarasti, "Pour une narratologie de Chopin," *International Review of the Aesthetics
and Sociology of Music* 15 (1984): 53–75; Kallberg, "Chopin's Last Style"; Jim Samson, *The
Music of Chopin* (London: Routledge, 1985; reprint., Oxford: Clarendon Press, 1994), 200–
211; Samson, "The Composition-Draft of the Polonaise-Fantasy: the Issue of Tonality," in
Samson, ed., *Chopin Studies* (Cambridge: Cambridge University Press, 1988), 41–58; Nicholas Cook, *A Guide to Musical Analysis* (London: J. M. Dent & Sons, 1987), 335–43; John Rink,
"Schenker and Improvisation," *Journal of Music Theory* 37/2 (1993): 1–55; Newcomb, "Issues
of Musical Narrative."

approaches op. 61 from a Schenkerian perspective; more speculatively, he extends his voice-leading analysis to Chopin's sketches. Newcomb raises questions of formal function, formal ambiguity, and (like Tarasti) narrativity. Finally, in a wide-ranging study of ambiguity in Chopin's music, Edward T. Cone devotes a stimulating paragraph to the relation between hypermeter, phrase structure, and formal function in mm. 24–152.[5]

There must be a reason why, in the space of a decade, this work has assumed a central place in Chopin studies. Probably the spate of interest reflects trends in musicology and in the humanities in general. From the unapologetic "structuralism" of Rink to the "post-modernism" of Cook and Newcomb, scholars are struggling anew with basic questions of unity and disunity, "organic" necessity and historical contingency, internal structure and external reference. A work as resistant to interpretation as the Polonaise-Fantasy—Cook terms it a "problem piece"—offers a virtual Rorschach test for attitudes toward these questions. Cook has been the most radical in renouncing the search for unity in the work, claiming that the music is welded together from two separate pieces—one in A♭ major, the other in B major—that stubbornly refuse to fuse. Rink upholds the Schenkerian ideal of organic unity amidst apparent disorder—the paradox that underlay Schenker's fascination with the fantasy genre[6]—while Newcomb comes down somewhere in the middle, pointing to shifting invocations of disparate formal schemata within a master "plot" governed by narrative principles (although Newcomb leaves these largely undefined).

The present study focuses rather narrowly on questions of musical form. Like Newcomb, I will argue that multiple formal paradigms are invoked in op. 61; unlike him, I will suggest that these paradigms are far from equal in their significance for the work's large-scale shape. However intricate the pathways that Chopin takes, both formally and tonally, I will assert, with Rink, that there is a unifying plan at work. Since I am largely in agreement with Rink's view of the work's tonal organization, I will focus on its formal plan, a topic that Rink mostly avoids. I will also explore the connection between the Polonaise-Fantasy and the slightly earlier Polonaise in A♭ Major, op. 53. Topics that I will leave largely unaddressed—with no intention of slighting their importance—include the work's compositional history, its mixture of genres, and its expressive semiosis. My subject is not the fantastic element in the Polonaise-Fantasy, but the firm ground from which fantasy takes wing. A truly comprehensive view of the work is surely impossible; as with any masterpiece, this is an ideal that can at best be approached asymptotically.

---

5. Edward T. Cone, "Ambiguity and Reinterpretation in Chopin," in *Chopin Studies 2*, 140–60. See p. 152.

6. See Heinrich Schenker, *J. S. Bach's Chromatic Fantasy and Fugue*, trans. and ed. Hedi Siegel (New York: Longman, 1984); also "The Art of Improvisation," trans. Richard Kramer, in Schenker, *The Masterwork in Music*, vol. 1, ed. William Drabkin (Oxford: Oxford University Press, 1995), 2–19. Edward Laufer's "On the Fantasy" (*Intégral* 2 [1988], 99–133) is an important study of the same subject, as is Rink's article "Schenker and Improvisation."

II

Most descriptions of op. 61 identify a large ternary form (ABA). The middle section is, of course, the *più lento* (in some sources, *poco più lento*) in B major; the final section is an apotheosis—to use Edward Cone's now-standard term—of both main themes in the tonic key, A♭ major.[7] The enharmonically spelled minor third separating the two tonics is outlined in m. 1, as several authors have noted.

In a brilliant analysis of Chopin's Fantasy, op. 49—another work usually said to be in ternary form—Carl Schachter has identified a different and peculiarly Romantic formal idea.[8] Schachter views op. 49 as a modified strophic form, in which the slower central section interrupts the second of three "cycles." Although Schachter does not use these terms, one could speak here of an *underlying form* (strophic) that is overlaid with a *surface form* (ternary); the surface form arises at a level closer to the musical foreground. An analogous situation exists in the F-Minor Ballade, op. 52, where a set of variations is overlaid with a sequence of events that is clearly patterned after sonata form. Much of the Ballade's surface form—including the "second theme," the "development," and much of the "recapitulation"—arises as a series of interpolations within individual variations.[9]

The *Polonaise-Fantasy* is another formal hybrid, with underlying and surface forms of different types. The surface form—a sprawling ternary structure with extensive transitions, including briefly stable passages of lyrical character—has been described by several authors.[10] The underlying form is identified here for the first time. As in the op. 49 Fantasy, the slow middle section is part of an interpolation, or interruption, within the underlying form. In op. 61 that form is a *quatrain*, a common song form composed in the pattern AABA.[11] That such a modest form undergirds a work as ambitious as op. 61 is remarkable, to say the least.

The most famous example of quatrain form is probably Beethoven's "Ode to Joy." Beethoven's *musical* quatrain does not correspond precisely to Schiller's *poetic* quatrains, because each of Beethoven's "lines" corresponds to one of Schiller's couplets (half of a quatrain). Each musical "line" is four measures long; the second half of the form is repeated (this is a common occurrence).

Another quatrain form, almost as famous, is the song "I Want to Hold Your Hand" by John Lennon and Paul McCartney. This example is noteworthy because

---

7. Edward T. Cone, *Musical Form and Musical Performance* (New York: Norton, 1968), 83–84.

8. Schachter, "Chopin's Fantasy op. 49: the Two-Key Scheme," in *Chopin Studies*, 221–53.

9. See my "Ambiguity in the Themes of Chopin's First, Second, and Fourth Ballades," *Intégral* 8 (1994): 1–50.

10. See especially Samson's chart in "The Composition-Draft," 52. Samson calls this chart a "crude synopsis."

11. See the discussion of quatrain form in my *Phrase Rhythm in Tonal Music* (New York: Schirmer Books, 1989), 107–8 and 256–57.

the four "lines" (hereafter "segments") of the quatrain are relatively long—twelve, twelve, eleven, and fifteen measures respectively—and because, unusually, all three A segments end with perfect authentic cadences in the tonic key.[12]

The intrusion of popular song into this discussion should not surprise. The use of quatrain form in European art music almost certainly arose as an imitation of popular song; indeed, the term "quatrain" was first used by the musicologist Dénes Bartha to describe the form of folk songs.[13] In the twentieth century, quatrain form became almost the invariable choice for Broadway songs and jazz "standards." The form's third or contrasting segment is commonly called the "bridge" by popular musicians; I will adopt this term.[14] The four segments of a quatrain will thus be called Antecedent, Consequent 1, Bridge, and Consequent 2. In simple quatrains, such as the "Ode to Joy," the music of Consequents 1 and 2 is identical.

A clear example of quatrain form in Chopin's music is the principal section (mm. 3–26) of the A♭-Major Nocturne, op. 32, no. 2. Chopin uses the same formal pattern as Beethoven: a quatrain with segments of four measures each, with the second half repeated. Consequents 1 and 2 are virtually identical. The series of cadences is the same as Beethoven's, alternating half cadences (in the Antecedent and Bridge) with perfect authentic cadences (in the two Consequents), all in the tonic key. I am not arguing that Beethoven's quatrain influenced Chopin's—merely that both represent a formal type that was nearly as ubiquitous in the nineteenth century as it came to be in the twentieth.

The quatrain form of most immediate relevance to the *Polonaise-Fantasy* is that of the A♭-Major Polonaise, op. 53, which shows Chopin working to enlarge the dimensions of the form.[15] The principal section, mm. 17–80, is a quatrain with segments of sixteen measures each; segments end at mm. 32, 48, 64, and 80. Even the introduction is sixteen measures long, subdivided in the manner of a Schoenbergian sentence: 4 + 4 + (2 + 2 + 4). Like the introduction, each segment of the quatrain is subdivided into smaller groups, often of four measures. These subdivisions are especially apparent in the Bridge, where each four-measure group ends with an authentic cadence.

---

12. See Walter Everett, *An Analytical History of the Music of the Beatles* (Oxford: Oxford University Press, forthcoming).

13. See Bartha's contribution to Jens Peter Larsen, Howard Serwer, and James Webster, eds., *Haydn Studies: Proceedings of the International Haydn Conference* (New York: Norton, 1981), 353–55.

14. The bridge is also called the "release." In *Phrase Rhythm in Tonal Music*, I used the term "contrasting phrase" for this segment of a quatrain. Since, however, the bridge often comprises merely an extended dominant harmony, the term "phrase" may not always be strictly applicable to it (see *Phrase Rhythm*, chapter 1 and pp. 228–29.) On the use of quatrain form in jazz, see Steve Larson, "Schenkerian Analysis of Modern Jazz" (Ph.D. diss., University of Michigan, 1987), 52–53.

15. It is interesting to note that Chopin used the quatrain form—which is not a very common formal pattern in his music—for three works in the same key, A♭ major.

The polonaise's middle section, in the flatted submediant (F♭ major, spelled enharmonically as E major), begins as though it were destined to become a second quatrain, one with proportions quite as ample as those of the first. Two sixteen-measure segments, corresponding to Antecedent and Consequent 1, are heard (mm. 85–100 and 105–20); each is introduced by a four-measure "vamp." The Bridge begins much as it did in the principal section, with a four-measure statement and its repetition a third higher. But mm. 127–28 already diverge from the model, and the succeeding passage (mm. 129–54) brings a meandering retransition to A♭ major. Thus the second quatrain is never completed, although that fact becomes apparent to a listener only gradually.[16] Once the principal section returns, only a single sixteen-measure segment is heard. This segment is slightly extended at its end, so that the cadence—imperfect authentic—falls in the seventeenth measure, a hypermetrical downbeat (this is also the beginning of the coda). All earlier cadences have been hypermetrically weak, as is usual in polonaises; the typical "polonaise cadence" is weak both metrically (the tonic falls on the third beat) and hypermetrically (it occurs at the end of a hypermeasure).

Chopin expands the quatrain form still further in op. 61, using several means to achieve additional breadth. First, he expands segments of the quatrain—each of which is, in principle, sixteen measures long, as in op. 53—with interpolated material, so that the *surface length* of each segment becomes unpredictable. Second, he adds a modulatory transition between Consequent 1 and the Bridge, and adds transitions at other points as well. Third, he applies the idea of truncation—used in the middle section of op. 53—to Consequent 2, the final segment of the quatrain, so that the form is cut short after it has come very close to completion. (The finality of Consequent 2 is undercut in other ways too, as we shall see.) The non-fulfillment of the form, at so late a stage, is used to generate expectation for its eventual completion—much as, in Schenkerian theory, the interruption of a fundamental line at its penultimate note, $\hat{2}$, creates the expectation that the line will be resumed and led to its natural goal, the tonic. Much of the central portion of op. 61, including the *più lento*, represents an interpolation prior to the resumption and completion of the quatrain. The apotheosis, beginning at m. 242, thus represents more than a synthesis of two themes, and more than a passage of triumphal rhetoric: it is also the long-delayed statement, complete and rhetorically heightened, of the quatrain's fourth and final segment. The quotation of the *più lento* theme within the apotheosis is another interpolation, but one with a venerable ancestry: it functions as a cadenza in the precise meaning of the term—that is, an expansion of the cadential $^{6-5}_{4-3}$.

---

16. Compare Wagner's use of truncated quatrains in act II of *Lohengrin*; the passages are analyzed in *Phrase Rhythm*, 291–94. Truncated and otherwise transformed formal schemata figure importantly in Anthony Newcomb's writings on nineteenth-century music; see especially "Those Images That Yet Fresh Images Beget," *Journal of Musicology* 2 (1983): 227–45.

III

Example 1 is a durational reduction of the *Polonaise-Fantasy*, including all of the piece except the introduction; the example thus begins with m. 24, the beginning of the principal theme. The introduction is omitted because it stands outside the expanded quatrain, and because its hypermeter is highly unstable. The hypermeter of the rest of the work is remarkably regular, except for several ambiguities in the *più lento*.[17] Even there, ambiguities emerge only at levels larger than two measures; that is, it is sometimes unclear how—or even whether—two-measure units join to form hypermeasures of larger size.

The reduction itself is straightforward. Each $\frac{3}{4}$ measure of the score has been reduced to a unit of $\frac{3}{8}$; the resulting units have been joined into compound measures, mostly of $\frac{12}{8}$. A $\frac{12}{8}$ measure in the reduction thus represents a hypermeasure of four bars. Dotted bar lines are used occasionally to indicate two-bar subdivisions, especially for long "measures" of $\frac{18}{8}$. The two-bar level of hypermeter is uninterrupted from m. 24 to the end; thus, each measure in Example 1 is some whole multiple of $\frac{6}{8}$. Hypermeasure numbers are given at the beginning of each line of Example 1; the corresponding measure numbers are shown in parentheses.

Other symbols used in the example refer to elements connected with the music's form, phrase rhythm, and voice leading. Terms in capital letters mark the beginnings of formal segments. Table 1 summarizes this information more concisely. Segments of the underlying quatrain are given in boldface, other segments in regular type. The truncation of Consequent 2 creates the need for an additional consequent, Consequent 3; as indicated earlier, this is the passage commonly known (since Cone) as the apotheosis.

Parentheses enclosing entire passages in Example 1 denote internal expansions within formal segments. Since it would be tedious to describe in detail how these expansions have been determined, I offer instead an example (Ex. 2) that excises these passages, along with all transitions and other interpolations; only the underlying quatrain remains. The scale of reduction is the same as in Example 1—each measure represents a hypermeasure of four bars—but each of the quatrain's four segments appears in its *basic length* of four $\frac{12}{8}$ measures (equivalent to sixteen measures in the score).[18] For the quatrain's final segment, Consequent 3 has been used in place of the incomplete Consequent 2. Overlaps—which occur between the Antecedent and Consequent 1, between the Bridge and Consequent 2, and between Consequent 3 and the Coda— have been eliminated by recomposing slightly the ends of the appropriate segments (the Antecedent, the Bridge, and Consequent 3). Part of Chopin's purpose in creat-

---

17. Edward Cone has remarked upon the regular hypermeter of mm. 24–152 (see note 5).

18. On the concept of basic length, see *Phrase Rhythm*, 106–7. I used the term "structural time-span" to denote the same concept in my "Rhythm and the Theory of Structural Levels" (Ph.D. diss., Yale University, 1981). See also Carl Schachter, "Rhythm and Linear Analysis: Durational Reduction," in Felix Salzer and Carl Schachter, eds., *The Music Forum*, vol. 5 (New York: Columbia University Press, 1980): 197–232.

Table 1

Chopin: *Polonaise-Fantasy*, op. 61: Quatrain Form		

Formal segment	begins at hypermeasure no.	= measure no.
Antecedent (1st segment of quatrain)	1	24
Consequent 1 (2nd segment of quatrain)	6	44
Codetta becomes Transition	11	66
Bridge (3rd segment of quatrain)	17	94
Consequent 2 (4th segment of quatrain, truncated)	20	108
Transition	22	116
Middle section: Motto	30	148
Middle section: Antecedent	31	152
Middle section: Consequent	35	168
Transition	45	214
Consequent 3 (4th segment of quatrain, complete)	52	242
Cadenza (part of Consequent 3)	55	254
Coda	58	268

ing these overlaps can be seen if Examples 1 and 2 are compared. Not only do the overlaps enhance the music's continuity, something that Chopin often sought to do in his later music;[19] they also serve to place the cadence of each segment on or very near a hypermetrical downbeat, in contrast to the doubly weak "polonaise cadence" described earlier. (The "polonaise cadence" is heard only once in op. 61, at m. 70.)

Circled bass notes in Example 1 mark some of the main events in the music's middleground structure. That structure is shown more succinctly in Example 3, which is similar in important respects to Rink's middleground analysis.[20] Notice that the Antecedent comprises an ascending fifth-progression in the bass, from A♭ to e♭; Consequent 1 leads this progression to its logical conclusion, the authentic cadence V-I. This same bass motion—an ascending fifth-progression from I to V, followed by an authentic cadence—is reproduced, greatly enlarged, in the bass of the entire piece (not including the introduction). The two fifth-progressions are even harmonized similarly. In the Antecedent, each step of the progression except $\hat{4}$ supports a root-position triad ($\hat{4}$ supports II⁶). In the larger fifth-progression, *every* step supports a root-position triad: however, $\hat{2}$ (B♭) now supports a major rather than a minor triad, and ♭$\hat{3}$ is used in place of ♮$\hat{3}$(C♮). The latter substitution reflects the pervasive use of modal mixture throughout the piece.

---

19. See *Phrase Rhythm*, chapter 9.
20. See Rink, "Schenker and Improvisation," 31, Ex. 11.

Example 1. Chopin: *Polonaise-Fantasy*, op. 61: durational reduction.

As in op. 53, Chopin respells the middle section enharmonically: B major takes the place of C♭ major. In op. 61, however, the enharmonic situation is much more complex. In the Polonaise, the common-tone modulation from A♭ major to "E major" (mm. 80–81) makes it immediately clear that the latter harmony represents ♭VI, not ♯V. In the Polonaise-Fantasy, the middle section's B major is both approached and left in such a way that it sounds like B♮, not C♭. This is evident in mm. 214–15, where the progression from B♮ to C represents a diatonic and not a chromatic half

Example 1 cont'd.

step, like A♭-B♭♭ in mm. 1–2. In the transition to B major, the whole step from the E♮ of m. 128 (♯IV in B♭ major) to the F♯ of m. 134 (the new dominant) tells us that the B♭ tonic has ascended to B♮ and not—in the foreground, at least—to C♭.[21] (The ascent

21. Chopin's spelling of the diminished-seventh chord in m. 134 reflects neither its function in B♭ major—♯IV°⁷—nor its function in B minor—VII°₃⁴—but rather a compromise between the two. The chord is arrived at by descending-third motion from the B♭ of m. 124: I–VI–♯IV in B♭ major.

Example 1 cont'd.

from E♮ to F♯ is repeated in mm. 136–38, now as ♭II⁶–V in B minor.) And yet the
ascending pattern of the bass *as a whole* leads inescapably, I think, to the conclusion
that B major ultimately represents a mediant harmony, ♭III, within the long ascent
from I to V. The long stability of "B major," and the audibly transitional function of
C♮ in m. 215, indicate that it is C♭ and not C♮ that represents the third scale degree.
This enharmonic transformation of B♮ into C♭, *across* structural levels, is part of the
piece's deep-seated mystery.[22]

---

22. For a stimulating discussion of enharmonicism in nineteenth-century music—specifically, in Wagner's *Tristan und Isolde*—see John Rothgeb, "The Tristan Chord: Identity
and Origin," *Music Theory Online* 1, no. 1 (1995); also on-line responses to Rothgeb by Richard
Cohn, Eytan Agmon, and Allen Forte (the last in vol. 1, no. 2).

Example 1 cont'd.

IV

The twin pillars of the *Polonaise-Fantasy* are the quatrain form (see Table 1 and Ex. 2) and the ascending fifth-progression in the bass (Ex. 3). As I indicated earlier, however, other formal paradigms are also invoked. The outlines of ternary form are obvious and require no further comment. As several authors have noted, there are also traces of sonata form. These traces are most significant in what is roughly the first third of the work, the sections up to and including Consequent 2.

Example 1 cont'd.

    The initial pairing of Antecedent and Consequent 1 (mm. 24–66) forms a closed group in A♭ major. This is quite a lengthy tonic group—longer, certainly, than the first group of a typical sonata exposition. The use of antecedent-consequent form is very common in first groups (see the first movements of Chopin's Sonatas op. 35 and op. 58), but the internal shape of *this* tonic group is highly unusual. How many first groups build to a *fortissimo* climax (m. 56) and then twice come to a complete halt (mm. 62–63), only to end with a perfect authentic cadence in the tonic? The first movements of Chopin's last two Sonatas, op. 58 and op. 65, offer useful points of comparison. The first group in the B-Minor Sonata is comparably rhapsodic and contains as much chromatic detail as the tonic group in op. 61, but it is more compact and—most important—it never cadences in the tonic; its brilliant passages (beginning at m. 19) act as a transition to the subordinate key, D major.[23] The first group in the Cello Sonata comes closer to op. 61: it is extremely long, both in absolute terms and in proportion to the movement as a whole; it hews closely to the tonic key (with strong tonicizations of the subdominant); and it ends without having modulated. On the other hand, it contains multiple themes and ends with a half cadence (not an authentic cadence) in the tonic, and its overall form is asymmetrical. In short, the closed, symmetrical form of mm. 24–66 does not suggest that we are hearing a sonata exposition in the first part of op. 61.

    The following phrase, mm. 66–70, has the character of a codetta, as Newcomb has pointed out.[24] (This is where the lone "polonaise cadence" occurs.) But the evolu-

---

23. Compare mm. 68–80 in the F-Minor Ballade.

24. Newcomb, "Issues of Musical Narrative," 93.

tion of this codetta into a transition—by means of a sequence in ascending major thirds—suggests the possibility of a very broadly scaled sonata exposition: such a leisurely transition seems appropriate after a long introduction and first group. The prospect of sonata form is seemingly confirmed when V of V arrives at m. 92, along with a right-hand flourish and a new, nocturne-like accompaniment figure: it sounds as though a lyrical second theme were being prepared.[25] It is at this moment that a listener is most likely to entertain the idea of sonata form; the piece is, as it were, threatening to become a sonata on an immense scale. Since second groups are normally longer than first groups, the prospect is almost alarming.

What follows is not a new theme in the dominant (E♭ major) but the passage that I have labeled the Bridge. Leichtentritt and Newcomb call it a development, or part of a longer development; Samson and Kallberg simply call it a transformation of the principal theme. These descriptions are not entirely at odds, because the bridge in a quatrain frequently exhibits a developmental character, often using material from earlier segments (the Antecedent and Consequent 1). A bridge differs from a development, however, in that it is typically the same length as those earlier segments, often subdividing—like them—into symmetrical subphrases (for example, 2 + 2 or 1 + 1 + 2 measures). On the surface, this Bridge is shorter than either the Antecedent or Consequent 1, but the quatrain's four segments all share the same basic length, as shown in Example 2. In that example, the Bridge is seen to subdivide into subphrases of 1 + 1 + 2 "measures," just like the Antecedent and Consequent 3. (Consequent 1 has a slightly more complex subphrase structure.)

The return of the principal theme at m. 108 is another crucial juncture in the form. Samson sees this as another transformation of the theme, without distinguishing it from the earlier transformation at m. 94. This is, I think, a serious error. Kallberg discusses the return at length, and he alone does justice to its simultaneous hints at real return—with the implication of impending formal closure—and open-ended continuation. Tonally, we have finally arrived on V of A♭, having delayed this arrival through almost the entire Bridge.[26] Since the principal theme began with a V harmony, its return naturally does likewise. The sense of return is undercut, however, not only by the truncation of this segment (Consequent 2), but in three additional ways: first, by the minor mode; second, by the triplet accompaniment, which contin-

---

25. In Classical piano sonatas—those of Mozart and Beethoven in particular—the second group's accompaniment figure is frequently initiated at the half cadence (generally on V of V) that marks the goal of the transition. This anticipation of the second group frequently causes the two hands to sound in different hypermeters. See Roger Kamien, "Conflicting Metrical Patterns in Accompaniment and Melody in Works by Mozart and Beethoven: A Preliminary Study," *Journal of Music Theory* 37 (1993): 311–48. This conflict explains the difference between my reading of this passage (in Ex. 1) and that of Cone; I have followed the melody, Cone the accompaniment.

26. The E♭ harmony of m. 97 occurs in the middle of a sequence; it is therefore not a strong arrival.

Example 2. Chopin: *Polonaise-Fantasy*, op. 61: underlying quatrain.

ues the pattern begun in m. 92; third, by the *agitato* character of the passage, which suggests formal as well as emotional turbulence.

It is interesting to note that, at one point in his sketches, Chopin let the return play itself out at greater length; he broke it off only at the dominant of C minor, at a point corresponding to the end of m. 34.[27] Thus he restated fully eleven measures of

---

27. A facsimile of the sketch appears in Samson, *The Music of Chopin*, 208; it is transcribed in Kallberg, 291–92.

the Antecedent's basic sixteen (see Ex. 2). While it is speculative to reason from the sketches to the finished piece, this substantial restatement suggests that Chopin *did* think of this as a formal return, albeit a frustrated one.[28] Chopin's decision to keep Consequent 2 very short—only seven of the "original" sixteen measures are heard— makes the decisive return at m. 242 that much more powerful. Ultimately, though, Chopin's decision may have rested on linear factors. As Example 3 shows, Consequent 2 is in the *key* of Ab minor, but it never establishes the tonic *harmony* of Ab (major or minor) at a middleground level; instead it prolongs Eb (V of Ab).[29] Eb is led to F (V of Bb) at m. 116, in preparation for the firm arrival on Bb at m. 124. Chopin curtails Consequent 2 precisely where the bass has returned to Eb (mm. 114–15).[30]

V

None of the many analysts who have written on op. 61 has paid much attention to the internal structure of mm. 148–213, the *più lento*. This section, harmonically self-contained, has a form of its own: it is an expanded parallel period. The tonal content of the section is encapsulated in its opening motto, mm. 148–52; this content can be seen in Example 3 (the segment labeled "B major").[31] There are four voice-leading strands here, all of them significant. Ab "soprano" voice descends, $\hat{3}$–$\hat{2}$–$\hat{1}$; an "alto" descends chromatically from $\hat{5}$ to $\hat{3}$, in parallel sixths with the soprano; a "tenor" ascends by step from $\hat{5}$ to $\hat{8}$; the bass arpeggiates I–V–I. As Example 3 shows, all four of these strands return, transposed to Ab major, in the final cadence of Consequent 3 (this is also the close of the work's fundamental structure). There are some differences: the soprano's descent is now from $\hat{5}$ rather than from $\hat{3}$, and the bass arpeggiation lacks an initial tonic. Otherwise the final cadence is a faithful transposition of the earlier B-major cadence, which is itself foreshadowed in the motto and then expanded to comprehend the whole of the B-major section.

Example 4 portrays the voice leading of this section in somewhat greater detail. The motto begins by arpeggiating from f#¹ to d#², connecting the "alto" and

---

28. The decision to lead Consequent 2 into what is now the Bb-major section (it was originally sketched in B major) had apparently been made by the time Chopin made the sketch cited in note 27.

29. On the important distinction between tonic key and tonic harmony, see Carl Schachter, "Analysis by Key: Another Look at Modulation," *Music Analysis* 6 (1987): 289–318.

30. Even in the sketch, Chopin abandoned the thematic restatement just *before* the primary tone, eb² ($\hat{5}$), was reached. (In the Antecedent, $\hat{5}$ arrives over the C-minor harmony at the end of m. 35.) Thus it appears that he never intended to reestablish the primary tone above a consonant harmony. Instead, Eb appears in a dominant-seventh chord on F (m. 123); its resolution is overlapped by f², as shown in Ex. 3.

31. A similarly pregnant motto is used at the beginning of the Bb-major section in the F-Minor Ballade; see mm. 80–84. The featured tonal content is the tetrachord descending from I to V (Bb–A–G–F).

Example 3. Chopin: *Polonaise-Fantasy*, op. 61: middleground structure.

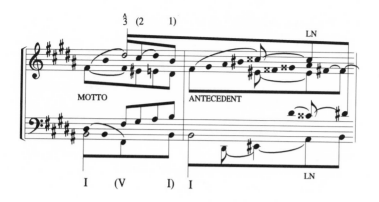

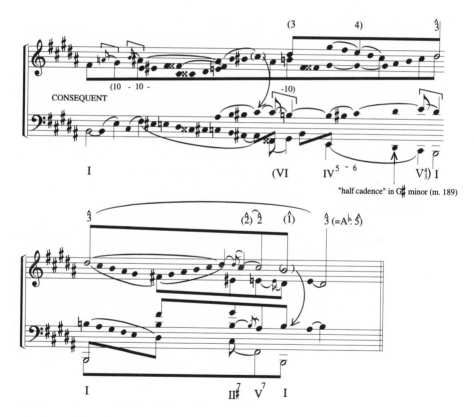

Example 4. Chopin: *Polonaise-Fantasy*, op. 61: voice leading in mm. 148–213.

"soprano" voices shown in Example 3. The antecedent of the period moves through the same sixth, seeking to retrace the motto's initial arpeggiation. Starting from f#¹, the melody succeeds in climbing only as far as c×², however; the final step is taken an octave lower (mm. 167–68), where it is covered by f#¹ for the beginning of the consequent. (The emphasis on the neighboring harmony, A♯ major, is surely intended to remind listeners of the preceding music in B♭.)

The consequent is much expanded. As Example 4 shows, it moves through the entire ascending sixth and then cadences, reproducing all four strands of the motto in the process. The ascent is again fraught with difficulties and setbacks. A series of reachings-over—or overlappings—leads from f#¹ to (a♮¹)–g#¹ to (b¹)–a♯¹; the next step, (c#²)–b¹, appears an octave lower. This time, however, the transferred tone—b¹—also appears in its "proper" register, where it is covered by d#², the very tone that is to serve as the goal of the ascent. The harmony is "wrong," however: G♯ minor (VI), another referential harmony, alluding now to the principal tonic; a plaintive new theme is heard in this key. The final ascent from b¹ to d#² occurs in mm. 187–90, where d#² finally appears above the tonic of B major. From here the sixth is retraced quickly downward, back to f#¹, and then even more quickly upward, as if to summarize the journey thus far; the regained d#² becomes a suspended ninth at m. 196. The final cadence ensues, prolonged by the famous multiple trills, but $\hat{1}$ of B major is immediately covered by $\hat{3}$, d#¹—which is to say, by the $\hat{5}$ of the fundamental line, an octave below its obligatory register. (The latter will be regained only with the e♭² of m. 254.)

From this perspective—largely a linear one—it will be seen that the mysterious G♯-minor theme is an incident within the period's consequent segment. To say this is, of course, to say far too little. The theme's texture and rhythm recall the earlier B♭-major music, as several authors have pointed out (Samson calls the two passages "first nocturne" and "second nocturne"). The recurrence of the new theme in F minor, following the B-major cadence and the recollection of mm. 1–2, helps to keep the middle section from sounding entirely self-contained. Notice, however, that in both of its appearances the theme helps to prolong a harmony *other* than its local tonic: B major (♭III of A♭ major) within the middle section; C major (III♮ of A♭) just after it. B♭ major was not enclosed within an analogous prolongation. This fact alone gives the later theme—the "second nocturne"—a special quality of distance and twilight not shared by the "first nocturne."[32] To me, it always sounds like a snatch from some half-remembered opera.

VI

I will conclude by discussing two motivic issues that touch upon aspects of form. The first concerns a feature shared by several segments of the quatrain. Example 5

---

32. Compare Schachter's analysis of mm. 77–84 in the op. 49 Fantasy; "Chopin's Fantasy," p. 237 and Example 10.

details this resemblance. Its focus is the third hypermeasure in each of four segments: the Antecedent, Consequent 1, Consequent 3, and the cadenza within Consequent 3. (Consequent 2 is cut short before reaching its third hypermeasure.) The continuation of each segment—beyond its third hypermeasure—is sketched, but without rhythmic values. Important middleground events in both melody and harmony are indicated.

Each of these four segments contains an ascending sequence in its first two hypermeasures (compare Ex. 1). The apex is reached at or near the beginning of the third hypermeasure, and the melody descends from there. In the Antecedent, the descent includes the tones G–F–E♭–D♭–C–B♮, accompanied mostly by a 10–8 linear-intervallic pattern (see the bracket in the first system of Ex. 5). This is very much a foreground progression: on a larger scale, the upper voice is in the midst of an initial ascent from a♭^{1} (m. 27) to the primary tone, e♭^{2} (m. 35; see Ex. 3).

It is the foreground descent, however, that is emulated by each of the consequents in turn (excepting, of course, Consequent 2). Consequent 1 reproduces the descent very imperfectly, turning it into a chromatic progression in parallel tenths. Chopin notates the third hypermeasure of Consequent 3 in B major, an obvious reference to the *più lento*. (The descending sixth in m. 250, from d♯$^#$ to f♯^{3}, is a less obvious reference but just as real.) The enharmonic notation is symbolic, but the passage actually prolongs G♭, a chromatic passing tone within a bass ascent from V to I (the "I" is itself a passing event at a higher level; see Ex. 3). When the passage is renotated in flats—as it is in both Examples 1 and 5—the resemblance to the Antecedent is striking. The first five tones of the original descent have been transposed down a chromatic semitone, to G♭–F♭–E♭♭–D♭♭–C♭; the linear-intervallic pattern is now 7–5 instead of 10–8. There is the same reaching-over to (f^2)–e♭^{2}, although this is now doubled an octave higher. The regaining of $\hat5$ prepares the descent of the fundamental line, which occurs in the cadenza.

The cadenza reproduces the Antecedent's descent almost perfectly so far as the upper voice is concerned. The descent now ends, appropriately, with the diatonic b♭^{1} instead of the chromatic b♮^{1}; the outer voices move mostly in parallel tenths. The chromatic deflection of Consequent 3 has been rectified. The apotheosis has incorporated references both to the key of the middle section, B major, and to its tonal content, the four-voice cadence first heard in the motto.

The second issue is so large that I can only sketch it here. It concerns the saturation of the piece with references to the enharmonic pair F♭/E♮, or ♭6/♯5—particularly in contrast to F♮, the diatonic form of $\hat6$. Fortunately, this issue has been touched upon by other authors, notably Cook.[33] The coda's obsessive repetition of F–E♭ is an attempt to exorcise the influence of ♭$\hat6$, but the attempt is vain: the recurrence of the descending minor tetrachord, in the inner voice of mm. 281–85, gives F♭ the last word. Is this a final glimpse of the worm in the apple, or a reminiscence of adversities overcome? I am strongly inclined to the former interpretation, although I will admit some plausibility to the latter.

---

33. See especially Cook, p. 337, Figure 165.

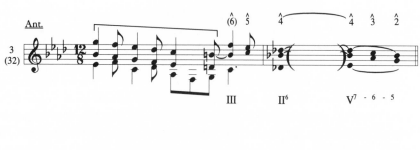

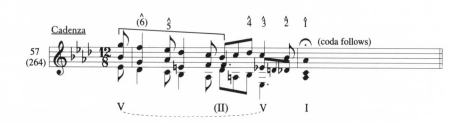

Example 5. Chopin: *Polonaise-Fantasy*, op. 61: continuations from the third hypermeasure in four sections.

Timothy Jackson has noted that enharmonic pairs themselves tend to come in pairs: a primary pair is often linked to a secondary pair a perfect fifth away.[34] Here the primary pair is ♭6̂/♯5̂; the secondary pair is ♭3̂/♯2̂. Translated into A♭ major, the

---

34. See Timothy Jackson, "Bruckner's Metrical Numbers," *Nineteenth-Century Music* 14 (1990): 121–22; also "The Enharmonics of Faith: Enharmonic Symbolism in Bruckner's *Christus factus est* (1884)," in Othmar Wessely, ed., *Bruckner-Jahrbuch 1987/88* (Anton Bruckner Institut Linz), 7–20.

secondary pair is C♭/B♮, defining the background-foreground conflict of the middle section. The flatted half of each pair grows naturally out of the extensive mixture between A♭ major and its parallel minor; this is present, of course, from the beginning of the piece.

Chopin focuses most of his attention on the F♭/E♮ pair in the early part of the work. The first arpeggio (m. 1) is capped by f♭^{4}–e♭^{4}. The F♭-major triad in m. 8 is given an especially lush scoring (not given in all editions), virtually inviting the pianist to take extra time; this is followed by a lengthy tonicization of "E major" (mm. 12–17). The expansion of the Antecedent is based on a harmonic deflection to V of F minor, with f^2–e♮^{2} featured prominently in the soprano (mm. 39–41). The latter note is corrected to the diatonic (minor) f♭^{2} in m. 42; the dyad is then transformed into the major-mode f^1–e♭^{1} (m. 43). Consequent 1 also gravitates toward F♭/E♮, its *fortissimo* climax peaking on f♭^{3} (mm. 56–57), its harmony coming briefly to rest on ♭II^6/V (F♭ major, m. 60). The curious halting motion in mm. 62–63 seems to represent an inability to overcome F♭, although the following cadence leads f♮^{1} calmly upward to g^1–a♭^{1} (mm. 65–66). It is as though the music were trying to deny the reality of the chromatic/enharmonic struggle.

The ascending major thirds of the transition introduce E♮, both as the third of a C-major triad (mm. 72–76) and as the "tonic" of E major (mm. 80–83). The early part of the Bridge brings F♮ to the fore; the music then reverts to A♭ minor, restoring F♭ and C♭, the latter in the melody itself (compare m. 60). Consequent 2 continues to stress C♭ in the melody, F♭ in the accompaniment. In the B♭-major passage, the repeated ornamental use of B♮ (mm. 117–25) foreshadows the large-scale transformation of C♭ into the B♮ of the *più lento*.[35] The final cadence of the B-major section repeatedly covers its own tonic degree with $\hat{4}$–$\hat{3}$, written as e^1–d♯^{1} (mm. 206–12) but functioning in a larger sense as f♭^{1}–e♭^{1} (♭$\hat{6}$–$\hat{5}$ in A♭). Thus the motive of m. 1 returns in a distant tonal landscape, providing motivation for the direct quotation that follows. The transition to Consequent 3 is perhaps the climax of confusion regarding the whole complex of upper neighbors to $\hat{5}$: E♮ (♯$\hat{5}$), F♭ (♭$\hat{6}$), and F♮ (♮$\hat{6}$). The upper voice of Example 3 summarizes this vacillation.

Chopin's preoccupation with enharmonic puns is another feature that op. 61 shares with op. 53, the A♭-Major Polonaise, and the tones involved are the same: the complex of upper neighbors to $\hat{5}$.[36] The punning is more obvious in op. 53, owing to the setting of the middle section in "E major." A glance at the Polonaise's introduction will confirm that F♭ is an important presence from the outset. This being a much

---

35. ♭$\hat{6}$ and ♯$\hat{5}$ are juxtaposed within B♭ major as well; see m. 125, left hand.

36. Preoccupation with this chromatic/enharmonic complex is prominent in much nineteenth-century music. See, for example, Beethoven's "Emperor" Concerto, op. 73, and his Piano Sonata op. 81a ("Das Lebewohl"). Edward Cone's well-known article "Schubert's Promissory Note," in Walter Frisch, ed., *Schubert: Analytical and Critical Studies* (Lincoln: University of Nebraska Press, 1986), 13–30, explores the same topic in Schubert's *Moment musical* no. 6, D. 780. Later examples include works by Brahms (for instance, the B♭-Major Piano Concerto, op. 83) and Dvořák (the E♭-Major Piano Quartet, op. 87).

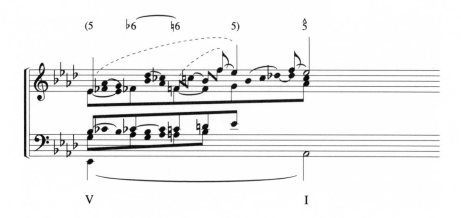

Example 6. Chopin: Polonaise, op. 53: Introduction.

more optimistic work than op. 61, F♯ prevails within the introduction itself, and F♮–E♭ becomes the leading motive of the principal theme (see the sketch in Ex. 6). There is similar use of E♮ as the third of C major, the altered mediant (see mm. 51–52, 58–63, and 145–51). As in op. 61, the coda stresses F♭ as well as F♮, and the chromatic upper neighbor—spelled here as ♯5̂, but functioning melodically as ♯6̂—has the final word (mm. 179–80). But there is nothing disquieting about this ending—nothing like the literally sinister buzzing in the analogous passage of op. 61 (mm. 282–85). The emphasis here is on unanimity, not conflict. All possible upper neighbors have been sounded and resolved securely to 5̂. The Devil has been tamed; nothing can deter the final march to victory.

VII

Much has been written about the fusion of genres in the Polonaise-Fantasy, especially the two genres from which Chopin ultimately fashioned the title of the work.[37] It is no secret that op. 49 figures importantly in the prehistory of op. 61, but the equal role of op. 53 has not been sufficiently appreciated. It seems that, in the Polonaise-Fantasy, Chopin was revisiting formal and motivic issues from two earlier works—*one* polonaise and *one* fantasy—in order to resolve them in a new way.[38] In so doing,

---

37. We know from Chopin's letters that he had difficulty deciding upon a suitable title. See Kallberg, "Chopin's Last Style," 267–75.

38. It is true that the F♯-Minor Polonaise, op. 44, also evoked from Chopin a juxtaposition of the terms "fantasy" and "polonaise" (Ibid., 269–72). Except for a preoccupation with the descending tetrachord 8̂–7̂–6̂–5̂ —a preoccupation shared by several other of Chopin's later works, including ops. 49, 52, and 61—the links between ops. 44 and 61 seem more superficial than those between op. 61 and ops. 49 and 53.

he created a work that is far more complex, ambiguous, and troubling than either of its models. As for the specifically formal issue—the expansion of simple song forms (ternary and quatrain) into a relatively vast and certainly imposing structure—Chopin probably felt that he had taken this to its limit in op. 61. Only time and a measure of health could have permitted him to pursue his formal experiments further, but it is difficult not to feel that op. 61 represents not the beginning of a new road for Chopin (as has often been maintained) but the end of an old one.[39] Further "progress" would have to start from radically new premises.

39. The same seems to be true of Chopin's phrase rhythm in his late works. See my "Phrase Rhythm in Chopin's Nocturnes and Mazurkas," in *Chopin Studies*, 115–41.

Chasing the Scent:
The Tonality of
Liszt's *Blume und Duft*

Robert P. Morgan

I

In a groundbreaking article on Liszt's "experimental idiom" published in 1987, Allen Forte distinguishes between two general types of Lisztian music:

> the traditional music of triadic tonality and the experimental music, which represents innovational departures from the norms of tonal syntax. In the latter there is an increasingly stronger movement toward a different sphere of sonic organization, one that came into full view some twenty years after Liszt's death in the new music of Bartók, Schoenberg, Webern, Scriabin, and Stravinsky.[1]

Avoiding issues of influence, Forte makes no claim for a direct line connecting Liszt's experimental music to these later figures; indeed, he does not even suggest that "this emergent phase" of twentieth-century musical development gave rise to "any kind of orderly evolutionary progression" (210–11). What interests him is simply Liszt's "precursory role," and that the music he wrote which is "most closely related to . . . the early twentieth century . . . include[s] not only the late work, but also segments of earlier works, extending back into the pre-Weimar period, before 1848" (210).

Among the earlier works Forte considers is the song *Blume und Duft,* one of Liszt's most beautiful and elusive creations, composed in 1860. (A complete score appears as Ex. 1.) Since he is concerned exclusively with the octatonic features of the

---

This article was originally presented in different form as the Keynote Address for the 1988 annual meeting of the Texas Society for Music Theory at the University of Texas, Arlington. I would like to thank Karen Painter for reading this earlier version and for her many helpful suggestions.

1. Allen Forte, "Liszt's Experimental Idiom and Music of the Early Twentieth Century" *Nineteenth-Century Music* 11 (1987): 210. All subsequent page references within the text are to this article.

Blume und Duft.

Franz Liszt.

Example 1. Liszt: *Blume und Duft.*

Example 1 cont'd.

song, Forte confines his comments to the two segments in which these figure prominently: (1) the opening four-measure introduction, where a pair of third-related dominant-seventh sonorities, the pitch-class set 4–27, is presented (mm. 1–2) and then sequenced a minor third higher (mm. 3–4); and (2) the climax (mm. 15–20), where this introductory harmonic succession recurs in a more heavily scored and differently configured form, now with added voice, but beginning with what was originally the second chord-pair (mm. 3–4 = 15–17) and sequenced up by half step rather than minor third (mm. 18–20). Moreover, whereas in the introduction each chord-pair formed only a six-note octatonic subset, the two together producing the octatonic septad, at the climax the first pair plus voice alone produces the septad, while the second generates the complete octatonic collection. The climactic moment is thus marked not only by such surface features as louder dynamics, fuller texture, and expanded registration, but by increasing collectional density, attaining its maximum—the full octatonic—in its final three-measure segment.

Forte's remarks thus draw attention not only to the octatonicism of two of the song's critical formal moments, the opening measures and climax, but also to the ubiquity of set 4–27, the "dominant-seventh" sonority, which completely defines their harmonic content, each segment consisting of four such chords in succession. Forte, consistent with his octatonic perspective, rejects a tonal interpretation of these chords, noting that his "reading avoids the obvious 'dominant-seventh' label that might be attached to the four verticals, a label that has no analytical consequences whatsoever since the sonorities so designated play no functional role within a tonality, explicit or implied" (215).

Since Forte deals only with these two portions of the song, and thus not with the relationships between these octatonic "dominants" and other features of the music, he leaves open the question of what their actual meaning might be. Having left the door ajar, however, he seems to invite the reader to continue without him; and that is what I propose to do here.

II

Perhaps the first thing to note in turning to the song as a whole is how little the octatonicism of mm. 1–4 and 15–20 influences the remainder. At the same time, the saturation of these two passages with a sonority so closely tied to classical tonality (indeed, perhaps its most emblematic representative), the dominant-seventh, produces strong associations with what happens elsewhere in the song, as the chord-type pervades much of the rest of the music.[2] In addition, all the other significant

---

2. For purposes of identification I will refer to this chord throughout as a "dominant-seventh," regardless of its spelling, and without making any claims concerning its actual functional role. The justification for doing so will become apparent, I hope, during the course of the analysis.

verticals likewise conform to standard late eighteenth- and early nineteenth-century harmonic vocabulary. Taking voice and accompaniment into consideration, dominant-sevenths are projected in mm. 5, 7, 8 (here preceded by a $^6_4$ chord), 21, 23, 26–27, 28 (over a nonharmonic pedal), and 30, accounting (along with those in the introduction and climax) for 19 of the song's 31 measures. And of the remaining twelve measures, six display major triads (mm. 6, 9, 11, 13, 29, and 31), one a minor triad (m. 22), two augmented triads (mm. 10 and 12), two diminished sevenths (mm. 24 and 25), and one a half-diminished seventh (m. 14). Measured on a chord-by-chord basis, then, *Blume und Duft* is consistently triadic; and even the chord-by-chord successions, taken individually, are not unusual by nineteenth-century standards. Yet if the whole is considered, striking anomalies emerge relative to functional conventions, making the piece—as Forte states—decidedly resistant to standard tonal interpretation. On the other hand, one must add that, taken as a whole, it is equally resistant to an octatonic one. How then should one proceed?

A good place to start is with a consideration of the overall form and its relationship to the song's text, written by the German poet and dramatist Friedrich Hebbel (1813–63). The basic design is quite simple: following a four-measure piano introduction, three varied strophes appear in mm. 5–9, 10–20, and 21–27, the second distinguished by significant extension, after which there is a four-measure piano postlude (mm. 28–31). Since Hebbel's text has only two four-line verses (each with abab rhyme scheme), however, the first strophe sets the opening two lines of the first verse and the third strophe the closing two lines of the second, while the middle strophe encompasses both the closing two lines of the first verse and opening two of the second. The middle strophe thus cuts across the poem's formal structure, a point that will be discussed later. This disparity between poetic and musical division can be displayed as follows:

		Blume und Duft	*Flower and Scent*
		First Strophe	
V	1.	In Frühlings Heiligtume,	In springtime's holy realm,
E	2.	wenn dir ein Duft ans	when a scent touches you most
R		Tiefste rührt,	deeply,
S			
E			
		Second Strophe	
1	3.	da suche nicht die Blume,	don't look for the flower,
	4.	der ihn ein Hauch entführt	from which a breath of air
			stole it
V	1.	Der Duft lässt Ew'ges ahnen,	The scent reveals eternity,
E	2.	von unbegrenztem Lebenvoll;	full of unbounded life;
R			
S		Third Strophe	
E	3.	die Blume kann nur mahnen,	the flower can only remind,
2	4.	wie schnell sie welken soll.	how quickly it will fade.

The strophic quality stems mainly from the opening of the three strophes, where the voice part has essentially the same music, untransposed in the first and third and a half step higher in the second. Thereafter the strophes develop independently, although the piano postlude, rather than returning to material from the introduction, brings back music closely related to the first strophe.

In many respects the song projects strong A♭ centricity. Not only does it end on an A♭ root-position triad (m. 31), preceded by a bass A♭ in m. 28 and A♭ triad in m. 29, but A♭-rooted chords also figure prominently at the beginning (the introduction opens and closes with A♭ dominant-seventh chords and the first strophe returns to an A♭ $^6_4$ in m. 6), and at the climax (where an A♭ dominant-seventh reappears as the goal harmony associated with the prominent formal articulation at mm. 16–17). Yet despite this A♭ emphasis, there is no dominant *to* A♭ anywhere in the piece, whereas A♭ is itself represented as frequently by dominant sonorities as by major triads (three times each). In addition, none of the dominant-sevenths in the octatonically structured introduction and climax resolves according to normal functional practice, nor does the heavily emphasized dominant on E in m. 29, which moves back to A♭ in the following measure.[3]

Two other dominant-sevenths, on the other hand, do appear in contexts that affirm their functional status: one on C♯ in m. 8, which resolves to F♯ major in m. 9, producing an authentic cadence (the only one in the song); and two on C in mm. 21 and 23, which appear in a well-defined (though not cadentially confirmed) F-minor context, the first (V$^4_2$) resolving to I^6, but the second (V$^4_3$) proceeding chromatically in a motion ultimately leading back to A♭. Functional relationships are thus by no means entirely avoided. Simply to say, then, that emphasis on A♭ at the beginning and end creates the sort of nonhierarchical "tonality-by-assertion" found in much twentieth-century music is to ignore the critical matter of how the two tonal areas receiving functional articulation are integrated into the larger structure. But this leaves us with the question: how is one to reconcile the peculiar behavior of so many

---

3. Respelled as F♭–A♭–B–D, the chord corresponds in type and function to an augmented-sixth chord identified by Mark DeVoto as "Swiss": one in which the augmented sixth resolves outward to the fifth degree of the tonic chord without intervening dominant. Mark DeVoto, "Alban Berg and Creeping Chromaticism," in David Gable and Robert P. Morgan, eds., *Alban Berg: Historical and Analytical Perspectives* (Oxford: Oxford University Press, 1991), 59. The double half-step resolution of this chord is one of a series of such resolutions, almost all in contrary motion, between adjacent chord pairs found throughout the piece, forming an associative voice-leading network that plays a significant cohesive role: G♭–F/A♭–A , mm. 1–2; A–A♭/B–C, mm. 3–4; E–E♭/G–A♭, mm. 5–6; G–F♯/C–C♯, mm. 7–8; E♯–F♯/A–A♯, mm. 10–11; mm. 15–19 (where the progression from mm. 1–2 returns, now with voice exchanges); and E–F/D♭–C, mm. 21–22. The idea is then intensified in the completely chromatic voice leading of mm. 24–26, after which it returns with m. 27's "Swiss sixth" and the reprise of mm. 5–6 in mm. 28–29 and 30–31. A double leading-tone motion also straddles the move back to the beginning of the third strophe, from the A7 in m. 19 to C$^4_2$ in m. 21: A–B♭/C♯–C .

"wrong" dominants, plus the total absence of the "right" one, with passages in which the conventions of traditional tonality are still clearly in operation?

A quasi-Schenkerian graph offers one kind of answer—a linear analysis that shows the prolongation of an A♭ chord throughout the song, elaborated by various contrapuntal motions (see Ex. 2). In my view this represents the most comprehensive (but, as we shall see, not unproblematic) account of the overall pitch structure, relating all details of the voice leading to a single background framework and integrating the events on each level with those on the others.

The analysis is most easily read from the lowest (most background) level to the highest. (Note that accidentals have been altered in the bottom three graphs to clarify the larger voice-leading and prolongational connections). The lowest graph, level a, displays the sort of non-Schenkerian background sometimes encountered in nineteenth-century music: a single triad (A♭-major) is unfolded through passing and neighbor motions rather than a dominant divider, while the top voice prolongs a single pitch (here scale-degree $\hat{3}$). It also reveals that the influence of nonfunctional dominant-seventh sonorities, so prominent on the foreground (where they might be said to play a "motivic" or "associational" role), extends down to this relatively background level: note the emphasis on the lowered seventh degree, G♭, which provides consonant support for the passing parallel third B♭–D♭ in the upper voices (corresponding to m. 9 of the song); and the substitution of a dominant-seventh for the tonic triad that results from this G♭ being suspended as an inner voice when the upper-voice B♭-D♭ third resolves to C–E♭ (corresponding to m. 16). After an upper-neighbor B♮ chord, the A♭ chord returns, delayed by a 6–5 exchange (F–E♭), the origin of the F-minor passage in the third strophe, elaborated by a chromatic passing-tone F♭. The lowered-seventh G♭ of the previous music is resolved by the F of this exchange, and from this point it remains absent.

The subsequent graphs show elaborations of this underlying structure. At level b the inner-voice G♭ of level a is connected to the returning A♭ bass by a series of descending thirds, outlining a (minor) seventh chord; and the passing F♭ elaborating the 6–5 exchange is projected into the bass (respelled E♮). On level c the opening A♭ triad is composed out through an elaborated arpeggiated motion in the lowest voice, the G♭-major chord is tonicized with an authentic cadence, and the first of the downward third successions connecting the inner-voice G♭ to the bass A♭ is filled in with passing motion. The first-inversion F-minor triad produced by the 6–5 exchange is also tonicized, giving rise to a descending stepwise motion in the bass connecting A♭ to E. In addition, the upper-neighbor sonority on B♮, like the chord it elaborates a dominant-seventh type, is itself embellished by a dominant-seventh a minor third higher, producing a sequence up by half step of the chords associated with the bass's preceding C♭–A♭ (the last of the succession of descending thirds). Finally, level d reveals the source of the G♭ emphasis and the A♭ dominant-sevenths: the opening A♭-major triad is embellished by a succession of four dominant- sevenths, the first and last rooted on A♭. This succession, based on two falling-third root progressions, A♭–F and B–A♭ (= C♭–A♭), prepares the G♭ to A♭ arpeggiation by descending thirds first

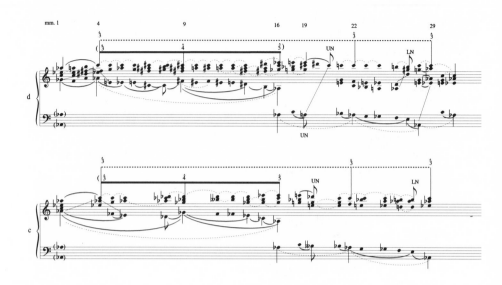

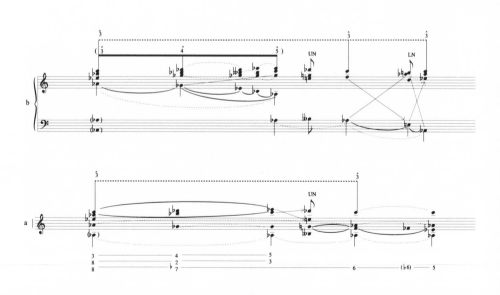

Example 2. A quasi-Schenkerian analysis of *Blume und Duft*.

encountered at level b; and the second pair (mm. 3–4), as mentioned, anticipates the content (but not the registral layout) of the final link of this arpeggiation (mm. 15–16). In both cases the falling-third progression brings about a return to A♭ following a departure. Since the other level-d embellishments are relatively straightforward, they require no additional comment.

There is much that seems convincing in this analysis. It helps explain the unconventional turn to F♯ (G♭) major and the ubiquitous dominant-type sonorities by subsuming them within a comprehensible larger structure that is ultimately controlled by a pure A♭-major triad. It is also consistent with the formal layout of the song: the introduction (mm. 1–4) states and prolongs the A♭ dominant-seventh sonority through two sequential descending-third progressions; the first strophe establishes A♭ major as a triadically-centered key and modulates to G♭ major; the second strophe (including its extension in mm. 14–20) brings the G♭–A♭ bass arpeggiation, plus an upper-neighbor embellishment of the goal harmony; the third strophe (mm. 21–27) presents the F-minor portion of the 6–5 exchange and its dissolution; and the coda provides the return to A♭.

In addition to supporting the song's strophic structure, however, the principal pitch motions also project a single unfolding progression that—while formally articulated—is ultimately indivisible and spans the entire song, transcending the strophic features to support a second formal design layered over the strophic one: an overall wave-like motion of a type much favored in nineteenth-century music. Thus the song can be seen as defining a continuous, developmental gesture, rising in intensity to a climactic point at mm. 19–20, followed by a denouement characterized by formal dissolution and expressive relaxation (mm. 21–31). This explains why the three strophes are more like variations than simple repetitions (all three are radically different harmonically, for example); and why the second especially, but also the third, are extended in the specific manner they are (each in response to its own particular position in the overall wave).

There are nevertheless two significant aspects of the song that run counter to the reading of Example 2, both of which concern the analytically problematic second strophe. There is a definite impression at the opening of this strophe that it represents a varied restatement of the first, transposed up a half step to A major. Since it sequences the first strophe almost exactly, the vocal line especially supports this, even though Liszt obscures the connection by beginning in F♯ (= G♭) major rather than A. As the strophe unfolds, moreover, F♯ does in fact prove to be VI♯ of A major (no doubt explaining Liszt's F♯ spelling). And when A major arrives in m. 13 it has something of the quality of a cadential arrival: the text reaches the end of the first verse, completing an idea whose opening portion ended with the previous cadence (m. 9), underscored by the rhyme between *rührt* and *führt*; there is relatively strong rhythmic closure in the voice; and most importantly, a sense of resolution is produced by the association between the first strophe's top-voice C, heard in conjunction with A♭ major, and the C♯ in m. 13, now heard in conjunction with A major.

Forward motion nevertheless does not reach an entirely convincing close at

m. 13. The A-major chord is in $^6_4$ position and its harmonic definition is weak, preceded by an augmented triad that contains two of its three pitches. The accompanimental pattern and descending bass motion of the preceding segment also continue through m. 14 and beyond,[4] and the voice eventually returns with an upbeat figure that extends both of the linear strands it initiated in mm. 10–13 (see Ex. 3), thus carrying on the rising line. Though there is definitely a formal "comma" at m. 13, there is no real cadence.

Both rhythmic and linear motion continue until m. 17, where for the first time the accompanimental pattern ceases, coinciding with the return of A♭ in the bass (consistent with the analysis in Ex. 2). The slight variation in texture in mm. 15 and 16 (echoing an alteration first made at the cadence in mm. 8–9), along with the crescendo, fermata, and cessation of accompanimental pattern, suggest that this must be the principal arrival (also subsequently supported by the pitch relationship associating the voice line here with that beginning the final strophe, m. 22, where the structural top-voice C returns, an association reinforced by the *ahnen/mahnen* rhyme).

But in what is perhaps the most extraordinary moment in a piece full of surprises, the entire cadential gesture of mm. 15–17 is repeated up a half step in mm. 18–20 (slightly elaborated in the voice), again with altered textural pattern, continuing crescendo, fermata (now two of them, one on the high E in m. 19, one after the C♯ in m. 20), and cessation of the accompanimental pattern in the third measure (after which the accompaniment is not heard again in complete form). This seems to suggest that mm. 18–20, not mm. 15–17, complete the second strophe.

But if so, what does this say about the analysis in Example 2, in which the end of the second strophe is associated with an upper-neighbor chord, tacked on the end of an extensive A♭ prolongation, rather than with the completion of that prolongation? Or is A major perhaps the real structural goal? And if so, should it not relate more deeply to what precedes it?

Such questions suggest an alternate reading, given in Example 4 (in somewhat less detail than the previous one, and with enharmonic respellings). The second strophe is here shown to be controlled by a prolongation of A major, linking the A-major $^6_4$ chord of the subsidiary arrival (m. 13) to the A dominant-seventh at the end (mm. 19). According to this reading, the F♯ (= G♭) chord is subordinate to the A$^6_4$, while the A♭ dominant becomes a lower neighbor resolving back to an A chord (represented by the dominant chord at m. 19). The entire strophe is thereby realized within a single middleground motion, its completion coinciding with the end of the prolongation. This lends considerably greater weight to the upper-neighbor A at the background level: no longer a relatively isolated event, it defines the song's principal prolongation, which governs the entire second strophe (see especially level b).

---

4. Although the accompanimental pattern also continues through m. 9 and beyond, thus overlapping the first strophe as well, there the V–I cadence, supported by slight textural variation at the V^7 chord (beat three of m. 8), and the descending melodic line produce a much stronger sense of closure.

Example 3. Analysis of vocal part of *Blume und Duft,* mm. 5–19.

There are nevertheless distinct disadvantages with this reading as well. It fails to account for the prominence of the F#-major chord in m. 9, and thus also for its connection with the pervasive "dominant" coloring of the tonic scale degree. And although it better accounts for the sense of subsidiary arrival at m. 13, it downplays the even stronger arrival at mm. 16–17—and thus the quality mm. 18–20 unmistakably project as an "added" limb extending the second strophe (even if, after the fact, they can be grasped differently).

Similar questions arise concerning the structural upper voice. The first reading indicates a motion through the A♭-major triad: from A♭ (m.1) through C (mm.4–7) to E♭ (mm. 15–17), relegating the prominent C# of mm. 8–14 to a mere passing note, and the climactic E of m. 19, the culminating note closing the steadily rising motion of the introduction and first strophe, to an upper neighbor. It also suppresses the role of this climactic E as the termination of two overlapping octatonic scale segments, the first—A♭–A–B–C—spanning the introduction, and the second—C#–D#–E—the first two strophes, a line that connects the two consistently octatonic segments stressed by Forte, the introduction and climax, and is the piece's only prominent octatonic element that transcends these two.

Which of the two readings given in Examples 2 and 4 is better, then? The question, of a type commonly encountered in considerations of functionally tonal music, seems out of place here, since neither reading does justice to—nor is indeed fully consistent with—critical features of the composition, which defies any single, unequivocal structural orientation. Both are valid, if only to a degree; and both are helpful in responding to features of the second strophe that—according to conventional analytical assumptions—are in conflict with one another, yet here seem to exist in a kind of delicate balance.

Even when combined, however, these analyses—while revealing important aspects of the linear structure and their ordering within a prolongational framework, fail to address critical questions relating to the song's tonality and the music's overall expressive character. I want to consider two of these, both tied to the persisting role of functional tonality. One concerns the F-minor area that controls the opening of the third strophe. In Schenkerian terms, evident in both linear analyses, F minor emerges as a middleground displacement of the final A♭-major chord, and thus apparently as an isolated detail (though the resolution of the middleground G♭ to the F of the 6–5 exchange, shown in level a of Example 2, defines a linear motion that spans the entire piece—another reason for favoring that reading). But the F-minor area, in addition to delaying the return of the final tonic, also participates in a network of F-minor connections that extends back to the introduction. Though the latter is shown in both linear analyses to define an A♭ prolongation, articulated by opening and closing harmonies rooted on A♭, it can also be heard as projecting an F–A♭ bass arpeggiation, articulated by the two-chord progression that moves first to a root-position chord on F and then, sequenced upwards by minor third, to a root-position chord on A♭.

This reading promotes the possibility of hearing a root progression arpeggiating through an F-minor triad: from F in m. 2, to A♭ in m. 4, to C in m. 5. If one substitutes an F-minor chord for A♭ in m. 6, it becomes evident just how strongly that key is suggested—indeed, sufficiently to make the A♭⁶₄ of m. 6 sound almost "deceptive." When C major returns in the next measure (m. 7), moreover, the possibility continues that the strophe may conclude on F minor. The voice implies F minor at least as much as A♭ major throughout mm. 5–7; and the sudden, functionally defined turn toward F♯ major in mm. 8–9 would represent a move to the Neapolitan of the tonic F—one consistent with the voice's sequential repetition of the opening of the first strophe a half step higher. When C then returns as V⁴₃ of F in m. 21, it again follows an A♭ dominant-seventh (mm. 16–17), itself inflected up a half step to an A dominant-seventh (mm. 18–19). The latter is elaborated by a C dominant-seventh (m. 19), making an easily audible connection with the C chord in m. 21, which *does* resolve to F minor, thus realizing a long-latent potentiality. The 6–5 resolution to A♭ ⁵₃ can thus be heard as the final link in a chain of associations going back to the opening measures of the song. Even when A♭ returns in the postlude, it still reverberates with F-minor resonances: as in the initial strophe, C dominants usurp the role of the real dominant (mm. 28 and 30, corresponding to mm. 5 and 7), so that the conclusion is thus anything but emphatic. A final F-minor resolution remains a possibility, and from a strictly functional point-of-view, would provide perhaps an even stronger, if no doubt less satisfying, one than the close on A♭.

The second matter relates to the association of the tonic A♭ with dominant-seventh sonorities. As mentioned, only three of six A♭ chords in the song are pure triads (mm. 6, 29, and 31), and of these the first two are in ⁶₄ position. This leaves the closing chord as the sole root-position tonic triad (though it might be argued that the low bass A♭ of m. 28 is still present by implication in m. 29, and even in mm. 30–31). The other three A♭ chords (mm. 1, 4, and 16), are all dominant-sevenths, all appearing at critical formal junctures: at the opening and closing measures of the introduction and at what seems to be (but ultimately turns out not to be) the close of the climactic ascent of the second strophe (m. 16). We have seen that the dominant quality of A♭ extends to the most background level; and in addition, the upper-neighbor motion in the middle segment associates the structural A♭ seventh with a chord—an A♮ (or B♭♭) dominant-seventh—that relates to it like a conventional (German) augmented-sixth to a dominant, a connection underlined by the immediate juxtaposition of mm. 15–17 with their sequential repetition a half step higher (mm. 18–20).

Add to the dominant aura of A♭ the absence of a single dominant *to* A♭, and we understand how tenuous the tonality is, despite the relatively clear prolongational structures graphed in Examples 2 and 4. Indeed, one might wonder whether A♭ should not be taken as an *actual* dominant, the V of a suppressed D♭ tonic, offering a more radical version of those tonal structures (not uncommon in late nineteenth-century music) in which the tonic, implied by a prolonged V^7, does not appear until the closing measures—more radical here in that the tonic does not appear at all.[5] Finally, however, I think not, both because the harmonic elements traditionally associated with D♭ play such a minor role in the song (except for the V^7 chord itself), and because the lowered seventh degree associated so strongly with Ab in the first half disappears almost entirely in the second. The only G♭ (or F♯) heard after m. 16, roughly the midpoint, is the passing bass note in m. 24, introduced as a chromatic alteration of the second degree of F minor. Yet the ambiguity inherent in this possibility contributes significantly to the unstable quality of the work, which seems to hover uncertainly even in closing, as if suspended in some rarefied tonal realm. Especially telling is the retention of C as structural top voice, a note that is at once static, since it is present so much in the opening and, especially, closing portions of the piece, yet also mobile, since it undergoes constant harmonic reinterpretation. The quality of weightlessness persists even to the final bass A♭, which, although it supports the music's sole A♭$^5_3$ chord (m. 31), also supplies the final note of the principal melodic figure (here placed below the accompaniment for the first time), a dual responsibility that deprives it of much of its harmonic force.[6]

The song's tonal uncertainty is of course inseparable from its expressive character and is, more particularly, closely tied to Hebbel's beautiful text, which implicitly evokes the idea of suspension in reference to the flower's scent (*Duft*), treated as an image of eternity (*Ew'ges*) and unbounded life (*unbegrenztem Leben*). Liszt places these images at the climactic conclusion of the second strophe, mm. 15–20, thereby grouping the first half of the second verse with the second half of the first. Though this contradicts the poem's formal structure, as was previously noted, it upholds its semantic design, which stresses in the first six lines the power of the flower's scent—

5. The *locus classicus* is Brahms's Intermezzo in B♭ major, op. 76, no. 4, although other examples are not difficult to find (in Scriabin and Debussy, for example). Analyses of Liszt pieces (though not *Blume und Duft*) that offer a functional tonal reading despite the absence of a tonic chord can be found in James M. Baker, "The Limits of Tonality in the Late Music of Franz Liszt," *Journal of Music Theory* 34 (1990): 145–73.

6. It should be clear from what has been said that *Blume und Duft* does not project what I have elsewhere called a "dissonant prolongation," though it leans far in that direction. There is a prolonged dissonance in the song, the A♭ dominant-seventh chord; but it is ultimately resolved, though not by means of the conventional dominant-to-tonic harmonic progression but by the voice-leading motion ♭7–6–5. See Robert P. Morgan, "Dissonant Prolongations: Theoretical and Analytical Precedents," *Journal of Music Theory* 20 (1976): 49–91. Liszt graphically symbolizes the emergence of A♭ as a more stable reference by inserting a four-flat key signature before the final four measures (just as he symbolized the music's previous instability by withholding a signature).

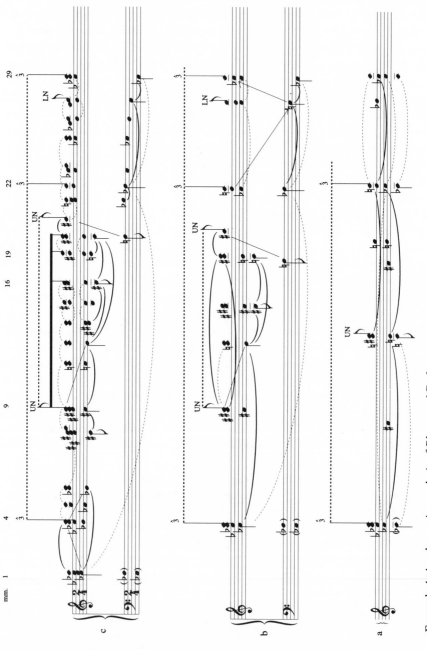

Example 4. An alternative analysis of *Blume und Duft*.

its "spirit"—to transcend the flower's materiality, while relegating to the final two the latter's impermanence.

Significantly, these last two lines are set to the only sustained functional progression, the song's most earthbound moment, in a progression that breaks up precisely as the last line ends (m. 24). A tonal dissolution then accompanies a more fragmented repetition of the same line (mm. 25–27), leading back to the hovering "eternity" of the A♭ area, which reemerges—now "purely musically"—in the piano postlude.

The constant off-beat accompanimental pattern, which makes its own contribution to the weightless quality of the music and which remains unbroken until the climactic moment, returns during the F-minor segment but represented solely by its heavier, on-beat (left-hand) component, while the lighter off-beat portion returns alone to accompany the A♭ of the postlude, where it continues to the end of the piece, including even the final (ostensibly cadential) measure.

The quality of Hebbel's poem is perfectly reflected in the focused yet fragile tonality of Liszt's setting. Its suggestion that real significance lies in the immaterial essence of things, not in their physical embodiment, must have appealed to Liszt, so deeply committed to the ideals of musical Romanticism. (Hebbel, incidentally, contributed to another masterful composition hanging on the edges of tonality: the first of Berg's Four Songs, op. 2.) His poem might also be taken as a warning to those analyzing this music: the true meaning cannot be literally defined but at best only intuited and suggested. What epitomizes *Blume und Duft* is not the emphatic statement of an unequivocal proposition (here, for example, an explicit key), but the way it skirts an implied assertion, never overtly stated, which must be inferred from its traces rather than comprehensively grasped. To hear and analyze such music requires response to momentary suggestion, pursuit of avenues dimly perceived, exploration of alternative paths.[7]

---

7. This does not mean that all analytical approaches to this music are equally valid. Two analyses of *Blume und Duft* that appeared together some years ago in an issue of *In Theory Only* (also referred to by Forte in his Liszt article) are instructive in this connection. One, by Howard Cinnamon, assumes an essentially orthodox Schenkerian view, modified to fit this unorthodox music. Though Cinnamon makes a number of interesting observations, especially about how the chromatic details of the first six measures might be derived from a diatonic and functionally tonal model, his attempt to preserve as much Schenker as possible in analyzing the overall structure is problematic. By forcing the music to conform to a triadic arpeggiation derived from the Schenkerian prototype I–III–V–I, altered to I–III♯–♯V♯–I, he distorts the song's rhythmic and formal shape. The III♯ (C major), for example—Cinnamon's principal prolonging harmony (since he views the ♯V♯ as III♯ of III♯)—must be extracted from a passing moment within the climactic phrase: m. 18, whose CV[7] chord, though clearly subordinate to the AV[7] in the following measure, is connected—across its AV[7] resolution—to CV$^4_2$ in m. 21, which in turn is connected—across its own I[6] resolution—to EV[7] (C major's

III

In closing the introductory segment of his Liszt article, Forte modestly characterizes his analytical remarks on individual pieces as no more than a "brief description of some of the general surface characteristics of the experimental idiom intended only as the most casual kind of introduction to this extraordinary music" (210). In the concluding section he goes on to mention two fruitful questions for further investigation—when did the experimental features first appear in Liszt, and what is their degree of prevalence?—and to add that the study of these and other such questions will contribute to "a larger and more precise picture of the development of Liszt's musical thought, not only as it pertains to the experimental idiom . . . but also to the entire range of his diversified output" (227–28).

It is to this final, larger injunction, embracing the full range of Liszt's compositional practice, that I hope to have responded in suggesting that, at least in this one instance (though I am convinced there are many others), the two Lisztian compositional idioms, the one experimental and the other traditional, work hand-in-hand, producing music that is at once triadic and still (somehow) tonal yet significantly independent of the norms of traditional tonal syntax. This attempt at tonal-atonal reconciliation, devoted to the music of Liszt, is offered as tribute to my friend and colleague Allen Forte, who has taught us so much about this composer.[8]

III♭) in m. 27. Howard Cinnamon, "Tonal Structure and Voice-Leading in Liszt's 'Blume und Duft,'" *In Theory Only* 6 (1982): 12–24.

Although the other analysis, by Edwin Hantz, does not attempt to reduce the song to a Schenkerian background, it too is largely linear in orientation. Much of what Hantz says about local motivic matters (including the rising octatonic top voice, though it is not identified as such) is convincing; and his view of the main linear configurations as comprising three neighbor relationships—A♭–A, C–C♯, and E♭–E—accords well with the tonal features of the song discussed here. But Hantz's idea that the A♭–A dyad is the least important of the three is puzzling, as is his contention that the "home chord" is an augmented triad (stemming from his view that A♭, C, and E are the three primary tones of the three neighbor-note pairs)—this despite the subordinate role played by augmented triads on the surface. Hantz, like Cinnamon, ultimately goes astray, I feel, because he misreads the larger form, which he describes as a "rounded binary" with principal division following m. 13. Edwin Hantz, "Motivic and Structural Unity in Liszt's 'Blume und Duft,'" *In Theory Only* 6 (1982): 3–11.

8. And not only through his comments on *Blume und Duft:* Forte has himself addressed questions of tonal-atonal interaction in another major figure in the evolution of modern music, Alban Berg. See his study of the Symphonic Epilogue from Berg's *Wozzeck,* "The Mask of Tonality," in Gable and Morgan, eds., *Alban Berg,* 151–200. Forte's elegant, quasi-Schenkerian tonal graphs of the epilogue, notwithstanding their intent to demonstrate the greater precision of an atonal reading over a tonal one, significantly illuminate critical and otherwise puzzling and recalcitrant features of this complex, multifaceted music—a point I have personally conveyed to Professor Forte on more than one occasion, eliciting what I humor myself to be a not wholly negative, and certainly not unfriendly, response.

Reflections on a Few Good Tunes: Linear Progressions and Intervallic Patterns in Popular Song and Jazz

Steven E. Gilbert

What makes a good tune? It depends on whom you ask. And even the same person may give different answers depending on the tune's intended purpose. In the literal sense, it would be a memorable melody—one with a clear sense of direction, with distinct highs and lows, with just the right gesture at a climactic moment. A different perspective comes into play when considering those songs that have been fertile ground for jazz improvisation.

This perspective is demanded even when a song is equally distinguished in both respects, reflecting both the various ways the song is treated and the structural features that make it attractive in one respect or the other. A snapshot of these differences can be seen in George and Ira Gershwin's "I Got Rhythm," whose melodic high point does not come until the downbeat of a two-bar tag at the end of the refrain. This, the penultimate "more," would be an important moment in any straightforward vocal performance, whereas in a typical jazz treatment it would be omitted. Most notably, it is omitted in what have become known to the jazz world as "rhythm changes." A tune with rhythm changes has the harmonic and metric framework of the refrain of "I Got Rhythm," with the aforementioned last two bars excised: a 32–bar chorus in AABA form, with identical A sections that begin and end on the tonic.

Rhythm changes are featured prominently in the music of Charlie Parker, who used them in "Crazeology," and, with Dizzy Gillespie, in "Anthropology" and "Shaw 'Nuff."[1] In "Ornithology" (a verbal reference to Parker's nickname), his model is Morgan Lewis's "How High the Moon"; in "Ko-Ko" (not to be confused with the Duke Ellington composition of the same name), Ray Noble's "Cherokee."

The practice, exemplified above, of fitting a preexisting framework of chord changes and period structure with a new melody, a faster tempo, and a different

---

1. Excerpts from "Anthropology" and "Shaw 'Nuff," preceded by the original score of "I Got Rhythm," are cited for teaching purposes in Charles Burkhart, ed., *Anthology for Musical Analysis*, 5th ed. (Fort Worth: Harcourt Brace College Publishers, 1994), 543–52.

title—a latter-day parody technique, if you will—was common in the bebop style, and is itself not the subject of this study.[2] The question to be explored here is why songs such as these have been attractive to improvisers, as opposed to the question of what may have accounted for their initial attractiveness as songs. Though there are no doubt other factors in the equation, much of the why and wherefore can be traced to two structural attributes: the linear progression and the linear intervallic pattern.

LINEAR PROGRESSION

A linear progression is a stepwise melodic motion, ascending or descending, that lies beneath the musical surface. The concept goes to the very heart of the theory of tonal structure set forth by Heinrich Schenker. Schenker's fundamental line, a stepwise descent from the third, fifth, or octave of the tonic scale, is in effect a linear progression at the deepest structural level, the background. Linear progressions proper, which occur in the middleground and foreground, may likewise span a third, fifth, or octave—indeed, they may replicate the fundamental line itself. They may also encompass other intervals: the fourth, the sixth, and occasionally the seventh.[3] To be valid in the Schenkerian sense, the interval spanned by a linear progression in any of the upper voices should be a part of the concurrently prolonged harmony. Linear progressions in the bass are somewhat different, tending instead to be connectors of harmonies.

Regardless of period or place of origin, there are melodies that are eloquent and those that are not; and richness in linear progression is a major indication of melodic eloquence.

Most song refrains are built in units of eight measures, which in the beguines characteristic of Cole Porter become sixteen. A single linear progression can govern an entire period, as in "I've Got You Under My Skin," where, in the key of E♭, the descending octave from b♭[1] to b♭ (that is from the B♭ above to that below middle C) is traced over each of the refrain's two A sections (mm. 1–16 and 17–32). Despite the change of scale occasioned by the momentary diversion to C major in the second of these periods, the overall path traced by each remains the same. This path, an octave in both cases, would in Schenkerian terms be called an octave-progression—more specifically, a descending octave-progression (Ex. 1).

Another notable linear progression can be heard in the refrain of George and Ira Gershwin's "Love Walked In" (one of the very last songs they wrote together),

2. See John H. Wilson, "Great American Song Writers and the Be-Bop Revolution," *Music Theory: Explorations and Applications*, Duquesne University School of Music, 3 (1994): 27–33.

3. On linear progressions, see Heinrich Schenker, *Free Composition (Der freie Satz)*, trans. and ed. Ernst Oster (New York and London: Longman, 1979), 43–45, 73–82. See also Allen Forte and Steven E. Gilbert, *Introduction to Schenkerian Analysis* (New York and London: W. W. Norton, 1982), 235–49.

Example 1. Descending octave-progressions.

beginning with g¹ and culminating with e♭². These notes, both of the same duration and both accompanying the word "love," embrace the interval of a sixth. The result, in the above terminology, is an ascending sixth-progression: from g¹ to a¹ and b♭¹ (mm. 3–4), to c² and d² (mm. 7–8), and finally to e♭² (m. 9) (Ex. 2).[4]

The progressions in Examples 1 and 2 fulfill Schenker's definition in that the interval spanned by each one is structurally relevant to its harmonic support, namely the tonic triad of E♭. Other melodies are characterized by linear progressions that are as least as strong, anchored to other harmonic functions.

One of these is the refrain of "Fools Rush In" (1940) by Rube Bloom. At every other measure, starting with a¹ at m. 1, the tune's main pitches move downward along the tonic C-major scale with unflagging certainty, reaching d¹ on the downbeat of m. 9 (Ex. 3). The first time around, this line descends another step prior to changing register for the first ending on d². At its second statement, beginning in m. 17, the register change takes place immediately thereafter, with an arpeggiated ninth to e² followed by the close, d²–c². Both times this progression suggests a prolongation of II, in the chords that support it at start and finish, and in the interval encompassed by the descending line. The role of II is at once familiar and unexpected: as preparation for V on the one hand, and as the main event on the other.

---

4. A more detailed analysis appears in Steven E. Gilbert, *The Music of Gershwin* (New Haven and London: Yale University Press, 1995), 14.

Example 2. Ascending sixth-progression.

Hoagy Carmichael's "Stardust," sounding quite modern for 1929, also begins on a dominant preparation—not II exactly, but IV with an added sixth. Here too, amidst the celebrated surface meanderings of this famous melody, there is a descending linear progression. As with "Fools Rush In," in the same key of C, the progression spans a fifth—not a^1–d^1 defining II, but d^2–g^1 defining V, which supports the progression at its conclusion (Ex. 4).[5]

Examples 1 through 4, all abstracted from great tunes in the literal sense, exhibit differences that affect the suitability of their respective sources for jazz improvisation. In the colloquial sense in which jazz players use the term, two of these songs are better "tunes"—and of those two, one is better still. The crucial factor in these differences is the other concept to be addressed in this study: the linear intervallic pattern.

LINEAR INTERVALLIC PATTERN

A linear intervallic pattern is a repeating succession of vertical intervals, typically between the outer voices, or between the bass and a prominent inner voice.[6] Also typically, a linear intervallic pattern will involve a stepwise progression in at least one of its components. Most germane to the present discussion are the patterns that alternate sevenths and tenths, 7–10 and 10–7. These patterns can and do often work together. In an excerpt from classical music, an episode from a Mozart rondo (Ex. 5),[7] the tenths formed by descant and bass are accompanied by sevenths in alto and

---

5. For a complete discussion, see Allen Forte, *The American Popular Ballad of the Golden Era 1924–50* (Princeton: Princeton University Press, 1995), 275–83.

6. Schenker frequently drew attention to linear intervallic patterns in his analyses; the term, however, was first used by Allen Forte in *Tonal Harmony in Concept and Practice*, 2d ed. (New York: Holt, Rinehart & Winston, 1974); see ibid., 3d ed. (New York: Holt, Rinehart & Winston, 1978), 363–76. The topic is covered more completely in Forte and Gilbert, *Introduction to Schenkerian Analysis*, 83–102.

7. This example was previously cited in Forte and Gilbert, *Introduction to Schenkerian*

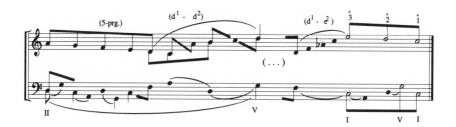

Example 3. Descending fifth-progression prolonging II.

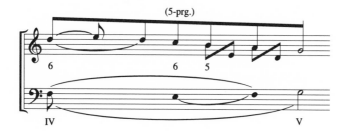

Example 4. Descending fifth-progression prolonging V.

bass, and vice versa. A second version of this pattern puts the descant down an octave, whereby it exchanges roles with the alto (Ex. 6).

The same pattern, extended to twice its original length, underlies the first half of the refrain of Jerome Kern's "All the Things You Are." This continuous 10–7 pattern occupies the first two A sections of the refrain's AABA form (Ex. 7a), while the bridge—the B section—is based on a closely related pattern, 7–10–7 (Ex. 7b). At the point where the reprise of the first A section departs from the original, a series of parallel tenths takes over, leading to the 10–7 of the final cadence (Ex. 7c). Another departure in these closing measures is that the upper component of the linear intervallic pattern shifts from the main thread of the melody to an inner voice.

An instance such as this, where a single linear intervallic pattern controls virtually an entire composition, is literally a textbook case (indeed, this article is not the first to cite it),[8] with the respective variants of the pattern each showing a different facet. If nothing else, example 7a illustrates the sheer downward force of the 10–7

Analysis, 96. Its source, Mozart's Rondo in F major, K. 494, is usually performed as the finale of a sonata whose first two movements have their own Köchel number, 533. The caption "K. 533, III" in Forte and Gilbert is not quite accurate in that regard.

8. Without mentioning it by name, Jerry Coker uses "All the Things You Are" as a model for improvisation in *Improvising Jazz* (Englewood Cliffs, N.J.: Prentice-Hall, 1964), 58–59.

Example 5. a) Mozart: Rondo in F major, K. 494, mm. 95–99; b) Linear intervallic pattern 7–10 (over 10–7).

Example 6. Linear intervallic pattern 10–7 (over 7–10).

pattern, which was evidently so strong that the composer continued it for the second A section instead of starting over. Here the pattern persists independently of whether the tenths and sevenths are major or minor. The same holds for example 7c, whose closing half additionally illustrates how a linear intervallic pattern can operate without an accompanying melodic sequence.

    Intervallic quality is a factor, however, in Example 7b, whose 10–7–10 pattern, in each of its two iterations, is minor tenth–minor seventh–major tenth. These intervals

Donald Johns cites the entire refrain as an exemplar of "*Funnel* Tonality in American Popular Music, ca. 1900–70," *American Music* 11, no. 4 (1993): 466–67. And John H. Wilson cites its reincarnation as the jazz composition "Prince Albert" in "Great American Song Writers," 30. Most recently, "All the Things You Are" is covered in Forte, *American Popular Ballad*, 73–79.

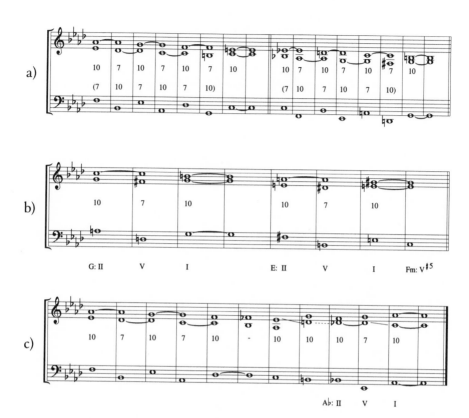

Example 7. a) Linear intervallic patter 10–7 (over 7–10); b) Linear intervallic pattern 10–7–10; c) Reprise of (a) and final cadence.

correspond to the harmonic progression II–V–I, with I being a temporary, major tonic; the latter, in this instance, proceeds at the interval of the minor third, from G to E.

The same pattern is operative in another exemplary standard, described by Alec Wilder as "virtually the 'bop' hymn," and as what "for years. . .was the most played tune in jazz."[9] Composed by Morgan Lewis in 1940 for the Broadway revue *Two for the Show*, "How High the Moon," as mentioned earlier, served as the structural source for "Bird" Parker's self-signatory parody piece, "Ornithology." Flatting the third of the tune's initial G-major tonic produces the minor tenth of the first 10–7–10; applying the same procedure to the latter (major) tenth gives rise to the next representation of 10–7–10. The two in succession produce a descending chromatic scale

9. Alec Wilder, *American Popular Song: The Great Innovators, 1900–1950* (New York: Oxford University Press, 1972), 502.

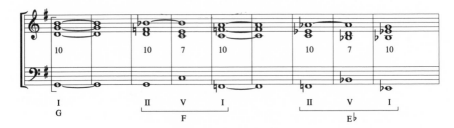

Example 8. Linear intervallic pattern 10–7–10 in sequence.

in the descant against whole steps in the bass (Ex. 8). By way of comparison, example 7b has descending whole steps supported by a harmonic descent of a minor third.

With the pattern 10–7–10 as a building block, Examples 7b and 8 produce two distinct, but related results. The latter, drawn from the main body of a song as opposed to the bridge, is the more fertile of the two. "How High the Moon" may be its most famous representation, and is certainly exemplary in its melodic focus on the chromatically descending line—a feature that also comes through in its derivative, "Ornithology," whose head opens with a sequence of arpeggiations emphasizing first b^1, then bb^1, a^1, ab^1, and g^1. This is identical to the opening melodic thread of "How High the Moon," whose path subsequently reverses itself with the ascending progression g^1–a^1–bb^1–b^1. The last two notes, the lone chromaticism in this otherwise diatonic figure, relate quite obviously to the conflict between B♮ and B♭ at the very beginning of the song.

FUNCTIONAL HARMONY

A key property of the linear intervallic pattern is its ability to go on indefinitely. And though one may label each vertical with a roman numeral, it is typically when the pattern ceases or changes that real harmonic movement takes place. The pattern in Example 5, from the Mozart rondo, prolongs F minor through its fourth measure, after which it dissolves in a weak progression to A♭. Example 7, from "All the Things You Are," also lands on A♭ eventually, but in a vastly different, more significant way. There too, the progression to A♭ involves a departure from the original pattern.

The return of 10–7–10 in an inner voice, accompanying the II–V–I that marks the final cadence, subtly evokes the common thread that ties the A and B sections together. Yet the above discussion reveals a basic difference despite the obvious relatedness of the two patterns: namely, that 10–7 (like the reverse pattern, 7–10) operates without regard to specific intervallic quality and harmonic function, while 10–7–10 tends toward just the opposite. Indeed, it is this link with harmonic progression that most likely accounts for its prevalence in a wide variety of compositions that have proved hospitable to jazz improvisation.

"Cherokee," written two years before "How High the Moon" by the British bandleader Ray Noble, is an equally good example. Also a jazz favorite, "Cherokee" was the source for another Parker parody, "Ko-Ko" (not to be confused with the Duke Ellington piece of the same name, to which it bears no relation). Its bridge, which works its way from a rather audacious B major back to the dominant of the home key of B♭, is built on a sequence parallel to the one used in "How High the Moon." Here as well, the local II–V–I resolutions produce a bass that descends in whole tones—now one step further, resulting in the span of a tritone (resolutions on B, A, G, F) instead of a major third (Ex. 9). But while the 10–7–10 pattern may still be found between the bass and an inner voice, the ambitus of the descant is oriented around the ninth above the bass.

This last feature, particularly when combined with the abrupt change from a scale with flats to one with sharps, makes the bridge of "Cherokee" a striking aural event, signaling a potential new direction for popular songs and for the improvisations they would inspire. An outstanding and universally admired example is David Raksin's motion-picture theme "Laura" (1945), fitted with lyrics by Johnny Mercer.[10]

"Laura" opens with a progression almost identical to the bridge of "Cherokee." It starts on a different pitch level and adds chromatic passing notes in the descant; otherwise it is the same both vertically and horizontally (Ex. 10). It differs in its position relative to the song's home key (C major), which, like that of "All the Things You Are," is not reached until the very end.[11] Not least, it shows how an underlying linear intervallic pattern, the 10–7–10 between inner voice and bass, can persist past the point where the melodic sequence in the descant ends. It also extends into the second of the four sections of the refrain, whose form (like "Fools Rush In" and "How High the Moon") is ABAC rather than AABA.

One must keep in mind, meanwhile, that performance practice plays a much larger role in popular song than in so-called art music, where the score we see is a fair blueprint of the sound we get. Even a straightforward interpretation of a standard takes liberties unheard of in the world of classical music: notes are characteristically sung ahead of the beat, and even the most respecting of pianists will impart a few personal stylistic touches. George Gershwin, for example—obviously a stylistically faithful interpreter of his own music—meant something similar when he wrote, "Playing my songs as frequently as I do at private parties, I have naturally been led to compose numerous variations upon them, and to indulge the desire for complication and variety that every composer feels when he manipulates the same material over and over again."[12]

---

10. Wilder, *American Popular Song*, 514–15.

11. Like "All the Things You Are," "Laura" gets special attention in Donald Johns, "*Funnel* Tonality." See p. 461 along with Johns's Example 7, p. 464. The latter shows a parallel between the openings of "Laura" and Beethoven's Piano Sonata, op. 53 ("Waldstein").

12. Preface to *George Gershwin's Song Book* (New York: Simon & Schuster, 1932), reprinted on the inside front cover of *Gershwin at the Keyboard: 18 Song Hits Arranged by the Composer* (New York: Warner Brothers Publications [n.d.]).

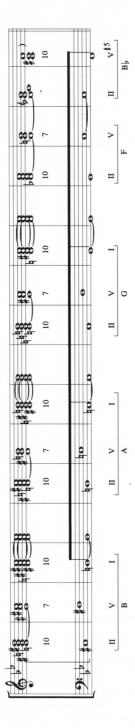

Example 9. Linear intervallic pattern 10–7–10 in sequence.

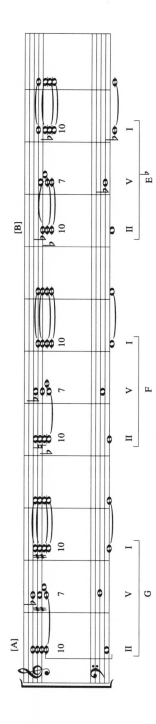

Example 10. Linear intervallic pattern 10–7–10 in sequence.

In the common practice of jazz and popular piano technique, the key result of this tendency is not complication so much as it is clarification, with voicings and chord changes that are readily understood by the players with whom one performs. The concept of the linear intervallic pattern, though not articulated as such in popular music parlance, is vital—as witness the prominent 7–10s in the left hand of the great bebop pianist Bud Powell (who played both "Cherokee" and its Parker parody "Ko-Ko").

The 7–10 pattern is at the heart of the local progression II–V, which pervades the mainstream of jazz and popular piano style. One may well "learn" a tune—by ear or through a lead sheet in a fake book[13]—without ever having seen the original sheet music. And the more modern tunes (that is, post-bebop or post-1950, certainly those post-1960), particularly those intended expressly for jazz, tend to be composed with this reality in mind. "Joy Spring," by trumpeter Clifford Brown (1930–56), a bebop player of a slightly later generation, uses II–V to effect a rapid shift from F to G♭ for the first and second A sections respectively.[14] The bridge begins in G major with the same progression as "How High the Moon" through its fifth downbeat on E♭, after which it changes course to move to G♭ and back to the home key of F—all by means of the local II–V–I and the concomitant 10–7–10 (Ex. 11).

Of the four songs cited for their linear progressions (Ex. 1–4), only the first, "I've Got You Under My Skin," is of comparable interest vertically. "Fools Rush In" (Ex. 3) abounds in the II–V–I progression—indeed, is governed by it at the deepest level—but the pattern mostly repeats its resolution on the tonic, moving only to the closely related functions of submediant and dominant.

On the other side of the ledger, "Love Walked In" and "Stardust" are lacking in either the use or the applicability of linear intervallic patterns. Melodically perfect as written, they are best suited to straightforward performance. At the same time, there is a place in jazz literature for a ballad that remains recognizable, albeit embellished. Charlie Parker never composed a bebop parody for Gershwin's "Embraceable You" or for Rodgers and Hart's "I Didn't Know What Time It Was," for example, although he gave memorable interpretations of both.

Victor Young's "Stella by Starlight" (1946), with lyrics by Ned Washington, compares with David Raksin's "Laura" in a number of ways. Young, a violinist, moved to Hollywood in 1935 and, like Raksin, built a career as a film composer.[15]

---

13. For decades, jazz performers have relied on lead sheets—melodies with chord symbols—collected in so-called fake books, whose quality, authenticity, and legality are often questionable. Probably the best and most widely used of these collections is *The Real Book* (n.p., n.d.), whose entries are in a uniform professional hand and represent a good cross-section of the mainstream jazz repertoire. Popular standards, of course, are most authentically represented by the original, fully notated sheet music. With tunes composed expressly for jazz, on the other hand, the lead sheet found in a fake book may well be all that was ever written down. In either event, one could argue that an accurate lead sheet in a well-circulated fake book is a fair representation of what most jazz players have at their disposal.

14. "Joy Spring," *The Real Book*, 246.

15. Young's theme song for the 1950s television series *Medic* was very popular at that time,

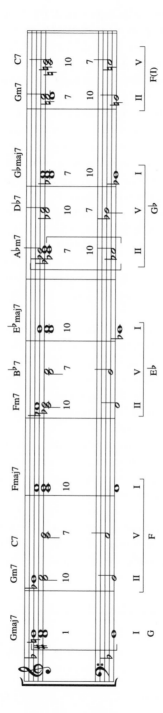

Example 11. Linear intervallic pattern 10–7–10 in sequence.

"Stella" attained considerable respect among jazz musicians, from Harry James, who first played it, to Miles Davis in his vintage years (see his recording with pianist Herbie Hancock in *My Funny Valentine*). It shares with "Laura" (and for that matter, "All the Things You Are") the trait of confirming the tonic with its final cadence and not before;[16] likewise, it abounds in linear intervallic patterns of sevenths moving to tenths and vice versa.

What makes "Stella by Starlight" unique is the way its local II–V and II–V–I progressions engage in a virtual free association through three of its four eight-bar periods (Ex. 12). Only the last eight measures (the A' in an unusual ABCA' form) conform as a whole to a consistent harmonic sequence—and that, in contrast to the setting of the same melodic material in the A section, is a perfectly regular, descending cycle of fifths leading to the final B♭ tonic.

The schema in Example 12, a realization of the chord symbols above the staff,[17] focuses on the successions of tenths and sevenths that form the common thread throughout the refrain. There is, at any given time, at least one 7–10 or 10–7–10 pattern in effect. Every bass note is involved in either a local II–V or II–V–I, with the sole exception of ♭VII–I, which occurs twice on the tonic (A♭7–B♭maj7) and once on the dominant (E♭7–Fmaj7). The former constitute the only tonic arrivals prior to the refrain's final cadence.

Delayed tonics, linear intervallic patterns, discrete and interlocked II–V progressions—all of these contribute to a tune's success. Adding prefixes to applied dominants is so widespread in jazz, and in compositions intended for jazz performance, that to say drawing attention to it at this late date is anticlimactic would be an understatement. Far less attention, on the other hand, has been directed toward the elemental contrapuntal tension and release of the 7–10 pattern (and its variants) as the principal force behind these ostensibly harmonic progressions—and that, it is hoped, is where this essay has made some small contribution.

The answer to the question posed at the outset remains elusive. John Coltrane, whose style in the decade before his death in 1967 evolved from an advanced form of bebop to a very personal kind of free jazz, recorded his own "Giant Steps" in 1959, in which a sequence of II–V–I resolutions moves up an octave by successive major thirds.[18] The fast pace of information in this tune contrasts with Coltrane's hypnotic recasting of Rodgers and Hammerstein's "My Favorite Things" (current at the time he first recorded it, in 1960) over a tonic vamp. There he was likely drawn to the

---

both in and out of context. It was known in the latter capacity, with lyrics, as "Blue Star," although I heard an entertainer once quip that "Blue Cross" would have been more appropriate.

16. It is, in other words, an example of what Donald Johns, in the article cited in note 8, calls "funnel tonality."

17. *The Real Book*, 408.

18. See Joe Brumbeloe, "Symmetry, Ambiguity and John Coltrane's *Giant Steps*," *Music Theory: Explorations and Applications* 3 (1994): 34–44.

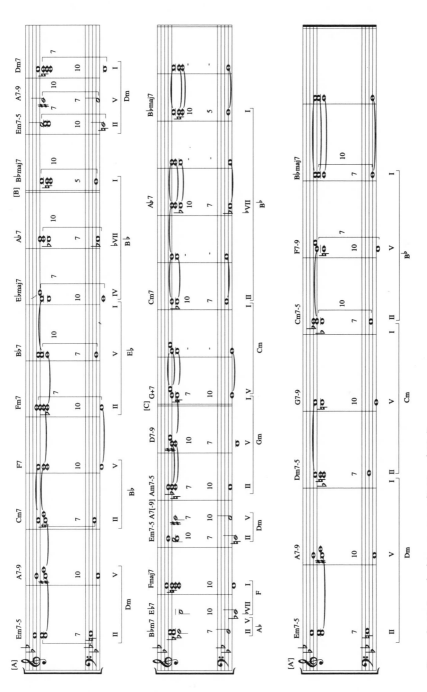

Example 12. Interlocking patterns 7–10 and 10–7.

angular melodic profile, whose fourths and fifths were extended, linked in various combinations, in his improvisation. Perhaps not coincidentally, the same intervals prevail in Sigmund Romberg's "Softly, As in a Morning Sunrise" (1928), a much older song with stronger European ties, recorded by Coltrane in 1961.

Bitonality, Pentatonicism, and Diatonicism in a Work by Milhaud

Daniel Harrison

D
arius Milhaud wrote his Second Chamber Symphony, subtitled "Pastorale," in 1918 during a return voyage to France after a stint in Brazil as a diplomatic secretary. The work is scored for string quartet augmented by flute, english horn, and bassoon. The first movement, all of thirty-three measures played at a rapid tempo, is a wonderfully vital piece, formally and rhythmically straightforward and without any pretense to complexity. Its pitch organization appears to have that distinctively bitonal sound image—the "double exposure" of structures from two different pitch centers—but this procedure discloses itself with only minimal analytic coaxing, so one might be able quickly to dispense with basic questions of large-scale pitch relations. All in all, the piece was neither intended nor received as an important intellectual achivement in twentieth- century composition. Indeed, considering the subtitle, adjectives such as "unsophisticated," "rustic," and perhaps even "earthy" could be deemed adequate descriptions of the piece.

Bitonality, so breezily invoked above, invites more searching investigation, if only because it has been subjected to such persistent ridicule by contemporary music theorists. Peter van den Toorn has gone so far as to dismiss it as one of the "horrors of the musical imagination," then beckoning in a footnote for Benjamin Boretz and Allen Forte to pile on.[1] Some of this ridicule surely arises from the association of bitonal music in the past with perverse pleasure and wit. Hugo Riemann, for example, recounted "with great amusement" Max Reger's playing the D-major Freischütz Waltz in the right hand while playing a C-major "Ach, du lieber Augustin" in the left.[2] Perhaps another source of disdain is the sense that bitonality is a very cheap way to create "modern," dissonant effects. Write some ditty in one key, write the accompaniment in another, and *voilà*—something that sounds as "bad" as the most studiously

---

1. Peter van den Toorn, "Some Characteristics of Stravinsky's Diatonic Music," *Perspectives of New Music* 14, no. 1 (Fall-Winter 1975): 105. Van den Toorn refers to Allen Forte's *Contemporary Tone-Structures* (New York: Columbia Teachers College Press, 1955), 137, and to Benjamin Boretz's "Metavariations: Part IV, Analytic Fallout," *Perspectives of New Music* 11, no. 1 (Fall-Winter, 1972): 149.

2. See Robert W. Wason and Elizabeth West Marvin, "Riemann's 'Ideen zu einer "Lehre von den Tonvorstellungen"': An Annotated Translation," *Journal of Music Theory* 36 (1992): 90.

atonal utterance of a real, hard-working composer.[3] Lastly, those who find bitonality compositionally meretricious can implicate those analysts whose efforts culminate in identifying the keys involved in a bitonal piece, as if this accomplishment were something more significant than identifying the one key of some tonal piece.

This last issue appears to open up the problem somewhat, since it exposes an unnecessary link between a compositional procedure of admittedly simple means and analytic efforts that are thought to be appropriate to it—that is, simplistic and artless. But to uncover compositional procedure is one thing; to analyze the effects and results of this procedure, as well as the conditions under which it flourishes, is quite another. The unfolding and deployment of the two centers perceived to be responsible for a bitonal composition—or of the combined tonal structure that these two centers create—is something rarely investigated. Bitonality, in other words, is quite under-theorized.[4]

Milhaud's Chamber Symphony movement thus invites analysis because it inhabits a particularly interesting bitonal environment, one much richer than that offered by "Ach du lieber Augustin" in one key and the Freischütz waltz in another. One source of its bitonal richness is the continually varying degree of "bi," while another results from ontological problems with the piece's "tonality." These matters are investigated by focusing first upon the melodic pitch material of the movement, which shares a common generating impulse that is channeled in various ways. Harmonic deployment of this material is then examined, which brings us to consider bitonal matters in the abstract. Finally, potentialities discussed in the previous sections are measured against compositional actuality—that is, we inquire into the way in which the precompositional tonal system set up by Milhaud is manifested in the piece.

MELODIC PITCH MATERIAL

The pitch-class material for the first movement of the symphony is based primarily on sets generated from cyclic application of T_5 (or T_7) operations. The pitch-class sets that result from this procedure will be called "5-cycle" sets, and the set of 5-cycle sets will be called the "5-cycle series." The trichordal through nonachordal elements are 3–9, 4–23, 5–35, 6–32, 7–35, 8–23, and 9–9. The 5-cycle series is symmetric, meaning that for any set class in the series, its complement is also in the series. This prop-

---

3. See William Thomson, *Schoenberg's Error* (Philadelphia: University of Pennsylvania Press, 1991), 14.

4. Some theoretical and analytical literature concerning bi- and polytonality includes Milhaud's own, somewhat unhelpful article "Polytonalité et Atonalité," *Revue Musicale* 4, no. 4 (1923): 29–44; Keith W. Daniel, "A Preliminary Investigation of Pitch-Class Set Analysis in the Atonal and Polytonal Works of Milhaud and Poulenc," *In Theory Only* 6, no. 6 (1982): 22–48; and Ann K. McNamee, "Bitonality, Mode, and Interval in the Music of Karol Szymanowski," *Journal of Music Theory* 29 (1985): 61–84.

erty results from the fact that 5-cycling from any starting pitch class eventually touches upon all twelve pitch classes. Stopping a 5-cycle at some point thus means creating a two-partition of the twelve-pitch-class aggregate into a 5-cycle set and its complement, which, by definition, is also a 5-cycle set.

Of the 5-cycle sets listed above, two are of great significance in traditional pitch-centered contexts: the diatonic collection, 7–35; and its complement, the anhemitonic pentatonic collection, 5–35. Although Milhaud composes a few straightforward diatonic and pentatonic figurations in the movement, we will find consistent use of many other 5-cycle sets, which implies a blurring of the distinction between pentatonic and diatonic collections. In fact, Milhaud often deploys the 5-cycle pitch material, as well as related material to be discussed below, in such a way as to problematize or even to prevent the formation of a sure tonal center.

Example 1, which shows the melody and bass for the opening phrase (without accompanying parts), provides a glimpse into the issue. Note that, for the bass in particular, it is difficult to pin down the "key" which would establish one of the two tonalities of the bitonal context. Position-finding[5] produces a number of candidates, and the three-note cycle occurring in a two-beat meter spreads the phenomenal accents around so that no one of the three notes is more accentually privileged than any other. To be sure, the role of A in both flute and bass invites comment, and I will address it—extensively, as it turns out—in due course. But, for this excerpt at least, we discover that the tonalities implicated in in the term "bitonality" may not be keys in a traditional sense, or in the sense that, say, the Freischütz waltz and "Ach, du lieber Augustin" are in keys.[6]

What about the bitonal aspect of the excerpt? The T_6 relationship between the opening figures of the flute and contrabass tunes seems primarily responsible. For one thing, the lack of common tones between the figures promotes their structural independence from each other, and, for another, the T_6 operation itself, from the standpoint of 5-cycle relationships, produces pitch-class relationships of maximum separation within the cycle. To these somewhat abstract reasons must be added a more concrete one that is a perhaps the cause (instead of a result) of the T_6 relationships: Milhaud deployed the pitches of the two figures so as to create pungent harmonic dissonances—an augmented fourth between the first pair of notes, a major seventh between the second pair, and a minor second between the third. In fact, with one exception, such harmonic dissonances—decidedly *not* part of the harmonic vocabulary of the 5-cycle series—occur on every strong beat of the phrase until the unison A of m. 4.[7]

---

5. This term was coined by Richmond Browne, "Tonal Implications of the Diatonic Set," *In Theory Only* 5, nos. 6–7 (July-August 1981): 3–21.

6. Daniel ("A Preliminary Investigation," 23) notes that "Milhaud tended to employ simple, folklike, diatonic melodies throughout his career."

7. The downbeat of m. 3 has a bass G set against a flute D♯. Although the spelling indicates a dissonance here (an augmented fifth)—one, moreover, that *sounds* like a dissonance in the context of the passage—this interval is enharmonically equivalent to the consonant minor sixth. The other harmonic dissonances mentioned in the passage do not have consonant equivalents.

Example 1. Chamber Symphony No. 2, I, mm. 1–4. This example was rerendered by University of Rochester Press from Milhaud 2. SYMPHONIE "Pastorale." Copyright 1922 by Universal Edition. Copyright renewed. All Rights Reserved. Used by permission of European American Music Distributors Corporation, sole US and Canadian agent for Universal Edition.

SERIES DERIVED FROM THE 5-CYCLE SERIES

The A at the end of the phrase is hardly a dissonance. What is more, its appearance in the flute tune is completely unexpected; for after sounding its initial 3–7, the flute melody begins to follow along the 5-cycle path, first forming 4–23 and then 5–35. Continuing along this path past the pentatonic collection would bring it to 6–32 by means of either A♯ or E, with the latter being more tonally satisfying given the context of the tune. The A in the flute at m. 4 surprises both harmonically and melodically. The harmonic result is to affirm A as the pitch center of the contrabass 3–7, which its initial, accented appearance in m. 1 had tentatively requested. The melodic result is rather less clear since the motivation for A's appearance is obscure. It is as if the flute tune were forced to conform to the A center of the bass.

The 6–33 the A creates, as well as other set classes used in the movement (including the opening 3–7), are related to the 5-cycle set classes in a remarkably consistent way, which Figure 1 reveals. The 5-cycle member sets from 3–9 to 9–9 are shown in the left column, with their interval vectors placed in the center column. The following typographical conventions are used in the notation of the 5-cycle interval vectors:

> 1. Underlined digits in the interval-class (ic)5 position in the vector highlight the generative role which that interval class plays in the formation of the series; a continual and integral increase in ic5 value is an obvious indication of the the serial cycling of ic5s that creates the series.
> 2. Boldfaced "1"s, which appear in various ic positions in the vector up to 7–35, denote ics that appear for the first time in the series. Each 5-cycling up to 7–35 brings about a hitherto unused ic.

In the right column is another series of sets whose interval vectors are aligned with those of the 5-cycle in the middle column. The typographical conventions for this series are different.

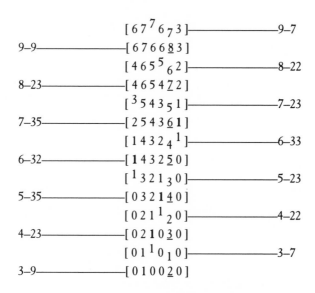

Figure 1. Interval vectors of 5-cycle set members and related sets.

1. The subscripted digit in the ic5 position in the interval vector shows that, compared to the 5-cycle set of the same cardinality, which appears immediately below, the set in question is down one ic5 value.

2. The superscripted digit appearing in various ic positions shows a new ic salient compared to the 5-cycle set of the same cardinality.

For example, comparing 3–9 with 3–7, we see that 3–7 has an ic5 value of 1 while 3–9 has an ic5 value of 2. It can be useful to think that the value "debited" from ic5 is used to "credit" another ic value. Thus, the value taken from ic5 in 3–9 is given to ic3 in 3–7, and so on up the figure. Notice that each debit from an ic5 account credits an ic value that would appear for the first time in the next 5-cycle set, hence the alignment of bold- face 1s in the 5-cycle sets with superscripted digits from sets in the right column. The right-column series thus contains what might be called "anticipatory" set classes between members of the 5-cycle set, in that they prepare the introduction of new ics in the 5-cycle set up to 7–35. Because it derives from 5-cycle relationships, the series in the right column will be called the (5-cycle) "first derivative series."[8]

---

8. An identical situation, *mutatis mutandis*, obtains with respect to the 1–cycle series, which involves an integral increase in ic1 values and new ic saliants appearing successively at ic2, 3, 4, 5 and 6 as set-class cardinality increases. A 1–cycle first derivative series can be constructed along the same lines as the 5-cycle derivative series. Considerations of space, as well as the limited relevance of this matter to the to the present compositional context, discourage its further exploration in this essay.

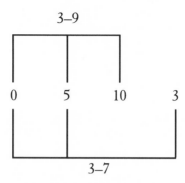

Figure 2. Comparison of 5-cycle structure for 3–9 and 3–7.

Another way to view the relationship between the two series is to recognize that, from the standpoint of cyclic generation, the first derivative series skips over what would be the first or last pitch class in some 5-cycle operation and alights instead on the next pitch class, as Figure 2 illustrates, using 3–7 and 3–9 as examples. The skipping over accounts for the lowering of the ic5 content compared to the 5-cycle set, and the alighting upon the next pitch class in the series accounts for the salient created in the other area of the interval vector, since the pitch class in question will appear in the next generation of the 5-cycle series.

An outstanding feature of the derivative series that deserves comment is subset relationships, which are shown in Table 1. Sets in the 5-cycle series are shown in the leftmost column. The top row contains sets from the two series—roman for a 5-cycle series, and bold for a first derivative series. The digits beneath each series set indicate the number of times distinct forms of a series set are found in the pertinent 5-cycle set listed in the leftmost column. It is perhaps surprising to note that 5-cycle subsets of 5-cycle supersets are not the most prevalent; the sets in the derivative series are.[9] The effect of this scarcity in distinct 5-cycle subset forms is to increase the (potential) structural prominence of the derivative-series subsets. That is, a set such as 3–7 can be heard as being more suggestive of the sound of, say, 7–35 than 3–9 because 7–35 has many more distinct 3–7s than 3–9s. This description harmonizes neatly with the portrayal above of sets from first derivative series as "anticipatory" of 5-cycle sets.

At this point, we have related all the sets in Example 1 to an underlying 5-cycle principle. Set classes in roman type are 5-cycle sets, and those in bold are first derivative sets. A more complex passage, shown in Example 2, brings other sets and issues to the fore. Use of sets from the two series, which are again notated in roman (5-cycle) and bold (derived), is frequent and deep. Two other set types manifest them-

---

9. The fact that 5-cycle sets have two degrees of symmetry, while derivative sets have only one, is responsible for this state of affairs.

Table 1. Subset relationships in 5-cycle and First Derivative Series

	3–9	3–7	4–23	4–22	5–35	5–23	6–32	6–33	7–35	7–23
4–23	2	2								
5–35	3	4	2	2						
6–32	4	6	3	4	2	2				
7–35	5	8	4	6	3	4	2	2		
8–23	6	10	5	8	4	6	3	4	2	2
9–9	7	12	6	10	5	8	4	6	3	4

selves. The major triad, 3–11, is used at two different levels of transposition, although, in both cases, the triads emphasize an underlying 3–7 root motion.[10] (Notice, for example, the coordination of flute and english horn with the bassoon.) It is tempting in the present context to capitalize on the fact that 3–11 can be construed as a member of a series defined by taking two skips after the first pitch class in a 5-cycle series (that is, 0,[5],[10],3,8), which opens up the possibility for yet another derived series. Milhaud's piece does not require such a gambit, although the theoretical issues involved are absorbing.[11] Another, special pitch-class set is marked in the bass part—special because it is quite dissimilar to the sets of the 5-cycle and derived series. Throughout the piece, such melodic "rogue" sets appear occasionally in various parts. They are all of different set classes and cardinalities, and their purpose appears to be one of contrast and relief, although, in the uniformly thick texture of the movement, it is hard for the rogue sets to make themselves heard.

HARMONIC RELATIONSHIPS AMONG 5-CYCLE AND DERIVED SERIES

Bitonality in this piece, when it appears as an obvious structural component, essentially results from a double projection of 5-cycle and related sets, by which I mean that the melodic pitch material discussed above is focused along two segments of a 5-cycle. In light of comments above about the difficulties in determining pitch centers for various 5-cycle sets, I pointedly avoid the image of focusing upon two *points* of a 5-cycle, which terminology would imply that these points were, in fact, pitch centers or tonics. 5-cycle material in general (set class 7–35 in particular) is the stuff from which keys and tonics are made; in this piece, however, it is deployed so as to avoid

---

10. This feature will be discussed in connection with Figure 3 below.

11. A brief and tantalizing report can suffice here. A derivative series defined by taking two skips after the first pc in a 5-cycle series is, in contrast to the first derivative series, not symmetric. The set classes in question are: 3–11, 4–14, 5–29, 6–Z47, 7–27, 8–26, and 9–7. However, the complements to these sets are found in a series formed by taking *one skip after the second pc* in a 5-cycle series: 3–7, 4–26, 5–27, 6–Z25, 7–29, 8–14, and 9–11.

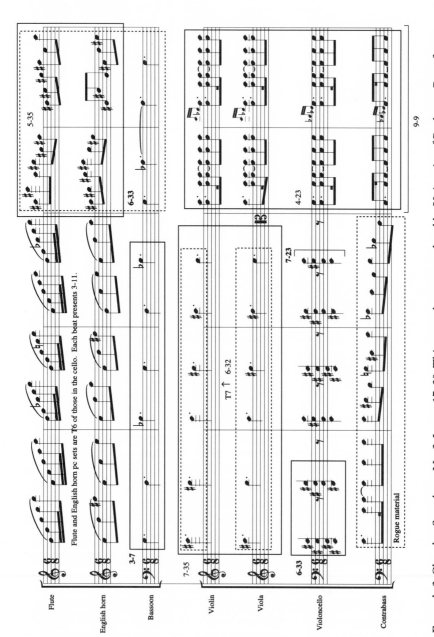

Example 2. Chamber Symphony No. 2, I, mm. 17–20. This example was rerendered by University of Rochester Press from Milhaud 2. SYMPHONIE "Pastorale." Copyright 1922 by Universal Edition. Copyright renewed. All Rights Reserved. Used by permission of European American Music Distributors Corporation, sole US and Canadian agent for Universal Edition.

creating keys and central tonal points. In their stead are tonal regions without sure centers.

The two 3–7s in Example 1, for instance, were discussed as such regions without centers. Their double projection resulted from T_6 separation between them. The same T_6 relationship also is found between the woodwinds and cello sets—3–11 both—in Example 2. From the standpoint of 5-cycle set structure, as well as set structure of the derived series, a T_6 relationship between sets ensures maximum distance between clusters of series fragments, resulting in maximum pitch-class variance among T_6 related sets. A T_1 relationship results in the next largest gap between series fragments, and there are important T_1 relationships to be found in the piece, as Figure 3 below will illustrate. But from the standpoint of *harmonic* relationships in this piece, T_6 is superior to T_1 because the tritone (that is, T_6 of some pitch class) is a common harmonic interval in musical styles in which 5-cycle relationships figure prominently—such as diatonic tonal music—whereas the semitone (T_1 [or T_{11}] of some pitch class) is not. In other words, T_6 can be used to create harmonic effects that have a "conservative," tonal cast to them, while T_1 can create effects of a more "radical" kind. T_6 has another advantage in the present context because it can create a single bitonal "signature set," 6–30, out of two trichords important to the piece, 3–7 and 3–11. Either of these trichords can form 6–30 if combined with itself at T_6.[12]

So far, bitonality seems a simple matter of applying T_6, T_1, or T_{11} to some 5-cycle series trichords. But the issues presented by Milhaud's piece are more complicated than that. Notice that the last two measures of Example 2 form a complete 5-cycle nonachord, 9–9. Where here is double projection? We encounter in this passage a consequence of Milhaud's composing with sets larger than trichords: as sets become larger and use more pitch-class space, the zone of separation between clusters of series fragments decreases. If the sets are sufficiently large, the zone disappears and, from a pitch-class perspective alone (that is, not attending to instrumentation or melodic presentation), bitonality essentially disappears, as happens at the end of Example 2.

The subsegmentation of those two measures suggests a way to preserve two clusters by creating a timbral zone of separation— that is, by attending to obvious 5-cycle structure of the string material (4–23 {7,9,0,2}) and counterposing that with the treble woodwinds material (5–35 {8,10,1,3,5}). The union of these two sets is the nonachord discussed above, their respective 5-cycle structures joined at 0 (from 4–23) and 5 (from 5–35). The fact that the two pitch-class sets—segmented by instrument class—do not intersect creates the possibility for maintaining two separate

---

12. This method of forming 6–30 from two 3–11s is used by Stravinsky in *Petrushka* (near the beginning of the Second Tableau, rehearsal 49) and is a kind of *locus classicus* of bitonality; Forte cites the passage in *The Structure of Atonal Music* (18), mentioning that it is "well known." Arthur Berger, in "Problems of Pitch Organization in Stravinsky" (*Perspectives of New Music* 2, no. 1 [Fall-Winter, 1963]: 22–24) would rather that it be understood as manifesting octatonic organization.

clusters of 5-cycle material, although the zone of separation is not determined by pitch-class content but by timbre.

Unfortunately, the results of employing this analytical tactic for the rest of the piece are disappointing, since Milhaud does not feel the need consistently to separate pitch-class clusters. This, of course, reproblematizes the already devious nature of bitonality in this piece, and we must now look more closely to relationships within the piece to discover more about its particular tonal structure.

RELATIONSHIPS IN THE PIECE

Discussion up to now has taken place without much structural context—that is, without really working with the actual compositional deployment of materials. This gambit has been prompted largely by the interesting abstract nature of the pitch structures involved—series, clusters, and the like. A structural diagram of the piece, shown in Figure 3, lays out other issues and places the discoveries discussed above in a richer compositional context.

The piece breaks out into rather small segments; some are a mere two or three measures long. These segments are defined by surface texture, figuration, or rhetorical gesture. They do not, in other words, involve changes in overall pitch-class content, which, as we have seen, is generally consistent in both melodic and harmonic dimensions throughout the piece. The segments are given conventional names describing their structural functions, the exception being "stasis," which describes the two segments where pedal tones and short figurational patterns put a brake on forward motion and prepare for the following transitional passages. The transitions mark the seams of an overall ternary design. The first consists of the solo contrabass run in mm. 15–16, and the second precedes the recapitulation in mm. 25 ff.

In the "motivic content" row of Figure 3, three recurring ideas are noted. "Tune" refers to the flute theme discussed in connection with Example 1. Its structural purpose is largely to make the ternary design obvious. The expression "3–7 on X" denotes a structure illustrated in Example 3, a bass line melodically unfolding set-class 3–7 accompanied by major triads that use the pitch classes of the 3–7 bass line as roots. The expression "5th stack(x)" refers to a salient presentation of harmonic perfect fifths, the "(x)" denoting how many such fifths are stacked. For example, "5th stack(3)," which is found in the mm. 20–21 segment, describes the harmonic 4–23 found in the string parts of Example 2.

Attending to the succession of fifth-stacking motives and correlating them with salient T_6 relationships allows us considerable refinement of our previous observations about harmonic relationships. The bitonal aspect of the piece—that is, the T_6 and T_1 relationships among 5-cycle and derived sets—is presented in the first two segments, the second actually involving simultaneous T_6 and T_1 relationships. Measures 9–12, however have no prominent T_6 or T_1 relationships and present instead the first fifth stack. In this passage, Milhaud shifts attention away from two separate

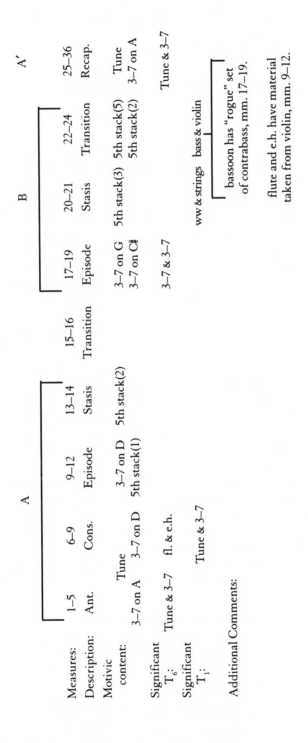

Figure 3. Structural Diagram, Chamber symphony No. 2, I.

Example 3. Definition of "3–7 on A" motive.

5-cycle clusters (bitonality) and towards the 5-cycle structure itself, made obvious by the fifth-stacking. It is instructive to investigate the pitch-class content of the passage, displayed in Figure 4, to see how this shift is made. A 5-cycle starting on pitch class 3 constitutes the row of integers, with the melodic content of each instrument (except for the cello's 3–11s over the contrabass's 3–7) marked by ticked brackets. Bitonality—that is, a double projection of 5-cycle sets—is not operative here because there is no zone of pitch-class separation. As was the case in Example 2, this lack of separation seems to promote instead the formation of chromatic aggregates. Unlike the situation in that passage, however, in which a resegmentation of the pitch-class material by timbre uncovered the double projection, in this passage there is no double projection; instead, bitonality seems to coast after the big push it received in the opening phrases, which is to say that Milhaud preserves aspects of the bitonal sound image but does not work towards a true bitonality. This reminiscence of bitonality is accomplished by heavily weighting certain parts of the complete 5-cycle and setting them against weakly weighted portions located at a distance of T_6. In particular, compare the weight given to {6,11,4,9,2} by the sounding of each pitch class by four different instruments to that given to {0,5,10,3}, in which each pitch class is sounded by only two instruments, except for pitch class 10, which is the sole property of the english horn.[13]

The mm. 13–14 segment, labeled "stasis" in Figure 3, has a structural profile similar to that in the previous segment in terms of pitch-class deployment: no zone of separation between sets, but enough coverage of the aggregate to be reminiscent of a bitonal sound image (see Fig. 5). In other words, as in the previous segement, perception of bitonality is still conditioned by the effects of the opening nine measures and not by the immediate pitch-class stimulus of mm. 13–14. Differences in pitch-class usage between the two segments are apparent, as some rogue sets (bassoon, english horn) appear along with sets from the derivative series (viola, flute). The "5th stack(3)" in the violin is represented by the 5-cycle set {4,9,2,7}.

The arc of the first section of the ternary form, mm. 1–14, thus appears to be one of an initially intense bitonality whose effects reverberate after the bitonal signal ceases in mm. 9–14. This relaxation is coincident with a gradual loss of forward momentum as the initial, clear-cut antecendent-consequent theme gives way to an episode and then to a static pedal-point passage. As echoes of the initial bitonal idea

---

13. Including the cello 3–11s does not substantially affect the sense of relative weighting.

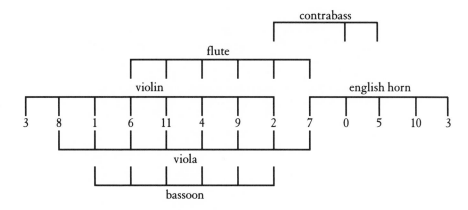

Figure 4. Pitch-class content of mm. 9–12.

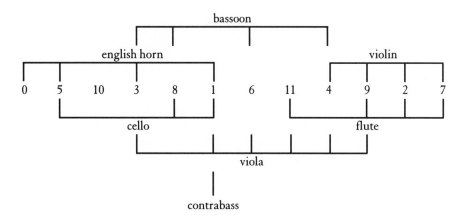

Figure 5. Pitch-class content of mm. 13–14.

and thematic structure die out, the 5-cycle pitch-class structure of the underlying tonal system is brought forward by means of fifth-stacking.

The contrabass solo in mm. 15–16 effects a transition between the first and second sections of the piece and, at the same time, re-energizes the T_6 relationship. The solo consists of an ascending scale (C♯ aeolian, but, in the present context, better described as 7–35) that starts on C♯ and concludes unexpectedly on G. The conclusion of the contrabass run elides with the beginning of the episode segment of mm. 17–19, which, along with mm. 20–21, appeared above as Example 2. In light of comments about the first section, we see in mm. 17–19 a renewal (and strengthening) of the bitonal idea by the double projection at T_6 of 3–7 motives, at C♯ and G—the two pitch classes emphasized by the contrabass run. But a similar process of bitonal entropy (that is, the strengthening of 5-cycle harmonic structure at the expense of bi-

Example 4. Chamber Symphony No. 2, I, mm. 22–24. This example was rerendered by University of Rochester Press from Milhaud 2. SYMPHONIE "Pastorale." Copyright 1922 by Universal Edition. Copyright renewed. All Rights Reserved. Used by permission of European American Music Distributors Corporation, sole US and Canadian agent for Universal Edition.

tonal structure) can also be uncovered here in the relationship of mm. 17–19 to mm. 20–21. In the latter measures, T_6 and T_1 are not operative, and a 5th–stack(3) occurs.

Although the segment in mm. 22–24 (Ex. 4) functions as a transition in terms of the overall ternary form, it also attempts a resolution of the 5-cycle and bitonal structural principles. By stacking five fifths in the string parts, Milhaud introduces a prominent T_1 relationship between lowest and highest elements in the stack, thereby co-opting it into the 5-cycle set principle. Each string chord forms the 5-cycle set 6–32.[14] Another compositional device makes an appearance here and is very striking in the context of this piece: material that appeared previously is reused. As Figure 3 noted, the bassoon repeats the "rogue" material that the contrabass had in mm. 17–19, and the top two woodwinds reuse the 5th–stack(2) material that the violin had in

14. On the last violin beat of m. 22, a G appears in the score, although it is most likely that this is a misprint for an intended G♯. Another misprint—more easily discerned because it is both suspect and does not appear in a later version of the figure—is a C♭ on the second eighth-note of m. 19; it should be a C.

mm. 9–12. Although reuse of material is about to be revealed as an important formal device in the next, recapitulatory segment, the particular form this device takes here is unusual; neither idea was especially prominent in its earlier manifestations, and neither is designed to integrate rhythmically or harmonically with what is happening in the strings. The incorporation of this material thus seems in service of the resolution of structural principles mentioned above. It represents in a concrete way the integration of different ideas, which concept is manifested in the integration of T_1 bitonality and 5-cycle set structure.

The recapitulation of the opening tune in mm. 25 ff. provides an obvious formal accent to the process of resolution just described. This time, the forcing of the tune into A at its conclusion is most clearly in the service of presenting A as the local pitch center, despite other, bitonal activity. This was suggested in the opening section, but it was not given time to solidify. Here, not only is the expected A given a boost by a thrice-avoided arrival, but, once it arrives in m. 33, all other instruments except the bassoon lock themselves into strong A- centered material, while the bassoon keeps alive a faint bitonal sound image by sounding E♭ and B♭, the T_6 and T_1 transforms, respectively, of A. At the final chord, the bassoon, too, settles into A.

CONCLUSION

A previous investigator, having found in various of Milhaud's works many of the same kinds of pentatonic, diatonic, and bitonal structures discussed in the present essay, concluded that pitch-class set theory was not a useful tool for analysis of Milhaud's music.[15] Here, I have argued to the contrary—that the theory is more than useful; the analytic employment of the theory, however, can be inappropriate. An important first step towards a good-faith analysis is to distinguish between bitonality as a parlor trick and bitonality as a complex set of abstract relationships among 5-cycle and related sets. As we have seen, these relationships can encounter problems in composition when buffer zones collapse and pitch-class space becomes saturated; the development of sophisticated compositional techniques thus becomes necessary to keep an established bitonal sound image reverberating after the source stops sending the signal.

These are not trivial matters, and the foregoing analysis of Milhaud's piece has opened up space for further, more searching investigations of the relevant abstract relationships and compositional techniques discovered here. I certainly will not use this opportunity to argue that the Chamber Symphony movement is now consecrated by complexity and can take its place alongside the atonal masterworks. The piece is, after all, a pastorale and—as the performance direction at the head of the score says—an expression of simple joy. But achieving this expression could hardly

---

15. Daniel, "A Preliminary Investigation," 27.

have been a simple matter; we should not assume that any observed degree of expressive complexity automatically reflects the same degree of technical complexity, or vice versa. Seriousness can always divulge any difficult technique that attends it; frolic, however, cannot. Milhaud's piece, with its surface simplicity, hides its machinery well. A more inviting summons for analysis is rarely found.

Signposts on Webern's Path to Atonality: The *Dehmel Lieder* (1906–08)

Robert W. Wason

I n a seminal study, Allen Forte has proposed an interpretation of Schoenberg's gradual move from tonal to atonal composition.[1] The present article, while it relies on analytical methods that are eclectic and relatively informal, has similar aims; and though of far more modest proportions than Forte's, it is part of a larger, ongoing effort to assess Webern's "path to atonality."[2] Because particular pieces of Schoenberg seem to have served as Webern's compositional models for much of his early music, Forte's subject and mine are closely related, even if our interpretations diverge. Webern's path to atonality certainly took essentially the same route as Schoenberg's, but since the younger composer was not carrying the weighty tonal baggage of his teacher, and his teacher's generation, he completed the journey much more quickly.

We have considerable evidence of the importance of vocal music in the transition from tonality to atonality. Webern and Schoenberg both spoke of the frequent dependence of early atonal works on texts or "programs."[3] And on the occasion of Dehmel's fiftieth birthday, Schoenberg wrote to him to say that "a Dehmel poem stands at almost every turningpoint in my musical development. . . ."[4] Indeed, Webern's vocal music has long been cited as a focal point of stylistic change throughout his career, and recent work continues to bear out the essential correctness of this view-

---

1. "Schoenberg's Creative Evolution: The Path to Atonality," *Musical Quarterly* 64, no. 2 (1978): 133–76.

2. The next installment of the story appears in my article "A Pitch-Class Motive in Webern's Op. 3 *George Lieder*," in *Webern Studies*, ed. Kathryn Bailey (Cambridge: Cambridge University Press, 1996), 111–34.

3. "All of the works created between the disappearance of tonality and the formulation of the new twelve-note law were short, strikingly short. The longer works written at the time were linked with a text which 'carried' them" (Anton Webern, *The Path to the New Music* [Bryn Mawr: Presser, 1963], 53). "I discovered how to construct larger forms by following a text or a poem. The differences in size and shape of its parts and the change in character and mood were mirrored in the shape and size of the composition . . ." (Arnold Schoenberg, "Composition with Twelve Tones (I)," in *Style and Idea*, ed. Leonard Stein [Berkeley and Los Angeles: University of California Press, 1984], 217).

4. Reinhard Gerlach, *Musik und Jugendstil der Wiener Schule, 1900–1908* (Laaber: Laaber Verlag, 1985), 175.

point, while filling in needed detail.[5] But if we look at the works that Webern himself designated for publication, with the intention of gaining a better understanding
of the transition from tonality to atonality, it is disappointing to find that only his
works op. 2 through op. 4—the choral work "Entflieht auf leichten Kähnen" (to a
George text) and the two groups of five *George Lieder*—offer us a window into this
period. The *Funf Sätze*, op. 5 (or at least the last four of them), mark the beginning of
Webern's "mature" atonal style. Further, even this limited sample becomes problematic when we consider one of the more dramatic results of recent Webern scholarship: the texts of the early music that have heretofore been taken as "authentic" were
revised by their author after he signed a contract with Universal in 1920 to publish
his early music. This is the music not only of the young, fledgling "atonal" composer,
but also of the seasoned professional adept at editing his works, and particularly
concerned with the sort of structural detail that his work with the new twelve-tone
method brought into strong focus.[6]

Fortunately, the music withheld by Webern but published in the sixties and
early seventies at the behest of Hans Moldenhauer is helpful in this study.[7] While
criticism could be (and much has been) directed at the nature and purpose of these
"performance" editions, and their (at best) uneven editorial policy, we can be thank-
ful for the public availability—in some form, at least—of works that both provide
additional detail with respect to Webern's composing on the borders of tonality and
atonality, and were not revised by their composer. The present study concentrates on

---

5. Anne C. Schreffler, "'Mein Weg geht jetzt vorüber': The Vocal Origins of Webern's
Twelve-tone Composition," *Journal of the American Musicological Society* 47 (1994): 275–339.

6. Elmar Budde dealt briefly with revisions to op. 3, no. 1 at the end of his *Anton Weberns
Lieder Op. 3* (Wiesbaden: Steiner, 1971). Soon thereafter Reinhold Brinkmann focused attention on the problem with his work on opp. 3 and 4; see "Die George-Lieder 1908/09 und
1919/23—ein Kapitel Webern-Philologie," in *Beiträge 1972/73*, Österreichische Gesellschaft
für Musik (Kassel/Basel: Bärenreiter, 1973). For a more recent study, see Felix Meyer's "Im
Zeichen der Reduktion; Quellenkritische und analytische Bemerkungen zu Anton Weberns
Rilke-Liedern op. 8" in *Quellenstudien I*, ed. Hans Oesch (Winterthur: Amadeus, 1991). Meyer
and I discussed the op. 8 revisions in our paper, "The Evolution of Webern's Op. 8" presented
at the Annual Meeting of the American Musicological Society in Oakland in 1990. Meyer
and Anne C. Schreffler have discussed revisions in various of the early pieces in "Rewriting
History: Webern's Revisions of His Early Works," a paper given at the International Musicological Society meeting in Madrid, 1992, "Webern's Revisions: Some Analytical Implications"
in *Music Analysis* 12 (1993): 355–80 and in "Performance and revision: the early history of
Webern's Four Pieces for violin and piano, Op. 7" in *Webern Studies* (see footnote 2), 135–69.
Wayne Alpern discusses analytical implications of Webern's revisions in his paper, "Aggre-
gation, Assassination, and an Act of God: The Impact of the Murder of Archduke Ferdinand
upon Webern's Op. 7, No. 3," presented at the Annual Meeting of the Society for Music
Theory, New York, 1995.

7. Hans and Rosaleen Moldenhauer, *Anton von Webern: A Chronicle of His Life and Work*
(New York: Alfred Knopf, 1979); see "Work List, Section B" for a complete list of posthumously published works.

five of the most important of these works dating from the crucial period, 1906 through 1908: the *Five Songs after Poems of Richard Dehmel*.[8] Thus we find out —not completely unexpectedly—that Dehmel's poetry stands at one of the "turning points" in Webern's compositional career as well.

Before getting into the songs themselves, a word must be said about the notion of recurrence of referential pitch material that I take to underlie much of Webern's music, in general, and that I shall stress in the present study. The word "signposts" in my title may be thought of as having a two-leveled significance: while the *Dehmel Lieder* are important signposts on Webern's path to atonality, the various referential entities we shall treat here are important signposts on the paths through each of these pieces. In the lectures he gave in the early 1930s Webern seems to have redis-covered the technique of repetition of referential collections in twelve-tone composi-tion: "The original form and pitch of the row occupy a position akin to that of the 'main key' in earlier music; the recapitulation will naturally return to it. We end 'in the same key!' This analogy with earlier formal construction is quite consciously fostered; here we find the path that will lead us again to extended forms."[9] It does seem that this compositional principle is almost—though not completely—absent in Webern's middle period music. There is no doubt, however, that referential pitch entities—which may take the form of particular referential pitch-classes, as well as particular intervallic shapes ("motives"), most often at "preferred" transpositional levels—are crucial to the understanding of the early "atonal" music. As with Schoenberg's early music, we move gradually along a continuum between "tonality" and "atonality"—not necessarily linearly nor without "regression," I might caution— to the extent that there often remains an important "tonal" dimension to the early

---

8. New York: Carl Fischer, 1966. The manuscripts for these pieces, unpublished in any other form, are in the Webern Collection of the Paul Sacher Foundation. Study and perfor-mance of the Carl Fischer edition of the Dehmel songs should be undertaken only after care-ful comparison of the score with Reinhard Gerlach's "Die Handschriften der Dehmel-Lieder von Anton Webern," *Archiv für Musikwissenschaft* 29, no. 2 (1972): 93–114, a complete critical report. There are significant questions and errors in the published edition of all five songs, though the scores are serviceable (corrections can be made without recopying the entire score; the most difficult error to correct in this fashion is a missing bar in number four; see fn. 20, below). Divergences between multiple "versions" of the same song (the case with numbers two and three, each of which exists in two manuscript versions) are problematic, since there was no final editing by Webern for publication. In the case of number three, one manuscript is incomplete and clearly preparatory to the other, complete one. The "first version" of num-ber two, however, is complete, and Gerlach includes it at the end of the critical report. (The printed edition is based upon the second, presumably "final" version.) For a discussion of the unusual status of these manuscripts that focuses on number two, see his "Kompositionsniederschrift und Werkfassung am Beispiel des Liedes 'Am Ufer' (1908) von Webern" in *Beiträge 1972/73,* Österreichische Gesellschaft für Musik (Kassel/Basel: Bärenreiter, 1973), 111–25.

9. Webern, *Path,* 54.

"atonal works;" and accordingly, analysis of these works should be more than simply tracking intervallic (motivic) shapes or unordered intervallic collections. We see the beginning of the process whereby motivic shapes replace conventional harmonies in the *Dehmel Lieder*: in the earliest song, stock cadential patterns become infused with idiosyncratic motivic shapes, lending them an individualized identity. The resulting idiosyncratic harmonic entities, to which I shall refer as "referential sonorities," begin to take over in the later songs, to the extent that the stock cadential patterns disappear, while the new motivic shapes move to the forefront.[10]

*   *   *

In our examination of the tonal structure of Webern's *Dehmel Lieder*, I shall proceed first to a brief review of the text, and Webern's interpretation of it, from which we can gain a sense of the overall structure of the song.[11] Even an analysis oriented towards tonal structure cannot avoid this first step, crucial when discussing the work of a composer who was extraordinarily sensitive to the declamation of the language, and for whom the text was a source of action to be expressed in music and inspiration for musical text painting, and even a determinant of form.

The five songs, as a group, show considerable variation in tonal structure: three end on the tonic (*not* the first three to be composed, incidentally), one finesses the final cadence by implying an unstated tonic at the end, while the last song ends on a dissonant chord. Moreover, the number of triadic arrival points through the course of the pieces—and even the number of triads used incidentally—varies considerably. This is hardly unexpected, for Webern composed the five songs over a two-year

---

10. The continuation of this technique can be seen in certain atonal pieces, such as Schoenberg's op. 16, no. 3, "Farben." The quasi-tonics in such pieces are most often register- and order-specific, as Hermann Erpf pointed out long ago with his notion of the *Klangzentrum*: "The essential characteristic of the technique of sound-center (Klangzentrum) is a chord that continually recurs after brief periods of absence, and is defined by an intervallic shape, registral positioning in pitch-space, and tone color. The chord—which generally is dissonant, and possesses a large number of tones as well as a definite sonic effect—achieves thereby, in a certain primitive sense, the character of a chord-center from which all development departs and to which it strives to return. The passages appearing between chord-centers are distinguished as contrasting, in a manner that is comparable to the dominant's departure from the tonic, so that a certain alternation tonic-nontonic-tonic comes into being. This informal relationship presents a final reference to functional harmony. The effect may be supported or weakened through rhythmic/metric relationships, tone color and register. Once it has been established, transformations—even of the chord center—are possible, without destroying the structural continuity" (Hermann Erpf, *Studien zur Harmonie- und Klangtechnik der neueren Musik* [Leipzig: Breitkopf und Härtel, 1927], 122).

11. See Elizabeth West Marvin and Robert W. Wason, "On the Analysis and Performance of Webern's Early Songs: A Collaborators' Dialogue, " *Theory and Practice* 20 (1995): 91–124, where I discuss this approach in a bit more detail.

span, which began, approximately, with Schoenberg's composition of his *Kammer-symphonie*, op. 9, and ended with his composition of much of *The Book of the Hanging Garden*, op. 15.[12] Though an overgeneralization, it is fair to say that the range of musical languages of the *Dehmel Lieder* is certainly closer to op. 9 than op. 15.[13] The latter marks Schoenberg's decisive move to a more abstract "atonal" language, in keeping with George's abstract and esoteric poetic technique, and it is certainly the inspiration for Webern's fourteen settings of George texts.

Richard Dehmel, on the other hand, never left the "naturalistic" style of the late nineteenth century completely behind.[14] Poetic images typical of the earlier pe-

---

12. Webern's dating of the *Dehmel Lieder* is far less exact than one would wish—as is the case with most of his early music (the mature twelve-tone composer, conscious of his place in history, was punctilious about such matters). The first song is dated "Easter, 1906," the fourth, "1907"; technical and stylistic features of the songs seem consistent with these earlier dates. The remaining songs are all dated "1908." An early cover for the group of songs exists, on which Webern refers to the latter four songs as composed in "1908," and isolates the first, perhaps planning to excise it; but ultimately he redated the fourth and included the first; see Gerlach, *Musik und Jugendstil*, 176f. In the 1972 critical report, Gerlach strongly implied that the order of composition of the 1908 songs was two, three, and five (making the order of composition of the whole cycle one, four, two, three, and five); presumably, Moldenhauer assigned his "Moldenhauer numbers" (which correspond to this order) based upon this report. Gerlach elaborates on his philological argument for this ordering (which the present discussion follows as well) in *Musik und Jugendstil*, 178.

13. Leonard Stein places these songs in the context of contemporaneous works by Schoenberg and Berg; see his "Webern's *Dehmel Lieder* of 1906–8" in *Anton von Webern; Perspectives*, compiled by Hans Moldenhauer, ed. Demar Irvine (1966; reprint, New York: Da Capo, 1978), 51–61. Despite its early date, this article remains a helpful introduction. Gerlach's *Musik und Jugendstil*, 176–215, is the most ambitious study of the *Dehmel Lieder*. The year 1908 is particularly critical: it is the same year that Webern finished op. 1, composed the op. 2 choral work, and composed all fourteen *George Lieder* (the five of opp. 3 and 4, as well as the four published posthumously as *Four Stefan George Songs* [New York: Carl Fischer, 1970]); unfortunately, he failed to provide exact dates for any of these works. Schoenberg's "Friede auf Erden" (finished "Mar. 9, 1907," according to Rufer [*Das Werk Arnold Schöenbergs* (Kassel: Bärenreiter, 1959), p. 10]) was certainly the model for op. 2. On the other hand, the third Dehmel song, "Himmelfahrt," shows the influence of Berg's Piano Sonata, op. 1, also composed in 1908.

14. Though virtually forgotten today, Dehmel was by far the most popular German poet at the turn of the century, and particularly so with composers; a contemporary biography tallies 550 musical settings of his poetry (by 1913), among which were twenty-three settings of "Helle Nacht," the text of the last of Webern's "Dehmel Lieder" (Julius Bab, *Richard Dehmel* [Berlin: 1926], 211; see Albrecht Dümling, *Die fremden Klänge der hängenden Gärten* [Munich: Kindler, 1981], 142). Dümling discusses philosophical and social attitudes that Schoenberg and Dehmel shared—an important source of Schoenberg's attraction to Dehmel's work (pp. 140–47). Though Webern had set three Dehmel texts in 1901 and 1903 (his cousin, Ernst Diez, gave him a volume entitled *Richard Dehmel, Ausgewählte Gedichte* [Berlin: 1901]), it seems clear that Schoenberg was the inspiration for the *Dehmel Lieder* of 1906–08, both with

riod appear , but in a charged, highly sensual atmosphere, and often in isolation, with larger contextual connections obscured. Likewise, in the harmonic language of the *Dehmel Lieder*, the most sensual clichés of nineteenth-century harmonic language survive precariously, their connection to the overall "key" and motivic detail often obscure. To be sure, in each of the *Dehmel Lieder*, except perhaps the last, the pure tonic major or minor triad is still a recognizable entity; but in all of them it seems irrelevant to the musical discourse—something merely to be postponed to the end of a phrase, or even the entire piece. However, Examples 1a and 1b show two tonic surrogates that appear at a number of points throughout these songs. They are the two (inversionally related) forms of the [0148] tetrachord: the "major triad with ♭6" ("+M7") and the "minor triad with leading tone" ("mM7").

These tonic surrogates offer an alternative to the perpetual avoidance of the tonic, as seen in *Tristan* and its followers: given a harmonic language in which the level of dissonance had been raised considerably, *any* triadic arrival point becomes increasingly "flat," and hence problematic. The "clouding" of the tonic with unresolved dissonance (or dissonances) manages to maintain the tonic and tonic-substitute arrival points, while at the same time expressing these arrivals with "chords" more consistent with the surrounding harmonic language.[15] After Schoenberg's "schwebende und aufgehobene Tonalität," such clouded tonics might be referred to as "suspended tonics," but since in one case the quasi-tonic is not the conceptual tonic (of the key signature), I have opted for the more neutral "referential sonority" (RS).

The first song, "Ideale Landschaft," composed a couple of months before Schoenberg's *Kammersymphonie*, is the most tonally conventional. Still, the tonic, E major, comes into such frequent conflict with the augmented triad resulting from the stepwise displacement of the tonic's triadic fifth that "E major" ultimately seems like an oversimplification, and one is tempted to propose as RS the pitch-class collec-

---

respect to musical language and choice of text. Dümling shows that all of the Dehmel texts that Schoenberg used come from two volumes of Dehmel's poetry, *Weib und Welt* and *Aber die Liebe*, and most come from the former; with Webern's *Dehmel Lieder*, all texts come from *Weib und Welt*, except for "Nächtliche Scheu," which comes from *Aber die Liebe*. Moreover, only the second text, "Am Ufer," appears in the volume given to him by Diez.

15. In Marra's opinion "the prominence of 4–19 [0148] and its complement 8–19 at some cadences (and its frequency throughout all four [early] songs) may be a reflection of Webern's proclivity towards employment of lowered submedient key relations" (James Marra, "Webern's 1904 Lieder: A Study in Late Tonal Practice," *Indiana Theory Review* 8, no. 2 (1987): 32). This is certainly the case if we are speaking of the major mode with lowered sixth (Hauptmann's "Moll-Dur"), which is the likely model "major scale" of much late-tonal practice, and which introduces the possible augmented fifth/diminished fourth ($^{♭6}_{3}$) into major. But the minor mode is even more likely to introduce "4–19" [0148]—the unfashionable "I$_7$" and "III$_7$" of dated harmony books. *All* of these possible 4–19s are suspensions of the tonic; certainly that is the most important reason for their frequent appearance in Webern's music.

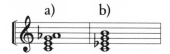

Example 1.

tion, E G♯ B C [0148]. The E G♯ B C collection has no registral or ordering specific-ity—unlike the "Farben Chord," for example—and is thus, except for the abiguity as to its "five-three" or "six-three" status, very close to the traditional notion of "tonic chord." Indeed, one might argue that the deepest structural level ultimately clarifies this ambiguity in favor of E major, for the "structural dominant" is articulated by a "cadential six-four" (mm. 23f.). Moreover, at the middleground level, the evocative setting of the second text line, "und eine hohe Abendklarheit war," to a T_3 cycle of "minor thirds" G (m. 15) B♭ (m. 16) C♯ (m. 17), likewise takes its point of departure from an implied overall E.[16]

So why not simply accept the E-major interpretation? The problem is that such an interpretation proves to be grossly oversimplified when we examine the ar-ticulations of "tonics" at the more surface levels of the piece, to which we turn now. First, we examine the text briefly in order to orient ourselves to the overall layout of the piece (see Fig. 1).[17] The poem, a simple concatenation of images with no articu-lated subsections (strophes, etc.), is straightforward: in essence, the iambic pentam-eter is largely undisturbed until the enjambment of the fourth line—"ins Licht, ins Licht" (which is prepared by the tetrameter of the third line), after which the pre-vailing meter returns for the last line. The enjambed line—the climax of the poem—likewise becomes the center of the musical form for Webern: the whole piece works up to "ins Licht" (last eighth of m. 21 through m. 23), which becomes remarkable through the melisma—four pitches spread over the duration of two complete mea-sures on only the word "Licht."[18] (The parallel with the only other melisma in m. 9, on "Glanz," which starts on the same highpoint, G5, is clear.) The big cadence is synchronized to occur at the end of the motivic buildup in piano.

16. This is an obvious debt to Hugo Wolf, whose influence begins to wane in the songs composed later.

17. There is no scholarly collection of Dehmel's works. All of the German texts of Dehmel's poems in the present article are taken from *Richard Dehmel Gesammelte Werke in drei Bänden* (Berlin: Fischer, 1913) (an abridgment of *Gesammelte Werke von Richard Dehmel (in zehn Bänden)* [Berlin: Fischer, 1908] that eliminates the prose works). The English translations are my own, though at some points they are indebted to the (uncredited) translations published in the Carl Fischer edition.

18. The analyst of Webern's vocal music quickly becomes sensitive to melismas; his text settings are generally syllabic—to the extent that poetic meter and form come close to being exclusive determinants of musical meter and form. For Webern, melismas suspend the progress of musical time: they are very rare—and always significant—events throughout his career.

Ideale Landschaft	Ideal Landscape
Du hattest einen Glanz auf deiner Stirn,	You had a gleam on your forehead,
Und eine hohe Abendklarheit war,	And it was a wonderfully clear evening,
Und sahst nur immer Weg von mir,	And you always looked away from me,
Ins Licht, ins Licht—	Into the light, into the light—
Und fern verscholl das	And the echo of my call
Echo meines Aufschreis.	Disappeared into the distance.

Figure 1.

After the initial tonic (mm. 1–2), there are four important local arrival points in the work that use the RS; three use the "tonic transposition," and one uses another one. The initial tonic and four subsequent locations are shown in Example 2. Example 2a shows the opening, in which the piano right hand announces the primary motive, which we shall call "M": $<$-6 +2 +1 -4$>$. The skip away from the pitch B tends to isolate it as chordal, but C arrives at the beginning of the next bar in the left hand; the dissonant harmonic support of the opening B, and the half-step voice leading (shown in the continuation of Ex. 2a), tend to make the C+ triad of m. 2 sound like a resolution (this is further supported by the relative stability of an entire bar consisting of only one clear tertian harmony).[19] Measure 3 does little to clarify, for both B and C are isolated and receive nearly equal support. Example 2b shows the next appearance of the RS (mm. 9–10), which articulates the entrance of voice (m. 9). Here, an apparent T_5 of M is in fact a "tonal" combination of T_5 and a shift to T_4, which, in effect preserves the E G♯ B C RS. Significantly, two clear harmonies support this appearance: C major and E major, though the position of the ambiguous B/C is reversed with respect to the harmonic support, effectively heightening the 5/♭6 ambiguity once again: B occurs against C major, C against E major. (B♭ receives so little support that it can be reduced out as an "appoggiatura.") The next appearance, at m. 23 (Ex. 2c), might appear to be an embellished T_7 (M), which brings in the structural dominant of the piece (mm. 24ff.). However, the "embellishing" G♯ is in fact chordal (the G♯ is doubled to make this clear), and it is not difficult to hear the RS (here as B2 E3 G♯3 C4) as the structural harmony of this bar—a kind of "cadential six-four"

19. This is certainly one reason why Gerlach, unconstrained by the analytical systems of American music theory, hears the C augmented triad as "tonic" of the work. See page 57 of his early article, "Die Dehmel-Lieder von Anton Webern; Musik und Sprache im Übergang zur Atonalität," in *Jahrbuch des Staatlichen Instituts für Musikforschung Preußischer Kulturbesitz 1970*, ed. Dagmar Droysen (Berlin: Verlag Merseburger, 1971), 45–100.

a)

b)

c)

d)

e)

Example 2.

permeated with the augmented triad (the skip to the C helps this hearing), which moves to a clear V^6_5. The next appearance occurs after a composing-out of the dominant (mm. 24–27) and arrival of the tonic pedal (m. 28). Here we return to a slightly embellished T_0 of M, but in a new harmonic setting. Measure 29 supports this motive harmonically with an inverted form of [0148], E2 C3 A3 G#4, a variant of the "pedal (IV)$^6_4$" that is typical of tonic pedal sections, once again containing the E augmented triad (see Ex. 2d). Now a composing-out of the tonic E-G# major third occurs in mm. 30–33. (This parallels the composing-out of the B-D# "dominant" major third in mm. 24–27, which ends with a "dominant" transposition of [0148] in m. 27; this composing-out was in turn a T_7 derivation of the tonic composing-out in mm. 1–6.) The E-G# bass motion of mm. 30–33 leads, in m. 34, to a modified restatement of mm. 9–10 (see Ex. 2e): at this point a C^6_4 arpeggiation, taken from the vocal line of m. 9, replaces the beginning of the primary motive, further emphasizing C, which makes its strongest appearance here; moreover, the final repeated statements of the C-G# skip (mm. 35ff.) emphasize the independence and importance of the C with the diminuendos and the simultaneous attack of both C and B in m. 36. Thus, though E major may be the larger, structural key, at the foreground and even middleground level, the competing support of C is of very great, if not equal, importance.

"Nächtliche Scheu," number four, and the next in order of composition, is perhaps the most reminiscent of Schoenberg's op. 9: it avoids triads over considerable spans, but resorts to them nevertheless to articulate the division between first and second formal sections (mm. 8–10), and the end of the third formal section (mm. 25ff.).[20] At the division between first and second section the "interlude" begins on

---

20. Before proceeding farther with the analysis of number four, the reader is reminded of the missing bar ("17") that Gerlach reintroduces after examining the manuscript (Gerlach, "Die Handschriften," 103), notated below:

Gerlach's missing bar "m. 17"

(second half of m. 16)

(Presumably, the left hand F# of m. 18 should be played an octave lower.)

"V," which in turn was clearly introduced by "III+^{6}/V" at the end of the previous vocal phrase (m. 7)—the clearest harmonic progression of the phrase. As "postlude" the same idea appears transposed down a fifth to articulate "I" (the progression from "III+^{6}" to I occurs between mm. 24 and 25, the postlude in mm. 25ff.). The three formal sections—the vocal music in mm. 1–7, 10–16, and 18–24, with corresponding piano interludes and postlude—align precisely with the text (see Fig. 2).

Webern avoids the periodicity that such articulations might seem to bring with them (as he continues to do in his later songs as well): first, the "interlude" consists of two prominent voices in double counterpoint, and the inversion of these starts off the second section (mm. 10–11), the vocal line a counterpoint against them; next, the "Kuss motive" of voice (m. 16) is elaborated by piano in a written-out ritardando (mm. 16–"17"—see fn. 20), which seems to be headed for V of D minor, but is abruptly terminated on III of that key (which acts enharmonically as "♭IV"). Each of the three sections is in turn divided into two subsections, the outer two of which are articulated by canonic imitation between voice, followed by piano left hand. (In the A section, the vocal phrase beginning "aus des Mondes" is imitated by piano left hand starting on the second beat of m. 5; in the returning A' section, the vocal phrase "und mit zaghafter . . ." is imitated by piano left hand starting on the second beat of m. 22.)

Given this interpretation of the song's formal structure for orientation, let us move on to tonal structure. We can proceed farther on this front if we note a formal correspondence that is now obvious: compare the musical setting of the first text line, "Zaghaft vom Gewölk ins Land," with the setting of the first line of the final strophe, "Hörst du, Herz?—Die Welle lallt." (The correspondence is that much clearer when we recall the comparison of settings of *second* couplets that we under-took in the previous paragraph.) Thus it seems sensible to call the third formal sec-tion an "altered reprise" of the first. This in turn allows us to see some interesting correspondences with respect to tonal structure: if the setting of "Gewölk ins Land" might have been regarded as an instance of our Example 1b, the parallel setting in mm. 18–19 makes the resemblance much more apparent. Thus one might well pro-pose the "suspended" tonic D F A C♯ as an RS that lurks throughout the piece until it is supplanted by a D-major triad at the end.

Unlike the referential sonorities that consist of a tonic plus ♭6, this one includes the augmented triad that functions as *dominant* in the key of I and ♭VI; thus it also links with the *other* whole-tone scale—the one which contains two-thirds of the domi-nant triad instead of two-thirds of the tonic. Still, though the referential sonority does not actually contain ♭6, it seems at a number of points ready to turn to VI. In-deed, this tendency is borne out almost immediately: in m. 4, when pitch-class D finally arrives to fill out the possible referential sonority (in both voice and piano), the harmony changes to B♭. In fact, (♭)VI remains an important tonal area in all of the songs.

The returning A section (mm. 18ff.) develops certain features of the initial A

Nächtliche Scheu		Nocturnal Hesitancy
	I	
Zaghaft vom Gewölk ins Land	a	Hesitantly, from the clouds into the countryside
fliesst des Lichtes Flut	b	Flows the flood of light
aus des Mondes bleicher Hand,	a	From the pale hand of the moon,
dämpft mir alle Glut.	b	Subduing all of my glow.
	II	
Ein verirrter Schimmer schwebt	c	A lost glimmer floats
durch den Wald zum Fluss,	d/b	Through the forest, to the river,
und das dunkle Wasser bebt	c	And the dark water quivers
unter seinem Kuss.	d/b	Beneath its kiss.
	III	
Hörst du Herz? Die Welle lallt:	e	Do you hear, my heart? the wave whispers:
küsse, küsse mich!	f	Kiss me!
Und mit zaghafter Gewalt,	e	and with hesitant force,
Mädchen, küss ich dich.	f	O maiden, I kiss thee.

Figure 2.

section. For example, the $B\flat^6_4$ reappears, this time as setting of the text "küsse mich."[21] In the next bar it is developed into the "sehr warm" $B\flat^6_4$ episode, which turns in quasi-Neapolitan fashion to E (V/V): indeed, the clearest triadic measure of the entire piece is there primarily as a direct means of text expression. The piece then lapses back to the even whole-tone harmony, thence to the dominant (second half of m. 24), and finally to the pure tonic, D major.

In "Am Ufer," composed in 1908, the assignment of referential sonority seems to be relatively clear: A2, A♭3, C4, E4—[0148]. Before we examine the tonal language in greater detail, however, let us look at the form of the piece—certainly the most sophisticated of all five songs.

The analysis on the text , taken from Gerlach,[22] presents some of the more obvious correspondences; one might continue, as Gerlach does, by pointing to the internal rhyme, "Blut, Glut, Flut"; or one might note the assonance in "Blut (erklingt)" and "Abgrund (sinkt)," or certainly the structural parallel in the refrains: the opposition, "*der* ferne Tag," and "*die* ferne Nacht" (which are nevertheless united by assonance, meter, and the repeated adjective, "ferne"), and the transcendent "*das* ewige Licht." The poem presents extraordinary possibilities to the composer, and it seems unlikely that they would have escaped Webern (see Fig. 3).

---

21. Gerlach's correction of the score turns the erroneous "C♯" into a D♮.

22. The analysis is taken from Gerlach, "Kompositionsniederschrift und Werkfassung"; also see *Musik und Jugendstil*, 194–99.

Am Ufer		On the Shore
Die Welt verstummt, dein Blut	a	The world falls silent, your blood resounds;
erklingt; in seinen hellen Abgrund	a	Into its bright abyss sinks
sinkt der ferne Tag,	b	The far-off day.
er schaudert nicht; die Glut	a	It shudders not; the glow embraces
umschlingt das höchste Land, im	a	The highest land, in the sea struggles
Meere ringt die ferne Nacht,	b/c	The far-off night,
sie zaudert nicht; der Flut	a	It hesitates not; from the tide rises
entspringt ein Sternchen, deine	a	A little star, your soul drinks
Seele trinkt das ewige Licht.	a/d	The eternal light.

Figure 3.

In Webern's musical setting, three refrains are particularly prominent, but they are not what we might expect from a study of the poem alone. The piano interludes at mm. 9 and 14 make it clear that Webern has returned the enjambed openings of the second and third strophes to the first and second respectively. This corresponds to the natural declamation of the poetry, completing the iambic tetrameter, and it clarifies as well the referents of "er schaudert nicht" (der Tag) and "sie zaudert nicht" (die Nacht), preserving the grammatical dualism as well. Thus the beginnings of Dehmel's second and third strophes seem to mark the *ends* of Webern's first and second musical sections, though in each case he introduces the slightest hesitation by separating them from the previous lines by two eighths' rest. On the other hand, at the end of the song, "das ewige Licht" follows directly upon "deine Seele trinkt," but seems to present a similar sectional marker. In fact, there are good musical reasons to hear these three passages as parallel. They are set as eighth pickups (with the appropriate triplet modification to account for "ewige") to the downbeat of the next bar; and further, the "evolution" of the intervallic setting of the three links them: <-2 -2 - 1> of "er schaudert nicht" becomes <-2 -2 -2> in "sie zaudert nicht," and <-2 -2 -2 - 1> in "das ewige Licht," the last filling out the fifth and producing the illusive "tonic." Indeed, the tonal support of all of this provided by the piano clarifies our incipient ABA further: the chromatic stepwise descent from the A pedal of the opening section leads to the low E2 that begins the second section in m. 16 together with a transposition on E of the "minor-major seventh chord" that had seemed to be a quasi-tonic on A during the first section. Measure 17 begins the canonic "tenor" imitations of the voice in piano, which seem to beg the question of the status of the bass line. But with the close of this section, and the obvious reiteration of the vocal E–D–C–B♭ in piano (in m. 14—the only time that such near-doubling occurs in the piece), the bass continues its descent and returns to the A pedal of the opening in m. 15ff. All of this then apparently dissolves vaguely into the ephemeral D of the last three measures.

But just as we assume that the formal case is closed with the announcement of this ABA, we note that the first A section overbalances the remaining sections with respect to number of syllables; previous experience tells us that such a preponderance of poetic feet will have inevitable repercussions at the level of overall form, given Webern's respect for poetic meter. Moreover, this overbalance is all the more pronounced due to the pacing of the text in the opening line of the poem: instead of the iambs that would emerge from a poetic reading, Webern sets the line as dactyls consistent with the $\frac{3}{4}$ meter signature of the whole (the two-beat melismas on "Welt," "stummt," "Blut," and "klingt" are particularly striking given the syllabic norm in Webern's vocal music). Further, motivic correspondences cut across our ABA formal boundaries: the second phrase ("in seinen hellen Abgrund sinkt . . .") presents motivic material that will be further developed in the "B section" proper: the alternating fourths and half steps that are so typical of Webern's melodic construction, throughout his compositional career. Meanwhile, the opening phrase, while it starts with the <-5 +1> motive that is picked up and developed here and in mm. 16ff., continues into the odd-whole-tone material that comes back with the returning A section, though curiously, the rhythmic setting of that opening never recurs. Indeed, if we were to divide the piece into two parts at m. 16, the first part would last 28 quarters, while the second would last 32, a discrepency that nearly vanishes when we consider the free rhythmic character of both the piano introduction and epilogue. (In fact, both sections last exactly 25 quarters when we substract the 3–quarter introduction and 7–quarter epilogue.) Thus it is certainly possible to conceive of the piece in two parts, each of which would consist in turn of an A phrase and B phrase, but in reverse order: AB/BA. Still, to this listener, the tonal articulation of form—as vague as it may be in this attenuated harmonic language—compels a hearing of the piece in three parts.

The operation of the referential sonority comes quite close to the way in which the "Farben Chord" operates in Schoenberg's op. 16, no. 3, since the registral ordering and position of the the chord is of importance.[23] This reading is made all the more convincing since the piece avoids *all* standard tonal triads and seventh chords, with the exception of two B♭$^6_4$ chords at the end of mm. 9 and second beat of m. 19. The referential sonority—which is *not* the implied tonic, but a "clouded" form of the dominant—is gradually put in place in the first incomplete measure and subsequent two measures through arpeggiation, starting from E6 downward.[24] Subsequently, it is "prolonged" by motion to the lower-neighbor augmented triad (through m. 4), which changes the set-type to the whole-tone tetrachord [0248] (see Ex. 3). This

---

23. Recall Erpf's *Klangzentrum* (fn. 10).

24. The problematic nature of this tonal structure cannot be allowed to pass without comment. While the goal of the vocal line up through m. 5 is D, the accompaniment fails to support it. When this material returns in m. 15, the piano extends the last part of the phrase with two canonic imitations to the final D, but it remains difficult to hear the "A minor with major 7th" as a "dominant."

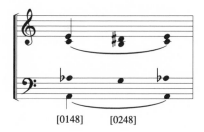

[0148]   [0248]

Example 3.

tetrachord recalls the late-nineteenth-century usage of whole-tone combinations as "dominant"-functioning entities, and thus works particularly well as the nontonic- "neighbor" chord. At m. 5, the bass pedal on A begins a descent, ultimately through a fourth to the E2 of m. 10, producing a long-range (incomplete) arpeggiation of the referential sonority. At the downbeat of m. 10, the arrival of the B section is announced tonally by T_7 of the referential sonority: E2 E♭4 G4 B4. This registrally expanded version of the chord also includes octave doublings, making the exact registral placements ambiguous, but the essential registral expansion of the chord remains clear. Through the piano left hand's abandonment of the new low register and its imitation of the vocal part as a new, left-hand "tenor" (starting in m. 11), E2 remains an implied pedal until m. 15, at which point A returns. Finally the work moves on to a "resolution" to D2 in m. 17.

Song number three, "Himmelfahrt," also composed in 1908, largely avoids triads as well, and thus the few triads that occur are of extraordinary interest. Again, we orient ourselves first with the text, given in Figure 4. The music is essentially a three-part form, which aligns with the text as indicated in the figure; the music exploits the dramatic content of the poem, rather than its poetic structure.[25] The "B section" (reminiscent of the development section of Berg's Piano Sonata written the same year) is demarcated by the dynamic extremes of the piece, beginning at pianisissimo dynamic (m. 14) and ending with the fortissimo and ritardando to the "sehr breit" of the beginning of the "recapitulation" (m. 31). This extraodinarily clear, and fairly regularly proportioned musical structure (a thirteen-bar A section, seventeen-bar B section, and seventeen-bar return) cuts across the poetic structure: of the five quatrains of the poem, the A section uses one, the B section two and one-half, and the modified return one and one-half. (There is no text repetition, as is almost always the case in Webern's music.) The musical delineation of these sections is particularly important to the notion of a referential sonority for the piece; we shall look at that now.

---

25. See Gerlach, *Musik und Jugendstil,* 186f., for an analysis of the text.

Himmelfahrt		Heavenly Journey
Schwebst du nieder aus den Weiten,	A	Do you float down from the distance,
Nacht mit deinem Silberkranz?		Night, with your silver garland?
Hebt in deine Ewigkeiten		Does the soft luster of darkness lift me
mich des Dunkels milder Glanz?		Into your eternities?
Als ob Augen liebend winken:	B	As though eyes beckon lovingly:
alle Liebe sei enthüllt!		Let all love be revealed!
Als ob Arme sehnend sinken:		As though arms reach longingly:
alle Sehnsucht sei erfülltt—		Let all longing be fulfilled!
Strahlt ein Stern mir aus den Weiten,		A star shines on me from afar,
alle Ängste fallen ab,		All fears melt away—
seligste Versunkenheiten,		most heavenly visions!—
strahlt und strahlt und will herab.		[It] shines and shines, and wants to descend,
und es treiben mich Gewalten		And forces push me
ihm entgegen, und er sinkt—		towards it, and it sinks—
und ein Quellen, ein Entfalten	A	And a streaming forth, a spreading out
seines Scheines nimmt und bringt		Of its light takes and brings
und erlöst mich in die Zeiten,		And releases me into those times
da noch keine Menschen sahn,		That no human yet perceived,
wie durch Nächte Sterne gleiten,		As stars glide through the nights,
wie den Seelen Rätsel nahn.		As mysteries approach souls.

Figure 4.

The opening motive and its harmonic support seem to point once again to the major triad with ♭6—this time, E♭ G B♭ C♭ (see Ex. 4a). But when the voice enters, this combination is enlarged by the addition of F♯, accented by the "B-major" arpeggiation that occurs in canon in piano, accompanying the voice's statement of the primary motive (Ex. 4b), This leads one to propose the union of E♭ major and B major, E♭ F♯ G B♭ B [01458], as the referential sonority.

The arrival point at m. 13 (voice) and m. 14 (piano) is simultaneously a cadence of the A section and the beginning of the B section. Appropriately, it also contains the longest sustained triadic harmony in the piece (other than the E♭-major harmonies at the beginning and ending), and significantly, that harmony is the "secondary harmony" of the referential sonority, C♭ major. Further, the beginning of the B section is marked by the conflicting B/B♭ (5/♭6) head-tone, first in piano and then in voice; the voice continues in canon with the piano throughout this opening vocal phrase of the section (through m. 17). The next vocal phrase plays on the parallel in

Example 4.

the text—the closest one in the poem ("als ob Augen liebend . . ."; "als ob Arme sehnend . . .," etc.), presenting the B section's first vocal phrase at T_2. The piano sneaks into the T_2 of its previous material on the second beat of m. 19 so that it once again preannounces the voice.

With the third vocal phrase of the B section (which begins the third text quatrain—"strahlt ein Stern"), the voice concentrates on the second phrase member of the earlier phrase ("alle Liebe"), just heard in its T_2 version (m. 20—"alle Sehnsucht"). The voice begins the third phrase by citing the first two notes a half step too low ("Strahlt ein Stern," which should be C–G#–B), but it corrects the citation in mm. 23–25 with its T_2 continuation ("alle Ängste . . ."). (The -1 -2 at the end of the motive is compressed to -1 -1 in "alle Ängste . . ."; throughout the rest of this development the -1 and -2 at the end of the motive is treated freely.) The piano begins to assert an ever greater independence, concentrating on the abbreviated and compressed form of the vocal motive, <-4 -1 -2 -1>, in counterpoint with the voice's assertion of the same motive, as shown in Example 4c. (This example shows the T_3 cyle of motivic transposition in piano, while the voice takes a stepwise ascent.) In essence, the piano takes over the primary role in the development, for it has the range to take the registral assent to the high B♭ (mm. 29ff.), which reintroduces the B♭ head-tone and prepares the recapitulation tonally. (The aural connection with the E♭ beginning of this activity in m. 23 is clear, as is the connection of this high B♭ with the piano B♭ that began the section in m. 14.)

But while the voice may be unable to match the registral ascent, it bears the responsibility for the motivic dimension of the recapitulation: after reaching its registral peak on F6 in m. 28, the beginning of the fourth quatrain (m. 29) registrally inverts the previous F–D♭, returning in the process to the B-section head motive < +8 +3 -4> ("und es treiben") in its original transposition (compare "alle Liebe"). Finally, just as the recapitulation begins, the voice again plays on a text parallelism ("und es treiben . . . ," "und er sinkt . . ."), presenting T_2 of the first < +8 +3> with the latter text (just as the earlier passage had). This in turn connects across the beginning of the recapitulation with its intervallic retrograde from the end of m. 32 into m. 33 ("und ein Quellen . . ."—another text parallel). The union of these two motives (G E♭ F♯/B♭ G B) is the referential sonority.

At least two additional features in the piano music in mm. 30–32 also serve to restore the referential sonority: (1) the apparent "error" in double counterpoint (the B♭–F♯–B right-hand soprano in m. 31, followed by B♭–G–B left-hand top voice in the next bar), which tends to set F♯ and G at the same level, the latter of which is supported by an E♭-major harmony; and (2) the other part in the double-counterpoint exchange, which, on the last beat of m. 32, shows its clear derivation from the "B-major arpeggiation" of the original vocal entrance in m. 5 (and other subsidiary contrapuntal voices in that bar).

Let us now look at the final six measures of the piece. Here, the "B-major" component becomes dominant to "♭II minor" (spelled as E minor) over a tonic pedal, leading us to consider enlarging the referential sonority still further to be E♭ E F♯ G B♭ B. But as striking as this effect is, its two-measure duration is shorter than that of ♭6, which lasts through yet one more augmented statement of the primary motive before it is resolved in the penultimate bar.

"Helle Nacht," probably composed last in the set, is certainly the most nontonal. Presumably, the conceptual tonic is D minor, but no D-minor triad ever appears, and, in fact, no vertical major or minor triads of any transposition ever occur. The formal layout of the piece has been handled in the secondary literature, since it is articulated clearly by triple counterpoint.[26] The three musical parts of the song correspond precisely to the three poetic strophes (see Fig. 5).

---

26. Wallace MacKenzie, "Webern's Technique of Choral Composition," and Leonard Stein, "Webern's *Dehmel Lieder* of 1906–8," in *Anton Webern: Perspectives* (fn. 14); Gerlach, *Musik und Jugendstil*, 206.

Helle Nacht	Luminous Night
Weich küsst die Zweige	Softly, the white moon
der weisse Mond.	Kisses the branches.
Ein Flüstern wohnt	A whisper lodges
im Laub, als neige,	In the leaves, as
als schweige sich der Hain zur Ruh—	The grove nodded, and became silent—
Geliebte du—	Beloved, you—
Der Weiher ruht, und	The pond is quiet, and
die Weide schimmert.	The willow glimmers.
Ihr Schatten flimmert	Its shadow flickers
in seiner Flut, und	In the water, and
der Wind weint in den Bäumen:	The wind weeps in the trees:
wir träumen—träumen—	We dream—dream—
Die Weiten leuchten	The distances illuminate
Beruhigung.	Peace.
Die Niederung	The plain
hebt bleich den feuchten	raises pallidly its moist
Schleier hin zum Himmelssaum:	veil to the edge of the heavens
O hin—O Traum—	upward—O dream—

Figure 5.

Each of the three six-line stanzas of the poetry is set to a different permutation of the three parts contained in voice, piano right hand, and piano left hand (mm. 4–14; mm. 15–25; mm. 25–35); the final three-measure "refrain" in each part is derived from the introduction, as is the "epilogue," which, however, is extended to be the same length as each of the sections (mm. 36ff.). And each of the refrains and the epilogue are set off from the rest of the poem.

The Introduction (mm. 1–3) consists of a Tristanesque figure, its repetition at T_2, and then a fragmentation of the T_2 statement. (The analogy with *Tristan* is made palpable by a number of features, including the motive's increasing textural density and the fact that it contains two chords, the second of which seems like a nonfinal "resolution" of the first.) There are a number of ways of parsing this succession. The strong beats of the piano right hand present a registral inversion of the opening C#5–A5 (as A4–C#5), replicated at T_2 as E♭5–B5 (and B4–E♭5). Chordal support of these intervals consists of [0248]-type tetrachords, and thus the union of strong-beat verticals is the odd whole-tone scale. Significantly, that whole-tone scale is the one that functions as dominant of the conceptual tonic, D minor. (Though the tonal interpretation of B F A C♯ is problematic, we wonder, could C♯ G B E♭ be VII⁷ of D Minor?) There is also an important sense in which the first harmonic tritone at the end of the first motive (B/F) is picked up as the melodic opening of the T_2 replication; once again, this leads to the whole-tone interpretation—this time split into its three tritones E♭/A, B/F, C♯/G (see Ex. 5a).

On the other hand, reading the "appoggiatura chords" in the right hand yields [0 3 4 7] ("major-minor") and [0 1 3 7] ("♭5") tetrachords (and their union, the [0 1 3 4 7] pentachord); meanwhile, chord types formed between hands are [0 2 3 6] and [0 2 5 8] ("dominant-seventh") tetrachords, the [0 2 3 6 8] pentachord, [0 1 3 4 6 9] hexachord, and finally the union of all of these pcs, the [0 1 3 4 6 7 9] septachord—seven-eighths of an octatonic scale (see Ex. 5b). Thus, all are octatonic set types that are immediately aurally distinguishable from the whole-tone cadence points. This characteristic is part of the reason why the last tetrachord of the introduction (C♯4 G4 D5 F♯5), which is neither octatonic nor whole-tone, sounds incomplete: its expected completion (F♯5/D5 moving to E♭5/B4) is taken by the vocal entrance, which overlaps the end of the introduction (voice on E♭ with piano C♭).

The entrance of the voice is remarkable in the way it seems to grow out of the piano introduction. This is in part because of the overlap of voice and piano on E♭, but also because the voice then presents a [0347] "major-minor" tetrachord at T_4 of the previous one presented in right hand, thus "pivoting" on the common E♭/F♯. Thereupon, the piano left hand continues in the manner of a "loose" mensuration canon, imitating the first vocal phrase (up to the F of m. 7). Given the imitation at the octave, the relative tonal "clarity" of at least the first vocal phrase—including the voice exchange that seems to highlight the B/F tritone once again (see the first beats of mm. 6 and 7, in piano left hand and voice)—is not entirely surprising. While the second phrase is more difficult to read, the notion of a detour to a "suspended" C-major $^6_4$ (in m. 11) rather than the expected E♭ continuation is not unconvincing. The problem is that any tonal interpretation of the two outer parts is undercut by the piano right-hand counterpoint to the mensuration canon, which consists, with the first vocal phrase, of three [0 1 3 7] "♭5" tetrachords (first as {11 3 5 6}, and then its T_1={0 4 6 7} and T_7={6 10 0 1}). The counterpoint to the second vocal phrase, like that phrase itself, is more difficult to read.

In the epilogue, the voice takes the A/E♭ tritone in imitation of the piano ("o hin"); it then takes the F/B tritone in imitation ("o Traum"). (Interestingly, the parallelism of the last two lines of text may well have furnished the initial inspiration of the primary motive of the introduction and its T_2 parallelism.)[27] While the voice takes the F/B tritone, the piano presents the interval pairs of the T_2 motivic state-

---

27. Leonard Stein proposes "geliebter Du" as the inspiration for the introductory motive in "Webern's *Dehmel Lieder*," 60. The form of the poem, and the visual appearance of this "refrain"—set off from the rest of the text each time—support Stein's point. This is one of many examples of the influence of poetic form on musical form and structure in the early atonal music.

a)

[0248]   [0248]

b)

[01347]   [0347]   [0137]

[0236]   [0258]   [013469]   [02368]   [0134679]

Example 5.

ment in double counterpoint. It then continues by returning to the original registral order of these pairs, after which it presents the original transposition of the motive in the original registral order. A registral inversion of the motive follows, and then finally a metrically augmented statement of the original motive in the original registral order, but with the bass F "subposed" under the B/F tritone. (The technique is similar to the one used at the end of the last song of op. 3, in which scale-degree 3 seems to substitute for the tonic—also in D minor.)

What of the notion of a "referential sonority" here? In the absence of any possible tonal reading, a contextually determined referential sonority becomes all that much more convincing. After all, this is the only song of the set in which the conceptual tonic, or even a substitute thereof, makes absolutely no appearance, even by implication. Instead, the referential sonority B F A C♯ [0248] at T_0 forms the goal of the opening motive (the *Grundgestalt?*), while its T_2 is the goal of the introduction, which recurs as a refrain after each verse. The T_0 level of the referential sonority proves to be the goal of the piece as a whole; indeed, the "epilogue" goes so far as to "restore" and extend the duration of T_0 after it earlier had achieved T_2. What has this referential sonority in common with the others of the *Dehmel Lieder*? Like the others, it is a dissonant chord that includes the F A C♯ we associate with the "D-minor tonics" we have seen—but without any D—a critical omission, to be sure. Instead, that hypothetical D is replaced by the "third substitutes" B at the beginning of the piece, and F at the end. Thus, with the referential sonority of the final song we have moved a long way from referential sonorities that may be heard as suspended conventional tonics, and very close indeed to the ad hoc combinations that one may find in the opp. 3 and 4 *George Lieder*.

*   *   *

Webern's *Dehmel Lieder* of 1906–08 are without doubt the most substantial musical compositions of any of the early vocal music published posthumously.[28] Indeed, I would argue that they would have made a stronger and more logical "op. 2" than the work he chose. As we have seen, they demonstrate a gradual evolution from the tonal language of op. 1 to the first "atonal" works. In choosing "Entflieht auf leichten Kähnen" (whose musical language is closest to the third Dehmel song, "Himmelfahrt"), Webern may well have wished to demonstrate the diversity of his composition— to stay away from one more set of *lieder*. But in so doing, he opted for a piece that was not unproblematic in performance.[29] The *Dehmel Lieder*, on the other hand, areeminently practical and successful in performance, and the fact that they are so little performed can only be explained by their absence from Webern's own "approved" list of works, and the many serious problems with the only published edition.

So why did Webern withhold them? Stein believes that their stylistic diversity may have been regarded by Webern as a weakness, and that this may have been the main reason.[30] But certainly we should consider the relatively late date at which

---

28. The other early songs all date from before Webern's study with Schoenberg, and are primarily of historical interest. They were edited by Rudolph Ganz and published in three sets, in the following order, as *Three Songs after Poems by Ferdinand Avenarius*, *Three Poems for Voice and Piano*, and *Eight Early Songs* (New York: Carl Fischer, 1961, 1965).

29. Webern returned to op. 2 in the mid 1920s and wrote an arrangement of it in which the chorus is accompanied by the "Pierrot Ensemble," with all attack points doubled by instruments. Certainly the difficulty of performing the piece a capella was a motivating factor. Interestingly, this arrangement may well have influenced his use of the same technique in the second movement of op. 19, where it adds an extraordinary sense of orchestrational "depth" to the piece.

30. But one must remember here that Stein, like many other commentators from the 1950s and 1960s, tends to hunt for stylistic homogeneity throughout Webern's career—to find harbingers of the "late-Webern" everywhere. For example, his opinion ("Webern's *Dehmel Lieder*," 59) that the third Dehmel song is "Schoenberg-like" and "probably the least successful of the entire set" is utterly untenable. On the contrary, it can be one of the most successful, though it may disappoint those who continually look for the late-Webern in his early works. The results of the most recent Webern research show him to have experimented with more diverse musical materials than once was thought (see Anne C. Schreffler, *Webern and the Lyric Impulse* [Oxford: Clarendon Press, 1994]; see especially chapter 6, "The Ostinato Fragments").

Webern was finally able to publish his early music (1920, coincidentally the year of Dehmel's death). By this time Dehmel's popularity was already fading, while George's was still strong. Webern, always the modernist in outlook—and in the 1920s, conscious of his status as a "pioneer" of atonality—might well have found both the aesthetic and the vestiges of tonality in these songs "dated." [31]

But the surviving title pages indicate that at some point (probably close to the composition of the pieces) Webern had found the pieces to be a "finished work"— even a "cycle," if you will, and probably contemplated their publication. In so doing, he changed their succession from the order of composition, and that is of particular interest.[32] That reordering was motivated, I believe, by aspects of the tonal language and the overall form of the pieces. First, by placing one of the two longest songs— and the most stable of those tonally—in the middle of five, he anchored the cycle around a stable midpoint. Further, the tonal effect of this is to place the E♭ major of song three between the relatively clear E minor of song one and the D minor of song four, a tonal arrangement that is prominent in op. 3, and suggests the sort of tonal "centering" that one finds in Schoenberg.[33] The repositioning of "Nächtliche Scheu" furthermore produces a particularly compelling connection between "Ideale Landschaft" and "Am Ufer" (now second): the C+ triad, a most significant subset of the RS of the first song (which comes out prominently in the postlude), is also the most significant subset of the RS of song two, and the one that starts off the piano introduction. (Moreover, it produces a particularly wonderful connection in the performance of these pieces: the low E–G♯ that finishes the first song seems to yield to "upper partials" E–C when the two songs are performed nearly attacca.) Song two then "preannounces" the D minor of the last two songs, but does it tentatively and unconvincingly. Indeed, only songs one, three, and four articulate tonics with clarity, while song five departs from the tonality of song four, but proceeds to muddy the waters considerably. Whether this was in fact the last song that Webern composed

---

31. One wonders also whether the publication of songs to Dehmel texts would not have made Webern's early dependence upon Schoenberg for compositional models a bit *too* clear.

32. Gerlach proposes an interesting, if rather esoteric, interpretation of the cylic character of these pieces, based upon the metaphor of "light," prevalent in the poems, and throughout Dehmel's poetry in general. He remarks that the choice of these particular poems was Webern's—that there is no single work in which Dehmel chose to place them even in close proximity. (This is in direct contrast to Webern's op. 3, I might add, in which the George texts were in fact printed contiguously, as I point out at the end of my article on op. 3.) Gerlach assembles the various words connected with "light," and orders them according to their "brightness" of vowel sound; he then shows that the five poems, taken in order of composition, concentrate on progressively "darker" vowel sounds. He seems to have little interest in Webern's decision to move the song composed second to the fourth position in the cycle; see *Musik und Jugendstil*, 212–14.

33. See David Lewin, "Inversional Balance as an Organizing Force in Schoenberg's Music and Thought," *Perspectives of New Music* 6, no. 2 (1967–68): 1–21.

before the "atonality" of op. 3 we shall probably never know. The ending of the cycle at a point of extreme tonal ambiguity is fitting, however. Indeed, one can almost hear the opening strains of op. 3, no. 1 as the next step in Webern's "creative evolution."

SOME NOTES ON
PIERROT LUNAIRE

DAVID LEWIN

xample 1 is a score for the first eleven measures of "Mondestrunken,"
the opening number of *Pierrot Lunaire*. Surveying the status of set
theory a decade ago, Allen Forte devoted particularly compelling
discussion to this music.[1] He offered an analysis based upon the notion of
basic cell, and another analysis taking into account more global features of the number as a whole, especially hexachords. He then showed how the approaches can be
integrated. Next, he drew attention to still another parsing of m. 1 in its own context,
a parsing shown in Figure 1.[2] In this parsing Forte called attention to the "rhythmically symmetric" patterning of the configuration, and to the symmetrical roles of the
augmented triad and the diminished triad therein. He related this parsing to his
earlier analyses, amply demonstrating that his systematics, far from being oblivious
to such foreground features of musical textures as those of Figure 1, rather respect
them, and provide richer contexts in which to situate and experience them.

I shall take Figure 1 as a point of departure to explore yet other contexts, particularly some which focus on transformations. I shall start with two salient observations that Forte made. First, there is some sense of symmetry about the motto figure;
second, the symmetry involves counterpoising the diminished triad against the augmented triad.

Indeed, the opening augmented triad of the measure seems to be associated
synecdochically with "major thirds" in the upper register, and with a suggestion of
the pertinent whole-tone hexachord; symmetrically, the diminished triad of the measure seems to be associated synecdochically with "minor thirds" or "major sixths" in
the lower register, and with a suggestion of the pertinent octatonic octachord. These
intuitions are fortified and developed by listening to the motto as suggested by Example 2. The structure exposed there coordinates effectively with other dichotomies
about the situation. The moon is above and before, with major thirds, augmented
triads, whole-tone formations; the poet is below and after, with minor thirds, diminished triads, octatonic formations; the motto streams down incessantly from the one
to the other in repeated wavelets. The example also shows how retrograde-inversional
structuring is analogous in the upper and lower registers. In the upper register the
ordered augmented triad is enchained with its RI_2–transform, thereby generating a

---

1. Allen Forte, "Pitch-Class Set Analysis Today," *Music Analysis* 4 (1985): 29–58.
2. Figure 1 is based on Example 5e in Forte, "Pitch-Class Set Analysis Today," 54.

1. Mondestrunken.

Arnold Schoenberg, Op. 21.

Example 1.

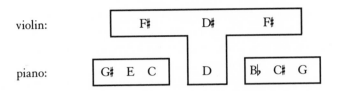

Figure 1.

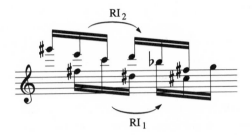

Example 2.

whole-tone hexachord; in the lower register the ordered diminished triad is analogously enchained with its RI_1–transform, thereby generating an octatonic hexachord.

The structure of Example 2—like so much else about Schoenberg's music—seems "obvious" once one hears it. One smacks one's forehead and wonders, "How could I never have heard THAT before?!" The reaction, I believe, manifests an essential feature of Schoenberg's compositional method, which is full of such suppression-creating gestures; the listener is often somehow encouraged not to notice the retrospectively "obvious" features of the material.[3] This line of thought is well worth pursuing, but the pursuit would lead us away from the present article (and the present piece). Here, it must suffice to explore those aspects of m. 1 which make it easy for a listener to listen through the structure of Example 2, without consciously noticing it.

First of all, the example cuts across the instrumentation; it takes the violin and the piano as one unit, rather than as two units in counterpoint. The point is enlightening, I think, for those who find it difficult (or a priori "wrong") to listen across Schoenberg's instrumentation in this way. For this example, the two-units-in-counterpoint are "the upper register" and "the lower register," in a fairly tricky sense of

---

3. Personally, I do not think that Schoenberg *consciously* tried to exploit the listener in this way. I think he was trying—even trying desperately—to make everything as clear and explicit as possible. Indeed, that is one reason why the phenomenon has such psychological power. One might say that when *every* thing is as explicit as possible, and when there are *many* things going on at once, then each *particular* thing is that much harder to grasp.

those words. I imagine that Schoenberg heard the registral articulation as sufficiently clear, so that he felt it would be tedious to overemphasize the idea by instrumentation as well, particularly when the little motto is repeated three times—an unusual sort of redundancy for Schoenberg. The instruments provide further information, rather than yet more redundancy, for the musical texturing; one does not quite grasp how the motto works, and one therefore listens to it several more times with added, rather than dissipating, interest.

Rhythm also makes the pattern of Example 2 difficult to hear. Instrumentation plays a strong role in this connection. The violin part suggests a definite metric grid for the stream of sixteenths, a grid wherein the sixteenths of the piano that attack together with the violin are strong and the others are weak. The meter complicates hearing Example 2. The first augmented triad of the example starts and ends on a weak sixteenth; the second augmented triad starts and ends on a strong sixteenth. That befits the idea of inversion (and retrograde inversion), but it makes the motivic correspondence of the two augmented triads cognitively elusive; one has a certain amount of difficulty hearing such a metric reversal, particularly in a context where so much else is going on. To complicate matters, the "analogous" events in the lower register are *not* completely analogous from this metric point of view. The first diminished triad starts and ends on a strong sixteenth; the second diminished triad starts and ends on a weak sixteenth. That is opposite from the way the augmented triads behave metrically. To make matters yet more difficult, the lower register "imitates" the upper, in Example 2, only one sixteenth later; that makes the analogy of the registers all the harder to pick up aurally. Imitation a sixteenth later recurs in the piano at m. 8 (with pickup), though there the rhythmically close imitation is much more straightforward pitchwise, and hence a good deal more audible. The metric reversal, from augmented to diminished trichords of the motto, puts the poet of the lower register "out of sync" with the moon of the upper register. That, happening at a time interval of only one sixteenth, projects a disoriented, out-of-focus character appropriate to the title "Mondestrunken."

Yet another feature makes Example 2 hard to hear: the skew play of the two different inversions. The inversions associated with the upper and the lower registers, respectively I_2 and I_1, are "a semitone apart" in the pitch-class world—that is, $I_1 = (T_{11})(I_2)$ in the operational sense. The "semitone-apart" seems a suggestive analogy for the rhythmic imitation "a sixteenth apart." Inversion I_1, organizing pitches in the lower register of Example 2, has the pitch pair F♯5/G5 as a center; those two pitches close the example (and the thematic motto, and the measure), so that their effect is strongly cadential as regards I_1. On the other hand I_2, not I_1, organizes pitches in the upper register, and I_2 there has the pitch C♯6 as a center; that pitch is absent from the example (and the thematic motto, and the measure), so that the RI_2 story is not as strongly closed inside the motto itself as is the RI_1 story. True, the last two sixteenths of the measure do reference the pitch *classes* C♯ and G, the two centers for I_2 as a pitch-class inversion. But the C♯ and the G do not make the RI_2 gesture balance in register. And, of course, the rival centers of inversion, for I_1 and for I_2, throw the structure of Example 2 inherently somewhat off balance, making the structure harder to take in at first hearing.[4]

In connection with the above discussion, we can focus upon two characteristic compositional motifs. There is *the motif of two adjacent inversions*; this is exemplified by the roles of I_2 and I_1 above. There is also *the motif of major/minor thirds*; this is exemplified in the pitch and pitch-class structure of Example 2, where it exfoliates into augmented/diminished triads, and into whole-tone/octatonic hexachords. The two motifs can be linked abstractly: if a minor third and a major third have a common tone, then the inversion that leaves the minor third invariant will be adjacent to the inversion that leaves the major third invariant. If I_n is one of the inversions, then the other will be $I_{(n+1)}$ or $I_{(n-1)}$.

Example 3a illustrates exactly this point, elaborating it in connection with the opening gesture of the voice part. The first tetrachord, here called the "*Wein* tetrachord," is I_7-symmetrical; the second tetrachord, which we shall call the "*Augen* tetrachord," is I_8-symmetrical. Operations I_7 and I_8 are adjacent inversions.[5] The *Wein* tetrachord spans and elaborates the minor third G♯-B (held invariant by I_7); the *Augen* tetrachord analogously spans and elaborates the major third G♯-C (held invariant by I_8). The two tetrachords are presented with the same rhythm and contour in the music, in the same metric positioning. Example 3b displays the ordered trichord held in common between the *Wein* and *Augen* tetrachords of Example 3a. We shall call this the "W/A trichord," generally considering it as unordered unless otherwise specified.

Example 4a, taking an enormous leap, shows how the W/A trichord is recalled and projected by the opening vocal phrase in "O alter Duft," the final number of *Pierrot*. It seems clear, regardless of disputes over how *Sprechstimme* is to be performed, that the singer will be sensitive to the recollection here, if only subliminally. It seems clear too that Schoenberg was sensitive to the recollection (possibly also subliminally), and that the recollection is central to the poetic theme of remembrance in the text for "O alter Duft." Example 4a includes the piano's cadential E-major $^6_4$ chord for the phrase; the cadence binds the melody of the W/A trichord here to the

---

4. In the pitch-class world, I_2 wants to balance with F♯/G, or with C/C♯; I_1 wants to balance "a semitone away" with G alone, or with C♯ alone. The last three pitches of Example 2 do reference three of the four pitch classes involved; to that degree there is a certain amount of closure. The F♯, G, and C♯ that one hears there finally summon the C at the flute entrance in m. 6.

5. The I_7/I_8 relation is "tritone related" to the I_1/I_2 relation in the motto (Ex. 2). We can imagine the "tritone" here in a number of ways. Most simply, we can just observe that $I_7 = (T_6)(I_1)$ and $I_8 = (T_6)(I_2)$. From a more sophisticated point of view, we can observe that the I-numbers 7 and 8 of Example 3 are respectively 6 more than the I-numbers 1 and 2 of Example 2. This enables us to assert a formal "isography" between some pertinent transformational networks. The interested reader can explore the basis for that formalism more precisely in David Lewin, "Klumpenhouwer Networks and Some Isographies that Involve Them," *Music Theory Spectrum* 12 (1990): 83–120 (88).

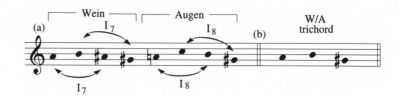

Example 3.

Example 4.

E-major tonality of "O alter Duft," strongly suggested both here and elsewhere. The W/A trichord is remembered not only "from long ago" in the cycle—that is, from song 1—but also through the filter (*Duft*) of tonality, which invokes a "long ago" even earlier than the opening of song 1. Again regardless of disputes over how *Sprechstimme* is to be performed, the relation of the vocal part here to the piano's E-major ambience is cemented by the doubling in the piano right hand at the opening of the piece. (This material is later recalled by the strings in mm. 26–27.)

Example 4b shows the piano part in mm. 24–25, carrying the penultimate cadence of the song (and of the cycle). The notes with stems up on the example show how the W/A trichord, now ordered as G♯–A–B, extends up to C at the cadence, producing the *Augen* tetrachord. In the third and fourth of the chords, the minor third {G♯,B} progresses directly to the major third {A♭,C}, manifesting even more directly the motif of the major/minor thirds which, at the opening of "Mondestrunken," characterized the progression of the *Wein* tetrachord to the *Augen* tetrachord (as on Ex. 3a). The last of the chords is marked with an asterisk and a parenthesized A♮. This pitch appears in the first complete autograph draft, but not in the fair copy *Stichvorlage*, or the first edition of the score, or Schoenberg's handwritten version *Handexemplar* for the first edition.[6] The pitch A♮ would project the *Augen* tetrachord even better than A♭. But A♮ would not project as well the expansion of the minor third {G♯,B} to the major third {A♭,C}. That major third seems better suited than

------

6. I am indebted to Reinhold Brinkmann for this information, which will appear in the *Revisionsbericht* for the forthcoming volume in the *Gesamtausgabe*.

does {A,C} for portraying the idea of looking *beyond* the minor third of the W/A trichord, "hinaus in selge Weiten."[7]

Such nostalgia and *Sehnsucht* are intensified by an association shown in Example 5. The passage is from mm. 24–25 of the Barcarole "Heimfahrt," the song that directly precedes "O alter Duft." As the example shows, the asterisked chord is highlighted there by its insistent recurrences, by its agogic accents, and by the text underlay. The text for the Barcarole involves Pierrot's sailing off into the distance, "in selge Weiten." The text underlay for Example 5 is the (complete) last verse of the poem. So the asterisked chord of Example 4b (with A♭) piles one nostalgia upon another, as it refers back to the nostalgic asterisked chords of Example 5.[8]

Having explored some ways in which the *Augen* tetrachord and related matters shape the final gestures of *Pierrot*, let us now return to the opening measures of the cycle, exploring how these matters exercise a constructive influence on the first phrases of "Mondestrunken." The left side of Example 6 displays again the *Wein* and *Augen* tetrachords, under upwards brackets. The rest of Example 6 shows the two subsequent vocal cadences, at "nieder" and at "Horizont." These cadences mark the ends of couplets in the text. They are articulated by rests—the only rests a quarter or longer for the voice in the first eleven measures, after the rest following "trinkt." And they project the only notes in the voice part that lie at middle C or below, emphasizing their cadential function in a most literal sense. One sees, and then hears, how the pair of cadences projects the *Augen* tetrachord in the lower octave (large lower bracket). The *Horizont* cadence by itself projects the W/A trichord in the ordering G♯–A–B (small lower bracket).

The *Wein* tetrachord is a chromatic tetrachord, 4–1 (0123); the *Augen* tetrachord is what we shall call an "octatonic tetrachord," 4–3 (0134).[9] The progression of the *Wein* tetrachord to the *Augen* tetrachord manifests an idea which we shall call *the motif of the chrom/octa tetrachords*. That is, in general, a progression whereby a chromatic tetrachord progresses to (or follows) an octatonic tetrachord with which it shares three common tones. The motif of chrom/octa tetrachords thus exfoliates from the motif of major/minor thirds; it also abstractly projects the motif of adjacent inversions (the inversion that leaves the chrom tetrachord invariant, and the inversion that leaves the octa tetrachord invariant). We shall soon explore chrom/octa tetrachord progressions in the first eleven measures of "Mondestrunken," beyond the progression of the *Wein* and *Augen* tetrachords themselves.

---

7. The idea of the poet's "looking" associates with the "Augen" of the *Augen* tetrachord in any case (whether one plays A♭ or A♮).

8. The auxiliary notes A3 and D4 for the trilled asterisked {G3,C♯4} in the strings coincide with the notes A3 and D4 in the left hand of Example 4b, notes from which asterisked G3 and D♭4 are approached in that example.

9. It will be convenient to reserve the term "octatonic tetrachord" for set class 4–3 only, even though the octatonic scale also contains 4–10 (0235) as a four-note scale segment. Set class 4–10 can then be referred to as the "Dorian tetrachord," for instance {D,E,F,G} or {A,B,C,D}.

Example. 5.

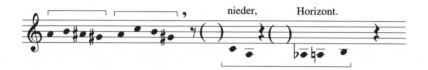

Example 6.

We must first, of course, hear some other constructive octatonic tetrachords in the music, beyond the *Augen* tetrachord itself. To focus our ears in this direction, Example 7 displays on three staves the pitches through the beginning of m. 6. The top staff shows all notes that lie above C6. The opening G♯6 and E6 are portrayed with open noteheads and beamed together, with an arrow pointing to their right; the reason for this will become clear later. The bottom staff of Example 7 shows all notes in the passage that lie below C♯5; the middle staff shows all notes that lie between C♯5 and C6 inclusive. At the left of the middle staff, beams portray the octatonic component of the opening motto in the manner of Example 2 earlier. The octatonic hexachord, isolated in the register between C♯5 and C6, suggests A5 and E5 to come, to complete the octatonic scale in that register.

The flute entrance in m. 3 presents the suggested A5, dwelling upon that note at some length. The notehead on Example 7 is opened, to suggest that length. In the example, the upward-beamed tetrachord A–B♭–F♯–G is marked "oct1"; the notes are adjacent in register and they sound on successive sixteenths over the last beat of m. 3. They sound again, in the same way, over the second beat of m. 4. Then the flute continues, over the last beat of m. 4, with A5–B♭5–A5–F♯5, continuing to elaborate the oct1 tetrachord. At the beginning of m. 5 the flute signs off on A4, shown on the low staff of Example 7; this note—the only nonvocal note on the low staff—ties the oct1 tetrachord together with the *Augen* tetrachord of the voice.

The next event on the middle staff of Example 7 is the new octatonic tetrachord oct2, presented by the left hand of the piano under a slur in mm. 5–6. Oct2 completes

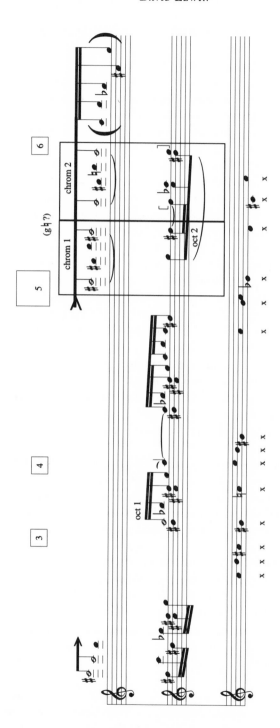

Example 7.

the diminution of the octatonic scale on the middle staff of the example. Oct2 and oct1 are I_1–partners; they invert into each other about their common tones F♯5/G5, the center of pitch inversion for the ambitus of the middle staff. The pitch pair F♯5/G5, we recall, was also the center of pitch inversion for the octatonic hexachord within the motto: the two beamed trichords at the left of Example 7 are related to each other by retrograde inversion about F♯5 and G5. The middle staff of Example 7 thus shows how the octatonic implications of the opening motto are fulfilled and elaborated by subsequent events in the "octatonic register" which they define. The example also shows how octatonic tetrachords become involved in that story. Oct2 specifically diminutes the {F♯,D♯} of the violin; that becomes very clear later in m. 6, when the violin resumes its ostinato pizzicatos on those notes directly after the end of oct2 in the piano left hand.

Toward the end of Example 7, new activity emerges in the upper register. The right hand of the piano encircles G♯6 with lower and upper neighbors; the G♯s are drawn with open noteheads. Then the right hand of the piano encircles E6 with lower and upper neighbors; the Es are also drawn with open noteheads. The encircled G♯s and Es begin a highly decorated statement of the motto, as suggested by the arrow coming into them from the left. Encircled G♯ and encircled E are beamed upwards, and the the beam continues on past the end of Example 7 proper, connecting with the continuation of the motto in the middle of m. 6—shown in parentheses to the right of the example.[10]

The boxes marked "chrom1" and "chrom2" display chromatic tetrachords governing the harmony in the piano during the indicated parts of the passage. (Chrom1 does not need G in the upper register to be manifest in the harmony.) The two chromatic tetrachords go together with the octatonic tetrachords oct1 and oct2, respectively. That is, chrom1 and oct1 project the motif of chrom/octa tetrachords; so do chrom2 and oct2.

The chrom sets provide a rationale for the ornamentation of G♯6 and E6 by their neighbors. Perhaps far-fetched, but to my ear utterly persuasive, is another aspect of the ornamentation. G♯–F♯–A, in the piano right hand over the first beat of m. 5, projects in order the pitch classes on which the instruments have so far entered the piece, G♯ in the piano (m. 1), F♯ in the violin (m. 1), A in the *Sprechstimme* (m. 2) and flute (m. 3).

Chrom1 and chrom2 invert into each other by I_0. One might thereby assert the adjacent-inversion motif, since oct1 and oct2 invert into each other by way of I_1. But the assertion seems strained. I find it easier to hear a T_9–relation between the chromatic tetrachords, following the descending minor third G5–E5 in the piano left hand during mm. 5–6. That minor third works in skew fashion against the open-notehead major third G♯6–E6 in the right-hand figuration. The pertinent motif here is that of the major/minor thirds. The idea of {G♯,E} versus {G,E} is reinforced

---

10. For this reason, I strongly prefer G♯6 to G6 in the middle of m. 5. Example 7, with a parenthesized G♮, indicates the possibility of that note. Pitch G♮ would make a complete chromatic tetrachord in the piano right hand. But I prefer the effect of G♯, as just discussed.

by the bracketed A♭–G of the violin at the end of the middle staff in Example 7. Pitch A♭ (G♯) sounds over the piano left-hand E of oct2; G sounds under the piano right-hand E at the opening of m. 6. The violin notes are bracketed because A♭ is the unique note, on the middle staff of Example 7, that does not belong to the pertinent octatonic scale; until this moment everything in the register C♯5–C6 has been octatonic diminution. Of course oct1 also transforms into oct2 by way of T_9, within their octatonic scale. The low note of oct1 is F♯5; the low note of oct2 is D♯5; the T_9–relation of the octatonic tetrachords thereby composes out the original F♯–D♯ minor thirds of the violin over mm. 1–4.

Example 8 inspects the vocal line as a whole over the first eleven measures. The *Wein* tetrachord is given an alternate label as "chrom0," and the *Augen* tetrachord as "oct0." We have already noted how oct0 recurs in the lowest register (middle C and below) at the cadences on "nieder" and "Horizont"; those cadences are marked on the example by brackets below with "oct0" labels.

The *Horizont* cadence, closing the passage, is approached through the highly symmetrical pitch set marked Y on the example. Set Y is inversionally symmetrical about the pitches E4 and G4, at its registral and temporal center. The E4 and G4 are all the more emphasized by being sung with full voice, rather than delivered with *Sprechstimme*. Pitch classes E and G engage the idea of the {E,G♯}/{E,G} relation, discussed a bit above in connection with the end of Example 7.[11]

In Example 8 we can hear that Y is approached from a chromatic set "chrom3." That set is {E♭,D,D♭,C}, here deployed in the upper register of the voice. As the example shows, chrom3 is also presented earlier in the voice, an octave lower (mm. 5–6). On that occasion it is combined with some whole-tone material that is not marked on the example. We shall explore the whole-tone material shortly; meanwhile let us turn our attention to the set, marked X, that bridges the two occurrences of chrom3 across the registral octave, bubbling up from "nieder" in the manner of "eine Springflut." Set X, like set Y, is an inversionally symmetrical pitch-class set. (It is pitch-class symmetrical about C: the high E♭ balances the low A about C, while D and B♭ also balance each other about C.) The lower staff of Example 8 shows the source for X in the music for the fourth, fifth, and sixth sixteenths of m. 3—the music surrounding the flute entrance.

Example 9 compares the symmetrical pcsets X and Y. Set X is I_0–symmetrical, and set Y is I_{11}–symmetrical. The progression from X to Y thus projects the motif of

---

11. One might even entertain the idea of a progression from the G♯–E that opens the piece, to the sung E–G, that heralds the cadence for the entire first section. It is interesting that the G♯–E is given the "E 6/4 harmonization" at "Wein," the first vocal downbeat of the piece (and indeed its first real downbeat of any sort). The arrows of Example 7 help one to listen for the big progression just proposed.

Whatever there is to that idea, the singer will enter very securely if she takes the B of "Wein" from the repeated G♯–E of the motto, and sings her preceding A as a pickup to that downbeat B.

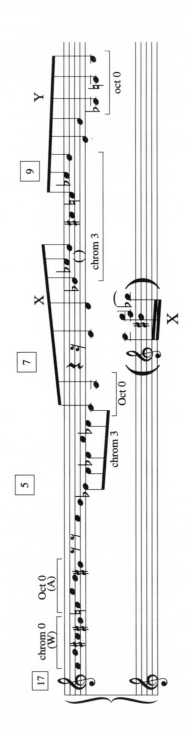

Example 8.

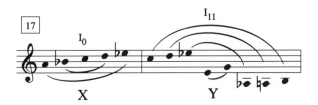

Example 9.

adjacent inversions. In this form of the motif, the I-number *decrements* by 1, which befits the cadential function of Y; in earlier projections of the motif the I-number *incremented* by 1, where the material was presenting "opening" ideas.

Example 10 explores relations among the chrom tetrachords of Example 8 (the voice part over mm. 1–11). The chrom3 tetrachord is in T_4–relation to the chrom0' tetrachord. Example 10 also articulates a "chrom0' tetrachord," with which chrom3 is T_3–related. Chrom0' is not as well articulated by the voice in mm. 1–4 as are chrom0 and oct0. Still, when chrom3 appears in the upper octave, the singer and the attentive listener will hear how the returning C5, at the bottom of chrom3, picks up the earlier C5 at the top of oct0, thereby making a gap-fill in the entire vocal line so far. The registral span E♭5–C5, spanning chrom3, thereby associates with the earlier registral span A4–C5. And that will synecdochically generate a cognitive chrom0', to diminute the A4–C5 span.

The T_3 and T_4 arrows of Example 10 manifest once more the major/minor third motif, now in a transformational setting. To a certain extent we can associate T_3 with the dyad A4–C5 (low notes of chrom0' and chrom3), while associating T_4 with the dyad G♯4–C5 (low notes of chrom0 and chrom3).

Example 11 analyzes the segment of the vocal part from mm. 1–11 so far not discussed. Example 11a shows the notes for "nachts der Mond in wogen nie-." A downwards beam connects the notes of chrom3. An upwards beam connects the "whole-tone idea" G–E♭–F–D♭, an idea which rides above chrom3 in register. The whole-tone idea, particularly in a local upper register, suggests material from the opening motto of the piece. Example 11c recalls the pertinent material, connected with a sixteenth-note type double beam: E–C–D–B♭. This material rides over the indicated *Sprechstimme*. In Example 11b the notes of 11c are compressed in register and reordered, the better to resemble Example 11a. One hears thereby that Example 11c is pc-transformed by T_3 into Example 11a. We have already seen how chrom0' is transformed by T_3 into chrom3; that is the "lower" part of the transformation on the example. The "upper" part maps the whole-tone idea of 11c into the whole-tone idea of 11a.

Example 11d shows how the piano responds to these relations. As soon as the voice's F (Ex. 11a) is heard, the piano launches a new version of the opening motto, transformed so as to begin with the pitch classes F–D♭–C that close Example 11a.

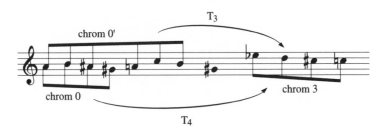

Example 10.

This is shown on the left side of Example 11d. The right side of 11d shows how the continuation of the transformed motto comes back to the original version, thereby cementing the association of Example 11c with Example 11a.

We have heard several times now how the T_3 relation of chrom0′ to chrom3 seems functional, related to the minor thirds that span the chromatic tetrachords. Example 12 expands on this notion. It helps us hear how chrom1, chrom2, and chrom3 participate in a chain of T_9–relations. (The three tetrachords then form a complete T_9–cycle along with chrom0′.) Chrom1 and chrom2, on the upper staff of the example, are projected as they were in earlier discussion (Ex. 7). The beam for chrom2 is extended to subsume the continuation of chrom2 in the F♯–D♯–F♯ of the violin, m. 6. Chrom3 then appears at the end of m. 6 in the manner indicated on the upper staff of Example 12, projecting a similar sort of texturing with a strong registral continuity. The lower staff of the example gives the notes of chrom3 in the voice, as they underlie the events of the upper staff.

The T_9 relations among chrom1, chrom2, and chrom3 can be heard as carried by their lowest notes, which are respectively F♯, D♯, and C. To the right of the double bar in the upper staff, those pitch classes appear configured as in the diminished triad of the opening motto. The play with the chromatic tetrachords can accordingly be heard as an elaboration of that diminished triad. We have already noted several times how the play with the chromatic tetrachords involves the violin's opening F♯–D♯ dyad, from within the diminished triad, in various ways.

Such matters associate with the octatonic set projected on the middle staff of Example 7 earlier. Example 13a shows the accompanimental pitches that sound during the fourth eighth of m. 6. The chord "summarizes" the octatonic register of Example 7: it projects the extremes of that register (C♯5 and C6) along with the means (F♯5 and G5). Pitches C♯5 and C6 define the ambitus of the octatonic scale at issue; F♯5 and G5 are the center of inversion for the scale. We have heard C♯5, F♯5, and G5 over and over again—this is how the motto ends. New to the picture is the added high C of the flute, provided by the second characteristic flute entrance.

That observation suggests examining aspects of the flute part in itself; Example 13b guides an exploration. The first flute entrance emphasizes A5–B♭5 during mm. 3–4; we have already seen (in Ex. 7) how those notes contribute to a projection of an

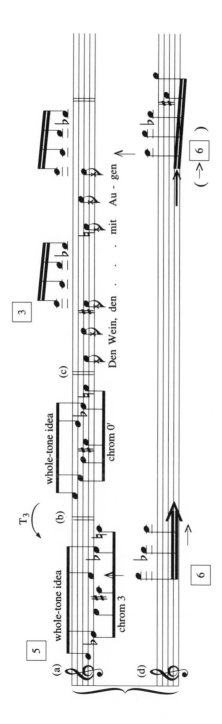

Example 11.

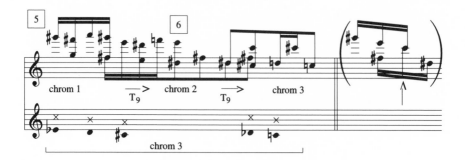

Example 12.

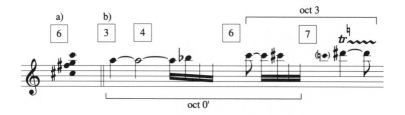

Example 13.

oct1 tetrachord. The second flute entrance (Ex. 13b, m. 6) emphasizes C6–C♯6 in a manner parallel to the earlier A5–B♭5. The lower bracket on Example 13b groups the rhyming dyads together, projecting oct0′, the octatonic tetrachord that "goes with" chrom0′ in our notational system. Oct0′ lies within the governing octatonic scale as a set of *pitch classes*; but one hears that the high C♯6 of oct0′ here breaches the *pitch* barrier of our "octatonic register" C♯5–C6. During the last eighth of m. 6 and almost the entire first quarter of m. 7, the flute leaves its high register—the rest of the music also leaves the high register alone. The flute picks up the high C6 again just before the second quarter of m. 7. Then that second quarter expands the upper range of the instrument in the piece yet a stage further, with the trill on D♯6(E6). The upper bracket on Example 13b groups the C6–C♯6 dyad of m. 6 with the D♯6–E6 trill of mm. 7–8; the two dyads project the tetrachord oct3 in the new upper register. (Oct3 is the tetrachord that goes with chrom3 in our system.)

We have already heard oct1 and oct2 tetrachords (as in Ex. 7); the new tetrachords oct0′ and oct3 complete the system of octatonic tetrachords within our octatonic scale. We now have an octatonic tetrachord to "go with" each of the chromatic tetrachords chrom0′, chrom1, chrom2, and chrom3. The three dyads of Example 13b project a T_3–chain, a gesture which recalls the T_9–chain of chromatic tetrachords earlier displayed in Example 12.

It seems poetically apt that the "octatonic register" of Example 7 expands upwards as shown in Example 13a. The original octatonic register was defined by the lower register of the motto, as shown in Example 2. That was the octatonic register of the poet, below the whole-tone register of the moon. Now the octatonic register expands upwards towards the moon, as the poet's thoughts and desires surge upwards in the "Springflut."

The chord of Example 13a is an instance of 4–9 (0167). From the C6–C#6 to the D#6–E6 of Example 13b, the music of the accompanying istruments manifests many fourths and tritones, characteristic intervals of (0167) sets. Without too much labor, we can find other (0167) sets embedded in this music. But the labor requires a bit too much intellectual sifting and winnowing of notes. The music can be more convincingly articulated, both intellectually and by ear, into 5–7 (01567) pentachords. Example 14 shows how.

The (01567) forms of Example 14 are all more or less contiguous in time and/or register. They cover all the accompaniment between the high C–C# and the high D#–E, except for the D–A in the piano, which will be discussed later. Having heard the (01567)s, we can now more easily focus our attention upon their (0167) subsets. Figure 2 arranges those sets in a suggestive format. Each column of the figure represents an (0167) set referenced by Example 14. The lower-case letters beneath the columns show to which (01567)s of the example the various (0167)s belong. Thus the set in the second column of Figure 2, the set {C,C#,F#,G}, belongs to both pentachord a and pentachord e of Example 14. Each column of the figure is T_{11} of the column to the left; the spatial layout of the figure thus portrays the (0167) tetrachords moving "down through a chromatic tetrachord" in a fashion that could readily be portrayed by a product network, in a sense I have explored elsewhere.[12] The transformational "chromatic tetrachord" is of course thematic here.

The progression of lower-case letters in the figure is also interesting. The alphabetic order of those letters represents the chronological order in which the music projects the completed (01567) sets (as indicated on Ex. 14). The induced order of (0167)s that one sees in Figure 2 is very systematic: the series of (0167)s moves consistently by T_{11} steps, except when there is a "carriage return" from set c to set d, going from the right side to the left side of the figure by way of T_3.

We must be cautious here, because (0167) is so symmetrical. We cannot distinguish the overall effect of T_{11} and T_5 on such a set, nor that of T_3 and T_9. The indicated pairs of operations are "contextual synonyms," in a sense defined elsewhere.[13] We could, in particular, describe the progression from c to d on the figure as "by way of T_9," or from a to b as "by way of T_5." (There are also contextually synonymous inversion operations to consider, but fortunately we need not do so here.) The sym-

---

12. David Lewin, *Generalized Musical Intervals and Transformations* (New Haven: Yale University Press, 1987), 204–06.

13. David Lewin, *Musical Form and Transformation: 4 Analytic Essays* (New Haven: Yale University Press, 1993), 80.

Example 14.

```
G#
G        G
         F#       F#
         F        F
                  F        F
                           E
D
C#       C#
         C        C
                  B        B
                           Bb

         a        b        c
d        e        fg
```

Figure 2.

metry of the (0167)s does not invalidate our discussion of Figure 2, but it does qualify it. To be precise, wherever we have referred to "T_{11}," we should instead refer to "T_{11} or some contextual synonym."

The "supplement" note of a (01567), the note beyond its (0167) tetrachord, plays an interesting role in this context. The supplement renders the pentachord *non*symmetrical. As regards (01567) pentachords, we *can* distinguish the effect of T_{11} from that of T_5, and the effect of T_3 from that of T_9. Thus in Figure 3, we see that the transformation from *pentachord* c to *pentachord* d is unambiguously by way of T_9, not by way of T_3. Likewise, the progression from pentachord d to e is unambiguously by way of T_5, not by T_{11}, and the progression from pentachord e to g is unambiguously by T_{11}, not by T_5. Pentachord f "anticipates" pentachord g with another (01567) form that shares the same (0167). Thus the supplements help us fill up the actual music, and parse its transformations unambiguously; the symmetrical (0167) subsets of the pentachords, without their supplements, help us group the transformations into contextual synonyms, arriving at the systematic structuring of Figure 2.[14]

14. An analogous situation, concerning a symmetrical pentachordal subset of a nonsymmetrical hexachord in Webern's op. 10, no. 2, is observed and critically discussed in Lewin, *Musical Form and Transformation*, 86–88.

F	D	G	F♯
E	C♯	F♯	F
C	A	D	C♯
B	G♯	C♯	C
B♭	G	C	B

$$T_9 \qquad T_5 \qquad T_{11}$$

c   d   e   g

Figure 3.

Figure 4 analyzes the progression of pentachords a, b, and c. The forms a′ and b′, not projected in the music, are aids for this analysis. The layout of the figure displays a sense in which a moves to b by the same transformation as b to c. Specifically, a goes to a′ by transformation J (to be explained shortly); then a′ goes to b by T_{11}. Analogously, b goes to b′ by way of transformation J; then b′ goes to c by way of T_{11}. The transformation J inverts any (01567) set by preserving its (0167) and moving the supplement note three semitones in such a way as not to cross any (0167) boundary.[15]

An interesting aspect of the (01567) pentachord, considering the present study, is that it can be analyzed as the set-theoretic union of a (0167) tetrachord with an "adjacent" 4–8 (0156) tetrachord. Figure 5 clarifies and sharpens the idea. The middle column of the figure shows those tetrachords that can be expressed as the product of a (01) dyad with some other dyad. Dyad (01) times (03), for example, yields a tetrachord (0134); (01) times (05) yields a tetrachord (0156).[16] The right-hand column of the figure shows pentachords that naturally combine various pairs of tetrachords that lie adjacent in the middle column. Thus tetrachords (0134) and (0145), adjacent in the middle column, combine to form the pentachord 5–3 (01345), shown at the appropriate location in the right-hand column.

At one extreme, at the top of the figure, we see that the chrom and oct tetrachords combine in this fashion, to form a chromatic pentachord. We are famil-

---

15. For example, the D of pentachord a can move "up" to the F of pentachord a′ without "crossing" either {C,C♯} or {F♯,G}. If the D of pentachord a were to move to B instead of F, the "boundary" {C,C♯} would have to be crossed moving "down," or the "boundary" {F♯,G} would have to be crossed moving "up." One could also define the J-inversion of a (01567) pentachord as that inversion which exchanges notes of constituent (0167)s that lie an ic5 apart—"1" with "6" and "0" with "7."

16. This idea invokes a notion systematically explored by Richard Cohn in "Transpositional Combination in Twentieth-Century Music" (Ph.D. diss., Eastman School of Music, 1987). Cohn's later article, "Inversional Symmetry and Transpositional Combination in Bartók," *Music Theory Spectrum* 10 (1988): 19–42, is more easily available, but more narrowly focused on the music of its one composer.

G	G			
F♯	F♯	F♯	F♯	
	F	F	F	F
	E	E		E
D				
C♯	C♯		C♯	
C	C	C	C	C
		B	B	B
				B♭

	J		T_{11}	J		T_{11}	
a		a'		b		b'	c

Figure 4.

the product of   is the   adjacent product tetras
(01) with   tetrachord;   combine to form pentachord

the product of (01) with	is the tetrachord;	adjacent product tetras combine to form pentachord
(02)	(0123) (chrom)	
		(01234)
(03)	(0134) (oct)	
		(01345)
(04)	(0145)	
		(01456)
(05)	(0156)	
		(01567) (Forte 5-7)
(06)	(0167)	

Figure 5.

iar with the phenomenon from many earlier contexts in this article—in particular from the way that the *Wein* and *Augen* tetrachords combine to form a chromatic pentachord for the opening vocal gesture. At the other extreme, at the bottom of the figure, we see that an (0156) tetrachord combines with an (0167) tetrachord in this fashion, to form a (01567) pentachord. We have just been exploring various (01567) pentachords and their (0167) subsets. What we see from Figure 5 is that such pentachords can be regarded as structurally "analogous" to chromatic pentachords, when regarded in the light shed by the figure. The combination of "adjacent" (0156) and (0167) tetrachords, in this fashion, specifically manifests something analogous to the motif of adjacent chrom/oct tetrachords. We may generalize the motif into a "motif of adjacent (01)-product tetrachords."[17]

17. The motif entails the motif of adjacent inversions: if X, for instance, is a (0156) tetrachord, and Y is an adjacent (0167) tetrachord, and I_n leaves X invariant, then either $I_{(n-1)}$ leaves Y invariant, or $I_{(n+1)}$ leaves Y invariant.

Another specific instance of the generalized motif can be heard in the vertical sonority halfway through m. 7. Pitches C, B, E, and D♯ manifest a (01)-product tetrachord of type 4–7 (0145); C, B, F, and E manifest an adjacent (01)-product tetrachord of type (0156); the combination of the two tetrachords projects a 5–6 (01456) pentachord in the manner sketched on Figure 5. In this connection it may not be coincidental that the sonority opening m. 7 recalls the combination of *Wein* and *Augen* tetrachords in its lower register. The G♯ and A in the flute, together with the B–C trill of the piano, project the *Augen* tetrachord in its original register; the low Bb of the violin completes the *Wein*-plus-*Augen* chromatic pentachord. The association is easier to hear than one might expect (Ex. 15).

Example 16a shows how the *Augen* tetrachord just cited is accompanied, during the music of m. 7, by an "organal" octatonic tetrachord five semitones higher. The *Augen* tetrachord is depicted in the example by solid noteheads, the organal tetrachord by open noteheads. The notes of the example portray all pitches in m. 7 that lie between G♯4 and F5 inclusive. The D–A fourth in the piano fits into this picture; it is an "organal" fourth just like the B–E fourth that precedes it in the piano part, along with the organal accessories C–F for the trills. The vertical B–E fourth then returns halfway through the measure, now in piano and violin.

The notion of "organal fourths" fits well with the idea that the (01567) pentachords arise from combination of (0167) sets with (0156) sets, the latter being products of semitones with ("organal") fourths. For instance, {B,C}-plus-{E,F}, in m. 7, is one such (0156) set. Example 16b gives a segment of the violin part from mm. 7–8. One hears how the organal tetrachord extends, by way of the C♮, into a (01345) pentachord. This manifests in another guise the motif of adjacent (01)-product tetrachords: {E,F}-plus-{C♯,D} combines with {E,F}-plus-{C,C♯}, forming the pentachord {C,C♯,D,E,F}.

Example 17a depicts the pitches of the *Springflut* in flute and violin, at the opening of m. 7, up through the flute's F5. The rising flurry of activity suggests ordering the pitches by register rather than chronology. One sees that the ordering is very symmetrical; the pitches fall into augmented triads below and above, with a chromatic tetrachord (chrom1) in the middle that bridges the augmented triads. The entire figure is symmetrical about G4 and G♯4.

The "welling-up" of this gesture suggests that we compare it to the "pouring-down" of the opening motto. Example 17b shows how a pitch-inverted form of the motto is essentially embedded in Example 17a. To get the complete inverted piano part of the original motto, we must include the E and B from the piano part at the opening of m. 7, with the E an octave lower. Those notes are marked by stems and a beam on the example. Example 17c shows how a transposed retrograde of the motto is also essentially embedded in Example 17a. To get the complete transposed retrograde for the piano part of the original motto, we must again include the E and B from the piano part at the opening of m. 7, with the E an octave lower.

If the entire motto (rather than just its piano part) were being inverted or retrograde-transposed, the transformed violin part of the entire motto would comprise

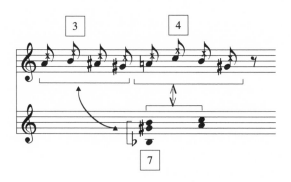

Example 15.

Example 16.

Example 17.

pitch classes C and E♭, to go with either Example 17b or Example 17c. Those pitch classes are found in m. 7, in the flute, immediately following the music of Examples 17a, b, and c. Example 17d indicates their presence there, inter alia completing the transformed-motto references.

We have considered the accompaniment music in the first half of m. 7 to be *Springflut* music. We can similarly consider the accompaniment music during mm. 7.5–9 to be *Überschwemmen* music. We exclude the flute trill and the piano chord at m. 7.5, which belong to the *Springflut*. As we shall see, we can consider the *Überschwemmen* to begin as early as the violin's C♯ in m. 7, and we can end the *Überschwemmen* with the first chord of m. 10. The accompaniment in the rest of m. 10 we shall call *Horizont* music.

Just when the first large section of the piece comes to its cadence, the piano part of the *Horizont* music projects major thirds, an augmented triad in a high register, and a whole-tone sonority, thus recalling whole-tone aspects of the original opening motto. And the octatonic aspects of the opening motto are recalled by the basically octatonic sound of the *Überschwemmen* music, that precedes and leads into the *Horizont*. The progression of the opening motto, as the piece begins, is from whole-tone to octatonic sound (as in Ex. 2); the progression from *Überschwemmen* to *Horizont*, at the biggest cadence so far, is from octatonic to whole-tone sound.

In the *Horizont*, flute and violin contribute to the major-third sound, with a major third from a whole-tone set different from the piano's. The sonority recalls aspects of the *Springflut*. Example 18a gives the *Horizont* pitches of flute, violin, and piano right hand. In Example 18b are copied pertinent "Springflut" pitches from Example 17a, to assert a T_5 relation; Example 18c copies pertinent *Springflut* pitches from Example 17a, to assert an I_8 relation. The I_8 relation seems easier to hear than the T_5 relation, because it matches the high B♭ of the *Horizont*, the highest note of the piece so far, with the low B♭ of the *Springflut*, the lowest metrically stressed note of the accompaniment so far. The low B♭ is stressed at the barline of m. 7, where the *Springflut* starts, and the low stressed B♭ returns at the barline of m. 10, just before the *Horizont* music, whose high B♭ is then easily heard as an echo. The matching low and high B♭s of Examples 18c and 18a are supported by the matching low and high B♭ augmented triads there.

We have observed that the *Überschwemmen* music is "basically octatonic." Specifically, the piano part of this music basically projects the complete octatonic scale which includes the familiar major third {G♯,E}; the familiar major third functions once more as an incipit, now for the piano figure of mm. 7–8. That octatonic scale also includes the minor third {E,G}, heard several times already in counterpoise to {E,G♯}. We hear that counterpoise once more at the beginning of m. 8, where E-G continues the incipit G♯-E of the melodic figure; E–G in the right hand also sounds in counterpoint against G♯-E in the left hand, imitating a sixteenth later. The melodic figure of m. 8 continues on within the octatonic scale until the right hand reaches the next G♯, halfway through the measure. Then C, which is not in the octatonic scale, obtrudes itself into the figure. After that C, and its immediate imitation in the left hand, the remainder of the piano part in m. 8 returns to and completes the octatonic scale. Indeed, the piano part of m. 9 remains within the scale, except for the F♯ auxiliary to the trill.

We shall return later to that F♯. Meanwhile let us devote some more attention to the "intruder" C in m. 8 of the piano part. Abstractly, C completes the augmented triad that includes the incipit {G♯,E}. The idea is a bit more than abstract, because the opening motto projected the augmented triad G♯-E-C in exactly that way. More concretely yet, the piano's C in the middle of m. 8 is approached from B-G♯ in the melodic figure. The succession B-G♯-C projects another highly thematic form of the major/minor third motif. It specifically references the progression from *Wein* to *Augen* tetrachords; in that connection the progression from {G♯,B} to {G♯,C} emerged particularly strongly on Examples 3a and 4b earlier.

Thus the piano figure of m. 8, with pickup, involves two thematic major/minor third segments, G♯–E–G and B–G♯–C; the latter segment assigns a thematic

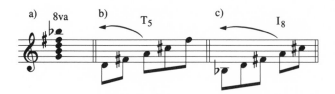

Example 18.

meaning to the intruder C. Between those two melodic segments we can hear another segment that projects a major/minor third, namely F–C♯–D. And that segment rhymes with the end of the figure in the right hand, going on into m. 9; there
we hear C♯–F–E (ignoring the auxiliary F♯ in this connection). Except for B♭–G in
m. 8, the entire piano figure thus parses into forms of the major/minor third motif.

The B♭–G segment of m. 8 is part of a diminished-triad arpeggiation, B♭–G–
C♯; the gesture recalls the same triad at the end of the opening motto (piano, end of
m. 1). While the piano is playing this segment, the violin plays the familiar F♯–D♯
alternation that constituted its contribution to the original motto (during m. 1). The
arpeggiated diminished triad B♭–G–C♯ that begins the third beat of m. 8 in the piano right hand rhymes with the arpeggiated diminished triad D–B–G♯ that begins
the second beat of the measure there. The rhyming diminished triads suture together various forms of the major/minor third segments. An analogous suture, during the first beat of the measure, is provided by the segment G–F–C♯ there. This
recalls aspects of the voice part in mm. 5–6 ("nachts . . . in Wogen"). Example 11a,
earlier, showed how this "whole-tone idea" fit into the overall shaping of the voice
part there. The G–F–C♯ suture returns at the end of m. 8 in the piano right hand,
now as G–C♯–F; in the imitating left hand, the F remains throughout m. 9.

It is time now to analyze the violin part during the *Überschwemmen* music.
Whether we start at the C♯ of m. 7, or at the following E, we shall find it plausible to
hear the part as projecting the same octatonic set as the piano, along with the same
"intruder" pitch class (C), and also an additional insertion of the F♯–D♯ dyad, during
mm. 8–9, quoted from the original motto material of m. 1. The intruder C at the first
beat of m. 8 fits into the augmented triad E–C–A♭ projected by the notes on the
quarter-note beats from the middle of m. 7 to the middle of m. 8; indeed the first
four notes of m. 8 transpose down by a major third the last three notes of m. 7, along
with the C that begins m. 8. After the inserted F♯–D♯ dyads are finished, the remaining notes of m. 9, up through the beginning of m. 10, return to the octatonic
scale, except for a second intruder C. These notes, C♯–D–B–G♯–C–G–B♭, refer back
to the melodic figure in the piano a measure earlier; there (piano, m. 8) we heard
C♯–D–B–G♯–C–B♭–G. As in the piano during m. 8, the intruder C of the violin
during m. 9 fits into the thematic segment B–G♯–C, now deployed with a different
registral contour.

Example 19.

The piano F♯ in m. 9, auxiliary to the trill there, picks up the preceding F♯ of the violin and sounds the pitch against the final D♯ of the violin, at the barline of m. 9. Example 19 shows how the original motto lies like a template behind the "basically octatonic" music of the *Überschwemmen*, in particular contributing the "intruder C" and the F♯–D♯ dyad that lie outside the particular octatonic scale at issue here. The top staff of the example locates inside the piano right-hand figure of m. 8 (with pickup) the pitches of the piano part from m. 1. The pitches are all there, and they are now presented in descending registral order, "*Überschwemmend*." On the bottom staff of the example appear the concomitant F♯–D♯ pitches of the violin. The fit of violin with piano part is somewhat different here from what it was in m. 1, but it is not so different as to obscure the reference to the opening motto. Everything else is octatonic filler, as already described, or imitative material in the piano left hand and in the violin part of m. 9, except for one particular intruder C, the one in the violin at the barline of m. 8. We have discussed this C in connection with the augmented triad outline E–C–A♭ provided by the strong eighths of the violin during mm. 7.5–8.5. The C also figures in a vertical projection of the augmented triad, whose pitch classes all sound together at the barline of m. 8 in violin and piano.

FORM AND IDEA IN SCHOENBERG'S *PHANTASY*

CHRISTOPHER F. HASTY

> *Form in Music* serves to bring about comprehensibility
> through memorability. Evenness, regularity, symmetry, sub-
> division, repetition, unity, relationship in rhythm and har-
> mony and even logic—none of these elements produces or
> even contributes to beauty. But all of them contribute to an
> organization which makes the presentation of the musical
> idea intelligible.[1]

P acked into this opening theoretical statement from the essay "Brahms
the Progressive" are several themes often encountered in Schoenberg's
writings. At the core of this statement and of Schoenberg's theoretical
reflection in general is the notion of *comprehensibility*.[2] It is only because of
our (shared) capacity to hold onto or grasp the complex character of a sequence of
sonic events that there can be such a thing as a "musical idea." Because musical ideas
appear to us only in passage, *memorability* is crucial for our ability to comprehend
these ideas and, more broadly, to make intelligible "the presentation of the idea" (for
Schoenberg, a unity in which ideas and their contrasts are comprehended or held

---

1. Arnold Schoenberg, "Brahms the Progressive," in *Style and Idea*, trans. Leo Black (London: Faber and Faber, 1975), 399. An illuminating interpretation of this passage is found in
Carl Dahlhaus, "Musical Prose," in *Schoenberg and the New Music*, trans. Derrick Puffett and
Alfred Clayton (Cambridge: Cambridge University Press, 1987), 105–106. Especially interesting is Dahlhaus's suggestion that "a musical idea—if the concept is to be neither fictitious
nor tautological—cannot be understood as anything other than the essence of the relationships by means of which a musical phrase reaches beyond itself and its immediate existence."
(106)
2. The physical, gestural connotations that can be felt in the word "comprehensibility" by
an English speaker who hears a connection with "prehensile" (or even "hand") or remembers
some Latin (the intensive *com* + *praehendere*, "to grasp") will be much more keenly felt by a
German speaker in the word *Fasslichkeit*. The same might be said of the relationship between "coherence" and *Zusammenhang*. The attempt to overcome oppositions of physical
and intellectual, feeling and thinking, was characteristic of Schoenberg's theoretical speculation and is a characteristic that I believe has great value both for the study of music and for

together in the imagination as variations of the "basic idea"). Schoenberg does not, however, identify beauty with comprehensibility; for the characteristics that enhance comprehensibility (evenness, regularity, symmetry, and so forth) can also lead to banal and tedious music—tedious, that is, to an "alert and well-trained mind." Although beauty cannot exist apart from comprehensibility, it exceeds mere comprehensibility in its aim for complexity of feeling and intensity of involvement.[3]

A leading idea of the Brahms essay is that regularity, symmetry, and repetition can be highly attenuated without leading to a failure of comprehension. Complexities of phrase division wedded to subtle motivic correspondences can result in music of high aesthetic rank in which heightened demands for comprehensibility are rewarded with a novel intensity and range of expression. Schoenberg does not, however, attempt to describe in any detail how this intensification is achieved or how it is to be reconciled with the demands of musical form. In his essay, brief analyses of phrases from music of Brahms and Mozart are suggestive but hardly engage the very complex theoretical and analytic problems raised by his thesis. But the more pressing question that emerges here and throughout Schoenberg's writings is precisely how comprehensibility is achieved in the style that Schoenberg himself devel-

---

our ability to relate music to more general questions of human experience. In the following essay I will not attempt to reconstruct Schoenberg's theoretical enterprise. Instead, I will take some of his comments from the late essay "Brahms the Progressive" as a point of departure for what might be called a "temporal-processive" analysis—a form of analysis that would attempt to include aesthetic categories (categories of feeling) among its distinctions. I should note, however, that a much more detailed understanding of the Schoenbergian concepts of "comprehensibility" and "coherence" (as well as the other concepts we shall explore here) has been made possible with the publication of Schoenberg's *Coherence, Counterpoint, Instrumentation, Instruction in Form,* trans. Severine Neff (Lincoln: University of Nebraska Press, 1994) and *The Musical Idea and The Logic, Technique, and Art of Its Presentation,* ed. and trans. Patricia Carpenter and Severine Neff (New York: Columbia University Press, 1995). Although, for reasons of space, I have not been able to incorporate this material into the present essay, I believe that many of Schoenberg's early formulations are fully compatible with the approach taken here.

3. Elsewhere, Schoenberg reserves for *form* a somewhat closer though still indirect connection to beauty. In "Eartraining through Composing" (published in 1946, a year before "Brahms the Progressive" was "fully reformulated" for publication), Schoenberg writes: "The principal function of form is to advance understanding. Music should be enjoyed. Undeniably, understanding offers man one of the most enjoyable pleasures. And though the object of form is not beauty, by providing comprehensibility, form produces beauty. An apple tree does not exist to give us apples, but it produces apples nevertheless." (*Style and Idea,* 380) And again in the essay, "Composition with Twelve Tones" (1948): "Form in the arts, and especially in music, aims primarily at comprehensibility. The relaxation which a satisfied listener experiences when he can follow an idea, its development, and the reasons for such development is closely related, psychologically speaking, to a feeling of beauty. Thus, artistic value demands comprehensibility, not only for intellectual, but also for emotional satisfaction. However, the creator's idea has to be presented, whatever mood he is impelled to evoke." (Ibid., 215)

oped—a style characterized by highly irregular phrase structures and (in general) by the studied avoidance of obvious or literal repetition. Although he points to cases of extreme imparity even in the music of Mozart, toward the end of the essay Schoenberg argues that "post-Wagnerian" composers (for instance, Mahler, Strauss, and Schoenberg himself) had pushed asymmetry and irregularity to a radically new level. "Musical prose" has now become a stylistic given which is to be accepted as a matter of course by progressive contemporary composers.

> Asymmetry and imparity of structural elements are no miracle in contemporary music, nor do they constitute a merit. A contemporary composer connects phrases irrespective of their size and shape, only vigilant of harmonic progression, of rhythmic and motival contents, fluency and logic. . . .
> Merits of contemporary compositions may consist of formal finesses of a different kind. It may be the variety and multitude of the ideas, the manner in which they develop and grow out of germinating units, how they are contrasted and how they complement one another; it may also be their emotional quality, romantic or unromantic, subjective or objective, their expression of moods and characters of illustration.[4]

To inquire into the "formal finesses" of this nontraditional kind in Schoenberg's music I would like to venture a close reading of the opening of one of his most eloquent chamber pieces. Like the *String Trio,* op.45 (1946), the *Phantasy for Violin with Piano Accompaniment,* op.47 (1949) attains a remarkably broad and intensely lyrical continuity while at the same time presenting a highly articulated surface marked by frequent discontinuity and extreme contrast. Both of these works quite magically unite the shock of discontinuity with glimpses of a wholeness in which the most diverse characters can succeed one another without confusion. Indeed, it is this fully "comprehensible" wealth of expression that Schoenberg takes to be the special merit of the new compositional style.

Following Schoenberg's example, I will parse the opening bars[5] of the *Phantasy* and attempt to trace some of the motivic connections that run through this music. But before embarking on this analysis I would like to discuss briefly the approach taken here and to explain the formal categories that my parsing will employ. In the first "section" (bars 1–24) I will identify two "phrase groups," five "large phrases," ten "small phrases" (ranging in duration from about six to twelve seconds), and thirty-three "phrase constituents" (or subphrases). Although these divisions will likely strike

---

4. Schoenberg, "Brahms the Progressive," 429.

5. In a departure from the convention followed in the other essays of this volume, I will refer to notated measures as "bars." This practice conforms to an important distinction drawn in my book *Meter as Rhythm* (Oxford University Press, forthcoming 1997) between "measure," which names a metrically (or "projectively") functional duration, and "bar," which names a score segment delimited by barlines. A measure may indeed correspond to a notated bar, but in the portion of the *Phantasy* we will consider here there are no clear correspondences of bar and measure.

most musicians as more or less plausible, I do not think that, presented simply as points of articulation, they will be more compelling than a number of other plausible divisions. (Nor do I think that such divisions, presented simply as points of articulation or as containers abstracted from content, will shed much light on the form of this piece.)[6] Like all rhythmic analysis, the analysis of phrase is notoriously controversial, especially in music such as Schoenberg's which lacks conventional cadential markings. However, our difficulty in reaching consensus does not necessarily point to a hopeless relativity of judgment or indeterminacy of musical meaning. Indeed, I would argue that our disagreements arise less from irreconcilable differences in hearing than from terminological confusions, oversimplifications, and failures of introspection—that is to say, from problems of description. Although an adequate discussion of these problems is far beyond the scope of this essay, we may be able to negotiate some of these problems tolerably well by keeping two factors in mind: first, the complexity and variety of musical articulation; and second, the processive, temporal nature of musical understanding. Taking these two factors together we should be encouraged to speak of the complex and quite fluid *formation of events* rather than the neat division into parts of a preexisting whole.

In our efforts to speak of formation, Schoenberg's notion of comprehensibility may help to remind us that if a "formal" analysis is to reflect an aural experience it must take very seriously the temporality of that experience. To comprehend is to act; and the act of comprehending is a holding together of discrete individuals—a *process* in which the many are united as one. Comprehension, since it is an act, is neither instantaneous nor predetermined; it is a creative process that cannot be detached from ongoing experience. But when, instead of formation, we speak of formed units we will tend to think of *products* rather than of process—of wholes and parts, or of phrases, periods, and sections as fully formed objects. And in speaking of such products it is difficult to avoid the image of spatially juxtaposed blocks of music. Moreover, if we concentrate our attention on the so-called "points" of articulation or the boundaries that enclose and separate these objects, we will come to see such "units" rather as boxes or containers abstracted from their contents. However, if we can speak of musical events (rather than products or objects) and their process of formation, articulation will be inseparable from content or "idea" and inseparable too from the expressive characters of events. If in the *Phantasy* form serves the comprehensibility of idea (as Schoenberg maintains), it is also true that idea serves the creation of form. To investigate this dialectic of form and idea, let us now turn to our first division and to the analytic representations shown in the annotated score that appears in Example 1.

---

6. Josef Rufer, in *Composition with Twelve Notes Related Only to One Another* (New York: Macmillan, 1954), identifies the following "thematic shapes" in the first twenty-four bars of the *Phantasy*, measured (approximately) in bars: (6 (3 + 3) + 3) + 4 + (4 + 7). This segmentation, in fact, corresponds quite closely to my analysis. Although Rufer does not comment on these divisions, I suspect our divergences may have less to do with hearing than with the limitations of expressing the subtleties of articulation in this section with such crude symbolisms.

The decision to label a second phrase or second event beginning in bar 2 should not require elaborate justification, apart perhaps from justifications for the use of the term "phrase."[7] We could simply point to differences between the two units: for example, to the alternation of hexachordal collections given to violin and piano or to changes of texture and pattern. However, such differences in themselves have little to say about the process through which a new phrase comes into being or when and how the first small phrase ("phrase 1") is completed. If we are to speak of process here, we should attempt to discover in the first phrase those aspects of completeness that prepare us for the emergence of a new beginning in bar 2, and we should attempt to discover in the early stages of the second phrase those features that support the closure of the first phrase by denying its continuation. This will mean analyzing each phrase in some detail or, what comes to the same thing, identifying smaller events that compose the phrase. In analyzing these phrases I will make a distinction between *constituents* ("A" and "B" in phrase 1) and *figures* or *motives* ("*a*," "*b*," "*c*," and so on).

Constituents are rather like very small phrases or "subphrases." Like phrases, they are continuous in the sense that there is no gap between the end of one and the beginning of its successor (though there may be silence, as there may be between successive phrases). However, they are different from phrases in that they are too brief to attain the degree of completeness or closure that we generally impute to phrases. In phrase 1, for example, two constituents, A and B, are identified. Incompleteness here is very clearly manifested in the ambiguity of beginning and end. Constituent A might include the violin's high F if we hear the following low G as a beginning that corresponds to the low B♭ that begins constituent A. On the other hand, the rhythmic parallel (short-long) of the opening B♭–B♭ and a second opening F–G has its own charms, and Schoenberg's *sforzando* on F may indicate an intention to keep this latter possibility alive. This sort of ambiguity is highly productive. It functions, as does such ambiguity in general, both to keep the larger phrase event open and to keep open a variety of "motivic" possibilities for the motivation of later events (and for their emotive particularity).

What I shall call *figures* are the smallest gestures that can be discriminated in the fabric of the phrase. However, at this level of detail it is difficult to determine with much certainty just which such individuals are in fact discriminated or even whether we can clearly decide among several possibilities. Although I have chosen to label five figures in phrase 1 (*a1, b1, c, a2* (or *d*), and *b2*) there are many other plausible candidates: for example, the violin line from the opening B♭ to the *sforzando* F (*a1 + c*); the descending figure, B–F–G; the single, concluding G; or even the non-contiguous B♭ and G that begin and end the phrase in the violin's low register. A precise location of boundaries will be considerably more elusive here even than in

---

7. For a justification of the use of the term "phrase" in this repertory that takes into account issues of perception, see my "Phrase Formation in Post-Tonal Music," *Journal of Music Theory* 28 (1984): 167–89.

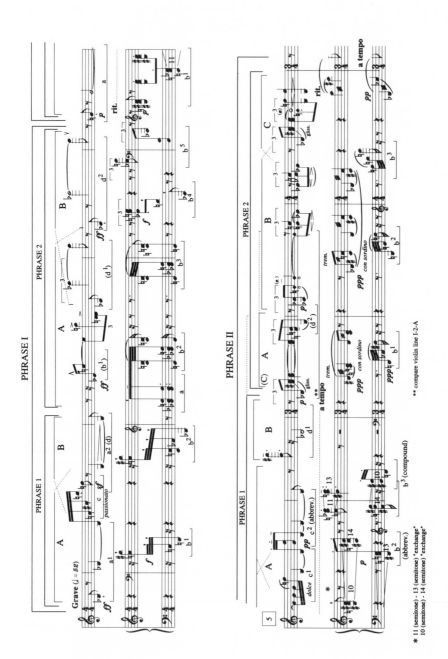

Example 1.

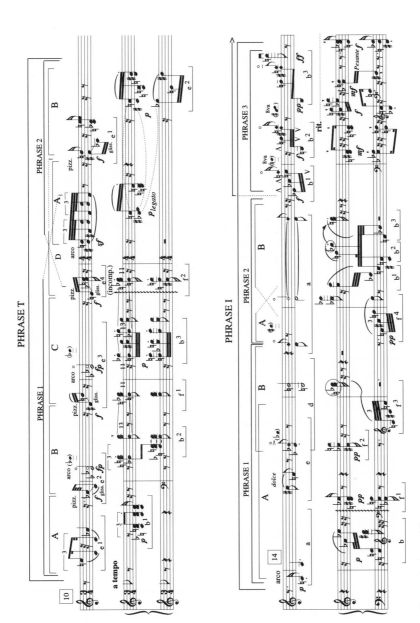

Example 1 cont'd.

the case of phrase constituents. The extreme mobility of these characters or shapes might be explained on psychological grounds as contents of "echoic" or "auditory sensory" memory—a brief and relatively unsegmented "store" of sense data that stands open for interpretation or "segmentation."[8] If there is a high degree of segmental indeterminacy in this realm of duration there is, nevertheless, an abundance of sonic distinctiveness. This most vivid and immediate aspect of our experience may with some justice be likened to a "surface" distinguished from a supporting, temporal "depth" (provided that we do not denigrate this "surface" or imagine that there can be depth apart from surface).

Although the traditional term "figure" seems appropriate enough for these relatively unstable discriminations, it is more customary to call such small units "motives." However, a limitation of the term "motive" in this regard is the requirement of repetition. Unless we are prepared to say that every segment that can be discriminated is a motive, we will need a broader term. Nevertheless, the concept of motive and its requirement for repetition may help us limit to some extent the unwieldy proliferation of figures presented to us on the "surface." On the assumption that our selection of detail is motivated in part by our recognition of features that have become familiar from past experience, motivic repetition will play a crucial role in our acts of segmentation. We might abbreviate this general observation in the principle of *segmentation by recognition*. Motivic correspondence will thus serve comprehensibility by guiding our search for more or less definite objects of attention—objects that can be held together as components of greater spans of attention. Obviously, analysis cannot hope to comprehend the extent or depth of such repetition in its particularity and detail. Simultaneous, overlapping, capable of subtle gradations of prominence and of protean transformation, motivic correspondences in this broadest sense are the very life of an experience of music and live only in an actual experience. Analysis can, however, hope to trace some of the more obvious strains of correspondence and attempt to weigh their contributions to the formation of such analytic objects as constituent, phrase, and section.

Of the many figures presented in phrase 1, only those that play a relatively clear motivic role in phrase formation are identified by lower-case letters.[9] Note that,

---

8. A brief summary of recent research concerning this category of memory can be found in Mark H. Ashcroft, *Human Memory and Cognition* (Glenview, Ill.: Scott, Foresman and Co., 1989), 105–14. For a more detailed account which favors the concept of "working memory," see Alan Baddeley, *Human Memory: Theory and Practice* (Boston: Allyn and Bacon, 1990). Although musical perception is hardly explained by current theories of memory, psychological research does, nevertheless, engage issues of temporality that music theory has characteristically neglected. Indeed, the approach taken here (and to some extent by Schoenberg in his theoretical writings) frankly acknowledges that there is no music apart from real acts of comprehension and, hence, from the particular capabilities of human memory.

9. In view of the evanescent nature of figures, the openness of their possible motivic efficacies, and the fact that such creatures are in reality utterly remote from the stable objects that a labeling of notes will invariably suggest, it must be admitted that the selection of "mo-

unlike the upper-case labels for phrase constituents, labels for motives indicate some identity through transformation. Thus, all "*b*'s," for example, are related by common ancestor, the first *b* of phrase 1. It must be understood, however, that in the course of generations clear resemblance to an ancestor may be lost—as, for example, in the relation of the first *b* figure of phrase 1 (*b*1 in bar 1) and the first *b* figure of the third small phrase (*b*1 in bars 4 and 5). Nevertheless, each of these figures resembles in its own way the second b figure of phrase 2 (*b*2 in bar 2). It remains to be seen how the repetitions of motive, either singly or gathered together in motivic complexes, serve comprehensibility by leading to the formation of larger events.

"SMALL" PHRASE

In phrase 1 repetitions are agents both for the overlapping of phrase constituents A and B and for the closure of the phrase as a whole. The return to the violin's low register in the sustained G at the end of bar 1 combined with the repetition of the piano's figure b1 in b2 creates a new beginning—in this case a *beginning-again,* since this beginning of the second constituent repeats in several respects the beginning of the phrase. And if, as this repetition gains more contextual depth, we can come to hear in the high *sforzando* F a rhythmic correspondence with the violin's first B♭, then the end of the first phrase constituent will have become overlapped with the beginning of a second constituent through figure *c* (anacrusis to the *sforzando* F). The label for this new figure, *a*2, reflects its repetition of *a1*. (The parenthetic label *d* identifies the novel, closing function of the figure which will be repeated in subsequent phrases.) The violinist here can either enhance or suppress the formation of this figure. Its enhancement will contribute to the comprehensibility of much larger

---

tives" displayed in our annotated score is hardly an adequate representation. Nevertheless, some form of labeling seems necessary if we are to take advantage of the opportunities a notated score can provide for testing musical perceptions. The system of labels employed here, though quite primitive, should provide a useful set of references for our discussion of the possibilities for rhythmic experience offered by this piece. In any case, I shall attempt to compensate for the apparent rigidity of labeled segments in my commentary.

It should be noted that in the alphanumeric notation of figures provided here, numerals label the order of succession in figures of the same "type" (a, b, c, etc.) *within each small phrase.* Where only one instance of a type occurs within a small phrase no numerical label appears. For example, in "small" phrase 2 of "large" phrase I (bars 2–4), since there is only one instance of figure-type a, this figure is labeled a rather than a1. This taxonomic convention should be kept in mind lest it be thought that figures with the same alphanumeric label (for example b2 in phrase 1 and b2 in phrase 2) participate in some special correspondence. (Incidentally, since the figure labeled a2 in the first small phrase of the piece is eventually interpreted as the first instance of a closing figure d, the very first figure, the repeated Bb in violin, might—from a perspective of greater "depth"—have been labeled *a* rather than *a1*. Such are the vagaries of references to "notes.")

gestures when the ending or cadential function of this motive reemerges in bar 3 (*d2*) and again in bar 6 (*d1*). But even if the violinist misses this opportunity, the connection will remain a more or less latent possibility whose influence can still be felt. However this overlapping of constituents is interpreted, the emergence of a correspondence between A and B is itself the promise of ending. Once *b2* is completed there is a sense in which nothing more needs to be done—constituent B will now have fulfilled its promise of repeating A. This degree of closure allows a new phrase to begin in bar 2 with minimal overlapping despite the fact that there is no overt break between the two phrases. Indeed, the articulation of the two constituents of phrase 1 is quite spacious compared to the suddenness with which the second phrase follows the first.

In noting the "internal" closure of the first phrase we should not ignore the importance of the beginning of a new phrase for the articulation of the end of phrase 1. Although this new beginning in bar 2 emerges very quickly, it is not instantaneous. At the very least, there must emerge some evidence of motive *a*—a gesture characterized by immediate pitch repetition and a durational pattern, short-long. What makes this figure so effective is its function of beginning again. As a repetition of Phrase 1's figure *a1* (and not *a2* or (*d*)), it is a second beginning and therefore the beginning of a second unit which now promises a phrase-event on the durational order of what has now become phrase 1.

In discussing the formation of a first phrase, I have argued for the articulative function of repetition. But there is another function of repetition and another aspect of articulation that must be considered: the creation of contrasts that enhance the definiteness or particularity of the event's character. The special urgency, intensity, and compression of the opening of the second small phrase are clearly dependent upon a multitude of contrasts with the opening of the first small phrase. Most immediately, this suddenness of the new beginning is a result of the metrical openness of *b2* in bar 1 and the fact that phrase 2 enters an eighth note too soon by comparison to constituents A and B of phrase 1.[10] But it is the contrast of the beginning of phrase 2 with constituent A of phrase 1 that gives this rush to phrase 2 its point. At the core of this gesture, figure a in bar 2 repeats *a1* of phrase 1 twice as fast, sharply distinguish-

---

10. By "metrical openness" here I mean that the final sixteenth note in figure *b2* at the end of bar 1 leads us to expect a new metrical beginning with bar 2. (Instead, we get an eighth-note rest.) By comparison, figure *b1* is relatively closed since the thirty-second notes lead to the beginning of an eighth-note *duration* that completes the first beat of bar 1. For a general discussion of metrical closure, see my *Meter as Rhythm*. The distinction I have made between metrical "closure" and "openness" is very close to Eugene Narmour's distinction of "cumulative" and "countercumulative" duration. See Narmour, *The Analysis and Cognition of Basic Melodic Structures* (Chicago: University of Chicago Press, 1990).

Because my theory of meter may not be available prior to the publication of this essay and cannot be usefully summarized here, I will not be able comment in any detail upon the contributions of meter to the form of this first section of the *Phantasy*. This is an unfortunate limitation, in part because Schoenberg's metrical/rhythmic invention is extraordinarily refined (especially in the late works) and not often appreciated. Ironically, it is because of

ing an anacrusis that in phrase 1 was latent or only faintly sensed. In rhythm and (inverted) contour the new violin entrance in bar 2 (*b1*) corresponds, at least initially, to the piano's figure *b1* in bar 1 to confirm the exchange of instruments in the new phrase. But, almost immediately, the piano responds with its own version of motive *b* (*b2*), freeing the violin to develop a more or less independent and novel line.

Some degree of tonal closure in the piano may also contribute to this opening of space for the violin. Note that in bar 2 the piano repeats in trichordal segmentation the pitch classes of the violin's opening hexachord—$H_0{}^a$ in Lewin's labeling.[11] Although we have little reason to hear the first three pitches of the violin in bar 1

Schoenberg's mastery of durational detail—because the metrical is so highly integrated with all other domains—that we can afford to dispense with an explicit analysis. However, by the same token, a close analysis of meter could greatly clarify our understanding of motive and phrase structure or form.

11. I refer to the labels David Lewin assigned to the ordered hexachordal collections of this piece in his "A Study of Hexachord Levels in Schoenberg's Violin Fantasy," *Perspectives of New Music* 6, no.1 (Fall–Winter 1967): 18–32; repr. in *Perspectives on Schoenberg and Stravinsky,* ed. Benjamin Boretz and Edward T. Cone (New York: W.W. Norton and Co., 1972), 78–92. Given below, together with their hexachord labels, are the two row forms (S_0 and I_0) used in bars 1–21. (Note that the labels "H" and "h" distinguish two complementary hexachordal collections of the 6–21 type, and that the superscripts "a" and "c" denote "antecedent" and "consequent.")

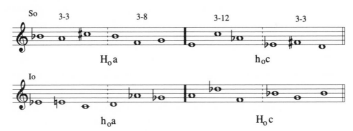

In bars 1–9 Schoenberg uses only the "antecedent" hexachords of S_0 and I_0—$H_0{}^a$ and $h_0{}^a$. Although the obvious relation between these collections is one of inversion, there are many correspondences that can arise from their combination. Below is a display of the violin's succession of pitches from bars 1–3. Here I have pointed to an additional correspondence through retrograde inversion. (Incidentally, there is also a small transposed retrograde B♭–A–C♯–B and F–G–E♭–E, but Schoenberg does not take advantage of this possibility here.)

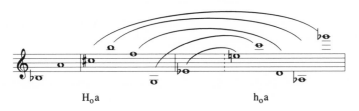

(B♭-A-C♯) as a figure, the last three (B-F-G) present a much better opportunity for grouping—in the sense, perhaps, of B as immediate anacrusis to the F-G figure and connected to F and G in an unbroken descending contour. In bar 2 this second trichord, in the piano, is displayed in precisely the same registral ordering that we encountered in the violin (bottom to top, G-F-B), thus reproducing exactly the set of intervals (modulo 12). Also preserved is the intervallic connection of B♭ to G in the bottom voice. This descending minor third, more or less clearly perceptible as a cadential figure in phrase 1, is brought into focus as it is repeated in bar 2, and this quick reminder in bars 2 and 3 may help to strengthen its "memorability" for later uses.[12] The brief repetition of the opening of the first phrase (*a1* + *b1*) in the complex figure that opens a second small phrase (*a* + (*b1*) + *b2*) clearly contributes to a sense of energy and compression in the beginning of the second phrase. This energy is sustained by the violin's continuation and by the imaginative turn of events that completes the second phrase and a larger phrase (phrase I) that will eventually comprehend phrases 1 and 2.

On comparison with phrase 1, the ingredients missing thus far from phrase 2 are a second constituent, which to match B in phrase 1 would feature something resembling figure *a2* (or *d*), and a transition between the two constituents—something like figure c. What we get in the violin is a descending three-note figure, C-D-A♭. This is an exact registral inversion (in retrograde) of the closing violin figure in phrase 1, B-F-G; and it is, of course, immediately preceded by a close registral inversion of the same set class in the piano.[13] However, on account of its rhythm this violin figure is blocked from reproducing the motivic genus of figure *a2* or *d* in phrase 1. Instead of a long duration on the low A♭ which might match the final G of phrase 1, there is a gigantic leap up to G♭ quickly followed by another *b* figure (*b3*) in piano. All this now matches the end of the first phrase—even a transition in the violin descent, C-D-A♭. By enclosing in parentheses the label *d1* I mean to assert that the leap to a sustained G♭ at the end of bar 2 is a more or less latent reproduction of figure *d* from bar 1 that becomes fully manifest in *d2* at the end of the phrase. At the end of the phrase the conjunction of *d2* in violin and *b5* in piano is a very explicit and grand revival of the final constituent of phrase 1 (B = *d* + *b2*).

Although there is a complex transition to this moment of ending by which it is seamlessly overlapped with a highly compressed beginning constituent A, constituent B in phrase 2 claims a degree of autonomy and independence from A that was not felt in the antecedent-consequent relation of A and B in phrase 1. This separation is due in part to the contrasting characters of A and B in phrase 2 in which B

---

12. As Allen Forte has pointed out in his linear analysis of the *Phantasy* in *Contemporary Tone-Structures* (New York: Columbia Teachers College, 1955) the significance and recognizability of this minor third G–B♭ as a "boundary" interval is considerably enhanced by the fact that there are no instances of interval class 3 formed by adjacent tones of the row.

13. Incidentally, as I have indicated in note 9, this set-class correspondence is not a product of the inversional relationship of hexachords H_0^a and h_0^a.

turns from the energetic confinement of A toward a stark deliberateness akin to but more exaggerated than that felt in the opening of the first phrase. The separation is also (in part) due to the *twofold* repetition of the motivic pair *b1–b2* from phrase 1 in phrase 2: *b2–b3* and *b4–b5*. The latter pair returns to the descending contours of phrase 1 but now introduces a great deceleration. The deceleration and the focus on a moment of (contextually defined) ending prepares us for a new beginning. That Schoenberg can avoid relaxation or loss of energy here is a mark of the virtuosity he commands throughout this piece.

Since my labeling so oversimplifies the composition of constituent B in phrase 2 and the overlapping of the two constituents, I would like to point out one other feature of constituent B that seems crucial for the form. In the middle of bar 3 violin and piano for the first time (and the only time in bars 1–6) come together in a simultaneous attack—that of the very high G♭ and the very low A♭. And here there is a very long suspension of activity relative to the surrounding music. This moment strikes me as the climax of the phrase and a remarkably energized arrest that, as it were, stores energy for a second large phrase (phrase II). Among the many factors that might contribute to such a perception, one tonal factor in particular is more effective for the ear than it may appear to the eye. In the violin line in constituent A (bar 2) there is a registral (half-step) connection of the low E♭ and low D-A♭, or at least the potential for such a connection. Although this figure, E♭-D-A♭, is certainly in some sense audible, so are many other complexes. But, again, this more or less latent possibility is strengthened (according to our hypothetical principle of segmentation by recognition) by the repetition in *b4* (bar 3)—E♭-D-A♭. A good analogy is the effect of rhyme—and not only end-rhyme—in verse. If there is such a rhyme here it will have definite rhythmic consequences: the violin sequence in bar 2 — E♭-D-A♭-G♭, involving a hiatus (relatively long and indirect) between E♭ and D will be brought into contrast with the lightning-fast figure of bar 3—E♭ to D in triplet eighths to A♭ and G♭ simultaneously. The long and metrically indefinite suspension of activity in the sustained high G♭ of the violin holds us in a moment of climax that is charged with expectancy. The concluding piano event, *b5,* only now draws the violin figure *d2* into a fully explicit repetition of the ending of phrase 1 (*d + b2*). And together with *b4,* figures *d2* and *b5* will prepare our ears for the following G of the second large phrase. To see the relation one need only rewrite the violin's G♭ as F♯ to produce in bar 4 a "French augmented sixth": A♭-D-C-F♯, from bottom to top. And although any trace of scale degree here is evanescent at best, the intervallic arrangement in constituent B subtly favors the convergence of A♭ and G♭ in the middle register G at the beginning of the next phrase.

"LARGE" PHRASE

If in constituent B of phrase 2 the deceleration and the reenactment of figures from phrase 1 heralds the end of a second phrase, this constituent also presents a gesture of opening. The contrast of the falling figure *d* at the end of phrase 1 (F-G) with the rising *d2* at the end of phrase 2 (A♭-G♭) creates a feeling of incompleteness or opening analogous, perhaps, to the close on dominant harmony in a half cadence. Indeed, the relatively sharp separation of the two phrases in bar 4 and the emergence of a new beginning that clearly resembles the beginning of the piece serve to intensify this openness in the phrase (or phrases) we are leaving behind. Here, as in the case of a half cadence, such openness is not for the continuation of the present event, but for the creation of a new event—in this case, for the creation of a second large phrase. Evidence of the formation of a first large phrase (I) will be the feeling that the beginning of a new phrase in bar 4 is a *second* (rather than simply a third) beginning — for by this new act of beginning the first two small phrases are united as a single event that will now have been made past.[14] Although our analysis of phrase 2 has pointed in many ways to the possibility for such an event, it must be remembered that phrase event I is not fully determined until it is made past by the beginning of a new phrase. And, as past, the definiteness of phrase I will contribute to the particular character of the newly emerging phrase II.

Again, the very close motivic resemblances between the beginnings of phrases I and II serve both to articulate the large phrases and to throw their contrasting characters into high relief. Schoenberg has designated these characters (at least the characters of motive *c*) as "*passionato*" and "*dolce*." Among the many qualities that might be said to characterize the opening of phrase II, I would like to comment here on its relaxation or leisureliness. Even before the ritardando can come into play, the initial eighth notes in the violin and piano will feel like a change of tempo compared with the immediately preceding figure *b5* (assuming, of course, an accurate performance). The effect of entering phrase II could be likened to suddenly passing into a more viscous medium where everything all at once moves much more slowly. But it is not only the tempo that slows down. The presentation of ideas is also more relaxed. If there is a sense in which the first small phrase of phrase I (abbreviated: I–1) is repeated in the first small phrase of phrase II (II–1), the latter presentation will be more than twice the duration of the former. In this comparison notice especially the violin figures: *a1, c,* and *d* in I–1–A and *a, c1, c2,* and *d1* in II–1–A. In phrase II–1 we simply have much more time than we did in I-1 to attend to these complex tonal gestures.

In terms of the relaxation that can be felt in phrase II–1, a comparison with the highly compressed and agitated first constituent in bar 2 (I–2–A) offers even

---

14. Throughout this essay the term "second" (from *sequi*, to follow) is used not simply as a numerical-ordinal category, but as a category for the description of immediate succession by which one event is made past and another event emerges as present. "Secondness" in this sense refers to the function (and act) of following or succeeding a first. In a succession of phrases, for example, each new phrase will end or make past the immediately preceding phrase. But the emergence of a "second" phrase group will make the preceding series of phrases *as a whole* past.

greater contrast. Indeed, many aspects of this second small phrase are repeated, transfigured in bars 4–6. The piano figure labeled *b1* in bar 4 is an extremely relaxed reincarnation of the piano figure *b2* in bar 2 (or perhaps of the figure-complex *a* + *b2*).[15] Further, the reiteration *d1–d2* in phrase I–2 (bars 3–4) provides some motivation for the repetitions *c1–c2, b1–b2* in phrase II–1. This sort of reiteration is new with the second small phrase (I–2) and creates, by the lengthening of figures *d1* and *d2*, a deceleration that leads to further deceleration in the beginning of the second large phrase. In phrase II–1 similar reiteration leads, by contrast, to an acceleration by the abbreviation of figures *c1* and *c2, b1* and *b2*. On the other hand, it would be a mistake to focus only on correspondence in the second large phrase, even in an attempt to locate contrasts. Phrase II–1, although bound to the same hexachordal collections and the same trichordal subcollections as phrases I–1 and I–2, presents novel registral orderings of trichords and therefore novel sonorities. The reader will remember that in phrase I the second trichord of H_0^a (in sequential order, B–F–G) was uniquely ordered in register—from bottom to top G–F–B in violin and piano. In phrase II–1 the registral ordering of this trichord is B–G–F, and this trichord appears now only in violin. This detail is worth mentioning because it plays a role in the overlapping of two small phrases that will come to compose Phrase II.

Unlike phrase I–1, phrase II–1 features no overlap in constituents A and B; that is to say, in II–1 figure *c2* (an abbreviated replica of *c1*) is completed prior to the presentation of a second constituent B (labeled also as figure *d1*). (Notice too in this connection the rhyming of *c2* and *d1* whereby *c2* is eventually assimilated to a closing figure.) In II–1 the transitional figure *b3* serves to articulate the completion of constituent A. (Note also that *b3* in II–1 combines the features of both "*b*-motives"— the down-up contour first heard in bar 2 (*b2*) and the down-down contour of bars 1 and 3.) This articulative function of figure *b3* (like that of *b5* in I–2 which articulates the completion of the first large phrase) is enhanced by its metrical detachment from the immediately preceding figures.

From a look at the score, it would appear that constituent B in bar 6 ends the small phrase, answering the ascending figure *d2* at the end of the first large phrase (bar 3) with a cadential descent in the figure *d1* (bar 6). But an attentive hearing will

---

15. Notice that although figure *b2* of phrase I–2 clearly corresponds to *b1* of phrase I–1 and figure *b1* of phrase II–1 corresponds to *b2* of phrase I–2, *b1* of II–1 does not in itself correspond to *b1* of I–1. Such an apparent breach of transitivity does not, however, compromise Schoenberg's "musical logic." Placed in the common environment of the violin figures *a1* (phrase I–1) and *a* (phrase II–1) and "genetically" linked through the figure complex *a* + *b2* in phrase I–2, figure *b1* in phrase II–1 is a true inheritor of the initial idea and one that bears witness to all the adventures that that idea has endured in the course of winning for the composition a greater duration. The logic of which Schoenberg speaks is the logic of the musical imagination, a poetic logic of particularity rather than of abstraction that is capable of the most fantastic of connections and obliged only to insure that each new addition enhance rather than detract from the depth or richness of feeling.

reveal a more subtle and complex articulation, one in which the music of bar 7 can be felt to continue the small phrase and to lead to a closure in bar 7 that recalls the closure at the end of bar 1. Only later will bar 7 be detached from a moment of ending to become the first constituent of a second small phrase (II–2) which will be the final phrase of a larger unit comprising bars 1–9. I have labeled the phrase constituent in bar 7 "(C)" as a continuation of phrase II–1 and "A" as the first constituent of phrase II–2. This overlapping of the two small phrases (II–1 and II–2) relies heavily on tonal relations in the violin. The violin line in bar 7 repeats in retrograde the pitch classes of the violin line in bars 4–6. Thus, the immediate repetition of the pitches A–C♯ and B♭ in similar registral ordering across bar 7 (as in the violin line in bar 1, from bottom to top: B♭–A–C♯) insures some feeling of continuity. At the end of bar 7 the B–F–G trichord reappears in the registral ordering it displayed throughout the first large phrase, and now we can hear in bars 6 and 7 a repetition of the cadential minor third descent B♭–G that closed the first small phrase in bar 1. Again, it is *because* of the first constituent in bar 1—because this "idea" is still effective through repetition—that bar 7 can continue phrase II in a gesture of closure. To reflect this closure I have labeled the concluding figure in bar 7 "(*d2*)." However, the next event beginning in bar 8 suddenly undercuts this potential closure to reinterpret the course of the large phrase. Very quickly bar 8 emerges as a repetition of bar 7 and a continuation of the music begun with bar 7—not as the beginning of a second small phrase. Only at this moment does bar 7 (now properly labeled A) definitely become the beginning of a second small phrase, II–2.

The result of this overlapping of II–1 and II–2 is a remarkably fluid transition in the second large phrase to a new and quite unexpected character in its second small phrase (II–2). To say that this character is novel is not to deny its appropriateness as a continuation of the large phrase. Certainly, its intimacy and delicacy match the character of the first small phrase II–1 and continue to complement the more violent character of the first large phrase. But there is a definite change in bar 7 to a more agitated expression and, eventually, to a curiously fragmented music in bars 8 and 9 (and to even greater fragmentation in bars 10–13). Constituent B in bar 8 begins as if to repeat constituent A (bar 7), and might do so were it not for a violin line that, instead of responding to the end of constituent A with a rhyme for figure (*d2*), seems to lose itself in languid and rather aimless half-step motions E–E♭ beneath a static C, as if drowsily recalling the piano's tremolo from bar 7. The interruptive or parenthetical character of this new violin figure breaks constituent B to create an extension of constituent A and thus an overlapping of A and B (shown above the score as a dotted line continuing A across the boundary of constituent B). As a result of this reorientation of the violin line, a larger violin figure emerges in bars 7 and 8, beginning with the B♭ in bar 7 and ending with the sustained high D in bar 8. I draw attention to this figure because it so closely resembles the six-note violin figure in bar 2 (I–2–A) in rhythm and contour. Notice in this connection how closely the piano figures in each case correspond to the matching violin figures (that is, figures *b2* and *b3* in phrase I–2, and figures *b1* and *b2* in phrase II–2). If these correspondences point to a sharpening of the analogy to a parallel period composed of the two large phrases I and II then we might look also to correspondences in the first small phrase of each—I–1 and II–1. We have already remarked on the very clear repetition of constituent A of phrase I–1 in constituent A of II–1. We might now point also to the similarity of the violin figures in constituent B of phrase I–1 and constituent B of phrase II–1. Yet I think it would be an oversimplification to carry this analogy too far. If noticing this similarity prevents us from also noticing, for example, the relation of figure *d2* in bar 3 and figure *d1* in bar 6 and the continuation of this latter figure in (*d2*) of bar 7, then we will have sacrificed some insight into the rich play of musical imagination in this piece for the doubtful consolations of schemata—or, worse, for taking a position on the virtues of "classical models." In any case, the end of phrase II–2 hardly presents us with an analogy for a tonal cadence.

As was mentioned above, the second constituent (B) of II–2 fails to develop its initial conformity to the first constituent (A) and, instead, slips into a relatively aimless reverie broken by the emergence of a third constituent C in bar 9. Constituent C in the violin repeats in condensation the violin figure of constituent A (now in precisely the same registral ordering as bar 1). However, there is little sense of closure here for the small phrase. For one thing, there is no figure resembling our "cadential" *d*. In fact, to the degree that we can hear in the violin a repetition of bar 7 and bar 1, the violin figure will sound especially incomplete with the F sounding simultaneously above G. And on the same comparison but from a rhythmic standpoint, it will seem that we are lacking a final beat—as if we were stuck on the *sforzando* F in bar 1 without being able to get to the concluding G. There is one other novelty worthy of mention here: this is the first time violin and piano are both given pitches from H_0^a. The only occasion in which violin and piano shared pitches was at the end of the first large phrase (I–2–B), and there the pitches comprised h_0^a. And although there is certainly no "internal" closure at the end of phrase II to match that at the end of phrase I, there may be a sense in which the end of phrase II, like the end of phrase I, offers an opening for the piece in this sustained, shimmering sonority so full of promise for continuation. Notice, moreover, how seamlessly constituents B and C are overlapped in bars 8 and 9 through the overlapping of pitches of hexachord H_0^a. The violin figure in constituent C seems almost to crystallize out of the preceding right hand tremolo at the catalytic touch of figure *b3*.

PHRASE GROUP

Although phrase II–2 is in many respects highly continuous (and continuous—by overlapping—with II–1), it is also very complex and, compared to the preceding phrases, rather anarchic. Already with the gradual emergence of this phrase a transition is being effected that will lead to a new character that contrasts very sharply with both of the first two large phrases. This new character appears quite clearly in the following large phrase in bars 10–13. But this event raises a new question. Should we call this event a third large phrase (III) or regard it as a second beginning whereby the first two phrases are together made past and "comprehended" as a single unit? There is no simple answer to this question. As we consider larger durations comprising groups of phrases, we must consider much broader contexts that contribute to feelings of articulation or closure. Furthermore, these contexts are not fixed arrangements but changing configurations in which what is in the process of becoming is adjusting to the demands of novelty and to a growing history of past events. In the present case, I will suggest that bars 10–13 function as a new event for bars 1–9 as a whole, but that with the advent of a large phrase in bars 14–17 which recalls the opening of the piece, bars 10–13 come to function as a transitional unit to a *second* phrase group in bars 14–24. In deference to the reader's patience and in the interest of space I will not undertake a highly detailed analysis of bars 10–13 ("phrase T") or of the remainder of the first section of this piece. It will be necessary, however, to consider somewhat more carefully the end of phrase II or, rather, the end of the first phrase group, and the beginning of the new phrase with bar 10.

The many contrasts introduced in bars 10–13 *vis à vis* the relative homogeneity of figures and figure-complexes in phrases I and II will, I think, lead us to feel that we have entered a new sort of music in bars 10–13, a music sufficiently different from all we have yet heard to make what we have heard in bars 1–9 *de facto* an "all" or a whole. But we do not have to wait very long for such contrast to emerge to feel a new beginning in bar 10. Nor, in spite of the lack of "internal" closure at the end of II–2 in bar 9 and the lack of an obvious rhythmic articulation, does there seem much sense of overlap in the articulation of end and beginning. Very effective for this articulation is the sudden change in the tonal domain. Beginning in bar 10 we enter a new tonal-intervallic world freshly contrasting with the tonal characters learned so well in bars 1–9. We are now presented with reorderings of the preceding hexachordal collections (H_0^a and h_0^a) in the new forms, h_0^c and H_0^c. The most striking novelty (indeed, the only set-class novelty in the trichordal partitions) is the introduction of the augmented triads—E–C–A♭ (in h_0^c) and A–D♭–F (in H_0^c). Each of these three-note groups is very clearly sounded in bar 10. However, it should also be observed that an augmented triad emerges for our attention at the end of bar 9 as the only such sonority in bars 1–9. This intervallic constellation of tremolo A–C♯ in piano and sustained high F in violin is not merely an analytic fabrication; its special coloration of this final sonority is quite sensible and contributes to the novelty and openness of this ending. But the appearance of the pitch group A–C♯(D♭)–F in bar 10 does not lead to an overlapping; if it accomplishes anything for the new phrase it is to focus our attention on the freshness of these new sonorities, isolated by silences and suspended in virtually ametrical isolation.

If the last small phrase of the fist phrase group, II–2, tended toward quirkiness, the new phrase begun in bar 10 quickly and unexpectedly turns this character into one of disjunction and fragmentation. Again, the separation of figures or constituents by silence and the suspension of meter here is in high contrast to the course of the preceding phrases, especially phrase II–1. Compared to bars 1–9, the new phrase could be called "defective" in its failure to hold constituents together in clearly defined larger gestures. Although I have identified two small phrases T–1 and T–2 (marked, in part, by a return to the prior hexachordal arrangement) and several constituents, a close analysis will reveal considerable ambiguity in grouping and a relatively loose motivic organization. Notice, for example, the static repetitions in components B and C (bars 11–12), or the incompleteness of constituent D which promises a repetition of motive "e." Though highly eccentric, the tiny shards of figures in the second phrase unit (T–2) begin to cohere as the phrase progresses. So intricately are these figures overlapped that it now becomes very difficult to isolate constituents. This consolidation leads to a quite effective cadence at the end as the various figures are drawn together in close repetition of sonorities familiar from phrase I. (Note especially the registral ordering of the final three trichords in piano and the falling contours.)

It is only with the revival of the opening gesture of the piece in the small phrase beginning with the anacrusis to bar 14 that the phrase labeled "T" (bars 10–13) will have become transition or a moment of waiting for a new and (for the piece) *second* beginning; for it is only now, with bar 14, that the claim for such a second beginning has been made. Bar 10 can no longer hold such a claim. However, merely to call phrase T "transitional" and to disparage the creature (as I did above) as deficient in comprehensibility is at the very least to lose sight of a positive contribution that exceeds the merely "formal." This is its expressive contribution, or its character. The phrase is a remarkable invention—whimsical, tragicomical, Harlequinesque, ridiculously mechanical with a pathetic turn toward animal warmth at the end (but introduced by the piano, not the violin). But this character, however we might wish to describe it, is not separate from, not other than, its "formal," transitional function. The relaxation of rhythm and the virtual suspension of forward drive that dissipate or "liquidate" the intense energy of the first group are inseparable from this expressive character *and* function to open a space for a second phrase group.

As noted before in connection with the formation of small and large phrase, there is another and equally important sense in which the character of a unit such as bars 10–13 is inseparable from the form. If expression-content-form are truly a whole, then this "formal" transition must also be a transition in feeling. Or to put the matter in more temporal-processive terms, whatever occurs in bars 10–13 will be part of the inheritance or history of the new event(s) that will succeed this phrase. As it happens, the new phrase does inherit many characteristics of phrase T. For instance, phrase constituents continue to be separated by relatively long silences, and there is a return in bars 14–16 to the hexachordal arrangements h_0^c and H_0^c of bars 10–12 and an introduction of the new motivic figures e and f into the familiar fabric of motives from the beginning of the piece. Again, a close analysis could sharpen our account of the novelty and particularity of this second opening. Here I would draw attention only to the assimilation of figure-type b to f in bars 14–15 and to the overlapping in bars 14–15 of figure e and the now almost archetypal closing figure d. In this connection one of the more remarkable transformations is the appearance in bars 15–16 of figure *a* in its original form—an op. 47 archetype of opening. There follows in the piano a novel sequence of three "*b*"-figures ending, suggestively, on the major third G–B (preceded by B♭ and beneath a sustained F♯ in violin). The section will end in bar 24 with a clearly corresponding three-part piano figure closing on the minor third G–(F♯)–B♭ (beneath a B♮ in violin). (See also the closing figure *d* in bars 14–15, the connection of the pitches B–B♭–G in violin in bars 5–7, and, of course, the connection B♭–G in bar 1.)

Since I will not here undertake a close analysis of the remainder of the section I have not thought it necessary to reproduce the music in bars 18–24. Suffice it to say that a second (bars 18–20) and a third (20–24) phrase complete the second phrase group. Each of these phrases comprises three "parts" (though the third phrase includes an extra "part"—the cadential piano figure I mentioned above). Are these "parts" small phrases? No, they are phrase constituents; but with the peculiar property of being much larger and more regular than the constituents we have thus far considered (each has a duration of four quarter notes). What is occurring, I believe, is that the proportions we have gotten used to are growing larger. The end of the first section is expanding—in a sense, slowing down—making room in its own peculiar way for a second section, or rather, for what will become a transition to a second section. Finally, the tripartite division of each of the two concluding phrases of the section (bars 18–20 and 20–24) continues a process of tripartite division initiated in the third small phrase beginning with the violin's upbeat to bar 17. Indeed, this development works to detach this small phrase from the large phrase begun in bar 14 and join it to the following two phrases to create a highly overlapped phrase group. Notice that this third small phrase itself issues directly out of the tripartite piano constituent (*b1–b2–b3*) that closes the second small phrase in bar 16. And, though the genealogy may be obscure, we may truly feel a progenitor for this development in the novel tripartite division introduced in bars 10–12 in the three constituents of T's first small phrase.

Although we have considered only a small part of the *Phantasy,* and only nine bars in much detail, we have had the opportunity to observe a remarkable diversity not only of character or expression but also of phrase formation. As the piece progresses there is no abatement in the novelty of either of these aspects of the composition. Whether overlapped, interrupted, or abandoned; whether expanding or contracting; whether diffuse or sharply focused, parts are joined to (and torn from) parts in an astonishing variety of manners. And since this variety can characterize even the smallest connections, the pace of Schoenberg's kaleidoscopic invention often reaches a speed or compression that calls for an unusual level of attentiveness from player and listener. Of course, this pace too is variable and cannot be abstracted from the form of the piece and its expression. If there is beauty in this music it is not a tame beauty of simple harmonies and mild contrasts or of easily predictable regularities. Rather, it is a highly adventurous and demanding beauty arising from "the variety and multitude of the ideas, the manner in which they develop and grow out of germinating units, how they are contrasted and how they complement one another."

Our attempt to apply Schoenberg's theoretical categories in the tiny laboratory of these few bars has, I hope, demonstrated to some extent the accuracy of his characterization of musical meaning and its production. However, there are two points in Schoenberg's argument that may be misleading. I have made my opposition to one of these thematic in the above analysis. Although Schoenberg is generally eager to dissolve or at least blur conventional oppositions such as mind and body, intellect and feeling, innovation and tradition (even horizontal and vertical), he generally reserves for "idea" an essential independence from "form" and in so doing draws what I believe is an artificial separation between content and form or between the "presence" (or omnipresence) of the idea and its "presentation" by means of an organization that packages the idea for human comprehension. I have argued throughout the present essay that form—conceived as the process through which individual events come to be created or formed—is nothing apart from the emerging particularity of these events and from their particular emotive characters. The postulation of such interdependence may help to explain why musicians often disagree so vehemently about questions of phrase structure and why there are not simple tests for the correctness of segmentations. If the events we call phrases are moments in a process rather than self-sufficient "blocks" of music and if their beginning and ending cannot be reduced to "points" then phrase articulation will not be an abstractable feature of the music that we could hear in isolation from an experience of the ongoing whole.

The other point of Schoenberg's I find questionable is his separation of form and beauty. His notion, as I understand it, is that form, by bringing comprehensibility to music, brings it alike to music of all grades or ranks: dull and interesting, superficial and deep, tame and adventurous, reactionary and progressive—however we wish to construct the differences. Again, form is divorced from "content" and emotion. But, if in reality there is no such separation, we must say that "form" in every case is constitutive of the type of beauty that is produced (and, if there is to be a ranking, judged). The question of beauty, of course, opens our inquiry quite dramatically to a category of experience that is not often broached in music analysis. And yet, was not Schoenberg right in mentioning beauty alongside comprehensibility, memorability, form, and idea?

Elision and Structural Levels in Peter Maxwell Davies's *Dark Angels*

Ann K. McNamee

Peter Maxwell Davies's contribution to contemporary music includes capturing techniques and devices from the distant past such as medieval chant, mensuration canons, parody technique, and magic squares and assimilating them into a harmonic language of the present. A case in point is *Dark Angels*, which revives elements of Medieval chant, Renaissance lute songs, and Baroque recitative. Composed in 1973, *Dark Angels* is a song cycle for mezzo-soprano and acoustic guitar made up of three pieces: the first and third, "The Drowning Brothers" and "Dead Fires" respectively, for voice and guitar, flanking the second, "Dark Angels," for guitar solo. This song cycle shows Davies's commitment to experimenting with various forms and with various small performing forces.[1] I view Davies's pieces as tightly organized, carefully crafted works of art with several distinct structural levels. The article that follows focuses not only on the forms of the pieces in *Dark Angels*, but also on the hierarchical structures that result from the interaction of several levels of melodic motives. An argument for the use of two different kinds of elision will be made, with regard to the deepest structural connections between verses of the first song, and with regard to large-scale melodic motives within the last song.

Taking the three pieces in order, I will first outline their formal subdivisions and then discuss the parallels found between the musical and poetic structures. Whereas the strophic organization of the music in "The Drowning Brothers" mirrors perfectly the verse structure of the poem, in "Dead Fires" Davies goes beyond a reflection of the text. He adds formal divisions in the music which do not appear in the poem, thereby bringing a new dimension to the poetry. In fact, a very different reading of the poem results because Davies's music imposes an interpretation upon the poem that is quite different from what one might garner from reading it unset to music.

For help with this article, I would like to thank my Swarthmore colleagues George Huber and Michael Marissen, my advanced music analysis seminar students, and my research assistant Lia Fernald.

1. A fine recording of *Dark Angels* has been made by Jan de Gaetani, mezzo-soprano, and Oscar Ghiglia, guitar, on Nonesuch Records (H-71342, 1977).

After discussing the balance between musical form and poetic form, I will present the structural intervals in these pieces and their formation into what I consider to be the central motive. More than one level of the central motive, and more than one form of it, are at work in *Dark Angels*, weaving a subtle musical texture. Because of the emphasis on the vocal line, and in view of the very light sound of the guitar, this work provides us with an excellent example for the study of melodic structure, relatively independent of the accompanimental harmony. Although a complete harmonic analysis of the three pieces will not be attempted, the hierarchical structures that the central motives form, and their crucial role in the music, both in the melody and in the accompaniment, will be presented. Even in light of the excellent current research concerning Davies' music, I hope these new ideas about elision, about deeper structural levels, and about the interaction of one level with another will also inform the listener.[2]

"The Drowning Brothers"

The following note from the composer provides essential background information concerning the subject matter of *Dark Angels*:

> The valley where I live, in a remote island off the north coast of Scotland, since Viking times a thriving crofting and fishing community, is now all but deserted. The islanders gradually left through the first half of this century, the contrasts between their own hard life and the comparatively easy life of the Scottish cities being too cruel. A few crofts were worked till quite recently, but there were ever fewer young people, and the final blow for the community was the drowning of the last two children—brothers—in the mid-'50's. . . .
>
> The two poems I have set by George Mackay Brown concern these events; the first, "The Drowning Brothers," relates the circumstance which led to the final exodus, and the second, "Dead Fires," is a litany of the deserted crofts. The title of the guitar solo separating the two settings, "Dark Angels," which I gave to the whole work, refers to the silent hills brooding around the deserted valley.[3]

In the first song, "The Drowning Brothers," four verses unequal in length delineate both the text and the music. Figure 1 contains the entire poem, with my subdivisions added; Example 1 provides the full score for the first verse, mm. 1–22. As Figure 1 illustrates, each verse of poetry has the following three subdivisions:

---

2. The following are examples of excellent research concerning Davies's music: Mike Seabrook, *Max: the Life and Music of Peter Maxwell Davies* (London: V. Gollancz, 1994); Stephen Pruslin, Peter Maxwell Davies: *Studies from Two Decades, Tempo* booklet, No. 2 (London: Boosey & Hawkes Music Publishers, 1979), Peter Owens, "Revelation and Fallacy: Observations on Compositional Technique in the Music of Peter Maxwell Davies," *Music Analysis* 13 (1994): 161–93; and Paul Griffiths, *Peter Maxwell Davies* (London: Robson Books Ltd., 1982).

3. Peter Maxwell Davies, jacket notes to Nonesuch recording of *Dark Angels*.

VERSE I   Section: A The boy said (his arm a long white stone)

                       B 'The burn is a fish in a net of fences . . .

                                The burn is a glancing shuttle . . .'

                       C A crofter turned a homing rudder.

                           Corn, a prodigal, stood in the door of the sun

                           Arrayed in harvest patches.

                           The crofter beached. The ripe hands of the wind

                           Throttled his haddocks.

                           He shouted the women from loom and fire.

VERSE II   A' The brother said (his thigh a struck gleam)

                      B' 'The burn is a lark in a cage. The silver tongue

                           Yearns on and out . . .'

                      C' The burn throbbed between hills and beach all day,

                           Pigeons fretted the stubble.

                           Women stooped to the sheaves with bronze throats.

VERSE III   a The first boy said (half marble and half flesh)

                      b 'The tinker burn hurries from field to field.

                           He begs for small things.

                           Heather to cornstalk to seaweed he burbles gossip.

                           He spreads his pack at every stone,

                           Torrents of sapphire and lace,

                           Among the reeds a swatch of green silk . . .'

                      c An oat, a can, a straw, left the slow valley.

                           Ikey slouched at the stubble edge,

                           Banished that day with larks, rats, fishermen.

VERSE IV   a' The brother said (his throat a sculpted psalm)

                      b' 'The burn is our angel. He praises.

                           He fills our pails.

                           He flames in the face of the drinking beasts.

                           He carries the valley filth

                           Out to the seven brightnesses of the bay.

                           He has turned a key.

                           Quick, now, follow the cold one.

                           They will drag us back to their old sweat and dung . . .'

                      c' Those hills, The Ward and Moorfea, brooded upon them

                           Dark angels.

                           The tractor throbbed with one urgent image, bread.

                           Heavy with images, the statues drowned.

Figure 1. Subdivisions of text in "The Drowning Brothers." Text from the book of poems *Fishermen with Ploughs* by George Mackay Brown © George Mackay Brown 1971. Text reprinted by permission of George Mackay Brown and the Hogarth Press.

Example 1. "The Drowning Brothers," verse I, mm. 1–22.

section A (A', a, and a'). Introduction of the character;
section B (B', b, and b'). Quotation from the character; and
section C (C', c, and c'). Description of landscape or event.

In the music (as shown in Ex. 1), the gestures which correspond to the textual subdivisions can be described as follows:

section A (A', a, and a'). Reciting tone, with embellishment;
section B (B', b, and b'). Another embellished reciting tone,
   higher in pitch than the first; and
section C (C', c, and c'). Angular, lyrical melody, beginning in a low register.

Relating the text in Figure 1 to the music shown in Example 1, one sees that section A spans mm. 1–2 and introduces an embellished reciting tone on A4; section B, mm. 3–8, presents another reciting tone, also embellished, at the higher pitch level of C5; and section C, mm. 9–22, begins with a dramatic shift in register and brings in the first lyrical moment in the piece, an angular melody. All of these musical characteristics recur in the three later verses. A brief description of the musical and poetic correspondences of each section follows.

Sections A, A', a, and a'

A comparison of Figure 1 and Example 2 reveals that the first line of each verse in Brown's poem alternately introduces the two characters, the "first boy" and the "brother." (The first and third verses introduce the "first boy," while the second and fourth refer to "the brother.")

The first line of each verse ends with a parenthetical phrase. For the first boy, the parenthetical phrases suggest images of marble, as follows:

verse I. "The boy said (his arm a *long white stone*)"; and
verse III. "The first boy said (*half marble* and half flesh)."

For the brother, the initial "th" sound of "thigh" and "throat" echoes the "th" in "brother" and connects these two parenthetical phrases, as follows:

verse II. "The bro*th*er said (his *thigh* a struck gleam)"; and
verse IV. "The bro*th*er said (his *throat* a sculpted psalm)."

All four of these opening lines closely correspond to each other with references to marble ("long white stone," "half marble," "struck gleam," and "sculpted") and with references to human flesh or parts of the body ("his arm," "half flesh," "his thigh," and "his throat"). The text suggests the dying, then dead boys, being placed beneath the marble headstones of their graves.

The tightly organized structure in the music parallels that of the poetry, as

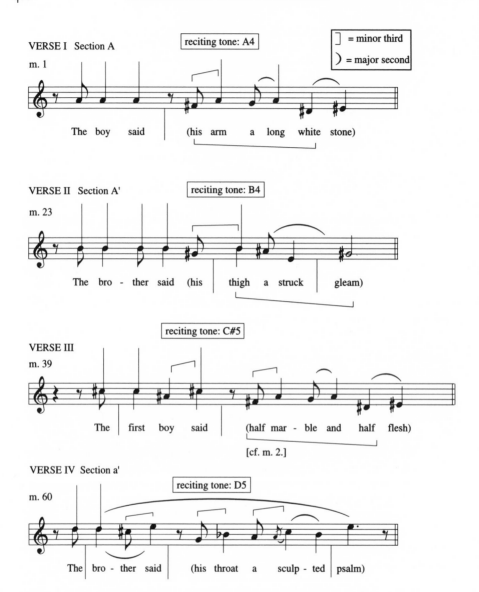

Example 2. Motivic elements in "The Drowning Brothers," sections A, A′, a, and a′.

shown in Example 2. Perhaps the two most distinctive musical gestures, which high-light these structural correspondences and which are characteristic of a great deal of Davies's music, are the use of the minor third, and the syllabic treatment of text. In all four verses, one may describe sections A, A′, a, and a′ as embellished reciting tones—highlighting Davies's interest in capturing musical elements from the distant past. In the first two verses, only a repeated reciting tone is used for the text, "The boy said" and "The brother said." With the opening of the parenthetical expression, a new interval appears, the minor third. All four verses begin the parenthetical phrase with an ascending third. In verses III and IV, the minor third also occurs earlier, for "boy said" and "brother said."

In addition to the minor third, another structural interval shapes *Dark Angels*, the interval of the major second. Verse I shows this most plainly, with the parenthetical phrase outlining a minor third followed by two major seconds. (See Ex. 2.) Note that Davies repeats this phrase exactly for the parenthetical phrase in verse III, section a. In verse II, the major second formed by A♯4–G♯4 will reappear as a middleground feature in the last two verses, as will be discussed below. And in verse IV, all of section a′ is framed by the major second D5 to E5. (In Ex. 2, and in the remaining examples, the use of the bracket graphically highlights the minor third, while the slur marks a major second.)

Sections B, B′, b, and b′

These sections (compare Exx. 1 and 3) are given over to the boys' speech. Textually, all four quotations end with an ellipsis, and mention "the burn," the stream which flows through the valley. Musically, all four link with section A by means of another embellished reciting tone, higher in pitch than that of the corresponding A section. Just as the text adds another dimension to the character by introducing a quote from that character, the music of section B intensifies that of section A with the use of a reciting tone higher in pitch. Other musical means of heightening expression include the quickened rhythm, the longer phrases, and a more densely textured guitar accompaniment.

As shown in Example 3, the pitch content itself also helps to intensify the drama. While minor thirds and major seconds continue to structure the music, the semitone B4–C5 also appears prominently, thereby appropriately adding tension to the music. As highlighted by asterisks in Example 3, the B4 functions at first as a lower-neighbor motion to C5 at the foreground level (C5–B4–C5). This embellished C5 is part of a structural major second, C5–D5. The D5 later returns in sections B′ and b, along with B4, to form a structural minor third, D5–B4. Exactly this ambiguity and these pitches, B4, C5, and D5, return at a deeper structural level as part of an elision, which will be discussed below.

Sections b and b′, although not shown in their entirety in Example 3, clearly reiterate the importance of the minor third and the major second in "The Drowning Brothers." The D5 discussed above with regard to the descending minor third, D5–

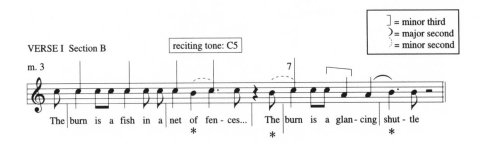

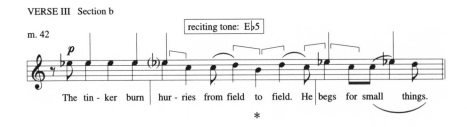

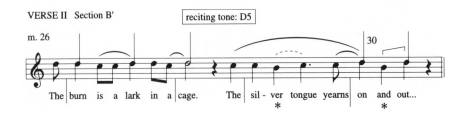

* The ambiguity of the m2 and the close interplay of the pitches B, C, and D will return in the large-scale elision.

Example 3. Motivic elements in "The Drowning Brothers," sections B, B′, b, and b′.

B4, is also used as a point of symmetry. In section b′, the same D5 defines part of an ascending minor third, D5–F5, thereby showing Davies's characteristic use of symmetrical pitch structures.

Sections C, C′, c, and c′

As illustrated in Example 4, both the text and the music in section C break away from the preceding gestures. Textually, the quotes disappear and are replaced by narratives, describing the landscape or events. Musically, the reciting tones disappear and are replaced by lyrical melodies. One important aspect of Davies's music is its emphasis upon the isolation of musical elements. Davies isolates the element of lyricism by contrasting it with reciting-tone passages.

With the marked shift in register for the voice and the change in melodic contour, the drama of the story unfolds: first, the embellished reciting tones heighten intensity with ascending transpositions; next, a plunge downward in register releases tension; finally, a new kind of intensity builds with new musical means, angular melodies.

In the midst of these striking changes in section C, the structural intervals of a minor third and a major second remain constant. As shown in Example 4, the first lyrical moment in the piece, "a crofter," begins with a minor third and continues with a major second. Although only the first few measures of sections C, C′, c, and c′ appear in Example 4, enough evidence is given to show the consistency and maintenance of the central intervals. "The Drowning Brothers," in both text and intervallic content, displays a remarkably clear and tight organization.

ELISION IN "THE DROWNING BROTHERS"

Davies's song cycle *Dark Angels* provides excellent examples of the use of elision in twentieth-century music.[4] More than one kind of elision technique occur in these songs, as will be discussed below. For clarity's sake, I will label one elision technique "elision/substitution" and the other "elision/contraction." For twentieth-century music, the concept of "expected harmony or event" must be expanded to include the linear as well as the vertical dimension.

---

4. The technique of elision shapes much tonal music. See Allen Forte, *Tonal Harmony in Concept and Practice*, 3d ed. (New York: Holt, Rinehart, and Winston, 1979), 504. With respect to twentieth-century music, Vincent Persichetti provides a clear description of elision techniques in his *Twentieth-Century Harmony: Creative Aspects and Practice* (New York: W.W. Norton & Co., 1961), 188, 236, and 274. The term elision describes more than one kind of musical event. On the one hand, elision can mean "substitution" or "extension," when a harmony other than the expected one occurs. On the other hand, elision can describe "contraction," when an expected harmony or event is omitted.

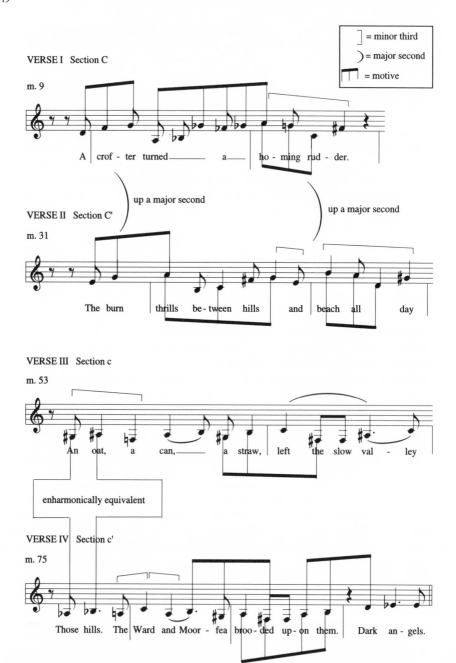

Example 4. Motivic elements in "The Drowning Brothers," sections C, C′, c, and c′.

In Davies's deft marriage of music with poetry, the forms of both the poem and the music easily reach the ear. As tension in the poetry builds, the music brings in higher and higher pitch levels of the reciting tones, thereby building excitement. This striking musical connection, the reciting tones at higher and higher pitch levels, can be heard both within each verse and between verses; intuitively, one gathers that a consistent pattern is at work.

The transpositions of the reciting tones appear in Figure 2. In verses I, II, and IV, the reciting tones *within each verse* are transposed up a minor third, from section A to section B (that is, in verse I, from A4 to C5). The only exception to this rule is in verse III, where the initial reciting tone C♯5 is transposed up a diminished third to E♭5. A different pattern, also shown in Figure 2, outlines the transpositions of reciting tones *from verse to verse*. From verse I, section A, to verse II, section A′ the transposition is up a major second (from A4 to B4). This pattern continues to section a of verse III, up another major second, from B4 to C♯5. However, the pattern breaks off at verse IV, section a′, with a semitone ascent from C♯5 to D5.

These patterns hold promise for establishing a very large-scale structure of "The Drowning Brothers," depending upon an adequate explanation of the anomalies. The first pattern of internal transposition by minor third breaks off in verse III, with an ascent of a diminished third, from C♯5 to E♭5. In verse IV, the pattern returns, with an ascent of a minor third from D5 to F5. How should one account for the "near miss"? The most obvious explanation is that the diminished third is enharmonically equivalent to the major second, and therefore both the minor third and the major second appear as both surface and large-scale events. In support of this argument, another instance of enharmonic respelling surfaces in verses III and IV, where the G♯4–A♯4 in section c is enharmonically equivalent to the A♭4–B♭4 in section c′. This argument is very convincing with respect to the sound at the surface of the music. Perhaps the asymmetry in the music here represents the uncertainty of the brothers' fate, or the horror of their final moments. As an operatic composer, Davies often brings compelling drama to his music; these moments of great strife may be felt by the asymmetry. But how do the last two verses, linked by this enharmonic respelling yet out of step with the first two verses, function with respect to the whole?

I offer the technique of elision/substitution as an explanation of the asymmetry. If, as Forte says, the concept of elision "affects larger contexts when it occurs where one expects a harmonic goal,"[5] what does one expect in the case of "The Drowning Brothers"? Perhaps an exact transposition from one verse to each of the others?

Figure 3 outlines the hypothetical structure of the four verses using exact transposition. Just as verse II transposes internal reciting tones up a minor third, so does verse III (from C♯5 to a hypothetical E5). Just as verse II transposes verse I up by an ascending major second, so does verse IV transpose verse III. The correspondences that result from this hypothetical outline, comparing Figures 2 and 3, are as follows:

5. Forte, *Tonal Harmony*, 504.

VERSE I	Section: A	Reciting Tone:	A4	⎤	minor third
	B	Reciting Tone:	C5	⎦	
	C	Angular Melody:	D4–F4		minor third
VERSE II					
	A′		B4	⎤	minor third
	B′		D5	⎦	
	C′		E4–G4		minor third
VERSE III					
	a		C♯5	⎞	diminished third (= major second)
	b		E♭5	⎠	
	c		G♯4–A♯4		major second
VERSE IV					
	a′		D5	⎤	minor third
	b′		F5	⎦	
	c′		A♭4–B♭4		major second (= G♯–A♯)

Figure 2. Large-scale melodic outline in "The Drowning Brothers."

VERSE I	Section: A	Reciting Tone:	A4	⎤	minor third
	B	Reciting Tone:	C5	⎦	
	C	Angular Melody:	D4–F4		minor third
					Each verse is transposed up a major second
VERSE II					
	A′		B4	⎤	minor third
	B′		D5	⎦	
	C′		E4–G4		minor third
VERSE III					
	a		C♯5	⎞	minor third
	b		E5	⎠	
	c		F♯4–A4		minor third
VERSE IV					
	a′		D♯5	⎤	minor third
	b′		F♯5	⎦	
	c′		G♯4–B4		minor third (G♯=A♭)

Figure 3. Hypothetical melodic outline, using exact transposition.

1) Verse III, section a, begins in both instances with C♯5.
2) Verse IV, section c', begins enharmonically equivalent, A♭4 and G♯4.

Not much insight is gained from attempting to read this type of elision.

One can invoke a different kind of elision/substitution, with a different expected goal, as shown in Figure 4. One can view the transposition by major second from verse II to verse III, not as a continuation of a pattern of transposition up by major second, but as an elision/substitution of an expected minor second, between B4 and C5. Exactly this elided pitch, C5, was heard prominently in the matter of the minor second/major second discussed previously.

Likewise, the elided C5 would continue the internal transpositions by minor third within verses. The minor third connections between sections A and B, and also between sections A' and B', would continue with the elided C5 in section a to the E♭5 in section b. The minor-third transposition is maintained in verse IV, with a progression from D5 to F5. The following correspondences result, comparing the elision argument outlined in Figure 4 with the actual music outlined in Figure 2:

1) In verse III, section b, the reciting tone is E5 in both cases;
2) In sections c and c', the G♯4 and A♭4 are enharmonically equivalent. In the hypothetical outline in Figure 4, A♭4 figures prominently in section c, and B♭4 appears prominently in section c'; and
3) In verse IV, the D5–F5 of section a' is identical to that of section b'.

Several factors strongly support this elision/substitution argument. One is the closeness of resemblance between both versions of verse IV, with sections a' and b' matching perfectly. Beyond this, the pitches that are enharmonically equivalent in section c of verse III and section c' of verse IV are G♯4–A♯4 (A♭4–B♭4)—exactly that major second which is central to the last two verses. Taking this correspondence one step further, one finds that the final B♭4 in section c' of verse IV appears in the same position. One could say that the piece "ends up in the same place," which is exactly the function of an elision/substitution.

The deciding factor, though, must be the text. While theorists most often use pitch structure, repetition, rhythmic emphasis, and harmonic progression as determining factors for analytical decisions, I believe that in this instance the *text* must outweigh them in importance.

Comparing Figures 2 and 4, one sees that verses II and IV relate to each other as follows: sections A' to a' and sections B' to b' link together, from B4 to D5, and from D5 to F5. Beyond this, verses II and IV are strongly related to each other by the text: both verses concern the brother.

Extending this textual relationship to verses I and III, which are both about the first boy, sections A to a and B to b link as follows, using elision/substitution: A4 to C5, and C5 to E♭5. With the elision/substitution of the C♯5 of section a, the same E♭5 appears in the same position of section b, and the textual relationship of the verses pertaining to the first boy is maintained.

VERSE I	Section:	A	Reciting Tone:	A4		minor third
		B	Reciting Tone:	C5	]	
		C	Angular Melody:	D4–F4		minor third
						Each pair of verses is transposed up a major second
VERSE II		A′		B4		minor third
		B′		D5	]	
		C′		E4-G4		minor third

// elision/substitution //

VERSE III		a		C5		minor third
		b		E♭5	]	
		c		F–A♭		minor third (A♭=G♯)
VERSE IV		a′		D5		minor third
		b′		F5	]	
		c′		G–B♭		minor third (B♭=A♯)

Figure 4. Hypothetical melodic outline, using elision/substitution.

The elision argument preserves the most fundamental structure, while the pitch levels at the surface are altered. Davies has a means of showing the boys' identities as two separate people, alongside their kinship. (One can recall the strong correlation between the opening phrases of verses I and II, the literal repetition of m. 2 in m. 41.) The composer constantly refers to both kinship and difference throughout the piece. Also, at some level, the concept of elision itself reflects the literal ellipses used extensively in the poetry. In these ways, the text can be a critical factor in making analytical decisions.

The Central Motive in Dark Angels

As shown in Examples 2, 3, and 4, the minor third and the major second appear most regularly as structural intervals. I view the central motive in this piece as the combination of the minor third and major second. This trichord can be heard most clearly in m. 9, the first lyrical moment in the piece, for the words "a crofter." (See Ex. 1.) After the monotones of "the boy" and "the burn," the expanded, three-syllable "a crofter" strikingly introduces this central motive at the surface level. Another poignant use of the central motive occurs at the very end of the first piece, for the words "statues drowned," at which point the descending version of this motive is sung, A♭4–F4–E♭4. (See "statues drowned" in Ex. 10.)

Many variations of the central motive occur, and at more than one level. Some of the possible variants are as follows: ascending m3–M2 (like "a crofter"); descending m3–M2 (like "statues drowned"); ascending M2–m3; descending M2–m3; any octave equivalence (register transfer); and any inversion. All of these forms are embraced by Allen Forte's designation of pitch-class set 3–7 [025].[6] Both (025) and (035), with all octaves and inversions, are represented by 3–7.

Another possible combination of minor third and major second results from an ascending minor third filled in by a descending major second, producing 3–2 [013]. Although a few of these sets appear at the surface of *Dark Angels*, they do not appear on deeper levels, and therefore do not receive the designation of "central motives," which will be reserved for the 3–7 sets.

The structural motives for verses I and II are illustrated in Examples 5 and 6. The notes graphically highlighted by boxes mark the central motive, while the brackets in the graph outline the minor third. For very large-scale motives, or where using boxes is graphically awkward, the 3–7 sets are beamed together.

To progress from one structural set to another, several types of connections are available. If any one of the three pitches remains constant while the other two shift, a common-tone pivot results. If the outer perfect fourth, (05), remains constant, while the inner note shifts from (025) to (035), a common-dyad pivot results.

All of the different forms of 3–7 found in this piece, and all of the possible progressions connecting them, work on more than one structural level. As illustrated in Examples 5 and 6, many beautiful examples of 3–7 at the surface level occur and recur throughout the piece, weaving a tightly knit texture. A fascinating variation on the surface level appears in verse III (Ex. 7), where the boxes are dotted to show that a *major* third and a major second are at work, temporarily replacing the central motive's minor third. This apparent inconsistency in fact complements the asymmetry of the transposition levels, and supports the concept of elision/substitution, also found in verse III. In both cases, a semitone difference marks the elision/substitution—in the difference between minor and major thirds (3–7 [025] and 3–8 [026]) and between the elided C5 and the actual C♯5.

While the "foreground" examples of 3–7, graphically highlighted by boxes, can easily be checked against Example 1, some of the larger-scale examples of the central motive, and the links between surface and deeper levels, need further explanation.[7]

---

6. Allen Forte, *The Structure of Atonal Music* (New Haven and London: Yale University Press, 1973).

7. Bibliographies for this relatively new direction in analyzing non-tonal and extended tonal music can be found at the end of Allen Forte, "New Approaches to the Linear Analysis of Music," *Journal of the American Musicological Society* 41 (1988): 315–48; and Allen Forte, "Concepts of Linearity in Schoenberg's Atonal Music: A Study of the Op. 15 Song Cycle," *Journal of Music Theory* 36 (1992): 285–382. Other excellent sources are Paul Wilson, *The Music of Béla Bartók* (New Haven and London: Yale University Press, 1992), Joseph N. Straus, *Introduction to Post-Tonal Theory* (Englewood Cliffs: Prentice Hall, 1991), and Pieter van den Toorn, *The Music of Igor Stravinsky* (New Haven and London: Yale University Press, 1983).

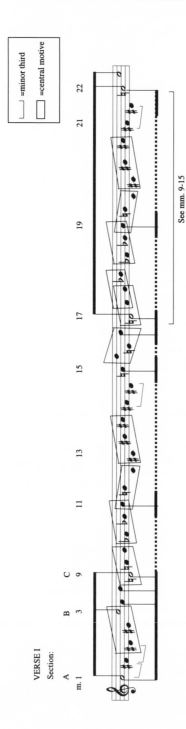

Example 5. "The Drowning Brothers," large-scale motivic structure, verse I.

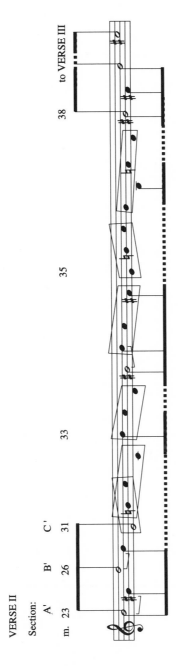

Example 6. "The Drowning Brothers," large-scale motivic structure, verse II.

The very first surface 3–7, D♯4–E♯4–C5, boxed at mm. 2–3 of Example 5, connects with a deeper level 3–7, A4–C5–D4, beamed with open noteheads in mm. 1–9. Initiating a "middleground" progression, this A4–C5–D4 connects section A's reciting tone and section B's reciting tone to the first note of section C. What initially sounds simply as a lovely intertwining of trichords at the surface level also contains more fundamental motives connecting all three sections of a particular verse.

Whereas the first surface set, C5–D♯4–E♯4, has a common-tone pivot with the "middleground" set A4–C5–D4, deeper-level motives between sections pivot by means of a common dyad. I view the entire first verse as a large-scale pivot between the original A4–C5–D4 and an A4–B4–D4 set. This same common-dyad pivot also structures the deepest connection between verse I and verse II, where the "middleground" 3–7 A4–C5–D4 links to the "middleground" B4 and D5 of verse II A4–B4–D5. (See Ex. 9.)

And yet again, this same pivot structures the largest-scale, elided form of the entire piece. As shown in Figures 2 and 4, the A4 reciting tone from verse I connects to the elided C5 reciting tone of verse III and to the D5 reciting tone in verse IV. This elided 3–7 pivots with the actual large-scale 3–7, formed from the initial A4 reciting tone from verse I, to the B4 reciting tone in verse II, to the D5 reciting tone in verse IV.

Another example of the interplay between structural levels involves the hinting at or echoing of various trichordal sets. For example, in mm. 15 and 16 in Example 5, the surface D5–E4–B4 set anticipates the much larger-scale set that structures verse II, illustrated in Example 6. The large-scale B4–D5–E4 set in mm. 23–31 connects all three sections in verse II, in a manner identical to verse I's A4–C5–D4 set.

In the third verse, illustrated in Example 7, the surface variants of major thirds plus major seconds (3–8 sets) are graphically highlighted by dotted boxes. At the same time, a deeper level of 3–7 sets continues to structure deeper levels of the piece. The connection between sections a, b, and c changes from the method used in the first two verses. In verse III, the C♯5 of section a links to the E♭5 of section b, then to the A♯3 (not the G♯3) of section c, thereby forming a large-scale 3–7 set, A♯–C♯–E♭. (Note that this 3–7 set is exactly T₁ of verse I's "middleground" set, A–C–D, maintaining another textual link between verses concerning "the first boy," and using the semitone in yet another variation.) As verse III begins the elision discussed above, this change in verse structure is not surprising. The importance of the G♯–A♯ dyad begins to emerge.

The G♯–A♯ dyad's central role continues in verse IV (see Ex. 8), where another means of linking sections a', b', and c' develops. One can follow the use of the G♯–A♯ dyad, enharmonically spelled as A♭–B♭, throughout the fourth verse, until the very last trichord for the last words of the song, "statues drowned" (A♭4–F4–E♭4).

To display the deepest structural level of all, the verse-to-verse connections, I have included Example 9. One readily sees the parallel structures in verses I and II, as well as this pattern breaking for the elision/substitution in verse III, the G♯–A♯ dyad emerging as a structural pivot, and the G♯–A♯ dyad continuing its central role to the very end of verse IV.

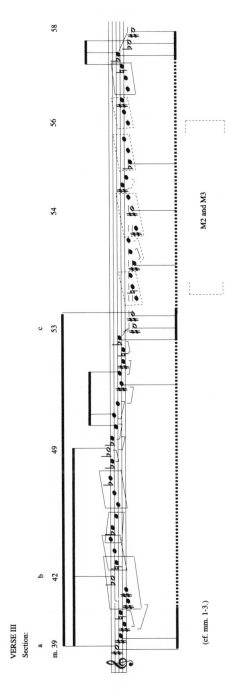

Example 7. "The Drowning Brothers," large-scale motivic structure, verse III.

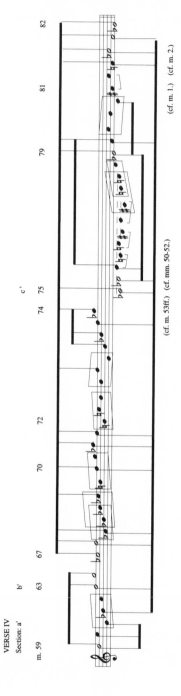

Example 8. "The Drowning Brothers," large-scale motivic structure, verse IV.

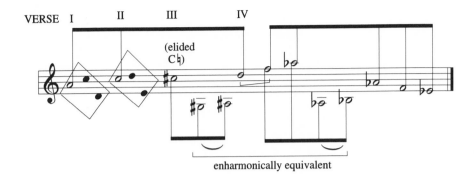

Example 9. "The Drowning Brothers," large-scale structure showing elision/substitution.

Speaking in his own terms about various sets and their function in his music, Davies uses the phrase "pitch transformations" and describes his compositional method in the following words:

> I find that the simpler one's basic concept—a very basic harmonic relationship between three, four, five pitches—the more complex the structure one can develop from it. I don't mean complex on paper: I mean complexity that the ear can actually perceive.[8]

My analysis of this piece shows a multilayered structure built on a very basic harmonic relationship between three pitches. The number three makes sense with regard to many dimensions of this cycle, as it reflects both the three-part structure of the poetry and, on the largest scale, the number of pieces in the song cycle itself. The number three also brings many religious connotations with it, which are indeed appropriate for this poetry.

The Guitar Accompaniment

To consider questions of harmony, harmonic support, and harmonic progressions, I have provided analyses of the guitar accompaniment in Examples 10, 11, and 12. The song cycle begins with the mezzo-soprano *a cappella*. When the guitar enters, it brings in the minor third, C3–E♭3. This C3–E♭3 presages the "elided" C-E♭ discussed above. As Example 10 illustrates, the transition from section A to section B in the poem coincides with the introduction of the guitar and forms a 3–7 set (035), which enharmonically includes the voice's D♯4–E♯4 for the text "white stone." Also shown in Example 10 is the last measure of "The Drowning Brothers," which marks a perceptible return of this central motive at the very end of the piece for the text "statues drowned."

---

8. Peter Maxwell Davies, "Symphony," *Tempo* 124 (March 1978): 2.

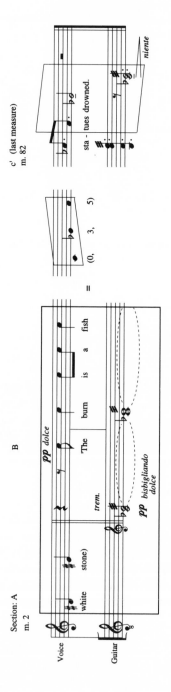

Example 10. "The Drowning Brothers," transition from section A to section B; also, last measure.

Back at the beginning of the piece at m. 7, the guitar adds another minor third, B3–D4, as shown in Example 11a. Again, the surface sound B3–D4 anticipates a large-scale inter-verse connection. And again, this sonority reappears in the last measure. The first complex verticality appears in m. 8 (Ex. 11b), and recurs in variations throughout the piece. Two possible ways of reading this sonority are shown in Examples 11c-d and 11e-f. The first reading shows two superimposed "diminished triads," with roots a major second apart. With this reading, the minor thirds are clearly highlighted; one can speak of an additive progression in the first eight measures of the guitar accompaniment, from one minor third, to two minor thirds, to four minor thirds. The minor thirds are related to each by a major second (F-E♭), nicely reflecting the central motive.

One can also read the complex verticality as four statements of a 3–7 set, as shown in Examples 11e and f. Both the (025) and the (035) forms appear, first with the perfect fourth outlined by E♭3–A♭3, then with the perfect fourth, G♭3–C♭4. At Example 11f, I have shown these 3–7 sets placed in the proper register for the guitar. Both readings make perfect sense with regard to the structural intervals of this song cycle.

As the first song intensifies with the narration of the tragic story of the drowning boys, the guitar part expands and develops. More forms of 3–7 occur, as illustrated in Example 12. (Compare with the full score, Ex. 1.) A wide variety of sets structures mm. 9–12, some using only the pitches of the guitar accompaniment, others including notes from the vocal part as well. An overwhelming amount of evidence shows the set 3–7 to be not only the central melodic motive for the voice, but also the structural harmonic set for the accompaniment, virtually saturating the music on all levels. How this first piece in the cycle relates to the other two will be discussed below.

"DARK ANGELS"

Made up of five distinct parts, the guitar solo uses pitch-class set 3–7 as a structural harmonic sound, yet in more subtle ways than in either of the vocal songs. As shown in Example 13 (score with analytical overlay), the guitar solo begins with a melodic major sixth, E♭3–C4, an inversion of the guitar's C3–E♭3, which begins and ends "The Drowning Brothers." (This also reminds us of the elided C-E♭ discussed above.) The opening melody is in two-part counterpoint with D3–E3, exactly the pitch classes to which the words "Dark angels" in the first song were set. (See Ex. 4, section c', m. 78.) In fact, the entire melody for part 1 of the guitar solo can be analyzed as spanning either minor thirds or major seconds. On a deeper level, the pitch C♯4 serves triple duty as a pivot in the opening texture, as part of an E♭3–G♭3–C♯4 set, as part of a C♯4–E4–B3 set, and as part of a C♯4–G♯3–B3 set. These specific transposition levels echo verse III of "The Drowning Brothers." (See Ex. 7, mm. 39–53.) In part 2, this C♯ is enharmonically D, and part of the large-scale 3–7 set, D♭4–E♭4–G♭3/G♭5, which

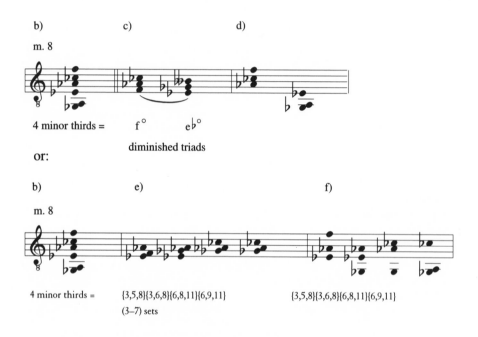

Example 11a–f. "The Drowning Brothers," section B, guitar part.

structures the melody. The D/C♯ pivot continues to link parts, as it connects to the G♯4 and A♯4 of part 3.

    More parallels can be drawn between the guitar solo and verses III and IV of "The Drowning Brothers." In the solo, part 3 obviously links with verses III and IV of "The Drowning Brothers" by means of the highlighted G♯4–A♯4. And just as the unusual G♯4–A♯4 dyads in both Verses III and IV link to the surrounding music by 3–7 sets, so does the G♯4–A♯4 dyad in the guitar solo, as illustrated in Example 13. A D♭5 occurs at the end of part 2 and reappears enharmonically as C♯5 at the beginning of part 4, making a convincing, symmetrical 3–7 link with the G♯4–A♯4 dyad in part 3. Davies seems to have taken the unique material in the first song, which grew out of the elision, and developed it here in the guitar solo.

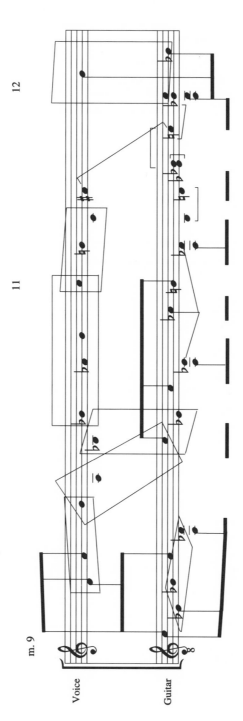

Example 12. "The Drowning Brothers," opening measures of section C.

Example 13. Analysis of "Dark Angels."

The sketch material for the guitar solo, reproduced in Example 14, shows some care seems to have been taken with the music at this point. The last notes written in the middle system of the sketch pertain to the published part 3, the G♯4–A♯4 dyad. Davies first writes an open notehead *B instead of A♯*. (The B is a minor third above G♯, an interval very much in keeping with the rest of the work.) Only later does the change to A♯ appear, in brackets. The most pivotal part in the guitar solo happens to be the part in the sketches with the most striking change.

Just as Davies isolates lyricism in the first song, he isolates intervallic elements in the guitar solo: the minor third in part 1; the 3–7 set in part 2; the major second in part 3; the symmetrical pivot to parts 4 and 5. And just as part 3 is an internal point of symmetry for the arch form of the guitar solo, the solo itself is the mid-cycle pivot for the entire work.

The use of the 3–7 set is especially appropriate to a piece for the guitar. The standard tuning of the guitar, from the bottom string up, is E2–A2–D3–G3–B3–E4. Taking the pitches of every other open string yields two collections of three notes each, E2–D3–B3 and A2–G3–E4—two forms of the 3–7 set! This relationship would seem much more than coincidental.

"DEAD FIRES"

The original published poem "Dead Fires" has very few irregular subdivisions. As shown in Figure 5, the first six lines of poetry are grouped 2 + 2 + 2. Throughout the rest of the poem, the lines of text are grouped in threes with no apparent hierarchy. One might view this repetitive phrase structure as perfectly apt for a litany. Davies, not Brown, adds a hierarchy, and further subdivides the text, by means of the musical form. When the musical form is overlaid onto the poetry, as in Figure 5, a new reading of the poem results.

Davies musically groups the first six lines of poetry 2 + 2 + 2, in keeping with the structure of the poetry. He then subdivides the following 27 lines, not into the equal groups of three found in Brown's poem, but into unequal multiples of three, 9 + 6 + 9 + 3, as shown in Figure 5. The new dimensions raise several questions. Why subdivide the poem in this way? Could Davies simply be avoiding a through-composed form, or is the resultant five-part form a perceptible reference to the guitar solo's five-part form?

Numerological schemes structure much of Davies's oeuvre.[9] As shown in Example 14, such a scheme may be at work in *Dark Angels*, evidence for which can be

---

9. Excellent research on Davies's predilection for numerological schemes can be found in Pruslin, *Studies from Two Decades*.

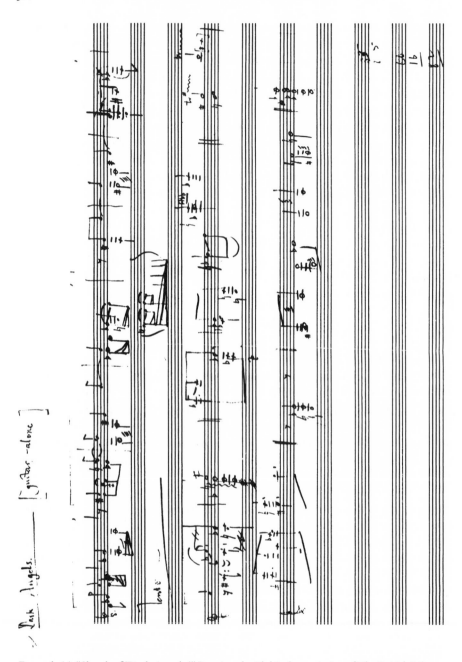

Example 14. "Sketch of 'Dark Angels.'" Reprinted with kind permission of The British Library.

VERSE I   Section: A   At Burnmouth the door hangs from a broken hinge
                            And the fire is out.

                            The windows of Shore empty sockets
                            And the hearth coldness.

                            At Bunertoon the small drains are choked.
                            Thrushes sing in the chimney.

                       B   Stars shine through the roofbeams of Scar.
                            No flame is needed
                            To warm ghost and nettle and rat.

                            Greenhill is sunk in a new bog.
                            No kneeling woman
                            Blows red wind through squares of ancient turf.

                            The Moss is a tumble of stones.
                            That one black stone
                            Is the stone where the heart fire was rooted.

VERSE II   A′   In Crawnest the sunken hearth
                            War an altar for priests of legend,
                            Old seamen from the clippers with silken beards.

                            The three-toed pot at the wall of Park
                            Is lost to woman's cunning.
                            A slow fire of rust eats the cold iron.

                       B′   The sheep drift through Reumin all winter.
                            Sheep and snow
                            Blanch fleetingly the black stone.

                            From that sacred stone the children of the valley
                            Drifted lovewards
                            And out of labour to the lettered kirkyard stone.

                            The fire beat like a heart in each house
                            From the first cornerstone
                            Till they led through a sagging lintel the last old one.

VERSE III   A″   The poor and the good fires are all quenched.
                            Now, cold angel, keep the valley
                            From the bedlam and cinders of A Black Pentecost.

Figure 5. Subdivisions of text in "Dead Fires." Reprinted with permission of the British Library. Text from the book of poems *Fishermen with Ploughs* by George Mackay Brown © George Mackay Brown 1971. Text reprinted by permission of George Mackay Brown and the Hogarth Press.

seen in the lower right-hand corner of the page of sketches of the guitar solo.[10] Therefore, it might not be too far-fetched to think that the central motive (a *second* plus a
third) is now echoed by the proportions on the deepest level, with the symbolic grouping of three sets of *two* lines (Section A = six lines), followed by groupings of three
sets of *three* lines (Section B = nine lines), and followed by *two* sets of *three* lines
(Section A' = six lines). The proportion of two to three also underpins the cycle as a
whole, with a pair of brothers, and a pair of poems, and a pair of performers performing a group of three pieces.

Perhaps a refinement of the sense of "litany" also occurs. ("Litany" is Davies's
choice of descriptive term, as quoted above, p. 482.) Litanies are not only repetitive,
but also responsorial, with the response by the congregation often being musically
less complicated. Davies's employment of a simpler, reciting-tone style in the B and
B' sections aptly reflects a litany's responsorial quality.

Palindromic considerations could also have affected the choice of form. The
first poem, "The Drowning Brothers," has nine lines of text in the first verse and six
lines of text in the second verse. Davies inverts this structure in the last song by joining the first six lines of text together in a 2 + 2 + 2 grouping, and the next nine lines
of text into a 3 + 3 + 3 grouping. The verse structure of the last song in this cycle
thereby bears a complementary relationship to that of the first song.

One can also describe the last song of *Dark Angels* as the culmination of the
solo/accompanist relationship. While the first song begins with voice alone, adding
very spare guitar, intensity builds throughout the piece, expanding the role of the
accompaniment. One might think of the vocal part as representing the boys and
earthly things, while the guitar part is more ethereal and of the world beyond. The
momentum builds up in the guitar part toward the end of the first song and reaches
a climax in the guitar solo (at which point the boys have died and the world beyond
has taken over). Continuing this momentum from the solo, the guitar alone begins
the third song. (See Ex. 15, the full score of "Dead Fires," mm. 1–22.) For the first
time in the cycle, an evenly balanced rapport between voice and guitar is evident, at
which point, the poetry states that the brooding hills (on earth) have become dark
angels ("Now, cold angel, . . ."). The achievement of balance between voice and guitar

---

10. This sketch is housed in the British Library as Add. 71.410. As shown in Example 14,
the lower right-hand corner of the sketch contains a list, which may be read as follows:

$$33$$
$$2 \qquad 5$$
$$66$$
$$16$$
$$82.$$

Two possible numerological inferences are: 33 x 2 = 66 and 66 + 16 = 82. The lone "5"
may refer to the five sections of the solo. One musical reference may be that there are sixteen
musical attacks in the last two sections of the guitar solo (shown as the entire last staff of
music in the sketch).

Example 15. "Dead Fires," verse I, mm. 1–22.

is dramatized by the text at this point. Just as Davies isolates other musical elements, he isolates the accompaniment and develops it in a dramatic way as the pieces and texts unfold.

In that it functions as a point of symmetry for the entire cycle, the guitar solo not only reflects material from the first song but also anticipates material in the last song. (See Ex. 16.) The crucial G♯–A♯ dyad, now spelled B♭2–A♭2 in the lowest register in m. 1, combines with F2 in m. 3 to form a 3–7 set, thereby continuing the echoes of elision/substitution in the first song.

Other forms of 3–7 that appear in the first two pieces reappear here. The very first vertical trichord in "The Drowning Brothers," E♮4–C3–E4, appears in mm. 2–5 of "Dead Fires," C4–F2–D♯4. As shown in Examples 15 and 16, several other forms overlap and intertwine in the vocal part of "Dead Fires" and mirror the previous pieces. The harmonic texture is in a rather transparent format in the third song, quite similar to the vocal part of the first. Another similarity between the first and third songs is that in both cases verse I is exactly 22 measures long.

However, there are also several important differences between the two vocal pieces. In the last song, Davies uses a different means of delineating the poetry. Whereas in the first song reciting tones were transposed up within verses and between succeeding verses, such transpositions do not appear in the third song. Rather, varied repetition at the same pitch level occurs, along with a different type of elision, as will be discussed below. (See Exx. 17, 18, 19a, and 19b.) Davies virtually repeats, or condenses, very large amounts of music into an arch: A B; A′ B′; A″ This five-part form echoes the five-part form of the guitar solo.

Sections A, A′, and A″

Example 17 displays the 3–7 sets in the opening of sections A, A′, and A″. Rather than the transposition process of "The Drowning Brothers," an unusual distillation process occurs in "Dead Fires." With each return of A material, not only does a shortening of the phrase length occur, thereby eliminating several pitches, but at the same time new forms of 3–7 are added. Various forms of 3–7 are outlined in the analytical graphs in Example 17, including large-scale common dyads. One can find most of the same forms of 3–7 in all verses; I have dotted the beam of the form in verse II that differs (C♭4–D♭4–E4). In verse III, further reduction occurs. Yet, at the same time, another new form of 3–7 appears, pivoting on the "common-tone" E♭ (E♭3–F♯4–C♯4).

Many connections, both surface and large-scale, can be made between the two vocal songs. The most obvious one is that the theme beginning the vocal line in sections A, A′, and A″ in the third song, for the words, "At Burnmouth," "At Crawsnest," and "The poor and," is transposed directly from the first lyrical moment in the first song, section C, for the words, "a crofter" (mm. 9–10). Not only are these two gestures similar on the surface level, but the pitch classes used in the third song for "At Burnmouth," etc., are A–C–D, *exactly* the pitch classes of the first large-scale set in

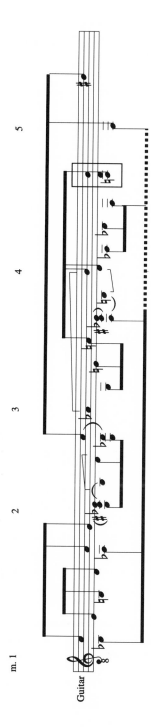

Example 16. "Dead Fires," mm. 1–5.

Example 17. "Dead Fires," beginnings of sections A, A', and A".

the first song connecting the three sections (sections A, B, and C) in verse I. (See the open noteheads in Ex. 5.)

Another connection between the two songs can heard in the largest-scale common-dyad set created in sections A and A′ of "Dead Fires." As shown in Example 17, a very large-scale 3–7 set, E♭-F-A♭, is created by one combination of three pairs of common dyads (C–F; E♭–A♭; E♭–F). This 3–7 set corresponds directly to the 3–7 set of the crucial words "statues drowned" in "The Drowning Brothers." (See Ex. 8.) The other 3–7 set shown in Example 8, C-E♭-F, corresponds exactly to the other possible combination of the common dyads in the third song! Thus, the interactions of surface and deeper levels span, not just one piece in the cycle, but the entire length of the cycle.

Sections B and B′

The order of presentation for the contrasting musical gestures of reciting-tone chant and lyrical melody is reversed between the two songs. In the last song, the lyrical melody appears first; a reciting-tone quality appears later in section B, as shown in Example 18. Perhaps this palindromic characteristic, along with other symmetrical structures, reflects the "from dust to dust" circle of life and death.

Many elegant overlappings of 3–7 occur in the two B sections. Also noteworthy is the reappearance of the G♯4–A♯4 dyad, as part of two G♯4–A♯4–C♯5 sets in mm. 27 and 64. Another echo of previous material is heard in the C♯4–D♯5–F♯5 set, spanning mm. 62–64, which is very important in both the first song and in the guitar solo.

Elision in "Dead Fires"

The large-scale structure of the vocal melody in the last song is analyzed in Examples 19a and 19b, where large-scale sets are graphically highlighted by beams and boxes. A large-scale pattern emerges, here called "Pattern WXYZ." One can easily trace the development of this pattern by comparing Examples 17 and 18 with Examples 19a and 19b. As shown in Example 19a, verse I, section A presents this pattern in order and in its entirety (WXYZ). The pattern is reversed in its entirety in section B (ZYXW). Such an arch form perfectly complements the many symmetrical structures in this cycle.

In verse II, section A′, the original pattern reemerges (WXYZ). However, in section B′ (Ex. 19b), an elision occurs: instead of the reversed pattern in its entirety (ZYXW), we hear a partial pattern (ZYW). Such an elision is of the elision/contraction type, in which an element is missing. (This differs from the elision/substitution type found in "The Drowning Brothers.")

In verse III, section A″ (Ex. 19b), my elision argument finds further support. The original pattern (WXYZ) is not heard in its entirety, but in an elided form (WYZ). Again, the type of elision is elision/contraction, and again the part of the pattern which is elided is the "X."

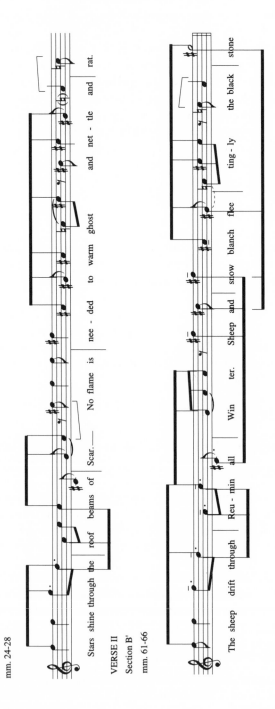

Example 18. "Dead Fires," beginnings of sections B and B′.

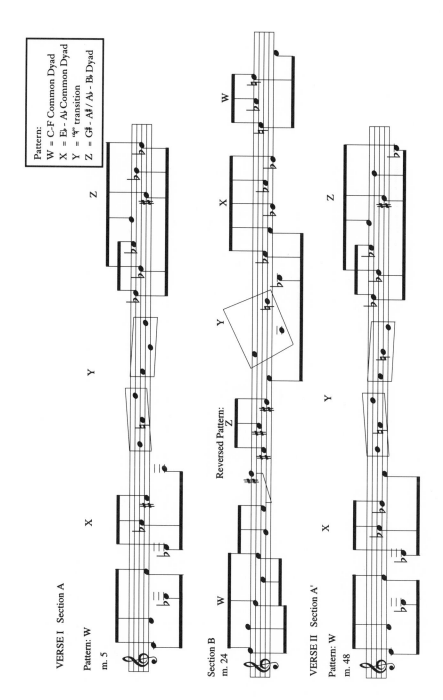

Example 19a. "Dead Fires," large-scale structural patterns.

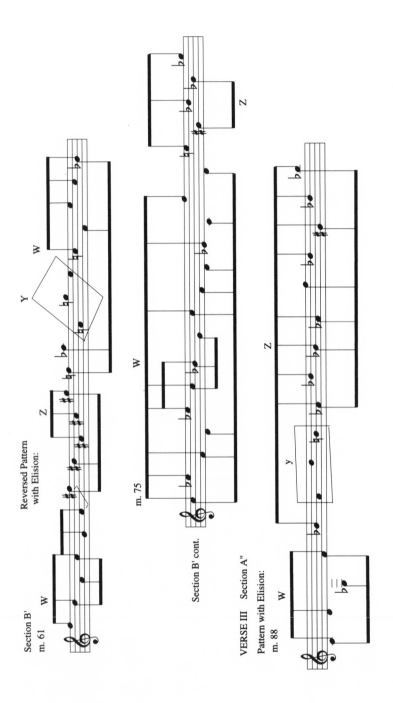

Example 19b. "Dead Fires," patterns with elided "X."

CONCLUSION

To place this Davies song cycle in historical perspective, one might consider its use of such traditional elements as the presence of memorable themes, lyricism, text painting, and interplay of solo and accompaniment. *Dark Angels* is "melodic," in the traditional sense of the term, in that certain contours and gestures, often forming a 3–7 set, are enough to recall "themes" that have been previously introduced. This is true even if the pitch relations aren't repeated exactly; the relationship is analogous to that of a tonal answer to the initial statement of an imitative subject.

Lyricism appears as a separate element in this piece. As registers shift dramatically to delineate the form, melodic shapes change simultaneously: from reciting tone to embellished reciting tone to dramatic angularity. The subtleties of text, of quotations and narratives, are elegantly complemented by the music.

Text painting of individual words—again, an element of the distant and not-so-distant past—is a technique sparingly used at the surface level. In "The Drowning Brothers," in m. 20, "Throttled," is embellished with a grace note; in m. 45, "burbled," also appears with a grace note; and in m. 71, "Quick now follow," creates a frantic quality by means of leaps, crescendos, and grace notes. On the other hand, text painting is often applied to entire phrases or moods, especially by means of the marked contrasts between sections of reciting-tone passages and lyrical passages, which may be viewed in "The Drowning Brothers" as a distillation of the recitative-aria procedure, or in "Dead Fires," its mirror image, as the call-and-response procedure of a litany.

Another musical characteristic which Davies isolates in this song cycle is the relationship between the soloist and the accompaniment. This relationship itself develops as the cycle proceeds. In the first song, the voice enters *a cappella*; the guitar's role is minimal throughout most of the piece. Toward the end of the first song, the intensity of the guitar's music increases, giving it sufficient momentum to flow into the next piece, the guitar solo. The roles of the two performers are reversed during the guitar solo, and at the beginning of the last song, the guitar begins alone. As the last song progresses, a perfect balance is achieved, with each part commenting on the other, each in turn taking the lead and retreating from prominence.

The two vocal songs are similar in terms of a consistent use of the set 3–7, but totally different in terms of form. Again, Davies's music isolates such musical elements as form distinct from harmonic development, contraction of phrase lengths while adding new harmonies, permutations of a trichord, and interchangeability of solo and accompanimental roles.

Paul Griffiths discusses the minor thirds and the symmetry in this piece, and sensitively describes the song cycle as follows:

> The two songs, which are separated by a guitar solo, [are] rooted in symmetrical, repetitive structures. There is, indeed, something of the fresh melancholy of so much Scottish folk music in this very attractive little work, which is a lament for the tragedy

of Rackwick, overshadowed by the "dark angels" of its guardian hills. It is in the first song, "The Drowning Brothers," that this tone of simple objective compassion is strongest, and particularly in its slow narrative chants, oscillating over a minor third, which set the scene for the tale of how the community lost its last two children in the burn and so withdrew to leave the "Dead Fires" of deserted dwellings that are the subject of the more passionate second song.[11]

Although many analyses are possible for this piece, I am convinced of the importance of a central motive, pitch-class set 3–7, and the existence of a multilayered structure at work, linking the 3–7 sets on several levels and in many variants. Particularly compelling to me are the "middleground prolongations," the composing-out of the 3–7 set over very long spans of music. The points of symmetry throughout the piece are heard at the surface, as the 3–7 sets pivot, and are heard at the deepest level, as the guitar solo serves as the center of a large arch form.

Dark Angels serves as an excellent example for the study of melodic structure and development and for the use of elision technique. In the first song, the forms of both the poetry and the music closely match, and the technique of elision/substitution can be used in a way relatively new to the analysis of twentieth-century music. In the third song, an added musical hierarchy brings a new reading to the poetry. A different kind of elision, elision/contraction, can be heard at work in the last two verses. The tightly organized, multilayered structure of this song cycle shows this twentieth-century composer's music to be a sophisticated and subtle work of classical art.

---

11. Griffiths, *Peter Maxwell Davies*, 86.

Index

Abbate, Carolyn, and Roger Parker: 200n, 215

Adorno, Theodor: 157, 158, 159, 169

Aesthetics: *See* Adorno, Theodor (*see also under* Stravinsky, Igor)

Alpern, Wayne: 410n

Annensky, Innokenty: 62

Babbitt, Milton: 11, 43–44, 46, 50, 136, 174, 242n

Bach, Johann Sebastian: 99, 144, 214n; Chorale No. 17, "Ach Gott, wie manches Herzeleid," 181–82, 182 ex. 1; Prelude, BWV 933, 184, 185 ex. 4; Prelude in B, *Well-Tempered Clavier* I, 309, 325–35

Bacon, Ernst: 18n, 21–23, 24n, 25, 29, 33

Baddeley, Allan: 466

Baker, James M.: 68n, 199n, 237n, 239n, 275n, 373n

Balmont, Konstantin: 57, 60n, 61n, 63

Bartha, Dénes: 340

Barthes, Roland: 159

Bartlett, James C., and W. Jay Dowling: 221n

Bartók, Béla: 45, 132n, 144n, 238n, 361, 451n, 495n; *Mikrokosmos*, "From the Isle of Bali," 278–82, 287–88; —, octatonic sets in, 278, 280, 282

Beach, Amy: String Quartet, first movement, 247 ex. 3b

Beach, David W.: 199n, 202, 212–13, 216, 238n, 239n, 304n, 311n, 312n, 320n, 324n, 329n

Beethoven, Ludwig van: 107n, 134, 142, 144, 200, 208; "An die ferne Geliebte," 209; Bagatelle, op. 126, no. 6, 186–96; —, hypermeter, 186n; —, parenthetical interpolation, 193, 195–96; —, motivic parallelism, 186, 188, 191–193; *Fidelio*, 215; Piano Concerto No. 5 ("Emperor"), op. 73, 207, 357n; Piano Sonata, op. 7, third movement, 312, 314 ex. 3, 315 fig. 3, 318, 322, 335; Piano Sonata, op. 26, third movement, 203n; Piano Sonata, op. 53 ("Waldstein"), 385n; —, "Introduzione," 202, 203 ex. 1, 208, 214, 311–12, 313 ex. 2, 313 fig. 2, 318, 335; Piano Sonata, op. 79, first movement, 322; Piano Sonata, op. 81a, 357n; Piano Sonata, op. 90, third movement, 182–84, 183 ex. 3; Piano Sonata, op. 106, first movement, 322; Piano Sonata, op. 111, first movement, 322; Piano Trio, op. 97, first movement, 322; String Quintet, op. 29, first movement, 322; Symphony No. 9, op. 125, first movement, 322; —, "Ode to Joy," quatrain form in, 339

Bely, Andrei: 54, 57, 69–70, 72n, 73, 74

Benjamin, William: 242n

Berg, Alban: 12n, 15, 37n, 40, 44n, 45, 47n, 48, 50, 254n, 275n, 366n, 413n; Four Songs, op. 2, 375; *Lulu*, 159; *Lyric Suite*, 40, 41; Piano Sonata, op. 1, 413, 423; *Wozzeck*, 376n

Berlioz, Hector: *Symphonie Fantastique*, 209

Bernard, Jonathan W.: 32n, 159n, 166, 168

Bernstein, David W.: 21n, 97n, 131n

Bever, Thomas: 217n, 233, 234n

Billington, James H.: 54n

Birtwistle, Harrison: 157, 159, 168–80; *Carmen arcadiae mechanicae perpetuum*, 172–73; *Duets for Storab*, "Urlar," 170, 171 ex. 5, 172 ex. 6; *Earth Dances*, 168; *Gawain*, 170; *The Mask of Orpheus*, 169–70; *Melencolia I*, 173, 174, 175 ex. 7, 176 ex. 8, 177 ex. 9, 178 ex. 10, 179; *Nomos*, 172; *Yan Tan Tethera*, 169

Bitonality: 393–95 (*see also under* Milhaud, Darius)

Blavatsky, Helena: 64, 65n, 66, 67, 68, 69, 85n, 88, 90, 95

Blok, Alexander: 55, 56, 57, 61n, 63, 69, 70n, 72

Bloom, Rube: "Fools Rush In," 379, 380, 385, 388

Boretz, Benjamin: 393

Boretz, Benjamin, and Edward T. Cone: 469n

Boss, Jack: 241n

Boulez, Pierre: 43, 161

Bowers, Faubion: 55n, 57n, 58n, 60n, 61n, 62n, 67n, 68n, 71n

Bowlt, John E.: 68n, 72n, 74n

Brahms, Johannes: 134, 142, 200n, 209; Intermezzo in B♭, op. 76, no. 4, 373n; Piano Concerto in B♭ Major, op. 83, 357n; Piano Quintet, op. 34, first movement, 322; String Sextet, op. 36, 108–28 passim; —, Schoenberg's analysis of, 114, 116–19, 121, 124, 127; Symphony No. 3, 144, 145 ex. 4

Brandenburg, Sieghard: 186n, 194n

Brinkmann, Reinhold: 410n, 438n

Bristol, Evelyn: 61n

Brodbeck, David: 205n

Brown, Clifford: "Joy Spring," 388

Brown, Helen: 228n

Browne, Richmond: 242n, 395n

Brumbeloe, Joe: 390n

Brumer, Cheryl: 218n

Bryusov, Valery: 55, 56, 57, 65n, 73

Budde, Elmar: 410

Bugayev, Nikolai: 73

Burkhart, Charles: 237n, 238n, 377n

Burliuk, David: 72

Campbell, Bruce F.: 65n, 66n, 68n

Capellen, Georg: 18, 21n

Carmichael, Hoagy: "Stardust," 380, 388

Carpenter, Patricia: 108n, 138

Carpenter, Patricia, and Severine Neff: 460n

Carter, Chandler: 263n

Carter, Elliott: 32n, 157, 159–68, 169, 170, 174, 175, 177, 179, 180; Double Concerto, 163; Duo for violin and piano, 163; *Enchanted Preludes*, 161, 162 ex. 1, 163, 164 ex. 2, 165 ex. 3, 166, 167 ex. 4, 168, 179; Oboe Concerto, 160; *Penthode*, 160–61, 166, 173; Second String Quartet, 159; *A Symphony of Three Orchestras*, 159–60, 168; *Triple Duo*, 159, 160, 161

Chapman, Alan: 238n

Chopin, Frédéric: 202n, 203n; Ballade in F Minor, op. 52, 348n, 351n; —, interpolations, 339; Fantasy, op. 49, 339, 358; —, surface/underlying form, 339; Mazurka, op. 17, no. 1, 203n; Mazurka, op. 17, no. 3, 203n; Polonaise in A Major, op. 40, no. 1, 203n; Polonaise in F♯ Minor, op. 44, 358n; Polonaise in A♭, op. 53, 338, 346, 348, 358; —, hypermeter, 341; *Polonaise–Fantasy,* op. 61, 337–59; —, durational reduction, 342, 344–48 ex. 1; —, hypermeter, 338, 342, 355, 356 ex. 5; —, interpolations, 341, 342; —, metrical expansion, 342, 354, 357, 359; —, underlying form (quatrain),

339, 347–51, 354, 359; Scherzo, op. 54, 208; Sonata, op. 58, 348; Sonata, op. 65, 348

Christensen, Jean and Jens: 124n

Christensen, Thomas: 98n

Chulkov, Georgy: 56, 60n, 63, 69, 72

Cinnamon, Howard: 375n, 376n

Cone, Edward T.: 207, 338, 339, 342n, 349n, 357n

Cohn, Richard: 238n, 272n, 278n, 348, 451n

Coker, Jerry: 381n

Coltrane, John: 392; "Giant Steps," 390

Cook, Nicholas: 337, 338, 355

Covach, John R.: 25n

Cowell, Henry: 29–31, 32n, 37, 50

Cranston, Sylvia: 64n

Crawford, Ruth: *Chant No. 2* ("To an Angel"), 249 ex.3f; *Diaphonic Suite No. 2*, 252 ex. 4d; —, transformational analysis of, 274 ex. 15; *Prelude No. 9*, 251 ex.4c

Cronen, L. M., and P. F. M. Kop: 221n, 223

Cuddy, Lola: 218, 221, 222, 223n, 232

Dahlhaus, Carl: 97n, 99n, 459n

Daniel, Keith: 394n, 395n, 407n

Darcy, Warren: 216n

Davies, Peter Maxwell: *Dark Angels*, 481–520; —, central motives, 482, 494–501, 503, 510, 520; —, elision, 481, 482, 487, 489–94, 498, 501 ex. 9, 503, 504, 512, 515, 518 ex. 19b, 520; —, large-scale motivic structures, 496 ex. 5, 497 ex. 6, 499 ex. 7, 500 ex. 8, 517 ex.19a; —, motivic elements, 486 ex.2, 488 ex.3, 490 ex.4, 494–501; —, numerological schemes, 507, 510; —, structural intervals, 482, 487, 489, 494, 503; —, symmetry, 489, 507, 510, 512, 519

Dehmel, Richard: 413, 415n, 431

Deliège, Irene, and Abdessadek El Ahmadi: 222n

Delville, Jean: 58, 68

Deutsch, Diana: 219n

DeVoto, Mark: 366n

Dibben, Nicola: 218n, 239n

Dowling, W. Jay: 218, 219n, 220–22, 223, 224, 227 ex. 2, 228n, 230–31

Dowling, W. Jay, and Diane S. Fugitani: 220, 227 ex. 2, 228, 231

Dubiel, Joseph: 43n, 242n

Dümling, Albrecht: 413n

Dunsby, Jonathan: 209

Dvořák, Anton: Piano Quartet in E♭, op. 87, 357n

Eimert, Herbert: 27n, 29n

Elsworth, J. D.: 54n, 66n

Epstein, David: 212

Erpf, Hermann: 412n, 422n

Everett, Walter: 340n

Fétis, François-Joseph: 99, 113

Fichte, Johann Gottlieb: 59, 60, 62, 66

Forte, Allen: 2n, 3, 4, 6, 7, 11, 12n, 44, 45, 46, 49–51, 75, 77, 90, 98, 146, 180, 199, 212, 216, 217, 237n, 238, 239n, 253n, 263n, 270n, 275–76, 282, 285n, 299n, 300, 304n, 306, 346n, 361, 364, 365, 375n, 376, 380n, 393, 401n, 409, 433, 470, 489, 491, 495; genera, 4, 199, 300–302; —, general formalization of, 302–03; K and Kh relations, 49, 275–76, 282–88, 297–304, 306

Forte, Allen, and Steven E. Gilbert: 378n, 380n, 381n, 382n

Friedmann, Michael: 218

Frisch, Walter: 15n, 142n, 205n, 357n

Garbusov, Nicolas A.: 31n

George, Stefan: 413, 431

Gerlach, Reinhard: 409n, 411n, 413n, 416n, 417n, 420, 423n, 431n

Gershwin, George: 32, 385; "Embraceable You," 388

Gershwin, George and Ira: "I Got Rhythm," 377; "Love Walked In," 378–79, 388

Gilbert, Steven E.: 32n, 378n, 379n, 380n

Gilliam, Bryan: 216n

Gippius, Zinaida: 62

Grass, Günter: 173, 174, 176; *From the Diary of a Snail*, 174

Greimas, A. J.: 208; semiotic square, 208, 209 fig. 1, 211, 213 fig. 2

Griffiths, Paul: 482n, 519, 520n

Grundgestalt: 107n, 117, 138, 144, 152, 153, 429

Hába, Alois: 28–31, 36, 37 ex. 8b, 47, 50

Hall, Michael: 168–69, 172n, 173n, 174

Hamburger, Paul: 337

Hancock, Herbie: 390

Hanson, Howard: 46–49

Hantz, Edwin: 376n

Harrison, Daniel: 21n

Harvey, Jonathan: 43n

Hasty, Christopher: 238n, 241n, 263n

Hauer, Josef: 17, 24–28, 50

Haydn, Franz Josef: *Chorale St. Antoni*, 309, 310 ex. 1, 311 fig. 1, 335; —, grouping structure, 310; —, metrical expansion, 310, 320, 324

Headlam, Dave: 24n, 37n

Heidenreich, Alfred: 69n

Heinemann, Stephen: 43n

Hill, Richard: 40, 41

Hindemith, Paul: 38–39, 49, 50, 51

Hull, Arthur E.: 14–16, 17, 31

Hummel, Johann Nepomuk: 205, 208; *Six German Dances*, 206

Hyde, Martha: 132n, 135n, 263n

Idson, W. L., and D. W. Massaro: 219n

Imberty, Michel: 218n

Ivanov, Vyacheslav: 54n, 56, 57, 71, 74

Jackson, Timothy: 356n

James, Harry: 390

Jameson, Fredric: 208

Johns, Donald: 382n, 385n, 390n

Jolivet, André: *Cinq danses rituelles*, "Danse initiatique," 248 ex. 3d

Jonas, Oswald: 182, 188, 322

Kalbouss, George: 71n

Kallberg, Jeffrey: 337, 349, 350n, 358n

Kamien, Roger: 349n

Kaminsky, Peter: 200, 201, 210, 212

Kandinsky, Vasily: 55, 56, 58, 68, 69, 72, 74

Kaplan, Richard: 275n, 277n, 279n, 304n

Katz, Adele: 237n

Kelkel, Manfred: 58n, 59, 60n, 66

Kerman, Joseph: 131n, 132n, 181n

Kern, Jerome: "All the Things You Are," 381, 382n, 384, 385, 390

Kidd, James C.: 97n

Kimura, Doreen: 233

Klein, Fritz Heinrich: 23n, 24n, 36, 37n, 38 ex.9a

Klumpenhouwer, Henry: 237n, 238n, 243n

Koblyakov, Lev: 43n

Komar, Arthur: 201, 204n, 212, 214

Korsyn, Kevin: 132n, 216n

Koussevitzky, Sergei: 57

Kramer, Lawrence: 173n, 338

Krebs, Harald: 202n

Krenek, Ernst: 40–42, 50; *Lamentatio Jeremiae Prophetae*, 41–42; *Symphonic Piece for String Orchestra*, 41

Krumhansl, Carol L. *et al.*: 222n

Kulbin, Nikolai: 71, 72, 74n

Lai, Eric: 258n
Lane, Anne: 60n, 61n, 70n
Lanner, Josef: *Ankunfts-Walzer*, op. 34, 205, 206; *Steyrische Tänze*, 208
Lansky, Paul: 13, 41
Larionov, Mikhail: 71n, 74
Larson, Steve: 237n, 340n
Laufer, Edward: 237n, 318n, 338n
Leichtentritt, Hugo: 337, 349
Lenormand, René: 14, 16, 17, 18
Lerdahl, Fred: 237n
Lerdahl, Fred, and Ray Jackendoff: 12n, 310n
Lester, Joel: 237n
Lewin, David: 4, 44–45, 46, 50, 51, 199, 212, 238n, 242n, 244n, 258n, 259n, 268n, 270n, 272, 272n, 431, 437n, 449nn, 450n, 469n
Lewis, Christopher: 200, 201, 214, 215
Lewis, Morgan: "How High the Moon," 377, 383, 384, 385, 388
Lincoln, W. Bruce: 63n, 69n, 90n
Liszt, Franz: 143, 337; "Blume und Duft," 361–76; —, octatonic sets in, 361, 364, 365, 366, 371; Sonata in B Minor, 209
Littlefield, Richard, and David Neumeyer: 208n
Loeb, David: 214n
Long, Rose-Carol Washton: 55n, 56n, 68n, 69n, 72n

M (or MI) operation: 307
Macdonald, Hugh: 53
Mackenzie, Wallace: 426n
Mahler, Gustav: 461
Marcozzi, Rudy T.: 216n
Markov, Vladimir: 62
Marra, James: 414n
Martino, Donald: 44
Marvin, Elizabeth West: 218, 393n

McCreless, Patrick: 199, 200, 201, 207, 208, 211, 214, 216n
McNamee, Ann: 394n
Mead, Andrew: 43n, 135n, 305
Medner, Emil: 57, 58n
Merezhkovsky, Dmitri: 54, 55n, 57, 62, 90n
Messiaen, Olivier: 22n, 39, 40n, 50; *Livre d'orgue* ("Les Mains de l'abîme"), 245 ex.2b
Meyer, Felix: 410n
Meyer, Leonard: 97n, 136n, 211, 212
Mihajlov, Mihajlo: 60n
Milhaud, Darius: Second Chamber Symphony, 393–408; bitonality, 399, 401, 404, 405, 407; five-cycle sets in, 394–99, 401–02, 404–07; pentatonic sets in, 395, 396, 407
Mikumo, Mariko: 218n
Miyazaki, Ken'ichi: 223n
Moldenhauer, Hans: 410, 413n
Morgan, Robert: 237n, 262n, 265, 267n, 366n, 373n
Morozova, Margarita: 58
Morris, Robert: 51, 218, 224, 228, 237n, 238n, 275n, 282n, 285n, 303n, 304n; KI relation, 277–82, 293, 298–303, 306
Morrison, Charles: 237n
Mozart, Wolfgang Amadeus: 208n, 209, 215, 349n, 460, 461; Fantasy in D Minor, K. 397, 312, 316 ex.14, 317 fig.4, 318, 335; Piano Concerto in C Minor, K. 491, 324; Piano Sonata in A, K. 331, 203; Rondo in F, K. 494, 380–81, 382 ex.5, 384

Narmour, Eugene: 468n
Nauert, Paul: 32n
Neff, Severine: 18n, 22n, 23n, 107n, 108n, 127n, 131n, 138, 460n
Neoclassicism: 131–156 passim
Nettl, Paul: 205n

Neumeyer, David: 197n; multi-move-
ment structure, theory of, 197–216
Neumeyer, David, and Susan Tepping:
238n
Newcomb, Anthony: 337, 338, 341n,
348, 349
Nietzsche, Friedrich: 60–61
Noble, Ray: "Cherokee," 377, 385, 388

octatonic: 22n, 73, 133, 144, 146, 147,
149, 150, 152-54, 156, 253n, 263n,
277, 278, 280, 282, 293, 296, 361, 364,
365, 371, 376n, 401n, 428n, 433, 435,
437, 439–43, 446, 448, 449, 453, 455,
456, 457
O'Donnell, Shaugn: 270n
Olcott, Henry: 64
Oster, Ernst: 202n, 238n, 309n, 310n,
322, 323n, 332, 334, 378n
Owens, Peter: 482n

Paddison, Max: 157n, 158
Panofsky, Edwin: 173n
Parker, Charlie: "Anthropology," 377;
"Crazeology," 377; "Ko–Ko," 377,
385, 388; "Ornithology," 377, 383,
384; "Shaw 'Nuff," 377
Parks, Richard: 301n
Parrinder, Geoffrey: 64
Pearsall, Edward: 238n
Perle, George: 24n, 40–41, 45n, 47, 50,
254n
Persichetti, Vincent: 51, 489n
Phrase rhythm: See under Beethoven,
Ludwig van (see also under Chopin,
Frédéric); interpolation/ insertion. See
under Beethoven, Ludwig van (see also
under Chopin, Frédéric); metrical
expansion. See under Chopin, Frédéric
(see also under Haydn, Franz Josef)
Plekhanov, Georgi: 62
Porter, Cole: "I've Got You Under My
Skin," 378, 388

Powell, Bud: 388
Pruslin, Stephen: 482n, 507n

Rahn, John: 22n, 51, 238n
Raksin, David: "Laura," 385, 388
Rameau, Jean-Philippe: 12, 14, 17, 98,
113
Reger, Max: 58n, 393
Reeve, F. D.: 65n, 74n
Richardson, William: 54n, 58n, 63n, 64n
Riemann, Hugo: 18, 21, 99, 182–184,
393
Rink, John: 337, 338, 343
Rodgers, Richard, and Oscar
Hammerstein II: "My Favorite
Things," 390
Rodgers, Richard, and Lorenz Hart: "I
Didn't Know What Time It Was,"
388
Roeder, John: 238n, 259n
Rogers, Lynne: 267n
Romberg, Sigmund: "Softly, As in a
Morning Sunrise," 392
Rosen, Charles: 209
Roslavets, Nicolai: Piano Piece, 246
ex.2c
Rothgeb, John: 182n, 238n, 322n, 346n
Rothstein, William: 322n, 339n, 340n,
341n, 342n, 343n
Rubtsova, V. V.: 58n
Russell, Tilden: 204n

Sabaneev, Leonid: 58, 74n
Salzer, Felix: 146, 147, 149, 237n, 320n
Salzer, Felix, and Carl Schachter: 342n
Samson, Jim: 337, 339n, 349, 350n, 354
Saslaw, Janna: 113n
Scarlatti, Domenico: Sonata in B♭,
L. 500, first movement, 322
Schachter, Carl: 206, 324, 339, 342n,
351n, 354
Schenker, Heinrich: 1, 2, 3, 5, 12, 51,
98n, 131n, 134, 172, 198, 201–02, 203,

204n, 208n, 211, 214 fig. 4, 237n, 238n, 272, 310n, 322, 323n, 338, 371, 375n, 378n, 379, 380n

Schenkerian concepts: 7, 84, 146, 149, 166, 181n, 186n, 197, 199, 200, 201, 202, 204, 211, 213, 239n, 338, 341, 375n, 376n; motivic parallelism, 186, 188, 191, 192

Schiff, David: 159–61, 166, 173, 179

Schillinger, Joseph: 32–37, 50

Schloezer, Boris de: 57, 58n, 59n, 60n, 62n, 64, 67, 70, 75, 79n, 80, 88, 95

Schmalfeldt, Janet: 12n, 43, 44n, 47n, 186n

Schoenberg, Arnold: 3, 4, 6, 12, 13n, 14, 15n, 16–17, 18, 24n, 26, 27, 28, 31, 35, 36n, 40, 41, 42, 44n, 45, 48, 50, 131, 132, 135, 136, 137, 142, 143, 144, 145, 146, 151, 152, 155, 199n, 212n, 218, 237n, 238n, 275n, 288n, 361, 409, 411, 430n, 431, 459, 460, 461; *Book of the Hanging Gardens*, op. 15, 413; Concept of Tonality, 97–129; *Drei Klavierstücke*, op. 11, 14; —, no. 1, transformational analysis of, 273 ex. 14; *Erwartung*, 14, 247 ex. 3a; *Five Orchestral Pieces*, op. 16, no. 3, 412n, 422; *Fünf Klavierstücke*, 14; *Kammersymphonie*, op. 9, 14, 413, 414, 417; *Klavierstück*, op. 33a, 39; *Little Piano Piece*, op. 19, no. 6, 270n; *Phantasy for Violin and Piano Accompaniment*, op. 47, 459–79; *Pierrot lunaire*, 151; —, "Mondestrunken," 433–57; —, chromatic sets in, 439, 442–43, 445– 46, 448–49, 451–53; —, octatonic sets in, 433–35, 437, 439–40, 442–43, 446, 448–49, 453, 455–57; —, symmetry in, 433, 437, 443, 449, 453; —, transformations in, 433–37, 443, 445–46, 449–50, 455; —, whole–tone sets in, 433–45, 445–56; Suite, op. 25, 27; Violin Concerto, op. 36, 42 ex. 10

Schreffler, Anne C.: 410n, 430n

Schubert, Franz: 200, 205, 208, 208n, 325; Fantasy in C Major ("Wan- derer"), op. 15, D. 716, 209; Im- promptu, op. 142, no. 2, D. 935/2, 182, 183 ex. 2; Impromptu, op. 142, no. 3, D. 935/3, 186, 187 exx. 7 and 8; *Moment musical* No. 6, D. 780, 357n; Piano Quintet in A ("Die Forelle"), op. 114, D. 667, second movement, 320, 321 fig. 6; Piano Sonata in A Minor, D. 537, first movement, 323; Piano Sonata in B♭, D. 960, third movement, 322, 323 fig. 7; Piano Trio in B♭, D. 898, first movement, 318, 319 fig. 5; —, second move- ment, 323, 324 fig. 8; String Quartet in G, D. 889, first movement, 325n; String Quintet in C, D. 956, first movement, 325n; Symphony No. 8 in B Minor ("Unfinished"), D. 759, second movement, 324; *Valses sentimentales*, D. 779, 204, 206, 207 ex. 4

Schumann, Robert: *Album for the Young*, op. 68, no. 30, 184, 185 exx. 5 and 6; *Carnaval*, 201, 210, 212; *Davidsbündlertänze*, 200, 210; *Dichterliebe*, 198, 200, 204, 205 exx. 2 and 3, 208, 212, 214; —, "Aus meinen Thränen spriessen," 203; —, "Im wunderschönen Monat Mai," 202; *Faschingsschwank aus Wien*, 210; *Kreisleriana*, 210; *Papillons*, 200, 210

Scriabin, Alexander: 43, 45, 53–96, 254n, 275n, 361, 373n; "Désir," op. 57, no. 1, 75, 76; "Ironies," op. 56, no. 2, 77, 77 ex.3; *Mysterium*, 67, 70–71, 79, 88; "Poem," op. 32, no. 2, 75; *Poem of Ecstasy*, op. 54, 60, 63, 64, 68, 70, 83–84, 89, 95; "Poème fantastique," op. 45, no. 2, 76 ex.2, 77; *Prefatory Action*, 70, 79, 88, 89n;

Prelude, op. 59, no. 2, 78–79, 80–81 ex. 5; Prelude, op. 74, no. 4, 249 ex. 3g; —, associative analysis of, 260 ex. 7a; —, transformational analysis of, 261 ex.7b; *Prometheus: The Poem of Fire*, op. 60, 68, 75, 83–90, 95, 96; Piano Sonatas: Third, op. 23, 80, 95; Fifth, op. 53, 70, 78, 78 ex. 4, 82 ex. 6, 82–85, 85 ex. 7, 95; Sixth, op. 62, 95; Seventh ("White Mass"), op. 64, 89, 91, 92 ex. 9a, 95; Ninth ("Black Mass"), op. 62, 70, 89, 90, 92 ex. 9b, 94 ex. 9d, 95 ex. 9d; Tenth, op. 70, 80, 89, 90, 93 ex. 9c, 95

Scriabine, Marina: 66n, 79n, 80n, 89n

Seabrook, Mike: 482n

Seeger, Ruth Crawford: *See* Crawford, Ruth

Set-complex theory: K and Kh relations. *See under* Forte, Allen; —, KI relation. *See under* Morris, Robert

Sets (chromatic). *See under* Schoenberg, Arnold; sets (diatonic), 395, 407 (*see also under* Stravinsky, Igor; Webern, Anton); sets (five-cycle). *See under* Milhaud, Darius; sets (octatonic). *See under* Bartók, Béla (*see also under* Liszt, Franz; Schoenberg, Arnold; Stravinsky, Igor; Varèse, Edgard); sets (pentatonic). *See under* Milhaud, Darius (*see also* under Stravinsky, Igor); sets (whole–tone). *See under* Schoenberg, Arnold (*see also under* Webern, Anton)

Sigogne, Emile: 67

Simms, Bryan: 17n, 24n, 25, 102n

Slonimsky, Nicolas: 35–36, 37 ex. 8a, 38 ex. 9b, 50, 57n

Sly, Gordon: 318n

Smith, Barbara H.: 104, 105n

Smith, Charles: 311n

Solie, Ruth A.: 97n, 131n

Sologub, Fyodor: 61, 71

Solovyov, Vladimir: 54, 56, 62, 63, 64, 69, 70

Stein, Leonard: 413n, 428n, 430

Steinberg, Ada: 57n, 73n

Steiner, Rudolf: 69

Stockhausen, Karlheinz: 32n, 43, 176

Straus, Joseph: 132n, 144n, 145n, 198, 199, 206, 208, 211, 216, 238n, 239n, 259n, 263n, 265n, 495n; near-inversion, 268, 272; near-transposition, 268, 270, 272

Strauss, Johann Sr.: 205n, 210

Strauss, Richard: 210, 215, 216, 461

Stravinsky, Igor: 43, 45, 53, 131, 176, 361, 393n; aesthetic of, 134; *Agon*, 254 ex. 5a, 256 ex. 5d; *Berceuses du chat*, transformational analysis of, 267 ex.11; *Concerto for Piano and Wind Instruments*, Schenker's analysis of, 237n, 263–65, 267, 268 ex. 12a; —, transformational analysis of, 269 ex. 12b; *Movements for Piano and Orchestra*, 43; *Oedipus Rex*, 151; *Orpheus*, 249 ex. 3e; *Petroushka*, 401n; *Pieces for String Quartet*, no. 2, 255 ex. 5b; —, no. 3, transformational analysis of, 271 ex. 13; *Rake's Progress*, 257 ex. 5e, 367 ex. 5c; *Rite of Spring*, 250 ex. 4b, 263n, 267n, 290; —, transformational analysis of, 266 ex. 10; *A Soldier's Tale*, 246 ex. 2d; *Symphonies of Wind Instruments*, 266n; *Symphony in C*, 150; *Symphony in Three Movements*, 132n, 133, 137–56; —, motives, 137–46, 147, 149, 152–53; —, Salzer's interpretation of, 146–49; —, diatonic sets in, 133, 149, 150, 152–54, 156; —, octatonic sets in, 133, 147, 149, 150, 152–54, 156; pentatonic sets in, 395, 396, 407; *Symphony of Psalms*, 150

Street, Alan: 215n

Sutton, Robert: 46, 48

Symbolism, Russian: 54–57, 59–63, 69–74

Takeushi, Annie, and Stewart Hulse: 223n
Taneyev, Sergei: 73
Tarasti, Eero: 337, 338
Taruskin, Richard: 134n, 145n
Theosophy: 58, 64–69, 74–85, 88–90, 95–96
Thomson, William: 394n
Tippett, Michael: *A Child of Our Time*, 173
Tovey, Donald Francis: 97
Travis, Roy: 237n, 263n, 267n
Treitler, Leo: 211
Trubetskoi, Prince Sergei: 58, 63, 64

Van den Toorn, Pieter: 144n, 147n, 149n, 263n, 393, 495n
Varèse, Edgard: 306; *Intégrales*, 290; *Octandre*, 288–99, 300, 302; —, octatonic sets in, 293, 296
voice leading (atonal): associational model, 198, 199, 200, 208, 211, 237, 240 ex. 1, 241, 242; prolongational model, 198, 199, 200, 237, 239, 240 ex. 1, 241, 263; transformational model, 238, 240 ex. 1, 242–74

Wagner, Richard: 58n, 71, 75, 99, 143, 199, 215, 216; *Lohengrin*, 341n; *Tristan und Isolde*, 346n, 414, 427
Wason, Robert: 13n, 98n
Wason, Robert, and Elizabeth West Marvin: 393n, 412n

Weber, Carl Maria Ernst von: 215
Webern, Anton: 24n, 45, 50, 218; *Bagatelles for String Quartet*, op. 9, 253n; —, no. 2, 256 ex. 5c; —, no. 5, 250 ex. 4a; *Dehmel Lieder*, 409–31; —, octatonic sets, 428; —, referential sonorities, 412, 419, 423, 424, 426, 429; —, whole–tone sets , 419; "Entflieht auf leichten Kähnen," 410, 430; *Five Pieces for Orchestra*, op. 10, 450n; *George Lieder*, 410, 430; Songs, op. 14, "Die Sonne," transformational analysis of, 258 ex. 6; *Five Movements for String Quartet*, op. 5, 304, 410; —, no. 2, 253 ex. 4e; transformational analysis of, 264 ex. 9a, 265 ex. 9b; —, no. 3, 245 ex. 2a, 248 ex. 3c; transformational analysis of, 262 ex. 8
Weitzmann, Carl Friedrich: 13n
West, James: 54n, 56n, 71n
Wilder, Alec: 383, 385
Wilson, John H.: 378, 382n
Wilson, Paul: 238n, 495n
Wolf, Hugo: 415

Yeston, Maury: 181n, 202n
Young, Victor: "Stella by Starlight," 388, 390

Zdanevich, Ilya, and Mikhail Larionov: 71n
Ziehn, Bernhard: 18, 19 ex. 2, 20 ex. 2, 21, 22, 23, 31n